collections

Copyright © 2017 by Houghton Mifflin Harcourt Publishing Company

All rights reserved. No part of this work may be reproduced or transmitted in any form or by any means, electronic or mechanical, including photocopying or recording, or by any information storage and retrieval system, without the prior written permission of the copyright owner unless such copying is expressly permitted by federal copyright law. Requests for permission to make copies of any part of the work should be addressed to Houghton Mifflin Harcourt Publishing Company, Attn: Intellectual Property Licensing, 9400 Southpark Center Loop, Orlando, Florida 32819-8647.

Houghton Mifflin Harcourt™ and Holt McDougal are trademarks of Houghton Mifflin Harcourt Publishing Company.

HISTORY®, A&E®, and Bio® branded videos © 2015 A&E Television Networks, LLC. All rights reserved. Used with kind permission.

A&E, Bio, HISTORY, the History "H" logo, and all associated trademarks and logos are the trademarks of A&E Television Networks, LLC.

Cover, Title Page Photo Credits: ©Tek Image/Getty Images

Printed in the U.S.A.

ISBN 978-1-328-66113-5

1 2 3 4 5 6 7 8 9 10   0868   24 23 22 21 20 19 18 17

4500649454   A B C D E F G

If you have received these materials as examination copies free of charge, Houghton Mifflin Harcourt Publishing Company retains title to the materials and they may not be resold. Resale of examination copies is strictly prohibited.

Possession of this publication in print format does not entitle users to convert this publication, or any portion of it, into electronic format.

collections

GRADE 8

Program Consultants:
Kylene Beers
Martha Hougen
Carol Jago
William L. McBride
Erik Palmer
Lydia Stack

About Our Program Consultants

Kylene Beers Nationally known lecturer and author on reading and literacy; 2011 recipient of the Conference on English Leadership Exemplary Leader Award; coauthor of *Notice and Note: Strategies for Close Reading*; former president of the National Council of Teachers of English. Dr. Beers is the nationally known author of *When Kids Can't Read: What Teachers Can Do* and coeditor of *Adolescent Literacy: Turning Promise into Practice*, as well as articles in the *Journal of Adolescent and Adult Literacy*. Former editor of *Voices from the Middle*, she is the 2001 recipient of NCTE's Richard W. Halley Award, given for outstanding contributions to middle school literacy. She recently served as Senior Reading Researcher at the Comer School Development Program at Yale University as well as Senior Reading Advisor to Secondary Schools for the Reading and Writing Project at Teachers College.

Martha Hougen National consultant, presenter, researcher, and author. Areas of expertise include differentiating instruction for students with learning difficulties, including those with learning disabilities and dyslexia; and teacher and leader preparation improvement. Dr. Hougen has taught at the middle school through graduate levels. Recently her focus has been on working with teacher educators to enhance teacher and leader preparation to better meet the needs of all students. Currently she is working with the University of Florida at the Collaboration for Effective Educator Development, Accountability, and Reform Center (CEEDAR Center) to improve the achievement of students with disabilities by reforming teacher and leader licensure, evaluation, and preparation. She has led similar efforts in Texas with the Higher Education Collaborative and the College & Career Readiness Initiative Faculty Collaboratives. In addition to peer-reviewed articles, curricular documents, and presentations, Dr. Hougen has published two college textbooks: *The Fundamentals of Literacy Assessment and Instruction Pre-K–6* (2012) and *The Fundamentals of Literacy Assessment and Instruction 6–12* (2014).

Carol Jago Teacher of English with 32 years of experience at Santa Monica High School in California; author and nationally known lecturer; and former president of the National Council of Teachers of English. Currently serves as Associate Director of the California Reading and Literature Project at UCLA. With expertise in standards assessment and secondary education, Ms. Jago is the author of numerous books on education, including *With Rigor for All* and *Papers, Papers, Papers*, and is active with the California Association of Teachers of English, editing its scholarly journal *California English* since 1996. Ms. Jago also served on the planning committee for the 2009 NAEP Framework and the 2011 NAEP Writing Framework.

William L. McBride Curriculum specialist. Dr. McBride is a nationally known speaker, educator, and author who now trains teachers in instructional methodologies. He is coauthor of *What's Happening?*, an innovative, high-interest text for middle-grade readers, and author of *If They Can Argue Well, They Can Write Well*. A former reading specialist, English teacher, and social studies teacher, he holds a master's degree in reading and a doctorate in curriculum and instruction from the University of North Carolina at Chapel Hill. Dr. McBride has contributed to the development of textbook series in language arts, social studies, science, and vocabulary. He is also known for his novel *Entertaining an Elephant*, which tells the story of a veteran teacher who becomes reinspired with both his profession and his life.

Erik Palmer Veteran teacher and education consultant based in Denver, Colorado. Author of *Well Spoken: Teaching Speaking to All Students* and *Digitally Speaking: How to Improve Student Presentations*. His areas of focus include improving oral communication, promoting technology in classroom presentations, and updating instruction through the use of digital tools. He holds a bachelor's degree from Oberlin College and a master's degree in curriculum and instruction from the University of Colorado.

Lydia Stack Internationally known teacher educator and author. She is involved in a Stanford University project to support English Language Learners, *Understanding Language*. The goal of this project is to enrich academic content and language instruction for English Language Learners (ELLs) in grades K-12 by making explicit the language and literacy skills necessary to meet the Common Core State Standards (CCSS) and Next Generation Science Standards. Her teaching experience includes twenty-five years as an elementary and high school ESL teacher, and she is a past president of Teachers of English to Speakers of Other Languages (TESOL). Her awards include the TESOL James E. Alatis Award and the San Francisco STAR Teacher Award. Her publications include *On Our Way to English, Visions: Language, Literature, Content,* and *American Themes,* a literature anthology for high school students in the ACCESS program of the U.S. State Department's Office of English Language Programs.

Additional thanks to the following Program Reviewers

Rosemary Asquino
Sylvia B. Bennett
Yvonne Bradley
Leslie Brown
Haley Carroll
Caitlin Chalmers
Emily Colley-King
Stacy Collins
Denise DeBonis
Courtney Dickerson
Sarah Easley
Phyllis J. Everette
Peter J. Foy Sr.

Carol M. Gibby
Angie Gill
Mary K. Goff
Saira Haas
Lisa M. Janeway
Robert V. Kidd Jr.
Kim Lilley
John C. Lowe
Taryn Curtis MacGee
Meredith S. Maddox
Cynthia Martin
Kelli M. McDonough
Megan Pankiewicz

Linda Beck Pieplow
Molly Pieplow
Mary-Sarah Proctor
Jessica A. Stith
Peter Swartley
Pamela Thomas
Linda A. Tobias
Rachel Ukleja
Lauren Vint
Heather Lynn York
Leigh Ann Zerr

COLLECTION 1
Culture and Belonging

ANCHOR TEXT	**SHORT STORY** My Favorite Chaperone	Jean Davies Okimoto		3
	PERSONAL ESSAY Bonne Année	Jean-Pierre Benoît		31
	RESEARCH STUDY A Place to Call Home	Scott Bittle and Jonathan Rochkind	▶	41
ANCHOR TEXT	**MEMOIR** from The Latehomecomer	Kao Kalia Yang	▶	53
MEDIA ANALYSIS	**DOCUMENTARY** New Immigrants Share Their Stories	Lisa Gossels	▶	71
	POEM The Powwow at the End of the World	Sherman Alexie		75

COLLECTION PERFORMANCE TASKS
Write an Informative Essay 79
Write a Personal Narrative 83

KEY LEARNING OBJECTIVES
- Make inferences.
- Analyze plot.
- Analyze characterization.
- Analyze allusion.
- Analyze imagery.
- Analyze central idea and details.
- Identify and analyze elements of a memoir.
- Analyze elements of a personal essay.
- Analyze use of text features and graphic aids.
- Determine use of figurative language.
- Analyze and evaluate elements of a documentary.

Close Reader

SHORT STORY
Golden Glass — Alma Luz Villanueva

ESSAY
What to Bring — Naisha Jackson

MEMOIR
Museum Indians — Susan Power

COLLECTION 2
The Thrill of Horror

ANCHOR TEXT	**SHORT STORY** The Tell-Tale Heart	Edgar Allan Poe		89
	ESSAY Scary Tales	Jackie Torrence		99
	SHORT STORY The Monkey's Paw	W. W. Jacobs	▶	105
MEDIA ANALYSIS	**FILM CLIP** from The Monkey's Paw	Ricky Lewis Jr.	▶	121
ANCHOR TEXT	**LITERARY CRITICISM** What is the Horror Genre?	Sharon A. Russell		125

COLLECTION PERFORMANCE TASKS
Present an Argument — 133
Write a Literary Analysis — 137

KEY LEARNING OBJECTIVES
Determine theme.
Identify use of suspense.
Identify and analyze foreshadowing.
Determine point of view.
Evaluate narrator.
Compare a written story to film.

Analyze elements of literary criticism.
Identify elements of author's style.
Analyze author's viewpoint.
Determine author's purpose.
Identify counterarguments.
Analyze filmmaker's choices.

Close Reader

SHORT STORY
The Outsider — H. P. Lovecraft

POEM
Frankenstein — Edward Field

ESSAY
Man-Made Monsters — Daniel Cohen

eBook *Explore It!*

Video Links

 Visit hmhfyi.com for current articles and informational texts.

COLLECTION 3
The Move Toward Freedom

ANCHOR TEXT	**AUTOBIOGRAPHY** from Narrative of the Life of Frederick Douglass, an American Slave	Frederick Douglass	▶	143
	BIOGRAPHY from Harriet Tubman: Conductor on the Underground Railroad	Ann Petry	▶	151
ANCHOR TEXT	**HISTORICAL FICTION** The Drummer Boy of Shiloh	Ray Bradbury	▶	167
	HISTORY WRITING from Bloody Times: The Funeral of Abraham Lincoln and the Manhunt for Jefferson Davis	James L. Swanson		177
	POEM O Captain! My Captain!	Walt Whitman		199

COLLECTION PERFORMANCE TASKS

Participate in a Collaborative Discussion — 203
Write a Literary Analysis — 207

KEY LEARNING OBJECTIVES

Identify elements of historical fiction.
Identify elements of elegy.
Identify and analyze extended metaphors.
Analyze mood.
Analyze elements of autobiography.
Identify methods of characterization in biography.

Analyze word choice and connotation.
Analyze author's craft.
Analyze compare-and-contrast organization.
Determine author's purpose.
Engage in collaborative discussion.

Close Reader

BIOGRAPHY
My Friend Douglass — Russell Freedman

SHORT STORY
A Mystery of Heroism — Stephen Crane

JOURNAL ENTRIES
Civil War Journal — Louisa May Alcott

eBook *Explore It!*

 Video Links   **Visit hmhfyi.com** for current articles and informational texts.

COLLECTION 4
Approaching Adulthood

ANCHOR TEXT	**SHORT STORY** Marigolds	Eugenia Collier	213
	POEMS Hanging Fire Teenagers	Audre Lorde Pat Mora	229 231
ANCHOR TEXT	**ARGUMENT** When Do Kids Become Adults?	Laurence Steinberg, Jenny Diamond Cheng, Jamie Lincoln Kitman, Barbara Hofer, Michael Thompson	235
COMPARE TEXTS	**ARTICLES** Is 16 Too Young to Drive a Car? Fatal Car Crashes Drop for 16-Year-Olds, Rise for Older Teens	Robert Davis Allison Aubrey	247 256
COMPARE MEDIA	**Persuading Viewers Through Ads** **PUBLIC SERVICE ANNOUNCEMENT FILM** Your Phone Can Wait **PUBLIC SERVICE ANNOUNCEMENT POSTER** Driving Distracted	 Stephanie Ramirez	263 263 266

COLLECTION PERFORMANCE TASKS
Write a Literary Analysis — 269
Produce a Multimedia Campaign — 273

KEY LEARNING OBJECTIVES
Make inferences.
Determine theme.
Analyze character motivation.
Identify speaker in poetry.
Determine central idea and details.
Evaluate reasoning.
Trace and evaluate an argument.
Analyze facts and interpretations in two texts.
Evaluate different mediums.

Close Reader

SHORT STORY
The Whistle — Anne Estevis

POEM
Identity — Julio Noboa Polanco

POEM
Hard on the Gas — Janet S. Wong

HISTORY ARTICLE
Much Too Young to Work So Hard — Naoki Tanaka

eBook *Explore It!*

Video Links   Visit hmhfyi.com for current articles and informational texts.

COLLECTION 5
Anne Frank's Legacy

ANCHOR TEXT	**DRAMA** The Diary of Anne Frank	Frances Goodrich and Albert Hackett	▶	279
	DIARY from The Diary of a Young Girl	Anne Frank		355
	LITERARY CRITICISM from Anne Frank: The Book, the Life, the Afterlife	Francine Prose		369
	SPEECH After Auschwitz	Elie Wiesel	▶	379
	POEM There But for the Grace	Wisława Szymborska		385

COLLECTION PERFORMANCE TASK

Research and Write an Informative Essay — 389

KEY LEARNING OBJECTIVES
Identify and analyze elements of drama.
Analyze flashback.
Analyze sound devices in poetry.
Make inferences.
Identify and analyze elements of a diary.
Analyze impact of word choice on tone.
Analyze persuasive techniques.
Determine use of rhetorical devices.
Determine author's viewpoint.

Close Reader

DRAMA

from The Diary of Anne Frank: Act I, Scenes 1 and 2

Frances Goodrich and Albert Hackett

eBook *Explore It!*

Video Links

 Visit hmhfyi.com for current articles and informational texts.

COLLECTION 6

The Value of Work

ANCHOR TEXT	**NOVEL** *from* The Adventures of Tom Sawyer	Mark Twain	395
	MEMOIR One Last Time	Gary Soto	405
	ARGUMENTS Teens Need Jobs, Not Just Cash Teens at Work	Anne Michaud	419 422
COMPARE ANCHOR TEXTS	**POEMS** Chicago Find Work My Mother Enters the Work Force	Carl Sandburg Rhina P. Espaillat Rita Dove	427 431 433

COLLECTION PERFORMANCE TASKS

Present a Narrative — 437
Write an Argument — 441

KEY LEARNING OBJECTIVES
Analyze point of view and narrator.
Determine and analyze style.
Determine use of figurative language.
Analyze rhyme scheme and meter.
Compare and contrast poetic structure.
Draw conclusions.
Analyze imagery.
Delineate and evaluate an argument.
Plan and present a narrative.

xvi   Grade 8

Close Reader

SHORT STORY
The Flying Machine — Ray Bradbury

GRAPHIC STORY
The Flying Machine — Ray Bradbury
illustrated by Bernard Krigstein

BIOGRAPHY
The Real McCoy — Jim Haskins

POEM
To Be of Use — Marge Piercy

POEM
A Story of How a Wall Stands — Simon J. Ortiz

eBook *Explore It!*

 Video Links   Visit hmhfyi.com for current articles and informational texts.

Student Resources

Performance Task Reference Guide R2
  Writing an Argument R2
  Writing an Informative Essay R4
  Writing a Narrative R6
  Conducting Research R8
  MLA Citation Guidelines R10
  Participating in a Collaborative Discussion R12
  Debating an Issue R14

Reading Informational Texts: Patterns of Organization R16
  1 Main Idea and Supporting Details R16
  2 Chronological Order R17
  3 Cause-Effect Organization R18
  4 Compare-and-Contrast Organization R19
  5 Problem-Solution Organization R21

Reading Arguments R22
  1 Analyzing an Argument R22
  2 Recognizing Proposition and Support Patterns R23
  3 Recognizing Persuasive Techniques R23
  4 Analyzing Logic and Reasoning R24
  5 Evaluating Persuasive Texts R27

Grammar R29
  Quick Reference:
    Parts of Speech R29
    The Sentence and Its Parts R31
    Punctuation R32
    Capitalization R35
  Grammar Handbook:
    1 Nouns R36
    2 Pronouns R36
    3 Verbs R39
    4 Modifiers R41
    5 The Sentence and Its Parts R43
    6 Phrases R44
    7 Verbals and Verbal Phrases R45
    8 Clauses R46
    9 The Structure of Sentences R47
    10 Writing Complete Sentences R48
    11 Subject-Verb Agreement R49

Vocabulary and Spelling R53
  1 Using Context Clues R53
  2 Analyzing Word Structure R54
  3 Understanding Word Origins R55
  4 Synonyms and Antonyms R57
  5 Denotation and Connotation R57
  6 Analogies R57
  7 Homonyms, Homographs, and Homophones R57
  8 Words with Multiple Meanings R58
  9 Specialized Vocabulary R58
  10 Using Reference Sources R58
  11 Spelling Rules R59
  12 Commonly Confused Words R62

Glossary of Literary and Informational Terms R64

Using the Glossary R79

Pronunciation Key R79

Glossary of Academic Vocabulary R80

Glossary of Critical Vocabulary R81

Index of Skills R85

Index of Titles and Authors R95

Acknowledgments R96

DIGITAL OVERVIEW

Connecting to Your World

Every time you read something, view something, write to someone, or react to what you've read or seen, you're participating in a world of ideas. You do this every day, inside the classroom and out. These skills will serve you not only at home and at school but eventually in your career.

The digital tools in this program will tap into the skills you already use and help you sharpen those skills for the future.

Start your exploration at my.hrw.com

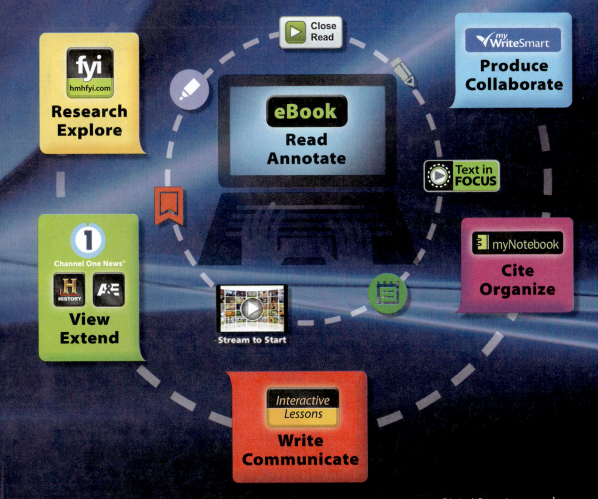

Digital Overview xix

INTERACTIVE LESSONS

Writing and Speaking & Listening

Communication in today's world requires quite a variety of skills. To express yourself and win people over, you have to be able to write for print, for online media, and for spoken presentations. To collaborate, you have to work with people who might be sitting right next to you or at the other end of an Internet connection.

Available Only in Your eBook

Interactive Lessons

These interactive lessons will help you master the skills needed to become an expert communicator.

Choosing Relevant Evidence

Choose the pieces of evidence that support the reason shown and drag them into the box.

Tip

Reality stars are often placed in situations that cause them to grow or change in a positive way.

One contestant who participated in a fashion reality show remarked, "The show made me a better designer." ✓

The winner of one cooking show won a million dollars.

According to Nielsen ratings for this season, 17 of the top 50 most popular TV shows for viewers between the ages of 18-49 were reality shows.

68% of former contestants on a popular weight-loss show have maintained their goal weight for five years post-show.

You've got it! This quotation shows how one contestant experienced personal growth.

Writing Arguments
Learn how to build a strong argument.

Interactive Lessons
1. Introduction
2. What Is a Claim?
3. Support: Reasons and Evidence
4. Building Effective Support
5. Creating a Coherent Argument
6. Persuasive Techniques
7. Formal Style
8. Concluding Your Argument

Writing Informative Texts
Shed light on complex ideas and topics.

Interactive Lessons
1. Introduction
2. Developing a Topic
3. Organizing Ideas
4. Introductions and Conclusions
5. Elaboration
6. Using Graphics and Multimedia
7. Precise Language and Vocabulary
8. Formal Style
9. Writing Business Documents

Writing Narratives
A good storyteller can always capture an audience.

Interactive Lessons
1. Introduction
2. Narrative Context
3. Point of View and Characters
4. Narrative Structure
5. Narrative Techniques
6. The Language of Narrative

Writing as a Process
Get from the first twinkle of an idea to a sparkling final draft.

Interactive Lessons
1. Introduction
2. Task, Purpose, and Audience
3. Planning and Drafting
4. Revising and Editing
5. Trying a New Approach

Producing and Publishing with Technology
Learn how to write for an online audience.

Interactive Lessons
1. Introduction
2. Writing for the Internet
3. Interacting with Your Online Audience
4. Using Technology to Collaborate

Conducting Research
There's a world of information out there. How do you find it?

Interactive Lessons
1. Introduction
2. Starting Your Research
3. Types of Sources
4. Using the Library for Research
5. Conducting Field Research
6. Using the Internet for Research
7. Taking Notes
8. Refocusing Your Inquiry

Evaluating Sources
Don't believe everything you read!

Interactive Lessons
1. Introduction
2. Evaluating Sources for Usefulness
3. Evaluating Sources for Reliability

Using Textual Evidence
Put your research into writing.

Interactive Lessons
1. Introduction
2. Synthesizing Information
3. Writing an Outline
4. Summarizing, Paraphrasing, and Quoting
5. Attribution

Participating in Collaborative Discussions
There's power in putting your heads together.

Interactive Lessons
1. Introduction
2. Preparing for Discussion
3. Establishing and Following Procedure
4. Speaking Constructively
5. Listening and Responding
6. Wrapping Up Your Discussion

Analyzing and Evaluating Presentations

Media-makers all want your attention. What are they trying to tell you?

Interactive Lessons
1. Introduction
2. Analyzing a Presentation
3. Evaluating a Speaker's Reliability
4. Tracing a Speaker's Argument
5. Rhetoric and Delivery
6. Synthesizing Media Sources

Giving a Presentation

Learn how to talk to a roomful of people.

Interactive Lessons
1. Introduction
2. Knowing Your Audience
3. The Content of Your Presentation: Argument
4. The Content of Your Presentation: Narrative
5. Style in Presentation
6. Delivering Your Presentation

Using Media in a Presentation

If a picture is worth a thousand words, just think what you can do with a video.

Interactive Lessons
1. Introduction
2. Types of Media: Audio, Video, and Images
3. Using Presentation Software
4. Practicing Your Presentation

DIGITAL SPOTLIGHT

Supporting 21st Century Skills

The amount of information people encounter each day keeps increasing. Whether you're working alone or collaborating with others, it takes effort to analyze the complex texts and competing ideas that bombard us in this fast-paced world. What can allow you succeed? Staying engaged and organized will. The digital tools in this program will help you to think critically and take charge of your learning.

Ignite your Investigation

You learn best when you're engaged. The **Stream to Start** video at the beginning of each collection is designed to inspire interest in the topics being explored. Watch it and then let your curiosity lead your investigations.

Learn How to Do a Close Read

An effective close read is all about the details; you have to examine the language and ideas a writer includes. See how it's done by accessing the **Close Read Screencasts** in your eBook. Hear modeled conversations about anchor texts.

long after we got here, Papa got a job driving a cab, and Mama worked cleaning people's houses. It was hard for them not to have the respect they were used to from holding government teaching jobs, but they had high regard for the food they could now easily buy at the store.

  Six months after we got here, the Boeing Company moved to Chicago and Mr. Bob Campbell got transferred there. When Aunt Madina left with him, it broke Mama's heart. Aunt Madina was the only person we knew from Kazakhstan, and it felt like our family just huddled together on a tiny island in the middle of a great American sea.

  I looked at the permission slip, wishing there were some special words I could say to get Mama and Papa to sign it. Around me, everyone in my homeroom was talking excitedly about the Spring Fling. Mama says she thinks the school is

Increase Your Understanding

TEXT IN FOCUS helps you dig deeper into complex texts by offering visual explanations of potential stumbling blocks. Look for **TEXT IN FOCUS** videos in anchor texts.

Annotate the Texts

Practice close reading by utilizing the powerful annotation tools in your eBook. Mark up key ideas and observations using highlighters and sticky notes. Tag unfamiliar words to create a personal word list in *my*Notebook.

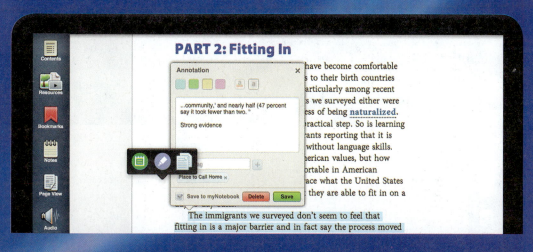

Find More Text Evidence on the Web

Tap into the *fyi* website for links to high-interest informational texts about collection topics. Synthesize information and connect notes and text evidence from any Web source by including it in *my*Notebook.

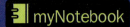 **Save and Organize Your Notes**

Save your annotations to *my*Notebook, where you can organize them to use as text evidence in performance tasks and other writing assignments. You can also organize the unfamiliar words you tagged by creating word lists, which will help you grow your vocabulary.

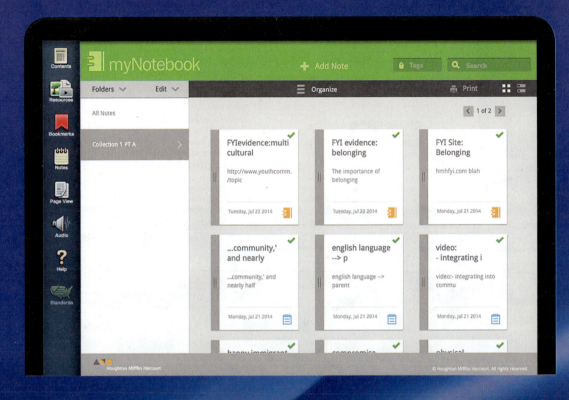

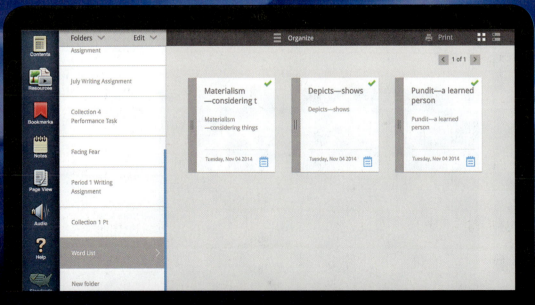

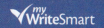

Create, Communicate, and Collaborate

Use the technology provided by the **myWriteSmart** tool to keep track of your writing assignments, create drafts, and collaborate and communicate with peers and your teacher. Use the evidence you've gathered in *my*Notebook to support your ideas.

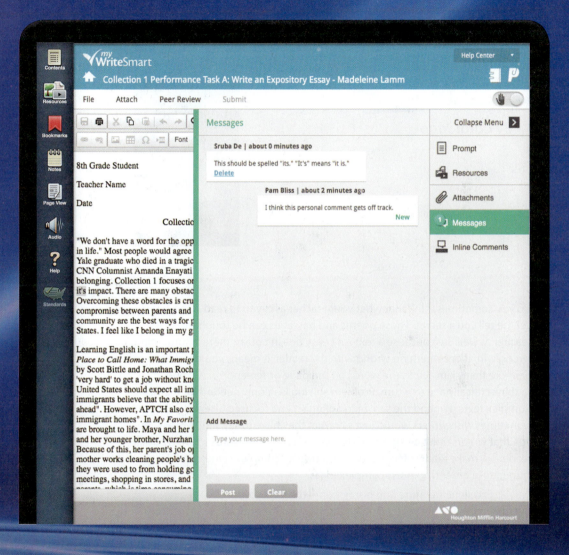

Digital Spotlight **xxix**

Making Meaning
in the 21st Century ...
or Don't Let Complex Texts Get You Down

By Carol Jago

Do you sometimes think that what your teacher asks you to read is too hard? Let me tell you a secret. Those poems and passages can be tough for your teacher as well. Just because a text isn't easy doesn't mean there is something wrong with it or something wrong with the reader. It means you need to do more than skim across the words on the page or screen. You will need to think critically at every turn. Problem solving isn't only needed for math. Complex texts demand the same kind of effort and focused attention. Do you sometimes wish writers would just say what they have to say simply? I assure you that writers don't use long sentences and unfamiliar words to annoy their readers or make readers feel dumb. They employ complex syntax and rich language in order to express complex ideas.

Excellent literature and nonfiction—the kind you will be reading over the course of the year—challenges readers in various ways. Sometimes the background of a story or the content of an essay is so unfamiliar that it is difficult to understand why characters are behaving as they do or to follow the argument a writer is making. By persevering, reading like a detective, and following clues in the text, you will find that your store of background knowledge grows. As a result, the next time you read about global issues, financial matters, political events, environmental news (like the California drought!) or health research, the text won't seem nearly as hard. The more you read, the better a reader you will become.

Good readers aren't put off by challenging text. When the going gets rough, they know what to do. Let's take vocabulary, a common measure of text complexity, as an example. Learning new words is the business of a lifetime. Rather than shutting down when you meet a word you don't know, take a moment to think about the word. Is any part of the word familiar to you? Is there something in the context of the sentence or paragraph that can help you figure out its meaning? Is there someone or something that can provide you with a definition? When reading literature or nonfiction from a time period other than our own, the text is often full of words we don't know. Each time you meet those words in succeeding readings you will be adding to your understanding of the word and its use. Your brain is a natural word-learning machine. The more you feed it complex text, the larger a vocabulary you'll have.

Have you ever been reading a long, complicated sentence and discovered that by the time you reached the end you had forgotten the beginning? Unlike the sentences we speak or dash off in a note to a friend, complex text is often full of sentences that are not only lengthy but also constructed in intricate ways. Such sentences require readers to slow down and figure out how phrases relate to one another as well as who is doing what to whom. Remember, rereading isn't cheating. It is exactly what experienced readers know to do when they meet dense text on the page. On the pages that follow you will find stories and articles that challenge you at the sentence level. Don't be intimidated. With careful attention to how those sentences are constructed, their meaning will unfold right before your eyes.

> "Your brain is a natural word-learning machine. The more you feed it complex text, the larger a vocabulary you'll have."

That same kind of attention is required for reading the media. Every day you are bombarded with messages—online, offline, everywhere you look. These, too, are complex texts that you want to be able to see through, that is, to be able to recognize the message's source, purpose, context, intended audience, and appeals. This is what it takes to be a 21st century reader.

Another way text can be complex involves the density of the ideas in a passage. Sometimes a writer piles on so much information that you think your head might explode if you read one more detail or one more qualification. At times like this talking with a friend can really help. Sharing questions and ideas, exploring a difficult passage together, can help you tease out the meaning of even the most difficult text. Poetry is often particularly dense, and for that reason it poses particular challenges. A seemingly simple poem in terms of vocabulary and length may express extremely complex feelings and insights. Poets also love to use mythological and Biblical allusions which contemporary readers are not always familiar with. The only way to read text this complex is to read it again and again.

You are going to notice a range of complexity within each collection of readings. This spectrum reflects the range of texts that surround us: some easy, some hard, some seemingly easy but in fact hard, some seemingly hard but actually easy. Whatever their complexity, I think you will enjoy these readings tremendously. Remember, read for your life!

COLLECTION 1

Culture and Belonging

“Culture is the widening of the mind and of the spirit.”
—Jawaharlal Nehru

COLLECTION 1

Culture and Belonging

In this collection, you will explore how people develop their own identity within a new culture.

COLLECTION
PERFORMANCE TASK Preview

At the end of this collection, you will have the opportunity to complete two performance tasks:

- In one, you will conduct research and write an informative essay on the best ways for newcomers to adjust to living in the United States.

- In the second, you will write a personal narrative about adjusting to a new situation or fitting in with different groups.

ACADEMIC VOCABULARY

Study the words and their definitions in the chart below. You will use these words as you discuss and write about the texts in this collection.

Word	Definition	Related Forms
contribute (kən-trĭb´yo͞ot) v.	to give or supply for a common purpose	contribution, contributor, contributing
immigrate (ĭm´ĭ-grāt´) v.	to enter and settle in a new country	immigrant, immigration, migrate, migratory
reaction (rē-ăk´shən) n.	a response to something	react, reactionary
relocate (rē-lō´kāt) v.	to move to a new place	relocated, relocation
shifting (shĭft´ĭng) adj.	changing attitudes, judgments, or emphases	shift, shifted

Background *In addition to being the author of more than a dozen novels for young adults,* **Jean Davies Okimoto** *(b. 1942) is a therapist. Perhaps that is why she has such insight into the characters that she portrays. Okimoto typically writes about the everyday problems and challenges faced by teenagers like Maya, the main character in "My Favorite Chaperone." Maya and her family have come to the United States from Kazakhstan, a country in Central Asia that used to be part of the Soviet Union.*

My Favorite Chaperone

Short Story by Jean Davies Okimoto

SETTING A PURPOSE As you read, pay attention to Maya's interactions with her family and her friends. How do these interactions help you to understand the challenges of being an immigrant in a new country?

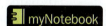

myNotebook

As you read, mark up the text. Save your work to *myNotebook*.
- Highlight details
- Add notes and questions
- Add new words to *myWordList*

In homeroom when Mr. Horswill handed out the permission slip for the Spring Fling, the all-school dance, I almost didn't take one. Why should I bother when I was sure the answer would be the same? Even though I'm in ninth grade now, it would still be the same. No. *Nyet* is what they say, and I don't want to hear this again. But I took a permission slip anyway. I don't know why I didn't just shake my head when this very popular girl Marcia Egness was handing them out. And even after I took one, I don't know why I didn't throw it away. Maybe I just couldn't give up hope. It's like that in America. It's a place where things can change for people, and many people always seem to have hope. At least that's how it seems to me. Maybe I was beginning to think this way, too, although my hope was very small.

We came to America through an international dating magazine. I don't mean that our whole family was in the magazine looking for dates, just Madina Zhamejakova, my aunt. Aunt Madina came after Kazakhstan broke away from the Soviet Union and things got very hard. Everyone's pay was cut and the *tenge*, our money, was worth less and less. Then my grandmother died. That was the worst part. She was the head of our family, and without her everything fell apart. That's when Aunt Madina started reading international dating magazines.

The next thing we knew, she had a beautiful photo taken of herself wearing her best outfit, a black dress with a scoop neck and a red silk band around the neck. Aunt Madina is very pretty. Mama says she looks like an old American movie star we saw on TV named Natalie Wood, except Aunt Madina looks more Kazakh with her dark, beautiful Asian eyes. She sent the photo to one of these magazines, and in a very short time a man from Seattle saw her picture. He started calling her, and they would talk on the phone for hours. I guess he had plenty of money for these calls, which Aunt Madina thought was a good sign. After about six months, he asked her to marry him.

His name was Bob Campbell and he'd been in the navy. He told Aunt Madina he never had a chance to meet anyone because he traveled so much. Maybe that was true, but Mama was worried.

"Madina, something must be wrong with this man if he has to find a wife through a magazine."

Mama was afraid for her, but Aunt Madina went to America anyway and married Mr. Bob Campbell. She phoned us a lot from America, and Mama admitted she sounded okay. Madina said Bob was a lot older and had less hair than in the picture he had sent her. He was also fatter than in the picture, but he was very nice. She sounded so good, Mama stopped worrying about Aunt Madina, but then things got so bad in Kazakhstan that she worried all the time about us. Papa and Mama lost their teaching jobs because the government was running out of money. Mama had to go to the market and sell many of our things: clothes, dishes, even some furniture. When Aunt Madina asked us to come to America for the hundredth time, we were running out of things to sell and my parents finally agreed. Aunt Madina **sponsored** us, and not

sponsor
(spŏn′sər) *v.* If you *sponsor* someone, you support his or her admission into a group.

long after we got here, Papa got a job driving a cab, and Mama worked cleaning people's houses. It was hard for them not to have the respect they were used to from holding government teaching jobs, but they had high regard for the food they could now easily buy at the store.

Six months after we got here, the Boeing Company moved to Chicago and Mr. Bob Campbell got transferred there. When Aunt Madina left with him, it broke Mama's heart. Aunt Madina was the only person we knew from Kazakhstan, and it felt like our family just huddled together on a tiny island in the middle of a great American sea.

I looked at the permission slip, wishing there were some special words I could say to get Mama and Papa to sign it. Around me, everyone in my homeroom was talking excitedly about the Spring Fling. Mama says she thinks the school is strange to have parties and events after school when students should be doing their homework. Ever since I've been at Beacon Junior High, the only slip they signed was for the gymnastics team. Papa loves sports. (I think he told Mama that giving permission for this activity was important for my education.) I can't find words to say how grateful I was he signed that slip. The gymnastics team is a fine, good thing in my life. I compete in all the events: vault, beam, floor exercise, and my favorite: the uneven bars. I love to swing up and up, higher and higher, and as I fly through the air, a wonderful thing happens and suddenly I have no worries and no responsibilities. I'm free!

But there's another reason why I love gymnastics. Shannon Lui is on the team. We became friends when she was a teaching assistant in my ESL class. We're the same age, but she says I'm like her little sister. Her grandparents came from China, and her parents speak perfect English. Everything about Shannon's family is very American. Her mother has a red coat with gold buttons from Nordstrom, and her father cooks and sometimes even washes dishes! (I couldn't believe this when I first saw it; no Kazakh man would do kitchen work.) Shannon encouraged me to try out for the gymnastics team, and the team has meant even more to me this year since I got put in the mainstream and had to leave ESL. Since I left ESL, I often feel like I'm in the middle of a game where I don't know the players, the rules, or even the object of the game.

In my next class, Language Arts, even though I knew it was foolish, I was dreaming of the Spring Fling. I really like Language Arts. Ms. Coe, our teacher, is also the gymnastics coach, and there's a guy in the class, Daniel Klein, who was my partner for a research project last semester. He encouraged me to talk and listened to what I had to say (he's also a very handsome guy), and I always look forward to this class so I can see him. I was trying to think of some ideas to convince Mama and Papa to give permission (and also sneaking glances at Daniel Klein) when Mr. Walsh, the vice-principal, came into our class. He whispered something to Ms. Coe and she nodded. And then I was **stunned** because she nodded and pointed to me!

"Maya, you're wanted in the office," Ms. Coe said. "You can go now with Mr. Walsh."

My fingers tingled with fear. What was wrong? What had I done? Mr. Walsh only comes for people when there's trouble.

Like a robot, I gathered my books and followed Mr. Walsh. As he closed the classroom door behind us, my heart began to bang and I felt like I needed to go to the bathroom. In the hallway he told me Ms. Johnson, the school counselor, wanted to speak with me.

"What is wrong?" My voice came out as a whisper. I felt such terror I could barely speak.

"What's that?" Mr. Walsh couldn't hear my whisper.

"What is wrong?" I tried to speak more loudly.

"She didn't say. She just asked me to find you since I was heading down the hall anyway."

I suddenly remembered Sunstar Sysavath, who was in my ESL class last year. Her family came from Cambodia, and on her first day at Beacon she was in the wrong line in the lunchroom. Mr. Walsh went to help her, and he tapped her on her shoulder to get her attention. When she felt the tap and saw him, she lifted her hands in the air as if she were being arrested and about to be shot. People who saw this in the lunchroom laughed, but it wasn't a joke. Sunstar was filled with terror.

I knew I wouldn't be shot, but walking with Mr. Walsh to the office seemed like one of the longest walks of my life. I often fill my mind with nice things, such as imagining myself at the Olympics winning a gold medal for the U.S.A.— especially on days like today, when we have a gymnastics meet

stun
(stŭn) *v.* To *stun* someone is to make him or her feel shocked or dazed.

after school. But now my mind was filled with nothing. It was empty, like a dry riverbed where there is only cracked, baked earth and nothing lives.

I walked into the main office, where Ms. Johnson was waiting for me. "Come with me, Maya." Ms. Johnson smiled at Mr. Walsh. "Thanks, Tom."

Like a person made from wood, a puppet, I followed Ms. Johnson through the main office down the hall to her office across from the principal's. She showed me in and closed the door behind us.

"Sit down, dear."

I sat in a chair across from her desk and clutched my books to my chest. I'd never been in her office before. She had many nice green plants in front of the window and a small fish tank in one corner. I stared at the brightly colored fish swimming back and forth, back and forth. Then Ms. Johnson spoke.

"I received a call from Mr. Shanaman, the principal at Evergreen Elementary, and your brother's been suspended for fighting."

"Nurzhan?"

"Yes. Nurzhan Alazova." She read his name from a pink message slip. "They haven't been able to locate your mother, so they called over here to see if you could help."

"Is Nurzhan all right?"

"Yes. And I believe the other boy wasn't seriously hurt."

"Who did Nurzhan fight?" It was a foolish question—I was sure of the answer. Ms. Johnson hesitated, so I just said, "Ossie Nishizono," and she nodded.

"What must I do?" I asked.

"The school policy on suspension requires that the parent or guardian must have a conference at school within twenty-four hours of the suspension. Can you help us locate your mother or your father?"

"Yes. I can do that."

"Do your parents speak English, Maya?"

"Just a little."

"Then perhaps you could attend the meeting and translate for them."

"Yes. I must always do this for my parents—at the store, at the doctor, things like that."

"Here's the phone. I'll step out to give you some privacy."

Ms. Johnson left the office, quietly closing the door behind her. I looked at the nameplate on her desk. CATHERINE JOHNSON, it said. Outside her window, the sky was gray and it had started to rain. I stared at the phone, wishing I didn't have to be the messenger with this bad news. Then I called the Northwest Cab Company and asked them to contact my father.

"Aibek Alazova. Cab 191. I'm his daughter, and there is a family problem I must speak with him about."

I stayed on the line while the **dispatcher** radioed Papa. I looked at the clock and felt my heart grow heavy. In a minute the bell would ring, school would be out, and the gymnastics meet would begin.

"Maya!" Papa's voice was alarmed. "What is wrong?"

"Nurzhan has been in a fight with another boy." Then I explained in Russian what had happened, and Papa said he had to drop his passenger at the Four Seasons Hotel downtown and then he'd come straight to Nurzhan's school. He'd be there about three-thirty.

Ms. Johnson came back into the office as I hung up the phone. "Did you get your mother?"

"I don't have the number where she works today, but I got my father. He will come to the school."

"Good."

dispatcher
(dĭs-păch´ər) *n.* A *dispatcher* is a person who sends out vehicles according to a schedule.

"Ms. Johnson?"

"Yes?"

"I will leave now for Evergreen. Will you tell Ms. Coe I have a family problem and I cannot attend the gymnastics meet?"

"Of course. And I'll call Mr. Shanaman at Evergreen now and let him know that you and your father will be there."

I went to my locker, got my coat, then walked quickly down the hall to the south door that opens onto the play field that joins our school with Evergreen. Poor Nurzhan, getting in such big trouble. I couldn't fault him for fighting with Ossie Nishizono. Such a mean boy—he'd been teasing Nurzhan without mercy for not speaking well and mispronouncing things. I hoped Nurzhan had given him a hard punch. But why did he have to make this fight today! I felt angry that I had to miss the meet because of Nurzhan. Would Ms. Coe still want me on the team? Would she think I wasn't reliable?

But as I neared Nurzhan's school—my old school—I only worried about Papa. Even though he didn't shout at me on the phone, that didn't mean he wasn't angry. He had a person in his cab and the dispatcher might have been hearing us. Probably the dispatcher didn't know Russian, but Papa wouldn't show his anger in the cab anyway. But Papa could be very, very angry—not just with Nurzhan but with me, too. He and Mama think it's my duty to watch out for Nurzhan and keep him out of trouble.

As I walked up to the front door, Mr. Zabornik, the custodian, waved to me. He was picking up papers and litter around the bushes next to the front walk. It was still raining lightly, and Mr. Zabornik's wet gray hair was pasted against his forehead.

"Hi, Maya."

"Hello, Mr. Zabornik."

"Here about your brother, I suppose."

"How did you know?"

"I was fixing the drainpipe when it happened." He pointed to the corner of the building by the edge of the play field. "That kid Ossie Nishizono was teasing Nurzhan something fierce. Telling him he could never be a real American, making fun of the way he talked." He bent down and picked up a candy wrapper. "Reminded me of how this bully used to treat me when my family came after the revolution."

"Oh." I think Mr. Zabornik could tell I didn't know what revolution this was.

"The Hungarian revolution, in 1956." He looked out over the play field and folded his arms across his chest. "Guess some things never change."

"Nurzhan's going to be suspended."

"Sorry to hear that. 'Course, the school can't allow fights, and this was no **scuffle**. But I can sure see how your brother lost his temper." Then he went back to picking up the litter. "Good luck."

"Thank you, Mr. Zabornik."

I went to the front office, where Ms. Illo, the head secretary, spoke to me in a very kind way. "Maya, Mr. Shanaman is waiting for you in his office. You can go right in."

Mr. Shanaman was behind his big desk, and Nurzhan was sitting on a chair in the corner. He looked like a rabbit caught in a trap. He had scrapes on his hands and on his cheek, and his eyes were puffed up. I couldn't tell if that was from crying or being hit.

"I understand your father will be coming. Is that right, Maya?"

I nodded.

"Just take a seat by your brother. Ms. Illo will bring your father in when he gets here."

Then Mr. Shanaman read some papers on his desk and I sat down next to Nurzhan and spoke quietly to him in Russian.

"*Neechevo, Nurzhan. Ya vas ne veenu.*" It's okay, Nurzhan. I don't blame you, is what I said.

Nurzhan's eyes were wet with tears as he nodded to me.

I stared out the principal's window. Across the street, the bare branches of the trees were black against the cement gray sky. The rain came down in a steady drizzle, and after a few minutes, I saw Papa's cab turn the corner. His cab is green, the color of a lime, and he always washes and shines it. I watched Papa park and get out of the cab. His shoulders are very broad underneath his brown leather jacket, and Papa has a powerful walk, like a large, strong horse that plows fields. He walked briskly, and as he came up the steps of the school, he removed his driver cap.

scuffle
(skŭf´əl) *n.* A *scuffle* is a disorderly fight.

It seemed like one thousand years, but it was only a minute before Ms. Illo brought Papa into the office. Nurzhan and I stood up when he entered, but he didn't look at us, only at Mr. Shanaman, who shook hands with him and motioned for him to have a seat.

Papa sat across the desk from Mr. Shanaman and placed his driver cap in his lap.

"We have asked Maya to translate, Mr. Alazova."

"Yes." Papa nodded. When he heard my name, he understood what Mr. Shanaman meant.

"Your son, Nurzhan, was involved in quite a nasty fight."

Papa looked at me, and I said to him in Russian, "Nurzhan was in little fight."

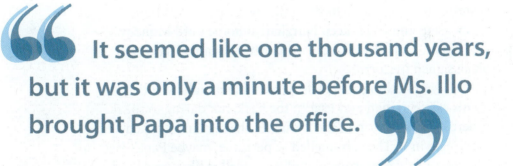

Mr. Shanaman continued. "The other boy, Ossie Nishizono, needed two stitches at the hospital."

"The other boy, Ossie Nishizono, was a little hurt," I told Papa.

Nurzhan's eyes became wide as he listened to my translation.

"We have a policy that anyone who fights must be suspended from school. Both boys will receive a two-day suspension."

"The other boy, who is very bad," I translated for Papa, "is not allowed to come to school for two days and his parents must punish him. Nurzhan must stay home, too. But he should not be punished so much."

Papa nodded.

Then Mr. Shanaman said, "We've been told the other boy was teasing your son. We'd like you to help Nurzhan find ways to handle this situation without resorting to violence. We're working with the other boy to help him show respect for all students."

I looked at Papa and translated: "The other boy was teasing Nurzhan in a violent manner. This boy will be punished and must learn to respect all students. We understand how Nurzhan became so angry, and we ask that you punish him by not allowing him to watch television."

"Yes, I will punish my son as you suggest," Papa said in Russian.

I looked at Mr. Shanaman. "My father says he will teach Nurzhan not to fight by giving him a very serious punishment."

"We are glad you understand the serious nature of this situation," Mr. Shanaman said. Then I told Papa in Russian the exact words of Mr. Shanaman.

Mr. Shanaman held out a form on a clipboard. "We require you to sign this to show that we've discussed the suspension and you'll keep Nurzhan at home until Monday."

Again, I told Papa exactly what Mr. Shanaman said, and Papa signed the form.

We said nothing as we left the school and followed Papa to his cab. Nurzhan and I sat in the back, not daring to speak. There was a small rip in the leather of the seat and I poked my finger in it. The cab smelled of perfume; maybe Papa's last ride was a lady who wore a lot of it. It smelled like some kind of flower, but I couldn't name it. I wished so much I was in a beautiful meadow right then, surrounded by sweet-smelling flowers, lying in the soft grass, looking up at the clouds. I tried to calm myself by thinking about this meadow, but I just kept feeling scared—scared Papa might somehow find out I'd changed what Mr. Shanaman said.

Maybe I should've felt bad about changing Mr. Shanaman's words, but I didn't. I only felt afraid. I don't mean that I think changing words like that is okay; I have to admit it's sort of like telling lies. But I think maybe some lies are okay, like in the play we read last semester about Anne Frank and how the people who were hiding her family lied and said no one was in the attic when they really were. They lied to save Anne's family from the Nazis. Maybe I wasn't saving Nurzhan from death, but I was sure scared to death of what Papa might have done if I hadn't changed the words. I stared at the back of Papa's thick neck. It was very red, and he drove in silence until he pulled up in front of our building. Papa shut off the engine. Then he put his arm across the top of the seat and turned his face to us, craning his neck.

His dark eyes narrowed and his voice was severe. "I am ashamed of this! To come to this school and find you in trouble, Nurzhan! This does not seem like much punishment to me, this no watching television. You will go to bed tonight without dinner." He clenched his teeth. "I have lost money today because of you. And Maya, you must keep your brother out of trouble!" Then he waved us away furiously, like shooing away bugs. "Go now! Go!"

We went in the house, and Nurzhan marched straight to the table in the kitchen with his books. He seemed to be in such a hurry to do his work, he didn't even take off his jacket.

"Take off your jacket and hang it up, Nurzhan."

"Okay."

I began peeling potatoes for dinner, while Nurzhan hung up his jacket. Then he sat back down at the table.

"Maya, I—"

"Don't talk. Do your work."

"But I—"

"I missed the gymnastics meet because of you!"

"Watch the knife!" Nurzhan looked scared.

I glanced at my hand. I was holding the knife and I'd been waving it without realizing it.

"I wasn't going to stab you, stupid boy."

"I was only going to say thank you." Nurzhan looked glumly at his book.

I went back to peeling the potatoes. I'd had enough of him and his troubles.

"For changing what Mr. Shanaman said when you told Papa," he said in a timid voice, like a little chick peeping.

"It's okay, Nurzhan." I sighed. "Just do your work."

A few minutes before six, we heard Mama get home. She came straight to the kitchen, and when she saw Nurzhan sitting there doing his work, a smile came over her tired face.

"Oh, what a good boy, doing his work."

"Not so good, Mama. Nurzhan got in trouble." I didn't mind having to tell her this bad news too much (not like when I had to call Papa). Then I explained about the fight and how Papa had to come to the school.

"Oh, my poor little one!" Mama rushed to Nurzhan and examined his hands. Tenderly, she touched his face where it had been cut. Then she turned sharply toward me.

"Maya! How could you let this happen?"

"Me! I wasn't even there."

"On the bus, when this boy is so bad to Nurzhan. You must make this boy stop."

"No, Mama," Nurzhan explained. "He would tease me more if my sister spoke for me."

"I don't understand this. In Kazakhstan, if someone insults you, they have insulted everyone in the family. And everyone must respond."

"It's different here, Mama."

Mama looked sad. She sighed deeply. Then the phone rang and she told me to answer it. Mama always wants me to answer because she is shy about speaking English. When her work calls, I always speak on the phone to the women whose houses she cleans and then translate for Mama. (I translate their exact words, not like with Mr. Shanaman.)

But it wasn't for Mama. It was Shannon, and her voice was filled with worry.

"Maya, why weren't you at the meet? Is everything all right?"

"Everything's okay. It was just Nurzhan." Then I explained to her about what had happened. "I hope I can still be on the team."

"Ms. Coe is cool. Don't worry, it won't mess anything up."

Shannon was right. The next day at practice Ms. Coe was very understanding. Practice was so much fun I forgot all about Nurzhan, and Shannon and I were very excited because Ms. Coe said we were going to get new team leotards.

After practice we were waiting for the activity bus, talking about the kind of leotards we wanted, when two guys from the wrestling team joined us. One was David Pfeiffer, a guy who Shannon talked about all the time. She always said he was so cute, that he was "awesome" and "incredible" and things like that. She was often laughing and talking to him after our practice, and I think she really liked him. And today he was with Daniel Klein!

"Hey, Maya! How was practice?"

"Hi." I smiled at Daniel, but then I glanced away, pretending to look for the bus because talking to guys outside class always made me feel embarrassed and shy.

The guys came right up to us. David smiled at Shannon. "Wrestling practice was great! We worked on takedowns and escapes, and then lifted weights. How was your practice?"

"Fun! We spent most of it on the beam."

"I'm still pumped from weight training!" David grinned and picked up a metal trash can by the gym door. He paraded around with the can, then set it down with a bang right next to Shannon. Everyone was laughing, and then David bent his knees and bounced up and down on his heels and said, "Check this out, Daniel! Am I strong or what?" The next thing we knew, David had one arm under Shannon's knees and one arm under her back and he scooped her up. Shannon squealed and laughed, and I was laughing watching them, when all of a sudden Daniel scooped me up too!

"*Chort*!" I shouted, as he lifted me. I grabbed him around his neck to hang on, and my head was squished against his shoulder. He strutted around in a circle before he let me down. I could feel that my face was the color of borscht, and I flamed with excitement and embarrassment and couldn't stop laughing from both joy and nervousness.

"That's nothing, man." David crouched like a weight lifter while he was still holding Shannon and lifted her as high as his shoulders.

It was exciting and crazy: Daniel and David showing each other how strong they were, first picking up Shannon and me, then putting us down, then picking us up and lifting us higher, as if Shannon and I were weights. After a few times, whenever Daniel picked me up, I was easily putting my arms around his neck, and I loved being his pretend weight, even though Shannon and I were both yelling for them to put us down. (We didn't really mean it. Shannon is a strong girl, and if she didn't like being lifted up and held by David, there was no way it would be happening.) I couldn't believe it, but I began to relax in Daniel's arms, and I laughed each time as he slowly turned in a circle.

Then Shannon and I tried to pick them up, and it was hilarious. Every time we tried to grab them, they did wrestling moves on us and we ended up on the grass in a big heap, like a litter of playful puppies. I couldn't remember a time in my life that had been so fun and so exciting. We lay on the grass laughing, and then David and Daniel jumped up and picked Shannon and me up again.

But this time when we turned, as my face was pressed against Daniel's shoulder, I saw something coming toward the school that made me tremble with fear.

"Daniel, please. Put me down!" My voice cracked as my breath caught in my throat.

But Daniel didn't hear. Everyone was shouting and laughing, and he lifted me up even more as the lime green cab came to a halt in front of the school. The door slammed. Papa stood like a huge bull in his dark leather jacket and flung open the back door of the cab.

"MAYA ALAZOVA!" His voice roared across the parking lot. He pointed at me the way one might identify a criminal. "*EDEE SUDA!*" he shouted in Russian. COME HERE!

Daniel dropped me and I ran to the cab, **whimpering** and trembling inside like a dog caught stealing a chicken.

Papa didn't speak. His silence filled every corner of the cab like a dark cloud, slowly suffocating me with its poisonous rage. Papa's neck was deep red, and the skin on the back of my hands tingled with fear. I lay my head back against the seat and closed my eyes, squeezing them shut, and took myself far away until I was safe on the bars at a beautiful gymnastics meet in the sky. I swung back and forth, higher and higher, and then I released and flew to the next bar through fluffy white clouds as soft as goose feathers, while the air around me was sweet and warm, and my teammates cheered for me, their voices filled with love.

whimper
(hwĭm′pər) *v.* To *whimper* is to sob or let out a soft cry.

We screeched to a stop in front of our building. My head slammed back against the seat. When I struggled from the taxi, it was as though I had fallen from the bars, crashing down onto the street, where I splintered into a million pieces. And as hard as I tried, I couldn't get back on the bars any more than I could stop the hot tears that spilled from my eyes. Papa roared in front of me, and as he charged toward the door in his glistening dark leather jacket, he again seemed transformed to a creature that was half man and half bull.

"Gulnara!" He flung open the door, shouting for Mama, his voice filled with anger and blame.

"Why are you here? What has happened, Aibek?" Mama came from the kitchen as Nurzhan darted to the doorway and peeked around like a little squirrel.

I closed the front door and leaned against it with my wet palms flat against the wood, like a prisoner about to be shot.

"Is this how you raise your daughter! Is this what you teach her? Lessons to be a toy for American boys!" Papa spat out the words.

The color rose in Mama's face like a flame turned up on the stove, and she spun toward me, her eyes flashing. "What have you done?"

"Your daughter was in the arms of an American boy."

Mama looked shocked. "When? H-how can this be?" she stammered.

"Outside the school as I drove by, I found them at this. Don't you teach her anything?"

"Who let her stay after school? Who gives permission for all these things? You are the one, Aibek. If you left it to me, she would come home every day. She would not have this permission!"

Mama and Papa didn't notice that I went to the bathroom and locked the door. I huddled by the sink and heard their angry voices rise and fall like the pounding of thunder, and then I heard a bang, so fierce that the light bulb hanging from the ceiling swayed with its force. Papa slamming the front door. Then I heard the engine of the cab and a sharp squeal of tires as he sped away.

I imagined running away. I would run like the wind, behind the mini-mart, sailing past the E-Z Dry Cleaner, past the bus stop in an easy gallop through the crosswalk. As I ran, each traffic light I came to would turn green, until there would be a string of green lights glowing like a necklace of emeralds strung all down the street. And then I would be at the Luis' house. Mrs. Lui would greet me in her red Nordstrom coat with the gold buttons. She would hug me and hold me close. Then Mr. Lui would say, "Hi, honey," and make hamburgers. "Want to use the phone, Maya?" Mrs. Lui would say. "Talk as long as you want—we have an extra line for the kids."

"Oh, by the way," Mr. Lui would say, "Shannon is having David and some other kids over Friday night for pizza and videos. It's fine if there's a guy you want to invite, too."

"Maya! Open this door. Do you want more trouble?" Mama rattled the doorknob so hard I thought she'd rip it off.

"I'm coming." My voice caught in my throat. I felt dizzy as I unlocked the door and held my stomach, afraid I would be sick.

"You have brought shame to your father and to this family." Mama glared at me.

"Mama, it was just kids joking. Guys from the wrestling team pretending some of us were weights."

"I don't know this weights."

"It was nothing, Mama!"

"Do not tell me 'nothing' when your father saw you!" she screamed.

The next morning Papa was gone when I woke up. And even though Mama hadn't yet left for work, it was like she was gone, too. She didn't speak to me and didn't even look at me, except once when she came in the kitchen. I was getting *kasha*, and she stared at me like I was a stranger to her. Then she turned and left. Not only was Mama not speaking to me, but she didn't speak to Nurzhan, either. This never happens. Even when he was punished for the fight with Ossie Nishizono and had to stay home, Mama still spoke to him. But as I was getting dressed in my room, I heard Nurzhan try to talk to her. I put my ear to the door to listen.

"It's different here, Mama. I'm sure Maya and those guys were playing. Joking, like in a game."

"Quiet, boy! You know nothing of these things!"

I was shocked. Mama hardly ever says a harsh word to her precious boy. Then I heard her rush by, and then *bam*! The door slammed. The *kamcha* that hung by the door trembled with the force. We brought our *kamcha* when we came to

America. It looks like a riding crop with a carved wooden handle and a leather cord, decorated with some horsehair. It's an old Kazakh tradition to put the *kamcha* inside the house next to the door because it's believed to bring good fortune and happiness. But our *kamcha* was not bringing us good fortune today. Mama left without a word of goodbye to either one of us.

> **I didn't feel happy that Nurzhan got yelled at; I felt bad about the whole thing.**

I came out of my room and Nurzhan and I just looked at each other. I didn't feel happy that Nurzhan got yelled at; I felt bad about the whole thing.

"Did you hear?"

I nodded.

"She won't listen."

"Thank you for trying, Nurzhan."

"It did no good," he said with sadness. "They don't know about things here, only their own ways. They are like stone."

I wondered how long this tension and anger would stay in our home. I was afraid it might be a long time, because Mama and Papa were so upset. But gradually, in the way that winter becomes spring, there was a slight thaw each day. Perhaps because we huddled together like a tiny Kazakh island in the middle of the great American sea, we couldn't allow our winter to go on and on, and by the next week, things in my family were almost calm.

But it was not to last. On Wednesday afternoon of the following week, Mama was waiting to talk to me when I got home from school. I was afraid when I saw her. Her ankle was taped up, and she sat on the couch with her leg up on a chair. Next to it was a pair of crutches!

"Mama, what happened?"

"I fell at work. Mrs. Hormann took me to the emergency room. I can't work for six weeks until it heals. I must keep my foot up as much as possible."

"I'll start dinner." My eyes filled with tears, I felt so bad for her. And I felt bad that I'd made them so upset when my father saw me and Daniel. Even though I knew I hadn't done anything wrong, it still bothered me that I'd been the cause of such trouble in our house.

It was decided that I'd take Mama's jobs for her while she couldn't work. I wouldn't go to gymnastics practice; instead, right after school I'd go straight to the houses Mama cleaned. The people Mama worked for agreed to this, and I worked at each house from three-thirty until six-thirty, when Papa came to pick me up. I wasn't able to clean their entire houses in this amount of time, but they told me which rooms were the most important, and I was able to clean those. Bathrooms were on the list at every house.

I didn't mind doing Mama's jobs. Although I did get very tired, and I was scared sometimes that I might break something when I dusted (especially at Mrs. Hathaway's house, because she had a lot of glass vases and some small glass birds), but I didn't mind vacuuming, mopping, dusting, cleaning cupboards, counters, stoves, and refrigerators. I didn't even mind cleaning toilets. It was as if all the work I did at Mama's jobs was to make up for the problems I'd caused. And besides, our family needed the money.

When I finished working for Mama, as soon as I got home I had to make dinner for everyone. Each day I got more tired, and on Friday, when I was peeling potatoes, I cut my finger. I thought it was just a little cut, so I washed it off and continued to peel.

Nurzhan looked up from the table, where he was doing his work. "What's wrong with the potatoes?"

"Nothing," I said automatically, with my eyes half-closed.

"They're red!"

"What?"

"The potatoes, Maya. They look like you painted them with red streaks."

I looked down and saw my finger bleeding on the potatoes, and it scared me to be so tired that I hadn't seen this. "It's just blood, Nurzhan. I cut myself. It'll wash off."

"Oh, yuck."

"Quiet, boy! I said I would wash it off."

That night at dinner, Nurzhan refused to eat the potatoes, even though there was no sign of blood on them, and I wanted to take the whole dish and dump them on his head.

The next week I was so tired after going to school and cleaning Mrs. Hathaway's house that I burned the chicken. After I put it in the oven, I sat at the table with Nurzhan to do my homework. I rested my head on my book for just a minute, and the next thing I knew, Nurzhan was pounding on my arm.

"Maya! The oven!" he shouted.

I woke to see smoke seeping from the oven. "Oh, no!"

I leaped up and grabbed a dishtowel and pulled the pan from the oven. The chicken was very dark but not black, although all the juice at the bottom of the pan had burned and was smoking. "It's okay, Nurzhan. We can still eat it."

"Good."

Nurzhan didn't mind the almost-burned chicken that night, but Papa did.

"This tastes like my shoe!" Papa grumbled.

"Aibek, I have to keep my foot up, and Maya is doing the best she can. It is not easy. She must go to school, then do my work, then cook for us. She is just a young girl."

I looked at Mama and felt tears in my eyes. I couldn't remember another time when Mama spoke on my behalf, and my tears were the kind you have when you know someone is on your side.

The next evening as dinner was cooking, I sat with Nurzhan at the kitchen table and helped him with his spelling words. While I waited for him to think how to spell *admire*, I took the permission slip for the Spring Fling from my notebook and stared at it. I'd never thrown it away.

"A-D-M-I-E-R."

"Almost, Nurzhan. It's this," I said as I wrote the correct spelling on the top of the permission slip and turned it for him to see.

"A-D-M-I-R-E," he spelled. Then he looked closely at the slip. "What's this for?"

"It's a permission slip for the Spring Fling, the all-school dance, but it is only good for scratch paper to help you with spelling. Papa will never let me go. I don't know why I trouble myself to keep such a thing."

Nurzhan took the slip and put it in his notebook.

"What are you doing with it?"

"Let me try."

"Try what?"

"Let me try to get permission for you from Papa."

I laughed. "Oh, Nurzhan. Don't be foolish. You waste your time. Papa will never change his thinking because of you."

"I will try anyway. When he comes home tonight, I will speak to him myself. I have a plan."

I could only smile a sad smile at the idea of little Nurzhan trying to change the mind of Papa, who is a man like a boulder.

After dinner I went to my room to study, leaving Nurzhan to talk with Mama and Papa. I was afraid to really hope that any good thing could come from Nurzhan's plan. To hope and then be disappointed seemed to be worse. It was better not to hope and to live my dreams through Shannon. I could at least hear every little detail of her experience at the dance and be happy for her, giving up the idea that I'd ever be the one who goes to the dance, too.

But I comforted myself thinking about the dream in my life that really had come true—the gymnastics team. I still had that, and I was warming my heart with thoughts of the team when Nurzhan burst into the room.

"Maya! You can go!" Nurzhan jumped up and down like a little monkey, and I stared at him in disbelief.

"Don't joke with me about such a thing, boy!" I snapped.

"No! It's true. Look!" He waved the permission slip in front of my face.

I stared at the slip, still in disbelief. *Aibek Alazova*... Papa's name and Papa's writing. *It was true*! I was still staring at the slip, still afraid to completely believe that such a thing could be true, when Mama and Papa came in.

"We give permission for this, Maya, because Nurzhan will go, too," Mama said.

"He will not leave your side," Papa announced in a most serious tone. "He is your *capravazhdieuushee*."

"Chaperone." I said the English word. I knew this word because the parents who help the teachers supervise the kids at school activities are called this. But I hadn't heard of a little boy being a chaperone.

"Thank you, Mama. Thank you, Papa."

"It is Nurzhan you must thank," Mama said.

I thanked Nurzhan, too, and Mama and Papa left our room. Then I heard the front door close and I knew Papa had left for work.

That night Nurzhan and I whispered in our beds after Mama had gone to sleep.

"Nurzhan, what will I tell my friends when you come to the dance?"

"Don't worry. I thought about that problem. You will tell them you must baby-sit for me."

"But at a dance?"

"I think it will work. At least it is better than to say I am your chaperone."

"That is true."

I watched the orange light of the mini-mart sign blink on and off, and I heard Nurzhan's slow breathing as he fell asleep.

"Thank you, Nurzhan," I whispered as I began to dream of the dance.

The morning of the dance, Mama came into the kitchen while Nurzhan and I were eating *kasha*. Mama still had a wrap on her ankle, but she was walking without her crutches now. She was happier, and I could tell she felt better. It was better for me, too. When Mama was happier, I didn't feel so worried about her.

"Maya, I have something for you." Mama came to the table and put a small package wrapped in tissue paper in front of me. "Open." She pointed at the package.

I looked up at her, my face full of surprise.

"Open."

Carefully, I unfolded the tissue paper and let out a gasp when I saw a small gold bracelet lying on the folds of the thin paper.

"You wear this to the dance." Mama patted my shoulder.

"Oh, Mama." I wanted to hug her like we hug on the gymnastics team, but I was too shy. We don't hug in our family.

"I forget sometimes when there is so much work that you are just a young girl. This bracelet my mother gave to me when I was sixteen. Girls and boys dance younger here, Maya. So you wear this now."

"Thank you, Mama. I will be careful with it."

"I know. You're a good girl. And Nurzhan will be right there. Always by your side."

"Yes, Mama." Nurzhan nodded.

Shannon and I met in the bathroom after school, and she loaned me her peach lip-gloss. I can't remember ever being so excited about anything, and so nervous, too.

Nurzhan was waiting by the gym door when we got out of the bathroom. Shannon and I said hi to him, and he followed us into the gym. Nurzhan found a chair next to the door and waved to us while we joined Leslie Shattuck and her sister Tina and Faith Reeves from the gymnastics team. The gym got more and more crowded, and everywhere you looked there were flocks of boys and flocks of girls, but no boys and girls together, as if they were birds that only stayed with their own kind.

Then a few ninth-grade guys and girls danced together. They were very cool and everyone watched them, except some seventh-grade boys who were pushing each other around in an empty garbage can.

Shannon and I were laughing at those silly boys when Daniel and David came up to us. I was so happy to see Daniel, even though I was embarrassed about my face, which I knew was once again the deepest red, like borscht. But the next thing I knew, Daniel had asked me to dance, and Shannon was dancing with David!

Daniel held my hand and put his arm around my waist, and I put my hand on his shoulder just the way Shannon and I had practiced so many times. It was a slow dance, and Mama's bracelet gleamed on my wrist as it lay on Daniel's shoulder.

"My little brother's here. I had to baby-sit."

"Want to check on him?" Daniel asked.

"Sure."

We danced over near Nurzhan, who sat on the chair like a tiny mouse in the corner, and I introduced him to Daniel.

"Are you doing okay?" I asked Nurzhan.

"Yes. It's a little boring though."

"I'm sorry you have to be here."

"It's not that bad. The boys in the garbage can are fun to watch. I would enjoy doing that if I came to this dance."

Then we danced away and danced even more slowly, and Daniel moved a little closer to me. I looked over, afraid that Nurzhan was watching, but all I saw was an empty chair. And then we danced closer.

Daniel and I danced four more times that afternoon (two fast and two *very* slow), and each time Nurzhan's chair was empty and he seemed to have disappeared. I didn't think too much about Nurzhan during the rest of the dance, and on the bus going home, while Shannon and I talked and talked, reliving every wonderful moment, I almost forgot he was there.

But that night when Nurzhan and I were going to sleep and I was thinking about how that day had been the best day of my life, I thanked him for making it possible for me to go to the dance.

"There's just one thing I wondered about," I whispered as the mini-mart sign blinked on and off.

"What's that?"

"Where did you go when I danced with Daniel?"

"To the bathroom."

"The bathroom?"

"Yes."

"You are an excellent chaperone."

Nurzhan and I giggled so loud that Mama came in and told us to be quiet. "Shhh, Nurzhan, Maya. Go to sleep!" She spoke sharply to both of us.

After she left, Nurzhan fell asleep right away like he usually does. But I lay awake for a while and I looked over at Nurzhan and was struck by how much things had changed. I looked at the table by my bed and saw the gold bracelet shining in the blinking light of the mini-mart sign, and I imagined Mama wearing it when she was sixteen, and I treasured what she'd said as much as the bracelet: "Girls and boys dance younger here, Maya. So you wear this now."

And I thought of Daniel, who I think is quite a special boy with a good heart. *Kak horosho.* How wonderful. Thinking of him made me smile inside. Then I closed my eyes, hoping very much that Nurzhan would like to chaperone at the next dance.

COLLABORATIVE DISCUSSION Do you think life in the United States is more challenging for Maya, for her brother, or for their parents? With a partner, discuss the story events that support your answer.

Analyze Stories: Plot

From simple fairy tales to complex novels, most stories contain a **plot,** a series of events that occur in stages of development. Most plots focus on a **conflict,** or problem faced by the main character. The five stages of plot development are

- **exposition,** in which the characters, setting, and conflict are introduced
- **rising action,** in which the character takes steps to solve the problem even while complications might be introduced
- **climax,** or point of greatest tension in the story, in which the conflict begins to be resolved
- **falling action,** in which the effects of the climax become clear
- **resolution,** in which the end of the story reveals the final outcome

To analyze a plot, examine the way events and actions in each stage increase or help to resolve the conflict.

Identify the conflict Maya faces in "My Favorite Chaperone." What is the turning point that begins to resolve her conflict?

Analyze Stories: Character

Characters are the people, animals, or imaginary creatures who take part in the action of a story. **Characterization** is the way an author reveals the traits and personality of the characters. An author may choose to reveal a character by

- describing what a character looks like
- having a narrator make direct comments about him or her
- presenting the character's thoughts, speech, and actions
- presenting other characters' thoughts, speech, and actions

Characters' speech is revealed in **dialogue,** the written conversation between two or more people in a story. Look back at Maya's dialogue with Ms. Johnson in lines 150–180. What do you learn about Maya from this conversation?

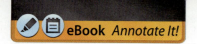

Analyzing the Text

Cite Text Evidence Support your responses with evidence from the story.

1. **Identify** What do you learn about Maya and the conflict she faces in lines 1–14?

2. **Infer** In lines 126–136, Maya tells a story about a student who immigrates to the United States from Cambodia. How does this story advance, or add details to, the plot's rising action?

3. **Draw Conclusions** Reread lines 295–337. Complete a chart like this one to show how Maya's translation changes the meaning of what the principal says. Why does she make these changes?

Principal's Words	Maya's Translation	Effect

4. **Compare** Reread the dialogue involving Maya, her mother, and Nurzhan in lines 396–413. What does this dialogue reveal about how the mother's relationship with Maya differs from her relationship with Nurzhan?

5. **Analyze** What complications does Maya face as she attempts to resolve her conflict? List at least two.

6. **Interpret** Reread lines 527–541, in which Maya's parents are arguing about her. What does Maya's reaction tell you about what she wants?

7. **Analyze** What role does Nurzhan play in resolving the conflict?

PERFORMANCE TASK

Writing Activity: Summary Write a summary of "My Favorite Chaperone." To summarize, briefly retell the plot of the story in your own words.

- Introduce the major characters and state the conflict.
- Summarize the major events in the rising action of the story.
- Identify and describe the climax of the story.
- Describe how the conflict is resolved.

Critical Vocabulary

sponsor   stun   dispatcher   scuffle   whimper

Practice and Apply Use your understanding of the Vocabulary words to answer each question.

1. If someone agreed to **sponsor** you, would you be annoyed or grateful? Why?

2. Would getting a homework assignment or getting a special award be more likely to **stun** you? Why?

3. If you were a **dispatcher**, would you need to speak to people or write to them? Why?

4. Would people be more likely to have a **scuffle** if they were angry, or if they were lost? Why?

5. If you heard someone **whimper**, would you think he or she was feeling lucky, or scared? Why?

Vocabulary Strategy: Context Clues

The **context** of a word is made up of the punctuation marks, words, sentences, and paragraphs that surround the word. When you encounter an unfamiliar word, its context may provide you with clues that can help you understand its meaning. Look at the following example:

> Mr. Walsh, the vice-principal, came into our class. He whispered something to Ms. Coe and she nodded. And then I was <u>stunned</u> because she nodded and pointed at me!

From the context clues, you can figure out that *stunned* describes how Maya felt. The exclamation point at the end of the sentence suggests that she did not expect the principal would call her out of class. Feeling stunned probably means "to feel surprised or shocked."

Practice and Apply Review "My Favorite Chaperone" to find the following words. Complete a chart like the one shown.

Word	Context Clues	My Guessed Definition	Dictionary Definition
huddled (line 66)			
mispronouncing (line 217)			
drizzle (line 280)			
emeralds (line 553)			

Language Conventions: Imperative Mood

The **mood of a verb** refers to the manner in which the action or state of being is expressed. A verb is in the **imperative mood** when it is part of a command or request. In an imperative sentence, the subject is always implied or understood to be *you*. These sentences from "My Favorite Chaperone" are in the imperative mood.

> "Take off your jacket and hang it up, Nurzhan."

> "Let me try to get permission for you from Papa."

In the first sentence, Maya is giving her brother a command. In the second sentence, Nurzhan is requesting something from his sister, Maya. Note that the subject of both sentences (you) is not stated, but is understood.

Imperative Mood	Understood Subject	Command or Request?
Do your homework.	(You) do your homework.	command
Please help me get this done.	(You) please help me get this done.	request

Practice and Apply Rewrite each sentence so that it is in the imperative mood. Label each sentence as a command or a request.

1. I do not want you to ask her about the permission slip again.
2. You should call my father and tell him what happened.
3. I think you should stop teasing my brother.
4. You should punish your son so that he never fights like this again.
5. I'm telling you to sit at the kitchen table and do your homework.
6. Will you please tell your parents that they must sign this form?
7. I want you to quit asking me if you can go.
8. I would like it if you would help your mother do her work.

Background *Haiti is a small country located on the island of Hispaniola in the Caribbean Sea. In the late 1950s, the ruthless dictator François "Papa Doc" Duvalier took control of the country. Haitians like author* **Jean-Pierre Benoît** *(b.1957) and his parents began to immigrate to the United States to escape the tyrannical government. This immigration increased in the 1970s during the brutal rule of Duvalier's son, Jean-Claude "Baby Doc" Duvalier. By the 2000s, hundreds of thousands of Haitians were living in the United States.*

BONNE ANNÉE

Personal Essay by Jean-Pierre Benoît

SETTING A PURPOSE *Bonne Année* is a French phrase that means "Happy New Year." As you read, pay attention to how the author feels about the country in which he was born and the country in which he lives now. Write down any questions you have during reading.

It is the 1960s, a cold New Year's day in New York. The men are huddled but it is not for warmth; if anything, the Queens apartment is overheated. Important matters are to be discussed. The women are off to the side, where they will not interfere. The location of the children is unimportant; they are ignored. I am in the last category, ignored but overhearing. French, English, and *Kreyòl* commingle. French, I understand. My English is indistinguishable from that of an American child. *Kreyòl*, the language of my birthplace, is a mystery. *Kreyòl* **predominates**, but enough is said in French and English for me to follow. He is leaving. Any day. Father Doctor. Papa Doc. Apparently he is the reason we are

predominate
(prĭ-dŏm´ə-nāt´) *v.*
If ideas or things *predominate*, they are the most common.

in New York, not Port-au-Prince.[1] And now he is leaving. And this will make all the difference. My father is clear. We are returning to Haiti. As soon as this man leaves. No need to await the end of the school year, although my schooling is otherwise so important.

I have no memory of Haiti. No memory of my crib in Port-au-Prince, no memory of the neighbors' children or the house in which we lived. My friends are in New York. My teachers are in New York. The Mets[2] are in New York. I do not know Papa Doc, but our destinies are linked. If he leaves, I leave. I do not want him to leave.

Another January first, another gathering. If it is the beginning of a new year, that is at best incidental. January first is the celebration of Haitian independence. A glorious day in world history, even if someone seems to have forgotten to tell the rest of the world. But it is not bygone glory that is of the moment. A new independence is dawning. It is more than just a rumor this time. Someone has inside information. It is a matter of months, weeks, maybe days, before Duvalier falls. I am one year older now, and I understand who Duvalier is. An evil man. A thief and a murderer. A monster who holds a nation prisoner. A man who tried to have my father killed. A man who will soon get his justice. My father is adamant, Duvalier's days are numbered. And then we will return. Do I want to leave? I am old enough to realize that the question is unimportant.

Go he must, but somehow he persists. A new year and he is still in power. But not for long. This time it is true. The signs are unmistakable, the gods have finally awoken. Or have they? After so many years, the debates intensify. Voices raised in excitement, in agitation, in Haitian cadences. Inevitably, hope triumphs over history. Or ancient history triumphs over recent history. Perhaps there will be a **coup**, Haitian exiles landing on the shores with plans and weapons, a well-timed assassination.

We are not meant to be in this country. We did not want to come. We were forced to flee or die. Americans perceive

coup (ko͞o) *n.* A *coup* is the sudden overthrow of a government by a group of people.

---

[1] **Port-au-Prince** (pôrt′ ō-prĭns′): the capital of Haiti.
[2] **The Mets:** a professional baseball team in New York City.

desperate brown masses swarming at their golden shores, wildly inventing claims of **persecution** for the opportunity to flourish in this prosperous land. The view from beneath the bridge is somewhat different: reluctant refugees with an aching love of their forsaken homeland, of a homeland that has forsaken them, refugees who desire nothing more than to be home again.

Then there are the children. Despite having been raised in the United States, I have no special love for this country. Despite the searing example of my elders, I am not even sure what it means to love a country. Clearly, it is not the government that one is to love. Is it then the land, the dirt and the grass, the rocks and the hills? The people? Are one people any better than another? I have no special love for this country, but neither do I desire a return to a birthplace that will, in fact, be no real return at all. If nothing else, the United States is the country that I know, English is my daily language. Another New Year, but I am not worried; we will not be back in Port-au-Prince anytime soon. With their crooked ruler the adults can no longer draw a straight line, but I can still connect the dots and see that they lead nowhere.

persecution
(pûr´sĭ-kyōō´shən) *n.*
Persecution is the harsh treatment of others, often due to race or religion.

> **We are not meant to be in this country. We did not want to come. We were forced to flee or die.**

II

The Haitian sun has made the cross-Atlantic journey to shine on her **dispossessed** children. This time it is not just wispy speculation, something has changed. It is spring 1971 and there is death to celebrate. The revolutionaries have not landed on the coast, the assassin's poison has not found its blood. Nonetheless, Duvalier is dead. Unnaturally, he has died

dispossess
(dĭs´pə-zĕs´) *v.* To *dispossess* someone is to deny him or her possession of something.

of natural causes. Only his laughable son remains. *Bébé*[3] Doc, Jean-Claude Duvalier. Everyone agrees that *Bébé* Doc will not be in power long enough to have his diapers changed.

Laughable *Bébé* Doc may be, but it turns out to be a long joke, and a cruel one. The father lasted fourteen years, the son will last fifteen. Twenty-nine years is a brief time in the life of a country, but a long time in the life of its people. Twenty-nine years is a very long time in the life of an exile waiting to go home.

Three years into *Bébé* Doc's terrible reign there is news of a different sort. For the first time, Haiti has qualified for the World Cup. The inaugural game is against eternal powerhouse Italy. In 1974 there are not yet any soccer moms, there is no ESPN all-sports network. Americans do not know anything of soccer, and this World Cup match will not be televised. Yet America remains a land of immigrants. For an admission fee, the game will be shown at Madison Square Garden on four huge screens suspended in a boxlike arrangement high above the basketball floor. I go with my younger brother. In goal, Italy has the legendary Dino Zoff. Together they have not been scored upon in two years. The poor Haitians have no hope. And yet, Haitians hope even when there is no hope. The trisyllable cry of "HA-I-TI" fills the air. It meets a response, "I-TA-LIA," twice as loud but destined to be replaced by an even louder HA-I-TI, followed by IT-A-LIA and again HA-I-TI in a spiraling crescendo. The game has not even started.

My brother and I join in the cheer; every time Haiti touches the ball is cause for excitement. The first half ends scoreless. The Italian fans are nervous, but the Haitian fans are feeling buoyed. After all, Haiti could hardly be expected to score a goal, not when the Germans and the English and the Brazilians before them have failed to penetrate the Italian defense. At the same time, the unheralded Haitian defenders have held. The second half begins. Less than a minute has gone by and Emanuel Sanon, the left-winger for Haiti, has the ball. Less than twenty-four hours earlier he had foolhardily predicted that he will score. Zoff is fully aware of him. Sanon shoots. There is a split second of silence and then madness.

---

[3] *Bébé* (bə-bā´): French word that means "baby."

Madison Square Garden is an indoor arena in New York City where games, concerts, boxing matches, and other sports and entertainment activities take place. It is shown here with the Haitian flag.

The ball is in the back of the net, Sanon has beaten Zoff. The Italians are in shock. The world is in shock. Haiti leads 1–0.

"HA-I-TI, HA-I-TI." Half of Madison Square Garden is delirious, half is uncomprehending. The Haitians are beating the Italians. Haiti is winning. Haiti is winning. For six minutes. Then the Italians come back to tie the score, 1–1. The Italians score again. And then again. The Haitians cannot respond. Italy wins 3–1.

Still. Still, for six minutes Haiti is doing the impossible, Haiti is beating Italy. Italy, which twice has won the World

Cup. Six minutes. Perhaps the **natal** pull is stronger than it seems. For that one goal, that brief lead, those six minutes, mean more to me than all the victories of my favorite baseball team.

natal
(nāt′l) *adj.* If something is *natal*, it relates to birth.

III

February 7, 1986, amid massive protests in Haiti, Jean-Claude flees the country. There is a blizzard in New York, but this does not prevent jubilant Haitians from taking to the snowy streets, waving flags, honking horns, pouring champagne. Restaurants in Brooklyn serve up free food and drink. The Duvalier regime has finally come to an end. The New Year's prediction has finally come true. If he leaves, I leave. In July, I fulfill my destiny, more or less. I return to Haiti, on an American passport, for a two-week visit.

In October the Mets win their second World Series. The city celebrates with a tickertape parade attended by over two million people. A pale celebration indeed, compared to the celebrating that took place earlier in the year.

COLLABORATIVE DISCUSSION With a partner, discuss whether a person's homeland is the country where he or she is born, or the country where he or she is raised. Cite evidence from the text to support your ideas.

Determine Central Idea and Details

The **central idea** of an essay is the main point that the author wants to communicate to readers. Sometimes an author may directly state his or her central idea. Often, however, readers must figure it out based on what the author has written. To determine what the central idea is, ask:

- Who or what does the author tell most about?
- What does the author seem to think about that person or thing?
- What overall idea do the details in the selection support?

Supporting details are the facts, opinions, examples, and anecdotes that the author provides to make his or her point. Look at these examples from "Bonne Année":

Fact	Opinion	Anecdote
"My friends are in New York. My teachers are in New York. The Mets are in New York." (lines 20–21)	"Despite having been raised in the United States, I have no special love for this country." (lines 56–57)	The author describes watching the World Cup soccer match between Haiti and Italy. (lines 85–128)

What is the central idea of "Bonne Année"? Identify at least one additional detail that supports this idea.

Analyze Text: Personal Essay

A **personal essay** is a short work of nonfiction in which an author expresses an opinion or provides insight based on personal experiences. By connecting a topic to his or her own life, authors can make others more aware of it.

An author may use **chronological order,** or describe a sequence of events in time order. Telling things in chronological order is an easy way to help readers understand how the ideas in an essay are connected. In "Bonne Année," the author explains how things change from one New Year's Day to another:

> **Another January first, another gathering. If it is the beginning of a new year, that is at best incidental. January first is the celebration of Haitian independence.**

The author also uses time clues, such as dates, to make the order of events clear. Look back at the selection and find two other time clues that help you understand when the events in this selection take place.

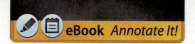

Analyzing the Text

Cite Text Evidence   Support your responses with evidence from the essay.

1. **Cause/Effect**   When discussing Papa Doc in lines 18–23, the author says "our destinies are linked." What does his statement mean?

2. **Infer and Cite Evidence**   Reread lines 1–23. What details from the text explain why it is New York rather than Haiti that feels like home?

3. **Compare**   How do the author's feelings about Haiti differ from the feelings of the older generation, including his father's?

4. **Draw Conclusions**   In your own words, describe the author's account of the World Cup soccer match between Italy and Haiti, and explain his reaction to this event.

5. **Compare**   Using a timeline like the one shown, identify main events in the essay in chronological order. Compare the narrator's shifting hopes for returning to Haiti as each new year arrives and his understanding grows.

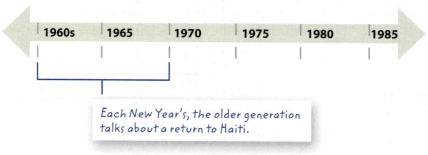

6. **Analyze**   Situational **irony** is a contrast between what a reader, character, or person expects and what actually happens. What is ironic about the situation the author describes in lines 129–137?

7. **Analyze and Synthesize**   How does the last paragraph of the selection relate to the central idea? Consider the details about sports and celebrations that appeared earlier in the essay.

PERFORMANCE TASK

Speaking Activity: Narrative   Present a story about a real-world event in the news that affected your life.

- Research the event.
- Explain the event and identify key people or places involved in it.
- Describe how you are connected to the people or places involved in the event.
- Explain how the event changed some part of your life.

Critical Vocabulary

predominate   coup   persecution   dispossess   natal

Practice and Apply Explain which vocabulary word is most closely related to another word you know.

1. Which Vocabulary word goes with *relocate*? Why?
2. Which Vocabulary word goes with *baby*? Why?
3. Which Vocabulary word goes with *government*? Why?
4. Which Vocabulary word goes with *bullying*? Why?
5. Which Vocabulary word goes with *outweigh*? Why?

Vocabulary Strategy: Using a Glossary

A **glossary** is a list of specialized terms and their definitions. A text may have more than one glossary if it refers to multiple types of specialized terms.

- When a printed book contains a glossary, words are listed in the back of the book in alphabetical order.
- An electronic glossary allows readers to click on a word in the text to see its definition and hear its pronunciation.

Notice the parts of this glossary entry for the word *natal*.

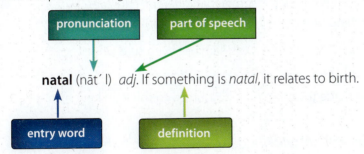

Practice and Apply This literature program contains multiple glossaries. Use the table of contents and the glossaries to answer the following questions.

1. In which glossary would you expect to find a listing for the Critical Vocabulary words that are highlighted in each selection?
2. Which glossary would you use to learn definitions for the literary terms that are used in the instruction?
3. Use the glossaries to look up *predominate* and *chronological order*. What differences do you notice between the two entries?
4. According to the glossary, what is the part of speech for the word *persecution*?

Language Conventions: Participles

A verb usually shows action. A **verbal** is a word that is formed from a verb but is used as a noun, an adjective, or an adverb. A **participle** is one kind of verbal. A participle is a verb form that is used as an adjective, which modifies a noun. Writers use participles to help create vivid descriptions.

- A present participle ends in *-ing*. A past participle can have different endings, such as *-d*, *-ed*, or *-en*.

    Present participle: The **deafening** cheers shook the stadium.

    Past participle: The **disgraced** regime comes to an end.

- A participle can come before or after the noun or pronoun that it modifies, or describes.

    Before the noun it modifies: The **fallen** dictator flees the country.

    After the noun it modifies: Haitians, **smiling**, celebrated in New York.

Practice and Apply Read these sentences from "Bonne Année." Identify each participle and the noun that it modifies.

1. The view from beneath the bridge is somewhat different: reluctant refugees with an aching love of their forsaken homeland.

2. Despite the searing example of my elders, I am not even sure what it means to love a country.

3. The Haitian sun has made the cross-Atlantic journey to shine on her dispossessed children.

4. It meets a response, "I-TA-LIA," twice as loud but destined to be replaced by an even louder HA-I-TI, followed by IT-A-LIA and again HA-I-TI in a spiraling crescendo.

5. At the same time, the unheralded Haitian defenders have held.

Background *Public Agenda is a nonprofit organization that does research to find out people's opinions on important issues. It hopes that by making people's opinions heard, government leaders will be better able to find good solutions to some of our nation's biggest problems. Public Agenda has done research on a variety of topics, including immigration, education, healthcare, and the economy.*

A Place to Call Home:
What Immigrants Say Now About Life in America

Research Study by Scott Bittle and Jonathan Rochkind

SETTING A PURPOSE As you read, pay attention to the immigrants' attitudes about their decisions to come to the United States. What do you find surprising about the information presented?

Introduction

It's a cliché to say that America is a nation of immigrants, but like most clichés, this one began as a statement of simple truth. Another truth is that if we're going to overhaul immigration policy, it only makes sense to listen to the people who will be most affected by it: immigrants. To craft a just and practical policy, we need to see America through the immigrant's eyes. That's true whether you favor an open door or a higher fence. You can't hope to implement sound strategies unless you understand what brings people to the United States and what they think about the nation once they get here.

That's what Public Agenda hopes to accomplish with A PLACE TO CALL HOME: WHAT IMMIGRANTS SAY NOW ABOUT LIFE IN AMERICA, the follow-up to our pioneering 2002 survey of immigrants, NOW THAT I'M HERE.

Part 1: The Right Move

Overall, immigrants say they're quite satisfied with life in the United States, for themselves and their children. Discrimination against immigrants doesn't seem to be part of their daily lives. Although majorities say it exists, majorities also say they haven't personally experienced much of it. Right now, the biggest concern for immigrants is much the same as for native-born Americans: the economy and their own financial well-being. The economic **tumult** in our society may be shaping some of their perceptions—and motivations.

For any decision in life, whether it involves a job accepted or lost, a marriage made or ended, a school selected or a vote cast, the evaluation comes down to one question: Would you do it all over again? There may be regrets or dissatisfactions; that's part of the human condition. But if life came with a time machine or a reset button, would you make the same choice?

By that standard, immigrants in America are clearly happy with their choice. More than 7 in 10 (71 percent) report that if they could do it all over again, they'd still come to the United States. Nor are they likely to give up and go home; indeed, equally large numbers (70 percent) say that they intend to make the United States their permanent home.

That goes for their children as well. About three-quarters of immigrant parents (74 percent) say it's unlikely their children will want to live in their birth country, with a strong 58 percent saying it's "very unlikely."

The reasons for this seem straightforward: Immigrants buy in to American society. There's always been a fierce debate among pundits and political scientists about "American exceptionalism," the idea that the United States is unique among nations. Some find this idea ennobling, others **pernicious**. Maybe it's no surprise, since immigrants have volunteered to build their lives here, but the people we surveyed have very little doubt: 76 percent say the United States is "a unique country that stands for something special in the world." Only 20 percent disagree, saying that the United States is "just another country that is no better or worse than any other."

---

tumult
(tōō′mŭlt′) *n*. A *tumult* is a disorderly disturbance.

pernicious
(pər-nĭsh′əs) *adj*. If something is *pernicious*, it is very harmful or destructive.

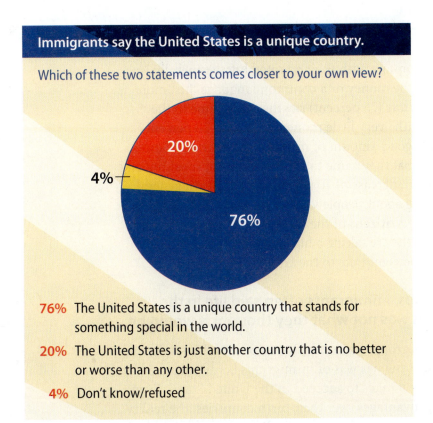

Immigrants say the United States is a unique country.

Which of these two statements comes closer to your own view?

- **76%** The United States is a unique country that stands for something special in the world.
- **20%** The United States is just another country that is no better or worse than any other.
- **4%** Don't know/refused

PART 2: Fitting In

Most immigrants say that they have become comfortable in the United States quickly, yet ties to their birth countries have become stronger since 2002, particularly among recent immigrants. Most of the immigrants we surveyed either were citizens already or were in the process of being **naturalized**. For most of them, citizenship is a practical step. So is learning to speak English, with most immigrants reporting that it is difficult to get ahead or keep a job without language skills.

Immigrants clearly buy into American values, but how long does it take them to feel comfortable in American society? Although immigrants embrace what the United States stands for, this is no guarantee that they are able to fit in on a day-to-day basis.

The immigrants we surveyed don't seem to feel that fitting in is a major barrier and in fact say the process moved quickly. More than three-quarters (77 percent) say that it takes fewer than five years to "feel comfortable here and part of the

naturalize
(năch´ər-ə-līz´) v.
When governments *naturalize* people, they grant them full citizenship.

community," and nearly half (47 percent) say it took fewer than two.

Such easy comfort with their adopted home generally isn't being propelled by money or a common language. Just more than three-quarters (76 percent) say that they came to the United States with "very little money," and only 20 percent say they had "a good amount of money to get started." Some 45 percent say that they came to this country not speaking any English at all, an increase of 10 points since 2002. In general, we aren't talking about people who move freely between nations, so-called citizens of the world. We're talking about people who say they're taking a big financial and cultural gamble when they emigrate to the United States.

In focus groups, immigrants often said life in the United States was not what they thought it would be.

In the focus groups we conducted as part of this study, one of the consistent themes was of immigrants being surprised by how much work it takes to succeed in the United States. Even with all of its advantages over their birth countries, the reality for many immigrants is that it can be difficult to live in the United States and achieve a good standard of living.

> *"There's the assumption that when you come here you will become wealthy very fast and very easily. I have to work 12, 16 hours a day to make a living. [In my birth country] . . . they work, like, from nine until two and then go home."*
> — A woman in the Detroit, Michigan, focus group

Her sentiment is partly borne out by the survey, which also asked how often immigrants found themselves living "paycheck to paycheck." Some 70 percent of immigrants reported doing so "always," "most of the time" or "sometimes." When Newsweek asked the same question of the general public in January 2009, only 59 percent said they lived paycheck to paycheck.

Among our focus groups, there was a general sense that America has no better publicist than Hollywood on this point—although movies and television often broadcast a misleading picture.

> "All the movies [are] just great propaganda . . . like it's a lot of fun and [you have] a lot of money and all that. You don't think about, like, you have to pay [the] mortgage. You don't know."
> —A man in New York

> "When I came here, the first thing I imagined was I want to live la vida loca, the great life. When I recently arrived here, I wound up in an area that was very bad, in a two-bedroom apartment where 12 people were living. They were sharing their rent, and I said, 'What have I gotten myself into?' With time, I wound up renting another apartment. I didn't imagine it would be like this."
> —A woman in the Los Angeles focus group

Immigrants report closer ties to their birth country than they did seven years ago. They spend more time with people from their birth country and are more likely to call home and send money.

There's some suggestion, however, that when it comes to being "comfortable" in communities, other immigrants play a critical role. Compared with results from 2002, more immigrants say that they spend time with people from their birth country and have closer ties there.

Half of the immigrants we surveyed (51 percent) say they spend "a lot" of time with people from their birth country, a jump of 14 points from 2002. Other kinds of birth-country ties have strengthened as well. One is the simple act of telephoning. The number of immigrants who tell us that they call home at least once a week rose 12 points (40 percent from 28 percent). Granted, this may be partly because **telecommunications** is better and cheaper than even a few years ago. Cell phones are common, international calling is less expensive and innovations like Skype and instant messaging make it easier to keep in touch.

telecommunications (tĕl´ĭ-kə-myōō´nĭ-kā´shəns) *n.* *Telecommunications* are the electronic systems that telephones and other electronic devices use to send information.

These strengthened ties are not merely emotional, either; they're financial. While there's been no real change in the number of immigrants who say they send money to their birth country regularly, the number who say they do so "once in a while" increased 14 points, to 44 percent. And the number who say they never send money fell from 55 percent to 37 percent.

About one-quarter of our sample was made up of more recent immigrants, those who arrived since 2001. On the whole, their ties to the United States aren't as strong. For example:

- One-third say they will go back to live in their birth country someday.

- Three in ten (32 percent) say it is likely that their children will one day want to live in their birth country (compared with 18 percent of those here before 2001).

- One-third (34 percent) say that if they had it to do over, they would either stay where they were born (26 percent) or pick a different country (8 percent).

- Six in ten (61 percent) say that they spend a lot of time with people from their birth country, compared with 47 percent of immigrants here before 2001.

- More than twice as many (66 percent compared with 29 percent) telephone home at least once a week.

The recent immigrants in A PLACE TO CALL HOME do seem to have different attitudes on these points than those who were recent arrivals in our 2002 study, NOW THAT I'M HERE—in other words, those who were new and still adjusting to American life in the 1990s as opposed to the 2000s. When we compare immigrants who arrived between 2001 and 2009 with those from the 2002 study who arrived between 1990 and 2001, we find:

- The 2001–2009 group are more likely to spend a lot of time with people from their birth country (61 percent versus 35 percent in the 2002 survey).

- They're also more likely to call their birth country at least once a week (66 percent compared with 38 percent).

- And, of those who came to the United States knowing little or no English, they're more likely to say they speak their native language most of the time at home (86 percent compared with 55 percent).

At least as far as perceptions go, a majority of the immigrants we surveyed in 2009 (57 percent) suggest that recent immigrants "have the same respect for American laws and customs as immigrants like you." About a third (32 percent) say that recent immigrants have less respect, though only 15 percent of immigrants who have arrived after 2001 agree.

Among our focus groups, there was a strong sense that American culture is a difficult force to resist. Many immigrants mentioned the materialism often associated with America as a drawback, although how they responded to it depended greatly on their personal beliefs.

Significant numbers of immigrants came to the United States without being able to speak English, and more than half still consider their language skills fair or poor. However, they consider speaking English important for getting ahead, and most say they've taken classes to improve their ability.

One of the **perpetual** flashpoints in the immigration debate has been over language: to what extent immigrants speak English and to what extent the nation should accommodate those who don't. As mentioned above, a sizable number of immigrants (45 percent) come to the United States with no knowledge of English. Overall, about half of them (52 percent) report that they can read a book or newspaper "a little" or "not at all." Even more of them, 63 percent, consider their ability to speak English to be "fair" or "poor."

This is a barrier, and immigrants know it. More than half of immigrants (52 percent) say it is "very hard" to get a job

perpetual
(pər-pĕch′ o͞o-əl) *adj.*
If something is *perpetual*, it lasts for a very long time.

without knowing English (although, interestingly, that's a 10-point decline from 2002), and more than half (56 percent) say that the United States should expect all immigrants to learn English.

Immigrants are willing to take practical steps to address this. Seven in ten of those who came to this country knowing very little or no English at all say that they've taken classes to improve their English, a jump of 23 percent from 2002. Nearly three-quarters (74 percent) of immigrants overall say that it is more important for schools to teach immigrant children English as quickly as possible than it is to teach them other subjects in their native language. Some 88 percent of those with school-age children consider their child's English to be "excellent" or "good."

Despite this, English isn't the primary language in many immigrant homes. Nearly two-thirds (64 percent) of those who came to the United States speaking little or no English say that they mostly speak their native language at home, a 25-point increase from 2002.

There's also a significant difference based on when immigrants came here and how much money they have. Ninety percent of those who still don't speak English well came to the country with very little money. Recent immigrants (since 2001) are more likely to have arrived already knowing how to speak English (30 percent compared with 22 percent), but the recent immigrants who did not are also much more likely to speak their native language in the home (86 percent compared with 55 percent). These immigrants are also more doubtful about their skills, with 75 percent reporting that their English is "fair" or "poor," compared with 58 percent of immigrants who have been here a while.

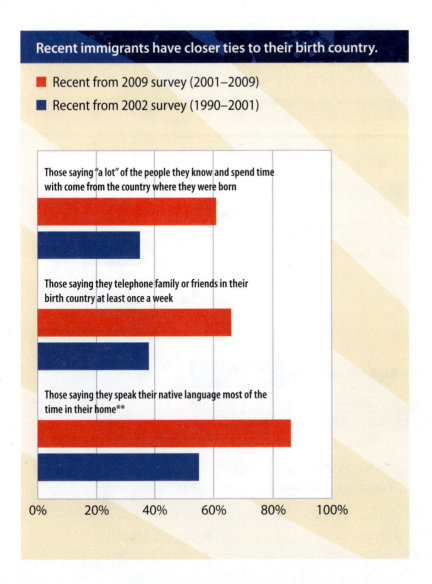

COLLABORATIVE DISCUSSION How do the immigrants surveyed for this study feel about the United States? Compare and contrast their attitude about living in the United States to your own.

A Place to Call Home

Analyze Nonfiction Elements

Text features are design elements such as headings, subheadings, and graphs that authors use to organize information, identify key ideas, and help guide readers through a text. Various types of text features are used for different purposes:

- The **heading** is the title of a text. A **subtitle,** or an additional part of a title, may tell more about what the piece is about.

- **Subheadings** are headings within the text that introduce a new topic or section. They are usually larger, darker, or more colorful than regular text.

- A **bulleted list** (like the one you're reading now) is a list of related and equally important points or ideas.

Review the text and identify all the subheadings. What does each subheading suggest about the kind of information in that section?

Information can also be transmitted visually through **graphic aids,** which include graphs, charts, diagrams, photographs, and other visuals. **Graphs** are used to illustrate statistical information, and they are helpful in showing numerical relationships. Various types of graphs are used for different purposes:

- A **circle graph** is a circular shape that shows how the parts of something compare to the whole. The parts of the circle represent percentages of the whole.
- A **bar graph** is a graph that uses dark or colored bars to display amounts or percentages. Bar graphs are helpful when showing how things change over time. They often include keys, or explanations of how to read the graph.

Find the circle graph in this selection. Identify what question the respondents, or the people who participated in the study, were asked. What was the most common answer? Find the bar graph in this selection. What is being compared?

Analyzing the Text

Cite Text Evidence   Support your responses with evidence from the text.

1. **Infer** What does the use of the word *now* in the selection's subtitle suggest about the information provided in the text?

2. **Interpret** In lines 1–14, what does it mean "to see America through the immigrant's eyes"? Explain why the authors believe that this is important.

3. **Summarize** Are people generally happy or unhappy once they immigrate to the United States? Support your answer by explaining in your own words the information in lines 15–51.

4. **Draw Conclusions** To **draw conclusions** is to make a judgment based on evidence, experience, and reasoning. Study the circle graph that shows immigrants' views about the United States. What conclusion can you draw about the immigrants' choice to come to the United States from the evidence shown here and the information provided in the text?

5. **Cause/Effect** Reread lines 100–110. What contributes to immigrants' false impressions of what life in the United States will be like?

6. **Compare** How do the attitudes of the immigrants who have arrived here recently compare to those who arrived earlier? In a chart like the one shown, gather information from the bulleted list and bar graphs in Part 2. Then explain how immigrants' thoughts about their country of birth and their relationships with others from their birth country are shifting.

	Immigrants Surveyed in 2002	Immigrants Surveyed in 2009
Thoughts about Country of Birth		
Relationships with Others from Birth Country		

PERFORMANCE TASK

Research Activity: Explanation Do research to discover where recent immigrants to the United States came from.

- Choose one or more years to research.
- Identify the number of immigrants who settled in the United States as well as their birth countries.
- Compare the number of immigrants who came from various countries.
- Create a bar graph or a circle graph to show your findings.
- Explain why you chose to use the graphic aid you did.

Critical Vocabulary

tumult   pernicious   naturalize   telecommunications   perpetual

Practice and Apply Complete each sentence in a way that shows the meaning of the Vocabulary word.

1. There was **tumult** in the neighborhood when . . .
2. Advertisements can be **pernicious** if . . .
3. A government may **naturalize** an immigrant if . . .
4. Advanced **telecommunications** systems make it possible for Armando to . . .
5. One **perpetual** challenge people have when they relocate is . . .

Vocabulary Strategy: Using Greek Prefixes

Many English words are made from word parts that come from the Greek language. A **prefix** is a word part that is added to the beginning of a base word or a word root. Knowing the meaning of a prefix can often help you figure out the meaning of a new word. Look at this example from "A Place to Call Home":

> **Granted, this may be partly because <u>telecommunications</u> is better and cheaper than even a few years ago.**

If you know that the Greek prefix *tele-* means "distance," it will help you understand that *telecommunications* is "electronic communication over a distance."

Practice and Apply Use the meaning of the prefix *tele-* to help you complete a chart like the one shown.

Word	Word Meaning
teleconference	
telemarketer	
televise	
telescope	
telephoto	

Background The Hmong (hmông) are an ethnic group from southern China, Laos, Vietnam, and Thailand. In the 1970s, war and conflict caused many of the Hmong people in Laos to flee to refugee camps in Thailand. Author **Kao Kalia Yang** (b. 1980) was born in one of these camps. She moved with her family, including her older sister Dawb, to Minnesota in 1987. Four other siblings were born in the United States, where all the Yang children received their educations.

from The Latehomecomer

Memoir by Kao Kalia Yang

SETTING A PURPOSE As you read, notice the challenges and the opportunities that life in a new country presents Kao Kalia Yang and her family. How does Yang react to her situation?

We had been in America for almost ten years. I was nearly fifteen, and Dawb had just gotten her driver's license. The children were growing up. We needed a new home—the apartment was too small. There was hardly room to breathe when the scent of jasmine rice and fish steamed with ginger mingled heavily with the scent of freshly baked pepperoni pizza—Dawb's favorite food. We had been looking for a new house for nearly six months.

10   It was in a poor neighborhood with houses that were ready to collapse—wooden planks falling off, colors chipping away, sloping porches—and huge, old trees. There was a realty sign in the front yard, a small patch of green in front of the white house. It was one story, with a small open patio and a single wide window framed by black panels beside a black door. There was a short driveway that climbed up a

little hill. No garage. It looked out of place in the east side of St. Paul. In fact, it looked out of time. The house should have been on the prairie, in the early days of Minnesota. It looked like it belonged to Laura and Mary Ingalls and a time when girls wore cotton skirts with little flowers and bonnets to keep the sun away and carried pails with their sandwiches inside. The team of two old trees in the front yard dwarfed the house. From the car, my imagination took flight. I never thought I would get a chance to live in a house that belonged to storybooks.

I asked my mom, "Are you sure this is only $36,500?"

"It was really $37,000 on the paper, but Dawb asked the man to lower the price for us, and he agreed."

"It looks like at least $70,000 to me."

I couldn't wait to get out of the car. We had been looking for houses a long time—some we had liked well enough; most we couldn't afford. Now, this one that looked like a real antique, was only $36,500. The deal was incredible. It felt like a miracle.

Together, we had scoured the city looking for a suitable home. My mother, father, and Dawb in the front, and the rest of us in the back, all our knees touching. We had looked all summer long, driving up and down the avenues, the corridors, the smaller streets, and the busy thoroughfares of St. Paul. On days of fruitless hunting, my father would drive us past the mansions on Summit Avenue for inspiration. We were awed and discussed the merits of owning the structures before us, humongous and intimidating, haunting and invincible. We marveled at the bricks and the green lawns and the ivy climbing up the walls and windows.

Dawb and I posed creative arguments for why owning such behemoths would never work for our family. These were the homes that we saw on television, the ones with the ghosts and the gun dramas, the ones with the 1980s movie stars and their loose-fitting suits. These were the homes with the secret drug addicts and the eating disorders. We'd much rather live in places where men carried beverages in brown bags and walked lopsided up and down the sidewalks and a child could kick an empty beer bottle just as conveniently as a rock. We had fun with our talk, but sometimes Mom and Dad got annoyed. These houses were supposed to inspire us to work extra hard in school.

The small house before us would work. It would be our first piece of America, the first home we would buy with the money our parents earned. We were full of eagerness. Some of our cousins had purchased houses already; others were looking, just like us. It felt like we were joining the future with the past, our dreams and our lives coming together. This would be the home that the children would dream about for years to come.

Up close, we could see that the wood of the house was falling apart in places. White paint had been applied to the parts where the old paint had chipped. The floor of the porch was rotting. The black panels on either side of the window made it look bigger than it was. But that afternoon there was a feeling like the house was special, like it would be ours for a long time. I walked through the front door, into a space that was small, like an elevator. Then I made a left and entered our first home in America: 437 East York Avenue.

The house had the simplest design I had ever encountered. After the elevator-sized reception area, there were three bigger rooms all connected, each with a small bedroom to the right. There was a single bathroom in between the second and third bedrooms. The first room was a designated living room. The second was an "anything-you-need-me-to-be" room (that would be used to full capacity as bedroom, playroom, study room, and eating room). The third was a kitchen with enough room in the center for a round dining table (a remnant of the old owners). Off the kitchen there was a door leading to an enclosed porch area that my father liked because there was an old pencil sharpener nailed into the wall. The realtor had said that the sharpener still worked. Also off the kitchen there was a small room with just enough space for a washing and drying machine and the **requisite** heavy-duty sink. The total area of the house was 950 square feet, and it was built in 1895. It was called a two-and-a-half bedroom house because the middle room had no closet. The entire structure smelled old, like the thrift shops we were frequenting less and less.

My mother and father were in disagreement over the house. My mother kept on hoping for better. My father's position was that we had to make do with what was before us. But they both felt that they could not afford better for us.

My father said, "We can hide from the rain and the snow in here."

requisite
(rĕk´wĭ-zĭt) *adj.*
Something that is *requisite* is needed or essential.

"Ah-huh," we answered in various octaves.

"Someday maybe we can do better."

We all knew he was referring to education. Someday when Dawb and I became educated, and the kids grew up and did well in school too, and my mother and father no longer had to work so hard just to get enough food and pay the heating bill. That is the someday my father was waiting for. It was the someday we were all waiting for.

We moved into the house in the fall, my first year of high school. Dawb was already attending Harding High School, an inner-city school where nearly fifty percent of the student body was multicultural—many of whom were Hmong. Naturally, I would attend Harding with her. She had helped me choose my classes; I would take all the International Baccalaureate classes that I could get into, and where I couldn't, I'd take the advanced placement or college prep courses. I had gone to a small junior high school, a math and science magnet, in a white neighborhood with few Hmong kids. There I had done well in my classes; I discovered a formula I thought quite sacred: do the homework, go to class every day, and when in class, follow the teacher with your eyes. I was still whispering in school, but the teachers took it in stride. I felt ready for the life changes that high school would bring my way.

I was feeling a strong push to reinvent myself. Without my realizing, by the time high school began, I had a feeling in the pit of my stomach that I had been on simmer for too long. I wanted to bubble over the top and douse the confusing fire that burned in my belly. Or else I wanted to turn the stove off. I wanted to sit cool on the burners of life, lid on, and steady. I was ready for change, but there was so little in my life that I could adjust. So life took a blurry seat.

I knew that the parameters of our life would continue, but I pushed against the skin that contained me. There would be school or work during the day and then a return to the children and babysitting. The drama of a changing body had taken me by surprise but had taken care of itself smoothly. … Dawb drove around the block, often with me beside her in the passenger seat. We were both growing up, we were big sisters, and we took care of the children, and my mother and father were convinced of our status as good daughters with good grades. High school was important because it meant that we were closer to college. It did not **resonate** in my family that high school was a time to be young or to be old or that it was a time to sneak peeks into different worlds. Such ideas hit against the closed lids of my consciousness.

Dawb and I had decided long before that when the time came, we would strive for the University of Minnesota. We were hearing of Hmong doctors and lawyers, both men and women, all excelling in America, building successful lives for themselves, their mothers and fathers, grandmothers and grandfathers. I had never actually met a Hmong doctor or lawyer, but they had clan names I recognized as clearly as I did my own: Vue, Thao, Vang, Xiong, Lee, Lor, Moua, Cha, Hang, Chang, Khang, Her, Chue, Pha, Kong, and Khue. Dawb and I wanted to add to the success of our clan in this growing list of Hmong people who had made lives for themselves and their families in America. We wanted to make the life journeys of our family worth something. Our ambitions had grown: we contemplated changing not simply our own lives but the lives of poor children all over the world. And the key, we believed, was in school. But how far we could strive in school was unknown. We didn't tell anyone about our secret dreams.

Dawb had teachers who supported her all the way through. She had the kind of intelligence that a teacher could

resonate
(rĕz´ə-nāt´) v. When ideas *resonate*, they have a great effect or impact.

see (she looked every part the interested learner), could hear (her English had no accent), and could support (she soaked up information and processed it into her world for her use). I was lost, perpetually biting my lower lip: I didn't speak well or easily, and the link between what we were learning from books and living in life was harder for my mind to grasp.

In high school, this changed. I met a teacher who changed the way I saw myself in education. Her name was Mrs. Gallentin, and she opened up a possibility that I was special. She taught ninth-grade English, where we read *Romeo and Juliet* and *Nectar in the Sieve*, as well as other literary classics. I sat near the front of the class and absorbed the books. Mrs. Gallentin had a red face and a dry sense of humor. She had little patience for kids who giggled or were fussy in their seats—students who didn't pay close attention to lessons and did not do their assignments on time. I had overly curvy, confident handwriting that was hard to read, and I did not have a computer, so reviewing my work was a slow process. She may have noticed me initially because of this, and her interest was compounded by both my silence and my serious approach to literature.

Mrs. Gallentin became impressed with me because I could tell the important parts of a book. I knew how to anticipate the questions on her tests. At first, I was convinced I could read her mind. But after a few thought experiments in class, I realized I was picking up understanding from the books, not from her. It was in this class that I wrote my first real essay in response to the question: Is the story of Romeo and Juliet a story of love or lust?

It took me all night long to think about the essay. I had no personal experience with love, or lust. Some of my friends said that they were in love, but I was not convinced. The phone conversations they had with their boyfriends were mostly just listening to each other's breathing. After many false beginnings, I wrote about what mattered to me. I wrote about the love I felt I knew: Love is the reason why my mother and father stick together in a hard life when they might each have an easier one apart; love is the reason why you choose a life with someone, and you don't turn back although your heart cries sometimes and your children see you cry and you wish out loud that things were easier. Love is getting up each day and fighting the same fight only to sleep that night in the same bed beside the same person because long ago, when you were younger and you did not see so clearly, you had chosen them.

I wrote that we'll never know if Romeo and Juliet really loved because they never had the chance. I asserted that love only happened in life, not in literature, because life is more complex. As soon as I wrote the essay, I started worrying about it—what if she didn't like it, what if she didn't agree, what if I had it all wrong. That was my first understanding of how writing worked, how it mattered to the writer, personally and profoundly.

I had written the essay out by hand first. I stayed up all night typing the essay on our gray typewriter at the dining table (it was the only surface in our house that was steady enough for us to really spread out our books and papers), slowly, with my index fingers (mistakes were costly). The sound of slow keys being clicked, first the right and then the left, eyes looking from keyboard to the page. Flexing careful fingers every few minutes. Trying to find a rhythm and a beat in the clicking of the keys, the mechanical whirl at the end of each line, the changing of paper. It took me a long time to think it through and follow the letters to the words, but the writing calmed something inside of me, it cooled my head: like water over a small burn in the pit of my mind. I watched eagerly as the third then fourth then fifth page filled with typed letters.

My mother and father came home early in the morning. They had changed their work schedules entirely to the graveyard shift (the **nominal** increase in their wages was necessary to maintain the new house). They saw my eyes closing over my work and became convinced that I was their hardest working daughter. My heavy eyes followed the way they walked so tired around the kitchen, and I grew confident that I really did know love—that I had always known it. By morning, the exhausting work of writing was done. I turned it in to Mrs. Gallentin.

Mrs. Gallentin caught me in the hall later that day and said that my essay was beautiful. She said that I wrote more than an answer to the question; I was telling her the ways in which questions come from life and end in life. I had never thought of myself as a good writer. I liked stories, and in elementary school I had written gory tales about intestines coming out. I thought I was good at math and science (what my junior high

nominal
(nŏm′ə-nəl) *adj.*
Something that is *nominal* is small or insignificant.

school had been good at), but Mrs. Gallentin said that I had talent for literature. I didn't see it, but it pleased me to hear her say this. In the course of a semester, she opened up a real possibility that I could excel in high school and college because they were all about good reading and good writing.

I began to see a truth that my father had been asserting for a long time, long before America. In Ban Vinai Refugee Camp, I had sat on my father's shoulders, my hands secured in his hair, and I listened to him talk about how we might have a brother, how we would become educated, and how our lives would go places far beyond the horizons we saw—in America. I looked at our lives, and how could I not believe? Beyond all the spoken wishes, a dream had even come true: eight years into America and we owned a house of our own. I wanted to **recap** this journey with Grandma. I waited enthusiastically for her summer visit.

recap
(rē-kăp´) v. To *recap* an event is to retell or summarize it.

She didn't come.

In 1996, welfare reform was in the news. The program was ending. Families living on welfare had to learn how to work "within the system." This meant that my uncles in California could no longer farm on the side and raise their families with the help of the government. This meant that my grandma's sons were in danger. What's more, she herself could be at risk. She was not a citizen; there was no way she could pass the citizenship test or speak enough English to prove her loyalty, to pledge, "I will fight for America if it were ever in danger." It was fighting that all the Hmong in America had done with the lives that had fallen to the jungle floor, the spirits that had flown high into the clouds again, that had fled life and refused to return—despite all the urgings, the pleas, the crying. But we were refugees in this country, not citizens. It was not our home, only an asylum. All this came crashing down.

In American history we learned of the Vietnam War. We read about guerilla warfare and the Vietcong. The Ho Chi Minh Trail and communism and democracy and Americans and Vietnamese. There were no Hmong—as if we hadn't existed at all in America's eyes.[1]

---

[1] **In American history... in America's eyes:** When the United States' war with Vietnam spread to neighboring Laos, Laotian Hmong people fought with the United States. After the war, Hmong people had to flee from the governments of Vietnam and Laos. These governments saw them as enemies.

And yet Hmong were all over America. An exodus from California began. Minnesota was softer in the process of change. Welfare programs would not be terminated as quickly. Measures would be taken to ensure that old people received their benefits. A bill was being considered that would allow veterans of the Vietnam War, Hmong with documents, to apply for citizenship, and take the examination in Hmong. There was crazy studying everywhere. Aunt and Uncle Chue hovered over pages that he read with his French accent as she tried to make out the letters of the alphabet one at a time, through her thick reading glasses.

My own mother and father questioned themselves out loud, "What if we try to become Americans and fail?"

On the phone, Grandma said, "Lasting change cannot be forced, only inspired."

For the Hmong, inspiration came in those that were born in this country, the ready-made Americans in our arms, the little faces of boys and girls who spoke Hmong with American stiffness.

We could not remain just Hmong any longer. For our children, we could not fail. We had to try, no matter what. Even if it meant moving. Thousands of Hmong families moved from the farming lands of California to the job possibilities in Minnesota companies and factories. Aunt and Uncle Chue, despite their lack of English, studied for the citizenship exam, took it, failed, despaired, studied some more, and tried again. Eventually they succeeded, and they inspired my parents to try for citizenship, too. We had no more lands to return to. After nearly fifteen years, my family knew this. The camps in Thailand had closed. Hmong people there were **repatriated**, sometimes without knowledge, back into Laos. Families went missing in the process. Lives were lost. Children were killed. Ours were only beginning to raise their eyes to a country of peace, where guns at least were hidden and death did not occur in the scalding of grass or rains that drizzled death. We could not handle any more death. In wanting to live, we were willing to try becoming Hmong Americans.

    A new chapter of our lives unfolded as we strived to become Americans. We sank our roots deep into the land, took stake in the ground, and prayed to the moon that one day the wind would carry us away from our old moldy house, into a new stronger home that could not be taken away, that would not fall down on us, that would hold us safe and warm.

    Grandma and the uncles from California came to live with us in Minnesota. I felt caught in the larger context of being Hmong. We were only one family in the over two hundred thousand that lived in America. We all came from the same history. I burned for our stories, our poverty, and our cause. I was only in high school, and there was very little I could do. My father **chided** my impatient heart.

    He said, "Patience is the slow road to success."

    My father was a poet, and had a poet's heart. He carried love songs about the falling apart of a country. He made music of the loneliness in Thailand. He sang traditional song poetry about the earth grumbling and the sky crumbling, the leaves of the human heart fluttering all the while. I was his daughter, and I could not see poetry in the mold that grew wild on our walls—no matter how much my mother, Dawb, or I scrubbed, it never stopped, no matter how many layers of paint we applied. I couldn't understand why the Hmong people had to run for their children, how their children had to make lives, again and again, in different soils, to know belonging. Why it was that our house, so cute on the outside, rotted on the inside.

---

repatriate
(rē-pā′trē-āt′) *v.* To *repatriate* people is to return them to the country in which they were born.

chide
(chīd) *v.* To *chide* is to scold or correct in some way.

Why couldn't Grandma live with us now that we were all in one state? Why couldn't she live with any of her sons permanently? Because their homes were small. Because at one home, her heart yearned for another, and because all their homes together could never be like the country of her home in Laos, in the imagination and the stories she told all of us. In the world we lived in, our grandma carried her bags from one house to the next, sharing all our beds.

All this made me sick. My stomach cramped, and I could no longer eat. My bones hurt. I was tired. In the night, my heart squeezed itself, and I woke up incapable of crying the pain away. I remember one night, falling asleep looking at how the car lights from the street reflected on my wall. I could hear the pounding of my heart in my ears, very loud and deep, like a hollow cry from my chest. I felt like needles were twisting their way into my chest. I remember thinking that the pain was teasing me but realizing soon that it wasn't a joke. The air in my lungs caught in my throat. I struggled for escape, my hands reaching for my heart, beating frantically within me. I remember trying to cry out but finding a lack of air, a thickening tongue. I kicked desperately on the hard wall. First one, then a sad two, a final three: thinking in red: Mom and Dad, help me, I'm dying. I'm Hmong and I'm your daughter and I'm dying in the room beside yours. The thoughts were on repeat. Sweat. I could feel it breaking out on my forehead. Skin: I could feel the cold settling in. Heaving inside of myself. My eyes growing tight in the darkness, light streaming in. The door opened, slamming with force against the wall. My mom and dad rushed to my side, and I remember seeing myself twisting and turning, all out of color and out of breath, but still moving with nervous life. My father tried to hold me and I could hear my mom's voice panicking and Dawb running for the phone, and then I felt **expiration** come. I stilled. Air flowed in. My vision cleared. It was slowly over.

No ambulance was called. It was too fast. What seemed like forever was little more than five minutes on a dark Minnesota night. No one knew what happened. In the doctor's office, days later, I said: perhaps it was a heart attack. The doctor didn't think so: I was too young for a heart attack. My mom and dad were eager to believe the doctor. We didn't want to pursue the idea, and so we came home happy that it was all over.

expiration
(ĕk´spə-rā´shən) *n.*
Expiration is the act of exhaling or breathing out.

In the month that followed, I lost twenty pounds. The doctors didn't know what was wrong. My mother and father hovered over me. My siblings watched me grow pale and weak; the bones on my hips jutted out, and the bags under my eyes took permanent residence.

Was I making myself sick? Looking for fundamental changes in my life? I loved the children, and I was happy to take care of them after school. All this time, I had been feeling like I was pushing against my skin: was it possible that I was pushing against my very own heart? The idea was a little preposterous. I didn't really believe it, but it nudged at me. But if indeed my heart did need changing, then what part of it? There was a clear division: the Hmong heart (the part that held the hands of my mom and dad and grandma protectively every time we encountered the outside world, the part that cried because Hmong people didn't have a home, the part that listened to Hmong songs and fluttered about looking for clean air and crisp mountains in flat St. Paul, the part that quickly and effectively forgot all my school friends in the heat of summer) or the American heart (the part that was lonely for the outside world, that stood by and watched the fluency of other parents with their boys and girls—children who lingered in the clubs and sports teams after school waiting to be picked up later by parents who could—the part that wondered if forgetting my best friends to life was normal and necessary). My body was surely whole. The doctors said so. What was broken in me must be something doctors couldn't see.

I worried. The more I thought about it, the sicker I became: how does one change what one is becoming?

My grandma worried over me. She tried calling my spirit home. My rebellious, independent spirit hated the moldy house and refused to return. She tried her healing herbs. Their smell and taste took my soul far away to Thailand, to other times and places, but could not locate me in the present. Grandma grew **despondent**.

Something was wrong inside me, and its location was murky, like the origins of the Hmong home long, long ago and far, far away.

despondent
(dĭ-spŏn′dənt) *adj.*
Someone who is *despondent* feels a loss of hope or confidence.

One day, I lay on the sofa—another day absent from school (my grades were dropping slowly)—looking up at the wall. Grandma and Dawb had gone shopping. My mother was in the kitchen preparing rice porridge for me. I heard the key in the lock. I heard them come in. I turned and saw that my grandmother had a gift for me.

There was something glittery in her hands. Her uneven gait came closer. She presented a thin silver bracelet made of elephants, bigger mother ones and smaller baby ones, circling together, tusks entwined. It was the most beautiful gift anyone had ever gotten me. She told me that the man at the store had taken off a few of the elephants to fit my small wrist. Grandma put the bracelet on me and said, "Elephants protect their babies by forming a circle around them. You are sick, and I cannot protect you. I bought this for you so that the power of the elephants will protect you and make you well again."

I wore the bracelet every day. I started to eat a little bit of food and took the medicines the doctors gave me (after all of the tests and retests, the doctors said that baby lupus would explain my symptoms). I wore the bracelet and grew stronger in its hold. The idea of a divided heart slowly lost merit: if there was no resolution that I could willingly and happily pick, then why not just live with it? Isn't this how all of life happens anyway? I looked at the glittering bracelet on my wrist and decided that a divided heart can be a good thing. One side can help the other. Why couldn't my chest expand to hold my heart? My father was always telling me that I needed to stiffen the walls of my heart, so it would not waver after the passage of people and places in my life. Maybe the softness of my heart, which I thought would cushion whatever may come, had been my biggest weakness. I had the help of elephants. I wore the bracelet every day and felt better.

One day, the tusks of two elephants lost their hold on each other. I placed the bracelet in a small bag, and I promised myself that I would eventually put the tusks back together again. Or, if that was impossible, I would have another one made, just like it.

I grew well again, but I understood that my body, like every other body in the world, could die. It could be healthy or not. If it carried life, then it could lose it. I was a child of war, and I should have known that we have no choice about when and where we die. When we do, we simply comply as bravely as we can. Getting up in the morning became harder than it had been. But each day, I did get up. That was the point. That had always been the point in the Hmong life, and even the American one. I grew satisfied with myself. Slowly, the sickness eased away.

COLLABORATIVE DISCUSSION Which of the author's experiences seems to have had the greatest effect on her? With a partner, discuss the reasons for your response. Cite specific evidence from the text to support your ideas.

Analyze the Meanings of Words and Phrases

Kao Kalia Yang conveys her family's situation by using language that creates striking images or suggests strong emotions. Her writing includes

- **imagery,** descriptions that appeal to the senses of sight, sound, smell, feeling, or taste to create an effect or evoke emotion
- **figurative language,** words and phrases that suggest meaning beyond the literal meanings of words themselves. Certain types of figurative language, such as similes and metaphors, can create comparisons between ideas that are otherwise unconnected.

	Definition	Example	Effect
imagery	vivid descriptions that appeal to one or more of readers' five senses	"… the scent of jasmine rice and fish steamed with ginger mingled heavily with the scent of freshly baked pepperoni pizza."	The scents suggest the mixing of Hmong and American cultures.
simile	a comparison of two unlike things using the words *like*, *as*, or *as if*	"I could hear the pounding of my heart in my ears, very loud and deep, like a hollow cry from my chest."	The comparison suggests the author's pain and implies a warning that it is serious.
metaphor	a comparison between two unlike things without the use of the words *like* or *as*	"We sank our roots deep into the land, took stake in the ground…"	Comparing the family to plants shows their strong desire to be part of America.

Find an example of each use of language in *The Latehomecomer*.

Analyze Text: Memoir

The Latehomecomer is a **memoir,** a true story of a person's life that focuses on personal experiences and observations about people or events. Memoirs often give readers insight into the impact of historical events on people's lives.

Yang shares her insights by making comparisons between the people or things she knows best and new ideas or feelings. For example, in lines 290–304, Yang reveals the frustrations of Hmong refugees seeking citizenship by comparing them to the Hmong children—like her own siblings—born in the United States.

What other comparisons does Yang make?

Analyzing the Text

Cite Text Evidence   Support your responses with evidence from the text.

1. **Interpret** In lines 17–22, Yang uses an **allusion,** a reference to a famous person, place, event, or literary work. What does the reference to the characters from *The Little House on the Prairie,* a classic American children's book, suggest about how Yang has begun to see herself? How does the family's first house contribute to that self-image?

2. **Draw Conclusions** To what does the author compare herself in the metaphor in lines 124–131? Explain what the comparison shows about Yang's shifting feelings at this point in her life.

3. **Infer** The author says that writing "cooled my head: like water over a small burn in the pit of my mind." What does this simile explain about why Yang became a writer?

4. **Draw Conclusions** Read lines 359–384 to review the imagery the author uses to describe the onset of her illness. What idea or feeling does "I could feel the cold settling in" convey?

5. **Analyze** In the memoir, the author bases her essay on *Romeo and Juliet* on her own life experiences. What does this insight teach her about herself as a writer?

6. **Compare** In lines 398–421, what conflict does the author feel she is facing? How does she resolve that conflict?

7. **Analyze** How does the author's recovery from her illness change her?

PERFORMANCE TASK

Writing Activity: Informative Report Research the Laotian Hmongs' involvement in the Vietnam War, and explain how the relationship between the United States and the Hmong led families like the Yangs to immigrate to the United States.

- Use print or digital sources for your research.
- Identify why the United States recruited Hmong people for the war.
- Explain how and where the Hmong people lived after the war.
- Write a short report and share it with the class.

Critical Vocabulary

| requisite | resonate | nominal | recap |
| repatriate | chide | expiration | despondent |

Practice and Apply Use what you know about the Vocabulary words to answer the following questions.

1. When might you explain that you have the **requisite** skills for a task?
2. If a new idea **resonates** with you, how might you react?
3. Does a new car cost a **nominal** amount of money? Explain.
4. Why might you **recap** an event for a friend?
5. Could you **repatriate** to another country? Why or why not?
6. How do you react to having a teacher **chide** you about your behavior?
7. What could you do to help someone who has difficulty with **expiration**?
8. What might you say or do for someone who is **despondent**?

Vocabulary Strategy: Using Latin Prefixes

Prefixes—word parts added to the beginning of a root or base word—often provide clues about the meaning of a word. For example, in the following sentence from *The Latehomecomer*, knowing that the Latin prefix *re-* usually means "again" or "back" helps you to understand the word *reinvent*. Yang wants to invent herself again, or have a new beginning.

> "I was feeling a strong push to <u>reinvent</u> myself."

When you encounter an unfamiliar word, follow these steps:
- Look for familiar word parts, such as prefixes.
- Identify the meaning of the prefix.
- Apply the meaning to define the word.

Practice and Apply Identify the *re-* word or words in the following sentences. Use the prefix meaning to define the word. Check a dictionary to confirm your definition.

1. Every Monday, my friends and I recap the weekend's events.
2. After the war, some Hmong people were repatriated back into Laos.
3. The family had to relocate after a fire destroyed their home.
4. Most students find it helpful to review a chapter before a test.
5. Getting new information can help to reform or rethink an opinion.

Language Conventions: Active and Passive Voice

The **voice of a verb** shows whether its subject performs or receives the action expressed by the verb. When the subject performs the action, the verb is in the **active voice.** When the subject is the receiver of the action, the verb is in the **passive voice.**

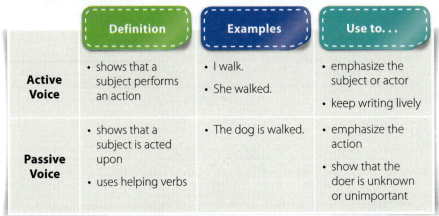

	Definition	Examples	Use to...
Active Voice	• shows that a subject performs an action	• I walk. • She walked.	• emphasize the subject or actor • keep writing lively
Passive Voice	• shows that a subject is acted upon • uses helping verbs	• The dog is walked.	• emphasize the action • show that the doer is unknown or unimportant

A writer uses **active voice** to show that a subject performs the verb's action. In this example from *The Latehomecomer*, Kalia Kao Yang uses active voice to emphasize the role she and her sister had in the process of searching for a house:

> **Dawb and I posed creative arguments for why owning such behemoths would never work for our family.**

Writers use **passive voice** to show that a subject is being acted upon. Passive voice uses forms of *be* such as *am, is, are, was, were,* or *will be* to emphasize the receiver of the action, as in this example from *The Latehomecomer*.

> **These houses were supposed to inspire us to work extra hard in school.**

Practice and Apply Identify the voice of the verb in each sentence and tell if the subject performs or receives the action. Then rewrite the sentence in a different voice.

1. The people of Laos were affected by the Vietnam War.
2. The war changed their country and their lives forever.
3. New leaders took harsh actions against the Hmong people.
4. The Hmong were uprooted from their homes by the war and its aftermath.

Background A collaboration between two very different New York schools is at the heart of the Building Bridges project. Newcomers High School in Queens, New York, is dedicated to teaching recent immigrants, while St. Luke's is a private middle school in Manhattan where students have many advantages.

MEDIA ANALYSIS

New Immigrants Share Their Stories

Documentary directed by Lisa Gossels

SETTING A PURPOSE Through letter writing, video diaries, and interviews, the English learners from Newcomers tell their personal immigration stories with support and encouragement from their St. Luke's "buddies." Together the students hope to change stereotyped ideas about immigrants, highlight their reasons for coming to America, and share their goals and dreams for the future. The documentary *New Immigrants Share Their Stories* chronicles the students' project.

As you view the film, pay attention to the interviews between the immigrant students and their "buddies." Listen to the questions asked and the answers given. Also watch the facial expressions and gestures of the individuals. Think about what you learn about the two groups from these conversations. Write down any questions you have as you view.

MEDIA

Format: Documentary
Running Time: 7:47

AS YOU VIEW The documentary you are about to view includes interviews and video diaries. An interview is a conversation or dialogue in which one person, the interviewer, asks specific questions of another person, the interviewee. A video diary is a video recording that shares a subject's personal views and on-the-spot reactions over a period of time. In these video diaries, the individual featured narrates his or her own diary.

As you view the documentary, consider the director's choice of scenes, words, and images in the video diaries and interviews and how they work together to tell about the thoughts and lives of the students who have recently arrived in their new country.

COLLABORATIVE DISCUSSION Which of the student interviews and video diaries had the greatest impact on you? With a partner, discuss concepts or ideas people might learn from the students' conversations.

Analyze Media

New Immigrants Share Their Stories is a **documentary,** a nonfiction film that presents, or documents, information about people or events. A documentary's **purpose** is the intent for which it is made: to inform, entertain, persuade, or express the feelings or opinions of the documentarian.

Documentary filmmakers use visual and sound techniques to present information in a way that meets their purpose and appeals to viewers. These techniques can include:

- **Voice-over**—the voice of an unseen commentator or narrator. The narrator explains or clarifies images or scenes shown on film and provides important new information. *New Immigrants Share Their Stories* uses several narrators, including an unidentified commentator and the teachers. In the video diaries, the students themselves are the narrators.
- **Stills**—images that are motionless, such as illustrations or photographs. Documentaries are composed mainly of moving images but often include stills. The students' video diaries include photographs from their years growing up in other countries.
- **Animation**—the process of creating images that appear to move and seem alive. *New Immigrants Share Their Stories* includes an animated graphic of travel across the globe.

Documentary filmmakers usually have a **motive,** or underlying reason for telling their story. The motive is why they feel the story is worth telling, and in telling it, they want to convey certain insights or angles on the subject. Here are some examples of motives and how they are revealed in a documentary.

Motive	How Motive Is Revealed
Social	Focus is on the interaction of people or on changing behaviors or attitudes
Commercial	Focus is on a product and encouraging viewers to buy it
Political	Focus is on support or opposition to government or laws

To **evaluate** a documentary, you examine the film's techniques and content to judge its value or worth. In evaluating, ask questions like these:

- What is the filmmaker's motive for making the film? How is the motive revealed?
- What techniques caught my interest? What made them effective?
- What is the main message of the film?

Analyzing the Media

Cite Text Evidence   Support your responses with evidence from the media.

1. **Summarize**   The documentary includes students' video diaries. Choose one of the video diaries and summarize the events shown and described.

2. **Analyze**   What do you think is the purpose of this documentary and the filmmakers' motive in making it? What is the film's central message?

3. **Evaluate**   What elements of the documentary reveal the filmmakers' motive and the film's message? How effectively are they revealed?

4. **Analyze**   Complete a chart like the one shown to identify three of the techniques the filmmakers use. Explain what each technique emphasizes.

Technique	Scene from the Documentary
1. Voice-over	
2. Stills	
3. Animation	

5. **Critique**   What information do you gain from the interviews included in the documentary? Is this information effective in helping to convey the documentary's overall message? Why or why not?

6. **Compare and Evaluate**   Consider what you have read and viewed about immigration. What are the advantages of using a documentary format to present the topic of immigration? What are the disadvantages?

PERFORMANCE TASK

Media Activity: Video   Work in small groups to create videos of your own personal stories.

- Prepare for your video by choosing a brief personal story to tell. It might be an immigration story, or it could be a story about another important event in your life. Write down a few notes or an outline of your story. Use it as a guide in your interview.

- Choose a "buddy" in the group to interview. Prepare a list of questions to ask your buddy. Use the types of interview questions from *New Immigrants Share Their Stories* to guide you in writing your questions. Remember to keep them general and open-ended.

- Record the interviews, modeling techniques you saw in the film.

Background *Award-winning author and poet* **Sherman Alexie** *(b. 1966) was born on the Spokane Indian Reservation in the state of Washington. Salmon have long played an important role in the economic and spiritual life of Native Americans in the Washington area. The building of dams in the 20th century destroyed the population of the once plentiful salmon and the way of life of the people who depended upon them. Many of Alexie's poems and stories deal with how the Native American community has been affected by this destruction.*

The Powwow at the End of the World

Poem by Sherman Alexie

SETTING A PURPOSE As you read, pay attention to the details Alexie presents about the river and salmon. How do these details show his feelings about the dams and their effects on the lives of Native Americans?

I am told by many of you that I must forgive and so I shall
after an Indian woman puts her shoulder to the Grand Coulee
    Dam[1]
and topples it. I am told by many of you that I must forgive
and so I shall after the floodwaters burst each successive dam
5 downriver from the Grand Coulee. I am told by many of you
that I must forgive and so I shall after the floodwaters find
their way to the mouth of the Columbia River as it enters the
    Pacific
and causes all of it to rise. I am told by many of you that I
    must forgive

---

[1] **Grand Coulee Dam:** a dam built across the Columbia River in the 1930s to provide hydroelectric power and irrigation.

and so I shall after the first drop of floodwater is swallowed by
that salmon
waiting in the Pacific. I am told by many of you that I must
forgive and so I shall
after that salmon swims upstream, through the mouth of the
Columbia
and then past the flooded cities, broken dams and abandoned
reactors
of Hanford.[2] I am told by many of you that I must forgive and
so I shall
after that salmon swims through the mouth of the Spokane
River
as it meets the Columbia, then upstream, until it arrives
in the shallows of a secret bay on the reservation where I wait
alone.
I am told by many of you that I must forgive and so I shall
after
that salmon leaps into the night air above the water, throws
a lightning bolt at the brush near my feet, and starts the fire
which will lead all of the lost Indians home. I am told
by many of you that I must forgive and so I shall
after we Indians have gathered around the fire with that
salmon
who has three stories it must tell before sunrise: one story will
teach us
how to pray; another story will make us laugh for hours;
the third story will give us reason to dance. I am told by many
of you that I must forgive and so I shall when I am dancing
with my tribe during the powwow at the end of the world.

COLLABORATIVE DISCUSSION With a partner, discuss Alexie's feelings about the effects of the dam. Do his feelings seem justified? Cite specific evidence from the text to support your ideas.

---

[2] **reactors of Hanford:** a series of abandoned nuclear reactors along the Columbia River.

Determine Meaning of Words and Phrases

Each word in a poem contributes to its overall meaning and effect. One way poets create meaning is through the use of **imagery,** descriptions that appeal to the senses of sight, sound, smell, taste, and touch. Notice the way Sherman Alexie appeals to the senses of sight and touch with this image, which communicates feelings of power and importance:

> . . . after / that salmon leaps into the night air above the water, throws / a lightning bolt at the brush near my feet, and starts the fire . . .

Another way poets can communicate meaning is through the use of **allusions,** or references to a famous person, place, event, or work of literature. Alexie creates a connection to the culture of Northwest Native Americans by alluding to characters and places that are important in their history. For example, "The Powwow at the End of the World" contains several references to salmon. Salmon have special significance to Northwest Coast peoples and are part of many traditional myths and ceremonies.

Identify at least one additional image and one allusion in "The Powwow at the End of the World" and explain how each creates an effect or contributes to the poem's meaning.

Make Inferences

When you **make inferences** about a poem, you combine clues from the text with your own knowledge and experience of the world to make educated guesses about meaning. Making inferences is sometimes called "reading between the lines," and it can be especially important in poetry, where much can be said in relatively few words. The diagram below shows one inference that can be made about "The Powwow at the End of the World."

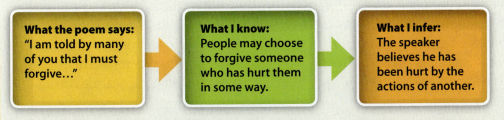

The **speaker** of a poem is the voice that talks to the reader. Who is the speaker being asked to forgive? Tell what the poem says and what you already know that helps you make this inference.

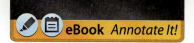

Analyzing the Text

Cite Text Evidence   Support your responses with evidence from the poem.

1. **Infer** The poem begins with an allusion to the Grand Coulee Dam, built on the Columbia River in the mid-20th century and widely considered to be an engineering marvel. Reread lines 1–3. What is the speaker's view of the mighty dam? Tell what image helps you understand the speaker's feelings about the dam.

2. **Interpret** Identify the imagery in lines 4–5. To what senses does it appeal? Explain what this image suggests about the power of the speaker's feelings.

3. **Analyze** The technique in which a sound, word, or phrase is repeated for emphasis as well as to create rhythm is called **repetition.** Identify the phrase that is repeated in this poem. What is the effect of this repetition?

4. **Infer** When will the speaker show forgiveness? Identify the lines in the poem that help you answer.

5. **Draw Conclusions** Powwows are gatherings where Native Americans of North America share dancing, music, and other cultural traditions. What phrases from the poem suggest what will happen at "The Powwow at the End of the World"?

6. **Evaluate** The **tone** of a poem expresses the speaker's attitude toward the subject being addressed. Here are some words that can describe tone: *lighthearted, humorous, sharp, gloomy, angry, grateful, defiant, reflective, energetic, ironic*. What word describes the tone of this poem? Explain your choice. Then read part of the poem aloud to express the tone.

PERFORMANCE TASK

Speaking Activity: Discussion The speaker in the poem makes allusions to stories about salmon. Do research to locate a retelling of a salmon myth originating among the Native Americans of the Northwest Coast.

- Find a retelling of a myth such as "Salmon Boy," "The Legend of the Lost Salmon," or "How Salmon Came to the Squamish."
- After reading the myth, compare and contrast its ideas about the significance of salmon with those mentioned in the poem. How does the poem reflect traditional ideas in a new way?
- Discuss your conclusions with your classmates.

COLLECTION 1
PERFORMANCE TASK A

Interactive Lessons
To help you complete this task, use
- *Writing Informative Texts*
- *Writing as a Process*

Write an Informative Essay

This collection focuses on immigration and its impact. You read texts about adjusting to a new culture. In this activity, you will research and write a short informative essay on the best ways for people from other countries to adjust to living in the United States.

A successful informative essay
- provides an introduction that catches the reader's attention and clearly introduces the topic or thesis statement
- develops the topic using facts, definitions, examples, and quotations
- logically organizes main ideas and supporting evidence
- uses appropriate transitions to connect ideas
- provides a conclusion that summarizes and supports the topic or thesis statement

Visit hmhfyi.com to explore your topic and enhance your research.

Mentor Text Notice how this example from "A Place to Call Home" develops its topic with facts.

> Half of the immigrants we surveyed (51 percent) say they spend "a lot" of time with people from their birth country, a jump of 14 points from 2002.

myNotebook
Use the annotation tools in your eBook to find evidence to support your ideas. Save each piece of evidence to your notebook.

PLAN

Determine Your Topic Review the selections and make a list of the issues that seem common to the characters and people in them. Choose one or more immigration-related issues to focus on.

Formulate Ideas Prepare for research by jotting down questions that you will answer in your essay, such as:
- Where can people go to find tips for adjusting to life in the United States?
- What are some obstacles to adjusting to life in a new country?
- What sources are available to immigrants when they arrive?

ACADEMIC VOCABULARY

As you write your essay, be sure to use the academic vocabulary words.

contribute
immigrate
reaction
relocate
shifting

Collection Performance Task A   **79**

Conduct Research Use print and digital sources to find additional definitions, information, and quotations from experts.

- Use a search engine or Internet directories to find online sources. Find library books using keywords or subject searches.
- Search government immigration websites.
- Cite real-life examples of people who have faced this issue.
- Copy information about the sources you use so you can give them credit in your essay.

Organize Your Ideas Create an outline showing the information in each paragraph. Organize your ideas in a logical sequence, making sure they flow smoothly and are connected.

> **I.** Use Roman numerals for main topics.
>   **A.** Indent and use capital letters for subtopics.
>   1. Indent and use numbers for supporting facts and details.
>   2. Indent and use numbers for supporting facts and details.

Interactive Lessons
For help in organizing your essay, use
- Writing Informative Texts: Organizing Ideas

Consider Your Purpose and Audience Think about who will read or listen to your essay and what you want them to understand. Keep your audience in mind as you prepare to write.

PRODUCE

Write Your Essay Review your notes and your outline as you begin your draft.

- Begin your essay with an unusual comment, fact, quote, or personal anecdote in order to grab your reader's interest.
- Make clear the thesis statement or controlling idea.
- Support your thesis statement with details, including facts, statistics, examples, and quotations from experts.
- Include website links that offer helpful resources.
- Prepare a conclusion that summarizes your main idea and provides your reader with a memorable insight.

Write your rough draft in *my*WriteSmart. Focus on getting your ideas down, rather than on perfecting your choice of language.

Interactive Lessons
For help in drafting your essay, use
- Writing Informative Texts: Elaboration

Prepare Visuals Add charts, graphs, photos, or statistical data to your essay. These visuals can be included in a sidebar.

REVISE

Review Your Draft Have your partner or group of peers review your draft. Use the following chart to revise your draft.

Have your partner or a group of peers review your draft in *my*WriteSmart. Ask your reviewers to note any details that do not support your ideas.

Questions	Tips	Revision Techniques
Is the thesis statement clear?	**Underline** the thesis statement.	**Add** a thesis statement.
Does each paragraph have a main point related to the thesis?	**Highlight** the main point of each paragraph.	**Delete** unrelated ideas, or **rearrange** information into separate paragraphs.
Are there relevant supporting details for each point?	**Underline** facts, statistics, examples, and quotations that support each point.	**Add** more facts, statistics, examples, and quotations from your notes.
Are ideas organized logically? Do transitions connect ideas?	**Highlight** transitional words and phrases.	**Rearrange** sentences to organize ideas logically. **Add** transitions.
Does the conclusion summarize the topic and support the information presented?	**Underline** the summary. **Highlight** sentences that support information in the essay.	**Add** a summary of the topic. **Insert** supporting sentences.

Interactive Lessons
For help in revising your essay, use
- Writing as a Process: Revising and Editing
- Writing Informative Texts: Precise Language and Vocabulary

Language Conventions: Connecting Ideas

Look for places where you can use coordinating **conjunctions** to create **compound sentences**. A compound sentence has more than one independent clause. Read the passage below from "A Place to Call Home."

> ❝ Most say that they have become comfortable in the United States quickly, yet ties to their birth countries have become stronger since 2002, particularly among recent immigrants. ❞

Notice how the conjunction *yet* combines clauses and connects their ideas.

PRESENT

Create a Finished Copy Finalize your essay and choose a way to share it with your audience. Consider these options:

- Present your essay as a speech to the class.
- Post your essay as a blog on a classroom or school website.

Collection Performance Task A

PERFORMANCE TASK A RUBRIC
INFORMATIVE ESSAY

	Ideas and Evidence	Organization	Language
4	• The introduction is appealing, is informative, and catches the reader's attention; the thesis statement is clearly identified. • The topic is well developed with clear main ideas supported by facts, details, definitions, and examples from reliable sources. • The conclusion effectively summarizes the information presented.	• The organization is effective and logical throughout the essay. • Transitions logically connect related ideas. • Conjunctions combine clauses to create compound and complex sentences.	• The writer maintains a formal style throughout the essay. • Language is strong and precise. • Sentences vary in pattern and structure. • Spelling, capitalization, punctuation, and other mechanics are correct. • Grammar and usage are correct.
3	• The introduction could be more appealing and engaging; the thesis statement is clearly identified. • One or two important points could use more support, but most main ideas are well supported by facts, details, definitions, and examples from reliable sources. • The conclusion summarizes the information presented.	• The organization of main ideas and details is confusing in a few places. • A few more transitions are needed to connect related ideas. • Some conjunctions combine clauses to create compound sentences.	• The writing style is inconsistent in a few places. • Language is too vague or general in some places. • Sentences vary somewhat in pattern and structure. • Some spelling, capitalization, and punctuation mistakes occur. • Some grammar and usage errors are repeated.
2	• The introduction is only partly informative; the thesis statement is unclear. • Most important points could use more support from relevant facts, details, definitions, and examples from reliable sources. • The conclusion is unclear or only partially summarizes the information presented.	• The organization of main ideas and details is logical in some places, but it often doesn't follow a pattern. • More transitions are needed throughout to connect related ideas. • Few conjunctions are used to combine clauses.	• The writing style becomes informal in many places. • Language is too general or vague in many places. • Sentence pattern and structure hardly vary; some fragments or run-on sentences occur. • Spelling, capitalization, and punctuation are often incorrect but do not make reading difficult. • Grammar and usage are often incorrect, but the writer's ideas are still clear.
1	• The introduction is missing or confusing. • Supporting facts, details, definitions, or examples are unreliable or missing. • The conclusion is missing.	• The organization is not logical; main ideas and details are presented randomly. • No transitions are used, making the essay difficult to understand. • Conjunctions are not used.	• The style is inappropriate for the essay. • Language is too general to convey the information. • Sentence structure is repetitive and monotonous; fragments and run-on sentences make the essay hard to follow. • Spelling, capitalization, and punctuation are incorrect and distracting throughout. • Many grammatical and usage errors obscure the meaning of the writer's ideas.

COLLECTION 1
PERFORMANCE TASK B

Interactive Lessons
To help you complete this task, use *Writing Narratives.*

Write a Personal Narrative

Like the characters in "My Favorite Chaperone" and *The Latehomecomer,* many people struggle to adjust to new situations or to fit in with different groups. Think about a time when you faced that type of challenge and write a personal narrative about your own experience.

A successful personal narrative
- establishes a situation and introduces a narrator and characters
- organizes a well-structured event sequence
- uses narrative techniques such as dialogue, pacing, relevant descriptive details, and reflection to develop experiences
- provides a conclusion that reflects on the narrated experiences and events

Mentor Text See how this example from "My Favorite Chaperone" establishes a context and point of view.

> " In homeroom when Mr. Horswill handed out the permission slip for the Spring Fling, the all-school dance, I almost didn't take one. Why should I bother when I was sure the answer would be the same? Even though I'm in ninth grade now, it would still be the same. No. *Nyet* is what they say, and I don't want to hear this again. "

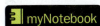 myNotebook

Use the notebook in your eBook to record examples of narrative techniques in the selections that show pacing or descriptive details.

PLAN

Establish the Situation Think about the following to help you choose an event to write about.

- When did you struggle to fit into a new group or adjust to new situation, such as going to a new school or joining a new club or team?
- What challenges did you face?
- What did you learn from your struggle?

List the Events Tell your story in an order that will make sense to readers.

ACADEMIC VOCABULARY

As you prepare your narrative, be sure to use the academic vocabulary words.

contribute
immigrate
reaction
relocate
shifting

Collection Performance Task B   **83**

A graphic organizer, such as a flow chart, can help you describe the event in a logical way.

Interactive Lessons
To help you establish a context, use
• Narrative Context

Brainstorm Images Think about your mental images of the event. Describe the images using words and phrases that convey

- vivid colors
- specific sounds
- scents, tastes, or feelings

Consider Your Purpose and Audience Consider your audience as you prepare to write. Keep in mind that your wording and tone may be different for a group of classmates or friends than it would be for a group of adults.

Mentor Text Look for the images in this excerpt from "My Favorite Chaperone" that bring the scene to life.

> Papa didn't speak. His silence filled every corner of the cab like a dark cloud, slowly suffocating me with its poisonous rage. Papa's neck was deep red, and the skin on the back of my hands tingled with fear. I lay my head back against the seat and closed my eyes, squeezing them shut, and took myself far away until I was safe on the bars at a beautiful gymnastics meet in the sky.

PRODUCE

Write Your Personal Narrative Review your notes and your graphic organizer as you begin your draft.

- Begin with an attention-grabbing comment or some dialogue that will catch readers' interest. Provide any background on your experience that readers may need.
- Include descriptive details to capture your experience for readers.
- Conclude by reflecting on what made the experience significant for you. Explain what you learned from it or how the experience had an impact on your life.

Write your rough draft in *myWriteSmart*. Focus on getting your ideas down, rather than on perfecting your choice of language.

Interactive Lessons
To help you organize your narrative, use:
• Narrative Structure

REVISE

Review Your Draft Have your partner or group of peers review your draft. Use the following chart to revise your draft.

Ask your reviewers to note any parts of the story that are confusing or that could benefit from more descriptive details.

Questions	Tips	Revision Techniques
Does the essay narrate a clear, coherent, incident?	**Underline** details that show when and where the experience happened.	**Add** details about where and when the event took place.
Is the first-person point of view used consistently?	**Note** anywhere the point of view changes.	**Change** any third-person pronouns to first-person pronouns, as necessary.
Are well-chosen descriptive details included?	**Highlight** sensory details.	**Elaborate** with sensory details. **Delete** irrelevant details.
Is the dialogue relevant to the purpose?	**Note** any dialogue that seems unnecessary.	**Add** dialogue that reveals character and advances the action.
Does the narrative reveal why the incident is significant?	**Underline** details that show why the experience is meaningful.	**Add** a statement that explains the event's importance, if necessary.

Language Conventions: Details and Sensory Language

Look for places where you can add descriptive details and sensory language to bring your experiences to life. Read the following passage from *The Latehomecomer*.

> " There was hardly room to breathe when the scent of jasmine rice and fish steamed with ginger mingled heavily with the scent of freshly baked pepperoni pizza—Dawb's favorite food. "

Note how Yang uses specific details that appeal to the sense of taste and smell to describe a scene of a house too small for its companions and the contrasting flavors of their food.

PRESENT

Create a Finished Copy Choose a way to share your narrative with your audience. Consider these options:

- Present your personal narrative as a speech to the class.
- Post your personal narrative as a blog on a school website.
- Dramatize your personal narrative in a one-person show.

PERFORMANCE TASK B RUBRIC
PERSONAL NARRATIVE

	Ideas and Evidence	Organization	Language
4	• The narrative establishes the situation using well-chosen details. • Dialogue and description are used effectively. • The conclusion unfolds naturally and reflects on the significance of the experience.	• The narrative has a coherent sequence that builds to a logical conclusion. • Well-chosen events result in effective pacing. • Transitions logically connect the sequence of events.	• The narrative successfully weaves in sensory language and vivid details. • The writer's word choice develops or enhances his or her voice. • Grammar, usage, and mechanics are correct.
3	• The narrative conveys a real experience. • Some well-chosen details are included. • More dialogue or description could be used. • The conclusion could be strengthened.	• The narrative includes some extraneous events, resulting in ineffective pacing. • More transitions would make the sequence of events clearer.	• The narrative includes sensory language and descriptive details. • The writer's word choice is effective. • Some errors in grammar, usage, or mechanics create distractions.
2	• The narrative conveys a real experience but needs more development. • Details are lacking or irrelevant. • Dialogue and description are limited or lacking. • The conclusion is ineffective.	• The narrative has a confusing sequence caused by extraneous events or the lack of transitions. • Missing events or information creates ambiguity.	• The narrative needs more sensory language and descriptive details. • The writer's word choice needs improvement. • Multiple errors in grammar, usage, or mechanics create distractions.
1	• The narrative has no identifiable experience. • Details are vague or omitted. • Dialogue and description are not included. • A conclusion is not included.	• The narrative has no apparent organization.	• The narrative lacks sensory language and descriptive details. • The writer's word choice is vague or confusing. • Significant errors in grammar, usage, or mechanics create confusion and misunderstanding.

COLLECTION 2

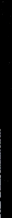

The Thrill of Horror

"There is a . . . horror story that is only two sentences long: The last man on Earth sat alone in a room. There was a knock at the door."

—Frederick Brown

COLLECTION 2
The Thrill of Horror

In this collection, you will examine why the horror genre both terrifies and fascinates.

Stream to Start

Channel One News

COLLECTION
PERFORMANCE TASK Preview

At the end of this collection, you will have the opportunity to complete two performance tasks:

- In one, you will present a speech arguing whether a classic horror story is appropriate for your age group to read.
- In the second, you will write a literary analysis that examines how the fiction in the collection meets the criteria for the horror genre.

ACADEMIC VOCABULARY

Study the words and their definitions in the chart below. You will use these words as you discuss and write about the texts in this collection.

Word	Definition	Related Forms
convention (kən-vĕn´shən) n.	a practice or procedure widely used by a group; a custom	conventional, conventionally
predict (prĭ-dĭkt´) v.	to tell about in advance, especially on the basis of special knowledge	prediction, predictable, predictive
psychology (sī-kŏl´ə-jē) n.	the study of mental processes and behaviors	psychological, psychologist
summary (sŭm´ə-rē) n.	a condensed, or shorter, report that includes the main points of a text or event	summarize, summation
technique (tĕk-nēk´) n.	the systematic or orderly procedure by which a task is accomplished	technical

Edgar Allan Poe (1809–1849) *was born in Boston to parents who were traveling actors. Orphaned by the time he was three, he moved to Virginia where friends of his family raised him. As a young man, Poe worked as a journalist while writing the stories and poems that would earn him the title "father of the modern mystery." After his young wife died, Poe fell into despair. He passed away two years later. His dark and sometimes horrifying works perhaps mirror the darkness and sadness of his own short life.*

The Tell-Tale Heart

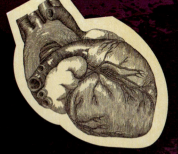

Short Story by Edgar Allan Poe

SETTING A PURPOSE As you read, pay attention to the way the narrator describes himself. What makes him unusual?

myNotebook

As you read, save new words to *myWordList*.

True!—nervous—very, very dreadfully nervous I had been and am! but why *will* you say that I am mad? The disease had sharpened my senses—not destroyed—not dulled them. Above all was the sense of hearing acute. I heard all things in the heaven and in the earth. I heard many things in hell. How, then, am I mad? Hearken! and observe how healthily—how calmly I can tell you the whole story.

It is impossible to say how first the idea entered my brain; but once **conceived**, it haunted me day and night. Object there was none. Passion there was none. I loved the old man. He had never wronged me. He had never given me insult. For his gold I had no desire. I think it was his eye! yes, it was this! He had the eye of a vulture—a pale blue eye, with a film over it. Whenever it fell upon me, my blood ran cold; and so by degrees—very gradually—I made up my mind to take the life of the old man, and thus rid myself of the eye forever.

Now this is the point. You fancy me mad. Madmen know nothing. But you should have seen *me*. You should have seen

conceive
(kən-sēv´) *v.* When you *conceive* an idea, you think of it.

how wisely I proceeded—with what caution—with what foresight—with what dissimulation[1] I went to work!

I was never kinder to the old man than during the whole week before I killed him. And every night, about midnight, I turned the latch of his door and opened it—oh, so gently! And then, when I had made an opening sufficient for my head, I put in a dark lantern, all closed, closed, so that no light shone out, and then I thrust in my head. Oh, you would have laughed to see how cunningly I thrust it in! I moved it slowly—very, very slowly, so that I might not disturb the old man's sleep. It took me an hour to place my whole head within the opening so far that I could see him as he lay upon his bed. Ha!—would a madman have been so wise as this? And then, when my head was well in the room, I undid the lantern cautiously—oh, so cautiously—cautiously (for the hinges creaked)—I undid it just so much that a single thin ray fell upon the vulture eye. And this I did for seven long nights—every night just at midnight—but I found the eye always closed; and so it was impossible to do the work; for it was not the old man who **vexed** me, but his Evil Eye. And every morning, when the day broke, I went boldly into the chamber, and spoke courageously to him, calling him by name in a hearty tone, and inquiring how he had passed the night. So you see he would have been a very profound old man, indeed, to suspect that every night, just at twelve, I looked in upon him while he slept.

Upon the eighth night I was more than usually cautious in opening the door. A watch's minute hand moves more quickly than did mine. Never before that night had I *felt* the extent of my own powers—of my sagacity.[2] I could scarcely contain my feelings of triumph. To think that there I was, opening the door, little by little, and he not even to dream of my secret deeds or thoughts. I fairly chuckled at the idea; and perhaps he heard me; for he moved on the bed suddenly, as if startled. Now you may think that I drew back—but no. His room was as black as pitch with the thick darkness (for the shutters were close fastened, through fear of robbers), and so I knew that he could not see the opening of the door, and I kept pushing it on steadily, steadily.

vex
(věks) *v.* If you *vex* someone, you annoy that person.

---

[1] **dissimulation** (dĭ-sĭm′yə-lā′shən): a hiding of one's true feelings.
[2] **sagacity** (sə-găs′ĭ-tē): sound judgment.

I had my head in, and was about to open the lantern, when my thumb slipped upon the tin fastening, and the old man sprang up in the bed, crying out—"Who's there?"

I kept quite still and said nothing. For a whole hour I did not move a muscle, and in the meantime I did not hear him lie down. He was still sitting up in the bed listening,—just as I have done, night after night, hearkening to the death watches[3] in the wall.

Presently I heard a slight groan, and I knew it was the groan of mortal terror. It was not a groan of pain or grief—oh, no!—it was the low, **stifled** sound that arises from the bottom of the soul when overcharged with awe. I knew the sound well. Many a night, just at midnight, when all the world slept, it has welled up from my own bosom, deepening, with its dreadful echo, the terrors that distracted me. I say I knew it well. I knew what the old man felt, and pitied him, although I chuckled at heart. I knew that he had been lying awake ever since the first slight noise, when he had turned in the bed. His fears had been ever since growing upon him. He had been trying to fancy them causeless, but could not. He had been saying to himself—"It is nothing but the wind in the chimney—it is only a mouse crossing the floor," or "it is merely a cricket which has made a single chirp." Yes, he has been trying to comfort himself with these suppositions; but he had found all in vain. *All in vain;* because Death, in approaching him, had stalked with his black shadow before him, and enveloped the victim. And it was the mournful influence of the unperceived shadow that caused him to feel—although he neither saw nor heard—to *feel* the presence of my head within the room.

When I had waited a long time, very patiently, without hearing him lie down, I resolved to open a little—a very, very little **crevice** in the lantern. So I opened it—you cannot imagine how stealthily, stealthily—until, at length, a single dim ray, like the thread of the spider, shot from out the crevice and fell full upon the vulture eye.

It was open—wide, wide open—and I grew furious as I gazed upon it. I saw it with perfect distinctness—all a dull blue, with a hideous veil over it that chilled the very marrow in my bones; but I could see nothing else of the old man's face

stifle
(stī´ fəl) *v.* If you *stifle* something, you smother it.

crevice
(krĕv´ ĭs) *n.* A *crevice* is a narrow crack.

---

[3] **death watches:** deathwatch beetles—insects that make a tapping sound with their heads.

or person: for I had directed the ray as if by instinct, precisely upon the damned spot.

And now have I not told you that what you mistake for madness is but over-acuteness of the senses?—now, I say, there came to my ears a low, dull, quick sound, such as a watch makes when enveloped in cotton. I knew *that* sound well too. It was the beating of the old man's heart. It increased my fury, as the beating of a drum stimulates the soldier into courage.

But even yet I refrained and kept still. I scarcely breathed. I held the lantern motionless. I tried how steadily I could maintain the ray upon the eye. Meantime the hellish tattoo[4] of the heart increased. It grew quicker and quicker, and louder and louder every instant. The old man's terror *must* have been extreme! It grew louder, I say, louder every moment!—do you mark me well? I have told you that I am nervous: so I am. And now at the dead hour of the night, amid the dreadful silence of that old house, so strange a noise as this excited me to uncontrollable terror. Yet, for some minutes longer I refrained and stood still. But the beating grew louder, louder! I thought the heart must burst. And now a new anxiety seized me—the sound would be heard by a neighbor! The old man's hour had come! With a loud yell, I threw open the lantern and leaped into the room. He shrieked once—once only. In an instant

---

[4] **hellish tattoo:** awful drumming.

I dragged him to the floor, and pulled the heavy bed over him. I then smiled gaily, to find the deed so far done. But, for many minutes, the heart beat on with a muffled sound. This, however, did not vex me; it would not be heard through the wall. At length it ceased. The old man was dead. I removed the bed and examined the corpse. Yes, he was stone, stone dead. I placed my hand upon the heart and held it there many minutes. There was no pulsation. He was stone dead. His eye would trouble me no more.

If still you think me mad, you will think so no longer when I describe the wise precautions I took for the concealment of the body. The night waned, and I worked hastily, but in silence. First of all I dismembered the corpse. I cut off the head and the arms and the legs.

I then took up three planks from the flooring of the chamber, and deposited all between the scantlings.⁵ I then replaced the boards so cleverly, so cunningly, that no human eye—not even *his*—could have detected anything wrong. There was nothing to wash out—no stain of any kind—no blood-spot whatever. I had been too wary for that. A tub had caught all—ha! ha!

When I made an end of these labors, it was four o'clock—still dark as midnight. As the bell sounded the hour, there came a knocking at the street door. I went down to open it with a light heart,—for what had I *now* to fear? There entered three men, who introduced themselves, with perfect suavity,⁶ as officers of the police. A shriek had been heard by a neighbor during the night: suspicion of foul play had been aroused; information had been lodged at the police office, and they (the officers) had been deputed to search the premises.

I smiled,—for *what* had I to fear? I bade the gentlemen welcome. The shriek, I said, was my own in a dream. The old man, I mentioned, was absent in the country. I took my visitors all over the house. I bade them search—search *well*. I led them, at length, to *his* chamber. I showed them his treasures, secure, undisturbed. In the enthusiasm of my confidence, I brought chairs into the room, and desired them *here* to rest from their fatigues, while I myself, in the wild **audacity** of my perfect triumph, placed my own seat upon the very spot beneath which reposed the corpse of the victim.

audacity
(ô-dăs´ ĭ-tē) *n.*
Audacity is shameless daring or boldness.

---

⁵ **scantlings:** small wooden beams supporting the floor.
⁶ **suavity** (swä´vĭ-tē): graceful politeness.

The officers were satisfied. My *manner* had convinced them. I was singularly at ease. They sat, and while I answered cheerily, they chatted of familiar things. But, ere long, I felt myself getting pale and wished them gone. My head ached, and I fancied a ringing in my ears: but still they sat and still chatted. The ringing became more distinct:—it continued and became more distinct: I talked more freely to get rid of the feeling: but it continued and gained definitiveness—until at length, I found that the noise was *not* within my ears.

No doubt I now grew *very* pale;—but I talked more fluently, and with a heightened voice. Yet the sound increased—and what could I do? It was *a low, dull, quick sound—much such a sound as a watch makes when enveloped in cotton*. I gasped for breath—and yet the officers heard it not. I talked more quickly—more **vehemently**; but the noise steadily increased. I arose and argued about trifles, in a high key and with violent gesticulations,[7] but the noise steadily increased. Why *would* they not be gone? I paced the floor to and fro with heavy strides, as if excited to fury by the observation of the men—but the noise steadily increased. What *could* I do? I foamed—I raved—I swore. I swung the chair upon which I had been sitting, and grated it upon the boards, but the noise arose over all and continually increased. It grew louder—louder—*louder!* And still the men chatted pleasantly, and smiled. Was it possible they heard not?—no, no! They heard!—they suspected!—they *knew!*—they were making a *mockery* of my horror!—this I thought, and this I think. But anything was better than this agony! Anything was more tolerable than this **derision**! I could bear those **hypocritical** smiles no longer! I felt that I must scream or die!—and now—again!—hark! louder! louder! *louder!*—

"Villains!" I shrieked, "dissemble[8] no more! I admit the deed!—tear up the planks!—here, here!—it is the beating of his hideous heart!"

vehemently
(vē´ə-mənt-lē) *adv.*
If you do something *vehemently*, you do it with intense emotion.

derision
(dĭ-rĭzh´ən) *n.*
Derision is jeering laughter or ridicule.

hypocritical
(hĭp´ə-krĭt´ĭ-kəl) *adj.*
If someone is *hypocritical*, the person is false or deceptive.

COLLABORATIVE DISCUSSION "The Tell-Tale Heart" is a well-known classic. With a partner, discuss what makes the story—and its narrator—so thought provoking. Cite specific evidence from the text to support your ideas.

---

[7] **gesticulations** (jĕ-stĭk´yə-lā´shəns): energetic gestures of the hands or arms.
[8] **dissemble**: pretend.

Analyze Point of View

Point of view is the method of narration used in a short story, novel, narrative poem, or work of nonfiction. In a story told from the **third-person point of view,** the **narrator,** or the voice that tells the story, is an outside observer. In a story told from **first-person point of view,** the narrator is a character in the story and uses the pronouns *I* and *me.*

Just as you can't believe everything everyone tells you, you can't always believe everything you learn from a first-person narrator. An **unreliable narrator** is a narrator whose assessment of events cannot be trusted for some reason—he or she might be purposefully lying, mentally unstable, or too young or unsophisticated to fully understand events. In order to determine whether or not a narrator is reliable, consider his or her actions, attitudes, and statements, and then decide whether he or she is generally trustworthy.

Do you think the narrator of "The Tell-Tale Heart" is reliable? Review the story and identify the lines that help you decide.

Analyze Suspense

Suspense is the sense of growing tension, fear, and excitement felt by the reader. When a story is suspenseful, the reader becomes increasingly curious about what will happen next. Writers use different techniques to create suspense in fiction. Notice these examples from "The Tell-Tale Heart."

Technique	Example
Describing a character's anxiety or fear	"... groan of mortal terror ... it was the low, stifled sound that arises from the bottom of the soul when overcharged with awe."
Using vivid words to describe dramatic sights, sounds, or feelings	"He had the eye of a vulture—a pale blue eye with a film over it. Whenever it fell upon me, my blood ran cold."
Repeating words, phrases, or characters' actions	the actions the narrator repeated as he entered the old man's room each night

As you analyze "The Tell-Tale Heart," look for additional examples of each technique.

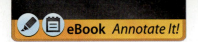

Analyzing the Text

Cite Text Evidence   Support your responses with evidence from the text.

1. **Infer** Does the narrator's opinion of himself in lines 1–16 make him seem more or less reliable? Explain your choice.

2. **Analyze** What prevents the narrator from killing the old man during the first seven nights? Explain how his inaction contributes to the suspense.

3. **Interpret** In what way does the author's repeated image of the "eye of a vulture" help to create suspense?

4. **Draw Conclusions** Reread lines 88–105. What do readers learn from this first-person narration about the narrator's subjective, or personal, experience?

5. **Analyze** In lines 151–160, the narrator makes his case to the police and thinks he has convinced them of his innocence. What happens next that leads the narrator to finally confess? Tell what this suggests about his mental state.

6. **Evaluate** Do you think the reader's ability to trust the narrator increases the suspense in this story? Explain your answer.

Speaking and Listening

Working alone or with one or more partners, act out a scene from "The Tell-Tale Heart" that you consider especially suspenseful. Be prepared to identify the techniques or conventions that create suspense in the scene.

PERFORMANCE TASK

Writing Activity: Narrative Criminals sometimes undergo a psychiatric evaluation during which their mental health is reviewed by a psychologist. Based on details from the story, write a narrative about the evaluation of the narrator by a mental health expert. Consider the following questions:

- What crime did the narrator commit?
- What was his motive? Was he insane, enraged, seeking revenge, or something else?
- Would the narrator take responsibility for his crimes?
- Why or why not?
- What might a mental health expert say about the narrator's state of mind?

Critical Vocabulary

| conceive | vex | stifle | crevice |
| audacity | vehemently | derision | hypocritical |

Practice and Apply Use what you know about the Vocabulary words to answer these questions.

1. Would it **vex** you if someone were **hypocritical**? Why?
2. Why does it take **audacity** to **vehemently** deny that you told a lie?
3. What method can you **conceive** to get something out of a **crevice**?
4. What can you do to **stifle derision** of another student?

Vocabulary Strategy: Use a Thesaurus

A **thesaurus** is a reference source that provides synonyms for many words. Writers use **synonyms,** or words that have a similar meaning as another word, to make writing precise and to avoid repeating the same word.

A good writer does not simply choose the first synonym provided in the thesaurus. He or she chooses the synonym that conveys the precise, or exact, meaning intended for a sentence. Look at the synonyms a thesaurus provides for the word *terror*:

fear, horror, fright, dread, shock, panic, alarm

Think about how each synonym might fit in this sentence from "The Tell-Tale Heart."

I knew it was a groan of mortal terror.

Does *a groan of terror* mean exactly the same as *a groan of alarm*? Which word conveys the idea of concern? Which conveys the idea of complete and total fear?

Practice and Apply Read these sentences. Use a print or digital thesaurus to replace the underlined words. Check that the synonym you chose fits the precise meaning of the sentence.

1. The narrator at first appears calm. By the end of the story, he is no longer <u>calm</u>.
2. As the story continues the narrator becomes increasingly nervous. His inability to stop talking shows how <u>nervous</u> he is.
3. "The Tell-Tale Heart" is a suspense-filled story. The narrator builds <u>suspense</u> as he reveals his carefully constructed plan to kill an old man.

Language Conventions: Using Dashes

A writer's use of punctuation not only helps readers understand the writer's message, it can also signal how the writer wants the text to be read. A **dash** (—) is a horizontal line that is longer than a hyphen. Writers may use a dash for different purposes, as noted in the following chart.

Purpose	Example
to signal a sudden break in thought	"I did so for seven long nights—every night just after midnight—but found the eye always closed..."
to signal the reader to pause and pay attention	"I resolved to open a little—a very, very little crevice in the lantern."
to let the reader better hear a narrator's thoughts	"I went down to open it with a light heart—for what had I *now* to fear?"

Notice that when the interrupting thought appears in the middle of the sentence, one dash appears at the beginning of the thought and one dash appears at the end. Look at this example from "The Tell-Tale Heart":

> **He had the eye of a vulture—a pale blue eye, with a film over it. Whenever it fell upon me, my blood ran cold; and so by degrees—very gradually—I made up my mind to take the life of the old man, and thus rid myself of the eye forever.**

The dash after "vulture," signals the reader to pause and pay attention. The two dashes surrounding "very gradually" emphasize the slow, gradual process the narrator went through before deciding to kill the old man. Poe uses dashes not only to indicate pauses, but also to let the reader hear the excited, irrational voice of the narrator.

Practice and Apply Working with a partner, write a paragraph in which your narrator tells readers about him- or herself. Use dashes to

- set off a sudden break in thought.
- signal the reader to pause and pay attention.
- let the reader better hear your narrator's voice.

Jackie Torrence (1944–2004) *spent much of her childhood on a North Carolina farm, where she grew up listening to traditional stories told by her grandfather. Years later, while working as a librarian, she was asked to read stories to some young children. She agreed, and the children were instantly captivated. Before long, Torrence was invited to tell stories in local and neighboring communities. Torrence, who was later dubbed "The Story Lady," went on to gain national prominence as a storyteller.*

SCARY TALES

Essay by Jackie Torrence

SETTING A PURPOSE As you read, pay attention to the points the author makes about scary tales. Would most people agree with her ideas?

I guess I like scary tales so much because my granddaddy liked scary tales. He'd have to tell one if it killed him. He was sick a lot, but if visitors came, he'd prop himself up in an armchair and put a quilt on his lap. So nobody could see his nightshirt. Then he'd put his derby hat on, he loved that derby, and somebody would say, "Mr. Jim, tell us about that time when the fire dog followed you down through the wheat field." And my grandma would say, "Hold it, let me leave the room, lightning's going to strike." She always said Granddaddy was the biggest liar God ever blew breath into. So she'd leave, but not me. I'd get closer to Pa 'cause I wanted to watch the people listening to him.

There used to be an old man who came to our house named Hall. I would hear people say, "Mr. Hall wears a rug." I didn't know what a rug was. I'd lay down on the floor and Grandma would say, "What are you doing?" "I'm trying to find Mr. Hall's rug." And Grandma would say, "Get up, *get up!* That ain't nice." Well, one day Mr. Hall was there and Grandpa started into one of his scary stories. There was a piece of wood burning in the fireplace, sort of sticking out, and Pa spotted it. I watched him put his tobacco way back in his mouth so he could get a good long shot. At just the right moment in the story, he threw his head forward and that tobacco came out and hit that wood just right; it fell off on the floor and the fire sparked up. Somebody threw a baby on the floor, men ran out, and Mr. Hall ran out too. When he passed us, Mr. Hall's scalp was as naked as the palm of my hand. *Jesus have mercy!* Granddaddy scared the hair right off Mr. Hall's head! Well, I went over to his chair, and there in Mr. Hall's hat was his scalp! I picked it up. "Grandma! Is this Mr. Hall's rug?" Grandma said, "Put that thing down and go wash your hands." Oh, I loved those days when Grandpa told his scary stories.

So when I started telling stories in school, that's what I chose, scary tales. I've got storytelling friends who'd rather be killed than go to junior high. But not me, I love junior high.

That's sixth, seventh, and eighth grade, and those kids can't believe they're going to have to sit there and listen to me tell a story. So I do just what Grandpa said, "If you want to get the attention of a mule who's too stubborn to listen, you take the branch off a tree and come right down across the top of his head." What is my branch? A good scary story. When I tell those kids, "I'm going to scare you," when I start to give them a little bit of fear, well, they're ready to listen.

A lot of people have told me I really shouldn't tell children scary things. Well, children can frighten themselves without your help. When they're alone in bed they hear things and they see things. So I just help them along. "It's *daaaaaaark*," I say. And there's a strange voice, "Where's Myy Haaairy Toe…" That's all they need. They remember the dark and they're scared again and that's good.

Children need to be frightened. We all do. It's an emotion that was given to all of us and it should be exercised. When you don't exercise it, you lose your sense of fear. That's why my granddaddy told me scary stories. He wanted me to know that only fools rush in where angels fear to tread. You should be a little hesitant sometimes, his stories were saying, you should think twice before you go into the woods, there just might be a hairy man and you need to be cautious.

My grandfather scared me to death. Grandma would say, "Get up on your granddaddy's lap and kiss him good night." I'd throw my arms around him and say, "I'm going to bed." And he'd say, "It's dark up there." And I'd say, "I know." "You know what's in the dark?" "Nooooo." "Monsters," he'd say. "What do monsters do?" "They'll drag you off the bed and put you in the keyhole," he'd say. Well, I yelled and screamed going up the stairs. My grandmother would say to me on the way up, "*Would you stop crying*? There's not a keyhole big enough to put you in." So I remained fat for the rest of my life. That's why no monsters have ever bothered me.

COLLABORATIVE DISCUSSION With a partner, discuss whether you agree with Torrence's ideas about scary tales. Cite specific evidence from the text to support your ideas.

Determine Author's Viewpoint

Why does Jackie Torrence feel the way she does about scary tales? In order to answer, you have to determine her viewpoint. An **author's viewpoint** is the unique combination of ideas, values, feelings, and beliefs that influence the way the writer looks at a topic. To determine an author's viewpoint, consider

- the opinions an author holds about a topic
- the details that suggest why he or she thinks a certain way
- the reasons offered in support of a certain view
- the way the author's background might affect his or her outlook

A good writer anticipates and acknowledges opposing views and responds to them. A **counterargument** is an argument made to oppose an alternative view. In "Scary Tales," Jackie Torrence includes this counterargument when discussing whether or not it's a good idea for children to experience fear:

> It's an emotion that was given to all of us and it should be exercised.

Review "Scary Tales" and identify at least two more counterarguments.

Analyze the Meanings of Words and Phrases

Style is a manner of writing. It involves *how* something is said rather than *what* is said. Writers show style through the choices they make about the following elements:

Elements of Style	Examples
Word choice and imagery are the use of specific words. Writers might choose elegant, specialized words or vivid, blunt language.	"... there in Mr. Hall's hat was his scalp!"
Syntax refers to the way words are put together to form phrases and sentences. The length of a writer's sentences and the use of formal or informal grammar all contribute to style.	"And Grandma would say, 'Get up, get up! That ain't nice.'"
Figurative language is language used imaginatively in ways that go beyond literal definitions. The kinds and amount of images writers use can help define his or her style.	"My grandfather scared me to death."

Style can be described with words such as *formal, conversational, sophisticated,* and *humorous*. How would you describe the style in which "Scary Tales" is written? Review the selections and find examples to support your answer.

Analyzing the Text

Cite Text Evidence   Support your responses with evidence from the text.

1. **Interpret**   What does the author's grandma mean in lines 8–9 when she says, "Hold it, let me leave the room, lightning's going to strike"?

2. **Summarize**   Tell what happens when Mr. Hall comes to visit.

3. **Analyze**   An **analogy** is an extended comparison of two things that are alike in some way. Examine lines 39–42. What two things is the author comparing? Explain what this comparison reveals about the author's **tone,** or attitude, toward storytelling.

4. **Interpret**   What does Grandpa Jim mean when he tells his granddaughter that "only fools rush in where angels fear to tread"? Explain what lesson scary stories can help teach.

5. **Analyze**   Use a chart like the one shown to record examples of the word choice, syntax, and figurative language that contribute to Torrence's style.

Elements of Style	Examples
Word choice	
Syntax	
Figurative language	

6. **Draw Conclusions**   How would you describe Torrence's viewpoint on scary tales? Explain how her values, beliefs, and background contribute to the way she thinks about this topic.

7. **Evaluate**   Are the author's counterarguments effective in proving her own view? Explain why or why not.

PERFORMANCE TASK

Speaking Activity: Debate   Is it a good idea for middle school students to hear scary stories? Have a debate about this topic.

- Working with a partner, decide which viewpoint you will argue: Is it a good idea for young people to hear scary stories, or is it a bad idea?

- List reasons that support your viewpoint. Include evidence from "Scary Tales."
- Prepare for counterarguments.
- Practice your arguments orally. Then debate another pair of students who have chosen the opposite position.

Scary Tales   103

Language Conventions: Subject-Verb Agreement

The subject and verb in a sentence or clause must agree in number. **Agreement** means that if the subject is singular, the verb must also be singular; if the subject is plural, the verb must also be plural. In this sentence from "Scary Tales," both the subject and the verb are plural.

Children need to be frightened.

Notice how the verb changes when the subject is singular:

A child needs to be frightened.

Add -s or -es to most verbs in the present tense to agree with a singular subject. Do not add -s if the subject is *I* or *you*.

Singular Subjects and Verbs	Plural Subjects and Verbs
I scream.	We scream.
You scream.	You scream.
He/She/It scream<u>s</u>.	They scream.
Jacob scream<u>s</u>.	My cousins scream.

Sometimes, other words in a sentence come between the subject and the verb. When this happens, first identify the subject, and then make sure the verb agrees with it.

My <u>friends</u> in the neighborhood <u>like</u> scary stories.

Use a plural verb with most compound subjects joined by the coordinating conjunction *and*.

The <u>students and their teacher</u> <u>watch</u> a horror movie.

When the parts of a compound subject are joined by *or*, *nor*, or the correlative conjunctions *either...or* or *neither...nor*, the verb should agree with the noun or pronoun nearest the verb.

<u>Neither the pupils nor Ms. Chen</u> <u>believes</u> that the house is really haunted.

Practice and Apply Choose the correct verb in parentheses to agree with its subject.

1. Grandma and friends (listen, listens) to Grandpa Jim's stories.
2. Visitors, who come to the house to visit, (see, sees) the image.
3. People not far from the author (run, runs) out of the room.
4. She (watch, watches) the commotion with interest.
5. Neither the grandmother nor the guests (love, loves) the scary tales.

William Wymark Jacobs (1863–1943) *grew up in London near the waterfront wharfs. As a boy, Jacobs absorbed the tales of strange, distant lands told by passing sailors. As a young man, Jacobs worked at a bank—a job that he hated—and wrote stories in his spare time. He eventually became a popular writer of humor. Ironically, his best-known work, "The Monkey's Paw," became a classic of the horror genre.*

The Monkey's Paw

Short Story by W. W. Jacobs

SETTING A PURPOSE As you read, pay attention to the relationships among the members of the White family. How does the appearance of the monkey's paw affect those relationships?

Part I

Without, the night was cold and wet, but in the small parlor of Laburnum Villa the blinds were drawn and the fire burned brightly. Father and son were at chess; the former, who possessed ideas about the game involving radical changes, putting his king into such sharp and unnecessary **perils** that it even provoked comment from the white-haired old lady knitting placidly by the fire.

"Hark at the wind," said Mr. White, who, having seen a fatal mistake after it was too late, was amiably desirous of preventing his son from seeing it.

"I'm listening," said the latter, grimly surveying the board as he stretched out his hand. "Check."

peril
(pĕr´əl) *n.* A *peril* is something that is dangerous.

"I should hardly think that he'd come tonight," said his father, with his hand poised over the board.

"Mate," replied the son.

"That's the worst of living so far out," bawled Mr. White, with sudden and unlooked-for violence; "of all the beastly, slushy, out-of-the-way places to live in, this is the worst. Pathway's a bog,[1] and the road's a torrent.[2] I don't know what people are thinking about. I suppose because only two houses in the road are let,[3] they think it doesn't matter."

"Never mind, dear," said his wife soothingly; "perhaps you'll win the next one."

Mr. White looked up sharply, just in time to intercept a knowing glance between mother and son. The words died away on his lips, and he hid a guilty grin in his thin gray beard.

"There he is," said Herbert White, as the gate banged loudly and heavy footsteps came toward the door.

The old man rose with hospitable haste, and opening the door, was heard **condoling** with the new arrival. The new arrival also condoled with himself, so that Mrs. White said, "Tut, tut!" and coughed gently as her husband entered the room, followed by a tall, burly man, beady of eye and rubicund of visage.[4]

"Sergeant-Major Morris," he said, introducing him.

The sergeant-major shook hands, and taking the proffered seat by the fire, watched contentedly while his host brought out drinks and stood a small copper kettle on the fire.

He began to talk, the little family circle regarding with eager interest this visitor from distant parts, as he squared his broad shoulders in the chair and spoke of wild scenes and doughty[5] deeds; of wars and plagues and strange peoples.

"Twenty-one years of it," said Mr. White, nodding at his wife and son. "When he went away, he was a slip of a youth in the warehouse. Now look at him."

"He don't look to have taken much harm," said Mrs. White politely.

"I'd like to go to India myself," said the old man, "just to look round a bit, you know."

condole
(kən-dōl´) v. If you *condole* with someone, you express sympathy or sorrow.

---

[1] **bog:** a swamp.
[2] **torrent** (tôr´ənt): a swift-flowing stream.
[3] **let:** rented.
[4] **rubicund** (roō´bĭ-kənd) **of visage** (vĭz´ĭj): with a ruddy complexion.
[5] **doughty** (dou´tē): brave.

"Better where you are," said the sergeant-major, shaking his head. He put down the empty glass, and sighing softly, shook it again.

"I should like to see those old temples and fakirs and jugglers," said the old man. "What was that you started telling me the other day about a monkey's paw or something, Morris?"

"Nothing," said the soldier hastily. "Leastways nothing worth hearing."

"Monkey's paw?" said Mrs. White curiously.

"Well, it's just a bit of what you might call magic, perhaps," said the sergeant-major off-handedly.

His three listeners leaned forward eagerly. The visitor absent-mindedly put his empty glass to his lips and then set it down again. His host filled it for him.

"To look at," said the sergeant-major, fumbling in his pocket, "it's just an ordinary little paw, dried to a mummy."

He took something out of his pocket and proffered it. Mrs. White drew back with a **grimace**, but her son, taking it, examined it curiously.

"And what is there special about it?" inquired Mr. White as he took it from his son, and having examined it, placed it upon the table.

"It had a spell put on it by an old fakir," said the sergeant-major, "a very holy man. He wanted to show that **fate** ruled people's lives, and that those who interfered with it did so to their sorrow. He put a spell on it so that three separate men could each have three wishes from it."

His manner was so impressive that his hearers were conscious that their light laughter jarred somewhat.

"Well, why don't you have three, sir?" said Herbert White cleverly.

The soldier regarded him in the way that middle age is wont to regard presumptuous youth. "I have," he said quietly, and his blotchy face whitened.

"And did you really have the three wishes granted?" asked Mrs. White.

"I did," said the sergeant-major, and his glass tapped against his strong teeth.

"And has anybody else wished?" persisted the old lady.

grimace
(grĭm´ĭs) *n.* A *grimace* is a facial expression of pain or disgust.

fate
(fāt) *n. Fate* is a power that is thought to determine the course of events.

"The first man had his three wishes. Yes," was the reply; "I don't know what the first two were, but the third was for death. That's how I got the paw."

His tones were so grave that a hush fell upon the group.

"If you've had your three wishes, it's no good to you now, then, Morris," said the old man at last. "What do you keep it for?"

> "His tones were so grave that a hush fell upon the room."

The soldier shook his head. "Fancy, I suppose," he said slowly. "I did have some idea of selling it, but I don't think I will. It has caused enough mischief already. Besides, people won't buy. They think it's a fairy tale, some of them; and those who do think anything of it want to try it first and pay me afterward."

"If you could have another three wishes," said the old man, eyeing him keenly, "would you have them?"

"I don't know," said the other. "I don't know."

He took the paw, and dangling it between his forefinger and thumb, suddenly threw it upon the fire. White, with a slight cry, stooped down and snatched it off.

"Better let it burn," said the soldier solemnly.

"If you don't want it, Morris," said the other, "give it to me."

"I won't," said his friend doggedly. "I threw it on the fire. If you keep it, don't blame me for what happens. Pitch it on the fire again like a sensible man."

The other shook his head and examined his new possession closely. "How do you do it?" he inquired.

"Hold it up in your right hand and wish aloud," said the sergeant-major, "but I warn you of the consequences."

"Sounds like the *Arabian Nights*,"[6] said Mrs. White, as she rose and began to set the supper. "Don't you think you might wish for four pairs of hands for me?"

---

[6] *Arabian Nights*: a famous collection of Asian stories.

Her husband drew the talisman[7] from his pocket, and then all three burst into laughter as the sergeant-major, with a look of alarm on his face, caught him by the arm.

"If you must wish," he said gruffly, "wish for something sensible."

Mr. White dropped it back in his pocket, and placing chairs, motioned his friend to the table. In the business of supper the talisman was partly forgotten, and afterward the three sat listening in an enthralled fashion to a second installment of the soldier's adventures in India.

"If the tale about the monkey's paw is not more truthful than those he has been telling us," said Herbert, as the door closed behind their guest, just in time for him to catch the last train, "we shan't make much out of it."

"Did you give him anything for it, Father?" inquired Mrs. White, regarding her husband closely.

"A trifle," said he, coloring slightly. "He didn't want it, but I made him take it. And he pressed me again to throw it away."

"Likely," said Herbert, with pretended horror. "Why, we're going to be rich, and famous, and happy. Wish to be an emperor, Father, to begin with; then you can't be henpecked."

He darted round the table, pursued by the maligned Mrs. White armed with an antimacassar.[8]

Mr. White took the paw from his pocket and eyed it dubiously. "I don't know what to wish for, and that's a fact," he said slowly. "It seems to me I've got all I want."

"If you only cleared the house, you'd be quite happy, wouldn't you?" said Herbert, with his hand on his shoulder. "Well, wish for two hundred pounds, then; that'll just do it."

His father, smiling shamefacedly at his own **credulity**, held up the talisman, as his son, with a solemn face, somewhat marred by a wink at his mother, sat down at the piano and struck a few impressive chords.

"I wish for two hundred pounds," said the old man distinctly.

A fine crash from the piano greeted the words, interrupted by a shuddering cry from the old man. His wife and son ran toward him.

credulity
(krĭ-dōō´ lĭ-tē) *n.*
Credulity is a tendency to believe too readily.

---

[7] **talisman** (tăl´ ĭs-mən): an object thought to have magical powers.
[8] **antimacassar** (ăn´tĭ-mə-kăs´ər): a cloth placed over an arm or the back of a chair.

"It moved," he cried, with a glance of disgust at the object as it lay on the floor. "As I wished, it twisted in my hand like a snake."

"Well, I don't see the money," said his son, as he picked it up and placed it on the table, "and I bet I never shall."

"It must have been your fancy, father," said his wife, regarding him anxiously.

He shook his head. "Never mind, though; there's no harm done, but it gave me a shock all the same."

They sat down by the fire again. Outside, the wind was higher than ever, and the old man started nervously at the sound of a door banging upstairs. A silence unusual and depressing settled upon all three, which lasted until the old couple rose to retire for the night.

"I expect you'll find the cash tied up in a big bag in the middle of your bed," said Herbert, as he bade them goodnight, "and something horrible squatting up on top of the wardrobe watching you as you pocket your ill-gotten gains."

He sat alone in the darkness, gazing at the dying fire, and seeing faces in it. The last face was so horrible and so simian[9] that he gazed at it in amazement. It got so vivid that, with a little uneasy laugh, he felt on the table for a glass containing a little water to throw over it. His hand grasped the monkey's paw, and with a little shiver he wiped his hand on his coat and went up to bed.

Part II

In the brightness of the wintry sun next morning as it streamed over the breakfast table he laughed at his fears. There was an air of **prosaic** wholesomeness about the room which it had lacked on the previous night, and the dirty, shriveled little paw was pitched on the sideboard[10] with a carelessness which betokened no great belief in its virtues.[11]

"I suppose all old soldiers are the same," said Mrs. White. "The idea of our listening to such nonsense! How could wishes be granted in these days? And if they could, how could two hundred pounds hurt you, father?"

prosaic
(prō-zā´ĭk) *adj.* If something is *prosaic*, it is dull or ordinary.

---

[9] **simian** (sĭm´ē-ən): monkey- or ape-like.
[10] **sideboard:** a piece of furniture used to store linens and dishes.
[11] **virtues:** powers.

"Might drop on his head from the sky," said the frivolous[12] Herbert.

"Morris said the things happened so naturally," said his father, "that you might if you so wished attribute it to coincidence."

"Well, don't break into the money before I come back," said Herbert as he rose from the table. "I'm afraid it'll turn you into a mean, avaricious[13] man, and we shall have to disown you."

His mother laughed, and following him to the door, watched him down the road; and returning to the breakfast table, was very happy at the expense of her husband's credulity. All of which did not prevent her from scurrying to the door at the postman's knock, when she found that the post brought a tailor's bill.

"Herbert will have some more of his funny remarks, I expect, when he comes home," she said, as they sat at dinner.

"I dare say," said Mr. White, "but for all that, the thing moved in my hand; that I'll swear to."

"You thought it did," said the old lady soothingly.

"I say it did," replied the other. "There was no thought about it; I had just—What's the matter?"

His wife made no reply. She was watching the mysterious movements of a man outside, who, peering in an undecided fashion at the house, appeared to be trying to make up his mind to enter. In mental connection with the two hundred pounds, she noticed that the stranger was well dressed, and wore a silk hat of glossy newness. Three times he paused at the gate, and then walked on again. The fourth time he stood with his hand upon it, and then with sudden resolution flung it open and walked up the path. Mrs. White at the same moment placed her hands behind her, and hurriedly unfastening the strings of her apron, put that useful article of apparel beneath the cushion of her chair.

She brought the stranger, who seemed ill at ease, into the room. He gazed at her furtively, and listened in a preoccupied fashion as the old lady apologized for the appearance of the room, and her husband's coat, a garment which he usually reserved for the garden. She then waited patiently for him to broach his business, but he was at first strangely silent.

---

[12] **frivolous** (frĭv´ə-ləs): inappropriately silly.
[13] **avaricious** (ăv´ə-rĭsh´əs): greedy.

"I—was asked to call," he said at last, and stooped and picked a piece of cotton from his trousers. "I come from Maw and Meggins."

The old lady started. "Is anything the matter?" she asked breathlessly. "Has anything happened to Herbert? What is it? What is it?"

Her husband interposed. "There, there, mother," he said hastily. "Sit down, and don't jump to conclusions. You've not brought bad news, I'm sure, sir;" and he eyed the other wistfully.

"I'm sorry—" began the visitor.

"Is he hurt?" demanded the mother wildly.

The visitor bowed in assent. "Badly hurt," he said quietly, "but he is not in any pain."

"Oh!" said the old woman, clasping her hands. "Thank goodness for that! Thank—"

She broke off suddenly as the sinister meaning of the assurance dawned upon her and she saw the awful confirmation of her fears in the other's averted face. She caught her breath, and turning to her slower-witted husband, laid her trembling old hand upon his. There was a long silence.

"He was caught in the machinery," said the visitor at length in a low voice.

"Caught in the machinery," repeated Mr. White, in a dazed fashion, "yes."

He sat staring blankly out at the window, and taking his wife's hand between his own, pressed it as he had been wont to do in their old courting days nearly forty years before.

"He was the only one left to us," he said, turning gently to the visitor. "It is hard."

The other coughed, and rising, walked slowly to the window. "The firm wished me to convey their sincere sympathy with you in your great loss," he said, without looking round. "I beg that you will understand I am only their servant and merely obeying orders."

There was no reply; the old woman's face was white, her eyes staring, and her breath inaudible; on the husband's face was a look such as his friend the sergeant might have carried into his first action.

"I was to say that Maw and Meggins disclaim all responsibility," continued the other. "They admit no liability at all, but in consideration of your son's services, they wish to present you with a certain sum as **compensation**."

Mr. White dropped his wife's hand, and rising to his feet, gazed with a look of horror at his visitor. His dry lips shaped the words, "How much?"

"Two hundred pounds," was the answer.

Unconscious of his wife's shriek, the old man smiled faintly, put out his hands like a sightless man, and dropped, a senseless heap, to the floor.

compensation (kŏm′ pən-sā′ shən) n. *Compensation* is something, such as money, that is received as payment.

Part III

In the huge new cemetery, some two miles distant, the old people buried their dead, and came back to a house steeped in shadow and silence. It was all over so quickly that at first they could hardly realize it, and remained in a state of expectation as though of something else to happen—something else which was to lighten this load, too heavy for old hearts to bear.

But the days passed, and expectation gave place to **resignation**—the hopeless resignation of the old, sometimes miscalled apathy. Sometimes they hardly exchanged a word, for now they had nothing to talk about, and their days were long to weariness.

It was about a week after that the old man, waking suddenly in the night, stretched out his hand and found himself alone. The room was in darkness, and the sound of subdued weeping came from the window. He raised himself in bed and listened.

resignation (rĕz′ ĭg-nā′shən) n. *Resignation* is the acceptance of something that is inescapable.

"Come back," he said tenderly. "You will be cold."

"It is colder for my son," said the old woman, and wept afresh.

The sound of her sobs died away on his ears. The bed was warm, and his eyes heavy with sleep. He dozed fitfully, and then slept until a sudden wild cry from his wife awoke him with a start.

"*The paw!*" she cried wildly. "The monkey's paw!"

He started up in alarm. "Where? Where is it? What's the matter?"

She came stumbling across the room toward him. "I want it," she said quietly. "You've not destroyed it?"

"It's in the parlor, on the bracket," he replied, marveling. "Why?"

She cried and laughed together, and bending over, kissed his cheek.

"I only just thought of it," she said hysterically. "Why didn't I think of it before? Why didn't *you* think of it?"

"Think of what?" he questioned.

"The other two wishes," she replied rapidly. "We've only had one."

"Was not that enough?" he demanded fiercely.

"No," she cried triumphantly; "we'll have one more. Go down and get it quickly, and wish our boy alive again."

The man sat up in bed and flung the bedclothes from his quaking limbs. "You are mad!" he cried, aghast.

"Get it," she panted; "get it quickly, and wish—Oh, my boy, my boy!"

Her husband struck a match and lit the candle. "Get back to bed," he said unsteadily. "You don't know what you are saying."

"We had the first wish granted," said the old woman feverishly; "why not the second?"

"A coincidence," stammered the old man.

"Go and get it and wish," cried his wife, quivering with excitement.

He went down in the darkness, and felt his way to the parlor, and then to the mantelpiece. The talisman was in its place, and a horrible fear that the unspoken wish might bring his mutilated son before him ere he could escape from the room seized upon him, and he caught his breath as he found that he had lost the direction of the door. His brow cold with sweat, he felt his way round the table, and groped along the wall until he found himself in the small passage with the unwholesome thing in his hand.

Even his wife's face seemed changed as he entered the room. It was white and expectant, and to his fears seemed to have an unnatural look upon it. He was afraid of her.

"*Wish!*" she cried, in a strong voice.

"It is foolish and wicked," he faltered.

"*Wish!*" repeated his wife.

He raised his hand. "I wish my son alive again."

The talisman fell to the floor, and he regarded it fearfully. Then he sank trembling into a chair as the old woman, with burning eyes, walked to the window and raised the blind.

He sat until he was chilled with the cold, glancing occasionally at the figure of the old woman peering through the window. The candle-end, which had burned below the rim of the china candlestick, was throwing pulsating shadows on the ceiling and walls, until, with a flicker larger than the rest, it expired. The old man, with an unspeakable sense of relief at the failure of the talisman, crept back to his bed, and a minute or two afterward the old woman came silently and apathetically beside him.

Neither spoke, but lay silently listening to the ticking of the clock. A stair creaked, and a squeaky mouse scurried noisily through the wall. The darkness was oppressive, and after lying for some time gathering up his courage, he took the box of matches, and striking one, went downstairs for a candle.

At the foot of the stairs the match went out, and he paused to strike another; and at the same moment a knock, so quiet and stealthy as to be scarcely audible, sounded on the front door.

The matches fell from his hand. He stood motionless, his breath suspended until the knock was repeated. Then he turned and fled swiftly back to his room, and closed the door behind him. A third knock sounded through the house.

"*What's that?*" cried the old woman, starting up.

"A rat," said the old man in shaking tones—"a rat. It passed me on the stairs."

His wife sat up in bed listening. A loud knock resounded through the house.

"It's Herbert!" she screamed. "It's Herbert!"

She ran to the door, but her husband was before her, and catching her by the arm, held her tightly.

"What are you going to do?" he whispered hoarsely.

"It's my boy; it's Herbert!" she cried, struggling mechanically. "I forgot it was two miles away. What are you holding me for? Let go. I must open the door."

"Don't let it in," cried the old man, trembling.

"You're afraid of your own son," she cried, struggling. "Let me go. I'm coming, Herbert; I'm coming."

There was another knock, and another. The old woman with a sudden wrench broke free and ran from the room. Her husband followed to the landing, and called after her appealingly as she hurried downstairs. He heard the chain rattle back and the bottom bolt drawn slowly and stiffly from the socket. Then the old woman's voice, strained and panting.

"The bolt," she cried loudly. "Come down. I can't reach it."

But her husband was on his hands and knees groping wildly on the floor in search of the paw. If he could only find it before the thing outside got in. A perfect fusillade[14] of knocks reverberated through the house, and he heard the scraping of a chair as his wife put it down in the passage against the door. He heard the creaking of the bolt as it came slowly back, and at the same moment he found the monkey's paw, and frantically breathed his third and last wish.

The knocking ceased suddenly, although the echoes of it were still in the house. He heard the chair drawn back, and the door opened. A cold wind rushed up the staircase, and a long loud wail of disappointment and misery from his wife gave him courage to run down to her side, and then to the gate beyond. The streetlamp flickering opposite shone on a quiet and deserted road.

COLLABORATIVE DISCUSSION Mr. White decides to make a wish, even though he says he already has everything he wants. Discuss with a partner whether his wish is more for himself or for his family. Use evidence from the text to support your ideas.

---

[14] **fusillade** (fyoo´sə-läd´): discharge from many guns; a rapid outburst.

Determine Theme

One reason people read literature is to learn how to avoid or understand common problems. Literature conveys these lessons through **themes,** the messages about life or human nature that writers share with readers.

- In some stories, the theme is stated directly in the text.
- In most cases, readers must **infer,** or make an educated guess about, the theme based on clues in the text.
- One way to determine a story's theme is to ask, "What lesson does the main character learn that applies to real people's lives?"

Contemporary literature often draws on the themes and patterns of events that have been expressed in myths and traditional stories passed down through the centuries. For example, you've probably been told many stories in which a theme about greed is revealed through the granting of three wishes. When the same message can be found in the literature of different cultures and in different time periods like this, it's called a **universal theme.**

Review "The Monkey's Paw" and identify the traditional pattern of events that reveals a universal theme.

Analyze Stories: Foreshadowing

Foreshadowing occurs when a writer provides hints that suggest future events in a story. Writers use this technique to create suspense and propel the action by making readers eager to find out what happens next.

Clues about future events may appear in dialogue, descriptions of events, or imagery. Think about how these examples from "The Monkey's Paw" foreshadow what will occur later in the story.

Dialogue (lines 97–98)	"I did have some idea of selling it, but I don't think I will. It has caused enough mischief already."
Event (lines 106–107)	"He took the paw, and dangling it between his forefinger and thumb, suddenly threw it upon the fire."
Imagery (lines 176–182)	"He sat ... at the dying fire ... seeing faces in it. The last face was so horrible ... that he gazed at it in amazement. It got so vivid that, with a little uneasy laugh, he felt on the table for a glass containing a little water to throw over it. His hand grasped the monkey's paw and with a little shiver he wiped his hand on his coat and went to up to bed."

As you analyze "The Monkey's Paw," look for an additional example of each kind of foreshadowing.

Analyzing the Text

Cite Text Evidence Support your responses with evidence from the text.

1. **Infer** In what way does the setting described in lines 1–21 suggest or foreshadow later events?

2. **Analyze** Reread lines 110–119 and identify the **allusion,** or reference to a well-known work that Mrs. White makes. What does the allusion suggest about Mrs. White's view of the paw?

3. **Compare and Analyze** Complete the chart to identify how Morris's and Mr. White's views about the monkey's paw are different. Then explain how these differing points of view add to the suspense in the story.

Sergeant-Major Morris's View	Mr. White's View

4. **Draw Conclusions** Examine lines 271–281 to review the Whites' reaction as they realize what has happened to their son. What do they assume about the two hundred pounds they will receive "as compensation"?

5. **Compare** What do the actions of Mr. and Mrs. White at the end of the story reveal about their different expectations for wishes made on the monkey's paw? Identify what hopes or fears these expectations reveal.

6. **Analyze** What is the theme of "The Monkey's Paw"? Give examples of how the author develops the theme through the characters and plot.

7. **Connect** There are many traditional stories in which characters are granted three wishes. What theme do many of them share? Tell what makes "The Monkey's Paw" different from the others.

PERFORMANCE TASK

Writing Activity: Report Review lines 39–56. What ideas and attitudes about India are expressed here? Do research to learn more about the historical relationship between Britain and India. Write a short report in which you

- explain how Britain came to rule India, including the role of the British East India Company

- describe the attitudes the two peoples had toward one another during British rule

Then share your findings with the class. Be prepared to discuss the ways the attitudes in the story reflect the historical context.

Critical Vocabulary

| peril | condole | grimace | fate |
| credulity | prosaic | compensation | resignation |

Practice and Apply Explain what is alike and different about the meanings of the words in each pair.

1. peril/risk
2. grimace/frown
3. compensation/wages
4. fate/outcome
5. credulity/trust
6. resignation/acceptance
7. condole/encourage
8. prosaic/dull

Vocabulary Strategy: Latin Roots

A word **root** is a word part that contains the core meaning of a word. A root is combined with other word parts, such as a prefix or a suffix, to form a word. The root of many English words comes from Latin. Read this sentence from "The Monkey's Paw."

> His mother laughed, and following him to the door, watched him down the road; and returning to the breakfast table, was very happy at the expense of her husband's credulity.

The word *credulity* includes the Latin root *cred*, which means "believe" or "trust." You can use the meaning of the root *cred* as a clue to figure out that *credulity* means "a disposition to believe too readily."

Practice and Apply Find the word in each sentence that includes the Latin root *cred*. Use context and the meaning of the root to help you write a definition of the word. Then verify each of your definitions by finding the word's precise meaning in a print or digital dictionary.

1. Herbert was incredulous when he heard the sergeant-major's tale.
2. A person must have the proper credentials to enter a foreign country.
3. Mrs. White didn't give any credence to the notion that the monkey's paw moved.
4. Were the sergeant-major's stories about India credible?
5. One witness may discredit the story that another person tells.

Language Conventions: Subjunctive Mood

The **mood** of a verb shows a writer's judgment or attitude about a statement he or she makes. The **subjunctive mood** is used to express a recommendation, a requirement, a wish or hypothetical situation, or a condition that is contrary to fact. The subjunctive mood is generally used only in very formal English.

- Use the subjunctive base form of a verb in clauses beginning with *that* to express a recommendation or a requirement.

  Morris suggests that Mr. White burn the monkey's paw.
  (*burn* not *burns*)

  It is important that he think carefully before making a wish.
  (*think* not *thinks*)

- Use the subjunctive *be* in clauses beginning with *that* to express a recommendation or a requirement.

  Mrs. White insists that another wish be made.
  (*be* not *is*)

  I recommend that all students be required to read this story.
  (*be* not *are*)

- Use the subjunctive *were* to express a wish or hypothetical situation, or to state a condition that is contrary to fact.

  I wish Herbert were here with us.
  (*were* not *was*)

  The monkey's paw moved, as though it were alive.
  (*were* not *was*)

Practice and Apply One verb in each sentence is not correct. Rewrite each sentence correctly, using the subjunctive mood.

1. The Whites recommend that Morris is seated by the fire.
2. My teacher suggests that the class predicts what will happen next in the story.
3. Mrs. White acted as though she was mad.
4. Mr. White insists that his wife keeps the door closed.
5. If Mrs. White was taller, she could reach the bolt on the door.
6. I move that each student is required to write a story summary after reading.

Background *The film* The Monkey's Paw *is an adaptation of the short story of the same name. The film's writer and director, Ricky Lewis Jr. had read the story as a child. He decided to make it into a movie because his "morbid curiosity wanted to see it." While other film adaptations of the story had modernized it, Lewis thought it was important that the film be set in the past, "when odd things were sure to happen." He chose to "let a little darkness" into his film to create its gloomy, sometimes spooky mood.*

MEDIA ANALYSIS

from THE MONKEY'S PAW

Film by Ricky Lewis Jr.

SETTING A PURPOSE The film clip you will view deals with the ending of the short story "The Monkey's Paw." Keep your reading of the short story in mind as you view the film, and pay attention to any differences you notice between the content of the text version of the story and the content of the film. Think about how any differences affect the story being told. Also consider your own reaction to each version and how the choices made by the author of the short story and the director of the film helped bring about your reaction. Write down any questions you have during viewing.

MEDIA

Format: Film
Running Time: 6:02

AS YOU VIEW Directors use many different techniques to make stories come alive on the screen. As you view *The Monkey's Paw*, notice the lighting and camera angles the director uses. Notice how they vary or change as the scenes change. Think about the techniques being used and why Ricky Lewis Jr. chose those particular techniques to tell the story.

COLLABORATIVE DISCUSSION Review the ending of the print version of the short story. Then consider the ending of the film clip. With a partner, compare and contrast the two endings and decide how the film ending differs from the ending of the short story. Discuss why the director might have chosen to tell parts of the story in a different way. Cite specific evidence from the text and the film to support your ideas.

Evaluate Media

Like many movies, the film clip of *The Monkey's Paw* is based on a written story. When a film director decides to make a movie, he or she must make choices about how closely to follow the written work. Will the film

- include all of the same characters?
- have the same setting?
- show all of the same events?

Think about how the director's choices affect the content of the film clip of *The Monkey's Paw*.

Writers and directors use different techniques to create suspense and to tell the story.

- Writers use words to describe the rising action or the characters' struggles.
- Directors use a combination of visual and sound techniques.

For example, directors may use different camera shots to convey ideas, to track characters' emotions, or to show a situation from a character's viewpoint. Directors also use other techniques to build suspense.

Camera Shot	What It Is	Why It Is Used
Close-up shot	a shot that focuses on a character's face	to convey a character's emotions or thoughts
Low-angle shot	a shot in which the camera looks up at a subject	to create the impression of height or distance; to make a subject look more menacing
High-angle shot	a shot in which the camera looks down on a subject	to show a character in relation to his or her surroundings; to make a subject look unprotected or exposed
Point-of-view shot	a shot that shows what a character sees	to let viewers see what is happening from a character's point of view

- **Lighting** can create moods that are gloomy, mysterious, or scary. Suspenseful movies often use minimal lighting with frequent use of shadows.
- **Camera filters** are glass or plastic disks that are inserted in front of a camera lens. These filters can change the way that images appear, making them clearer, brighter, darker, or fuzzier.
- **Music** can signal dramatic events or tense moments. Music sometimes foreshadows, or hints at, what is going to happen.

As you analyze the film clip, **evaluate,** or make judgments about the different film techniques the director uses in *The Monkey's Paw*.

Analyzing the Media

Cite Text Evidence Support your responses with evidence from the media.

1. **Summarize** The film clip shows several scenes from the short story "The Monkey's Paw." Summarize the events shown and described in the film.

2. **Compare** Has the director remained faithful to the written story? Name some of the ways that the story you read and the film clip are the same. Then name some of the ways that they are different.

3. **Evaluate** Complete a chart like the one shown to identify three of the techniques the director used. Then explain which one you found most effective and why.

Technique	Part in the Film
1.	
2.	
3.	

4. **Analyze** Consider the ways the director uses lighting in the film. What is the effect of the lighting in the scene where Herbert returns to the house?

5. **Analyze** How do the camera angles and camera filters that the director uses affect the mood of the film? How do they affect the impact of the final scenes at the cemetery?

6. **Compare and Evaluate** You have read a story and viewed a film clip of that story. What are some of the advantages of the written version of the story? What are some of the advantages of the film version?

PERFORMANCE TASK

Media Activity: Storyboard Work with a partner to create a storyboard for your own film retelling of a scene from "The Monkey's Paw." A storyboard is a device filmmakers use to plan the shooting of a movie. It serves as a map that includes images and descriptions.

- Decide whether you will stay faithful to the short story or depart from the text.
- Draw a series of at least 12 separate frames. Sketch the characters and scene for each frame.
- Underneath each frame, write descriptions of shots—such as close-up, medium, or distance shots—and write a line of dialogue or describe what characters will say.
- Consider what kind of music you will add and write where you'll include it.

Sharon A. Russell (b. 1941) *is a retired professor of Communication and Women's Studies at Indiana State University, where she taught courses on film and television. Russell has published extensively on horror film and literature and detective fiction. She is the author of* Stephen King: A Critical Companion, *a book that analyzes several of King's famous horror novels and in which this essay appears.*

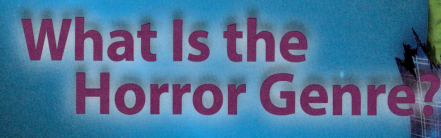

What Is the Horror Genre?

Literary Criticism by Sharon A. Russell

SETTING A PURPOSE As you read, pay attention to the points the author makes about horror stories. Do her ideas make you think about horror stories in new ways?

Many people define horror by its subjects. We all think of creatures like Frankenstein's monster, Dracula, and the wolfman[1] as monsters in the horror genre. Each one of these creatures has a history and developed over a period of time. But we also know that horror covers more than just these monsters. We could all make long lists of the kind of creatures we identify with horror, especially when we think of films as well as literature. The minute we would start to make such a list we would also realize that not all monsters are alike and that not all horror deals with monsters. The subject approach is not the clearest way to define this genre.

---

[1] **Frankenstein's monster, Dracula, and the wolfman:** legendary monsters. "Frankenstein's monster" is the creature created by Dr. Victor Frankenstein in Mary Shelley's novel; "Dracula" is the vampire in Bram Stoker's novel; in folklore, the wolfman is a man who can become a wolf.

Some students of this genre find that the best way to examine it is to deal with the way horror fiction is organized or structured. Examining the organization of a horror story shows that it shares certain traits with other types of fiction. Horror stories share the use of suspense as a tactic with many other kinds of literature. The tension we feel when a character goes into the attic, down into the basement, or just into the abandoned house is partially a result of suspense. We don't know what is going to happen. But that suspense is **intensified** by our knowledge of the genre. We know that characters involved in the world of horror always meet something awful when they go where they shouldn't. Part of the tension is created because they are doing something we know is going to get them in trouble. Stephen King refers directly to our anticipation of horror. In *Salem's Lot*[2] Susan approaches the house which is the source of evil. "She found herself thinking of those drive-in horror movie epics where the heroine goes venturing up the narrow attic stairs…or down into some dark, cobwebby cellar…and she…thinking: …*I'd never do that!*" Of course Susan's fears are **justified**. She does end up dead in the basement, a victim of the vampire.

If the horror genre uses the character's search for information to create suspense, it controls when and where we get our knowledge. Because we are outside of the situation we usually know more than the characters. Our advance knowledge creates suspense because we can anticipate what is going to happen. The author can play with those expectations by either confirming them or surprising us with a different outcome. When suspense is an important element in fiction we may often find that the plot is the most critical part of the story. We care more about what happens next than about who the characters are or where the story is set. But setting is often considered a part of the horror genre. If the genre has traditional monsters, it also has traditional settings. Only authors who want to challenge the tradition place events in bright, beautiful parks. We expect a connection between the setting and the events in this genre. We are not surprised to find old houses, abandoned castles, damp cellars, or dark forests as important elements in the horror story.

intensify
(ĭn-tĕn´sə-fī´) *v.* If you *intensify* something, you make it grow in strength.

justify
(jŭs´tə-fī´) *v.* If you *justify* something, you prove it is right or valid.

---

[2] **Salem's Lot:** a horror fiction novel written by Stephen A. King.

The actor Boris Karloff as the monster in the 1931 film *Frankenstein,* based on the novel

The actor Lon Chaney as a werewolf in the 1941 film *The Wolf Man*

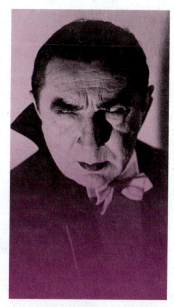

The actor Bela Lugosi as Dracula in the 1931 film by the same name

Some people make further distinctions based on how the stories are organized. We can divide stories into different categories based on how we come to believe in the events related and how they are explained to us. Stories that deal with **parallel** worlds expect us to accept those worlds without question. We just believe Dorothy is in Oz; we accept Oz as a parallel world separate from ours. Other times events seem to be supernatural but turn out to have natural explanations: the ghosts turn out to be squirrels in the attic, or things that move mysteriously are part of a plot to drive someone crazy. Sometimes the supernatural is the result of the way the central character sees the world, as in stories told from the point of view of a crazy person. But at times we are not sure, and hesitate about believing in the possibility of the supernatural. When I first read Dracula I seriously considered hanging garlic on my windows because I believed that vampires could exist. This type of hesitation, when we almost believe, falls into the general category of the "fantastic" (Todorov 25).[3] Often horror has its greatest effect on us because we almost

parallel
(păr´ə-lĕl´) *adj.*
If things are *parallel*, they have comparable or similar parts.

---

[3] **Todorov 25:** the author is following MLA style to cite her source for the information just stated: page 25 of a work by an author named Todorov.

believe, or believe while we are reading the book or watching the film, that the events are possible.

Yet another way of categorizing works of horror is by the source of the horror. Some horror comes from inside the characters. Something goes wrong inside, and a person turns into a monster. Dr. Frankenstein's need for knowledge turns him into the kind of person who creates a monster. Dr. Jekyll also values his desire for information above all else, and creates Mr. Hyde.[4] In another kind of horror story the threat to the central character or characters comes from outside. An outside force may invade the character and then force the evil out again. The vampire attacks the victim, but then the victim becomes a vampire and attacks others. Stories of ghosts or demonic possession also fall into this category.

We can also look at the kinds of themes common to horror. Many works concentrate on the conflict between good and evil. Works about the fantastic may deal with the search for forbidden knowledge that appears in much horror literature. Such **quests** are used as a way of examining our attitude toward knowledge. While society may believe that new knowledge is always good, the horror genre may question this assumption, examining how such advances affect the individual and society.

quest
(kwĕst) *n.* A *quest* is a search.

COLLABORATIVE DISCUSSION With a partner, discuss how Russell's ideas about horror stories compare with your own knowledge of this genre.

---

[4] **Dr. Jekyll ... and ... Mr. Hyde:** the good and evil sides of the same character in a novella by Robert Louis Stevenson.

Analyze Text: Literary Criticism

One of the pleasures of reading literature is thinking about it afterward. **Literary criticism** is writing that examines, analyzes, and interprets a piece of literature or a general aspect of literature.

In literary criticism, the **author's purpose**—or the reason he or she is writing—is often to inform or to persuade other readers to view a text in a certain way. The chart shows some specific purposes an author might have when writing literary criticism.

Purpose	What the Author Does
To define a genre	explains the characteristics of a type of writing using specific examples as evidence
To categorize works of literature	defines and classifies works of literature based on certain **criteria,** or standards
To examine the structure of a work of literature	analyzes the organization of a piece of literature
To analyze an author's technique	explains and evaluates the effectiveness of literary techniques, such as using an unreliable narrator, recurring imagery, or flashbacks

What is the purpose of the work of literary criticism you have just read?

Summarize Text

A good way to check your comprehension and remember what you read is to summarize the text. When you **summarize,** you briefly retell the central ideas and most important details of a piece of writing in your own words. You can summarize a section of a text or an entire work.

- Begin with a clear, brief statement of the central idea of the section or work.
- Present the most important details that support the idea in the order in which they appear in the text.
- Write in your own words, but be careful not to change the author's meaning.

Summarize the first paragraph of "What Is the Horror Genre?"

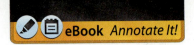

Analyzing the Text

Cite Text Evidence   Support your responses with evidence from the text.

1. **Identify**   Reread the first paragraph, lines 1–11. Why does the author reject characters or subjects as a way to categorize the horror genre?

2. **Infer**   Reread the first two paragraphs of the essay, lines 1–32. What does the opening suggest about the author's purpose in writing this essay?

3. **Cause/Effect**   In lines 20–21, the author says that in horror stories "suspense is intensified by our knowledge of the genre." What knowledge is the author referring to? Explain why it increases suspense.

4. **Analyze**   Events described in the horror genre often defy everyday reality. According to Russell, what are three different reactions the reader might have to supernatural events depicted in horror stories?

5. **Interpret**   In line 87, what does the author mean by "the search for forbidden knowledge"?

6. **Summarize**   After reading this essay, what is your response to its title: "What Is the Horror Genre?" To answer, summarize the text.

7. **Synthesize**   Consider your own knowledge of the horror genre. Which of Russell's proposed categories do you consider the most useful for gaining new understanding about these stories? Explain your answer by referring to horror stories with which you're familiar.

PERFORMANCE TASK

Speaking Activity: Discussion   Use the characteristics of the horror genre described in the essay to categorize the horror stories you have read and the horror films you have seen.

- Work with a small group to create a list of stories and films.
- Review the characters, setting, events, structure, and organization of the stories and films.
- Decide how to categorize the stories and films. What creates the suspense in each one? Do they have similar themes or settings? Are the sources of horror alike in some way?
- Be prepared to explain your categories as you share your final list with the class or a small group.

Critical Vocabulary

intensify   **justify**   **parallel**   **quest**

1. Which Vocabulary word goes with *similar*? Why?
2. Which Vocabulary word goes with *strengthen*? Why?
3. Which Vocabulary word goes with *search*? Why?
4. Which Vocabulary word goes with *defend*? Why?

Vocabulary Strategy: Using Suffixes

A **suffix** is a word part that is added to the end of a word. The suffix *-ied* is added to verbs that end in the letter *-y* and are preceded by a consonant. Adding *-ied* to such verbs changes the verb from the present to the past tense.

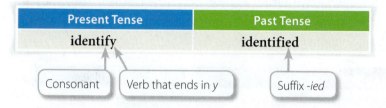

For example, to change a verb like *identify* to the past tense, you drop the *-y* and add *-ied*. Look at the sentences from "What Is the Horror Genre?" that show how the author uses the verbs *intensify* and *justify* in the past tense.

But that suspense is <u>intensified</u> by our knowledge of the genre.

Of course, Susan's fears are <u>justified</u>.

In the case of both *justify* and *intensify*, the author dropped the *-y* and added *-ied* to show the past tense.

Practice and Apply Read the sentences. Change the verbs in parentheses to the past tense by adding the suffix *-ied*.

1. In the horror story, the main character (rely) on her brother for help.
2. She was (mystify) when her calls to him were not answered.
3. She (hurry) to check that all her house doors were securely locked.
4. She was (petrify) when she thought she saw someone looking in the window.
5. Now she was (worry) that her brother would not show up to help her.

Language Conventions: Using Commas

A writer's use of punctuation not only helps readers understand the writer's message, but also signals how the writer wants the text to be read. In your writing, you can use commas to signal a break or a pause to the reader. When you write, read your sentences out loud, noticing where you pause. The parts where you pause probably need to be punctuated by a comma. Look at these examples from "What Is the Horror Genre?"

> **So, she does end up dead in the basement, a victim of the vampire.**

> **This type of hesitation, when we almost believe, falls into the general category of the "fantastic."**

Read the two sentences out loud, noticing where you pause. The commas after "So" and "basement" in the first sentence signal the reader to pause. The commas before and after "when we almost believe" do the same thing. They also signal a break in thought and make the sentence easier to understand. Additional examples are shown in the following chart.

Purpose of Comma	Example
to signal a break in thought	"Often horror has its greatest effect on us because we almost believe, or believe while we are reading the book or watching the film, that the events are possible."
to signal the reader to pause	"If a genre has traditional monsters, it also has traditional settings."

Practice and Apply These sentences include words, phrases, and clauses that need to be punctuated with commas. Rewrite the sentences, inserting the needed punctuation. If you get stuck, try reading the sentence out loud.

1. Yes I absolutely love horror stories.
2. You know of course that the main purpose of horror stories is to inspire fear and dread.
3. If Frankenstein is frightening he is also sympathetic.
4. The long movie was terrifying so much so that several times I just closed my eyes and blocked my ears.
5. Writing a horror story a big dream of mine will take a lot of thought and hard work.

COLLECTION 2
PERFORMANCE TASK A

Interactive Lessons
To help you complete this task, use
- Writing Arguments
- Delivering a Presentation

Present an Argument

The horror genre is intended to inspire terror. In this activity, you will give a speech arguing whether a classic of the horror genre, "The Tell-Tale Heart," is appropriate for your age group to read.

A successful argument

- contains an engaging introduction that establishes the claim
- supports the claim with reasons and relevant evidence from a variety of credible sources
- emphasizes key points in a focused, coherent manner
- uses language that effectively conveys ideas and adds interest
- concludes by leaving the audience with a lasting impression

Mentor Text Note how this section from "Scary Tales" argues that students should read scary stories.

> " Children need to be frightened. We all do. It's an emotion that was given to all of us and it should be exercised. When you don't exercise it, you lose your sense of fear. That's why my granddaddy told me scary stories...You should be a little hesitant sometimes, his stories were saying, you should think twice before you go into the woods, there just might be a hairy man and you need to be cautious. "

Visit hmhfyi.com to explore your topic and enhance your research.

PLAN

Choose Your Position Reread "The Tell-Tale Heart," and think about its effects on you as a reader. What kind of lasting impression does it create? Decide whether the story is appropriate reading for students your age. Choose a position and write out your claim in a statement.

Gather Information Focus on "The Tell-Tale Heart." Jot down details that provide reasons and evidence that support your claim.

- Identify quotations from the story that you can use as examples to support your claim.
- What might others say to oppose your claim?

Use the annotation tools in your eBook to find text evidence that supports your claim.

ACADEMIC VOCABULARY

As you take notes, be sure to use the academic vocabulary words.

conventions
predict
psychology
summary
technique

Do Further Research Use additional print and digital sources to find solid, credible evidence for your argument.

- Search for facts, quotations, and statistics about the horror genre that support your claim.
- Anticipate arguments against your claim and develop counterclaims to refute them.

Organize Your Ideas Use a graphic organizer, such as a hierarchy chart, to help you present your ideas logically.

Interactive Lessons
For help in organizing your ideas, use
- Writing Arguments: Building Effective Support

Consider Your Purpose and Audience Who will listen to your speech? Decide which specific ideas will be most convincing. Your tone and word choices should be appealing and targeted toward your listeners.

PRODUCE

Draft Your Speech As you draft your speech, keep the following in mind:

- Introduce your claim in an attention-grabbing way.
- Organize your reasons and evidence logically.
- Include facts, details, and examples from your sources.
- Use transitional words and phrases to clarify relationships among your claim, reasons, and evidence.
- Vary the length and type of sentences in your speech to create a lively flow of ideas.
- Summarize your main points in a concluding statement.

Prepare Visuals Think about using multimedia resources to create pictures or charts to clarify and strengthen your claims. Plan how you will integrate these visuals into your speech.

Write your rough draft in *my*WriteSmart. Focus on getting your ideas down, rather than on perfecting your language.

REVISE

Practice Your Speech Present your speech aloud. Try speaking in front of a mirror or recording your speech and listening to it. Use your voice effectively, varying your pitch and tone. Maintain eye contact with the members of your audience.

Evaluate Your Speech Use the following chart to revise your draft.

Have your partner or a group of peers review your draft in *my*WriteSmart. Ask your reviewers whether your claim, reasons, and evidence are clear.

Interactive Lessons
For tips on giving a presentation, use
• Giving a Presentation: Delivering Your Presentation

Questions	Tips	Revision Techniques
Does the introduction grab the audience's attention?	**Underline** questions or statements that would interest the audience.	If needed, **add** an attention-grabber to your introduction.
Do at least two reasons support my opinion statement?	**Highlight** the reasons that support your opinion.	**Add** reasons that support the opinion statement.
Does at least one piece of evidence support each reason?	**Highlight** evidence that supports each reason.	**Elaborate** on pieces of evidence by adding details.
Does the conclusion restate my position?	**Underline** your conclusion.	**Add** a restatement of your position.

Language Conventions: Using Transitions

To clarify relationships among your claim, reasons, and evidence, use **transitions**. These words and phrases will help make your argument stronger and more cohesive. See the following examples from "What Is the Horror Genre?"

To show cause and effect "Part of the tension is created because they are doing something we know is going to get them in trouble."

To reinforce ideas "Yet another way of categorizing works of horror is by the source of the horror."

PRESENT

Deliver your Speech Finalize your argument and present it to the class. Consider these additional options:

- Debate someone who makes an opposing argument.
- Publish your speech as a podcast and share it with classmates.

PERFORMANCE TASK A RUBRIC
ARGUMENT

	Ideas and Evidence	Organization	Language
4	• The introduction immediately grabs the audience's attention; the claim clearly states the speaker's position on an issue. • Logical reasons and relevant evidence convincingly support the speaker's claim. • Opposing claims are anticipated and effectively addressed. • The concluding section effectively summarizes the claim.	• The reasons and evidence are organized logically and consistently throughout the speech. • Transitions logically connect reasons and evidence to the speaker's claim.	• The speech is written and delivered in a consistent formal style. • Sentence beginnings, lengths, and structures vary and have a rhythmic flow. • Grammar, usage, and mechanics are correct.
3	• The introduction could do more to grab the audience's attention; the speaker's claim states a position on an issue. • Most reasons and evidence support the speaker's claim, but they could be more convincing. • Opposing claims are anticipated but need to be addressed more thoroughly. • The concluding section restates the claim.	• The organization of key points and supporting details is confusing in a few places. • A few more transitions are needed to clarify the relationships between ideas.	• The style is inconsistent in a few places. • Sentence beginnings, lengths, and structures vary somewhat. • Some grammatical and usage errors are repeated in the speech.
2	• The introduction is ordinary; the speaker's claim identifies an issue, but the position is not clearly stated. • The reasons and evidence are not always logical or relevant. • Opposing claims are anticipated but not addressed logically. • The concluding section includes an incomplete summary of the claim.	• The organization of reasons and evidence is logical in some places, but it often doesn't follow a pattern. • Many more transitions are needed to connect reasons and evidence to the speaker's claim.	• The style is inconsistent in many places. • Sentence structures barely vary, and some fragments or run-on sentences are present. • Grammar and usage are incorrect in many places, but the speaker's ideas are still clear.
1	• The introduction is confusing. • Supporting reasons and evidence are missing. • Opposing claims are neither anticipated nor addressed. • The concluding section is missing.	• A logical organization is not used; reasons and evidence are presented randomly. • Transitions are not used, making the speech difficult to understand.	• The style is completely inconsistent or inappropriate for the speech. • Repetitive sentence structure, fragments, and run-on sentences make the speech hard to follow. • Many grammatical and usage errors obscure the meanings of ideas.

COLLECTION 2
PERFORMANCE TASK B

Interactive Lessons
To help you complete this task, use
- Writing as a Process
- Using Textual Evidence

Write a Literary Analysis

In this activity, you will write a literary analysis of one or both of the fictional horror stories in this collection. Use the criteria for horror explained in "What Is the Horror Genre?" by Sharon A. Russell to support your analysis. Think about the structure of horror fiction and the tools its authors use, such as suspense and plot. As you analyze the story or stories, pay attention to setting, events, and details that make the work both believable and entertaining.

A successful literary analysis

- provides an introduction that captures the reader's attention and clearly states the topic
- cites textual evidence that strongly supports the writer's ideas
- clearly organizes ideas and concepts
- conveys key points through the analysis of relevant content
- provides a strong conclusion that summarizes the analysis

Mentor Text In this selection from "What Is the Horror Genre?" the writer includes a specific example to support her idea.

> Some horror comes from inside the characters. Something goes wrong inside, and the person turns into a monster. Dr. Frankenstein's need for knowledge turns him into the kind of person who creates a monster.

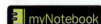

Use the annotation tools in your eBook to note the criteria in Sharon A. Russell's piece and to apply it to the story or stories you will analyze.

PLAN

Choose a Story for Analysis
Refresh your memory of "What Is the Horror Genre?" as well as "The Tell-Tale Heart" and "The Monkey's Paw."

- Take notes about the criteria for horror that are explained in "What Is the Horror Genre?"
- Reread "The Tell-Tale Heart" and "The Monkey's Paw." Identify aspects of the stories that impress—and horrify—you.
- Decide whether you will analyze one or both stories.

ACADEMIC VOCABULARY

As you share what you have learned about the horror genre, be sure to use the academic vocabulary words.

conventions
predict
psychology
summary
technique

Consider Audience and Purpose Think about what your readers need to know to understand your literary analysis.

- Determine if you need to provide information about the techniques related to horror storytelling, such as suspense.
- Decide what you want your audience to know about the horror genre, and about the story or stories you are analyzing.

Identify Your Criteria Use your notes about "What Is the Horror Genre?" to plan your analysis.

- Decide what your thesis statement will be. This statement contains the main point you want to make, so the criteria and textual evidence you discuss should relate to it.
- Create a graphic organizer for each of the criteria you identify.
- List story details that are relevant for each of your criteria.

Interactive Lessons
For help in planning your essay, use
- Writing as a Process: Task, Purpose, and Audience

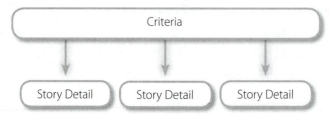

PRODUCE

Write Your Literary Analysis Use your notes and your graphic organizers to draft your literary analysis.

- You may wish to discuss each of your chosen criteria with examples from the story or stories. Another option would be to organize around the sequence of events in the story.
- Include a brief summary of the story or stories you will discuss.
- Include concrete details and quotations to support your ideas. Use precise language to explain key concepts.
- Use transitions to show relationships between your ideas and the textual evidence that supports them.
- Condense related ideas into a single sentence when possible.
- Conclude your analysis with a summary of your main points and your own insights about the appeal of the horror genre.

Write your rough draft in *my*WriteSmart. Concentrate on getting your ideas down rather than on crafting perfect sentences.

Interactive Lessons
For help in drafting your essay, use
- Using Textual Evidence: Summarizing, Paraphrasing, and Quoting

Language Conventions: Condensing Ideas

Look for places where you can condense ideas by combining them into one sentence. Read this sentence from "What Is the Horror Genre?"

> "In *Salem's Lot* Susan approaches the house which is the source of evil."

The writer condenses ideas about Susan and the house in a precise, detailed sentence. Condensing ideas helps communicate clearly with your audience.

REVISE

Review Your Draft Have your partner or group of peers review your draft. Use the following chart to revise your draft.

Ask your reviewers to note any points that need clarification or better support from the texts.

Interactive Lessons
For help in revising your essay, use
- Writing as a Process: Revising and Editing

Questions	Tips	Revision Techniques
Have I written a clear, coherent thesis statement?	**Highlight** your thesis statement.	**Rewrite** your statement to make it clearer, if needed.
Have I supported my points with details from the text?	**Underline** each detail or quotation from the text.	**Add** details or quotations wherever support is needed.
Have I organized the information in a logical way?	**Highlight** transitions between ideas.	**Add** transitions that show the relationships between your ideas.
Have I condensed ideas to create precise, detailed sentences?	**Underline** sentences that combine two or more clauses to condense ideas.	**Combine** related sentences to condense related ideas.
Does the conclusion include a summary of my analysis and an original insight?	**Highlight** the summary of your analysis. **Underline** your original insight.	**Add** a summary of your analysis and an original insight, if needed.

PRESENT

Create a Finished Copy Choose a way to share your literary analysis with your audience. Consider these options:

- Combine your analysis with those of your classmates to create a "Literary Review: Horror Edition" for your school's library.
- Present your analysis as an advertisement for the horror genre.
- Organize a panel discussion on the horror genre.

PERFORMANCE TASK B RUBRIC
LITERARY ANALYSIS

	Ideas and Evidence	Organization	Language
4	• The thesis statement presents a specific idea about the work(s). • Concrete, relevant details support the key points. • The concluding section summarizes the analysis and offers an insight.	• Key points and supporting details are organized effectively and logically throughout the literary analysis. • Transitions successfully show the relationships between ideas.	• Language is precise and captures the writer's thoughts with originality. • Ideas are condensed in precise, detailed sentences. • Grammar, usage, and mechanics are correct.
3	• The thesis statement sets up criteria for the analysis. • Some key points need more support. • The concluding section summarizes most of the analysis but doesn't offer an insight.	• The organization of key points and supporting details is mostly clear. • A few more transitions are needed to clarify the relationships between ideas.	• Most language is precise. • Some ideas are condensed in precise, detailed sentences. • Some errors in grammar, usage, and mechanics occur.
2	• The thesis statement only hints at a main point. • Details support some key points but often are too general. • The concluding section gives an incomplete summary without insight.	• Most key points are organized logically, but many supporting details are out of place. • More transitions are needed throughout the literary analysis to connect ideas.	• Language is repetitive or too general at times. • Few ideas are condensed in precise, detailed sentences. • Many errors in grammar, usage, and mechanics occur, but the writer's ideas are still clear.
1	• The thesis statement is missing. • Details and evidence are irrelevant or missing. • The literary analysis lacks a concluding section.	• A logical organization is not apparent. • Transitions are not used.	• Language is inaccurate, repetitive, and too general. • Ideas are not condensed. • Errors in grammar, usage, and mechanics obscure the meaning of the writer's ideas.

COLLECTION **3**

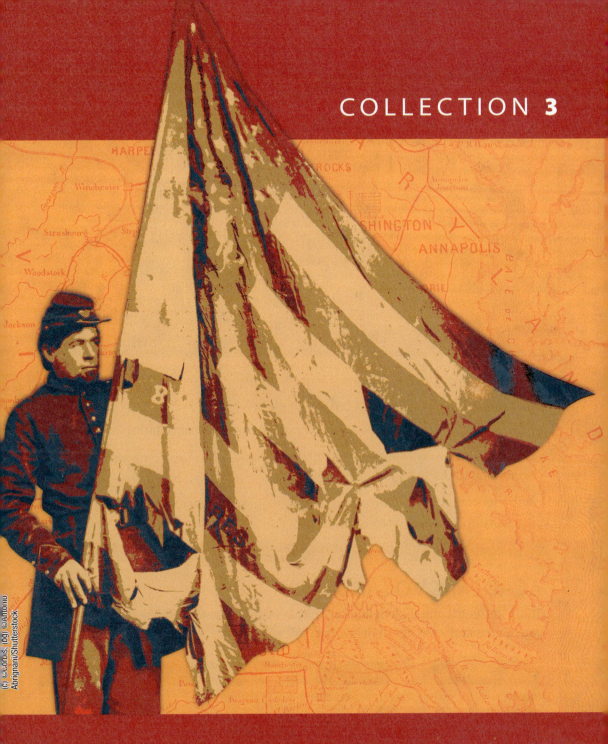

The Move Toward Freedom

" I should fight for liberty as long as my strength lasted. "
—Harriet Tubman

COLLECTION 3

The Move Toward Freedom

In this collection, you will focus on the quest for freedom that led to the American Civil War.

COLLECTION
PERFORMANCE TASK Preview

At the end of this collection, you will complete two performance tasks:

- In the first, you will participate in a collaborative discussion about how people responded to the struggle against slavery.

- In the second, you will write a literary analysis in which you consider the symbolism in a story in light of its historical context.

ACADEMIC VOCABULARY

Study the words and their definitions in the chart below. You will use these words as you discuss and write about the texts in this collection.

Word	Definition	Related Forms
access (ăk´sĕs) n.	a way of approaching or making use of	accessible, accessed
civil (sĭv´əl) adj.	of, or related to, citizens and their relations with each other and the state	civilization, civilian, civil rights
demonstrate (dĕm´ən-strāt´) v.	to show clearly and deliberately	demonstration, demonstrable
document (dŏk´yə-mənt) n.	written or printed paper that provides evidence or information	documentary, documentation
symbolize (sĭm´bə-līz´) v.	to serve as a symbol of, or represent something else	symbol, symbolic, symbolism

Frederick Douglass (1818–1895) *was born into enslavement in Maryland at a time when slavery was still legal in many states in the Union. As Douglass grew up, he tried to escape several times. Finally, in 1838, he succeeded. Douglass went on to become a famous speaker and writer, fighting to abolish, or end, slavery. His autobiography,* Narrative of the Life of Frederick Douglass, an American Slave, *became a best seller in the United States and Europe.*

from Narrative of the Life of Frederick Douglass, an American Slave

Autobiography by Frederick Douglass

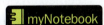

SETTING A PURPOSE As you read, consider why Frederick Douglass chose these particular events to write about. Think about what his focus on these events reveals about his character and his struggle for freedom.

myNotebook

As you read, mark up the text. Save your work to *my*Notebook.
- Highlight details
- Add notes and questions
- Add new words to *my*WordList

I lived in Master Hugh's family about seven years. During this time, I succeeded in learning to read and write. In accomplishing this, I was compelled to resort to various stratagems. I had no regular teacher. My mistress, who had kindly commenced to instruct me, had, in compliance with the advice and direction of her husband, not only ceased to instruct, but had set her face against my being instructed by any one else. It is due, however, to my mistress to say of her, that she did not adopt this course of treatment immediately. She at first lacked the depravity[1] indispensable to shutting me up in mental darkness. It was at least necessary for her to have

---

[1] **depravity** (dĭ-prăv´ĭ-tē): moral corruption.

some training in the exercise of irresponsible power, to make her equal to the task of treating me as though I were a brute.

My mistress was, as I have said, a kind and tender-hearted woman; and in the simplicity of her soul she **commenced**, when I first went to live with her, to treat me as she supposed one human being ought to treat another. In entering upon the duties of a slaveholder, she did not seem to perceive that I sustained to her the relation of a mere chattel,[2] and that for her to treat me as a human being was not only wrong, but dangerously so. Slavery proved as injurious to her as it did to me. When I went there, she was a pious warm, and tender-hearted woman. There was no sorrow or suffering for which she had not a tear. She had bread for the hungry, clothes for the naked, and comfort for every mourner that came within her reach. Slavery soon proved its ability to divest her of these heavenly qualities. Under its influence, the tender heart became stone, and the lamblike disposition gave way to one of tigerlike fierceness. The first step in her downward course was in her ceasing to instruct me. She now commenced to practise her husband's precepts.[3] She finally became even more violent in her opposition than her husband himself. She was not satisfied with simply doing as well as he had commanded; she seemed anxious to do better. Nothing seemed to make her more angry than to see me with a newspaper. She seemed to think that here lay the danger. I have had her rush at me with a face made all up of fury, and snatch from me a newspaper, in a manner that fully revealed her **apprehension**. She was an apt woman; and a little experience soon demonstrated, to her satisfaction, that education and slavery were incompatible with each other.

From this time I was most narrowly watched. If I was in a separate room any considerable length of time, I was sure to be suspected of having a book, and was at once called to give an account of myself. All this, however, was too late. The first step had been taken. Mistress, in teaching me the alphabet, had given me the *inch*, and no precaution could prevent me from taking the *ell*.

commence
(kə-měns′) *v.* When things *commence*, they begin or start.

apprehension
(ăp′rĭ-hĕn′shən) *n.* *Apprehension* is the fear or dread of the future.

---

[2] **chattel** (chăt′l): a property or slave.
[3] **precepts** (prē′sĕpts′): a rule or principal regarding action or conduct.

"Slavery proved as injurious to her as it did to me."

The plan which I adopted, and the one by which I was most successful, was that of making friends of all the little white boys whom I met in the street. As many of these as I could, I converted into teachers. With their kindly aid, obtained at different times and in different places, I finally succeeded in learning to read. When I was sent of errands, I always took my book with me, and by going one part of my errand quickly, I found time to get a lesson before my return. I used also to carry bread with me, enough of which was always in the house, and to which I was always welcome; for I was much better off in this regard than many of the poor white children in our neighborhood. This bread I used to bestow upon the hungry little urchins, who, in return, would give me that more valuable bread of knowledge. I am strongly tempted to give the names of two or three of those little boys, as a testimonial of the gratitude and affection I bear them; but **prudence** forbids;—not that it would injure me, but it might embarrass them; for it is almost an unpardonable offence to teach slaves to read in this Christian country. It is enough to say of the dear little fellows, that they lived on Philpot Street, very near Durgin and Bailey's ship-yard. I used to talk this matter of slavery over with them. I would sometimes say to them, I wished I could be as free as they would be when they got to be men. "You will be free as soon as you are twenty-one, *but I am a slave for life!* Have not I as good a right to be free as you have?" These words used to trouble them; they would express for me the liveliest sympathy, and console me with the hope that something would occur by which I might be free.

I was now about twelve years old, and the thought of being *a slave for life* began to bear heavily upon my heart. Just about this time, I got hold of a book entitled "The Columbian Orator."[4] Every opportunity I got, I used to read this book. Among much of other interesting matter, I found in it a dialogue between a master and his slave. The slave was

prudence
(prōōd´ns) *n.*
Prudence is the wise handling of practical matters.

---

[4] **"The Columbian Orator":** a collection of political essays, poems, and dialogues that were used to teach reading and speaking at the beginning of the 19th century.

represented as having run away from his master three times. The dialogue represented the conversation which took place between them, when the slave was retaken the third time. In this dialogue, the whole argument in behalf of slavery was brought forward by the master, all of which was disposed of by the slave. The slave was made to say some very smart as well as impressive things in reply to his master—things which had the desired though unexpected effect; for the conversation resulted in the voluntary emancipation of the slave on the part of the master.

In the same book, I met with one of Sheridan's mighty speeches on and in behalf of Catholic emancipation.[5] These were choice documents to me. I read them over and over again with **unabated** interest. They gave tongue to interesting thoughts of my own soul, which had frequently flashed through my mind, and died away for want of utterance. The moral which I gained from the dialogue was the power of truth over the conscience of even a slaveholder. What I got from Sheridan was a bold **denunciation** of slavery, and a powerful **vindication** of human rights. The reading of these documents enabled me to utter my thoughts, and to meet the arguments brought forward to sustain slavery; but while they relieved me of one difficulty, they brought on another even more painful than the one of which I was relieved. The more I read, the more I was led to abhor and detest my enslavers. I could regard them in no other light than a band of successful robbers, who had left their homes, and gone to Africa, and stolen us from our homes, and in a strange land reduced us to slavery. I loathed them as being the meanest as well as the most wicked of men. As I read and contemplated the subject, behold! that very discontentment which Master Hugh had predicted would follow my learning to read had already come, to torment and sting my soul to unutterable anguish. As I writhed under it, I would at times feel that learning to read had been a curse rather than a blessing. It had given me a view of my wretched condition, without the remedy. It opened

unabated
(ŭn´ə-bā´tĭd) *adj.*
If something is *unabated*, it keeps its full force without decreasing.

denunciation
(dĭ-nŭn´sē-ā´shən) *n.*
A *denunciation* is the public condemnation of something as wrong or evil.

vindication
(vĭn´dĭ-kā´shən) *n.*
Vindication is the evidence or proof that someone's claim is correct.

---

[5] **one of Sheridan's mighty speeches on and behalf of Catholic emancipation:** Richard Brinsley Sheridan (1751–1816) was an Irish playwright and politician who made speeches about the rights of people who practiced the Roman Catholic religion in Britain and Ireland.

my eyes to the horrible pit, but to no ladder upon which to get out. In moments of agony, I envied my fellow-slaves for their stupidity. I have often wished myself a beast. I preferred the condition of the meanest reptile to my own. Any thing, no matter what, to get rid of thinking! It was this everlasting thinking of my condition that tormented me. There was no getting rid of it. It was pressed upon me by every object within sight or hearing, animate or inanimate. The silver trump of freedom had roused my soul to eternal wakefulness. Freedom now appeared, to disappear no more forever. It was heard in every sound, and seen in every thing. It was ever present to torment me with a sense of my wretched condition. I saw nothing without seeing it, I heard nothing without hearing it, and felt nothing without feeling it. It looked from every star, it smiled in every calm, breathed in every wind, and moved in every storm.

COLLABORATIVE DISCUSSION Frederick Douglass describes his ability to read as a curse. With a partner, discuss why he comes to think this way after working so hard to learn to read. Cite specific evidence from the text to support your ideas.

Analyze Text: Autobiography

Narrative of the Life of Frederick Douglass is an **autobiography,** an account of the writer's own life. Almost all autobiographies
- are told from the first-person point of view using the pronouns *I* and *me*
- focus on the most significant events and people over a period of time in the author's life

Authors of autobiography often have a **purpose,** or reason for writing, beyond informing readers about what happened to one individual. For example, writers might also want to shed light on the time period in which they lived, or on an issue that has shaped their lives as well as the lives of others. Sometimes writers state their purpose directly, but often you must infer it by paying attention to what topics they come back to repeatedly and the thoughts, attitudes, and beliefs about these topics that they reveal.

What topic does Frederick Douglass focus on in this excerpt of his autobiography?

Analyze Structure

In an autobiography, authors often choose to focus on events that are related by **cause and effect,** which means that one event brings about another event or creates a change in attitude. The first event is the cause, and what follows is the effect. Paragraphs may be structured to show these cause-and-effect relationships.

For example, review the second paragraph of this selection. Douglass begins by saying his mistress was "a kind and tender-hearted woman," and he gives examples to support his statement. Then he explains how slavery caused her to change. "Under its influence, the tender heart became stone, and the lamblike disposition gave way to one of tigerlike fierceness." He supports this description of slavery's effects by giving examples. "Nothing seemed to make her more angry than to see me with a newspaper.... I have had her rush at me with a face made all up of fury, and snatch from me a newspaper."

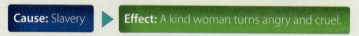

Review the autobiography and find another paragraph that explains a cause-and-effect relationship.

Analyzing the Text

Cite Text Evidence Support your responses with evidence from the text.

1. **Cause/Effect** Read lines 14–48. Did the mistress's initial kindness or her eventual cruelty have a greater effect on Frederick Douglass? Explain.

2. **Interpret** When describing how he paid his child tutors, Douglass says, "This bread I used to bestow upon the hungry little urchins, who, in return, would give me that more valuable bread of knowledge." In what way is knowledge "bread"?

3. **Cause/Effect** Douglass reads a dialogue between a master and his slave as well as a speech by Sheridan. In a chart like the one shown, list several effects that resulted from reading these documents.

4. **Analyze** Why does Douglass say in line 121, "I have often wished myself a beast"?

5. **Evaluate** Reread lines 105–112. What words reveal Douglass's perspective on, or view of, slaveholders?

6. **Analyze** What is Douglass's purpose for writing? Identify three events in this selection that help him achieve his goal.

Speaking and Listening

In lines 116–117, Douglass says "I would at times feel that learning to read had been a curse rather than a blessing." With a partner or small group, discuss Douglass's statement and examine whether people today might share his attitude. Be sure to support your views with evidence from the text.

PERFORMANCE TASK

Writing Activity: Literary Analysis
How does the tone of Douglass's autobiography help him achieve his purpose? Write a short literary analysis.

- With a partner, discuss the author's purpose for writing. Identify the **tone** of the piece, or the writer's attitude toward his subject.
- Next, find examples where Douglass's choice of words helps establish the tone.
- When you write, begin by stating your view. Then support that view with evidence from the text.

Critical Vocabulary

commence   apprehension   prudence
unabated   denunciation   vindication

Practice and Apply Use what you know about the Vocabulary words to answer the following questions.

1. If a criminal receives **vindication,** will he feel relieved or upset?
2. Which demonstrates **prudence,** saving an allowance or spending it all?
3. To **commence** baking a cake, would you stir the batter or study the recipe?
4. Which is a type of **denunciation,** praise or criticism?
5. Would you feel **apprehension** about taking a test or about getting an A?
6. If your interest in Frederick Douglass is **unabated,** will you read many books about him or just one?

Vocabulary Strategy: Use Context Clues

Context clues are the words, phrases, and sentences surrounding a word that provide hints about a word's definition. These clues can be found either before or after the unfamiliar word. Look at this example:

> She seemed to think that here lay the danger. I have had her rush at me with a face made all up of fury . . . in a manner that fully revealed her apprehension.

The first sentence says that the subject perceives some danger. This provides a clue to the meaning of the word *apprehension*, which you can infer is a feeling of fear or dread that often arises in the face of danger. The dictionary definition confirms this guess.

Practice and Apply Find the following words in Douglass's autobiography. Look at the surrounding words, phrases, and sentences for clues to each word's meaning. On a separate piece of paper, fill out a chart like the one shown.

Word	Context Clues	Guessed Definition	Dictionary Definition
divest (line 26)			
apt (line 39)			
bestow (line 61)			
console (line 75)			

Background Before the Civil War, many enslaved people fled north to freedom along the Underground Railroad, a secret network of safe houses. One of the Underground Railroad's most famous "conductors" was Harriet Tubman.

Ann Lane Petry (1908–1997) *grew up in a small town in Connecticut, where she and her family were the only African American residents. Much of her writing focused on the important contributions of African Americans.*

from
HARRIET TUBMAN:
Conductor on the Underground Railroad

Biography by Ann Petry

SETTING A PURPOSE As you read, look for clues about the kind of person Harriet Tubman was. What qualities led others to trust her as a leader? Write down any questions you have.

The Railroad Runs to Canada

Along the Eastern Shore of Maryland, in Dorchester County, in Caroline County, the masters kept hearing whispers about the man named Moses, who was running off slaves. At first they did not believe in his existence. The stories about him were fantastic, unbelievable. Yet they watched for him. They offered rewards for his capture.

They never saw him. Now and then they heard whispered rumors to the effect that he was in the neighborhood. The woods were searched. The roads were watched. There was never anything to indicate his whereabouts. But a few days afterward, a goodly number of slaves would be gone from the plantation. Neither the master nor the overseer had heard or seen anything unusual in the quarter.¹ Sometimes one or the other would vaguely remember having heard a whippoorwill call somewhere in the woods, close by, late at night. Though it was the wrong season for whippoorwills.

Sometimes the masters thought they had heard the cry of a hoot owl, repeated, and would remember having thought that the intervals between the low moaning cry were wrong, that it had been repeated four times in succession instead of three. There was never anything more than that to suggest that all was not well in the quarter. Yet when morning came, they invariably discovered that a group of the finest slaves had taken to their heels.

Unfortunately, the discovery was almost always made on a Sunday. Thus a whole day was lost before the machinery of pursuit could be set in motion. The posters offering rewards for the fugitives could not be printed until Monday. The men who made a living hunting for runaway slaves were out of reach, off in the woods with their dogs and their guns, in pursuit of four-footed game, or they were in camp meetings saying their prayers with their wives and families beside them.

Harriet Tubman could have told them that there was far more involved in this matter of running off slaves than signaling the would-be runaways by imitating the call of a whippoorwill, or a hoot owl, far more involved than a matter of waiting for a clear night when the North Star was visible.

In December, 1851, when she started out with the band of fugitives that she planned to take to Canada, she had been in the vicinity of the plantation for days, planning the trip, carefully selecting the slaves that she would take with her.

She had announced her arrival in the quarter by singing the forbidden spiritual—"Go down, Moses, 'way down to Egypt Land"²—singing it softly outside the door of a slave cabin, late at night. The husky voice was beautiful even when it was barely more than a murmur borne³ on the wind.

Once she had made her presence known, word of her coming spread from cabin to cabin. The slaves whispered to each other, ear to mouth, mouth to ear, "Moses is here." "Moses has come." "Get ready. Moses is back again." The ones

---

¹ **quarter:** the area in which enslaved people lived.
² **"Go down, Moses, 'way down to Egypt Land":** a line from an African American folk song.
³ **borne:** carried.

who had agreed to go North with her put ashcake and salt herring in an old bandanna, hastily tied it into a bundle, and then waited patiently for the signal that meant it was time to start.

There were eleven in this party, including one of her brothers and his wife. It was the largest group that she had ever conducted, but she was determined that more and more slaves should know what freedom was like.

She had to take them all the way to Canada. The Fugitive Slave Law[4] was no longer a great many incomprehensible words written down on the country's lawbooks. The new law had become a reality. It was Thomas Sims, a boy, picked up on the streets of Boston at night and shipped back to Georgia. It was Jerry and Shadrach, arrested and jailed with no warning.

She had never been in Canada. The route beyond Philadelphia was strange to her. But she could not let the runaways who accompanied her know this. As they walked along she told them stories of her own first flight, she kept painting vivid word pictures of what it would be like to be free.

But there were so many of them this time. She knew moments of doubt when she was half-afraid, and kept looking back over her shoulder, imagining that she heard the sound of pursuit. They would certainly be pursued. Eleven of them. Eleven thousand dollars' worth of flesh and bone and muscle that belonged to Maryland planters. If they were caught, the eleven runaways would be whipped and sold South, but she— she would probably be hanged.

They tried to sleep during the day but they never could wholly relax into sleep. She could tell by the positions they assumed, by their restless movements. And they walked at night. Their progress was slow. It took them three nights of walking to reach the first stop. She had told them about the place where they would stay, promising warmth and good food, holding these things out to them as an incentive to keep going.

When she knocked on the door of a farmhouse, a place where she and her parties of runaways had always been welcome, always been given shelter and plenty to eat, there

---

[4] **Fugitive Slave Law:** a law by which enslaved people who escaped could be recovered by their owners.

was no answer. She knocked again, softly. A voice from within said, "Who is it?" There was fear in the voice.

She knew instantly from the sound of the voice that there was something wrong. She said, "A friend with friends," the password on the Underground Railroad.

The door opened, slowly. The man who stood in the doorway looked at her coldly, looked with unconcealed astonishment and fear at the eleven **disheveled** runaways who were standing near her. Then he shouted, "Too many, too many. It's not safe. My place was searched last week. It's not safe!" and slammed the door in her face.

She turned away from the house, frowning. She had promised her passengers food and rest and warmth, and instead of that, there would be hunger and cold and more walking over the frozen ground. Somehow she would have to **instill** courage into these eleven people, most of them strangers, would have to feed them on hope and bright dreams of freedom instead of the fried pork and corn bread and milk she had promised them.

They stumbled along behind her, half-dead for sleep, and she urged them on, though she was as tired and as discouraged as they were. She had never been in Canada but she kept painting wondrous word pictures of what it would be like. She managed to **dispel** their fear of pursuit, so that they would not become hysterical, panic-stricken. Then she had to bring some of the fear back, so that they would stay awake and keep walking though they drooped with sleep.

Yet during the day, when they lay down deep in a thicket, they never really slept, because if a twig snapped or the wind sighed in the branches of a pine tree, they jumped to their feet, afraid of their own shadows, shivering and shaking. It was very cold, but they dared not make fires because someone would see the smoke and wonder about it.

She kept thinking, eleven of them. Eleven thousand dollars' worth of slaves. And she had to take them all the way to Canada. Sometimes she told them about Thomas Garrett, in Wilmington. She said he was their friend even though he did not know them. He was the friend of all fugitives. He called them God's poor. He was a Quaker[5] and his speech was a little different from that of other people. His clothing was

---

[5] **Quaker:** a member of a religious group called the Society of Friends.

disheveled
(dĭ-shĕv´əld) *adj.*
When something is *disheveled*, it is messy or untidy.

instill
(ĭn-stĭl´) *v.* When you *instill* something, you supply it gradually.

dispel
(dĭ-spĕl´) *v.* When you *dispel* something, you drive it away.

Harriet Tubman

130 different, too. He wore the wide-brimmed hat that the Quakers wear.

She said that he had thick white hair, soft, almost like a baby's, and the kindest eyes she had ever seen. He was a big man and strong, but he had never used his strength to harm anyone, always to help people. He would give all of them a new pair of shoes. Everybody. He always did. Once they reached his house in Wilmington, they would be safe. He would see to it that they were.

She described the house where he lived, told them about
140 the store where he sold shoes. She said he kept a pail of milk and a loaf of bread in the drawer of his desk so that he would have food ready at hand for any of God's poor who should

suddenly appear before him, fainting with hunger. There was a hidden room in the store. A whole wall swung open, and behind it was a room where he could hide fugitives. On the wall there were shelves filled with small boxes—boxes of shoes—so that you would never guess that the wall actually opened.

While she talked, she kept watching them. They did not believe her. She could tell by their expressions. They were thinking, New shoes, Thomas Garrett, Quaker, Wilmington—what foolishness was this? Who knew if she told the truth? Where was she taking them anyway?

That night they reached the next stop—a farm that belonged to a German. She made the runaways take shelter behind trees at the edge of the fields before she knocked at the door. She hesitated before she approached the door, thinking, suppose that he, too, should refuse shelter, suppose—Then she thought, Lord, I'm going to hold steady on to You and You've got to see me through—and knocked softly.

She heard the familiar guttural voice say, "Who's there?"

She answered quickly, "A friend with friends."

He opened the door and greeted her warmly. "How many this time?" he asked.

"Eleven," she said and waited, doubting, wondering.

He said, "Good. Bring them in."

He and his wife fed them in the lamplit kitchen, their faces glowing, as they offered food and more food, urging them to eat, saying there was plenty for everybody, have more milk, have more bread, have more meat.

They spent the night in the warm kitchen. They really slept, all that night and until dusk the next day. When they left, it was with reluctance. They had all been warm and safe and well-fed. It was hard to exchange the security offered by that clean warm kitchen for the darkness and the cold of a December night.

"Go On or Die"

Harriet had found it hard to leave the warmth and friendliness, too. But she urged them on. For a while, as they walked, they seemed to carry in them a measure of contentment; some of the serenity and the cleanliness of that big warm kitchen **lingered** on inside them. But as they walked farther and farther away from the warmth and the light, the

linger
(lĭng′gər) *v.* When you *linger,* you remain or stay longer.

cold and the darkness entered into them. They fell silent, **sullen**, suspicious. She waited for the moment when some one of them would turn mutinous. It did not happen that night.

Two nights later she was aware that the feet behind her were moving slower and slower. She heard the irritability in their voices, knew that soon someone would refuse to go on.

She started talking about William Still and the Philadelphia Vigilance Committee.[6] No one commented. No one asked any questions. She told them the story of William and Ellen Craft and how they escaped from Georgia. Ellen was so fair that she looked as though she were white, and so she dressed up in a man's clothing and she looked like a wealthy young planter. Her husband, William, who was dark, played the role of her slave. Thus they traveled from Macon, Georgia, to Philadelphia, riding on the trains, staying at the finest hotels. Ellen pretended to be very ill—her right arm was in a sling, and her right hand was bandaged, because she was supposed to have rheumatism. Thus she avoided having to sign the register at the hotels for she could not read or write. They finally arrived safely in Philadelphia, and then went on to Boston.

No one said anything. Not one of them seemed to have heard her.

She told them about Frederick Douglass, the most famous of the escaped slaves, of his **eloquence**, of his magnificent appearance. Then she told them of her own first vain effort at running away, **evoking** the memory of that miserable life she had led as a child, reliving it for a moment in the telling.

But they had been tired too long, hungry too long, afraid too long, footsore too long. One of them suddenly cried out in despair, "Let me go back. It is better to be a slave than to suffer like this in order to be free."

She carried a gun with her on these trips. She had never used it—except as a threat. Now as she aimed it, she experienced a feeling of guilt, remembering that time, years ago, when she had prayed for the death of Edward Brodas, the Master, and then not too long afterward had heard that great wailing cry that came from the throats of the field hands, and knew from the sound that the Master was dead.

sullen
(sŭl´ən) *adj.* Sullen people show silent resentment.

eloquence
(ĕl´ə-kwəns) *n.* Eloquence is the ability to speak powerfully and persuasively.

evoke
(ĭ-vōk´) *v.* When you *evoke* something, you summon it.

---

[6] **Philadelphia Vigilance Committee:** fundraising organization that helped people who escaped enslavement.

A stop on the Underground Railroad

One of the runaways said, again, "Let me go back. Let me go back," and stood still, and then turned around and said, over his shoulder, "I am going back."

She lifted the gun, aimed it at the despairing slave. She said, "Go on with us or die." The husky low-pitched voice was grim.

He hesitated for a moment and then he joined the others. They started walking again. She tried to explain to them why none of them could go back to the plantation. If a runaway returned, he would turn traitor, the master and the overseer would force him to turn traitor. The returned slave would disclose the stopping places, the hiding places, the cornstacks they had used with the full knowledge of the owner of the farm, the name of the German farmer who had fed them and sheltered them. These people who had risked their own security to help runaways would be ruined, fined, imprisoned.

She said, "We got to go free or die. And freedom's not bought with dust."

This time she told them about the long agony of the Middle Passage[7] on the old slave ships, about the black horror of the holds, about the chains and the whips. They too knew these stories. But she wanted to remind them of the long hard

---

[7] **Middle Passage:** sea route along which enslaved Africans were transported to the Americas.

way they had come, about the long hard way they had yet to go. She told them about Thomas Sims, the boy picked up on the streets of Boston and sent back to Georgia. She said when they got him back to Savannah, got him in prison there, they whipped him until a doctor who was standing by watching said, "You will kill him if you strike him again!" His master said, "Let him die!"

Thus she forced them to go on. Sometimes she thought she had become nothing but a voice speaking in the darkness, **cajoling**, urging, threatening. Sometimes she told them things to make them laugh, sometimes she sang to them, and heard the eleven voices behind her blending softly with hers, and then she knew that for the moment all was well with them.

cajole
(kə-jōl´) v. When you *cajole*, you coax or urge gently.

She gave the impression of being a short, muscular, indomitable woman who could never be defeated. Yet at any moment she was liable to be seized by one of those curious fits of sleep, which might last for a few minutes or for hours.

Even on this trip, she suddenly fell asleep in the woods. The runaways, ragged, dirty, hungry, cold, did not steal the gun as they might have, and set off by themselves, or turn back. They sat on the ground near her and waited patiently until she awakened. They had come to trust her implicitly, totally. They, too, had come to believe her repeated statement, "We got to go free or die." She was leading them into freedom, and so they waited until she was ready to go on.

Finally, they reached Thomas Garrett's house in Wilmington, Delaware. Just as Harriet had promised, Garrett gave them all new shoes, and provided carriages to take them on to the next stop.

By slow stages they reached Philadelphia, where William Still hastily recorded their names, and the plantations whence they had come, and something of the life they had led in slavery. Then he carefully hid what he had written, for fear it might be discovered. In 1872 he published this record in book form and called it *The Underground Railroad*. In the foreword to his book he said: "While I knew the danger of keeping strict records, and while I did not then dream that in my day slavery would be blotted out, or that the time would come when I could publish these records, it used to afford me great satisfaction to take them down, fresh from the lips of fugitives on the way to freedom, and to preserve them as they had given them."

William Still, who was familiar with all the station stops on the Underground Railroad, supplied Harriet with money and sent her and her eleven fugitives on to Burlington, New Jersey.

Harriet felt safer now, though there were danger spots ahead. But the biggest part of her job was over. As they went farther and farther north, it grew colder; she was aware of the wind on the Jersey ferry and aware of the cold damp in New York. From New York they went on to Syracuse, where the temperature was even lower.

In Syracuse she met the Reverend J. W. Loguen, known as "Jarm" Loguen. This was the beginning of a lifelong friendship. Both Harriet and Jarm Loguen were to become friends and supporters of Old John Brown.[8]

From Syracuse they went north again, into a colder, snowier city—Rochester. Here they almost certainly stayed with Frederick Douglass, for he wrote in his autobiography:

> On one occasion I had eleven fugitives at the same time under my roof, and it was necessary for them to remain with me until I could collect sufficient money to get them to Canada. It was the largest number I ever had at any one time, and I had some difficulty in providing so many with food and shelter, but, as may well be imagined, they were not very fastidious in either direction, and were well content with very plain food, and a strip of carpet on the floor for a bed, or a place on the straw in the barnloft.

Late in December, 1851, Harriet arrived in St. Catharines, Canada West (now Ontario), with the eleven fugitives. It had taken almost a month to complete this journey; most of the time had been spent getting out of Maryland.

---

[8] **Old John Brown:** anti-slavery leader who was executed.

St. Catharines, Prince Edward Island, Canada

That first winter in St. Catharines was a terrible one. Canada was a strange frozen land, snow everywhere, ice everywhere, and a bone-biting cold the like of which none of them had ever experienced before. Harriet rented a small frame house in the town and set to work to make a home. The fugitives boarded with her. They worked in the forests, felling trees, and so did she. Sometimes she took other jobs, cooking or cleaning house for people in the town. She cheered on these newly arrived fugitives, working herself, finding work for them, finding food for them, praying for them, sometimes begging for them.

Often she found herself thinking of the beauty of Maryland, the mellowness of the soil, the richness of the plant life there. The climate itself made for an ease of living that could never be duplicated in this bleak, barren countryside.

In spite of the severe cold, the hard work, she came to love St. Catharines, and the other towns and cities in Canada where black men lived. She discovered that freedom meant more than the right to change jobs at will, more than the right to keep the money that one earned. It was the right to vote and to sit on juries. It was the right to be elected to office. In Canada there were black men who were county officials and members of school boards. St. Catharines had a large colony of ex-slaves, and they owned their own homes, kept them neat and clean and in good repair. They lived in whatever part of town they chose and sent their children to the schools.

When spring came she decided that she would make this small Canadian city her home—as much as any place could be said to be home to a woman who traveled from Canada to the Eastern Shore of Maryland as often as she did.

In the spring of 1852, she went back to Cape May, New Jersey. She spent the summer there, cooking in a hotel. That fall she returned, as usual, to Dorchester County, and brought out nine more slaves, conducting them all the way to St. Catharines, in Canada West, to the bone-biting cold, the snow-covered forests—and freedom.

She continued to live in this fashion, spending the winter in Canada, and the spring and summer working in Cape May, New Jersey, or in Philadelphia. She made two trips a year into slave territory, one in the fall and another in the spring. She now had a definite crystallized purpose, and in carrying it out, her life fell into a pattern which remained unchanged for the next six years.

COLLABORATIVE DISCUSSION What did you find most interesting about Harriet Tubman? With a partner, discuss the characteristics that surprised or impressed you. Cite specific evidence from the text to support your ideas.

Analyze Text: Biography

A good way to gain an understanding of a historical figure is to read his or her **biography,** a true account of a person's life told by someone other than the subject, usually in the third-person point of view. Biographers thoroughly research the people they write about. They then use the research to give readers access to their subjects through one or more methods of **characterization,** techniques that reveal a person's qualities and personality.

To analyze the biography you have just read, examine how the author characterizes the subject.

- Look at what the author says about Harriet Tubman's hopes, thoughts, and worries.
- Consider what Harriet Tubman says and does. What is her motivation, or reason, for her words and actions?
- Think about how others behave toward Harriet Tubman.

Analyze Structure

Author's craft refers to the methods authors use to make their writing come alive. Notice how Ann Petry combines the techniques below to develop and refine ideas about Harriet Tubman in the paragraphs cited in these examples. Review the text to find an additional example of each technique.

Technique	Definition	Examples
word choice	the author's use of specific words to impact the reader	"The man who stood in the doorway looked at her coldly, looked with unconcealed astonishment and fear."
sentence variety and punctuation	variations in sentence length and use of dashes for dramatic effect	"She had never used it—except as a threat."
parallelism	similar grammatical constructions used to express ideas that are related or equal in importance	"When she knocked on the door of a farmhouse, a place where she and her parties of runaways had always been welcome, always been given shelter."
syntax	the arrangement of words and phrases in sentences used to convey accurate meaning and tone	"Sometimes the masters thought they heard the cry of a hoot owl, repeated, and would remember having thought the intervals between the low moaning cry were wrong."

Harriet Tubman: Conductor on the Underground Railroad

 eBook *Annotate It!*

Analyzing the Text

Cite Text Evidence   Support your responses with evidence from the text.

1. **Infer** Reread lines 1–16. What does the description suggest about the qualities of the person called Moses?

2. **Interpret** Reread lines 28–32. What is the effect of the author's use of the phrase "in pursuit of four-footed game"?

3. **Interpret** Identify the parallelism in lines 47–49. How does this technique contribute to the effectiveness of these lines?

4. **Infer** In lines 59–70, the author describes the difficulty of the task facing Harriet Tubman. What is Tubman's response? Explain what her words and actions reveal about her.

5. **Analyze** Reread lines 258–265. Find and explain three examples of the techniques the author uses to make the events come alive in this paragraph.

6. **Draw Conclusions** Based on the characterization of Harriet Tubman in this biography, how would you describe her? Fill out a chart like the one shown with examples from the selection, and then write a one-sentence description of this famous woman.

What Harriet Tubman thinks	
What Harriet Tubman does	
What Harriet Tubman says	
What others think and say about her	

PERFORMANCE TASK

Speaking Activity: Speech Imagine that Harriet Tubman will be honored at a "Hall of Fame" for those who fought slavery. Prepare and give a speech explaining why she is a heroic figure. Consult sources in addition to the selection. Consider the following:

- What kind of person was Harriet Tubman?
- What was Tubman's motivation for bringing enslaved people to freedom?
- What examples demonstrate Tubman's heroism?
- How do historians judge Tubman's impact on the quest for freedom prior to the Civil War?

Critical Vocabulary

disheveled	**instill**	**dispel**	**linger**
sullen	**eloquence**	**evoke**	**cajole**

Practice and Apply Use what you know about the Vocabulary words to answer the following questions.

1. Would you **linger** at a party if you were **disheveled**? Why or why not?
2. Could someone **instill eloquence** in you? Why or why not?
3. What might someone do to **evoke** a **sullen** response?
4. Would you **cajole** a friend to **dispel** a bad mood? Why or why not?

Vocabulary Strategy: Use Word Relationships

You can use relationships among words to help you figure out the meaning of an unfamiliar word. Look at this sentence from *Harriet Tubman*:

> "Sometimes she thought she had become nothing but a voice speaking in the darkness, cajoling, urging, threatening."

The words "cajoling, urging, threatening" are synonyms, or words that have similar meanings.

> Look at this sentence from *Harriet Tubman*:
>
> "She had promised her passengers food and . . . warmth, and instead of that, there would be hunger and cold . . ."

The phrase "instead of" provides a clue that the words *warmth* and *cold* are **antonyms,** or words that have opposite meanings. If you know the meaning of one word in a synonym or antonym pair, you can often guess the meaning of the other.

Practice and Apply For each sentence, write an S if the underlined word is a synonym and an A if it is an antonym. Identify the other word or words in the synonym or antonym pair. Then write a definition of the underlined word.

1. Instead of becoming discouraged, she grew more determined.
2. The effect of the Fugitive Slave Law was appalling, horrifying, and dismaying.
3. Her incentive for leading her first group north was the same as her reason for leading the tenth group: she wanted others to know freedom.

Language Conventions: Conditional Mood

The **mood** of a verb indicates the tone or attitude with which a statement is made. Writers use the **conditional mood** when they want to make a statement about what might happen if something else happens. The conditional mood often includes the words *might, could, would,* or *if*. Look at this example from *Harriet Tubman*. Notice that the sentence describes what might happen ("he would turn traitor") if something else happens ("If a runaway returned").

> <u>If</u> a runaway returned, he <u>would</u> turn traitor, the master and the overseer <u>would</u> force him to turn traitor.

If this happens it might cause . . .   **. . . this to happen**

Study these examples.

> <u>If</u> he did not forge ahead, he <u>would</u> not reach his goal.
>
> He <u>might</u> have succeeded <u>if</u> he had tried harder.
>
> She <u>could</u> have won the game <u>if</u> she had practiced.

Practice and Apply Read the sentences. Rewrite them so that they are in the conditional mood.

1. Max did not write a good report because he had not done enough research.
2. Kim did not study hard and did not do well on the test.
3. Maria wanted to succeed but decided to play computer games rather than to study.
4. To earn a good grade you have to do thorough research on the topic.
5. The weather has to be good in order for gym class to be held outside.

Background *Though **Ray Bradbury** (1920–2012) is best known as a science fiction writer, he's also written plays, mysteries, fantasies, realistic stories, and novels. In this story, Bradbury tells about a drummer boy on the night before the Battle of Shiloh in the Civil War. This two-day battle began on April 6, 1862, near the southwestern Tennessee church from which the bloody clash takes its name. More than 23,000 soldiers died during those two days. At that time, it was the bloodiest battle in American history.*

The Drummer Boy of Shiloh

Historical Fiction by Ray Bradbury

SETTING A PURPOSE As you read, pay attention to the details the author provides about the scene of the battle and about the men who were preparing to fight. What do the details suggest about the realities of war?

In the April night, more than once, blossoms fell from the orchard trees and lit with rustling taps on the drumskin. At midnight a peach stone left miraculously on a branch through winter, flicked by a bird, fell swift and unseen, struck once, like panic, which jerked the boy upright. In silence he listened to his own heart ruffle away, away, at last gone from his ears and back in his chest again.

After that, he turned the drum on its side, where its great lunar[1] face peered at him whenever he opened his eyes.

His face, alert or at rest, was **solemn**. It was indeed a solemn time and a solemn night for a boy just turned fourteen in the peach field near the Owl Creek not far from the church at Shiloh.

solemn
(sŏlʹəm) *adj.* If an event is *solemn*, it is deeply serious.

---

[1] **lunar** (lo͞oʹnər): of or relating to the moon.

The Drummer Boy of Shiloh   167

"... thirty-one, thirty-two, thirty-three ..."

Unable to see, he stopped counting.

Beyond the thirty-three familiar shadows, forty thousand men, exhausted by nervous expectation, unable to sleep for romantic dreams of battles yet unfought, lay crazily **askew** in their uniforms. A mile yet farther on, another army was **strewn** helter-skelter, turning slow, basting themselves with the thought of what they would do when the time came: a leap, a yell, a blind plunge their strategy, raw youth their protection and benediction.[2]

Now and again the boy heard a vast wind come up, that gently stirred the air. But he knew what it was, the army here, the army there, whispering to itself in the dark. Some men talking to others, others murmuring to themselves, and all so quiet it was like a natural element arisen from south or north with the motion of the earth toward dawn.

What the men whispered the boy could only guess, and he guessed that it was: Me, I'm the one, I'm the one of all the rest won't die. I'll live through it. I'll go home. The band will play. And I'll be there to hear it.

Yes, thought the boy, that's all very well for them, they can give as good as they get!

For with the careless bones of the young men harvested by night and bindled[3] around campfires were the similarly strewn steel bones of their rifles, with bayonets fixed like eternal lightning lost in the orchard grass.

Me, thought the boy, I got only a drum, two sticks to beat it, and no shield.

There wasn't a man-boy on this ground tonight did not have a shield he cast, riveted or carved himself on his way to his first attack, compounded of remote but nonetheless firm and fiery family devotion, flag-blown patriotism and cocksure immortality strengthened by the touchstone of very real gunpowder, ramrod, minnieball and flint.[4] But without these last the boy felt his family move yet farther off away in the dark, as if one of those great prairie-burning trains had chanted them away never to return, leaving him with this drum which was worse than a toy in the game to be played tomorrow or some day much too soon.

askew (ə-skyo͞o´) *adj.* When something is *askew*, it is off center.

strew (stro͞o) *v.* If you *strew* something, you spread it here and there, or scatter it.

---

[2] **benediction** (bĕn´ĭ-dĭk´shən): a blessing.

[3] **bindled:** fastened or wrapped by encircling, as with a belt.

[4] **ramrod, minnieball, and flint:** items used to fire a rifle.

The boy turned on his side. A moth brushed his face, but it was peach blossom. A peach blossom flicked him, but it was a moth. Nothing stayed put. Nothing had a name. Nothing was as it once was.

If he lay very still, when the dawn came up and the soldiers put on their bravery with their caps, perhaps they might go away, the war with them, and not notice him lying small here, no more than a toy himself.

"Well, by God, now," said a voice.

The boy shut up his eyes, to hide inside himself, but it was too late. Someone, walking by in the night, stood over him.

"Well," said the voice quietly, "here's a soldier crying *before* the fight. Good. Get it over. Won't be time once it all starts."

And the voice was about to move on when the boy, startled, touched the drum at his elbow. The man above, hearing this, stopped. The boy could feel his eyes, sense him slowly bending near. A hand must have come down out of the night, for there was a little rat-tat as the fingernails brushed and the man's breath fanned his face.

"Why, it's the drummer boy, isn't it?"

The boy nodded, not knowing if his nod was seen. "Sir, is that *you*?" he said.

"I assume it is." The man's knees cracked as he bent still closer.

He smelled as all fathers should smell, of salt sweat, ginger tobacco, horse and boot leather, and the earth he walked upon. He had many eyes. No, not eyes, brass buttons that watched the boy.

He could only be, and was, the General.

"What's your name, boy?" he asked.

"Joby," whispered the boy, starting to sit up.

"All right, Joby, don't stir." A hand pressed his chest gently, and the boy relaxed. "How long you been with us, Joby?"

"Three weeks, sir."

"Run off from home or joined **legitimately**, boy?"

Silence.

"Damn-fool question," said the General. "Do you shave yet, boy? Even more of a damn-fool. There's your cheek, fell right off the tree overhead. And the others here not much older. Raw, raw, damn raw, the lot of you. You ready for tomorrow or the next day, Joby?"

"I think so, sir.

legitimately
(lə-jĭt´ə-mĭt-lē) *adv.*
When you do something *legitimately*, you do it lawfully.

"You want to cry some more, go on ahead. I did the same last night."

"*You*, sir?"

"God's truth. Thinking of everything ahead. Both sides figuring the other side will just give up, and soon, and the war done in weeks, and us all home. Well, that's not how it's going to be. And maybe that's why I cried."

"Yes, sir," said Joby.

The General must have taken out a cigar now, for the dark was suddenly filled with the Indian smell of tobacco unlit as yet, but chewed as the man thought what next to say.

"It's going to be a crazy time," said the General. "Counting both sides, there's a hundred thousand men, give or take a few thousand out there tonight, not one as can spit a sparrow off a tree, or knows a horse clod from a minnieball. Stand up, bare the breast, ask to be a target, thank them and sit down, that's us, that's them. We should turn tail and train four months, they should do the same. But here we are, taken with spring fever and thinking it blood lust, taking our sulphur with cannons instead of with molasses[5] as it should be, going to be a hero, going to live forever. And I can see all of them over there nodding agreement, save the other way around. It's wrong, boy, it's wrong as a head put on hind side front and a man marching backward through life. It will be a double massacre if one of their itchy generals decides to picnic his lads on our grass. More innocents will get shot out of pure Cherokee enthusiasm than ever got shot before. Owl Creek was full of boys splashing around in the noonday sun just a few hours ago. I fear it will be full of boys again, just floating, at sundown tomorrow, not caring where the tide takes them."

The General stopped and made a little pile of winter leaves and twigs in the darkness, as if he might at any moment strike fire to them to see his way through the coming days when the sun might not show its face because of what was happening here and just beyond.

The boy watched the hand stirring the leaves and opened his lips to say something, but did not say it. The General heard the boy's breath and spoke himself.

---

[5] **taking our sulphur with cannons instead of with molasses:** sulphur was an ingredient in gunpowder that was used to fire cannons; at that time sulphur was also used as a tonic or medical treatment. Molasses is a thick, brown syrup, used to mask the unpleasant taste of medicines.

"Why am I telling you this? That's what you wanted to ask, eh? Well, when you got a bunch of wild horses on a loose rein somewhere, somehow you got to bring order, rein them in. These lads, fresh out of the milkshed, don't know what I know, and I can't tell them: men actually die, in war. So each is his own army. I got to make *one* army of them. And for that, boy, I need you."

"Me!" The boy's lips barely twitched.

"Now, boy," said the General quietly, "you are the heart of the army. Think of that. You're the heart of the army. Listen, now."

And, lying there, Joby listened.

And the General spoke on.

If he, Joby, beat slow tomorrow, the heart would beat slow in the men. They would lag by the wayside.[6] They would drowse in the fields on their muskets. They would sleep

 You're the heart of the army.

forever, after that, in those same fields, their hearts slowed by a drummer boy and stopped by enemy lead.

But if he beat a sure, steady, ever faster rhythm, then, then their knees would come up in a long line down over that hill, one knee after the other, like a wave on the ocean shore! Had he seen the ocean ever? Seen the waves rolling in like a well-ordered cavalry charge to the sand? Well, that was it, that's what he wanted, that's what was needed! Joby was his right hand and his left. He gave the orders, but Joby set the pace!

So bring the right knee up and the right foot out and the left knee up and the left foot out. One following the other in good time, in brisk time. Move the blood up the body and make the head proud and the spine stiff and the jaw **resolute**. Focus the eye and set the teeth, flare the nostrils and tighten the hands, put steel armor all over the men, for blood moving fast in them does indeed make men feel as if they'd put on steel. He must keep at it, at it! Long and steady, steady and long! Then, even though shot or torn, those wounds got in hot blood—in blood he'd helped

resolute
(rĕz´ə-lo͞ot´) *adj.*
If you are *resolute*, you are firm or determined.

---

[6] **lag by the wayside:** fall behind.

stir—would feel less pain. If their blood was cold, it would be more than slaughter, it would be murderous nightmare and pain best not told and no one to guess.

The General spoke and stopped, letting his breath slack off. Then, after a moment, he said, "So there you are, that's it. Will you do that, boy? Do you know now you're general of the army when the General's left behind?"

The boy nodded mutely.

"You'll run them through for me then, boy?"

"Yes, sir."

"Good. And, God willing, many nights from tonight, many years from now, when you're as old or far much older than me, when they ask you what you did in this awful time, you will tell them—one part humble and one part proud— 'I was the drummer boy at the battle of Owl Creek,' or the Tennessee River, or maybe they'll just name it after the church there. 'I was the drummer boy at Shiloh.' Good grief, that has a beat and sound to it fitting for Mr. Longfellow. 'I was the drummer boy at Shiloh.' Who will ever hear those words and not know you, boy, or what you thought this night, or what you'll think tomorrow or the next day when we must get up on our legs and *move!*"

The general stood up. "Well, then. God bless you, boy. Good night."

"Good night, sir."

And, tobacco, brass, boot polish, salt sweat and leather, the man moved away through the grass.

Joby lay for a moment, staring but unable to see where the man had gone.

He swallowed. He wiped his eyes. He cleared his throat. He settled himself. Then, at last, very slowly and firmly, he turned the drum so that it faced up toward the sky.

He lay next to it, his arm around it, feeling the tremor, the touch, the **muted** thunder as, all the rest of the April night in the year 1862, near the Tennessee River, not far from the Owl Creek, very close to the church named Shiloh, the peach blossoms fell on the drum.

muted
(myōō´tĭd) *adj.* When something is *muted*, it is softened or muffled.

COLLABORATIVE DISCUSSION Do you think the drummer boy regretted his decision to become part of the Army once he begins to realize what war is like? With a partner, discuss your impressions of him and the choice that he made. Cite specific evidence from the text to support your ideas.

Analyze Stories: Historical Fiction

Every story has a **setting,** the time and place in which the action occurs. In historical fiction such as "The Drummer Boy of Shiloh," the setting is usually a key aspect of the work.

Historical fiction refers to stories that are set in the past and include real places and events from the time period. Like other works of historical fiction, Ray Bradbury's story involves characters that may be based on real people, plot developments that reflect real events, and details that are historically accurate. Sometimes, you may not know whether elements of a work of historical fiction are based on something real unless you do some research.

Review "The Drummer Boy of Shiloh" for additional examples of historical details and references to actual events.

Determine Meanings of Words and Phrases

When you get a general sense of anxiety, sadness, giddiness, or some other emotion as you read a story, you are responding to the work's **mood,** the feeling or atmosphere that the writer creates for readers. Various elements work together to contribute to a story's mood.

Elements	How they create mood
Setting, where and when the events take place	The writer's choice of setting and the words he or she uses to describe it can create a mood.
Imagery, language that appeals to the five senses	What we see, hear, or otherwise sense can make us feel frightened, cheerful, or many other things.
Symbol, a person, place, object, or activity that stands for something beyond itself	The emotions evoked by a symbol or what happens to it can affect the overall feeling of a piece. For example, a wounded bird might contribute to a mood of vulnerability.
Allusion, or reference to a famous person, place, event, or work of literature	An allusion to a serious person can help set a somber mood, just as an allusion to a fanciful place can contribute to a whimsical mood.

Notice the author's use of symbols and allusions to create the mood as you analyze "The Drummer Boy of Shiloh."

Analyzing the Text

Cite Text Evidence Support your responses with evidence from the text.

1. **Analyze** In the description of the setting in lines 24–26, what does the special wind suggest about the locations of the two armies? Identify what mood this description helps create.

2. **Cite Evidence** What are the descriptive details that the author provides about the General in lines 77–80 that help make this historical fiction accurate for its time? What is the effect of providing these details?

3. **Interpret** Why does the General refer to the pace of the boy's drumming as "the heart of the army" in lines 141–157?

4. **Analyze** Henry Wadsworth Longfellow was a popular American author who wrote "Paul Revere's Ride" and other works immortalizing early American history. Identify the allusion to him in lines 177–188. What mood does this allusion help create in the last paragraph?

5. **Compare** What is the similarity between the General's talk with the drummer boy and the drummer boy's role in the next day's battle?

6. **Analyze** What do the peach blossoms symbolize in this story? Explain how this symbol contributes to the overall mood.

Speaking and Listening

Working with a partner, act out the scene in which the General discusses the boy's fears and his role in the coming battle. Prepare by discussing the General's motivation for the conversation and how that might affect the way the General speaks.

PERFORMANCE TASK

Speaking Activity: Informative Report Research the Battle of Shiloh, including the legend of the drummer boy. Find out how many people died and how the significance of the battle is viewed today. Discuss whether your reaction to the following parts of the story has changed as a result of your research:

- lines 98–101
- lines 106–124
- lines 151–157
- lines 181–190

Critical Vocabulary

solemn   askew   strew
legitimately   resolute   muted

Practice and Apply Use what you know about the Vocabulary words to answer the following questions.

1. When did you have to act in a **resolute** way to face a challenge?
2. When did you **legitimately** claim that someone owed you something?
3. When did you **strew** things across a room? Why did you do it?
4. When would you need to be **solemn** in a group of people?
5. When has your response to news been **muted**?
6. When has your hat been **askew** on your head?

Vocabulary Strategy: Interpret Figures of Speech

A **figure of speech** is a word or phrase that communicates meanings beyond the literal definition of the words. **Idioms,** or expressions in which the entire phrase means something different from the words in it, are one kind of figure of speech. Consider this idiom from the story.

> "These lads, fresh out of the milkshed, don't know what I know, and I can't tell them."

You can use nearby words and phrases, or **context,** to help you understand that "fresh out of the milkshed" implies that not long ago these lads were farmer hands milking cows. The phrase "don't know what I know" helps you understand that the General is using a figure of speech to express concern that his soldiers lack battle experience.

Practice and Apply Use context to explain the meaning of each underlined figure of speech below.

1. "Yes, thought the boy, that's all very well for them, they can give as good as they get! . . . Me, thought the boy, I only got a drum, two sticks to beat it, and no shield."
2. "There's a hundred thousand men, . . . not one as can spit a sparrow off a tree, or knows a horse clod from a minnieball . . . . should turn tail and train."
3. "He might at any moment strike fire to them to see his way through the coming days when the sun might not show its face."

Language Conventions: Indicative Mood

The **mood of a verb** shows the speaker's attitude toward what is being said. There are several moods for verbs.

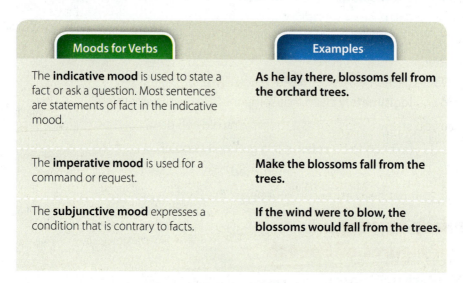

Moods for Verbs	Examples
The **indicative mood** is used to state a fact or ask a question. Most sentences are statements of fact in the indicative mood.	As he lay there, blossoms fell from the orchard trees.
The **imperative mood** is used for a command or request.	Make the blossoms fall from the trees.
The **subjunctive mood** expresses a condition that is contrary to facts.	If the wind were to blow, the blossoms would fall from the trees.

Notice how Ray Bradbury uses the indicative mood for effect. Read these sentences from the story aloud and hear how they use statements of fact to express difficult truths about the uncertainty of battle:

> "The boy turned on his side. A moth brushed his face, but it was peach blossom. A peach blossom flicked him, but it was a moth. Nothing stayed put. Nothing had a name. Nothing was as it once was. . . . the peach blossoms fell on the drum."

Practice and Apply Rewrite each sentence using the indicative mood.

1. I hope we have not lost the document that proves we own this land.
2. Stop crying and do something useful!
3. Try to get some sleep before the sun comes up.
4. If the troops guard the camp, everyone will be safer.
5. Don't charge until I give the order.
6. The cause may be lost if we do not succeed.
7. If the war ended sooner, many lives would have been saved.
8. Prepare for battle so you have a greater chance to survive it.

Background Confederate leaders believed that by abandoning their capitol in Richmond, they would be able to prolong the Civil War. But just a few days after they left Richmond, General Robert E. Lee was forced to surrender to the Union Army. Shortly after, the Civil War ended and President Lincoln was assassinated.

James L. Swanson has written several books about the Civil War and Abraham Lincoln. He has been fascinated with Lincoln's life since his tenth birthday, when he received an engraving of the pistol used to assassinate the president.

from BLOODY TIMES:
The Funeral of Abraham Lincoln and the Manhunt for Jefferson Davis

History Writing by James L. Swanson

SETTING A PURPOSE As you read, pay attention to the details the author provides about Abraham Lincoln and Jefferson Davis. What sorts of leadership qualities did each man possess?

Prologue

In the spring of 1865, the country was divided in two: the Union in the North, led by Abraham Lincoln, fighting to keep the Southern states from **seceding** from the United States. The South, led by its president, Jefferson Davis, believed it had the absolute right to quit the Union in order to preserve its way of life, including the right to own slaves. The bloody Civil War had lasted four years and cost 620,000 lives. In April 1865, the war was about to end.

secede
(sĭ-sēd´) *v.* When you *secede*, you formally withdraw from an organization or association.

Introduction

In April of 1865, as the Civil War drew to a close, two men set out on very different journeys. One, Jefferson Davis, president

Bloody Times 177

of the Confederate States of America,[1] was on the run, desperate to save his family, his country, and his cause. The other, Abraham Lincoln, murdered on April 14, was bound for a different destination: home, the grave, and everlasting glory.

Today everybody knows the name of Abraham Lincoln. But before 1858, when Lincoln ran for the United States Senate (and lost the election), very few people had heard of him. Most people of those days would have recognized the name of Jefferson Davis. Many would have predicted Davis, not Lincoln, would become president of the United States someday.

Born in 1808, Jefferson Davis went to private schools and studied at a university, then moved on to the United States Military Academy at West Point. A fine horseback rider, he looked elegant in the saddle. He served as an officer in the United States army on the western frontier, and then became a planter, or a farmer, in Mississippi and was later elected a United States Congressman and later a senator. As a colonel in the Mexican-American War, he was wounded in battle and came home a hero.

Davis knew many of the powerful leaders of his time, including presidents Zachary Taylor and Franklin Pierce. He was a polished speech maker with a beautiful speaking voice. Put simply, he was well-known, respected, and admired in both the North and the South of the country.

What Davis had accomplished was even more remarkable because he was often ill. He was slowly going blind in one eye, and he periodically suffered from malaria, which gave him fevers, as well as a painful condition called neuralgia. He and his young wife, Sarah Knox Taylor, contracted malaria shortly after they were married. She **succumbed** to the disease. More than once he almost died. But his strength and his will to live kept him going.

Abraham Lincoln's life started out much different from Jefferson Davis's. Born in 1809, he had no wealthy relatives to help give him a start in life. His father was a farmer who could not read or write and who gave Abe an ax at the age of nine and sent him to split logs into rails for fences. His mother died while Lincoln was still a young boy. When his father

succumb
(sə-kŭm´) v. To *succumb* is to give in to an overwhelming force.

---

[1] **Confederate States of America:** the government formed by the 11 southern states that seceded from the United States.

remarried, Abe's stepmother, Sarah, took a special interest in Abe.

By the time Abe Lincoln grew up, he'd had less than a year of school. But he'd managed to learn to read and write, and he wanted a better life for himself than that of a poor farmer. He tried many different kinds of jobs: piloting a riverboat, surveying (taking careful measurement of land to set up boundaries), keeping a store, and working as a postmaster.

He read books to teach himself law so that he could practice as an attorney. Finally in 1846 he was elected to the U.S. Congress. He served an unremarkable term, and at the end of two years, he left Washington and returned to Illinois and his law office. He was hardworking, well-off, and respected by the people who knew him—but not nearly as well-known or as widely admired as Jefferson Davis.

It may seem that two men could not be more different than Abraham Lincoln and Jefferson Davis. But in fact, they had many things in common. Both Davis and Lincoln loved books and reading. Both had children who died young. One of Davis's sons, Samuel, died when he was still a baby, and another, Joseph, died after an accident while Davis was the president of the Confederacy. Lincoln, too, lost one son, Eddie, at a very young age and another, Willie, his favorite, while he was president of the United States.

Both men fell in love young, and both lost the women they loved to illness. When he was twenty-four years old, Davis fell for Sarah Knox Taylor. Called Knox, she was just eighteen and was the daughter of army general and future president Zachary Taylor. It took Davis two years to convince her family to allow her to marry him—but at last he did. Married in June of 1835, just three months later both he and Knox fell ill with malaria, and she died. Davis was devastated. His grief changed him—afterward he was quieter, sterner, a different man.

Eight years later, he found someone else to love. He married Varina Howell, the daughter of a wealthy family. For the rest of his life, Davis would depend on Varina's love, advice, and loyalty. They would eventually have six children; only two would outlive Jefferson Davis.

Lincoln was still a young man when he met and fell in love with Ann Rutledge. Everyone expected them to get married, but before that could happen, Ann became ill and died. Lincoln himself never talked or wrote about Ann after her

Abraham Lincoln, president of the United States of America

death. But those who knew him at the time remembered how crushed and miserable he was to lose her. Some even worried that he might kill himself.

Abraham Lincoln recovered and eventually married Mary Todd. But their marriage was not as happy as that of Jefferson and Varina. Mary was a woman of shifting moods. Jealous, insulting, rude, selfish, careless with money, she was difficult to live with.

By far the greatest difference between Davis and Lincoln was their view on slavery. Davis, a slave owner, firmly believed that white people were superior to blacks, and that slavery was good for black people, who needed and benefited from having masters to rule over them. He also believed that the founding fathers of the United States, the men who had written the Constitution and the Declaration of Independence, a number of whom had owned slaves, had intended slavery to be part of America forever.

Lincoln thought slavery was simply wrong, and he believed that the founders hadn't intended it always to exist in the United States. Lincoln was willing to let slavery remain legal in the states where it was already permitted. But he thought that slavery should not be allowed to spread into the new states entering the Union in the American south and southwest. Every new state to join the country, Lincoln firmly believed, should prohibit slavery.

Lincoln explained his views in several famous debates during his campaign for Senate in 1858. The campaign debates between Lincoln and Stephen Douglas brought Lincoln to national attention for the first time. Though he lost that Senate race, his new visibility enabled Lincoln to win the presidential nomination and election in 1860. To the surprise of many, it was Abraham Lincoln who became the president of the United States by winning less than 40 percent of the popular vote. More people voted for the other three candidates running for president than for Lincoln.

Chapter One

On the morning of Sunday, April 2, 1865, Richmond, Virginia, capital city of the Confederate States of America, did not look like a city at war. The White House of the Confederacy was surprisingly close to—one hundred miles from—the White House in Washington, D.C. But the armies of the North had never been able to capture Richmond. After four years of war, Richmond had not been invaded by Yankees. The people there had thus far been spared many of the horrors of fighting. This morning everything appeared beautiful and serene. The air smelled of spring, and fresh green growth promised a season of new life.

As he usually did on Sundays, President Jefferson Davis walked from his mansion to St. Paul's Episcopal Church. One of the worshippers, a young woman named Constance Cary, recalled the day: "On the Sunday morning of April 2, a perfect Sunday of the Southern spring, a large congregation assembled as usual at St. Paul's." As the service went on, a messenger entered the church. He brought Jefferson Davis a telegram from Robert E. Lee.

The telegram was not addressed to Davis, but to his secretary of war, John C. Breckinridge. Breckinridge had sent it on to Davis. It told devastating news: The Union army was approaching the city gates, and the Army of Northern Virginia, with Lee in command, was powerless to stop them.

> Headquarters, April 2, 1865
>
> General J. C. Breckinridge:
>
> *I see no prospect of doing more than holding our position here till night. I am not certain that I can do that. . . . I advise that all preparation be made for leaving Richmond tonight. I will advise you later, according to circumstances.*
>
> R. E. Lee

On reading the telegram, Davis did not panic, but he turned pale and quietly rose to leave the church. The news quickly spread through Richmond. "As if by a flash of electricity, Richmond knew that on the morrow her streets would be crowded by her captors, her rulers fled… her high hopes crushed to earth," Constance Cary wrote later. "I saw many pale faces, some trembling lips, but in all that day I heard no expression of a weakling fear."

Many people did not believe that Richmond would be captured. General Lee would not allow it to happen, they told themselves. He would protect the city, just as the army had before. In the spring of 1865, Robert E. Lee was the greatest hero in the Confederacy, more popular than Jefferson Davis, who many people blamed for their country's present misfortunes. With Lee to defend them, many people of Richmond refused to believe that before the sun rose the next morning, life as they knew it would come to an end.

Jefferson Davis walked from St. Paul's to his office. He summoned the leaders of his government to meet with him there at once. Davis explained to his cabinet[2] that the fall of Richmond would not mean the death of the Confederate States of America. He would not stay behind to surrender the capital. If Richmond was doomed to fall, then the president and the government would leave the city, travel south, and set up a new capital in Danville, Virginia, 140 miles to the southwest. The war would go on.

Davis told the cabinet to pack their most important records and send them to the railroad station. What they could not take, they must burn. The train would leave tonight, and he expected all of them to be on it. Secretary of War John C. Breckinridge would stay behind in Richmond to make sure

---

[2] **cabinet:** a government leader's advisers.

the evacuation of the government went smoothly, and then follow the train to Danville. Davis ordered the train to take on other cargo, too: the Confederate treasury, consisting of half a million dollars in gold and silver coins.

After spending most of the afternoon working at his office, Davis walked home to pack his few remaining possessions. The house was eerily still. His wife, Varina, and their four children had already evacuated to Charlotte, North Carolina. His private secretary, Burton Harrison, had gone with them to make sure they reached safety.

Varina had begged to stay with her husband in Richmond until the end. Jefferson said no, that for their safety, she and the children must go. He understood that she wanted to help and comfort him, he told her, "but you can do this in but one way, and that is by going yourself and taking our children to a place of safety." What he said next was frightening: "If I live," he promised, "you can come to me when the struggle is ended."

On March 29, the day before Varina and the children left Richmond, Davis gave his wife a revolver and taught her how to use it. He also gave her all the money he had, saving just one five-dollar gold piece for himself. Varina and the children left the White House on Thursday, March 30. "Leaving the house as it was," Varina wrote later, "and taking only our clothing, I made ready with my young sister and my four little children, the eldest only nine years old, to go forth into the unknown." The children did not want to leave their father. "Our little Jeff begged to remain with him," Varina wrote, "and Maggie clung to him . . . for it was evident he thought he was looking his last upon us." The president took his family to the station and put them aboard a train.

While Jefferson Davis spent his last night in the Confederate White House, alone, without his family, he did not know that Abraham Lincoln had left his own White House several days ago and was now traveling in Virginia. Lincoln was visiting the Union Army.[3] The Union president did not want to go home until he had won the war. And he dreamed of seeing Richmond.

---

[3] **Union Army:** the land force of the military that fought for the northern states during the Civil War.

Chapter Two

On March 23 at 1:00 P.M., Lincoln left Washington, bound south on the ship *River Queen*. His wife, Mary, came with him, along with their son Tad. A day later the vessel anchored off City Point, Virginia, headquarters of General Grant and the Armies of the United States.

Lincoln met with his commanders to discuss the war. General William Tecumseh Sherman asked Lincoln about his plans for Jefferson Davis. Many in the North wanted Davis hanged if he was captured. Did Lincoln think so, too? Lincoln answered Sherman by saying that all he wanted was for the Southern armies to be defeated. He wanted the Confederate soldiers sent back to their homes, their farms, and their shops. Lincoln didn't answer Sherman's question about Jefferson Davis directly. But he told a story.

There was a man, Lincoln said, who had sworn never to touch alcohol. He visited a friend who offered him a drink of lemonade. Then the friend suggested that the lemonade would taste better with a little brandy in it. The man replied that if some of the brandy were to get into the lemonade "unbeknown to him," that would be fine.

Sherman believed that Lincoln meant it would be the best thing for the country if Jefferson Davis were simply to leave and never return. As the Union president, Lincoln could hardly say in public that he wanted a man who had rebelled against his government to get away without punishment. But if Davis were to escape "unbeknown to him," as Lincoln seemed to be suggesting, that would be fine.

At City Point Lincoln received reports and sent messages. He haunted the army telegraph office for news of the battles raging in Virginia. He knew that soon Robert E. Lee must make a major decision: Would he sacrifice his army in a final, hopeless battle to defend Richmond, or would he abandon the Confederate capital and save his men to fight another day?

In the afternoon of April 2, Lee telegraphed another warning to Jefferson Davis in Richmond. "I think it absolutely necessary that we should abandon our position tonight," he wrote. Lee had made his choice. His army would retreat. Richmond would be captured.

Davis packed some clothes, retrieved important papers and letters from his private office, and waited at the mansion.

Jefferson Davis, president of the Confederate States of America

Then a messenger brought him word: The officials of his government had assembled at the station. The train that would carry the president and the cabinet of the Confederacy was loaded and ready to depart.

Davis and a few friends left the White House, mounted their horses, and rode to the railroad station. Crowds did not line the streets to cheer their president or to shout best wishes for his journey. The citizens of Richmond were locking up their homes, hiding their valuables, or fleeing the city before the Yankees arrived. Throughout the day and into the night, countless people left however they could—on foot, on horseback, in carriages, in carts, or in wagons. Some rushed to the railroad station, hoping to catch the last train south. Few would escape.

But not all of Richmond's inhabitants dreaded the capital's fall. Among the blacks of Richmond, the mood was happy. At the African church, it was a day of **jubilation**. Worshippers poured into the streets, congratulated one another, and prayed for the coming of the Union army.

When Jefferson Davis got to the station, he hesitated. Perhaps the fortunes of war had turned in the Confederacy's

jubilation
(jōō´bə-lā´shən) *n.*
Jubilation is the act of celebrating.

favor that night. Perhaps Lee had defeated the enemy after all, as he had done so many times before. For an hour Davis held the loaded and waiting train in hopes of receiving good news from Lee. That telegram never came. The Army of Northern Virginia would not save Richmond from its fate.

Dejected, the president boarded the train. He did not have a private luxurious sleeping car built for the leader of a country. Davis took his seat in a common coach packed with the officials of his government. The train gathered steam and crept out of the station at slow speed, no more than ten miles per hour. It was a humble, sobering departure of the president of the Confederate States of America from his capital city.

As the train rolled out of Richmond, most of the passengers were somber. There was nothing left to say. "It was near midnight," Postmaster General John Reagan, on board the train, remembered, "when the President and his cabinet left the heroic city. As our train, frightfully overcrowded, rolled along toward Danville we were **oppressed** with sorrow for those we left behind us and fears for the safety of General Lee and his army."

The presidential train was not the last one to leave Richmond that night. A second one carried another cargo from the city—the treasure of the Confederacy, half a million dollars in gold and silver coins, plus deposits from the Richmond banks. Captain William Parker, an officer in the Confederate States Navy, was put in charge of the treasure and ordered to guard it during the trip to Danville. Men desperate to escape Richmond and who had failed to make it on to Davis's train climbed aboard their last hope, the treasure train. The wild mood at the station alarmed Parker, and he ordered his men—some were only boys—to guard the doors and not allow "another soul to enter."

Once Jefferson Davis was gone, and as the night wore on, Parker witnessed the breakdown of order: "The whiskey…was running in the gutters, and men were getting drunk upon it…. Large numbers of **ruffians** suddenly sprung into existence—I suppose thieves, deserters…who had been hiding." If the mob learned what cargo Parker and his men guarded, then the **looters**, driven mad by greed, would have attacked the train. Parker was prepared to order his men to fire on the crowd.

oppress
(ə-prĕs´) *v.* When you *oppress* someone, you overwhelm or crush them.

ruffian
(rŭf´ē-ən) *n.* A *ruffian* is a thug or a gangster.

looter
(loot´ər) *n.* A *looter* is someone who steals during a war or riot.

Before that became necessary, the treasure train got up steam and followed Jefferson Davis into the night.

To add to the chaos caused by the mobs, soon there would be fire. And it would not be the Union troops who would burn the city. The Confederates accidentally set their own city afire when they burned supplies to keep them from Union hands. The flames spread out of control and reduced much of the capital to ruins.

Union troops outside Richmond would see the fire and hear the explosions. "About 2 o'clock on the morning of April 3d bright fires were seen in the direction of Richmond. Shortly after, while we were looking at these fires, we heard explosions," one witness reported.

On the way to Danville, the president's train stopped at Clover Station. It was three o'clock in the morning. There a young army lieutenant, eighteen years old, saw the train pull in. He spotted Davis through a window, waving to the people gathered at the station. Later he witnessed the treasure train pass, and others, too. "I saw a government on wheels," he said. From one car in the rear a man cried out, to no one in particular, "Richmond's burning. Gone. All gone."

As Jefferson Davis continued his journey to Danville, Richmond burned and Union troops approached. Around dawn a black man who had escaped the city reached Union lines and reported what Lincoln and U. S. Grant, the commanding general of the Armies of the United States, suspected. The Confederate government had abandoned the capital during the night and the road to the city was open. There would be no battle for Richmond. The Union army could march in and occupy the rebel capital without firing a shot.

The first Union troops entered Richmond shortly after sunrise on Monday, April 3. They marched through the streets, arrived downtown, and took control of the government buildings. They tried to put out the fires, which still burned in some sections of the city. Just a few hours since Davis had left it, the White House of the Confederacy was seized by the Union and made into their new headquarters.

Chapter Three

The gloom that filled President Davis's train eased with the morning sun. Some of the officials of the Confederate government began to talk and tell jokes, trying to brighten the mood. Judah Benjamin, the secretary of state, talked about food and told stories. "[H]is hope and good humor [were] inexhaustible," one official recalled. With a playful air, he discussed the fine points of a sandwich, analyzed his daily diet given the food shortages that plagued the South, and as an example of doing much with little, showed off his coat and pants, both made from an old shawl, which had kept him warm through three winters. Colonel Frank Lubbock, a former governor of Texas, entertained his fellow travelers with wild western tales.

But back in Richmond, the people had endured a night of terror. The ruins and the smoke presented a terrible sight. A Confederate army officer wrote about what he saw at a depot, or warehouse, where food supplies were stored. "By daylight, on the 3d," he noted, "a mob of men, women, and children, to the number of several thousands, had gathered at the corner of 14th and Cary streets … for it must be remembered that in 1865 Richmond was a half-starved city, and the Confederate Government had that morning removed its guards and abandoned the removal of the **provisions**. . . . The depot doors

provisions
(prə-vĭzh´ənz) *n.*
Provisions are a stock of necessary supplies, such as food.

Richmond, Virginia shortly after Union forces entered the city on April 3, 1865.

were forced open and a demoniacal struggle for the countless barrels of hams, bacon, whisky, flour, sugar, coffee . . . raged about the buildings among the hungry mob. The gutters ran with whisky, and it was lapped up as it flowed down the streets, while all fought for a share of the plunder."

A Union officer wrote about what he saw as he entered the city in early morning, when it was still burning. "As we neared the city the fires seemed to increase in number and size, and at intervals loud explosions were heard. On entering the square we found Capitol Square covered with people who had fled there to escape the fire and were utterly worn out with fatigue and fright. Details were at once made to scour the city and press into service every able-bodied man, white or black, and make them assist in extinguishing the flames."

Constance Cary ventured outside to see her ruined and fallen city. Horrified, she discovered that Yankees had occupied the Confederate White House. "I looked over at the President's house, and saw the porch crowded with Union soldiers and politicians, the street in front filled with curious gaping negroes." The sight of ex-slaves roving freely about disgusted her. "It is no longer our Richmond," she complained, and added that the Confederate anthem still had the power to raise some people's spirits: "One of the girls tells me she finds great comfort in singing 'Dixie' with her head buried in a feather pillow."

All day on April 3, Washington, D.C., celebrated the fall of Richmond. The *Washington Star* newspaper captured the joyous mood: "As we write Washington city is in such a blaze of excitement and enthusiasm as we never before witnessed here. . . . The thunder of cannon; the ringing of bells; the eruption of flags from every window and housetop, the shouts of enthusiastic gatherings in the streets; all echo the glorious report. RICHMOND IS OURS!!!"

The Union capital celebrated without President Lincoln, who was still with the army. While Washington rejoiced, the secretary of war, Edwin Stanton, worried about Lincoln's safety. He believed that the president was traveling in enemy territory without sufficient protection. Stanton urged Lincoln to return to Washington. But Lincoln didn't take the warning. He telegraphed back:

> *Head Quarters Armies of the United States*
> *City-Point,*
> *April 3. 5 P.M. 1865*
>
> Hon. Sec. of War
> Washington, D.C.
>
> *Yours received. Thanks for your caution; but I have already been to Petersburg, stayed with Gen. Grant an hour & a half and returned here. It is certain now that Richmond is in our hands, and I think I will go there to-morrow. I will take care of myself.*
>
> *A. Lincoln*

President Davis did not arrive in Danville until 4:00 P.M. on the afternoon of April 3. It had taken eighteen hours to travel just 140 miles. The plodding journey from Richmond to Danville made clear an uncomfortable truth. If Jefferson Davis hoped to avoid capture, continue the war, and save the Confederacy, he would have to move a lot faster than this. Still, the trip had served its purpose. It had saved, for at least another day, the Confederate States of America.

On the afternoon and evening of Monday, April 3, the government on wheels unpacked and set up shop in Danville, Virginia. Jefferson Davis hoped to remain there as long as possible. In Danville he could send and receive communications so that he could issue orders and control the movements of his armies. It would be hard for his commanders to telegraph the president or send riders with the latest news if he stayed on the move and they had to chase him from town to town. In Danville he had the bare minimum he needed to continue the war.

The citizens of Danville had received word that their president was coming, and a large number of people waited at the station for his train. They cheered Jefferson Davis when he stepped down from his railroad car. The important people of the town opened their homes to the president and his government. But soon refugees fleeing from Richmond and elsewhere flooded into Danville. There was not enough room for everyone. Many slept in railroad cars and cooked their meals in the open.

But in Danville Davis and his government had little to do except wait for news. The future course of the war in Virginia depended upon Robert E. Lee and what was left of his army. Davis expected news from Lee on April 4, but none came. The president longed for action: He wanted to rally armies, send them to strategic places, and continue fighting. Instead, he had to sit still and wait for word from the Army of Northern Virginia.

"April 4 and the succeeding four days passed," noted Stephen R. Mallory, the secretary of the navy, "without bringing word from Lee or Breckinridge, or of the operations of the army; and the anxiety of the President and his followers was intense." Refugees from Richmond carried wild stories. Some said Lee had won "a glorious victory." Others said Lee was too busy fighting to send messengers. Jefferson Davis ignored the rumors.

On April 4, as Davis waited impatiently for news, Lincoln experienced one of the most thrilling days of his life. "Thank God that I have lived to see this!" he wrote. "It seems to me that I have been dreaming a horrid dream for four years, and now the nightmare is gone. I want to go to Richmond."

Admiral Porter, a Union navy admiral, agreed to take him there, "[i]f there is any of it left. There is black smoke over the city." On the *River Queen* they traveled up the river toward Richmond. When the water became too shallow for big boats, Porter transferred the president and Tad to his personal craft, the "admiral's barge." Despite the fancy name, it was no more than a big rowboat. But it allowed them to continue.

The city looked eerie. Lincoln and Porter peered at the rebel capital but saw no one. They saw smoke from the fires. The only sound was the creaking of the oars. "The street along the river-front was as deserted," Porter observed, "as if this had been a city of the dead." Although the Union army had controlled the city for several hours, "not a soldier was to be seen."

The oarsmen rowed for a wharf, and Lincoln stepped out of the boat. Admiral Porter described what happened next: "There was a small house on this landing, and behind it were some twelve negroes digging with spades. The leader of them was an old man sixty years of age. He raised himself to an upright position as we landed, and put his hands up to his eyes. Then he dropped his spade and sprang forward." The man knelt at Lincoln's feet, praising him, calling him the messiah[4] come to free his children from slavery. "Glory, Hallelujah!" he cried, and kissed the president's feet. The others did the same.

Lincoln was embarrassed. He did not want to enter Richmond like a king. He spoke to the **throng** of former slaves. "Don't kneel to me. That is not right. You must kneel to God only, and thank him for the liberty you will hereafter enjoy."

Before allowing Lincoln to leave them and proceed on foot into Richmond, the freed slaves burst into joyous song:

Oh, all ye people clap your hands,
And with triumphant voices sing;
No force the mighty power withstands
Of God, the universal King.

The hymn drew hundreds of blacks to the landing. They surrounded Lincoln, making it impossible for him to move. Admiral Porter recognized how foolish he had been to bring the president of the United States ashore without enough soldiers to protect him.

The crowd went wild. Some rushed forward, laid their hands upon the president, and collapsed in joy. Some, too awed to approach Father Abraham, kept their distance and, speechless, just stared at him. Others yelled for joy and performed somersaults. Lincoln spoke to them: "My poor friends, you are free—free as air. You can cast off the name of slave and trample upon it. . . . Liberty is your birthright. . . . But you must try to deserve this priceless **boon**. Let the world see that you merit it, and are able to maintain it by your good works. Don't let your joy carry you into excesses. Learn the laws and obey them. . . . There, now, let me pass on; I have but little time to spare. I want to see the capital."

Porter ordered six marines to march ahead of the president and six behind him, and the landing party walked toward downtown Richmond. The streets were dusty, and smoke from the fires still hung in the air. Lincoln could smell Richmond burning. By now thousands of people, blacks and whites, crowded the streets.

throng
(thrông) *n.* A *throng* is a large group of people.

boon
(bo̅o̅n) *n.* A *boon* is a gift or benefit.

---

[4] **messiah:** the savior or liberator.

> **The crowd went wild. Some rushed forward, laid their hands upon the president, and collapsed in joy.**

A beautiful girl, about seventeen years old, carrying a bouquet of roses, stepped into the street and advanced toward the president. Admiral Porter watched her struggle through the crowd. "She had a hard time in reaching him," he remembered. "I reached out and helped her within the circle of the sailors' bayonets, where, although nearly stifled with dust, she gracefully presented her bouquet to the President and made a neat little speech, while he held her hand. . . . There was a card on the bouquet with these simple words: 'From Eva to the Liberator of the slaves.'"

Porter spotted a sole soldier on horseback and called out to him: "Go to the general, and tell him to send a military escort here to guard the President and get him through this crowd!"

"Is that old Abe?" the trooper asked before galloping off.

Lincoln went on to the Confederate White House and entered Jefferson Davis's study. One of the men with him remembered watching Lincoln sit down and say, "This must have been President Davis's chair." Lincoln crossed his legs and "looked far off with a serious, dreamy expression." Lincoln knew the Confederate president had been here, in this room, no more than thirty-six hours ago. This was the closest Abraham Lincoln had ever come to Jefferson Davis.

One observer remembered that Lincoln "lay back in the chair like a tired man whose nerves had carried him beyond his strength." Sitting in the quiet study of the Confederate president, perhaps Lincoln weighed the cost—more than 620,000 American lives[5]—paid to get there. He did not speak. Then he requested a glass of water.

After Lincoln left the Confederate White House, he toured Richmond in a buggy. Blacks flocked to him and rejoiced, just

---

[5] **more than 620,000 American lives:** the number of deaths caused by the Civil War.

as they had done at the river landing. But not all of Richmond welcomed him to the ruined capital. Most whites stayed in their homes behind locked doors and closed shutters, with some glaring at the unwelcome conqueror through their windows.

It was a miracle that no one poked a rifle or a pistol through an open window and opened fire on the despised Yankee president. Lincoln knew the risk. "I walked alone on the street, and anyone could have shot me from a second-story window," he said. His Richmond tour was one of Lincoln's triumphs. It was the most important day of his presidency. It was also one of the most dangerous days of his life. No American president before or since has ever placed himself at that much risk.

Before Lincoln left Richmond, the Union general left in charge of the city asked Lincoln to tell him how he should deal with the conquered rebels. Lincoln's answer became an American legend. He replied that he didn't want to give any orders, but, "If I were in your place I'd let 'em up easy, let 'em up easy."

During his time in Richmond, Lincoln did not order arrests of any rebel leaders who stayed in the city, did not order their property seized, and said nothing of **vengeance** or punishment. Nor did he order a manhunt for Davis and the officials who had left the city less than two days ago. It was a moment of remarkable greatness and generosity. It was Abraham Lincoln at his best.

vengeance
(vĕn´jəns) *n.*
Vengeance is a punishment given in return for a wrong.

COLLABORATIVE DISCUSSION With a partner, discuss how Abraham Lincoln and Jefferson Davis demonstrated leadership qualities in the last days of the war. Cite specific evidence from the text to support your ideas.

Analyze Structure: Comparison and Contrast

The Civil War is a topic that lends itself to the examination of two sides. One way to do that in writing is through the use of **compare and contrast organization,** a pattern of organization in which an author compares two or more subjects by explaining how they are similar and contrasts them by explaining how they are different.

- Two subjects can be compared and contrasted within a single paragraph. In this example from *Bloody Times*, Swanson identifies ways that Abraham Lincoln and Jefferson Davis were alike:

    It may seem that two men could not be more different . . . But in fact, they had many things in common. Both . . . loved books and reading. Both had children who died young.

- A comparison and contrast can be made in two separate paragraphs, with one paragraph covering various aspects of the first subject and the next paragraph covering similar aspects of the second subject.
- A comparison and contrast can be made within larger sections of a piece, such as chapter by chapter.

Look for examples of each type of compare and contrast organization as you analyze *Bloody Times*.

Analyze Connotative Meanings

Word choice, an author's selection of words, can affect a reader's attitude toward a subject. For example, every word has a dictionary definition, or **denotation.** Words also have **connotations**—the feelings or ideas that people associate with that word. Words with a similar denotation can have a positive, neutral, or negative connotation.

Positive	Neutral	Negative
determined, resolute	firm	stubborn, obstinate

Study this sentence. How would your feelings about Lincoln be different if the author had used the word *stubbornly* instead of *firmly*?

Every new state to join the country, Lincoln firmly believed, should prohibit slavery.

Review *Bloody Times* to find another sentence whose meaning would change if a word with a similar denotation but different connotation was used.

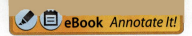

Analyzing the Text

Cite Text Evidence Support your responses with evidence from the text.

1. **Identify Patterns** Review the overall pattern of organization that author James Swanson used in this piece. How is the organizational pattern in the introduction different from each of the chapters?

2. **Interpret** Reread lines 74–82. Swanson writes that Davis was "sterner." How is the connotation of *stern* different from words such as *harsh* and *authoritarian* that have similar denotations?

3. **Compare** What does the author identify as the greatest difference between Davis and Lincoln? How did this difference affect the life course of these two men?

4. **Draw Conclusions** Reread lines 175–183. Describe Jefferson Davis's behavior. What does his conduct reveal about his character?

5. **Evaluate** When an author refers to another literary work without naming it, it is called an **allusion.** Identify several allusions to the Bible in lines 502–546. What do these suggest about the way Lincoln was viewed by the end of the Civil War?

Writing and Research

With a small group, conduct research and write a short report about how Lincoln's views on slavery and emancipation changed over time. Explain his thoughts about emancipation before, during, and after the Civil War, and describe what led to his changing attitudes. Share your findings with the class.

PERFORMANCE TASK

Writing Activity: Informative Essay Create a poster that compares and contrasts Abraham Lincoln and Jefferson Davis.

- First, draw a Venn diagram on your poster. Label each side of the diagram with one man's name and include an image to represent him.

- Next, revisit the text of *Bloody Times* to identify character traits of these two leaders. Write the traits in the appropriate sections of your Venn diagram.

- Finally, use the traits you identified to write a brief character sketch of each man below the corresponding parts of the diagram.

Critical Vocabulary

secede	succumb	jubilation	oppress
ruffian	looter	provisions	throng
boon	vengeance		

Practice and Apply Use your understanding of the Vocabulary words to complete each sentence.

1. A store owner might **succumb** to a **looter** because . . .
2. Some wanted **vengeance** against those who tried to **secede** because . . .
3. It would be scary to see a **throng** of **ruffians** because . . .
4. **Provisions** would be a **boon** to people following a hurricane because . . .
5. There is no **jubilation** when someone tries to **oppress** people because . . .

Vocabulary Strategy: Use Context Clues

Context clues are the words and phrases surrounding a word that provide hints about its meaning. Sometimes, you may find a context clue in the same sentence as the unfamiliar word you are trying to understand. The overall meaning of a sentence can also be a good context clue. Look at this example:

> If the mob learned what cargo Parker and his men guarded, then the looters, driven mad by greed, would have attacked the train.

If you didn't know what *looters* means, the words *greed* and *attacked* are clues. The overall meaning of the sentence is another context clue. Together, these hints can help you guess that looters are "robbers who use violent means during times of chaos." You can confirm your guess by checking a print or a digital dictionary.

Practice and Apply Find each of the following words in the selection and look for clues to the word's meaning. Then, complete a chart like the one shown.

Word	Context Clues	Guessed Definition	Dictionary Definition
fatigue (line 400)			
anthem (line 410)			
despised (line 583)			

Language Conventions: Gerunds

Recall that a **verbal** is a word that is formed from a verb but is used as a noun, an adjective, or an adverb.

A **gerund** is one type of verbal. It is a verb form ending in *-ing* that functions as a noun. In this sentence, the word *fighting* is a gerund:

> **He wanted to rally armies, send them to strategic places, and continue** *fighting.*

Gerunds can perform the same functions as nouns in a sentence.

Subject	**Fighting** changed the soldiers' lives forever.
Direct Object	The soldiers stopped **fighting**.
Object of Preposition	Many believed nothing could prevent the two sides from **fighting**.
Predicate Noun	For many the only solution was **fighting**.

Don't confuse gerunds with other kinds of words that end in *-ing*. A verb can end in *-ing*. A participle that modifies a noun or a pronoun can also end in *-ing*.

Gerund	Verb	Participle
Thinking became a torment for Davis.	The slaves were **thinking** about freedom.	Lincoln was a **thinking** person.

Practice and Apply Write each gerund. Label it *subject, direct object, object of preposition,* or *predicate noun* to explain its function in the sentence.

1. Reading gave Lincoln and Davis access to inspiring ideas.
2. The former slaves were demonstrating their joy by singing.
3. Davis and other promising leaders eventually stopped fleeing.
4. Studying was what allowed Lincoln to become a lawyer.
5. Vengeance meant losing because Lincoln believed it would destroy the healing nation.

Background On April 14, 1865, only five days after the Civil War ended, President Abraham Lincoln was assassinated at the Ford Theater in Washington, D.C., where he was watching a performance. Lincoln was shot by John Wilkes Booth, a famous actor and a Confederate sympathizer. Although Booth initially escaped, he was discovered days later by Union soldiers. Booth was killed while trying to avoid capture.

O Captain! My Captain!

Poem by Walt Whitman

Walt Whitman (1819–1892) *was a great admirer of President Lincoln. After the president was assassinated, Whitman wrote "O Captain! My Captain!" to capture the sense of tragedy that descended upon the country. Largely unknown to the public when he wrote this poem, Whitman eventually gained a reputation as one of the greatest American writers. "O Captain! My Captain!" is among his most famous works, and his book of poems,* Leaves of Grass, *is considered one of the masterpieces of American literature.*

SETTING A PURPOSE As you read, look for evidence of Whitman's feelings about Lincoln. Do others seem to share his feelings? Write down any questions you have as you read.

O Captain! My Captain!

O Captain! my Captain! our fearful trip is done,
The ship has weather'd every rack,[1] the prize we sought[2]
    is won,

The port is near, the bells I hear, the people all exulting,
5   While follow eyes the steady keel,[3] the vessel grim and daring:
        But O heart! heart! heart!
            O the bleeding drops of red,
                Where on the deck my Captain lies,
                    Fallen cold and dead.

10 O Captain! my Captain! rise up and hear the bells;
    Rise up—for you the flag is flung[4]—for you the bugle trills,
    For you bouquets and ribbon'd wreaths—for you the shores
        a-crowding,
    For you they call, the swaying mass, their eager faces turning;
15   Here Captain! dear father!
            This arm beneath your head!
                It is some dream that on the deck,
                    You've fallen cold and dead.

    My Captain does not answer, his lips are pale and still,
20 My father does not feel my arm, he has no pulse nor will,
    The ship is anchor'd safe and sound, its voyage closed
        and done,
    From fearful trip the victor ship comes in with object won;
        Exult O shores, and ring O bells!
            But I with mournful tread,[5]
                Walk the deck my Captain lies,
                    Fallen cold and dead.

COLLABORATIVE DISCUSSION What conflicting thoughts and feelings does this poem express about the end of the Civil War? With a partner, discuss whether you think many Americans shared Walt Whitman's feelings. Cite specific evidence from the text to support your ideas.

---

[1] **rack:** a mass of wind-driven clouds.
[2] **sought** (sôt): searched for; tried to gain.
[3] **keel:** the main part of a ship's structure.
[4] **flung:** suddenly put out.
[5] **tread** (trĕd): footsteps.

Determine Meaning of Words and Phrases

One way poets can help readers understand things in new ways is by using **figurative language,** or imaginative descriptions that are not literally true. A **metaphor** is a type of figurative language in which an author compares two things that are generally different but have some quality or qualities in common. In an **extended metaphor,** this comparison between two things is developed at some length and in different ways.

An extended metaphor in a poem may continue, or extend, through several lines or stanzas or throughout the entire poem. In "O Captain! My Captain!" Whitman uses an extended metaphor to express his feelings about Lincoln and the Civil War. Reread the poem and determine what is being compared.

Analyze Structure

Certain forms of poetry are associated with particular topics. For example, sonnets are often associated with love, and limericks are often associated with humor. "O Captain! My Captain!" is an elegy. An **elegy** is a poem in which the speaker reflects on death. In contrast to other forms of poetry, elegies often pay tribute to someone who has recently died.

Most elegies use formal, dignified language and are serious in **tone,** which is the writer's attitude toward the subject. Elegies may also express
- sorrow and grief
- praise for the person who has died
- comforting thoughts or ideas

In these lines from "O Captain! My Captain!," Whitman expresses his own sorrow.

> **But I with mournful tread,**
> **Walk the deck my Captain lies,**

Review "O Captain! My Captain!" and identify words and phrases that pay tribute to Lincoln's greatness.

Analyzing the Text

Cite Text Evidence   Support your responses with evidence from the text.

1. **Interpret** Reread lines 1–3. In Whitman's metaphor, what is the "fearful trip," the "ship," and the "prize" that was won? What is the "port"? Express your answer in a chart like the one shown.

Element	What It Represents
fearful trip	
ship	
prize	
port	

2. **Interpret** Examine lines 3–13. Describe the grand celebration that Whitman tells about in these lines. Why are the crowds rejoicing?

3. **Evaluate** When there is a contrast between appearance and reality, **irony** results. Why is it ironic that the crowds are celebrating in this poem?

4. **Cite Evidence** How does Whitman express his own grief about Lincoln's death? Cite three specific examples.

5. **Evaluate** Reread lines 20–21. What is the meaning of these lines in terms of Whitman's extended metaphor?

PERFORMANCE TASK

Speaking Activity: Respond by Speaking Work with a small group to present a choral reading of "O Captain! My Captain!"

- Begin by rereading the poem carefully. As a group, decide how each line should be read based on its message. Are the words expressing sorrow? praise? comfort?
- Next, decide who will read each line or part of a line. Should some words be read by one speaker? by two speakers? by your entire group?
- The choices you make about how the lines will be spoken should reflect your analysis of the poem. Be prepared to explain your choices.

COLLECTION 3
PERFORMANCE TASK A

Interactive Lessons
To complete this task, use *Participating in a Collaborative Discussion.*

Participate in a Collaborative Discussion

This collection focuses on slavery and the Civil War. Look back at the excerpt from *Narrative of the Life of Frederick Douglass,* and at the other texts you read. Prepare a response to the literature by making a generalization about the ways in which people respond to the Civil War or to the struggle for freedom. Then make your case in a collaborative discussion, citing evidence from the texts to support the points in your response.

An effective participant in a collaborative discussion

- makes a clear, logical generalization about the ways people respond to slavery or the Civil War in one of the selections
- uses quotations and specific examples to illustrate ideas
- responds politely to the moderator and other panel members
- evaluates other panel members' contributions
- summarizes the discussion by synthesizing ideas

PLAN

Get Organized Work with your classmates to prepare for a panel discussion.

- Join a group of four classmates and select one student to be the moderator for your discussion.
- As a group, choose three texts from the collection for your group to discuss. Each student who is not the moderator will be the expert on one of these texts. Decide which student will focus on each text.
- Create a format for your discussion—a schedule that shows the order in which members of the panel will speak and for how long. It will be the moderator's job to keep the discussion on schedule.
- Set rules regarding the times for the moderator, other group members, or the audience (your classmates) to ask questions.

Interactive Lessons
To help you plan your discussion, complete the following lesson:
- Establishing and Following Procedure

ACADEMIC VOCABULARY

As you share what you learned about your assigned text, be sure to use the academic vocabulary words.

access
civil
demonstrate
document
symbolize

Gather Evidence Analyze your assigned text and gather evidence for the discussion. Note details, examples, and quotations. Ask yourself these questions as you take notes:

- How does the struggle over slavery affect people in the text? How do they respond to it?
- How does a person's character or situation affect their actions?
- What generalization, or broad conclusion, can I make about people's responses to the struggle over slavery?

Use the annotation tools in your eBook to find evidence from the text to support your generalization. Save your evidence to *my*Notebook, in a folder titled *Collection 3 Performance Task*.

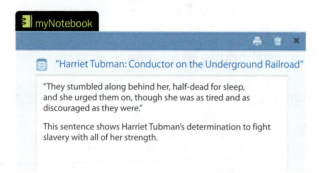

During this time, the moderator should make a list of relevant questions to be asked during the panel discussion.

PRODUCE

Write and Practice Work individually to write an outline of your response to your assigned text. Then practice with your group.

Write your outline in *my*WriteSmart. Focus on getting your ideas down, rather than on perfecting your choice of language.

- State a clear generalization about the ways people in your assigned text respond to the struggle over slavery.
- Write several central ideas that support your generalization.
- Match each piece of evidence with the idea it best supports.
- Present your ideas to your group. The moderator will ask questions about your ideas and examples, preparing you to "think on your feet" during the real discussion.
- If you are the moderator, decide how to introduce and conclude the discussion. Write a statement explaining the topic and format. Write notes for a concluding statement. Be ready to modify your remarks if new ideas emerge.

> **REVISE**

Reinforce Your Ideas Based on the practice session and the rubric on the following page, make changes to your written response to the texts. Consider the following questions:

- Were you able to defend your generalization? If not, revise your response so that it better reflects your textual evidence and your central ideas.
- Were you able to answer the moderator's questions without hesitation? If not, you may need to reorganize your response so that you can find information more quickly and easily.
- Did the moderator's questions help you see your text in a new light? If so, add new evidence to your response that you can share during the real discussion.

Have your partner or a group of peers review your outline in *my*WriteSmart. Ask your reviewers to note any evidence that does not support your generalization about how people respond to the struggle over slavery.

Interactive Lessons
To help you plan your discussion, complete the following lesson:
- Listening and Responding

> **PRESENT**

Have the Discussion Now it's time to present your panel discussion before the rest of the class. Have your outline at hand for reference during the discussion.

- Begin by having the moderator introduce the topic, the panelists, and the basic format for the discussion. The moderator will then ask the first question and continue to facilitate the discussion in the agreed-upon format.
- Use your writing to remind you of your main points, but try to speak directly to the panel and the audience. Don't just read from your paper.
- Listen closely to what all speakers say so that you can respond appropriately.
- Sustain a respectful tone toward your fellow panel members, even when you disagree with their ideas.
- When all the panelists have made their statements and discussed ideas amongst themselves, the moderator should invite panelists and audience members to ask questions.
- Conclude by having the moderator summarize the discussion and thank the panelists for their participation.

Summarize Write a summary of the main points from the discussion. Then explain whether the discussion made you rethink your generalization, and why.

PERFORMANCE TASK A RUBRIC
COLLABORATIVE DISCUSSION

	Ideas and Evidence	Organization	Language
4	• The panelist clearly states a valid generalization and supports it with strong, relevant ideas and well-chosen evidence from the texts. • The panelist carefully evaluates others' evidence and reasoning and responds with insightful comments and questions. • The panelist synthesizes the analysis of the texts to help listeners understand the generalization.	• The panelist's remarks are based on a well-organized outline that clearly identifies the generalization, the supporting ideas, and the evidence. • The panelist concludes with a statement that reinforces the generalization and includes the ideas that have emerged from the discussion.	• The panelist adapts speech to the context of the discussion, using appropriately formal English to discuss the texts and ideas. • The panelist consistently quotes accurately from the texts to support ideas. • The panelist consistently maintains a polite and thoughtful tone throughout the discussion.
3	• The panelist states a generalization and supports it with relevant ideas and evidence from the texts. • The panelist evaluates others' evidence and reasoning and responds with appropriate comments and questions. • The panelist synthesizes some ideas and links to the generalization.	• The panelist's remarks are based on an outline that identifies the generalization, supporting ideas, and evidence. • The panelist concludes with a statement that reinforces the generalization.	• The panelist mostly uses formal English to discuss literature and ideas. • The panelist mostly quotes accurately from the texts to support ideas. • The panelist maintains a polite and thoughtful tone throughout most of the discussion.
2	• The panelist states a reasonably clear generalization and supports it with some ideas and evidence. • The panelist's response to others' comments shows limited evaluation of the evidence and reasoning. • The panelist does not synthesize ideas but simply repeats the generalization in a vague way.	• The panelist's remarks reflect an outline that may identify the generalization but does not organize ideas and evidence very effectively. • The panelist makes a weak concluding statement that does little to reinforce the generalization.	• The panelist uses some formal and some informal English to discuss the texts and ideas. • The panelist's quotations and examples sometimes do not accurately reflect the texts. • The panelist occasionally forgets to maintain a polite tone when responding to others' comments and questions.
1	• The panelist's generalization is unclear; ideas and evidence are not coherent. • The panelist does not evaluate others' evidence and reasoning. • The panelist does not synthesize ideas.	• The panelist does not follow an outline that organizes ideas and evidence. • The panelist's remarks lack any kind of conclusion or summary.	• The panelist uses informal English and/or slang, resulting in a lack of clarity. • The panelist's quotations and examples do not accurately reflect the texts. • The panelist does not maintain a polite tone when responding to others' comments and questions.

COLLECTION 3
PERFORMANCE TASK B

Interactive Lessons
To help you complete this task, use:
- Writing Informative Texts
- Using Textual Evidence

Write a Literary Analysis

Ray Bradbury's "The Drummer Boy of Shiloh" invites readers to experience the night before a Civil War battle through the eyes of a young boy. In this activity, you will conduct research to learn how the historical details of the Battle of Shiloh are relevant to the story. Following a small-group discussion about your fresh insights into the story, you will write a literary analysis in which you offer an interpretation of the story's symbolism.

A successful literary analysis

- cites evidence from the text that strongly supports ideas and analysis
- is organized in a way that is appropriate to purpose and audience
- conveys ideas through the selection, organization, and analysis of relevant content

Visit hmhfyi.com to explore your topic and enhance your research.

PLAN

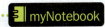

Use the annotation tools in your eBook to find details, descriptions, and events that support your impressions of the story.

Conduct Research
Use both print and digital sources to research the Battle of Shiloh.

- Find out why the battle was fought, and learn about the geography of the area, including the Peach Orchard.
- Identify the significance of the battle and its aftermath.
- Use relevant sources. Find books by using keyword or subject searches in the library. Use a search engine or Internet directories to find credible online sources.

Reread the Story
Develop fresh insights during a second reading of "The Drummer Boy of Shiloh." Look for

- events or descriptions that gain significance as a result of your research
- new or sharper understanding of symbols Ray Bradbury uses in the story

ACADEMIC VOCABULARY

As you share your insights into the symbolism in the story, be sure to use the academic vocabulary words.

access
civil
demonstrate
document
symbolize

Participate in a Group Discussion Join two or three classmates to discuss the story and its symbols. Focus on

- repeated events or images that may be symbols, such as peach blossoms, the drum, or even Joby himself
- how research affected your understanding of symbolism
- symbolism that was not apparent during your first reading

Plan Your Analysis Compile ideas for your literary analysis based on your research, reading, and discussion.

- Decide what your thesis statement, or controlling idea, will be. All of the ideas you discuss should relate or connect to it.
- Use a graphic organizer like the one shown to jot down ideas.

Symbol	Connection to the Battle	Effect in the Story

PRODUCE

Write Your Literary Analysis
Use your research, ideas from your group discussion, and your graphic organizer to draft a literary analysis of the symbolism in "The Drummer Boy of Shiloh."

- Decide on a logical way to organize your ideas. You might discuss symbols in the order they appear, or organize around story events.
- Include a brief summary of the story and of the Battle of Shiloh.
- Include details, quotations, or other examples from the story and your research to support your thesis statement. Use precise language.
- Consider using headers or other formatting to help readers understand how you have organized your ideas.
- Conclude your analysis with a summary of your main points and your own insights into the symbolism in the story.

Write your rough draft in *my*WriteSmart. Concentrate on supporting your main points and connecting ideas rather than on creating perfect sentences.

Interactive Lessons
For help in writing your essay, use
- Writing Informative Texts: Elaboration
- Using Textual Evidence: Summarizing, Paraphrasing, and Quoting

Language Conventions: Add Details

Look for places where you can include **nouns** and **noun phrases** to add details. A noun phrase includes a noun and the words that modify it. Read this passage from "The Drummer Boy of Shiloh."

> " And the voice was about to move on when the boy, startled, touched the drum at his elbow. The man above, hearing this, stopped. "

Note how the phrases "the drum at his elbow" and "the man above" add details, making it easier for the reader to picture.

REVISE

Review Your Draft
Have your partner or group of peers use the following chart to review your draft.

Questions	Tips	Revision Techniques
Is the thesis statement clear?	**Underline** the thesis statement.	**Add** a thesis statement. **Revise** the introduction to make the thesis clear.
Does the essay include background information?	**Highlight** details that provide background information.	**Add** details about the battle to help explain the analysis.
Is the analysis supported by details, quotations, and examples?	**Underline** facts, details, quotations, and examples that support main points.	**Add** examples from the text or research to support the analysis.
Are the ideas organized clearly and logically?	**Highlight** transitional words and phrases that connect ideas.	**Rearrange** sentences to organize ideas. **Add** transitions.
Does the conclusion summarize the main points and provide insight?	**Underline** the summary. **Highlight** sentences that provide insight.	**Add** a summary of the main points. **Insert** sentences that provide insight.

Have your partner or a group of peers review your draft in *my*WriteSmart and note any parts of your analysis that are unclear or that could be moved to improve your organization.

Interactive Lessons

To help you revise your essay, complete the following lessons in Writing Informative Texts:
- Precise Language and Vocabulary
- Formal Style

PRESENT

Create a Finished Copy
Finalize your literary analysis. Then choose a way to share it. Consider sharing your analysis in an oral report, or posting your analysis on a classroom or school website.

PERFORMANCE TASK B RUBRIC
LITERARY ANALYSIS

	Ideas and Evidence	Organization	Language
4	• The thesis statement is clearly presented and makes a strong statement about symbolism in the text. • Specific, relevant details support the key points. • The concluding section summarizes the analysis and offers an insight.	• Key points and supporting details are organized effectively and logically throughout the literary analysis. • Transitions successfully show the relationships between ideas.	• Language is precise and captures the writer's thoughts with originality. • Nouns and noun phrases add rich details. • Grammar, usage, and mechanics are correct.
3	• The thesis statement makes a point about symbols in the text. • Some key points need more support. • The concluding section summarizes most of the analysis but does not offer an insight.	• The organization of key points and supporting details is mostly clear. • A few more transitions are needed to clarify the relationships between ideas.	• Most language is precise. • Some nouns and noun phrases add details. • Some errors in grammar, usage, and mechanics occur.
2	• The thesis statement only hints at a main point. • Details support some key points but often are too general. • The concluding section gives an incomplete summary without insight.	• Most key points are organized logically, but many supporting details are out of place. • More transitions are needed throughout the literary analysis to connect ideas.	• Language is repetitive or too general at times. • Few nouns and noun phrases add details. • Several errors in grammar, usage, and mechanics occur, but the writer's ideas are still clear.
1	• The thesis statement is missing. • Details and evidence are irrelevant or missing. • The literary analysis lacks a concluding section.	• A logical organization is not apparent. • Transitions are not used.	• Language is inaccurate, repetitive, and too general. • No details are added by nouns or noun phrases. • Errors in grammar, usage, and mechanics obscure the meaning of the writer's ideas.

COLLECTION 4

Approaching Adulthood

"When you become a teenager, you step onto a bridge.... The opposite shore is adulthood."

—Gail Carson Levine

COLLECTION 4

Approaching Adulthood

In this collection, you will explore the passage from childhood to adulthood.

COLLECTION
PERFORMANCE TASK Preview

At the end of this collection, you will complete two performance tasks:

- You will write an essay to analyze how the theme of a story set in the past is relevant to the life of modern-day adolescents.

- You will create a campaign to recognize a certain life event—such as voting, getting a driver's license, or living independently—as the start of adulthood.

ACADEMIC VOCABULARY

Study the words and their definitions in the chart below. You will use these words as you discuss and write about the texts in this collection.

Word	Definition	Related Forms
debate (dĭ-bāt´) v.	to engage in arguments by discussing opposing points	debatable
deduce (dĭ-dōōs´) v.	to reach a conclusion or decision through reasoning	deduction, deductive, deducible
license (lī´səns) n.	a document that is issued as proof of legal permission to do something	licensed
sufficient (sə-fĭsh´ənt) adj.	being enough, or as much as needed	sufficiently
trend (trĕnd) n.	the general direction of something; a current style	trendy

Background *During the Great Depression of the 1930s, millions of Americans experienced poverty due to widespread unemployment. African Americans were particularly affected by the weak economy. In an age of racial segregation and prejudice, they generally had fewer job opportunities.*

Eugenia Collier (b. 1928) *was raised in Baltimore, Maryland. After working for the Department of Public Welfare, she became a college professor and began writing. "Marigolds" won the Gwendolyn Brooks Award for Fiction in 1969.*

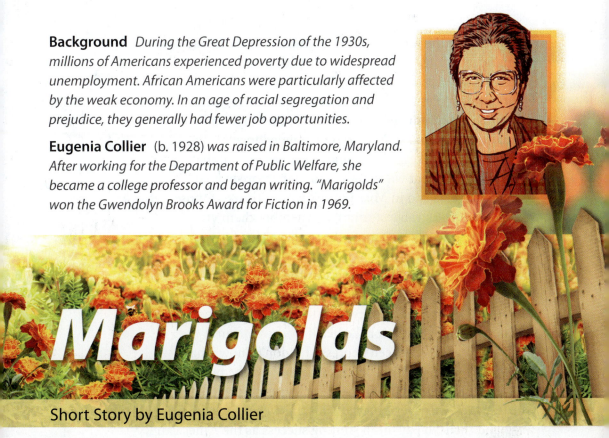

Marigolds

Short Story by Eugenia Collier

SETTING A PURPOSE As you read, notice the story details that suggest how the Great Depression influenced the life of the narrator and her family. Write down any questions you have when reading.

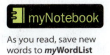

As you read, save new words to *my*WordList

When I think of the home town of my youth, all that I seem to remember is dust—the brown, crumbly dust of late summer—arid, sterile dust that gets into the eyes and makes them water, gets into the throat and between the toes of bare brown feet. I don't know why I should remember only the dust. Surely there must have been lush green lawns and paved streets under leafy shade trees somewhere in town; but memory is an abstract painting—it does not present things as they are, but rather as they *feel*. And so, when I think of that time and that place, I remember only the dry September of the dirt roads and grassless yards of the shanty-town where I lived. And one other thing I remember, another incongruity of memory—a brilliant splash of sunny yellow against the dust—Miss Lottie's marigolds.

Whenever the memory of those marigolds flashes across my mind, a strange nostalgia[1] comes with it and remains long after the picture has faded. I feel again the chaotic emotions of adolescence, illusive as smoke, yet as real as the potted geranium before me now. Joy and rage and wild animal gladness and shame become tangled together in the multicolored skein of 14-going-on-15 as I recall that devastating moment when I was suddenly more woman than child, years ago in Miss Lottie's yard. I think of those marigolds at the strangest times; I remember them vividly now as I desperately pass away the time waiting for you, who will not come.

I suppose that futile[2] waiting was the sorrowful background music of our impoverished little community when I was young. The Depression that gripped the nation was no new thing to us, for the black workers of rural Maryland had always been depressed. I don't know what it was that we were waiting for; certainly not for the prosperity that was "just around the corner," for those were white folks' words, which we never believed. Nor did we wait for hard work and thrift to pay off in shining success as the American Dream[3] promised, for we knew better than that, too. Perhaps we waited for a miracle, amorphous in concept but necessary if one were to have the grit to rise before dawn each day and labor in the white man's vineyard until after dark, or to wander about in the September dust, offering one's sweat in return for some meager share of bread. But God was chary[4] with miracles in those days, and so we waited—and waited.

We children, of course, were only vaguely aware of the extent of our poverty. Having no radios, few newspapers, and no magazines, we were somewhat unaware of the world outside our community. Nowadays we would be called "culturally deprived" and people would write books and hold conferences about us. In those days everybody we knew was just as hungry and ill-clad as we were. Poverty was the cage in which we all were trapped, and our hatred of it was still the

---

[1] **nostalgia** (nŏ-stăl´jə): bittersweet longing for things from the past.
[2] **futile** (fyōōt´l): having no useful result.
[3] **American dream:** the belief that through hard work one will achieve a comfortable and prosperous life.
[4] **chary** (châr´ē): sparing or stingy.

vague, undirected restlessness of the zoo-bred flamingo who knows that nature created him to fly free.

As I think of those days I feel most **poignantly** the tag-end of summer, the bright dry times when we began to have a sense of shortening days and the imminence of the cold.

By the time I was 14 my brother Joey and I were the only children left at our house, the older ones having left home for early marriage or the lure of the city, and the two babies having been sent to relatives who might care for them better than we. Joey was three years younger than I, and a boy, and therefore vastly inferior. Each morning our mother and father trudged wearily down the dirt road and around the bend, she to her domestic job, he to his daily unsuccessful quest for work. After our few chores around the tumbledown shanty, Joey and I were free to run wild in the sun with other children similarly situated.

For the most part, those days are ill-defined in my memory, running together and combining like a fresh watercolor painting left out in the rain. I remember squatting in the road drawing a picture in the dust, a picture that Joey gleefully erased with one sweep of his dirty foot. I remember fishing for minnows in a muddy creek and watching sadly as they eluded my cupped hands, while Joey laughed uproariously. And I remember, that year, a strange restlessness of body and of spirit, a feeling that something old and familiar was ending, and something unknown and therefore terrifying was beginning.

One day returns to me with special clarity for some reason, perhaps because it was the beginning of the experience that in some inexplicable way marked the end of innocence. I was loafing under the great oak tree in our yard, deep in some reverie which I have now forgotten except that it involved some secret, secret thoughts of one of the Harris boys across the yard. Joey and a bunch of kids were bored now with the old tire suspended from an oak limb which had kept them entertained for a while.

"Hey, Lizabeth," Joey yelled. He never talked when he could yell. "Hey, Lizabeth, let's us go somewhere."

I came reluctantly from my private world. "Where you want to go? What you want to do?"

The truth was that we were becoming tired of the formlessness of our summer days. The idleness whose

poignant
(poin´yənt) *adj.*
If something is *poignant*, it is profoundly moving or touching.

prospect had seemed so beautiful during the busy days of spring now had degenerated to an almost desperate effort to fill up the empty midday hours.

"Let's go see can we find some locusts on the hill," someone suggested.

Joey was scornful. "Ain't no more locusts there. Y'all got 'em all while they was still green."

The argument that followed was brief and not really worth the effort. Hunting locust trees wasn't fun any more by now.

"Tell you what," said Joey finally, his eyes sparkling. "Let's go over to Miss Lottie's."

The idea caught on at once, for annoying Miss Lottie was always fun. I was still child enough to scamper along with the group over rickety fences and through bushes that tore our already raggedy clothes, back to where Miss Lottie lived. I think now that we must have made a tragicomic spectacle, five or six kids of different ages, each of us clad in only one garment—the girls in faded dresses that were too long or too short, the boys in patchy pants, their sweaty brown chests gleaming in the hot sun. A little cloud of dust followed our thin legs and bare feet as we tramped over the barren land.

When Miss Lottie's house came into view we stopped, **ostensibly** to plan our strategy, but actually to reinforce our courage. Miss Lottie's house was the most ramshackle of all our ramshackle homes. The sun and rain had long since faded its rickety frame siding from white to a sullen gray. The boards themselves seemed to remain upright not from being nailed together but rather from leaning together like a house that a child might have constructed from cards. A brisk wind might have blown it down, and the fact that it was still standing implied a kind of enchantment that was stronger than the elements. There it stood, and as far as I know is standing yet—a gray rotting thing with no porch, no shutters, no steps, set on a cramped lot with no grass, not even any weeds—a monument to decay.

In front of the house in a squeaky rocking chair sat Miss Lottie's son, John Burke, completing the impression of decay. John Burke was what was known as "queer-headed." Black and ageless, he sat, rocking day in and day out in a mindless stupor, lulled by the monotonous squeak-squawk of the chair. A battered hat atop his shaggy head shaded him from the sun. Usually John Burke was totally unaware of everything

ostensible
(ŏ-stĕn′sə-bəl) *adj.*
If something is *ostensible*, it is apparent or supposed.

outside his quiet dream world. But if you disturbed him, if you intruded upon his fantasies, he would become enraged, strike out at you, and curse at you in some strange enchanted language which only he could understand. We children made a game of thinking of ways to disturb John Burke and then to elude his violent **retribution**.

But our real fun and our real fear lay in Miss Lottie herself. Miss Lottie seemed to be at least a hundred years old. Her big

retribution
(rĕt′rə-byōō′shən) *n.*
Retribution is something given in repayment, usually as a punishment.

frame still held traces of the tall, powerful woman she must have been in youth, although it was now bent and drawn. Her smooth skin was a dark reddish-brown, and her face had Indian-like features and the stern **stoicism** that one associates with Indian faces. Miss Lottie didn't like intruders either, especially children. She never left her yard, and nobody ever visited her. We never knew how she managed those necessities that depend on human interaction—how she ate, for example, or even whether she ate. When we were tiny children, we thought Miss Lottie was a witch and we made up tales, that we half believed ourselves, about her exploits. We were far too sophisticated now, of course, to believe the witch-nonsense. But old fears have a way of clinging like cobwebs, and so when we sighted the tumble-down shack, we had to stop to reinforce our nerves.

"Look, there she is," I whispered, forgetting that Miss Lottie could not possibly have heard me from that distance. "She's fooling with them crazy flowers."

"Yeh, look at 'er."

Miss Lottie's marigolds were perhaps the strangest part of the picture. Certainly they did not fit in with the crumbling decay of the rest of her yard. Beyond the dusty brown yard, in front of the sorry gray house, rose suddenly and shockingly a dazzling strip of bright blossoms, clumped together in enormous mounds, warm and passionate and sun-golden. The old black witch-woman worked on them all summer, every summer, down on her creaky knees, weeding and cultivating and arranging, while the house crumbled and John Burke rocked. For some **perverse** reason, we children hated those marigolds. They interfered with the perfect ugliness of the place; they were too beautiful; they said too much that we could not understand; they did not make sense. There was something in the vigor with which the old woman destroyed the weeds that intimidated us. It should have been a comical sight—the old woman with the man's hat on her cropped white head, leaning over the bright mounds, her big backside in the air—but it wasn't comical, it was something we could not name. We had to annoy her by whizzing a pebble into her flowers or by yelling a dirty word, then dancing away from her rage, reveling in our youth and mocking her age. Actually, I think it was the flowers we wanted to destroy, but nobody had

stoicism
(stō´ĭ-sĭz´əm) *n.*
Stoicism is indifference to pleasure or pain, or a lack of visible emotion.

perverse
(pər-vûrs´) *adj.* If something is *perverse*, it is stubbornly contrary, wrong, or harmful.

the nerve to try it, not even Joey, who was usually fool enough to try anything.

"Y'all git some stones," commanded Joey now, and was met with instant giggling obedience as everyone except me began to gather pebbles from the dusty ground. "Come on, Lizabeth."

I just stood there peering through the bushes, torn between wanting to join the fun and feeling that it was all a bit silly.

"You scared, Lizabeth?"

I cursed and spat on the ground—my favorite gesture of phony **bravado**. "Y'all children get the stones; I'll show you how to use 'em."

I said before that we children were not consciously aware of how thick were the bars of our cage. I wonder now, though, whether we were not more aware of it than I thought. Perhaps we had some dim notion of what we were, and how little chance we had of being anything else. Otherwise, why would we have been so preoccupied with destruction? Anyway, the pebbles were collected quickly, and everybody looked at me to begin the fun.

"Come on, y'all."

We crept to the edge of the bushes that bordered the narrow road in front of Miss Lottie's place. She was working placidly, kneeling over the flowers, her dark hand plunged into the golden mound. Suddenly "zing"—an expertly aimed stone cut the head off one of the blossoms.

"Who out there?" Miss Lottie's backside came down and her head came up as her sharp eyes searched the bushes. "You better git!"

We had crouched down out of sight in the bushes, where we stifled the giggles that insisted on coming. Miss Lottie gazed warily across the road for a moment, then cautiously returned to her weeding. "Zing"—Joey sent a pebble into the blooms, and another marigold was beheaded.

Miss Lottie was enraged now. She began struggling to her feet, leaning on a rickety cane and shouting, "Y'all git! Go on home!" Then the rest of the kids let loose with their pebbles, storming the flowers and laughing wildly and senselessly at Miss Lottie's **impotent** rage. She shook her stick at us and started shakily toward the road crying, "Git 'long! John Burke! John Burke, come help!"

bravado
(brə-vä′dō) *n.* *Bravado* is a false show of bravery.

impotent
(ĭm′pə-tənt) *adj.* If someone is *impotent*, he or she is lacking strength or vigor.

Then I lost my head entirely, mad with the power of inciting such rage, and ran out of the bushes in the storm of pebbles, straight toward Miss Lottie chanting madly, "Old witch, fell in a ditch, picked up a penny and thought she was rich!" The children screamed with delight, dropped their pebbles and joined the crazy dance, swarming around Miss Lottie like bees and chanting, "Old lady witch!" while she screamed curses at us. The madness lasted only a moment, for John Burke, startled at last, lurched out of his chair, and we dashed for the bushes just as Miss Lottie's cane went whizzing at my head.

I did not join the merriment when the kids gathered again under the oak in our bare yard. Suddenly I was ashamed, and I did not like being ashamed. The child in me sulked and said it was all in fun, but the woman in me flinched at the thought of the malicious attack that I had led. The mood lasted all afternoon. When we ate the beans and rice that was supper that night, I did not notice my father's silence, for he was always silent these days, nor did I notice my mother's absence, for she always worked until well into evening. Joey and I had a particularly bitter argument after supper; his **exuberance** got on my nerves. Finally I stretched out upon the palette in the room we shared and fell into a fitful doze.

exuberance
(ĭg-zo͞o′bər-əns) *n.*
Exuberance is a condition of unrestrained joy.

> " *The child in me sulked and said it was all in fun...* "

When I awoke, somewhere in the middle of the night, my mother had returned, and I vaguely listened to the conversation that was audible through the thin walls that separated our rooms. At first I heard no words, only voices. My mother's voice was like a cool, dark room in summer—peaceful, soothing, quiet. I loved to listen to it; it made things seem all right somehow. But my father's voice cut through hers, shattering the peace.

"Twenty-two years, Maybelle, twenty-two years," he was saying, "and I got nothing for you, nothing, nothing."

"It's all right, honey, you'll get something. Everybody's out of work now, you know that."

"It ain't right. Ain't no man ought to eat his woman's food year in and year out, and see his children running wild. Ain't nothing right about that."

"Honey, you took good care of us when you had it. Ain't nobody got nothing nowadays."

"I ain't talking about nobody else, I'm talking about me. God knows I try." My mother said something I could not hear, and my father cried out louder, "What must a man do, tell me that?"

"Look, we ain't starving. I git paid every week, and Mrs. Ellis is real nice about giving me things. She gonna let me have Mr. Ellis' old coat for you this winter—"

"Damn Mr. Ellis' coat! And damn his money! You think I want white folks' leavings? Damn, Maybelle"—and suddenly he sobbed, loudly and painfully, and cried helplessly and hopelessly in the dark night. I had never heard a man cry before. I did not know men ever cried. I covered my ears with my hands but could not cut off the sound of my father's harsh, painful, despairing sobs. My father was a strong man who would whisk a child upon his shoulders and go singing through the house. My father whittled toys for us and laughed so loud that the great oak seemed to laugh with him, and taught us how to fish and hunt rabbits. How could it be that my father was crying? But the sobs went on, unstifled, finally quieting until I could hear my mother's voice, deep and rich, humming softly as she used to hum to a frightened child.

The world had lost its boundary lines. My mother, who was small and soft, was now the strength of the family; my father, who was the rock on which the family had been built, was sobbing like the tiniest child. Everything was suddenly out of tune, like a broken accordion. Where did I fit into this crazy picture? I do not now remember my thoughts, only a feeling of great bewilderment and fear.

Long after the sobbing and the humming had stopped, I lay on the palette, still as stone with my hands over my ears, wishing that I too could cry and be comforted. The night was silent now except for the sound of the crickets and of Joey's soft breathing. But the room was too crowded with fear to allow me to sleep, and finally, feeling the terrible aloneness of 4 A.M., I decided to awaken Joey.

"Ouch! What's the matter with you? What you want?" he demanded disagreeably when I had pinched and slapped him awake.

"Come on, wake up."

"What for? Go 'way."

I was lost for a reasonable reply. I could not say, "I'm scared, and I don't want to be alone," so I merely said, "I'm going out. If you want to come, come on."

The promise of adventure awoke him. "Going out now? Where to, Lizabeth? What you going to do?"

I was pulling my dress over my head. Until now I had not thought of going out. "Just come on," I replied tersely.

I was out the window and halfway down the road before Joey caught up with me.

"Wait, Lizabeth, where you going?"

I was running as if the Furies[5] were after me, as perhaps they were—running silently and furiously until I came to where I had half-known I was headed: to Miss Lottie's yard.

The half-dawn light was more eerie than complete darkness, and in it the old house was like the ruin that my world had become—foul and crumbling, a grotesque caricature.[6] It looked haunted, but I was not afraid because I was haunted too.

"Lizabeth, you lost your mind?" panted Joey.

I had indeed lost my mind, for all the smoldering emotions of that summer swelled in me and burst—the great need for my mother who was never there, the hopelessness of our poverty and **degradation**, the bewilderment of being neither child nor woman and yet both at once, the fear unleashed by my father's tears. And these feelings combined in one great impulse toward destruction.

"Lizabeth!"

I leaped furiously into the mounds of marigolds and pulled madly, trampling and pulling and destroying the perfect yellow blooms. The fresh smell of early morning and of dew-soaked marigolds spurred me on as I went tearing and mangling and sobbing while Joey tugged my dress or my waist crying, "Lizabeth stop, please stop!"

degradation
(dĕg´rə-dā´shən) *n.* *Degradation* is the condition of being brought to a lower level or humiliated.

---

[5] **Furies:** In Greek and Roman mythology, the Furies were three goddesses of vengeance, or revenge.

[6] **a grotesque caricature** (grō-tĕsk´ kăr´ĭ-kə-choŏr´): a bizarre and absurdly exaggerated representation of something.

And then I was sitting in the ruined little garden among the uprooted and ruined flowers, crying and crying, and it was too late to undo what I had done. Joey was sitting beside me, silent and frightened, not knowing what to say. Then, "Lizabeth, look."

I opened my swollen eyes and saw in front of me a pair of large calloused feet; my gaze lifted to the swollen legs, the age-distorted body clad in a tight cotton night dress, and then the shadowed Indian face surrounded by stubby white hair. And there was no rage in the face now, now that the garden was destroyed and there was nothing any longer to be protected.

"M-miss Lottie!" I scrambled to my feet and just stood there and stared at her, and that was the moment when childhood faded and womanhood began. That violent, crazy act was the last act of childhood. For as I gazed at the immobile face with the sad, weary eyes, I gazed upon a kind of reality that is hidden to childhood. The witch was no longer a witch but only a broken old woman who had dared to create beauty in the midst of ugliness and sterility. She had been born in **squalor** and lived in it all her life. Now at the end of that life she had nothing except a falling-down hut, a wrecked body, and John Burke, the mindless son of her passion. Whatever verve there was left in her, whatever was of love and

squalor
(skwŏl´ər) *n. Squalor* is a filthy, shabby, and wretched condition, as from poverty.

beauty and joy that had not been squeezed out by life, had been there in the marigolds she had so tenderly cared for.

Of course I could not express the things that I knew about Miss Lottie as I stood there awkward and ashamed. The years have put words to the things I knew in that moment, and as I look back upon it, I know that that moment marked the end of innocence. People think of the loss of innocence as meaning the loss of virginity, but this is far from true. Innocence involves an unseeing acceptance of things at face value, an ignorance of the area below the surface. In that humiliating moment I looked beyond myself and into the depths of another person. This was the beginning of compassion, and one cannot have both compassion and innocence.

The years have taken me worlds away from that time and that place, from the dust and squalor of our lives and from the bright thing that I destroyed in a blind childish striking out at God-knows-what. Miss Lottie died long ago and many years have passed since I last saw her hut, completely barren at last, for despite my wild contrition she never planted marigolds again. Yet, there are times when the image of those passionate yellow mounds returns with a painful poignancy. For one does not have to be ignorant and poor to find that one's life is barren as the dusty yards of one's town. And I too have planted marigolds.

COLLABORATIVE DISCUSSION With a partner, discuss which aspects of Lizbeth's life contributed to her reaction to Miss Lottie's flowers.

Analyze Stories: Characters' Motivation

To fully understand a story, you need to think about the characters' **motivations,** or the reasons for their actions. Sometimes a narrator will state a character's motivations directly. For example, notice what the narrator of "Marigolds" says about why the children go to Miss Lottie's.

> . . . we were becoming tired of the formlessness of our summer days. The idleness . . . had degenerated to an almost desperate effort to fill up the . . . hours.
>
> "Tell you what," said Joey finally, his eyes sparkling. "Let's go over to Miss Lottie's."
>
> The idea caught on at once, for annoying Miss Lottie was always fun.

Other times, you will need to **infer,** or guess, a character's motivations. To do this, think about the character's personality, notice his or her reactions, and consider the situation. Then ask yourself what you might want to achieve if you were in his or her place.

Determine Theme

A **theme** is a message about life or human nature that a writer shares with the reader. Writers rarely state a story's theme directly. More often, readers deduce, or figure out, the writer's message by looking at clues, such as the symbols in a story. A **symbol** is a person, place, or thing that stands for something beyond itself. Other clues to a story's theme can be found in the following chart.

Clues to Theme	Questions to Ask
Plot and conflict	How are the conflicts resolved?
Characters	What lesson does the main character learn?
Setting	How does the setting affect the characters? What might the setting represent to readers?
Symbols	What might the symbol mean to the main character? What might it represent to the readers? What happens to the symbol?
Title	What idea or symbol does the title highlight?

Review "Marigolds" to identify clues to the story's theme.

Analyzing the Text

Cite Text Evidence Support your responses with evidence from the text.

1. **Infer** In lines 8–9, Collier writes that an abstract painting "does not present things as they are, but rather as they *feel*." What can you infer about the narrator's childhood experiences based on her description of her home town?

2. **Synthesize** What part do the "chaotic emotions of adolescence" (lines 17–18) play in motivating Lizabeth to taunt Miss Lottie?

3. **Infer** Reread lines 162–185. What might explain the children's reactions to the marigolds?

4. **Analyze** Review lines 257–293. How does the conversation between Lizabeth's parents motivate Lizabeth's later actions?

5. **Compare** How does the narrator's understanding of Miss Lottie at the end of the story compare to her feelings about the woman at the beginning of the story?

6. **Draw Conclusions** What is the story's theme? Note at least three clues that help you recognize the message the author is sharing.

7. **Analyze** What do the marigolds symbolize in this story? Explain how they contribute to the development of the story's theme.

8. **Draw Conclusions** What conclusions can you draw about the narrator's present life from the last paragraph in the story? Drawing on your understanding of the story's symbolism, paraphrase the last line.

PERFORMANCE TASK

Writing Activity: Literary Analysis Write a short essay in which you analyze how Lizabeth changes over the course of "Marigolds." Be sure to support your ideas with sufficient evidence from the text. Consider the following questions before you write.

- How aware is Lizabeth of her own surroundings and the wider world?
- What does Lizabeth's reflection at the end of the story suggest about her feelings toward the move into adulthood?

Critical Vocabulary

poignant	ostensible	retribution	stoicism
perverse	bravado	impotent	exuberance
degradation	squalor		

Practice and Apply Use your understanding of the Vocabulary words to answer each question.

1. Is it **perverse** to seek **retribution** for stolen property? Why?
2. Why might homeowners who feel **impotent** show **bravado** at an approaching wildfire?
3. Is suppressing a cry of pain showing **exuberance** or **stoicism**? Why?
4. Why might someone tell a **poignant** story about living in **squalor**?
5. What might be the **ostensible** reason for telling about **degradation**?

Vocabulary Strategy: Use Latin Suffixes

Suffixes—word parts added to the end of a root or base word—often provide clues about the meaning of a word. For example, knowing that the Latin suffix *-ation* usually means "state, condition, or quality of" helps you to understand the word *degradation* in the phrase below from "Marigolds":

> "... the hopelessness of our poverty and degradation ..."

When you break the longer word *degradation* into its parts (*degrad + ation*), it is easier to read and understand the word. The base word *degrade*, which means "to lower in dignity" combines with the suffix *-ation* to mean "the state of being lowered in dignity."

Practice and Apply Identify the *-ation* word or words in each of the following sentences. Use the base or root word and the suffix meaning to define the word. Check a dictionary to confirm your definition.

1. Lizbeth overheard her parents' heated conversation.
2. The combination of poverty and discrimination hurt Lizabeth's family.
3. The feeling of exhilaration from the release of rage and tension didn't last.
4. The desire to succeed filled Lizabeth with the determination to work hard.
5. Receiving the writing medal was affirmation of her hard work.

Language Conventions: Infinitives

Along with participles and gerunds, another kind of **verbal**—or verb form that is used as another part of speech—is the infinitive. An **infinitive** is a verb form that usually begins with *to* and functions as a noun, an adjective, or an adverb. An infinitive phrase consists of an infinitive plus its modifiers and complements.

In this example from "Marigolds," the author uses an infinitive phrase as an adverb modifying the adjective *sophisticated*:

> We were far too <u>sophisticated</u> now, of course, <u>to believe the witch-nonsense</u>.

Because *to*, the sign of the infinitive, precedes infinitives, it is usually easy to recognize them. However, sometimes *to* may be omitted, as in this example:

> Let no one dare [to] come into my garden.

Look at these examples of the uses of infinitives and infinitive phrases:

Uses of Infinitives	Examples
As a noun	<u>To taunt</u> is cruel. (subject)
	She wanted <u>to destroy the flowers</u>. (direct object)
	She wanted nothing except <u>to escape her room</u>. (object of preposition)
As an adjective	Now is the time <u>to grow up</u>. (modifies a noun)
	She was someone <u>to ridicule</u>. (modifies a pronoun)
As an adverb	<u>To escape</u>, jump out the window. (modifies a verb)
	The children were armed and ready <u>to do mischief</u>. (modifies an adjective)
	It was enough mischief <u>to do for one night</u>. (modifies an adverb)

Practice and Apply Identify the infinitive phrase in each sentence and tell whether it is being used as a noun, an adjective, or an adverb. Be careful not to confuse an infinitive with a prepositional phrase beginning with *to*.

1. To hurl stones at flowers is silly.
2. Lizabeth and Joey were free to run wild with the other children.
3. The road to Miss Lottie's was one to be avoided.
4. She loved to listen to her mother's soothing voice.
5. The children had too much time to do mischief.

HANGING FIRE
Poem by Audre Lorde

TEENAGERS
Poem by Pat Mora

Audre Lorde (1934–1992) *was born in New York City and found early success in writing poetry. Lorde used poetry as a means of expression and a way to communicate. She became a published author when a popular magazine published one of her poems while she was still in high school. In addition to poetry, Lorde also wrote acclaimed essays and novels. She won many important awards for her writing and worked to support several social causes close to her heart. Toward the end of her life, Lorde took the African name Gamba Adisa, which is believed to mean "she who makes her meaning clear."*

Pat Mora (b. 1942) *was born in El Paso, Texas. She comes from a Mexican American family and considers herself fortunate to be bilingual and have the ability to write in both Spanish and English. She has written several books of poetry, as well as children's books and essays. Mora takes pride in being a Hispanic writer. She says that she will continue to write and to struggle to say what no other writer can say in quite the same way she can. Family, Mexican American culture, and the desert are all important themes in Mora's work.*

SETTING A PURPOSE Both of these poems focus on communication during adolescence. As you read, think about the subject and how it is presented from two different points of view. How is the message in each poem communicated to readers?

Hanging Fire
Poem by Audre Lorde

I am fourteen
and my skin has betrayed me
the boy I cannot live without
still sucks his thumb
in secret
how come my knees are
always so ashy
what if I die
before morning
and momma's in the bedroom
with the door closed.

I have to learn how to dance
in time for the next party
my room is too small for me
suppose I die before graduation
they will sing sad melodies
but finally
tell the truth about me
There is nothing I want to do
and too much
that has to be done
and momma's in the bedroom
with the door closed.

Nobody even stops to think
about my side of it
I should have been on Math Team
my marks were better than his
why do I have to be
the one
wearing braces
I have nothing to wear tomorrow
will I live long enough
to grow up
and momma's in the bedroom
with the door closed.

Teenagers
Poem by Pat Mora

One day they disappear
into their rooms.
Doors and lips shut,
and we become strangers
5   in our own home.

I pace the hall, hear whispers,
a code I knew but can't remember,
mouthed by mouths I taught to speak.

Years later the door opens.
10 I see faces I once held,
open as sunflowers in my hands. I see
familiar skin now stretched on long bodies
that move past me
glowing
15 almost like pearls.

COLLABORATIVE DISCUSSION Both speakers address the idea of a lack of communication between parents and children. With a partner, discuss what might be the cause of this lack of communication. Cite specific evidence from the texts to support your ideas.

Make Inferences

Both "Hanging Fire" and "Teenagers" are poems about adolescence, but they offer starkly different points of view—in part because the speakers in the poems are quite different. In poetry, the **speaker** is the voice that "talks" to the reader and shares his or her point of view, similar to the narrator in a story. A poem's speaker may or may not be the poet.

Often readers must make an **inference,** or logical guess based on text clues and their own knowledge and experience, in order to identify a poem's speaker. For example, in "Teenagers," text clues help readers figure out that the speaker is an adult, probably a parent or guardian, commenting on the behavior of a child becoming a teen.

Text Clues	What You Know from Experience	Inference about the Speaker
"One day they disappear into their rooms. . . . and we become strangers."	Teens often spend time in their rooms. The adults in their lives don't understand them.	a parent or guardian who feels out of touch with a teenaged child

As you continue to analyze the two poems, think about what text-based inferences you can make about each speaker and his or her point of view.

Determine Theme

Readers also may need to make inferences about themes in a poem. A **theme** is a message about life or human nature that a writer shares with readers. A theme usually is developed over the course of a poem, rather than stated directly at the beginning or end. Sometimes the lesson a speaker or character learns is a sufficient clue to help readers determine theme. Other elements within the text should be considered as well.

- the poem's title
- important statements the speaker makes
- images and details that stand out
- repeated words and phrases

Pay attention to text details as you dig deeper into the poems. Use text clues to determine the themes in each poem and to analyze how those themes are developed through word choice, imagery, and the speaker.

Analyzing the Text

Cite Text Evidence   Support your responses with evidence from the texts.

1. **Infer**   Figurative language in which human qualities are given to an object, idea, or animal is called **personification.** What does the example of personification in the first stanza of "Hanging Fire" reveal about the speaker?

2. **Infer**   Reread lines 1–7 of "Hanging Fire." Based on these lines, what inferences can you make about the speaker of the poem?

3. **Analyze**   Reread lines 19–21 of "Hanging Fire." What does the contradiction or inconsistency expressed in these lines suggest about the speaker?

4. **Analyze**   Several themes are touched on in "Hanging Fire." Identify and explain one or two of these themes, using text evidence as support.

5. **Interpret**   A **simile** is a figure of speech that compares two unlike things using the word *like* or *as*. Identify a simile Mora uses in "Teenagers" that suggests what the speaker's grown children are like.

6. **Compare**   The speaker in each poem has a specific point of view, or position about the subject matter of the poem. Tell one way the points of view are similar and one way they are different.

Speaking and Listening

Work with a partner to prepare a dramatic reading of one of the poems. Begin by discussing the impact of the poet's word choices. Practice reading each line of your chosen poem in a way that conveys what you think it means. Then share your dramatic reading with the class.

PERFORMANCE TASK

Speaking Activity: Response to Literature   Compare and contrast the two poems.

- In a small group, work together to create Venn diagrams that show the similarities and differences between the poems' speakers, themes, and points of view.

- Then each group member should deliver a short speech in which she or he reflects on the advice the speaker in each poem might give to the other. Include text evidence from the poems to support your thoughts.

Language Conventions: Words Ending in *y*

The plurals of most nouns are formed by adding *-s* to the singular, as in *teenager/teenagers*. However, different rules may apply to nouns ending in *y*. Regular verbs follow similar spelling rules in order to agree with their subjects in number and to form verb parts.

Note these examples from the poems of correctly spelled words ending in *y*:

"I am fourteen / and my skin has <u>betrayed</u> me"
(past participle of the verb *betray*)

"I see / familiar skin now stretched on long <u>bodies</u>"
(plural form of the noun *body*)

Keep the following rules in mind for words ending in *y*:

Word Types	Rule	Example
words ending in *y* preceded by a vowel	Add *-s* to form the plural noun or to make a verb agree with a singular subject. Add *-ed* to form the past or past participle of a verb.	play/plays play/played
most words ending in *y* preceded by a consonant	Change the *y* to *i* and add *-es* to form the plural noun or to make a verb agree with a singular subject. Change the *y* to *i* before adding *-ed* to form the past or past participle.	cry/cries cry/cried

Practice and Apply   Rewrite these sentences, correcting any incorrectly spelled words.

1. Teenagers' emotions can swing from lofty peaks to deep vallies in a single day.

2. Children that once plaied board games with parents now disappeared into their rooms after dinner.

3. My sister is a drama queen. She flys into a panic if she isn't able to call her friends.

4. During my older brother's teen years, his moods varied quite a bit.

5. Work hard at your studys in high school if you want to be successful.

Background *"Room for Debate" is a weekly feature of the* New York Times *newspaper. Each week, the* Times *poses a question to a group of knowledgeable outside contributors about a news event or other timely issue. The contributors each bring different perspectives to the question and often offer conflicting opinions. Readers are invited to comment on the topic as well.*

When Do Kids Become Adults?

Arguments from "Room for Debate" in the *New York Times*

What the Brain Says about Maturity by Laurence Steinberg

Leave the Voting Age Alone by Jenny Diamond Cheng

Better Training for New Drivers by Jamie Lincoln Kitman

A Parent's Role in the Path to Adulthood by Barbara Hofer

Mandatory Service to Become an Adult by Michael Thompson

SETTING A PURPOSE As you read, pay attention to the points each writer makes about when and how children mature into adults. Why do you think it is so hard to define when this happens?

Is it time to rethink the age of adulthood? Do the age requirements for certain rights need to be lowered or raised? Shouldn't they at least be consistent?

What the Brain Says about Maturity
By Laurence Steinberg

Neuroscientists[1] now know that brain maturation continues far later into development than had been believed previously. Significant changes in brain anatomy and activity are still taking place during young adulthood, especially in prefrontal regions that are important for planning ahead, anticipating the future consequences of one's decisions, controlling impulses, and comparing risk and reward. Indeed, some brain regions and systems do not reach full maturity until the early or mid-20s. Should this new knowledge prompt us to rethink where we draw legal boundaries between minors and adults?

Maybe, but it's not as straightforward as it seems, for at least two reasons. First, different brain regions and systems mature along different timetables. There is no single age at which the adolescent brain becomes an adult brain. Systems responsible for logical reasoning mature by the time people are 16, but those involved in self-regulation are still developing in young adulthood. This is why 16-year-olds are just as competent as adults when it comes to granting informed medical consent, but still immature in ways that diminish their criminal responsibility, as the Supreme Court has noted in several recent cases. Using different ages for different legal boundaries seems odd, but it would make neuroscientific sense if we did it rationally.

Second, science has never had much of an influence on these sorts of decisions. If it did, we wouldn't have ended up with a society that permits teenagers to drive before they can see R-rated movies on their own, or go to war before they can buy beer. Surely the maturity required to operate a car or face combat exceeds that required to handle sexy movies or drinking. Age boundaries are drawn for mainly political reasons, not scientific ones. It's unlikely that brain science will have much of an impact on these thresholds, no matter what the science says.

---

[1] **neuroscientists:** people who study the brain and nervous system.

Leave the Voting Age Alone
By Jenny Diamond Cheng

The 26th Amendment, ratified in 1971, establishes 18 as the minimum voting age for both state and federal elections. Like all lines that divide legal childhood from adulthood, the voting age is essentially **arbitrary**. Indeed, in modern America 18-year-old voting has become **unmoored** from one of its more important original justifications, which was matching the minimum age for draft eligibility (itself also an arbitrary line). Despite this, raising or lowering the voting age, as some groups have suggested, seems a waste of time at best.

The American colonies mostly set their voting ages at 21, reflecting British common law.[2] This requirement went largely unchallenged until World War II, when several members of Congress proposed amending the Constitution to lower the age to 18. Between 1942 and 1970 federal legislators introduced hundreds of such proposals, but the issue lacked momentum until the late 1960s, when a **confluence** of factors—including the escalating war in Vietnam[3]—pushed 18-year-old voting closer to the surface of the national political agenda. The 26th Amendment itself was the culmination of some creative political maneuvering by Congressional advocates, with a crucial assist from the Supreme Court in Oregon v. Mitchell.[4]

As a historical matter, the significance of the soldier-voter link has been somewhat overstated. The amendment's passage was propelled by a small group of federal legislators whose motivations and rationales were considerably more complex than commonly thought. Still, the Vietnam-era slogan, "Old enough to fight, old enough to vote," was unquestionably a powerful claim, encompassing deeply embedded ideas about civic virtue, adulthood and fairness.

Tying voting to soldiering was always problematic, though, and it is even more so today. The contemporary U.S. military is an all-volunteer force and only a small fraction of Americans ever serve. Selective Service registration applies only to males and the possibility of an actual draft is remote.

arbitrary
(är´bĭ-trĕr´ē) *adj.*
If something is *arbitrary*, it is determined by chance or whim.

unmoor
(ŭn-mo͝or´) *v.* If you *unmoor* something, you release it from a place.

confluence
(kŏn´flo͞o-əns) *n.*
A *confluence* is a gathering or joining together in one place.

---

[2] **British common law:** the laws of England.
[3] **Vietnam:** a country in Southeast Asia where the United States fought a war in the 1960s and 1970s.
[4] **Supreme Court in Oregon v. Mitchell:** In this case, the Supreme Court decided that the U.S. Congress could set qualification rules for national elections.

Yet there is no life moment to which the voting age might be more obviously tethered, and any bright-line rule will inevitably seem unfair to some.

Interest in improving young adults' political participation would be better focused on attacking barriers like residency requirements that exclude college students and voter ID laws that disfavor young and mobile voters, sometimes **egregiously**. Tennessee's new law, for example, specifically disallows students, but not university employees, from using state university ID cards at the polls. More broadly, young Americans suffer from the same challenges to meaningful representation and governance that plague our democracy at all levels. The voting age is the least of their problems.

egregious
(ĭ-grē´jəs) *adj.*
If something is *egregious*, it is very bad or offensive.

Better Training for New Drivers
By Jamie Lincoln Kitman

Bright and early on the day I turned 17 you would have found me at the front of the line at the local New Jersey D.M.V. office, applying for a permit to drive. In due course, I got my full license and it wasn't long before I got my first ticket for speeding. And soon after that I got another for failing to observe a stop sign. After which failure, I'd turned without signaling and then traveled 40 mph in a 25 mph zone, a points cluster-bomb that resulted in the suspension of my license until I enrolled in a driver-training course. Which, I might add, like the driving instruction I'd received in school, was virtually useless.

Americans (with an assist from the automobile and oil industries) tend to treat driving like a right, rather than the privilege it most assuredly is. And now that I'm grown and I like to think a more responsible driver, two factors leave me convinced that the driving age shouldn't be lowered, indeed the right to drive should be doled out gradually to teens as it has been in New York since 2010.

The first problem is the utter **inadequacy** of our driver training. American states would do well to follow the example of European countries where licensing procedures require considerably more training and proven skill before new drivers are let loose on public roads. The second decider for me is the discovery by scientists that poor decision-making, the hallmark of many teenagers' existence, has its roots in biology.

So graduated licenses like we have in New York—where young drivers cannot drive past nightfall or with more than one unrelated person under the age of 21 in their car—make good sense.

Is it the case that many teenagers can and will drive responsibly, regardless the hour, number of young passengers or brain chemistry? Yes. Is there any inconsistency in the fact that a teen may work but not drive at night? Sure.

But, as every parent worth his or her salt[5] has reminded their child at least a hundred times, Sometimes, life isn't fair.

> **inadequate**
> (ĭn-ăd´ĭ-kwĭt) *adj.*
> If something is *inadequate*, it is insufficient or not enough.

---

[5] **worth his or her salt:** good at his or her job.

A Parent's Role in the Path to Adulthood
By Barbara Hofer

The transition to adulthood can be either clear or **diffuse**, depending on whether a culture chooses to offer all the privileges and responsibilities at one distinct age or spread them across time. In some countries, the ability to vote, drink, enter into legal contracts and serve in the military all occur at once. In the United States, these rights are not only spread out, but often without clear rationale. Serving in the military before one is considered responsible enough to purchase alcohol is one of the glaring inconsistencies. Some cultures also mark the transition formally, as in Japan, where "Coming of Age Day" (Seijin Shiki) is a national holiday to celebrate all who reached adulthood in the current year.

Becoming an adult is also a subjective experience, of course, and there is little doubt from recent research that individuals are taking longer to recognize themselves as adults. The age of first marriage and birth of a first child, often perceived by individuals as adult markers, are now occurring later than at any time in history in the U.S. (and greater numbers of individuals are also choosing to forge lives without either of these traditional markers). With increased numbers of individuals attending college and with the tremendous rise in the cost of education and the loans necessary for many, young people are also remaining dependent on parents financially far longer, often leaving them less likely to perceive themselves as adults.

Another psychological aspect of being an adult is feeling **autonomous**, and individuals whose autonomy is supported—at any age—are more personally motivated. As a college professor who studies adolescents and emerging adults, I am particularly concerned that college students are not getting the opportunities they need to grow into autonomous, healthily connected adults when parents are still hyper-involved in their lives. "Emerging adults"—whom Jeffrey Arnett[6] defines as individuals between 18 and 25—need opportunities to make their own choices, whether that's about their major, what courses to take, their social lives or summer plans, and

diffuse
(dĭ-fyōōs´) *adj.* If something is *diffuse*, it is very spread out or scattered.

autonomous
(ô-tŏn´ə-məs) *adj.* If someone is *autonomous*, the person is independent and not controlled by outside forces.

---

[6] **Jeffrey Arnett:** a doctor who studies emerging adulthood.

they need practice in making mistakes and recovering, and in owning the outcomes of their choices. They don't arrive in college fully formed as adults, but we hope they will use these years to make significant progress toward adult behavior, with all the support and safety nets that college can offer.

Yet my research with Abigail Sullivan Moore, reported in our book, shows that many college students are in frequent contact with their parents—nearly twice daily, on average—and that frequency of contact is related to lower autonomy. Parents who are using technology (calls, Skype, texting, e-mail, Facebook, etc.) to micromanage lives from afar may be **thwarting** the timely passage to adulthood. Not surprisingly, these college students are also not likely to see themselves as adults, nor fully prepared to take the responsibilities of their actions, nor even getting the benefits of college that they and their parents are paying for. One in five students in our study report parents are editing and proofing their papers, for example. College parents can help with the transition by serving as a sounding board rather than being directive, by steering their college-age kids to campus resources for help, by considering long-range goals rather than short-term ones and by giving their "kids" space to grow up.

thwart
(thwôrt) *v.* If you *thwart* something, you stop it from happening.

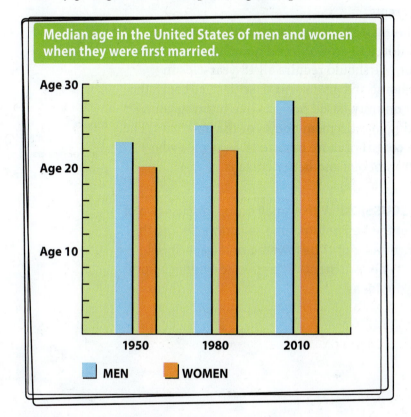

Median age in the United States of men and women when they were first married.

Mandatory Service to Become an Adult

By Michael Thompson

Children are so variable in their growth and the ways in which cultures understand child development are so different, it is futile to attempt to pin down the "right" age of majority. The Dutch, for example, allow children to drink at the age of 16 but not to drive until they are 19. Even if I thought it was a good idea to lower the drinking age and raise the driving age—and I do—I recognize that the U.S. would never embrace it.

I am more concerned with the issue of maturity than I am with the technical age of majority. Researchers and observers have noted that while our children are getting brighter (I.Q. scores have been going up for the last two decades), they are relatively immature for their ages in comparison to earlier generations. Over-protected by their parents and spending vast amounts of time in front of TV, computers and cellphones (over 50 hours a week by middle adolescence, according to the Kaiser Family Foundation), they are less skilled in the world, less able to build friendships and function in groups, and more reliant on their parents.

Instead of fiddling with the age of majority, we should encourage our children to grow up, and mandatory service would do just that. We should require all 18-year-olds in America to leave home and give a year to society, either in the military or in community-based projects like tutoring younger children or working in retirement homes or the inner city. The result would be a **cohort** of more mature 19-year-olds who would make better workers and better citizens.

cohort
(kō′hôrt′) *n.* A *cohort* is a group or band of people.

COLLABORATIVE DISCUSSION With a small group, discuss two of the questions posed at the beginning of the selection: Should the age requirements for certain rights be lowered or raised? Should these age requirements be consistent? Cite specific evidence from the texts to support your ideas.

Trace and Evaluate an Argument

Each writer who responded to the question "When Do Kids Become Adults?" presents an **argument,** or a claim supported with reasons and evidence. A **claim** is the writer's position on an issue or problem. There is usually one main claim in a text, but sometimes a writer may make multiple claims in a single piece of writing. **Evidence** is any information that helps prove a claim. Facts, quotations, examples, anecdotes, and statistics can all be used as evidence.

Look at this example of a claim made by Jamie Lincoln Kitman in "Better Training for New Drivers." The claim states the author's opinion:

> . . . the driving age shouldn't be lowered, indeed the right to drive should be doled out gradually to teens as it has been in New York since 2010.

To **trace,** or follow, the reasoning in an argument, you should
- Identify the claims that the author states directly or indirectly.
- Locate evidence that supports the claims.
- Identify **counterarguments,** statements that address opposing viewpoints. A good argument anticipates opposing views and provides counterarguments to disprove them.

Once you trace an author's argument, it's important to **evaluate** it by examining the support and deciding if it is valid and convincing.
- Consider whether the evidence is accurate and sufficient.
- Evaluate the evidence to determine if it is relevant. Evidence is **relevant** if it supports the claim in a logical way. It is **irrelevant** if it isn't based on sound reasoning or isn't clearly connected to the claim.
- Consider whether opposing viewpoints have been addressed.
- Identify persuasive techniques, such as exaggeration or appeals to a reader's emotions, that might distort a reader's views.

Here, Kitman presents personal experiences as relevant evidence to support his claim:

> . . . I got my full license and it wasn't long before I got my first ticket for speeding. And soon after that I got another for failing to observe a stop sign.

As you review each writer's argument in "When Do Kids Become Adults?" identify the main claim and prepare to evaluate it.

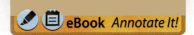 eBook *Annotate It!*

Analyzing the Text

Cite Text Evidence Support your responses with evidence from the text.

1. **Evaluate** In "What the Brain Says about Maturity," what is the main reason the author gives to support his claim?

2. **Analyze** In "Leave the Voting Age Alone," what counterargument does the author make to respond to people who want to lower the voting age in order to increase teenagers' participation in the political process?

3. **Evaluate** Evaluate the argument made in "Better Training for New Drivers." Does the author provide sufficient relevant evidence to support his claim? Explain why or why not.

4. **Cite Evidence** The author of "A Parent's Role in the Path to Adulthood" says people are "taking longer to recognize themselves as adults." What trends does she note to support this claim?

5. **Analyze** According to "A Parent's Role in the Path to Adulthood," how could parents promote autonomy in college-age students, and how do they limit autonomy? Record your answer in a chart.

Ways Parents Promote Autonomy	Ways Parents Thwart Autonomy

6. **Synthesize** The title of this selection asks, "When Do Kids Become Adults?" Based on what you have read, how would you answer this question?

PERFORMANCE TASK

Speaking Activity: Debate When are kids ready to assume adult responsibilities? Working with a group, choose one issue presented in the selection and have a debate.

- Assign one position on the issue to one half of your group, and assign the other position to the other half.
- Research the issue. Find answers to any questions you have.
- Decide on a claim. Prepare to support your claim with evidence from the selections as well as from your own research. Consider displaying your evidence in visuals, such as charts or graphs.
- When you debate, be sure to address counterarguments.
- As you listen to other groups, carefully evaluate each speaker's reasoning and evidence.

Critical Vocabulary

arbitrary   unmoor   confluence   egregious   inadequate
diffuse   autonomous   thwart   cohort

Practice and Apply Use your understanding of the Vocabulary words to answer each question.

1. What have you done that made you feel **autonomous**?
2. Have you ever disagreed with a decision that seemed **arbitrary**? Explain.
3. When did a **confluence** of events cause a change in your life?
4. When has something happened to **thwart** your progress? Explain.
5. When have you seen someone treated in an **egregious** way?
6. What trends in your school appear to be **diffuse**?
7. When have you felt **inadequate** to complete an assignment?
8. What is something you accomplished as part of a **cohort**?
9. When is a good time to **unmoor** from your family or classmates? Explain.

Vocabulary Strategy: Greek Roots

A word **root** is a word part that forms the basis of a word's meaning. A root is combined with other word parts, such as a prefix or a suffix, to make a word. Many English words have a root that comes from Greek. Look at this sentence from "When Do Kids Become Adults?":

> . . . Young Americans suffer from the same challenges . . . that plague our <u>democracy</u> at all levels.

The word *democracy* includes the Greek root *dem*, which means "people." The meaning of the root *dem* is a clue that can help you figure out that *democracy* means "a government by the people."

Practice and Apply Find the word in each sentence that includes the Greek root *dem*. Use the meaning of the root to help you write a definition of the word. Then check each definition you write against the dictionary definition.

1. In some areas, dropping out of school has reached epidemic levels.
2. Researchers feared the pandemic would spread rapidly among teenagers.
3. Certain cars are most popular with a younger demographic.
4. The demagogue convinced many that the voting age should be raised.
5. Is spending vast amounts of time texting endemic among adolescents?

Language Conventions: Shifts in Voice and Mood

Verbs have different voices and moods. The **voice of a verb** tells whether its subject performs or receives the action. A verb is in the **active voice** when the subject performs the action of the verb. A verb is in the **passive voice** when the subject receives the action of the verb.

Active Voice   Neuroscientists **study** the brain.

Passive Voice   The brain **is studied** by neuroscientists.

To change a verb from active to passive voice, use a form of the verb *be* with the past participle of the verb.

Active Voice   Politicians **write** laws about age.

Passive Voice   Laws **are written** about age.

The **mood of a verb** expresses a writer's judgment or attitude about a statement. The **indicative mood** is used when making a statement. The **imperative mood** is used in a request or a command.

Indicative Mood   Her teenage daughter **drives** responsibly.

Imperative Mood   Always **drive** responsibly!

A shift, or change, in verb voice or mood can make meaning unclear. It is usually correct to make the voice and mood in a sentence consistent.

Shift	Correct
From active to passive: They took driver training but very little was learned.	They took driver training but learned very little.
From imperative to indicative: Enroll in a good class, and it is helpful to learn traffic safety rules.	Enroll in a good class, and learn traffic safety rules.

Practice and Apply Write each item correctly by fixing the inappropriate shift in verb voice or mood.

1. When Liam turned 18, a voter registration form was filled out by him.
2. Classes were chosen by Lil after her mom made some suggestions.
3. Watch less TV and you should be tutoring young children instead.
4. Niki volunteers at a retirement home. Learn many valuable skills.

COMPARE TEXTS

Background *Although driver's licenses were required by some states by the early 1900s, age restrictions on drivers did not begin until later. These restrictions were motivated by the need to protect the public from young drivers, who were increasingly viewed as a problem on the highways. Some states selected 16 as the age at which people could drive, while others chose 18. Eventually, 16 became the recommended legal age for drivers. Although there are a few exceptions today, most states now allow teenagers to get a driver's license at the age of 16.*

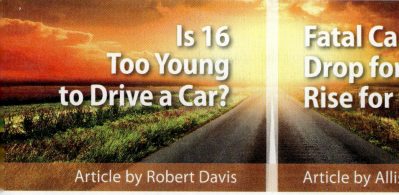

Is 16 Too Young to Drive a Car?
Article by Robert Davis

Fatal Car Crashes Drop for 16-Year-Olds, Rise for Older Teens
Article by Allison Aubrey

SETTING A PURPOSE As you read, think about the points each writer makes regarding the age requirements for drivers. Look for evidence that supports each point.

Raise the driving age. That radical idea is gaining momentum in the fight to save the lives of teenage drivers—the most dangerous on the USA's roads—and their passengers.

Brain and auto safety experts fear that 16-year-olds, the youngest drivers licensed in most states, are too immature to handle today's cars and roadway risks.

New findings from brain researchers at the National Institutes of Health explain for the first time why efforts to protect the youngest drivers usually fail. The weak link: what's called "the executive branch" of the teen brain—the part that weighs risks, makes judgments and controls impulsive behavior.

Scientists at the NIH campus in Bethesda, Md., have found that this vital area develops through the teenage years and isn't fully mature until age 25. One 16-year-old's brain might be more developed than another 18-year-old's, just as a younger teen might be taller than an older one. But evidence is mounting that a 16-year-old's brain is generally far less developed than those of teens just a little older.

The research seems to help explain why 16-year-old drivers crash at far higher rates than older teens. The studies have convinced a growing number of safety experts that 16-year-olds are too young to drive safely without supervision.

"Privately, a lot of people in safety think it's a good idea to raise the driving age," says Barbara Harsha, executive director of the Governors Highway Safety Association. "It's a topic that is emerging."

Americans increasingly favor raising the driving age, a USA TODAY/CNN/Gallup Poll[1] has found. Nearly two-thirds—61%—say they think a 16-year-old is too young to have a driver's license. Only 37% of those polled thought it was OK to license 16-year-olds, compared with 50% who thought so in 1995.

A slight majority, 53%, think teens should be at least 18 to get a license.

The poll of 1,002 adults, conducted Dec. 17–19, 2004, has an error margin of +/–3 percentage points.

Many states have begun to raise the age by imposing restrictions on 16-year-old drivers. Examples: limiting the number of passengers they can carry or barring late-night driving. But the idea of flatly forbidding 16-year-olds to drive without parental supervision—as New Jersey does—has run into resistance from many lawmakers and parents around the country.

Irving Slosberg, a Florida state representative who lost his 14-year-old daughter in a 1995 crash, says that when he proposed a law to raise the driving age, other lawmakers "laughed at me."

Bill Van Tassel, AAA's[2] national manager of driving training programs, hears both sides of the argument. "We have parents who are pretty much tired of chauffeuring their

---

[1] **Gallup Poll:** a survey done by the Gallup company to measure people's opinions.
[2] **AAA:** the American Automobile Association, an organization that provides benefits and information to drivers.

kids around, and they want their children to be able to drive," he says. "Driving is a very emotional issue."

But safety experts fear inaction could lead to more young lives lost. Some sound a note of urgency about changing course. The reason: A record number of American teenagers will soon be behind the wheel as the peak of the "baby boomlet" hits driving age.

Already, on average, two people die every day across the USA in vehicles driven by 16-year-old drivers. One in five 16-year-olds will have a reportable car crash within the first year.

In 2003, there were 937 drivers age 16 who were involved in fatal crashes. In those wrecks, 411 of the 16-year-old drivers died and 352 of their passengers were killed. Sixteen-year-old drivers are involved in fatal crashes at a rate nearly five times the rate of drivers 20 or older.

Gayle Bell, whose 16-year-old daughter, Jessie, rolled her small car into a Missouri ditch and died in July 2003, says she used to happily be Jessie's "ride." She would give anything for the chance to drive Jessie again.

"We were always together, but not as much after she got her license," Bell says. "If I could bring her back, I'd lasso the moon."

Most states have focused their fixes on giving teens more driving experience before granting them unrestricted licenses. But the new brain research suggests that a separate factor is just as crucial: maturity. A new 17- or 18-year-old driver is considered safer than a new 16-year-old driver.

Even some teens are acknowledging that 16-year-olds are generally not ready to face the life-threatening risks that drivers can encounter behind the wheel.

"Raising the driving age from 16 to 17 would benefit society as a whole," says Liza Darwin, 17, of Nashville. Though many parents would be inconvenienced and teens would be frustrated, she says, "It makes sense to raise the driving age to save more lives."

Focus on lawmakers

But those in a position to raise the driving age—legislators in states throughout the USA—have mostly refused to do so.

Adrienne Mandel, a Maryland state legislator, has tried since 1997 to pass tougher teen driving laws. Even lawmakers who recognize that a higher driving age could save lives, Mandel notes, resist the **notion** of having to drive their 16-year-olds to after-school activities that the teens could drive to themselves.

"Other delegates said, 'What are you doing? You're going to make me drive my kid to the movies on Friday night for another six months?'" Mandel says. "Parents are talking about inconvenience, and I'm talking about saving lives."

Yet the USA TODAY poll found that among the general public, majorities in both suburbs (65%) and urban areas (60%) favor licensing ages above 16.

While a smaller percentage in rural areas (54%) favor raising the driving age, experts say it's striking that majority support exists even there, considering that teens on farms often start driving very young to help with workloads.

For those who oppose raising the minimum age, their argument is often this: Responsible teen drivers shouldn't be punished for the mistakes of the small fraction who cause deadly crashes.

The debate stirs images of reckless teens drag-racing or driving drunk. But such flagrant misdeeds account for only a small portion of the fatal actions of 16-year-old drivers. Only about 10% of the 16-year-old drivers killed in 2003 had blood-alcohol concentrations of 0.10 or higher, compared with 43% of 20- to 49-year-old drivers killed, according to the Insurance Institute for Highway Safety.

Instead, most fatal crashes with 16-year-old drivers (77%) involved driver errors, especially the kind most common among **novices**. Examples: speeding, overcorrecting after veering off the road, and losing control when facing a roadway obstacle that a more mature driver would be more likely to handle safely. That's the highest percentage of error for any age group.

For years, researchers suspected that inexperience—the **bane** of any new driver—was mostly to blame for deadly crashes involving teens. When trouble arose, the theory went, the young driver simply made the wrong move. But in recent years, safety researchers have noticed a pattern emerge—one that seems to stem more from immaturity than from inexperience.

notion
(nō´shən) *n.* A *notion* is a belief or opinion.

novice
(nŏv´ĭs) *n.* A *novice* is a beginner.

bane
(bān) *n.* A *bane* is a cause of death, destruction, or ruin.

"Skills are a minor factor in most cases," says Allan Williams, former chief scientist at the insurance institute. "It's really attitudes and emotions."

A peek inside the brain

The NIH brain research suggests that the problem is human biology. A crucial part of the teen's brain—the area that peers ahead and considers consequences—remains undeveloped. That means careless attitudes and rash emotions often drive teen decisions, says Jay Giedd, chief of brain imaging in the child psychiatric unit at the National Institute of Mental Health, who's leading the study.

"It all comes down to impulse control," Giedd says. "The brain is changing a lot longer than we used to think. And that part of the brain involved in decision-making and controlling impulses is among the latest to come on board."

The teen brain is a **paradox**. Some areas—those that control senses, reactions and physical abilities—are fully developed in teenagers. "Physically, they should be ruling the world," Giedd says. "But (adolescence) is not that great of a time emotionally."

Giedd and an international research team have analyzed 4,000 brain scans from 2,000 volunteers to document how brains evolve as children mature.

paradox
(păr′ə-dŏks′) *n.* A *paradox* is a true statement that seems like it would not be true.

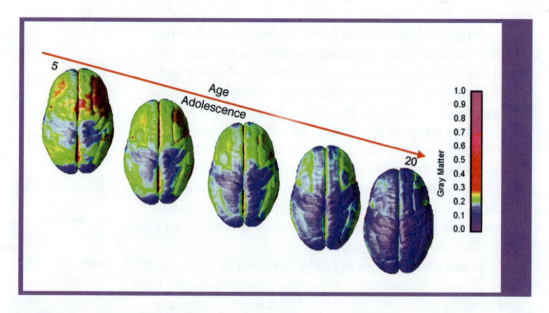

The human brain continues to develop throughout adolescence. As the brain prunes cells, there is an increase in reasoning skills.

In his office at the NIH, Giedd points to an image of a brain on his computer screen that illustrates brain development from childhood to adulthood. As he sets the time lapse in motion, the brain turns blue rapidly in some areas and more slowly in others. One area that's slow to turn blue—which represents development over time—is the right side just over the temple. It's the spot on the head where a parent might tap a frustrated finger while asking his teen, "What were you thinking?"

This underdeveloped area is called the dorsal lateral prefrontal cortex. The underdeveloped blue on Giedd's screen is where thoughts of long-term consequences spring to consciousness. And in teen after teen, the research team found, it's not fully mature.

"This is the top rung," Giedd says. "This is the part of the brain that, in a sense, associates everything. All of our hopes and dreams for the future. All of our memories of the past. Our values. Everything going on in our environment. Everything to make a decision."

When a smart, talented and very mature teen does something a parent might call "stupid," Giedd says, it's this underdeveloped part of the brain that has most likely failed.

"That's the part of the brain that helps look farther ahead," he says. "In a sense, increasing the time between impulse and decisions. It seems not to get as good as it's going to get until age 25."

This slow process plays a kind of dirty trick on teens, whose hormones are churning. As their bodies turn more adultlike, the hormones encourage more risk-taking and thrill-seeking. That might be nature's way of helping them leave the nest. But as the hormones fire up the part of the brain that responds to pleasure, known as the limbic system, emotions run high. Those emotions make it hard to quickly form wise judgments—the kind drivers must make every day.

That's also why teens often seem more **impetuous** than adults. In making decisions, they rely more on the parts of their brain that control emotion. They're "hotter" when angry and "colder" when sad, Giedd says.

When a teen is traveling 15 to 20 miles per hour over the speed limit, the part of his or her brain that processes a thrill is working brilliantly. But the part that warns of negative consequences? It's all but useless.

impetuous
(ĭm-pĕch´ōō-əs) *adj.*
If someone is *impetuous*, he or she acts without thinking things through.

"It may not seem that fast to them," Giedd says, because they're not weighing the same factors an adult might. They're not asking themselves, he says, " 'Should I go fast or not?' And dying is not really part of the equation."

Precisely how brain development plays out on the roads has yet to be studied. Giedd says brain scans of teens in driving simulations might tell researchers exactly what's going on in their heads. That could lead to better training and a clearer understanding of which teens are ready to make critical driving decisions.

In theory, a teen's brain could eventually be scanned to determine whether he or she was neurologically fit to drive. But Giedd says that ethical crossroad is too radical to seriously consider today. "We are just at the threshold of this," he says.

Finding explanations

The new insights into the teen brain might help explain why efforts to protect young drivers, ranging from driver education to laws that restrict teen driving, have had only modest success. With the judgment center of the teen brain not fully developed, parents and states must struggle to instill decision-making skills in still-immature drivers.

In nearly every state, 16-year-old drivers face limits known as "graduated licensing" rules. These restrictions vary. But typically, they bar 16-year-olds from carrying other teen passengers, driving at night or driving alone until they have driven a certain number of hours under parental supervision.

These states have, in effect, already raised their driving age. Safety experts say lives have been saved as a result. But it's mostly left to parents to enforce the restrictions, and the evidence suggests enforcement has been weak.

Teens probably appear to their parents at the dinner table to be more in control than they are behind the wheel. They might recite perfectly the risks of speeding, drinking and driving or distractions, such as carrying passengers or talking on a cell phone, Giedd says. But their brains are built to learn more from example.

For teenagers, years of watching parents drive after downing a few glasses of wine or while chatting on a cell phone might make a deeper imprint than a lecture from a driver education teacher.

The brain research raises this question: How well can teen brains respond to the stresses of driving?

More research on teen driving decisions is needed, safety advocates say, before definitive conclusions can be drawn. And more public support is probably needed before politicians would seriously consider raising the driving age.

In the 1980s, Congress pressured states to raise their legal age to buy alcohol to 21. The goal was to stop teens from crossing borders to buy alcohol, after reports of drunken teens dying in auto crashes. Fueled by groups such as Mothers Against Drunk Driving, public support for stricter laws grew until Congress forced a rise in the drinking age.

Those laws have saved an estimated 20,000 lives in the past 20 years. Yet safety advocates say politicians remain generally unwilling to raise the driving age.

"If this were forced on the states, it would not be accepted very well," Harsha says. "What it usually takes for politicians to change their minds is a series of crashes involving young people. When enough of those kind of things happen, then politicians are more likely to be open to other suggestions."

Determine Central Idea and Details

The **central idea** of a piece of writing is the main concept about a topic that a writer conveys. Entire pieces of writing can be based around a central idea, and so can individual paragraphs.

A central idea is supported by **details**—facts, statistics, or quotations—that tell more about it. Note these details from "Is 16 Too Young to Drive a Car?"

Detail	What It Is	Example
fact	a statement that can be proved	Many states have begun to raise the age by imposing restrictions on 16-year-old drivers.
statistic	information that deals with numbers	Already, on average, two people die every day across the USA in vehicles driven by 16-year-old drivers.
quotation by experts	an expert's exact written or spoken words	"Skills are a minor factor in most cases," says Allan Williams, former chief scientist at the insurance institute. "It's really attitudes and emotions."

It's important to remember that although facts, quotations by experts, and especially statistics can seem undeniable, there are often multiple ways to interpret them, depending on the information or attitudes a reader already has. For example, the statistic in the chart can be interpreted to mean

- Every day, 16-year-old drivers are to blame for deaths.
- 16-year-olds are driving in only a small percentage of fatal accidents that occur each day.

Readers have to decide how—or if—a statistic helps to support a central idea. Study the supporting details carefully as you analyze "Is 16 Too Young to Drive a Car?"

Analyzing the Text

Cite Text Evidence   Support your responses with evidence from the text.

1. **Draw Conclusions** What is the central idea of "Is 16 Too Young to Drive a Car?"

2. **Evaluate** Reread lines 101–125. Explain how the statistics the author provides support his central idea. Is there another way to interpret the statistics? Support your answer.

3. **Cause/Effect** Reread lines 155–173. Which details explain why teen drivers make poor decisions?

Fatal Car Crashes Drop for 16-Year-Olds, Rise for Older Teens
Article by Allison Aubrey

Terrified to see your teenager behind the wheel? You're not alone. But a new study finds tougher state licensing laws have led to a decrease in fatal accidents, at least among 16-year-olds. That's the good news.

But here's the rub. Some kids are waiting until they're 18-years-old to get their driver's licenses. At this point, they're considered adults, and they don't have to jump through the hoops required of younger teens. They can opt out of driver's ed. And they are not subject to nighttime driving restrictions or passenger restrictions.

"[Older teens] are saying, 'The heck with your more complicated process,'" says Justin McNaull, director of state relations for the American Automobile Association. At 18, teenagers can, in many cases, get their license in a matter of weeks.

It's one explanation for the latest findings published in the *Journal of the American Medical Association*. Researchers at the University of North Carolina and the California Department of Motor Vehicles analyzed more than 130,000 fatal teen crashes over 22 years.

They found that tougher licensing laws have led to 1,348 fewer fatal car crashes involving 16-year-old drivers. But during the same period, fatal crashes involving 18-year-old drivers increased. They were behind the wheel in 1,086 more fatal accidents.

States have made the licensing process more rigorous in many ways: longer permitting times, driver's ed requirements, and restrictions on nighttime driving and carrying fellow teenage passengers. Experts say all of these requirements help give teenagers the experience they need on the road. "In the last 15 years, we've made great strides in getting the licensing process to do a better job in helping teens get through it safely," says McNaull.

California has seen a big drop in 16-year-olds getting their driver's license. Back in 1986, 27 percent got licensed. By 2007, the figure dropped to 14 percent.

"We have more novices on the road at 18," says Scott Masten of the California DMV and an author of the study. And some of them may not have enough experience under their belts to face risky conditions. Masten says this may help explain the increase in fatal crashes.

It's not clear whether there are significantly fewer 16-year-olds behind the wheel in other states because there's no national database. But **anecdotally**, experts see this as a trend.

"There's a belief that graduated licensing has led to a delay," says Anne McCart, a senior vice president at the Insurance Institute for Highway Safety.

A survey of teens conducted by the Allstate Foundation found that there are many reasons teens are delaying the process of getting a license. Some say they don't have a car or can't afford it. Others report that their parents are not available to help them, or that they're too busy with other activities.

But parents who do want to be more proactive can refer to the tips the AAA has compiled on how to keep teens behind the wheel safe. And they might also consider another recent study, which showed that starting the school day a little bit later seems to reduce the accident rate for teen drivers.

anecdote
(ăn´ĭk-dōt´) *n.* An *anecdote* is a short account of an incident.

COLLABORATIVE DISCUSSION In your opinion, at what age should people begin driving? With a partner, discuss the reasons for your view. Cite specific evidence from the text to support your ideas.

Analyze Text

When you evaluate an author's conclusions, it's important to consider the **reasoning,** or logic, that links his or her ideas together. Two of the most commonly used methods of reasoning are deductive reasoning and inductive reasoning.

Deductive reasoning occurs when a person uses a general principle to form a conclusion about a particular situation or problem.

General principle	The situation being considered	Conclusion
To drive safely, new drivers must receive training.	High schools train students in many areas.	New drivers should get their license while in high school.

Inductive reasoning occurs when a person uses specific observations or examples to arrive at a general conclusion or statement.

Fact	Fact	Conclusion
Automobile accidents are more severe when cars are driven at high speeds.	Severe automobile accidents are more likely to occur on highways than on roads.	Lower speed limits on highways will save lives.

As you analyze "Fatal Car Crashes Drop for 16-Year-Olds, Rise for Older Teens," identify what kind of reasoning the author is using.

Analyzing the Text

Cite Text Evidence Support your responses with evidence from the text.

1. **Draw Conclusions** What conclusions can you draw about why there are fewer laws designed to restrict 18-year-old drivers or force them to take driver's education?

2. **Interpret** Reread lines 26–33. What kind of reasoning does the author use? Explain your answer.

3. **Analyze** What is the effect of the use of the word *belief* in this statement from the selection: "There's a belief that graduated licensing has led to a delay"?

COMPARE TEXTS

Analyze Information in Texts

A **fact** is a statement that can be proved. Most writers are careful to choose facts that support their central idea, while omitting facts that do not. However, similar facts can be used to support opposing ideas. That's because a fact can be **interpreted**—or understood—differently by different people.

It's important to identify when writers are supporting their ideas with facts and when they are supporting their ideas with interpretations of the facts, which you may or may not agree with. For example, look at this passage from "Is 16 Too Young to Drive a Car?"

> Scientists at the NIH campus in Bethesda, Md, have found that this vital area [the executive branch] develops through the teenage years and isn't fully mature until after age 25. — **fact**
>
> One 16-year-old's brain might be more developed than another 18-year-old's, just as a younger teen might be taller than an older one. But evidence is mounting that a 16-year-old's brain is generally far less developed than those of teens just a little older. — **fact**
>
> The research seems to help explain why 16-year-old drivers crash at far higher rates than older teens. — **interpretation**

Even if the executive branch of the brain is not fully developed, there may be other explanations of why 16-year-old drivers have more-frequent crashes than older teens, as "Fatal Car Crashes Drop for 16-Year-Olds, Rise for Older Teens" points out.

As you compare and contrast the two articles, read carefully to identify each writer's central idea and the facts and interpretations used to support it. Identify where the texts disagree on matters of fact and interpretation.

 eBook *Annotate It!*

Analyzing the Text

Cite Text Evidence Support your responses with evidence from the texts.

1. **Summarize** In your own words, explain the central idea of each selection.

2. **Compare** Identify similar facts that both selections use to support their central idea. What key facts on this topic are included in one selection but omitted in the other?

3. **Draw Conclusions** How does the study on brain development in the first article support the conclusions about the performance of 18-year-old drivers in the second selection?

4. **Compare** Reread lines 16–20 in "Fatal Car Crashes Drop for 16-Year-Olds, Rise for Older Teens." According to Allison Aubrey, what is one interpretation for the fact that there's been an increase in fatal car crashes among 18-year-olds? How does this interpretation conflict with the quotation in lines 133–135 of "Is 16 Too Young to Drive a Car?"

5. **Evaluate** Reread lines 19–20 in "Is 16 Too Young to Drive a Car?" Do the facts found in the other article support or conflict with this interpretation? Explain.

PERFORMANCE TASK

Writing Activity: Argument Which selection is most convincing to you?

- Review the two selections, and jot down notes to support your opinion.
- Meet with a small group to discuss which selection makes a stronger case by using sufficient details to prove its central idea. Use your notes to support your opinion.
- Next, write a paragraph or two to explain and give reasons for your opinion.
- Share your paragraph with the class. Discuss any opinions that you might not have considered during your group discussion.

Critical Vocabulary

notion   novice   bane   paradox
impetuous   anecdote

Practice and Apply Explain your response to answer each question.

1. Which Vocabulary word goes with *contradiction*?
2. Which Vocabulary word goes with *impulsive*?
3. Which Vocabulary word goes with *story*?
4. Which Vocabulary word goes with *idea*?
5. Which Vocabulary word goes with *nuisance*?
6. Which Vocabulary word goes with *beginner*?

Vocabulary Strategy: Domain-Specific Words

In some nonfiction texts, you may come across an unfamiliar word whose meaning is specific to its subject matter. As with any unfamiliar word, your first clue to the word's meaning should come from the surrounding text, or context. If context is not sufficient to help you define the word, you need to consult a dictionary. Read the following example:

> . . . Giedd points to an image of a brain on his computer screen. . . . the right side just over the temple. . . . is called the <u>dorsal lateral prefrontal cortex</u>.

The term *dorsal lateral prefrontal cortex* is not one you would know unless you were a doctor or a scientist. However, the nearby word *brain* is a clue to its meaning. Another clue is the phrase "the right side just over the temple." These clues allow you to guess that the term describes a section of the brain.

Practice and Apply Find the following terms in "Is 16 Too Young to Drive a Car?" On a separate piece of paper, fill out a chart like this one.

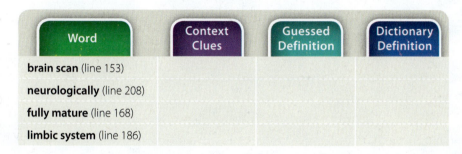

Word	Context Clues	Guessed Definition	Dictionary Definition
brain scan (line 153)			
neurologically (line 208)			
fully mature (line 168)			
limbic system (line 186)			

Language Conventions: Fragments

Usually, writers use grammatically correct sentences to make their meaning clear. However, they may occasionally include **fragments,** or incomplete sentences that lack a subject or predicate. Reasons for using fragments include

- to reproduce exactly what someone said in a quote
- to capture someone's voice or manner of speaking
- to emphasize particular ideas
- to avoid repeating sentence parts
- to craft a style of writing

Study this example from "Is 16 Too Young to Drive a Car?" The sentence fragments have been underlined.

> "This is the top rung," Giedd says. "This is the part of the brain that, in a sense, associates everything. <u>All of our hopes and dreams for the future. All of our memories of the past. Our values. Everything going on in our environment. Everything to make a decision.</u>"

These fragments define *everything*. They capture the speaker's exact words and emphasize the idea that the brain can associate the parts of our lives with each other.

Practice and Apply Read these fragments from the selections. In a chart like the one shown, tell what sentence part is missing and why the author used a fragment in each case.

1. "In a sense, increasing the time between impulse and decisions." (lines 178–179) [Selection 1]

2. " 'The heck with your more complicated process,'" (lines 11–12) [Selection 2]

Missing Part	Why Use the Fragment
1.	
2.	

COMPARE MEDIA

Background Ads are everywhere around us—on websites, in football and baseball stadiums, and even on clothing. Ads draw our attention to products or services and try to convince us to buy what we see advertised. Companies make billions of dollars from purchases made because ads were successful in persuading us.

One type of ad is not trying to sell something that costs money. Public service announcements, or PSAs, deliver a completely different kind of message—ideas that are for the public good.

MEDIA ANALYSIS

Persuading Viewers through Ads

Your Phone Can Wait
Public Service Announcement Film
by Stephanie Ramirez

Driving Distracted
Public Service Announcement Poster

SETTING A PURPOSE In this lesson, you will view and analyze two types of public service announcements—a film and a poster. Both try to convince people to change their attitudes and behaviors regarding aspects of driving in order to help them drive safely. Examine each public service announcement carefully to determine what particular points about safe driving it promotes and whom it is trying to persuade.

MEDIA

Your Phone Can Wait

Format: Public service announcement film
Running Time: 2:0 minutes

AS YOU VIEW The film you are about to view was created for the National Safety Council for a specific purpose and audience. Think about whom the filmmaker might have wanted to appeal to as you watch the film. How do the various parts of the film appeal to that audience? Also think about the specific message that the film delivers and the variety of techniques—verbal and visual—that the filmmaker uses.

Pause the video and write notes about techniques and ideas that impress you as you view. Also write down any questions you have during viewing. Replay or rewind the video as needed.

Analyze Ideas in Media

The creators of public service announcements like "Your Phone Can Wait" design them with a specific audience and purpose in mind. A **target audience** is the group that the creators want to appeal to. The individuals in the target audience may share certain attributes, such as age, gender, ethnic background, values, or lifestyle. The **purpose** of a film may be to share information or to persuade the audience to change behaviors or attitudes.

The creators of filmed public service announcements combine different techniques and elements to deliver their **message**—the idea that the film promotes.

- **Persuasive techniques** are methods used to convince viewers to agree with a message. Some language may appeal to viewers' sense of reason, while other words appeal to viewers' emotions. Repeated words help viewers remember the message.
- **Visual elements,** such as graphics or **animation**—the process of displaying images so they appear to move—can engage the audience. Fast-paced scene changes can convey excitement.
- **Sound elements** such as music or sound effects can emphasize a point or grab viewers' attention. A **narrator,** or the person who speaks and explains the message, also has an impact. An older voice may sound responsible and mature, while a younger voice may seem friendlier to a younger audience.

Consider how these elements are used in "Your Phone Can Wait."

Analyzing the Media

Cite Text Evidence Support your responses with evidence from the media.

1. **Identify and Infer** Review the public service announcement film and fill out a chart like this one.

Who is the target audience?	
What is the message of the announcement?	
What is the purpose of the announcement?	

2. **Evaluate** Which persuasive techniques, visual elements, and sound elements are used to deliver the film's message? How do these techniques and elements help make the message more appealing?

Driving Distracted

Format: Public service announcement poster

AS YOU VIEW In this poster, the writer and designer create a particular scene for a particular purpose. They include facts and figures as well as images. Think about how these visual and textual elements work together to convey the message.

Consider specific elements, such as
- the objects that are included
- the use of light and dark colors
- the content and placement of text and figures

What points do each of these elements make or emphasize?

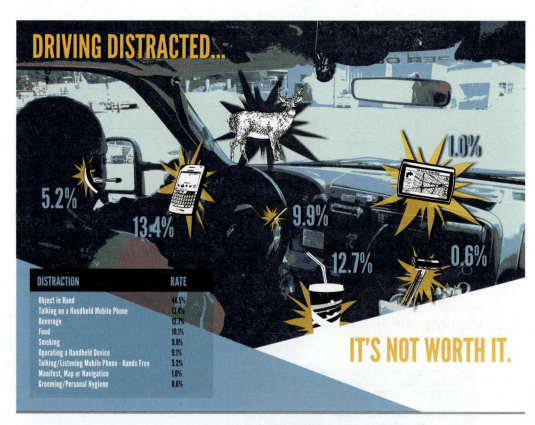

COLLABORATIVE DISCUSSION Evaluate how well the film and the poster work as public service announcements. Is the message in each announcement a powerful one? Why or why not?

Analyze Diverse Media

Public service announcements are communicated through various media, including magazines, billboards, or posters such as the "Driving Distracted" poster. These media use different elements to help make their messages more exciting.

Public service announcements quite often include **statistics,** mathematical information that is collected and analyzed to help people understand a situation or a trend. Statistics help make a message more convincing.

A public service poster, or any similar type of media, also includes visual elements, such as the following:

- **Graphics** are visual designs or elements that call attention to certain information. For example, the starbursts in the "Driving Distracted" poster call attention to the objects contained within.
- **Color** can be used to create certain feelings or to convey emphasis. For example, red can suggest danger, while blue can create a calm, peaceful feeling. Text in vivid colors will stand out more than text in darker colors. Viewers are more likely to read something bold or vivid because it catches their attention immediately.

Consider the impact of these elements as you analyze the "Driving Distracted" poster.

Analyzing the Media

Cite Text Evidence   Support your responses with evidence from the media.

1. **Infer** To what does the heading "Distraction/Rate" refer?

2. **Interpret** Each of the five yellow starbursts within the car contains an image with a percentage shown next to it. What does this use of visuals and statistics convey? What impact do these elements have on the message?

3. **Analyze** Why is the starburst containing the image of the deer placed within the windshield area? What message does this symbol and its placement convey?

COMPARE MEDIA

Evaluate Media

"Your Phone Can Wait" and "Driving Distracted" both deliver similar messages. However, because they are presented in different forms of media, they can emphasize different types of information to make their message clear.

- **Oral information** uses spoken language to make its point. While words can be logical and factual, some words can appeal to feelings and emotions. A speaker's tone or emphasis can also have an impact.
- **Quantitative information** conveys facts and details through numbers. It tells about information that is measurable.

Think about the techniques—or combination of techniques—each media form uses as you evaluate "Your Phone Can Wait" and "Driving Distracted."

Analyzing the Media

Cite Text Evidence   Support your responses with evidence from the media.

1. **Analyze** "Your Phone Can Wait" and "Driving Distracted" both provide quantitative information about the dangers of distracted driving. Complete a chart like this to gather details about the specific information each public service announcement provides. Which announcement more effectively conveys quantitative information?

Public Service Announcement	Quantitative Information	How Information Is Shared
Your Phone Can Wait		
Driving Distracted		

2. **Compare** "Your Phone Can Wait" includes a narrator who provides spoken information. It also includes an animated re-creation of a driving experience. Are these methods of conveying information more or less effective than the use of text and graphics in "Driving Distracted"? Explain.

PERFORMANCE TASK

Media Activity: Public Service Announcement   Work with your group to create your own print media public service announcement about safe driving for teenagers.

- Brainstorm with your group for ideas to include.
- Discuss the different techniques that would help you effectively deliver your message.
- Research the topic and gather statistics that will help make your message more persuasive.
- Create and lay out visuals that reflect your ideas.

COLLECTION 4
PERFORMANCE TASK A

Interactive Lessons
To help you complete this task, use
- Writing Informative Texts
- Writing as a Process
- Using Textual Evidence

Write a Literary Analysis

The transition from childhood to adulthood can be complicated. Write a literary analysis about what "Marigolds" reveals about that transition and explore how its theme relates to modern life.

A successful literary analysis

- cites evidence from the text that supports the writer's analysis
- is organized appropriately for the purpose and audience
- conveys ideas through the selection, organization, and analysis of relevant content

PLAN

 myNotebook

Use the annotation tools in your eBook to find evidence in the text that supports your ideas about the story's theme.

Analyze the Story Refresh your memory of "Marigolds."

- Reread "Marigolds" to review the lesson or theme that stands out for you. Consider Lizabeth's experiences as a teenager, as well as her view of those experiences as an adult.
- Take notes about evidence that reveals the story's theme. Remember to look for clues in the setting and in symbols that represent ideas or feelings.
- List some ways that the story's theme connects to modern trends or to the experiences of modern teens.

Consider Audience and Purpose Think about what your readers need to know to understand your analysis.

- Keep in mind that peers may be more in tune with experiences related to adolescence than older readers.
- Decide how you will appeal to readers who may have different views about the theme of the story.

Develop a Thesis Statement Use your notes about "Marigolds" to plan your analysis.

- Draft your thesis statement. This is the main point you want to make, so everything you discuss should relate to it.
- Decide what theme you will discuss, and identify evidence from the story that supports your thoughts.

ACADEMIC VOCABULARY

As you share what you learned about the transition to adulthood, be sure to use the academic vocabulary words.

debate
deduce
license
sufficient
trend

- Create a graphic organizer to plan your writing. Note how aspects of the story might resonate with modern teenagers.

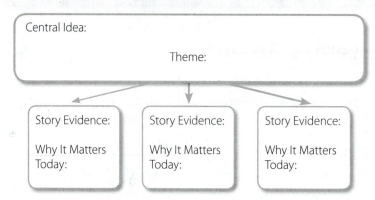

Interactive Lessons

For help in planning your essay, use
- Writing Informative Texts: Organizing Ideas
- Using Textual Evidence: Writing an Outline

PRODUCE

Write Your Literary Analysis
Use your notes and your graphic organizer to draft your literary analysis.

- Start with an attention-grabbing question or comment, and state your thesis to introduce your analysis. Provide a brief summary of the story.
- Organize your ideas. You may wish to discuss the theme along with related evidence, and then explain how the theme is relevant for today's young people. Another option would be to organize around the major events in the story, explaining how each one helps to reveal the theme and connects to today's teenagers.
- Include concrete details, quotations, or other examples from the story to support your ideas.
- Conclude with a summary and your own insights.

Write your rough draft in *my*WriteSmart. Focus on getting your ideas down, rather than on perfecting your choice of language.

Interactive Lessons

To help you draft your essay, complete the following lessons in Writing Informative Texts:
- Elaboration
- Introductions and Conclusions

Language Conventions: Connecting Ideas

Look for places where you can combine clauses to connect ideas. Read this passage from "Marigolds."

> "Whenever the memory of those marigolds flashes across my mind, a strange nostalgia comes with it and remains long after the picture has faded."

Note how the author connects the memory of the marigolds and the feeling of nostalgia. Her language choices show how the two ideas are related.

270 Collection 4

REVISE

Review Your Draft Have your partner or group of peers use the following chart to review your draft.

Questions	Tips	Revision Techniques
Does the introduction have a thesis statement and a summary of the story?	**Highlight** the thesis statement. **Underline** sentences that summarize the story.	**Add** a thesis statement. **Insert** a summary of the story.
Do the ideas in the body paragraphs support the thesis statement?	**Underline** the ideas that support the thesis statement.	**Revise** the body paragraphs to clearly explain their connections to the thesis statement.
Is there evidence to support each idea?	**Highlight** details, quotations, or other examples that support ideas.	**Add** details, quotations, or examples to ideas that do not have enough support.
Are the connections between ideas clear?	**Underline** sentences that combine two or more clauses to connect ideas.	**Combine** related sentences to show the connections between ideas.
Does the conclusion summarize the analysis and provide insight into the theme?	**Highlight** the sentences that summarize the analysis. **Underline** the sentences that provide insight into the theme.	**Add** a summary of the analysis. **Clarify** your insights into the theme.

Have your partner or a group of peers review your draft in *my*WriteSmart. Ask your reviewers to note any reasons that do not support the claim or that lack sufficient evidence.

Interactive Lessons
For help in revising your essay, use
• Writing as a Process: Revising and Editing

PRESENT

Create a Finished Copy Finalize your literary analysis. Then choose a way to share it with your audience. Consider these options:

- Present your literary analysis in a speech to your classmates.
- Send your analysis to a magazine that publishes articles of interest to adolescents.
- Organize a debate in which you and other classmates argue your views about the relevance of "Marigolds" for today's teenagers.

PERFORMANCE TASK A RUBRIC
LITERARY ANALYSIS

	Ideas and Evidence	Organization	Language
4	• The thesis statement clearly identifies the story's theme and its relevance. • Specific, relevant details support key points in the analysis. • The concluding section summarizes the analysis and offers an insight.	• Key points and supporting details are organized effectively and logically throughout the literary analysis. • Transitions successfully show the relationships between ideas.	• Language is precise and captures the writer's thoughts with originality. • Clauses are effectively combined to connect ideas. • Grammar, usage, and mechanics are correct.
3	• The thesis statement makes a point about the relevance of the theme. • Some key points need more support. • The concluding section summarizes most of the analysis but doesn't offer an insight.	• The organization of key points and supporting details is confusing in a few places. • A few more transitions are needed to clarify the relationships between ideas.	• Most language is precise and shows some originality. • Some clauses are combined to connect ideas. • Some errors in grammar, usage, and mechanics occur.
2	• The thesis statement only hints at a main point. • Details support some key points but often are too general. • The concluding section gives an incomplete summary without insight.	• Most key points are organized logically, but many supporting details are out of place. • More transitions are needed throughout the literary analysis to connect ideas.	• Language is repetitive or too general at times. • Few ideas are clearly connected. • Many errors in grammar, usage, and mechanics occur, but the writer's ideas are still clear.
1	• The thesis statement is missing. • Details and evidence are irrelevant or missing. • The literary analysis lacks a concluding section.	• A logical organization is not apparent. • Transitions are not used.	• Language is inaccurate, repetitive, and too general. • Ideas are not connected. • Errors in grammar, usage, and mechanics obscure the meaning of the writer's ideas.

COLLECTION 4
PERFORMANCE TASK B

Interactive Lessons
To help you complete this task, use
- Producing and Publishing with Technology
- Conducting Research

Produce a Multimedia Campaign

One selection in Collection 4 asks, "When Do Kids Become Adults?" In this activity, you will create a multimedia campaign to present your response to that age-old question. Your campaign will include an editorial along with messages in one or two other mediums.

A successful campaign

- presents an argument that supports claims with clear reasons and relevant evidence
- draws evidence from informational texts and from print and digital research
- integrates multimedia and visual displays to strengthen claims and to add interest

Visit hmhfyi.com to explore your topic and enhance your research.

PLAN

myNotebook
Use the annotation tools in your eBook to identify textual evidence from the collection that will help shape and support your argument.

Gather Information Review the selections in Collection 4 to find events or trends that may mark the beginning of adulthood.

- Identify the event, action, or age that reflects your position.
- Gather at least two pieces of evidence to support your position from selections in the collection.

Conduct Research Use both print and digital resources to gather information about the start of adulthood.

- If you have chosen to focus on an event such as obtaining a driver's license or voting for the first time, research the legal age for those events in the United States as well as in other countries.
- If your focus is on living independently, research laws or traditions that signal legal adulthood.
- Take notes and gather sufficient statistics to support your claim.

ACADEMIC VOCABULARY

As you share your ideas about the event or age that should mark the start of adulthood, be sure to use the academic vocabulary words.

debate
deduce
license
sufficient
trend

Consider Audience and Purpose Keep your intended audience in mind as you develop your campaign.

Collection Performance Task B **273**

- Your language and tone will generally be different for classmates and other peers than for adults.
- Your campaign will include an editorial, but you will also use other formats to present your ideas effectively. You might consider using a poster, a television or radio commercial, or a direct mail advertisement to effectively reach your audience.

Interactive Lessons
To help you revise your presentation, complete the following lessons in Conducting Research:
- Using the Library for Research
- Using the Internet for Research

Develop Your Argument Use your notes from your review of the collection and your research to plan your argument.

- Whether advertising a product or promoting a political candidate, a good campaign has a central message or claim. Plan how to deliver your message in writing for your editorial and in the other formats you choose.
- Create a graphic organizer like the one shown to develop an argument that includes a claim, supporting evidence, and a counterargument.

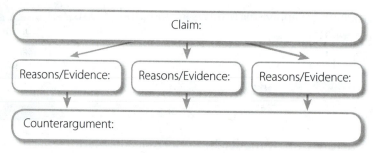

PRODUCE

Write Your Editorial Use your notes and your graphic organizer to draft your editorial.

- Use quotations or unexpected statistics to get your audience's attention, and state your position with a strong claim.
- Organize your ideas in a logical way. You might begin with the strongest reason and progress to less strong reasons. Another option would be to start with the least important reason and build to the most important.
- Be sure to include concrete details, quotations, or examples from the selections and your research to support your claim.
- Conclude your editorial by restating your claim and by encouraging readers to show their support for your argument.

Write your rough draft in myWriteSmart. Focus on getting your ideas down, rather than on perfecting your choice of language.

Design Other Formats The best campaigns use more than one medium to share their message. Using multimedia technology to mix visuals with sound is the latest trend, but something as "low-tech" as a poster, a T-shirt, or a bumper sticker may also reach a wide audience.

- Choose one or two other mediums to add to your campaign.
- Draft any necessary text and decide how to incorporate it with related visuals.
- Sketch out how you will display or present your visuals.
- Cite your research sources, following your teacher's choice of style.

REVISE

Review Your Draft Use the rubric on the next page to evaluate your draft. Work with a partner to determine whether you have presented a strong argument in your campaign. Consider the following:

Have your partner or a group of peers review the draft of your editorial in myWriteSmart. Ask your reviewers to note any reasons that do not support the claim or that lack sufficient evidence.

- Review your editorial to make sure you have clearly stated your claim and provided sufficient supporting reasons and evidence.
- Check that the other formats you have chosen clearly support your claim. Is each layout clear and easy to understand? Do all the visuals clearly represent your focus? Confirm that the text is easy to read and free of grammatical errors.
- Evaluate whether all the elements of your campaign send a unified message that will appeal to your audience.

PRESENT

Create a Finished Product Finalize all the parts of your campaign. Then choose a way to share it with your audience. Consider these options:

- Plan a campaign rally or kick-off event to share your ideas with classmates.
- Create a blog or website to share your argument with a wider audience.
- Organize a debate with classmates who claim a different age or event as the mark of adulthood.

PERFORMANCE TASK B RUBRIC
MULTIMEDIA CAMPAIGN

	Ideas and Evidence	Organization	Language
4	• All parts of the campaign clearly state a position and a call for action. • Logical reasons and relevant evidence support the claim. • Counterarguments are addressed. • The campaign's message is strong and unified throughout.	• The reasons and evidence are organized logically and consistently to persuasive effect. • Transitions connect reasons and evidence to the writer's claim.	• The editorial is presented in a consistent, formal style. • Grammar, mechanics, and usage are correct.
3	• A position is stated but could be more clear. • Reasons and evidence could be more convincing. • Responses to counterarguments need development. • The campaign's message is strong and mostly unified.	• The organization of reasons and evidence is confusing in places. • A few more transitions are needed to connect reasons and evidence to the claim.	• The style of the editorial becomes informal in a few places. • Some errors in grammar, usage, and mechanics occur.
2	• The writer's position is not clear. • Some reasons and evidence are not logical or relevant. • Opposing claims are not addressed logically. • The campaign's message is somewhat inconsistent.	• The organization of reasons and evidence is logical in some places, but it does not follow a clear pattern. • Many more transitions are needed to connect reasons and evidence to the claim.	• The style of the editorial becomes informal in many places. • Grammar, usage, and mechanics are incorrect in many places.
1	• No position is stated. • Reasons and evidence are missing. • Opposing claims are not anticipated or addressed. • The campaign lacks a unified message.	• A logical organization is not used; reasons and evidence are presented randomly. • Transitions are not used, making the argument difficult to understand.	• The style is inappropriate for the argument. • Errors in grammar, usage, and mechanics obscure the meaning of ideas.

COLLECTION 5

Anne Frank's Legacy

"I don't want to have lived in vain like most people… I want to go on living even after my death!"

—Anne Frank

COLLECTION 5

Anne Frank's Legacy

In this collection, you will learn about the lasting impact of a young girl and her diary.

COLLECTION
PERFORMANCE TASK Preview

At the end of this collection, you will research and write an informative essay comparing the experiences of Anne Frank and her family to those of other Jews hiding during World War II.

ACADEMIC VOCABULARY

Study the words and their definitions in the chart below. You will use these words as you discuss and write about the texts in this collection.

Word	Definition	Related Forms
communicate (kə-myōō´nĭ-kāt´) v.	to convey information or exchange ideas	communicated, communicable
draft (drăft) n.; v.	early versions or stages of a written document or plan; to write such a version	drafting, drafted
liberation (lĭb´ə-rā´shən) n.	the act of freeing or the state of being free	liberate, liberal
philosophy (fĭ-lŏs´ə-fē) n.	the underlying theory or set of ideas related to life as a whole	philosopher, philosophic
publish (pŭb´lĭsh) v.	to prepare and issue a book or other material to the public	publishing, publication, public

The Diary of Anne Frank

Drama by Frances Goodrich and Albert Hackett

Background Anne Frank and her family were Jewish citizens of Germany. When the Nazi party, led by Adolf Hitler, came to power in 1933, the Nazis blamed the country's problems on the Jews. Jews were stripped of their rights. Many were eventually sent to concentration camps, where more than 6 million died in what became known as the Holocaust. The Franks moved to the Netherlands to escape persecution, but the Nazis invaded that country in 1940. In order to survive, Anne's family went into hiding when she was 13 years old. They hid in attic rooms behind Mr. Frank's office, and several other Jews joined them. In this "Secret Annex," Anne kept a diary about her life in hiding. More than two years later, the group's worst fears came true when the Nazis found them. Everyone who had been living there was sent to concentration camps. Anne's diary was discovered later.

Frances Goodrich (1890–1984) and **Albert Hackett** (1900–1995) *were a married couple who worked together to write screenplays for movies. They wrote the play called* The Diary of Anne Frank *based on Anne's actual diary entries. Although the play differs from the diary in many ways, Anne's father, who survived the Holocaust, believed it captured the essence of his daughter's diary. The play won a Pulitzer Prize for Drama. It was later made into a movie.*

SETTING A PURPOSE As you read, think about what the play reveals about Anne Frank's philosophy of life. How are her thoughts communicated?

As you read, save new words to *myWordList*.

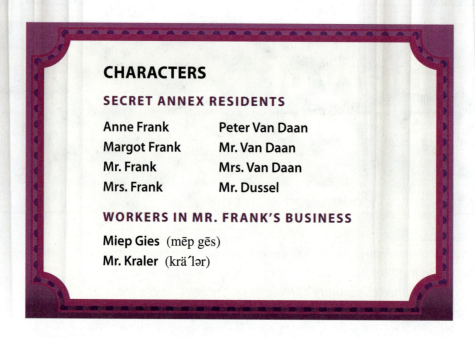

CHARACTERS

SECRET ANNEX RESIDENTS

Anne Frank
Margot Frank
Mr. Frank
Mrs. Frank
Peter Van Daan
Mr. Van Daan
Mrs. Van Daan
Mr. Dussel

WORKERS IN MR. FRANK'S BUSINESS

Miep Gies (mēp gēs)
Mr. Kraler (krä´lər)

The Time. *July 1942–August 1944, November 1945*

The Place. *Amsterdam, the Netherlands*

The scene remains the same throughout the play. It is the top floor of a warehouse and office building in Amsterdam, Holland. The sharply peaked roof of the building is outlined against a sea of other rooftops, stretching away into the distance. Nearby is the belfry of a church tower, the Westertoren, whose carillon rings out the hours. Occasionally faint sounds float up from below: the voices of children playing in the street, the tramp of marching feet, a boat whistle from the canal.

The three rooms of the top floor and a small attic space above are exposed to our view. The largest of the rooms is in the center, with two small rooms, slightly raised, on either side. On the right is a bathroom, out of sight. A narrow steep flight of stairs at the back leads up to the attic. The rooms are sparsely furnished with a few chairs, cots, a table or two. The windows are painted over, or covered with makeshift blackout curtains. In the main room there is a sink, a gas ring for cooking and a wood-burning stove for warmth.

The room on the left is hardly more than a closet. There is a skylight in the sloping ceiling. Directly under this room is a small steep stairwell, with steps leading down to a door. This is the only entrance from the building below. When the door is opened we see that it has been concealed on the outer side by a bookcase attached to it.

ACT ONE

Scene 1

The curtain rises on an empty stage. It is late afternoon November, 1945.

The rooms are dusty, the curtains in rags. Chairs and tables are overturned.

The door at the foot of the small stairwell swings open. Mr. Frank comes up the steps into view. He is a gentle, cultured European in his middle years. There is still a trace of a German accent in his speech.

He stands looking slowly around, making a supreme effort at self-control. He is weak, ill. His clothes are threadbare.

After a second he drops his rucksack on the couch and moves slowly about. He opens the door to one of the smaller rooms, and then abruptly closes it again, turning away. He goes to the window at the back, looking off at the Westertoren as its carillon strikes the hour of six, then he moves restlessly on.

From the street below we hear the sound of a barrel organ and children's voices at play. There is a many-colored scarf hanging from a nail. Mr. Frank *takes it, putting it around his neck. As he starts back for his rucksack, his eye is caught by something lying on the floor. It is a woman's white glove. He holds it in his hand and suddenly all of his self-control is gone. He breaks down, crying.*

We hear footsteps on the stairs. Miep Gies *comes up, looking for* Mr. Frank. Miep *is a Dutch girl of about twenty-two. She wears a coat and hat, ready to go home. She is pregnant. Her attitude toward* Mr. Frank *is protective, compassionate.*

Miep. Are you all right, Mr. Frank?

Mr. Frank (*quickly controlling himself*). Yes, Miep, yes.

Miep. Everyone in the office has gone home . . . It's after six. (*then pleading*) Don't stay up here, Mr. Frank. What's the use of torturing yourself like this?

Mr. Frank. I've come to say good-bye . . . I'm leaving here, Miep.

Miep. What do you mean? Where are you going? Where?

Mr. Frank. I don't know yet. I haven't decided.

Miep. Mr. Frank, you can't leave here! This is your home! Amsterdam is your home. Your business is here, waiting for you . . . You're needed here . . . Now that the war is over, there are things that . . .

Mr. Frank. I can't stay in Amsterdam, Miep. It has too many memories for me. Everywhere there's something . . . the house we lived in . . . the school . . . that street organ playing out there . . . I'm not the person you used to know, Miep. I'm a bitter old man. (*breaking off*) Forgive me. I shouldn't speak to you like this . . . after all that you did for us . . . the suffering . . .

Miep. No. No. It wasn't suffering. You can't say we suffered. (*As she speaks, she straightens a chair which is overturned.*)

Mr. Frank. I know what you went through, you and Mr. Kraler. I'll remember it as long as I live. (*He gives one last look around.*) Come, Miep.

(*He starts for the steps, then remembers his rucksack, going back to get it.*)

Miep (*hurrying up to a cupboard*). Mr. Frank, did you see? There are some of your papers here. (*She brings a bundle of papers to him.*) We found them in a heap of rubbish on the floor after . . . after you left.

Mr. Frank. Burn them.

(*He opens his rucksack to put the glove in it.*)

Miep. But, Mr. Frank, there are letters, notes . . .

Mr. Frank. Burn them. All of them.

Miep. Burn *this*?

(*She hands him a paperbound notebook.*)

Mr. Frank (*quietly*). Anne's diary. (*He opens the diary and begins to read.*) "Monday, the sixth of July, nineteen forty-two." (*to* Miep) Nineteen forty-two. Is it possible, Miep? . . . Only three years ago. (*As he continues his reading, he sits down on the couch.*) "Dear Diary, since you and I are going to be great friends, I will start by telling you about myself. My name is Anne Frank. I am thirteen years old. I was born in Germany the twelfth of June, nineteen twenty-nine. As my family is Jewish, we emigrated to Holland when Hitler came to power."

(*As* Mr. Frank *reads on, another voice joins his, as if coming from the air. It is* Anne's Voice.)

Mr. Frank and Anne. "My father started a business, importing spice and herbs. Things went well for us until nineteen forty. Then the war came, and the Dutch capitulation, followed by the arrival of the Germans. Then things got very bad for the Jews."

(Mr. Frank's Voice *dies out.* Anne's Voice *continues alone. The lights dim slowly to darkness. The curtain falls on the scene.*)

Anne's Voice. You could not do this and you could not do that. They forced Father out of his business. We had to wear yellow stars.[1] I had to turn in my bike. I couldn't go to a Dutch school any more. I couldn't go to the movies, or ride in an automobile, or even on a streetcar, and a million other things. But somehow we children still managed to have fun. Yesterday Father told me we were going into hiding. Where, he wouldn't say. At five o'clock this morning Mother woke me and told me to hurry and get dressed. I was to put on as many clothes as I could. It would look too suspicious if we walked along carrying suitcases. It wasn't until we were on our way that I learned where we were going. Our hiding place was to be upstairs in the building where Father used to have his business. Three other people were coming in with us . . . the Van Daans and their son Peter . . . Father knew the Van Daans but we had never met them . . .

(*During the last lines the curtain rises on the scene. The lights dim on.* Anne's Voice *fades out.*)

Scene 2

It is early morning, July, 1942. The rooms are bare, as before, but they are now clean and orderly.

Mr. Van Daan, *a tall, portly man in his late forties, is in the main room, pacing up and down, nervously smoking a cigarette. His*

---

[1] **yellow stars:** the six-pointed Stars of David that the Nazis ordered all Jews to wear for identification.

clothes and overcoat are expensive and well cut.

Mrs. Van Daan sits on the couch, clutching her possessions, a hatbox, bags, etc. She is a pretty woman in her early forties. She wears a fur coat over her other clothes.

Peter Van Daan is standing at the window of the room on the right, looking down at the street below. He is a shy, awkward boy of sixteen. He wears a cap, a raincoat, and long Dutch trousers, like "plus fours." At his feet is a black case, a carrier for his cat.

The yellow Star of David is conspicuous on all of their clothes.

Mrs. Van Daan (*rising, nervous, excited*). Something's happened to them! I know it!

Mr. Van Daan. Now, Kerli!

Mrs. Van Daan. Mr. Frank said they'd be here at seven o'clock. He said . . .

Mr. Van Daan. They have two miles to walk. You can't expect . . .

Mrs. Van Daan. They've been picked up. That's what's happened. They've been taken . . .

(*Mr. Van Daan indicates that he hears someone coming.*)

Mr. Van Daan. You see?

(*Peter takes up his carrier and his schoolbag, etc., and goes into the main room as Mr. Frank comes up the stairwell from below. Mr. Frank looks much younger now. His movements are brisk, his manner confident. He wears an overcoat and carries his hat and a small cardboard box. He crosses to the Van Daans, shaking hands with each of them.*)

Mr. Frank. Mrs. Van Daan, Mr. Van Daan, Peter. (*then, in explanation of their lateness*) There were too many of the Green Police[2] on the streets . . . we had to take the long way around.

(*Up the steps come Margot Frank, Mrs. Frank, Miep* [*not pregnant now*] *and Mr. Kraler. All of them carry bags, packages, and so forth. The Star of David is conspicuous on all of the* Franks' *clothing. Margot is eighteen, beautiful, quiet, shy. Mrs. Frank is a young mother, gently bred, reserved. She, like Mr. Frank, has a slight German accent. Mr. Kraler is a Dutchman, dependable, kindly.*

As Mr. Kraler *and* Miep *go upstage to put down their parcels,* Mrs. Frank *turns back to call* Anne.)

Mrs. Frank. Anne?

(Anne *comes running up the stairs. She is thirteen, quick in her movements, interested in everything, mercurial in her emotions. She wears a cape, long wool socks and carries a schoolbag.*)

Mr. Frank (*introducing them*). My wife, Edith. Mr. and Mrs. Van Daan (Mrs. Frank *hurries over, shaking hands with them.*) . . .

---

[2] **Green Police:** the Nazi police who wore green uniforms.

their son, Peter . . . my daughters, Margot and Anne.

(Anne *gives a polite little curtsy as she shakes* Mr. Van Daan's *hand. Then she immediately starts off on a tour of investigation of her new home, going upstairs to the attic room.* Miep *and* Mr. Kraler *are putting the various things they have brought on the shelves.*)

Mr. Kraler. I'm sorry there is still so much confusion.

Mr. Frank. Please. Don't think of it. After all, we'll have plenty of leisure to arrange everything ourselves.

Miep (*to* Mrs. Frank). We put the stores of food you sent in here. Your drugs are here . . . soap, linen here.

Mrs. Frank. Thank you, Miep.

Miep. I made up the beds . . . the way Mr. Frank and Mr. Kraler said. (*She starts out.*) Forgive me. I have to hurry. I've got to go to the other side of town to get some ration books[3] for you.

Mrs. Van Daan. Ration books? If they see our names on ration books, they'll know we're here.

Mr. Kraler. There isn't anything . . . } *Together*
Miep. Don't worry. Your names won't be on them. (*as she hurries out*) I'll be up later.

Mr. Frank. Thank you, Miep.

Mrs. Frank (*to* Mr. Kraler). It's illegal, then, the ration books? We've never done anything illegal.

Mr. Frank. We won't be living here exactly according to regulations. (*As* Mr. Kraler *reassures* Mrs. Frank, *he takes various small things, such as matches, soap, etc., from his pockets, handing them to her.*)

Mr. Kraler. This isn't the black market,[4] Mrs. Frank. This is what we call the white market . . . helping all of the hundreds and hundreds who are hiding out in Amsterdam.

(*The carillon is heard playing the quarter-hour before eight.* Mr. Kraler *looks at his watch.* Anne *stops at the window as she comes down the stairs.*)

Anne. It's the Westertoren!

Mr. Kraler. I must go. I must be out of here and downstairs in the office before the workmen get here. (*He starts for the stairs leading out.*) Miep or I, or both of us, will be up each day to bring you food and news and find out what your needs are. Tomorrow I'll get you a better bolt for the door at the foot of the stairs. It needs a bolt that you can throw yourself and open only at our signal. (*to* Mr. Frank) Oh . . . You'll tell them about the noise?

Mr. Frank. I'll tell them.

---

[3] **ration books:** books of stamps or coupons issued by the government in wartime. With these coupons, people could purchase scarce items, such as food, clothing, and gasoline.

[4] **black market:** a system for selling goods illegally, in violation of rationing and other restrictions.

Mr. Kraler. Good-bye then for the moment. I'll come up again, after the workmen leave.

Mr. Frank. Good-bye, Mr. Kraler.

Mrs. Frank (*shaking his hand*). How can we thank you? (*The others murmur their good-byes.*)

Mr. Kraler. I never thought I'd live to see the day when a man like Mr. Frank would have to go into hiding. When you think—(*He breaks off, going out.* Mr. Frank *follows him down the steps, bolting the door after him. In the interval before he returns,* Peter *goes over to* Margot, *shaking hands with her. As* Mr. Frank *comes back up the steps,* Mrs. Frank *questions him anxiously.*)

Mrs. Frank. What did he mean, about the noise?

Mr. Frank. First let us take off some of these clothes. (*They all start to take off garment after garment. On each of their coats, sweaters, blouses, suits, dresses, is another yellow Star of David.* Mr. and Mrs. Frank *are underdressed quite simply. The others wear several things, sweaters, extra dresses, bathrobes, aprons, nightgowns, etc.*)

Mr. Van Daan. It's a wonder we weren't arrested, walking along the streets . . . Petronella with a fur coat in July . . . and that cat of Peter's crying all the way.

Anne (*as she is removing a pair of panties*). A cat?

Mrs. Frank (*shocked*). Anne, please!

Anne. It's all right. I've got on three more. (*She pulls off two more. Finally, as they have all removed their surplus clothes, they look to* Mr. Frank, *waiting for him to speak.*)

Mr. Frank. Now. About the noise. While the men are in the building below, we must have complete quiet. Every sound can be heard down there, not only in the workrooms, but in the offices too. The men come at about eight-thirty, and leave at about five-thirty. So, to be perfectly safe, from eight in the morning until six in the evening we must move only when it is necessary, and then in stockinged feet. We must not speak above a whisper. We must not run any water. We cannot use the sink, or even, forgive me, the w.c.[5] The pipes go down through the workrooms. It would be heard. No trash . . . (Mr. Frank *stops abruptly as he hears the sound of marching feet from the street below. Everyone is motionless, paralyzed with fear.* Mr. Frank *goes quietly into the room on the right to look down out of the window.* Anne *runs after him, peering out with him. The tramping feet pass without stopping. The tension is relieved.* Mr. Frank, *followed by* Anne, *returns to the main room and resumes his instructions to the group.*) . . . No trash must ever be thrown out which might reveal that someone is living up here . . . not even a potato

---

[5] **w.c.:** water closet; toilet.

paring. We must burn everything in the stove at night. This is the way we must live until it is over, if we are to survive.

(*There is silence for a second.*)

Mrs. Frank. Until it is over.

Mr. Frank (*reassuringly*). After six we can move about . . . we can talk and laugh and have our supper and read and play games . . . just as we would at home. (*He looks at his watch.*) And now I think it would be wise if we all went to our rooms, and were settled before eight o'clock. Mrs. Van Daan, you and your husband will be upstairs. I regret that there's no place up there for Peter. But he will be here, near us. This will be our common room, where we'll meet to talk and eat and read, like one family.

Mr. Van Daan. And where do you and Mrs. Frank sleep?

Mr. Frank. This room is also our bedroom.

Mrs. Van Daan. That isn't right. We'll sleep here and you take the room upstairs.

Mr. Van Daan. It's your place.

} *Together*

Mr. Frank. Please. I've thought this out for weeks. It's the best arrangement. The only arrangement.

Mrs. Van Daan (*to* Mr. Frank). Never, never can we thank you. (*then to* Mrs. Frank) I don't know what would have happened to us, if it hadn't been for Mr. Frank.

Mr. Frank. You don't know how your husband helped me when I came to this country . . . knowing no one . . . not able to speak the language. I can never repay him for that. (*going to* Van Daan) May I help you with your things?

Mr. Van Daan. No. No. (*to* Mrs. Van Daan) Come along, *liefje.*[6]

Mrs. Van Daan. You'll be all right, Peter? You're not afraid?

Peter (*embarrassed*). Please, Mother.

(*They start up the stairs to the attic room above.* Mr. Frank *turns to* Mrs. Frank.)

Mr. Frank. You too must have some rest, Edith. You didn't close your eyes last night. Nor you, Margot.

Anne. I slept, Father. Wasn't that funny? I knew it was the last night in my own bed, and yet I slept soundly.

Mr. Frank. I'm glad, Anne. Now you'll be able to help me straighten things in here. (*to* Mrs. Frank *and* Margot) Come with me . . . You and Margot rest in this room for the time being. (*He picks up their clothes, starting for the room on the right.*)

Mrs. Frank. You're sure . . . ? I could help . . . And Anne hasn't had her milk . . .

Mr. Frank. I'll give it to her. (*to* Anne *and* Peter) Anne, Peter . . . it's best that you take off your

---

[6] ***liefje*** (lēf′yə) *Dutch:* little darling.

shoes now, before you forget. (*He leads the way to the room, followed by* Margot.)

Mrs. Frank. You're sure you're not tired, Anne?

Anne. I feel fine. I'm going to help Father.

Mrs. Frank. Peter, I'm glad you are to be with us.

490 **Peter.** Yes, Mrs. Frank.

(Mrs. Frank *goes to join* Mr. Frank *and* Margot.)(*During the following scene* Mr. Frank *helps Margot and* Mrs. Frank *to hang up their clothes. Then he persuades them both to lie down and rest. The Van Daans in their room above settle themselves. In the main room* Anne *and* Peter *remove their shoes.* Peter *takes his*
500 *cat out of the carrier.*)

Anne. What's your cat's name?

Peter. Mouschi.[7]

Anne. Mouschi! Mouschi! Mouschi! (*She picks up the cat, walking away with it. To* Peter.) I love cats. I have one . . . a darling little cat. But they made me leave her behind. I left some food and a note for the neighbors to take care
510 of her . . . I'm going to miss her terribly. What is yours? A him or a her?

Peter. He's a tom. He doesn't like strangers.

(*He takes the cat from her, putting it back in its carrier.*)

Anne (*unabashed*). Then I'll have to stop being a stranger, won't I? Is he fixed?

520 **Peter** (*startled*). Huh?

Anne. Did you have him fixed?

Peter. No.

Anne. Oh, you ought to have him fixed—to keep him from—you know, fighting. Where did you go to school?

Peter. Jewish Secondary.

Anne. But that's where Margot and I go! I never saw you around.

530 **Peter.** I used to see you . . . sometimes . . .

Anne. You did?

Peter. . . . in the school yard. You were always in the middle of a bunch of kids. (*He takes a penknife from his pocket.*)

Anne. Why didn't you ever come over?

Peter. I'm sort of a lone wolf. (*He*
540 *starts to rip off his Star of David.*)

Anne. What are you doing?

Peter. Taking it off.

Anne. But you can't do that. They'll arrest you if you go out without your star.

(*He tosses his knife on the table.*)

Peter. Who's going out?

Anne. Why, of course! You're right! Of course we don't need them any
550 more. (*She picks up his knife and starts to take her star off.*) I wonder

---

[7] **Mouschi** (mōō´shē)

what our friends will think when we don't show up today?

Peter. I didn't have any dates with anyone.

Anne. Oh, I did. I had a date with Jopie to go and play ping-pong at her house. Do you know Jopie de Waal?[8]

Peter. No.

Anne. Jopie's my best friend. I wonder what she'll think when she telephones and there's no answer? . . . Probably she'll go over to the house . . . I wonder what she'll think . . . we left everything as if we'd suddenly been called away . . . breakfast dishes in the sink . . . beds not made . . . (*As she pulls off her star, the cloth underneath shows clearly the color and form of the star.*) Look! It's still there! (Peter *goes over to the stove with his star.*) What're you going to do with yours?

Peter. Burn it.

Anne (*She starts to throw hers in, and cannot.*) It's funny, I can't throw mine away. I don't know why.

Peter. You can't throw . . . ? Something they branded you with . . . ? That they made you wear so they could spit on you?

Anne. I know. I know. But after all, it *is* the Star of David, isn't it?

(*In the bedroom, right,* Margot *and* Mrs. Frank *are lying down.* Mr. Frank *starts quietly out.*)

Peter. Maybe it's different for a girl.

(Mr. Frank *comes into the main room.*)

Mr. Frank. Forgive me, Peter. Now let me see. We must find a bed for your cat. (*He goes to a cupboard.*) I'm glad you brought your cat. Anne was feeling so badly about hers. (*getting a used small washtub*) Here we are. Will it be comfortable in that?

Peter (*gathering up his things*). Thanks.

Mr. Frank (*opening the door of the room on the left*). And here is your room. But I warn you, Peter, you can't grow any more. Not an inch, or you'll have to sleep with your feet out of the skylight. Are you hungry?

Peter. No.

Mr. Frank. We have some bread and butter.

Peter. No, thank you.

Mr. Frank. You can have it for luncheon then. And tonight we will have a real supper . . . our first supper together.

Peter. Thanks. Thanks.

(*He goes into his room. During the following scene he arranges his possessions in his new room.*)

Mr. Frank. That's a nice boy, Peter.

Anne. He's awfully shy, isn't he?

---

[8] **Jopie de Waal** (yō′pē də väl′)

Mr. Frank. You'll like him, I know.

Anne. I certainly hope so, since he's the only boy I'm likely to see for months and months.

(Mr. Frank *sits down, taking off his shoes.*)

Mr. Frank. Annele,[9] there's a box there. Will you open it? (*He indicates a carton on the couch. Anne brings it to the center table. In the street below there is the sound of children playing.*)

Anne (*as she opens the carton*). You know the way I'm going to think of it here? I'm going to think of it as a boarding house. A very peculiar summer boarding house, like the one that we—(*She breaks off as she pulls out some photographs.*) Father! My movie stars! I was wondering where they were! I was looking for them this morning . . . and Queen Wilhelmina! How wonderful!

Mr. Frank. There's something more. Go on. Look further. (*He goes over to the sink, pouring a glass of milk from a thermos bottle.*)

Anne (*pulling out a pasteboard-bound book*). A diary! (*She throws her arms around her father.*) I've never had a diary. And I've always longed for one. (*She looks around the room.*) Pencil, pencil, pencil, pencil. (*She starts down the stairs.*) I'm going down to the office to get a pencil.

Mr. Frank. Anne! No! (*He goes after her, catching her by the arm and pulling her back.*)

Anne (*startled*). But there's no one in the building now.

Mr. Frank. It doesn't matter. I don't want you ever to go beyond that door.

Anne (*sobered*). Never . . . ? Not even at nighttime, when everyone is gone? Or on Sundays? Can't I go down to listen to the radio?

Mr. Frank. Never. I am sorry, Anneke. It isn't safe. No, you must never go beyond that door.

(*For the first time* Anne *realizes what "going into hiding" means.*)

Anne. I see.

Mr. Frank. It'll be hard, I know. But always remember this, Anneke. There are no walls, there are no bolts, no locks that anyone can put on your mind. Miep will bring us books. We will read history, poetry, mythology. (*He gives her the glass of milk.*) Here's your milk. (*With his arm about her, they go over to the couch, sitting down side by side.*) As a matter of fact, between us, Anne, being here has certain advantages for you. For instance, you remember the battle you had with your mother the other day on the subject of overshoes? You said you'd rather die than wear overshoes. But in the end you had to wear them? Well now, you see, for as long as we are here you will never have to wear overshoes! Isn't that good? And the coat that

---

[9] **Annele/Anneke:** a nickname for Anne.

you inherited from Margot, you won't have to wear that any more. And the piano! You won't have to practice on the piano. I tell you, this is going to be a fine life for you!

(Anne's *panic is gone.* Peter *appears in the doorway of his room, with a saucer in his hand. He is carrying his cat.*)

Peter. I . . . I . . . I thought I'd better get some water for Mouschi before . . .

Mr. Frank. Of course.

(*As he starts toward the sink the carillon begins to chime the hour of eight. He tiptoes to the window at the back and looks down at the street below. He turns to* Peter, *indicating in pantomime that it is too late.* Peter *starts back for his room. He steps on a creaking board. The three of them are frozen for a minute in fear. As* Peter *starts away again,* Anne *tiptoes over to him and pours some of the milk from her glass into the saucer for the cat.* Peter *squats on the floor, putting the milk before the cat.* Mr. Frank *gives* Anne *his fountain pen, and then goes into the room at the right. For a second* Anne *watches the cat, then she goes over to the center table, and opens her diary.*

In the room at the right, Mrs. Frank *has sat up quickly at the sound of the carillon.* Mr. Frank *comes in and sits down beside her on the settee, his arm comfortingly around her.*

Upstairs, in the attic room, Mr. *and* Mrs. Van Daan *have hung their clothes in the closet and are now seated on the iron bed.* Mrs. Van Daan *leans back exhausted.* Mr. Van Daan *fans her with a newspaper.*

Anne *starts to write in her diary. The lights dim out, the curtain falls.*

In the darkness Anne's Voice *comes to us again, faintly at first, and then with growing strength.*)

Anne's Voice. I expect I should be describing what it feels like to go into hiding. But I really don't know yet myself. I only know it's funny never to be able to go outdoors . . . never to breathe fresh air . . . never to run and shout and jump. It's the silence in the nights that frightens me most. Every time I hear a creak in the house, or a step on the street outside, I'm sure they're coming for us. The days aren't so bad. At least we know that Miep and Mr. Kraler are down there below us in the office. Our protectors, we call them. I asked Father what would happen to them if the Nazis found out they were hiding us. Pim said that they would suffer the same fate that we would . . . Imagine! They know this, and yet when they come up here, they're always cheerful and gay as if there were nothing in the world to bother them . . . Friday, the twenty-first of August, nineteen forty-two. Today I'm going to tell you our general news. Mother is unbearable. She insists on treating me like a baby, which I loathe. Otherwise things are going better. The weather is . . .

(*As* Anne's Voice *is fading out, the curtain rises on the scene.*)

Scene 3

It is a little after six o'clock in the evening, two months later.

Margot is in the bedroom at the right, studying. Mr. Van Daan is lying down in the attic room above.

The rest of the "family" is in the main room. Anne *and* Peter *sit opposite each other at the center table, where they have been doing their lessons.* Mrs. Frank *is on the couch.* Mrs. Van Daan *is seated with her fur coat, on which she has been sewing, in her lap. None of them are wearing their shoes.*

Their eyes are on Mr. Frank, waiting for him to give them the signal which will release them from their day-long quiet. Mr. Frank, his shoes in his hand, stands looking down out of the window at the back, watching to be sure that all of the workmen have left the building below.

After a few seconds of motionless silence, Mr. Frank *turns from the window.*

Mr. Frank (*quietly, to the group*). It's safe now. The last workman has left. (*There is an immediate stir of relief.*)

Anne (*Her pent-up energy explodes*). WHEE!

Mrs. Frank (*startled, amused*). Anne!

Mrs. Van Daan. I'm first for the w.c. (*She hurries off to the bathroom.* Mrs. Frank *puts on her shoes and starts up to the sink to prepare supper.* Anne *sneaks* Peter's *shoes from under the table and hides them behind her back.* Mr. Frank *goes in to* Margot's *room.*)

Mr. Frank (*to* Margot). Six o'clock. School's over.

(Margot *gets up, stretching.* Mr. Frank *sits down to put on his shoes. In the main room* Peter *tries to find his.*)

Peter (*to* Anne). Have you seen my shoes?

Anne (*innocently*). Your shoes?

Peter. You've taken them, haven't you?

Anne. I don't know what you're talking about.

Peter. You're going to be sorry!

Anne. Am I? (Peter *goes after her.* Anne, *with his shoes in her hand, runs from him, dodging behind her mother.*)

Mrs. Frank (*protesting*). Anne, dear!

Peter. Wait till I get you!

Anne. I'm waiting! (Peter *makes a lunge for her. They both fall to the floor.* Peter *pins her down, wrestling with her to get the shoes.*) Don't! Don't! Peter, stop it. Ouch!

Mrs. Frank. Anne! . . . Peter! (*Suddenly* Peter *becomes*

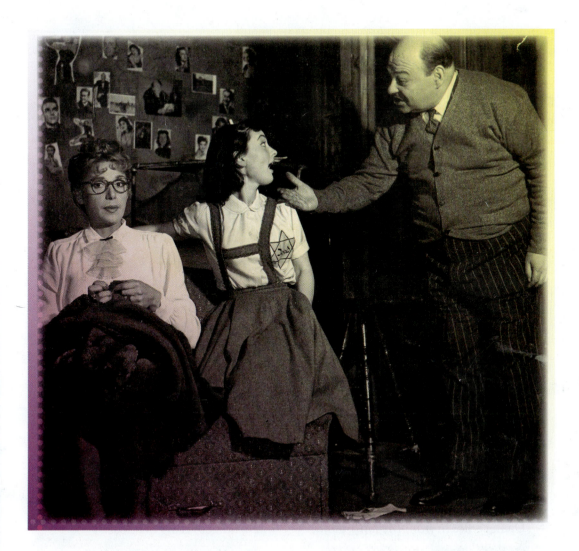

self-conscious. *He grabs his shoes roughly and starts for his room.*)

Anne (*following him*). Peter, where are you going? Come dance with me.

Peter. I tell you I don't know how.

Anne. I'll teach you.

Peter. I'm going to give Mouschi his dinner.

Anne. Can I watch?

Peter. He doesn't like people around while he eats.

Anne. Peter, please.

Peter. No! (*He goes into his room. Anne slams his door after him.*)

Mrs. Frank. Anne, dear, I think you shouldn't play like that with Peter. It's not dignified.

Anne. Who cares if it's dignified? I don't want to be dignified.

(Mr. Frank *and* Margot *come from the room on the right. Margot goes to help her mother. Mr. Frank starts for the center table to correct* Margot's *school papers.*)

Mrs. Frank (*to* Anne). You complain that I don't treat you like a grownup. But when I do, you resent it.

Anne. I only want some fun . . . someone to laugh and clown with . . . After you've sat still all day and hardly moved, you've got to have some fun. I don't know what's the matter with that boy.

Mr. Frank. He isn't used to girls. Give him a little time.

Anne. Time? Isn't two months time? I could cry. (*catching hold of* Margot) Come on, Margot . . . dance with me. Come on, please.

Margot. I have to help with supper.

Anne. You know we're going to forget how to dance . . . When we get out we won't remember a thing.

(*She starts to sing and dance by herself.* Mr. Frank *takes her in his arms, waltzing with her.* Mrs. Van Daan *comes in from the bathroom.*)

Mrs. Van Daan. Next? (*She looks around as she starts putting on her shoes.*) Where's Peter?

Anne (*as they are dancing*). Where would he be!

Mrs. Van Daan. He hasn't finished his lessons, has he? His father'll kill him if he catches him in there with that cat and his work not done.

(Mr. Frank *and* Anne *finish their dance. They bow to each other with extravagant formality.*) Anne, get him out of there, will you?

Anne (*at* Peter's *door*). Peter? Peter?

Peter (*opening the door a crack*). What is it?

Anne. Your mother says to come out.

Peter. I'm giving Mouschi his dinner.

Mrs. Van Daan. You know what your father says. (*She sits on the couch, sewing on the lining of her fur coat.*)

Peter. For heaven's sake, I haven't even looked at him since lunch.

Mrs. Van Daan. I'm just telling you, that's all.

Anne. I'll feed him.

Peter. I don't want you in there.

Mrs. Van Daan. Peter!

Peter (*to* Anne). Then give him his dinner and come right out, you hear? (*He comes back to the table.* Anne *shuts the door of* Peter's *room after her and disappears behind the curtain covering his closet.*)

Mrs. Van Daan (*to* Peter). Now is that any way to talk to your little girl friend?

Peter. Mother . . . for heaven's sake . . . will you please stop saying that?

Mrs. Van Daan. Look at him blush! Look at him!

Peter. Please! I'm not . . . anyway . . . let me alone, will you?

Mrs. Van Daan. He acts like it was something to be ashamed of. It's nothing to be ashamed of, to have a little girl friend.

Peter. You're crazy. She's only thirteen.

Mrs. Van Daan. So what? And you're sixteen. Just perfect. Your father's ten years older than I am. (*to Mr. Frank*) I warn you, Mr. Frank, if this war lasts much longer, we're going to be related and then . . .

Mr. Frank. *Mazeltov!*[10]

Mrs. Frank (*deliberately changing the conversation*). I wonder where Miep is. She's usually so prompt. (*Suddenly everything else is forgotten as they hear the sound of an automobile coming to a screeching stop in the street below. They are tense, motionless in their terror. The car starts away. A wave of relief sweeps over them. They pick up their occupations again.* Anne *flings open the door of* Peter's *room, making a dramatic entrance. She is dressed in* Peter's *clothes.* Peter *looks at her in fury. The others are amused.*)

Anne. Good evening, everyone. Forgive me if I don't stay. (*She jumps up on a chair.*) I have a friend waiting for me in there. My friend Tom. Tom Cat. Some people say that we look alike. But Tom has the most beautiful whiskers, and I have only a little fuzz. I am hoping . . . in time . . .

Peter. All right, Mrs. Quack Quack!

Anne (*outraged—jumping down*). Peter!

Peter. I heard about you . . . How you talked so much in class they called you Mrs. Quack Quack. How Mr. Smitter made you write a composition . . . "'Quack, quack,' said Mrs. Quack Quack."

Anne. Well, go on. Tell them the rest. How it was so good he read it out loud to the class and then read it to all his other classes!

Peter. Quack! Quack! Quack . . . Quack . . . Quack . . .

(Anne *pulls off the coat and trousers.*)

Anne. You are the most intolerable, insufferable boy I've ever met!

(*She throws the clothes down the stairwell.* Peter *goes down after them.*)

Peter. Quack, quack, quack!

Mrs. Van Daan (*to* Anne). That's right, Anneke! Give it to him!

Anne. With all the boys in the world . . . Why I had to get locked up with one like you! . . .

Peter. Quack, quack, quack, and from now on stay out of my room!

(*As* Peter *passes her,* Anne *puts out her foot, tripping him. He picks himself up, and goes on into his room.*)

Mrs. Frank (*quietly*). Anne, dear . . . your hair. (*She feels Anne's forehead.*) You're warm. Are you feeling all right?

Anne. Please, Mother. (*She goes over to the center table, slipping into her shoes.*)

---

[10] **Mazeltov!** (mä´zəl tôf´) *Hebrew*: Congratulations!

Mrs. Frank (*following her*). You haven't a fever, have you?

Anne (*pulling away*). No. No.

Mrs. Frank. You know we can't call a doctor here, ever. There's only one thing to do . . . watch carefully. Prevent an illness before it comes. Let me see your tongue.

Anne. Mother, this is perfectly absurd.

Mrs. Frank. Anne, dear, don't be such a baby. Let me see your tongue. (*As* Anne *refuses,* Mrs. Frank *appeals to* Mr. Frank.) Otto . . . ?

Mr. Frank. You hear your mother, Anne. (Anne *flicks out her tongue for a second, then turns away.*)

Mrs. Frank. Come on—open up! (*as* Anne *opens her mouth very wide*) You seem all right . . . but perhaps an aspirin . . .

Mrs. Van Daan. For heaven's sake, don't give that child any pills. I waited for fifteen minutes this morning for her to come out of the w.c.

Anne. I was washing my hair!

Mr. Frank. I think there's nothing the matter with our Anne that a ride on her bike, or a visit with her friend Jopie de Waal wouldn't cure. Isn't that so, Anne?

(Mr. Van Daan *comes down into the room. From outside we hear faint sounds of bombers going over and a burst of ack-ack.*)

Mr. Van Daan. Miep not come yet?

Mrs. Van Daan. The workmen just left, a little while ago.

Mr. Van Daan. What's for dinner tonight?

Mrs. Van Daan. Beans.

Mr. Van Daan. Not again!

Mrs. Van Daan. Poor Putti! I know. But what can we do? That's all that Miep brought us.

(Mr. Van Daan *starts to pace, his hands behind his back.* Anne *follows behind him, imitating him.*)

Anne. We are now in what is known as the "bean cycle." Beans boiled, beans en casserole, beans with strings, beans without strings . . .

(Peter *has come out of his room. He slides into his place at the table, becoming immediately absorbed in his studies.*)

Mr. Van Daan (*to* Peter). I saw you . . . in there, playing with your cat.

Mrs. Van Daan. He just went in for a second, putting his coat away. He's been out here all the time, doing his lessons.

Mr. Frank (*looking up from the papers*). Anne, you got an excellent in your history paper today . . . and very good in Latin.

Anne (*sitting beside him*). How about algebra?

Mr. Frank. I'll have to make a confession. Up until now I've managed to stay ahead of you in algebra. Today you caught up with me. We'll leave it to Margot to correct.

Anne. Isn't algebra *vile*, Pim!

Mr. Frank. Vile!

Margot (*to* Mr. Frank). How did I do?

Anne (*getting up*). Excellent, excellent, excellent, excellent!

Mr. Frank (*to* Margot). You should have used the subjunctive here . . .

Margot. Should I? . . . I thought . . . look here . . . I didn't use it here . . . (*The two become absorbed in the papers.*)

Anne. Mrs. Van Daan, may I try on your coat?

Mrs. Frank. No, Anne.

Mrs. Van Daan (*giving it to* Anne). It's all right . . . but careful with it. (Anne *puts it on and struts with it.*) My father gave me that the year before he died. He always bought the best that money could buy.

Anne. Mrs. Van Daan, did you have a lot of boy friends before you were married?

Mrs. Frank. Anne, that's a personal question. It's not courteous to ask personal questions.

Mrs. Van Daan. Oh I don't mind. (*to* Anne) Our house was always swarming with boys. When I was a girl we had . . .

Mr. Van Daan. Oh, God. Not again!

Mrs. Van Daan (*good-humored*). Shut up! (*Without a pause, to* Anne. Mr. Van Daan *mimics* Mrs. Van Daan, *speaking the first few words in unison with her.*) One summer we had a big house in Hilversum. The boys came buzzing round like bees around a jam pot. And when I was sixteen! . . . We were wearing our skirts very short those days and I had good-looking legs. (*She pulls up her skirt, going to* Mr. Frank.) I still have 'em. I may not be as pretty as I used to be, but I still have my legs. How about it, Mr. Frank?

Mr. Van Daan. All right. All right. We see them.

Mrs. Van Daan. I'm not asking you. I'm asking Mr. Frank.

Peter. Mother, for heaven's sake.

Mrs. Van Daan. Oh, I embarrass you, do I? Well, I just hope the girl you marry has as good. (*then to* Anne) My father used to worry about me, with so many boys hanging round. He told me, if any of them gets fresh, you say to him . . . "Remember, Mr. So-and-So, remember I'm a lady."

Anne. "Remember, Mr. So-and-So, remember I'm a lady." (*She gives* Mrs. Van Daan *her coat.*)

Mr. Van Daan. Look at you, talking that way in front of her! Don't you know she puts it all down in that diary?

Mrs. Van Daan. So, if she does? I'm only telling the truth!

(Anne *stretches out, putting her ear to the floor, listening to what is going on below. The sound of the bombers fades away.*)

Mrs. Frank (*setting the table*). Would you mind, Peter, if I moved you over to the couch?

Anne (*listening*). Miep must have the radio on.

(Peter *picks up his papers, going over to the couch beside* Mrs. Van Daan.)

Mr. Van Daan (*accusingly, to* Peter). Haven't you finished yet?

Peter. No.

Mr. Van Daan. You ought to be ashamed of yourself.

Peter. All right. All right. I'm a dunce. I'm a hopeless case. Why do I go on?

Mrs. Van Daan. You're not hopeless. Don't talk that way. It's just that you haven't anyone to help you, like the girls have. (*to* Mr. Frank) Maybe you could help him, Mr. Frank?

Mr. Frank. I'm sure that his father . . . ?

Mr. Van Daan. Not me. I can't do anything with him. He won't listen to me. You go ahead . . . if you want.

Mr. Frank (*going to* Peter). What about it, Peter? Shall we make our school coeducational?

Mrs. Van Daan (*kissing* Mr. Frank). You're an angel, Mr. Frank. An angel. I don't know why I didn't meet you before I met that one there.

Here, sit down, Mr. Frank . . . (*She forces him down on the couch beside* Peter.) Now, Peter, you listen to Mr. Frank.

Mr. Frank. It might be better for us to go into Peter's room. (Peter *jumps up eagerly, leading the way.*)

Mrs. Van Daan. That's right. You go in there, Peter. You listen to Mr. Frank. Mr. Frank is a highly educated man. (*As* Mr. Frank *is about to follow* Peter *into his room,* Mrs. Frank *stops him and wipes the lipstick from his lips. Then she closes the door after them.*)

Anne (*on the floor, listening*). Shh! I can hear a man's voice talking.

Mr. Van Daan (*to* Anne). Isn't it bad enough here without your sprawling all over the place? (Anne *sits up.*)

Mrs. Van Daan (*to* Mr. Van Daan). If you didn't smoke so much, you wouldn't be so bad-tempered.

Mr. Van Daan. Am I smoking? Do you see me smoking?

Mrs. Van Daan. Don't tell me you've used up all those cigarettes.

Mr. Van Daan. One package. Miep only brought me one package.

Mrs. Van Daan. It's a filthy habit anyway. It's a good time to break yourself.

Mr. Van Daan. Oh, stop it, please.

Mrs. Van Daan. You're smoking up all our money. You know that, don't you?

Mr. Van Daan. Will you shut up? (*During this,* Mrs. Frank *and* Margot *have studiously kept their eyes down. But* Anne, *seated on the floor, has been following the discussion interestedly.* Mr. Van Daan *turns to see her staring up at him.*) And what are you staring at?

Anne. I never heard grownups quarrel before. I thought only children quarreled.

Mr. Van Daan. This isn't a quarrel! It's a discussion. And I never heard children so rude before.

Anne (*rising, indignantly*). I, rude!

Mr. Van Daan. Yes!

Mrs. Frank (*quickly*). Anne, will you get me my knitting? (Anne *goes to get it.*) I must remember, when Miep comes, to ask her to bring me some more wool.

Margot (*going to her room*). I need some hairpins and some soap. I made a list. (*She goes into her bedroom to get the list.*)

Mrs. Frank (*to* Anne). Have you some library books for Miep when she comes?

Anne. It's a wonder that Miep has a life of her own, the way we make her run errands for us. Please, Miep, get me some starch. Please take my hair out and have it cut. Tell me all the latest news, Miep.

(*She goes over, kneeling on the couch beside* Mrs. Van Daan.) Did you know she was engaged? His name is Dirk, and Miep's afraid the Nazis will ship him off to Germany to work in one of their war plants. That's what they're doing with some of the young Dutchmen . . . they pick them up off the streets—

Mr. Van Daan (*interrupting*). Don't you ever get tired of talking? Suppose you try keeping still for five minutes. Just five minutes. (*He starts to pace again. Again* Anne *follows him, mimicking him.* Mrs. Frank *jumps up and takes her by the arm up to the sink, and gives her a glass of milk.*)

Mrs. Frank. Come here, Anne. It's time for your glass of milk.

Mr. Van Daan. Talk, talk, talk. I never heard such a child. Where is my . . . ? Every evening it's the same, talk, talk, talk. (*He looks around.*) Where is my . . . ?

Mrs. Van Daan. What're you looking for?

Mr. Van Daan. My pipe. Have you seen my pipe?

Mrs. Van Daan. What good's a pipe? You haven't got any tobacco.

Mr. Van Daan. At least I'll have something to hold in my mouth! (*opening* Margot's *bedroom door*) Margot, have you seen my pipe?

Margot. It was on the table last night. (Anne *puts her glass of milk on the table and picks up his pipe, hiding it behind her back.*)

Mr. Van Daan. I know. I know. Anne, did you see my pipe? . . . Anne!

Mrs. Frank. Anne, Mr. Van Daan is speaking to you.

Anne. Am I allowed to talk now?

Mr. Van Daan. You're the most aggravating . . . The trouble with you is, you've been spoiled. What you need is a good old-fashioned spanking.

Anne (*mimicking* Mrs. Van Daan). "Remember, Mr. So-and-So, remember I'm a lady." (*She thrusts the pipe into his mouth, then picks up her glass of milk.*)

Mr. Van Daan (*restraining himself with difficulty*). Why aren't you nice and quiet like your sister Margot? Why do you have to show off all the time? Let me give you a little advice, young lady. Men don't like that kind of thing in a girl. You know that? A man likes a girl who'll listen to him once in a while . . . a domestic girl, who'll keep her house shining for her husband . . . who loves to cook and sew and . . .

Anne. I'd cut my throat first! I'd open my veins! I'm going to be remarkable! I'm going to Paris . . .

Mr. Van Daan (*scoffingly*). Paris!

Anne. . . . to study music and art.

Mr. Van Daan. Yeah! Yeah!

Anne. I'm going to be a famous dancer or singer . . . or something wonderful. (*She makes a wide gesture, spilling the glass of milk on the fur coat in* Mrs. Van Daan's *lap.* Margot *rushes quickly over with a towel.* Anne *tries to brush the milk off with her skirt.*)

Mrs. Van Daan. Now look what you've done . . . you clumsy little fool! My beautiful fur coat my father gave me . . .

Anne. I'm so sorry.

Mrs. Van Daan. What do you care? It isn't yours . . . So go on, ruin it! Do you know what that coat cost? Do you? And now look at it! Look at it!

Anne. I'm very, very sorry.

Mrs. Van Daan. I could kill you for this. I could just kill you! (Mrs. Van Daan *goes up the stairs, clutching the coat.* Mr. Van Daan *starts after her.*)

Mr. Van Daan. Petronella . . . liefje! Liefje! . . . Come back . . . the supper . . . come back!

Mrs. Frank. Anne, you must not behave in that way.

Anne. It was an accident. Anyone can have an accident.

Mrs. Frank. I don't mean that. I mean the answering back. You must not answer back. They are our guests. We must always show the greatest courtesy to them. We're all living under terrible tension. (*She stops as* Margot *indicates that* Van Daan *can hear. When he is gone, she continues.*) That's why we must control ourselves . . . You don't hear Margot getting into arguments with them, do you? Watch Margot. She's always courteous with them. Never familiar. She keeps her distance. And they respect her for it. Try to be like Margot.

Anne. And have them walk all over me, the way they do her? No, thanks!

Mrs. Frank. I'm not afraid that anyone is going to walk all over you, Anne. I'm afraid for other people, that you'll walk on them. I don't know what happens to you, Anne. You are wild, self-willed. If I had ever talked to my mother as you talk to me . . .

Anne. Things have changed. People aren't like that any more. "Yes, Mother." "No, Mother." "Anything you say, Mother." I've got to fight things out for myself! Make something of myself!

Mrs. Frank. It isn't necessary to fight to do it. Margot doesn't fight, and isn't she . . . ?

Anne (*violently rebellious*). Margot! Margot! Margot! That's all I hear from everyone . . . how wonderful Margot is . . . "Why aren't you like Margot?"

Margot (*protesting*). Oh, come on, Anne, don't be so . . .

Anne (*paying no attention*). Everything she does is right, and everything I do is wrong! I'm the goat around here! . . . You're all against me! . . . And you worst of all!

(*She rushes off into her room and throws herself down on the settee, stifling her sobs.* Mrs. Frank *sighs and starts toward the stove.*)

Mrs. Frank (*to* Margot). Let's put the soup on the stove . . . if there's anyone who cares to eat. Margot, will you take the bread out? (Margot *gets the bread from the cupboard.*) I don't know how we can go on living this way . . . I can't say a word to Anne . . . she flies at me . . .

Margot. You know Anne. In half an hour she'll be out here, laughing and joking.

Mrs. Frank. And . . . (*She makes a motion upwards, indicating the Van Daans.*) . . . I told your father it wouldn't work . . . but no . . . no . . . he had to ask them, he said . . . he owed it to him, he said. Well, he knows now that I was right! These quarrels! . . . This bickering!

Margot (*with a warning look*). Shush. Shush.

(*The buzzer for the door sounds.* Mrs. Frank *gasps, startled.*)

Mrs. Frank. Every time I hear that sound, my heart stops!

Margot (*starting for* Peter's *door*). It's Miep. (*She knocks at the door.*) Father?

(Mr. Frank *comes quickly from* Peter's *room.*)

Mr. Frank. Thank you, Margot. (*as he goes down the steps to open the outer door*) Has everyone his list?

Margot. I'll get my books. (*giving her mother a list*) Here's your list.

(Margot *goes into her and* Anne's *bedroom on the right.* Anne *sits up, hiding her tears, as* Margot *comes in.*) Miep's here.

(Margot *picks up her books and goes back.* Anne *hurries over to the mirror, smoothing her hair.*)

Mr. Van Daan (*coming down the stairs*). Is it Miep?

Margot. Yes. Father's gone down to let her in.

Mr. Van Daan. At last I'll have some cigarettes!

Mrs. Frank (*to* Mr. Van Daan). I can't tell you how unhappy I am about Mrs. Van Daan's coat. Anne should never have touched it.

Mr. Van Daan. She'll be all right.

Mrs. Frank. Is there anything I can do?

Mr. Van Daan. Don't worry.

(*He turns to meet* Miep. *But it is not* Miep *who comes up the steps. It is* Mr. Kraler, *followed by* Mr. Frank. *Their faces are grave.* Anne *comes from the bedroom.* Peter *comes from his room.*)

Mrs. Frank. Mr. Kraler!

Mr. Van Daan. How are you, Mr. Kraler?

Margot. This is a surprise.

Mrs. Frank. When Mr. Kraler comes, the sun begins to shine.

Mr. Van Daan. Miep is coming?

Mr. Kraler. Not tonight.

(Kraler *goes to* Margot *and* Mrs. Frank *and* Anne, *shaking hands with them.*)

Mrs. Frank. Wouldn't you like a cup of coffee? . . . Or, better still, will you have supper with us?

Mr. Frank. Mr. Kraler has something to talk over with us. Something has happened, he says, which demands an immediate decision.

Mrs. Frank (*fearful*). What is it?

(Mr. Kraler *sits down on the couch. As he talks he takes bread, cabbages, milk, etc., from his briefcase, giving them to* Margot *and* Anne *to put away.*)

Mr. Kraler. Usually, when I come up here, I try to bring you some bit of good news. What's the use of telling you the bad news when there's nothing that you can do about it? But today something has happened . . . Dirk . . . Miep's Dirk, you know, came to me just now. He tells me that he has a Jewish friend living near him. A dentist. He says he's in trouble. He begged me, could I do anything for this man? Could I find him a hiding place? . . . So I've come to you . . . I know it's a terrible thing to ask of you, living as you are, but would you take him in with you?

Mr. Frank. Of course we will.

Mr. Kraler (*rising*). It'll be just for a night or two . . . until I find some other place. This happened so suddenly that I didn't know where to turn.

Mr. Frank. Where is he?

Mr. Kraler. Downstairs in the office.

Mr. Frank. Good. Bring him up.

Mr. Kraler. His name is Dussel . . . Jan Dussel.

Mr. Frank. Dussel . . . I think I know him.

Mr. Kraler. I'll get him. (*He goes quickly down the steps and out. Mr. Frank suddenly becomes conscious of the others.*)

Mr. Frank. Forgive me. I spoke without consulting you. But I knew you'd feel as I do.

Mr. Van Daan. There's no reason for you to consult anyone. This is your place. You have a right to do exactly as you please. The only thing I feel . . . there's so little food as it is . . . and to take in another person . . .

(*Peter turns away, ashamed of his father.*)

Mr. Frank. We can stretch the food a little. It's only for a few days.

Mr. Van Daan. You want to make a bet?

Mrs. Frank. I think it's fine to have him. But, Otto, where are you going to put him? Where?

Peter. He can have my bed. I can sleep on the floor. I wouldn't mind.

Mr. Frank. That's good of you, Peter. But your room's too small . . . even for *you*.

Anne. I have a much better idea. I'll come in here with you and Mother, and Margot can take Peter's room and Peter can go in our room with Mr. Dussel.

Margot. That's right. We could do that.

Mr. Frank. No, Margot. You mustn't sleep in that room . . . neither you nor Anne. Mouschi has caught some rats in there. Peter's brave. He doesn't mind.

Anne. Then how about *this*? I'll come in here with you and Mother, and Mr. Dussel can have my bed.

Mrs. Frank. No. No. *No!* Margot will come in here with us and he can have her bed. It's the only way. Margot, bring your things in here. Help her, Anne.

(*Margot hurries into her room to get her things.*)

Anne (*to her mother*). Why Margot? Why can't I come in here?

Mrs. Frank. Because it wouldn't be proper for Margot to sleep with a . . . Please, Anne. Don't argue. Please. (*Anne starts slowly away.*)

Mr. Frank. (*to Anne*). You don't mind sharing your room with Mr. Dussel, do you, Anne?

Anne. No. No, of course not.

Mr. Frank. Good. (*Anne goes off into her bedroom, helping Margot. Mr. Frank starts to search in the cupboards.*) Where's the cognac?

Mrs. Frank. It's there. But, Otto, I was saving it in case of illness.

Mr. Frank. I think we couldn't find a better time to use it. Peter, will you get five glasses for me?

(Peter *goes for the glasses. Margot comes out of her bedroom, carrying her possessions, which she hangs behind a curtain in the main room. Mr. Frank finds the cognac and pours it into the five glasses that Peter brings him. Mr. Van Daan stands looking on sourly. Mrs. Van Daan comes downstairs and looks around at all the bustle.*)

Mrs. Van Daan. What's happening? What's going on?

Mr. Van Daan. Someone's moving in with us.

Mrs. Van Daan. In here? You're joking.

Margot. It's only for a night or two . . . until Mr. Kraler finds him another place.

Mr. Van Daan. Yeah! Yeah!

(Mr. Frank *hurries over as* Mr. Kraler *and* Dussel *come up.* Dussel *is a man in his late fifties, meticulous, finicky . . . bewildered now. He wears a raincoat. He carries a briefcase, stuffed full, and a small medicine case.*)

Mr. Frank. Come in, Mr. Dussel.

Mr. Kraler. This is Mr. Frank.

Dussel. Mr. Otto Frank?

Mr. Frank. Yes. Let me take your things.

(*He takes the hat and briefcase, but* Dussel *clings to his medicine case.*) This is my wife Edith . . . Mr. and Mrs. Van Daan . . . their son, Peter . . . and my daughters, Margot and Anne.

(Dussel *shakes hands with everyone.*)

Mr. Kraler. Thank you, Mr. Frank. Thank you all. Mr. Dussel, I leave you in good hands. Oh . . . Dirk's coat.

(Dussel *hurriedly takes off the raincoat, giving it to* Mr. Kraler. *Underneath is his white dentist's jacket, with a yellow Star of David on it.*)

Dussel (*to* Mr. Kraler). What can I say to thank you . . . ?

Mrs. Frank (*to* Dussel). Mr. Kraler and Miep . . . They're our life line. Without them we couldn't live.

Mr. Kraler. Please. Please. You make us seem very heroic. It isn't that at all. We simply don't like the Nazis. (*to* Mr. Frank, *who offers him a drink*) No, thanks. (*then going on*) We don't like their methods. We don't like . . .

Mr. Frank (*smiling*). I know. I know. "No one's going to tell us Dutchmen what to do with our damn Jews!"

Mr. Kraler (*to* Dussel). Pay no attention to Mr. Frank. I'll be up tomorrow to see that they're treating you right. (*to* Mr. Frank) Don't trouble to come down again. Peter will bolt the door after me, won't you, Peter?

Peter. Yes, sir.

Mr. Frank. Thank you, Peter. I'll do it.

Mr. Kraler. Good night. Good night.

Group. Good night, Mr. Kraler. We'll see you tomorrow, (*etc., etc.*)

(Mr. Kraler *goes out with* Mr. Frank. Mrs. Frank *gives each one of the "grownups" a glass of cognac.*)

Mrs. Frank. Please, Mr. Dussel, sit down.

(Mr. Dussel *sinks into a chair.* Mrs. Frank *gives him a glass of cognac.*)

Dussel. I'm dreaming. I know it. I can't believe my eyes. Mr. Otto Frank here! (*to* Mrs. Frank) You're not in Switzerland then? A woman told me . . . She said she'd gone to your house . . . the door was open, everything was in disorder, dishes in the sink. She said she found a piece of paper in the wastebasket with an address scribbled on it . . . an address in Zurich. She said you must have escaped to Zurich.

Anne. Father put that there purposely . . . just so people would think that very thing!

Dussel. And you've been here all the time?

Mrs. Frank. All the time . . . ever since July.

(Anne *speaks to her father as he comes back*.)

Anne. It worked, Pim . . . the address you left! Mr. Dussel says that people believe we escaped to Switzerland.

Mr. Frank. I'm glad . . . And now let's have a little drink to welcome Mr. Dussel. (*Before they can drink,* Mr. Dussel *bolts his drink.* Mr. Frank *smiles and raises his glass.*) To Mr. Dussel. Welcome. We're very honored to have you with us.

Mrs. Frank. To Mr. Dussel, welcome.

(*The* Van Daans *murmur a welcome. The "grown-ups" drink.*)

Mrs. Van Daan. Um. That was good.

Mr. Van Daan. Did Mr. Kraler warn you that you won't get much to eat here? You can imagine . . . three ration books among the seven of us . . . and now you make eight.

(Peter *walks away, humiliated. Outside a street organ is heard dimly.*)

Dussel (*rising*). Mr. Van Daan, you don't realize what is happening outside that you should warn me of a thing like that. You don't realize what's going on . . . (*As* Mr. Van Daan *starts his characteristic pacing,* Dussel *turns to speak to the others.*) Right here in Amsterdam every day hundreds of Jews disappear . . . They surround a block and search house by house. Children come home from school to find their parents gone. Hundreds are being deported . . . people that you and I know . . . the Hallensteins . . . the Wessels . . .

Mrs. Frank (*in tears*). Oh, no. No!

Dussel. They get their call-up notice . . . come to the Jewish theatre on such and such a day and hour . . . bring only what you can carry in a rucksack. And if you refuse the call-up notice, then they come and drag you from your home and ship you off to Mauthausen.[11] The death camp!

Mrs. Frank. We didn't know that things had got so much worse.

Dussel. Forgive me for speaking so.

---

[11] **Mauthausen** (mout´hou´zən): a Nazi concentration camp in Austria.

Anne (*coming to* Dussel). Do you know the de Waals? . . . What's become of them? Their daughter Jopie and I are in the same class. Jopie's my best friend.

Dussel. They are gone.

Anne. Gone?

Dussel. With all the others.

Anne. Oh, no. Not Jopie!

(*She turns away, in tears. Mrs. Frank motions to Margot to comfort her. Margot goes to Anne, putting her arms comfortingly around her.*)

Mrs. Van Daan. There were some people called Wagner. They lived near us . . . ?

Mr. Frank (*interrupting, with a glance at Anne*). I think we should put this off until later. We all have many questions we want to ask . . . But I'm sure that Mr. Dussel would like to get settled before supper.

Dussel. Thank you. I would. I brought very little with me.

Mr. Frank (*giving him his hat and briefcase*). I'm sorry we can't give you a room alone. But I hope you won't be too uncomfortable. We've had to make strict rules here . . . a schedule of hours . . . We'll tell you after supper. Anne, would you like to take Mr. Dussel to his room?

Anne (*controlling her tears*). If you'll come with me, Mr. Dussel? (*She starts for her room.*)

Dussel (*shaking hands with each in turn*). Forgive me if I haven't really expressed my gratitude to all of you. This has been such a shock to me. I'd always thought of myself as Dutch. I was born in Holland. My father was born in Holland, and my grandfather. And now . . . after all these years . . . (*He breaks off.*) If you'll excuse me.

(Dussel *gives a little bow and hurries off after* Anne. *Mr. Frank and the others are subdued.*)

Anne (*turning on the light*). Well, here we are.

(Dussel *looks around the room. In the main room* Margot *speaks to her mother.*)

Margot. The news sounds pretty bad, doesn't it? It's so different from what Mr. Kraler tells us. Mr. Kraler says things are improving.

Mr. Van Daan. I like it better the way Kraler tells it.

(*They resume their occupations, quietly.* Peter *goes off into his room. In* Anne's *room,* Anne *turns to* Dussel.)

Anne. You're going to share the room with me.

Dussel. I'm a man who's always lived alone. I haven't had to adjust myself to others. I hope you'll bear with me until I learn.

Anne. Let me help you. (*She takes his briefcase.*) Do you always live all alone? Have you no family at all?

Dussel. No one. (*He opens his medicine case and spreads his bottles on the dressing table.*)

Anne. How dreadful. You must be terribly lonely.

Dussel. I'm used to it.

Anne. I don't think I could ever get used to it. Didn't you even have a pet? A cat, or a dog?

Dussel. I have an allergy for fur-bearing animals. They give me asthma.

Anne. Oh, dear. Peter has a cat.

Dussel. Here? He has it here?

Anne. Yes. But we hardly ever see it. He keeps it in his room all the time. I'm sure it will be all right.

Dussel. Let us hope so.

(*He takes some pills to fortify himself.*)

Anne. That's Margot's bed, where you're going to sleep. I sleep on the sofa there. (*indicating the clothes hooks on the wall*) We cleared these off for your things. (*She goes over to the window.*) The best part about this room . . . you can look down and see a bit of the street and the canal. There's a houseboat . . . you can see the end of it . . . a bargeman lives there with his family . . . They have a baby and he's just beginning to walk and I'm so afraid he's going to fall into the canal some day. I watch him . . .

Dussel (*interrupting*). Your father spoke of a schedule.

Anne (*coming away from the window*). Oh, yes. It's mostly about the times we have to be quiet. And times for the w.c. You can use it now if you like.

Dussel (*stiffly*). No, thank you.

Anne. I suppose you think it's awful, my talking about a thing like that. But you don't know how important it can get to be, especially when you're frightened . . . About this room, the way Margot and I did . . . she had it to herself in the afternoons for studying, reading . . . lessons, you know . . . and I took the mornings. Would that be all right with you?

Dussel. I'm not at my best in the morning.

Anne. You stay here in the mornings then. I'll take the room in the afternoons.

Dussel. Tell me, when you're in here, what happens to me? Where am I spending my time? In there, with all the people?

Anne. Yes.

Dussel. I see. I see.

Anne. We have supper at half past six.

Dussel (*going over to the sofa*). Then, if you don't mind . . . I like to lie down quietly for ten minutes before eating. I find it helps the digestion.

Anne. Of course. I hope I'm not going to be too much of a bother to you. I seem to be able to get everyone's back up.

(*Dussel lies down on the sofa, curled up, his back to her.*)

Dussel. I always get along very well with children. My patients all bring their children to me, because they know I get on well with them. So don't you worry about that.

(Anne *leans over him, taking his hand and shaking it gratefully.*)

Anne. Thank you. Thank you, Mr. Dussel.

(*The lights dim to darkness. The curtain falls on the scene.* Anne's Voice *comes to us faintly at first, and then with increasing power.*)

Anne's Voice. . . . And yesterday I finished Cissy Van Marxvelt's latest book. I think she is a first-class writer. I shall definitely let my children read her. Monday the twenty-first of September, nineteen forty-two. Mr. Dussel and I had another battle yesterday. Yes, Mr. Dussel! According to him, nothing, I repeat . . . nothing, is right about me . . . my appearance, my character, my manners. While he was going on at me I thought . . . sometime I'll give you such a smack that you'll fly right up to the ceiling! Why is it that every grownup thinks he knows the way to bring up children? Particularly the grownups that never had any. I keep wishing that Peter was a girl instead of a boy. Then I would have someone to talk to. Margot's a darling, but she takes everything too seriously. To pause for a moment on the subject of Mrs. Van Daan. I must tell you that her attempts to flirt with Father are getting her nowhere. Pim, thank goodness, won't play.

(*As she is saying the last lines, the curtain rises on the darkened scene.* Anne's Voice *fades out.*)

Scene 4

It is the middle of the night, several months later. The stage is dark except for a little light which comes through the skylight in Peter's room.

Everyone is in bed. Mr. and Mrs. Frank *lie on the couch in the main room, which has been pulled out to serve as a makeshift double bed.*

Margot *is sleeping on a mattress on the floor in the main room, behind a curtain stretched across for privacy. The others are all in their accustomed rooms.*

From outside we hear two drunken soldiers singing "Lili Marlene." A girl's high giggle is heard. The sound of running feet is heard coming closer and then fading in the distance. Throughout the scene there is the distant sound of airplanes passing overhead.

A match suddenly flares up in the attic. We dimly see Mr. Van Daan. *He is getting his bearings. He comes quickly down the stairs, and goes to the cupboard where the food is stored. Again the match flares up, and is as quickly blown out. The dim figure is seen to steal back up the stairs.*

There is quiet for a second or two, broken only by the sound of airplanes, and running feet on the street below.

Suddenly, out of the silence and the dark, we hear Anne *scream.*

Anne (*screaming*). No! No! Don't ... don't take me!

(*She moans, tossing and crying in her sleep. The other people wake, terrified.* Dussel *sits up in bed, furious.*)

Dussel. Shush! Anne! Anne, for God's sake, shush!

Anne (*still in her nightmare*). Save me! Save me!

(*She screams and screams.* Dussel *gets out of bed, going over to her, trying to wake her.*)

Dussel. For God's sake! Quiet! Quiet! You want someone to hear?

(*In the main room* Mrs. Frank *grabs a shawl and pulls it around her. She rushes in to* Anne, *taking her in her arms.* Mr. Frank *hurriedly gets up, putting on his overcoat.* Margot *sits up, terrified.* Peter's *light goes on in his room.*)

Mrs. Frank (*to* Anne, *in her room*). Hush, darling, hush. It's all right. It's all right. (*over her shoulder to* Dussel) Will you be kind enough to turn on the light, Mr. Dussel? (*back to* Anne) It's nothing, my darling. It was just a dream.

(Dussel *turns on the light in the bedroom.* Mrs. Frank *holds* Anne *in her arms. Gradually* Anne *comes out of her nightmare, still trembling with horror.* Mr. Frank *comes into the room, and goes quickly to the window, looking out to be sure that no one outside had heard* Anne's *screams.* Mrs. Frank *holds* Anne, *talking softly to her. In the main room* Margot *stands on a chair, turning on the center hanging lamp. A light goes on in the* Van Daan's *room overhead.* Peter *puts his robe on, coming out of his room.*)

Dussel (*to* Mrs. Frank, *blowing his nose*). Something must be done about that child, Mrs. Frank. Yelling like that! Who knows but there's somebody on the streets? She's endangering all our lives.

Mrs. Frank. Anne, darling.

Dussel. Every night she twists and turns. I don't sleep. I spend half my night shushing her. And now it's nightmares!

(Margot *comes to the door of* Anne's *room, followed by* Peter. Mr. Frank *goes to them, indicating that everything is all right.* Peter *takes* Margot *back.*)

Mrs. Frank (*to* Anne). You're here, safe, you see? Nothing has happened. (*to* Dussel) Please, Mr. Dussel, go back to bed. She'll be herself in a minute or two. Won't you, Anne?

Dussel (*picking up a book and a pillow*). Thank you, but I'm going to the w.c. The one place where there's peace! (*He stalks out.* Mr. Van Daan, *in underwear and trousers, comes down the stairs.*)

Mr. Van Daan (*to* Dussel). What is it? What happened?

Dussel. A nightmare. She was having a nightmare!

Mr. Van Daan. I thought someone was murdering her.

Dussel. Unfortunately, no.

(*He goes into the bathroom. Mr. Van Daan goes back up the stairs. Mr. Frank, in the main room, sends Peter back to his own bedroom.*)

Mr. Frank. Thank you, Peter. Go back to bed.

(*Peter goes back to his room. Mr. Frank follows him, turning* out the light and looking out the window. Then he goes back to the main room, and gets up on a chair, turning out the center hanging lamp.)

Mrs. Frank (*to* Anne). Would you like some water? (Anne *shakes her head.*) Was it a very bad dream? Perhaps if you told me . . . ?

Anne. I'd rather not talk about it.

Mrs. Frank. Poor darling. Try to sleep then. I'll sit right here beside you until you fall asleep.

(*She brings a stool over, sitting there.*)

Anne. You don't have to.

Mrs. Frank. But I'd like to stay with you . . . very much. Really.

Anne. I'd rather you didn't.

Mrs. Frank. Good night, then. (*She leans down to kiss* Anne. Anne *throws her arm up over her face, turning away.* Mrs. Frank, *hiding her hurt, kisses* Anne's *arm.*) You'll be all right? There's nothing that you want?

Anne. Will you please ask Father to come.

Mrs. Frank (*after a second*). Of course, Anne dear. (*She hurries out into the other room.* Mr. Frank *comes to her as she comes in.*) Sie verlangt nach Dir!¹²

Mr. Frank (*sensing her hurt*). Edith, Liebe, schau . . .¹³

Mrs. Frank. Es macht nichts! Ich danke dem lieben Herrgott, dass sie sich wenigstens an Dich wendet, wenn sie Trost braucht! Geh hinein, Otto, sie ist ganz hysterisch vor Angst.¹⁴ (*as* Mr. Frank *hesitates*) Geh zu ihr.¹⁵ (*He looks at her for a second and then goes to get a cup of water for* Anne. Mrs. Frank *sinks down on the bed, her face in her hands, trying to keep from sobbing aloud.* Margot *comes over to her, putting her arms around her.*) She wants nothing of me. She pulled away when I leaned down to kiss her.

Margot. It's a phase . . . You heard Father . . . Most girls go through it . . . they turn to their fathers at this age . . . they give all their love to their fathers.

Mrs. Frank. You weren't like this. You didn't shut me out.

Margot. She'll get over it . . . (*She smooths the bed for* Mrs. Frank *and sits beside her a moment as* Mrs. Frank *lies down. In* Anne's *room* Mr. Frank *comes in, sitting down by* Anne. Anne *flings her arms around him, clinging to him.*)

---

¹² **Sie verlangt nach Dir** (zē fer-längt´näкн dîr) *German*: She is asking for you.

¹³ **Liebe, schau** (lē´bə shou´) *German*: Dear, look.

¹⁴ **Es macht . . .** (ĕs mäкнt´ nĭкнts´! ĭкн dängk´ə dām lē´bən hĕr´gôt´, däs zē zĭкн´ vān´ĭкн-shtənz än dĭкн´ vĕn´dət, vĕn zē trôst´ brouкнt´! gā hĭn-īn´, ôt´tô; zē ĭst gänts hü-stĕr´ĭsh fôr ängst´) *German*: It's all right. I thank dear God that at least she turns to you when she needs comfort. Go in, Otto; she is hysterical with fear.

¹⁵ **Geh zu ihr** (gā´ tsoo îr´) *German*: Go to her.

In the distance we hear the sound of ack-ack.)

Anne. Oh, Pim. I dreamed that they came to get us! The Green Police! They broke down the door and grabbed me and started to drag me out the way they did Jopie.

Mr. Frank. I want you to take this pill.

Anne. What is it?

Mr. Frank. Something to quiet you.

(*She takes it and drinks the water. In the main room* Margot *turns out the light and goes back to her bed.*)

Mr. Frank (*to* Anne). Do you want me to read to you for a while?

Anne. No. Just sit with me for a minute. Was I awful? Did I yell terribly loud? Do you think anyone outside could have heard?

Mr. Frank. No. No. Lie quietly now. Try to sleep.

Anne. I'm a terrible coward. I'm so disappointed in myself. I think I've conquered my fear . . . I think I'm really grown-up . . . and then something happens . . . and I run to you like a baby . . . I love you, Father. I don't love anyone but you.

Mr. Frank (*reproachfully*). Annele!

Anne. It's true. I've been thinking about it for a long time. You're the only one I love.

Mr. Frank. It's fine to hear you tell me that you love me. But I'd be happier if you said you loved your mother as well . . . She needs your help so much . . . your love . . .

Anne. We have nothing in common. She doesn't understand me. Whenever I try to explain my views on life to her she asks me if I'm constipated.

Mr. Frank. You hurt her very much just now. She's crying. She's in there crying.

Anne. I can't help it. I only told the truth. I didn't want her here . . . (*then, with sudden change*) Oh, Pim, I was horrible, wasn't I? And the worst of it is, I can stand off and look at myself doing it and know it's cruel and yet I can't stop doing it. What's the matter with me? Tell me. Don't say it's just a phase! Help me.

Mr. Frank. There is so little that we parents can do to help our children. We can only try to set a good example . . . point the way. The rest you must do yourself. You must build your own character.

Anne. I'm trying. Really I am. Every night I think back over all of the things I did that day that were wrong . . . like putting the wet mop in Mr. Dussel's bed . . . and this thing now with Mother. I say to myself, that was wrong. I make up my mind, I'm never going to do that again. Never! Of course I may do something worse . . . but at least I'll never do *that* again! . . . I have a nicer side, Father . . . a sweeter, nicer side. But I'm scared to show it. I'm afraid that people are going to laugh at me if I'm serious. So the mean Anne comes to the outside and the good Anne stays on the inside, and I keep on trying to switch them around and have the good Anne outside and the bad Anne inside and be what I'd like to be . . . and might be . . . if only . . . only . . . (*She is asleep. Mr. Frank watches her for a moment and then turns off the light, and starts out. The lights dim out. The curtain falls on the scene.* Anne's Voice *is heard dimly at first, and then with growing strength.*)

Anne's Voice. . . . The air raids are getting worse. They come over day and night. The noise is terrifying. Pim says it should be music to our ears. The more planes, the sooner will come the end of the war. Mrs. Van Daan pretends to be a fatalist. What will be, will be. But when the planes come over, who is the most frightened? No one else but Petronella! . . . Monday, the ninth of November, nineteen forty-two. Wonderful news! The Allies have landed in Africa. Pim says that we can look for an early finish to the war. Just for fun he asked each of us what was the first thing we wanted to do when we got out of here. Mrs. Van Daan longs to be home with her own things, her needle-point chairs, the Beckstein piano her father gave her . . . the best that money could buy. Peter would like to go to a movie. Mr. Dussel wants to get back to his dentist's drill. He's afraid he is losing his touch. For myself, there are so many things . . . to ride a bike again . . . to laugh till my belly aches . . . to have new clothes from the skin out . . . to have a hot tub filled to overflowing and wallow in it for hours . . . to be back in school with my friends . . .

(*As the last lines are being said, the curtain rises on the scene. The lights dim on as* Anne's Voice *fades away.*)

Scene 5

It is the first night of the Hanukkah[16] celebration. Mr. Frank is standing at the head of the table on which is the Menorah.[17] *He lights the Shamos, or servant candle, and holds it as he says the blessing. Seated listening is all of the "family," dressed in their best. The men wear hats,* Peter *wears his cap.*

Mr. Frank (*reading from a prayer book*). "Praised be Thou, oh Lord our God, Ruler of the universe, who has sanctified us with Thy commandments and bidden us kindle the Hanukkah lights. Praised be Thou, oh Lord our God, Ruler of the universe, who has wrought wondrous deliverances for our fathers in days of old. Praised be Thou, oh Lord our God, Ruler of the universe, that Thou has given us life and sustenance and brought us to this happy season." (Mr. Frank *lights the one candle*

---

[16] **Hanukkah** (hä′nə-kə): a Jewish holiday, celebrated in December and lasting eight days.
[17] **Menorah** (mə-nôr′ə): a candleholder with nine branches, used in the celebration of Hanukkah.

of the Menorah *as he continues.*) "We kindle this Hanukkah light to celebrate the great and wonderful deeds wrought through the zeal with which God filled the hearts of the heroic Maccabees, two thousand years ago. They fought against indifference, against tyranny and oppression, and they restored our Temple to us. May these lights remind us that we should ever look to God, whence cometh our help." Amen. [Pronounced O-mayn.]

All. Amen.

(Mr. Frank *hands* Mrs. Frank *the prayer book.*)

Mrs. Frank (*reading*). "I lift up mine eyes unto the mountains, from whence cometh my help. My help cometh from the Lord who made heaven and earth. He will not suffer thy foot to be moved. He that keepeth thee will not slumber. He that keepeth Israel doth neither slumber nor sleep. The Lord is thy keeper. The Lord is thy shade upon thy right hand. The sun shall not smite thee by day, nor the moon by night. The Lord shall keep thee from all evil. He shall keep thy soul. The Lord shall guard thy going out and thy coming in, from this time forth and forevermore." Amen.

All. Amen.

(Mrs. Frank *puts down the prayer book and goes to get the food and wine.* Margot *helps her.* Mr. Frank *takes the men's hats and puts them aside.*)

Dussel (*rising*). That was very moving.

Anne (*pulling him back*). It isn't over yet!

Mrs. Van Daan. Sit down! Sit down!

Anne. There's a lot more, songs and presents.

Dussel. Presents?

Mrs. Frank. Not this year, unfortunately.

Mrs. Van Daan. But always on Hanukkah everyone gives presents . . . everyone!

Dussel. Like our St. Nicholas' Day.[18] (*There is a chorus of "no's" from the group.*)

Mrs. Van Daan. No! Not like St. Nicholas! What kind of a Jew are you that you don't know Hanukkah?

Mrs. Frank (*as she brings the food*). I remember particularly the candles . . . First one, as we have tonight. Then the second night you light two candles, the next night three . . . and so on until you have eight candles burning. When there are eight candles it is truly beautiful.

Mrs. Van Daan. And the potato pancakes.

---

[18] **St. Nicholas's Day:** December 6, the day that Christian children in the Netherlands receive gifts.

Mr. Van Daan. Don't talk about them!

Mrs. Van Daan. I make the best *latkes*[19] you ever tasted!

Mrs. Frank. Invite us all next year . . . in your own home.

Mr. Frank. God willing!

Mrs. Van Daan. God willing.

Margot. What I remember best is the presents we used to get when we were little . . . eight days of presents . . . and each day they got better and better.

Mrs. Frank (*sitting down*). We are all here, alive. That is present enough.

Anne. No, it isn't. I've got something . . .

(*She rushes into her room, hurriedly puts on a little hat improvised from the lamp shade, grabs a satchel bulging with parcels and comes running back.*)

Mrs. Frank. What is it?

Anne. Presents!

Mrs. Van Daan. Presents!

Dussel. Look!

Mr. Van Daan. What's she got on her head?

Peter. A lamp shade!

Anne (*She picks out one at random*). This is for Margot. (*She hands it to* Margot, *pulling her to her feet.*) Read it out loud.

Margot (*reading*).

---
[19] **latkes** (lät′kəz): potato pancakes.

"You have never lost your temper.
You never will, I fear,
You are so good.
But if you should,
Put all your cross words here."

(*She tears open the package.*)

A new crossword puzzle book! Where did you get it?

Anne. It isn't new. It's one that you've done. But I rubbed it all out, and if you wait a little and forget, you can do it all over again.

Margot (*sitting*). It's wonderful, Anne. Thank you. You'd never know it wasn't new.

(*From outside we hear the sound of a streetcar passing.*)

Anne (*with another gift*). Mrs. Van Daan.

Mrs. Van Daan (*taking it*). This is awful . . . I haven't anything for anyone . . . I never thought . . .

Mr. Frank. This is all Anne's idea.

Mrs. Van Daan (*holding up a bottle*). What is it?

Anne. It's hair shampoo. I took all the odds and ends of soap and mixed them with the last of my toilet water.

Mrs. Van Daan. Oh, Anneke!

Anne. I wanted to write a poem for all of them, but I didn't have time. (*offering a large box to* Mr. Van Daan) Yours, Mr. Van Daan, is really something . . . something you want more than anything. (*as she* *waits for him to open it*) Look! Cigarettes!

Mr. Van Daan. Cigarettes!

Anne. Two of them! Pim found some old pipe tobacco in the pocket lining of his coat . . . and we made them . . . or rather, Pim did.

Mrs. Van Daan. Let me see . . . Well, look at that! Light it, Putti! Light it.

(*Mr. Van Daan hesitates.*)

Anne. It's tobacco, really it is! There's a little fluff in it, but not much.

(*Everyone watches intently as Mr. Van Daan cautiously lights it. The cigarette flares up. Everyone laughs.*)

Peter. It works!

Mrs. Van Daan. Look at him.

Mr. Van Daan (*spluttering*). Thank you, Anne. Thank you.

(*Anne rushes back to her satchel for another present.*)

Anne (*handing her mother a piece of paper*). For Mother, Hanukkah greeting. (*She pulls her mother to her feet.*)

Mrs. Frank (*She reads.*) "Here's an I.O.U. that I promise to pay. Ten hours of doing whatever you say. Signed, Anne Frank." (*Mrs. Frank, touched, takes Anne in her arms, holding her close.*)

Dussel (*to Anne*). Ten hours of doing what you're told? *Anything* you're told?

Anne. That's right.

Dussel. You wouldn't want to sell that, Mrs. Frank?

Mrs. Frank. Never! This is the most precious gift I've ever had!

(*She sits, showing her present to the others. Anne hurries back to the satchel and pulls out a scarf, the scarf that Mr. Frank found in the first scene.*)

Anne (*offering it to her father*). For Pim.

Mr. Frank. Anneke . . . I wasn't supposed to have a present! (*He takes it, unfolding it and showing it to the others.*)

Anne. It's a muffler . . . to put round your neck . . . like an ascot, you know. I made it myself out of odds and ends . . . I knitted it in the dark each night, after I'd gone to bed. I'm afraid it looks better in the dark!

Mr. Frank (*putting it on*). It's fine. It fits me perfectly. Thank you, Annele.

(*Anne hands Peter a ball of paper, with a string attached to it.*)

Anne. That's for Mouschi.

Peter (*rising to bow*). On behalf of Mouschi, I thank you.

Anne (*hesitant, handing him a gift*). And . . . this is yours . . . from Mrs. Quack Quack. (*as he holds it gingerly in his hands*) Well . . . open it . . . Aren't you going to open it?

Peter. I'm scared to. I know something's going to jump out and hit me.

Anne. No. It's nothing like that, really.

Mrs. Van Daan (*as he is opening it*). What is it, Peter? Go on. Show it.

Anne (*excitedly*). It's a safety razor!

Dussel. A what?

Anne. A razor!

Mrs. Van Daan (*looking at it*). You didn't make that out of odds and ends.

Anne (*to* Peter). Miep got it for me. It's not new. It's second-hand. But you really do need a razor now.

Dussel. For what?

Anne. Look on his upper lip . . . you can see the beginning of a mustache.

Dussel. He wants to get rid of that? Put a little milk on it and let the cat lick it off.

Peter (*starting for his room*). Think you're funny, don't you.

Dussel. Look! He can't wait! He's going in to try it!

Peter. I'm going to give Mouschi his present! (*He goes into his room, slamming the door behind him.*)

Mr. Van Daan (*disgustedly*). Mouschi, Mouschi, Mouschi.

(*In the distance we hear a dog persistently barking.* Anne *brings a gift to* Dussel.)

Anne. And last but never least, my roommate, Mr. Dussel.

Dussel. For me? You have something for me? (*He opens the small box she gives him.*)

Anne. I made them myself.

Dussel (*puzzled*). Capsules! Two capsules!

Anne. They're ear-plugs!

Dussel. Ear-plugs?

Anne. To put in your ears so you won't hear me when I thrash around at night. I saw them advertised in a magazine. They're not real ones . . . I made them out of cotton and candle wax. Try them . . . See if they don't work . . . see if you can hear me talk . . .

Dussel (*putting them in his ears*). Wait now until I get them in . . . so.

Anne. Are you ready?

Dussel. Huh?

Anne. Are you ready?

Dussel. Good God! They've gone inside! I can't get them out! (*They laugh as* Mr. Dussel *jumps about, trying to shake the plugs out of his ears. Finally he gets them out. Putting them away.*) Thank you, Anne! Thank you!

Mr. Van Daan. A real Hanukkah! ⎫
Mrs. Van Daan. Wasn't it cute of her? ⎬ Together
Mrs. Frank. I don't know when she did it. ⎪
Margot. I love my present. ⎭

Anne (*sitting at the table*). And now let's have the song, Father . . .

please . . . (*to* Dussel) Have you heard the Hanukkah song, Mr. Dussel? The song is the whole thing! (*She sings.*) "Oh, Hanukkah! Oh Hanukkah! The sweet celebration . . ."

Mr. Frank (*quieting her*). I'm afraid, Anne, we shouldn't sing that song tonight. (*to* Dussel) It's a song of jubilation, of rejoicing. One is apt to become too enthusiastic.

Anne. Oh, please, please. Let's sing the song. I promise not to shout!

Mr. Frank. Very well. But quietly now . . . I'll keep an eye on you and when . . .

(*As* Anne *starts to sing, she is interrupted by* Dussel, *who is snorting and wheezing.*)

Dussel (*pointing to* Peter). You . . . You! (Peter *is coming from his bedroom, ostentatiously holding a bulge in his coat as if he were holding his cat, and dangling* Anne's *present before it.*) How many times . . . I told you . . . Out! Out!

Mr. Van Daan (*going to* Peter). What's the matter with you? Haven't you any sense? Get that cat out of here.

Peter (*innocently*). Cat?

Mr. Van Daan. You heard me. Get it out of here!

Peter. I have no cat. (*Delighted with his joke, he opens his coat and pulls out a bath towel. The group at the table laugh, enjoying the joke.*)

Dussel (*still wheezing*). It doesn't need to be the cat . . . his clothes are enough . . . when he comes out of that room . . .

Mr. Van Daan. Don't worry. You won't be bothered any more. We're getting rid of it.

Dussel. At last you listen to me. (*He goes off into his bedroom.*)

Mr. Van Daan (*calling after him*). I'm not doing it for you. That's all in your mind . . . all of it! (*He starts back to his place at the table.*) I'm doing it because I'm sick of seeing that cat eat all our food.

Peter. That's not true! I only give him bones . . . scraps . . .

Mr. Van Daan. Don't tell me! He gets fatter every day! Damn cat looks better than any of us. Out he goes tonight!

Peter. No! No!

Anne. Mr. Van Daan, you can't do that! That's Peter's cat.

Mrs. Frank (*quietly*). Anne.

Peter (*to* Mr. Van Daan). If he goes, I go.

Mr. Van Daan. Go! Go!

Mrs. Van Daan. You're not going and the cat's not going! Now please . . . this is Hanukkah . . . Hanukkah . . . this is the time to celebrate . . . What's the matter with all of you? Come on, Anne. Let's have the song.

Anne (*singing*). "Oh, Hanukkah! Oh, Hanukkah! The sweet celebration."

Mr. Frank (*rising*). I think we should first blow out the candle . . . then we'll have something for tomorrow night.

Margot. But, Father, you're supposed to let it burn itself out.

Mr. Frank. I'm sure that God understands shortages. (*before blowing it out*) "Praised be Thou, oh Lord our God, who hast sustained us and permitted us to celebrate this joyous festival."

(*He is about to blow out the candle when suddenly there is a crash of something falling below. They all freeze in horror, motionless. For a few seconds there is complete silence.* Mr. Frank *slips off his shoes. The others noiselessly follow his example.* Mr. Frank *turns out a light near him. He motions to* Peter *to turn off the center lamp.* Peter *tries to reach it, realizes he cannot and gets up on a chair. Just as he is touching the lamp he loses his balance. The chair goes out from under him. He falls. The iron lamp shade crashes to the floor. There is a sound of feet below, running down the stairs.*)

Mr. Van Daan (*under his breath*). God Almighty! (*The only light left comes from the Hanukkah* candle. *Dussel* comes from his room. Mr. Frank *creeps over to the stairwell and stands listening. The dog is heard barking excitedly.*) Do you hear anything?

Mr. Frank (*in a whisper*). No. I think they've gone.

Mrs. Van Daan. It's the Green Police. They've found us.

Mr. Frank. If they had, they wouldn't have left. They'd be up here by now.

Mrs. Van Daan. I know it's the Green Police. They've gone to get help. That's all. They'll be back!

Mr. Van Daan. Or it may have been the Gestapo,[20] looking for papers . . .

Mr. Frank (*interrupting*). Or a thief, looking for money.

Mrs. Van Daan. We've got to do something . . . Quick! Quick! Before they come back.

Mr. Van Daan. There isn't anything to do. Just wait.

(Mr. Frank *holds up his hand for them to be quiet. He is listening intently. There is complete silence as they all strain to hear any sound from below. Suddenly* Anne *begins to sway. With a low cry she falls to the floor in a faint.* Mrs. Frank *goes to her quickly, sitting beside her on the floor and taking her in her arms.*)

Mrs. Frank. Get some water, please! Get some water!

(Margot *starts for the sink.*)

Mr. Van Daan (*grabbing* Margot). No! No! No one's going to run water!

Mr. Frank. If they've found us, they've found us. Get the water. (Margot *starts again for the sink.* Mr. Frank, *getting a flashlight*) I'm going down.

(Margot *rushes to him, clinging to him.* Anne *struggles to consciousness.*)

Margot. No, Father, no! There may be someone there, waiting . . . It may be a trap!

Mr. Frank. This is Saturday. There is no way for us to know what has happened until Miep or Mr. Kraler comes on Monday morning. We cannot live with this uncertainty.

Margot. Don't go, Father!

Mrs. Frank. Hush, darling, hush. (Mr. Frank *slips quietly out, down the steps and out through the door below.*) Margot! Stay close to me.

(Margot *goes to her mother.*)

Mr. Van Daan. Shush! Shush!

(Mrs. Frank *whispers to* Margot *to get the water.* Margot *goes for it.*)

Mrs. Van Daan. Putti, where's our money? Get our money. I hear you can buy the Green Police off, so much a head. Go upstairs quick! Get the money!

Mr. Van Daan. Keep still!

Mrs. Van Daan (*kneeling before him, pleading*). Do you want to be dragged off to a concentration camp? Are you going to stand there

---

[20] **Gestapo** (gə-stä′pō): the Nazi secret police force, known for its terrorism and brutality.

and wait for them to come up and get you? Do something, I tell you!

Mr. Van Daan (*pushing her aside*). Will you keep still! (*He goes over to the stairwell to listen. Peter goes to his mother, helping her up onto the sofa. There is a second of silence, then Anne can stand it no longer.*)

Anne. Someone go after Father! Make Father come back!

Peter (*starting for the door*). I'll go.

Mr. Van Daan. Haven't you done enough?

(*He pushes Peter roughly away. In his anger against his father Peter grabs a chair as if to hit him with it, then puts it down, burying his face in his hands. Mrs. Frank begins to pray softly.*)

Anne. Please, please, Mr. Van Daan. Get Father.

Mr. Van Daan. Quiet! Quiet!

(*Anne is shocked into silence. Mrs. Frank pulls her closer, holding her protectively in her arms.*)

Mrs. Frank (*softly, praying*). "I lift up mine eyes unto the mountains, from whence cometh my help. My help cometh from the Lord who made heaven and earth. He will not suffer thy foot to be moved . . . He that keepeth thee will not slumber . . ." (*She stops as she hears someone coming. They all watch the door tensely. Mr. Frank comes quietly in. Anne rushes to him, holding him tight.*)

Mr. Frank. It was a thief. That noise must have scared him away.

Mrs. Van Daan. Thank God.

Mr. Frank. He took the cash box. And the radio. He ran away in such a hurry that he didn't stop to shut the street door. It was swinging wide open. (*A breath of relief sweeps over them.*) I think it would be good to have some light.

Margot. Are you sure it's all right?

Mr. Frank. The danger has passed. (*Margot goes to light the small lamp.*) Don't be so terrified, Anne. We're safe.

Dussel. Who says the danger has passed? Don't you realize we are in greater danger than ever?

Mr. Frank. Mr. Dussel, will you be still!

(*Mr. Frank takes Anne back to the table, making her sit down with him, trying to calm her.*)

Dussel (*pointing to Peter*). Thanks to this clumsy fool, there's someone now who knows we're up here! Someone now knows we're up here, hiding!

Mrs. Van Daan (*going to Dussel*). Someone knows we're here, yes. But who is the someone? A thief! A thief! You think a thief is going to go to the Green Police and say . . . I was robbing a place the other night and I heard a noise up over my head? You think a thief is going to do that?

Dussel. Yes. I think he will.

Mrs. Van Daan (*hysterically*). You're crazy! (*She stumbles back to* her seat at the table. Peter *follows protectively, pushing* Dussel *aside.*)

Dussel. I think some day he'll be caught and then he'll make a bargain with the Green Police . . . if they'll let him off, he'll tell them where some Jews are hiding!

(*He goes off into the bedroom. There is a second of appalled silence.*)

Mr. Van Daan. He's right.

Anne. Father, let's get out of here! We can't stay here now . . . Let's go . . .

Mr. Van Daan. Go! Where?

Mrs. Frank (*sinking into her chair at the table*). Yes. Where?

Mr. Frank (*rising, to them all*). Have we lost all faith? All courage? A moment ago we thought that they'd come for us. We were sure it was the end. But it wasn't the end. We're alive, safe. (Mr. Van Daan *goes to the table and sits.* Mr. Frank *prays.*) "We thank Thee, oh Lord our God, that in Thy infinite mercy Thou hast again seen fit to spare us." (*He blows out the candle, then turns to* Anne.) Come on, Anne. The song! Let's have the song! (*He starts to sing.* Anne *finally starts falteringly to sing, as* Mr. Frank *urges her on. Her voice is hardly audible at first.*)

Anne (*singing*). "Oh, Hanukkah! Oh, Hanukkah! The sweet . . . celebration . . . " (*As she goes on singing, the others gradually join in, their voices still shaking with fear.* Mrs. Van Daan *sobs as she sings.*)

Group. "Around the feast . . . we . . . gather

In complete . . . jubilation . . .

Happiest of sea . . . sons

Now is here. Many are the reasons for good cheer."

(Dussel *comes from the bedroom. He comes over to the table, standing beside* Margot, *listening to them as they sing.*)

"Together

We'll weather

Whatever tomorrow may bring."

(*As they sing on with growing courage, the lights start to dim.*)

"So hear us rejoicing

And merrily voicing

The Hanukkah song that we sing.

Hoy!"

(*The lights are out. The curtain starts slowly to fall.*)

"Hear us rejoicing

And merrily voicing

The Hanukkah song that we sing."

(*They are still singing, as the curtain falls.*)

The Curtain Falls.

Analyze Drama

A **drama,** or play, is a form of literature meant to be performed by actors for an audience. In a drama, the characters' words and actions tell the story. The author of a drama is called a **playwright,** and the text of the play is the **script.** The script for a drama includes several different elements:

- The **cast of characters** is a list of all the characters in the play. This list may also include a brief description of each character.
- **Stage directions** are instructions about how to perform the drama. They are often italicized, and they may also be set off with parentheses. They give readers, actors, and directors important details that explain what is happening. For example, these stage directions help readers imagine how Mr. Frank looks and feels when the play begins.

He stands looking slowly around, making a supreme effort at self-control. He is weak, ill. His clothes are threadbare.

- **Dialogue** is the written conversation between two or more characters. The name of a character is followed by the words that he or she speaks.

The **structure** of a text is the way in which it is arranged or organized. In a drama, the script is often divided into acts and scenes.

- An **act** is a major division within a play, similar to a chapter in a book.
- Each act may be divided into smaller sections, called **scenes.**
- A new act or scene often shows that the time or place of the action has changed.

As you review Act One, notice the important differences between Scene 1 and Scene 2. What does this difference help you to understand?

Analyzing the Text

Cite Text Evidence   Support your responses with evidence from the text.

1. **Draw Conclusions** Reread lines 679–706. What do the stage directions and dialogue reveal about Mr. Frank?

2. **Identify Patterns** How many scenes are there in Act One of this play? Why do the playwrights begin a new scene after line 785?

3. **Draw Conclusions** Examine lines 1339–1391. What do the stage directions and dialogue reveal about the characters?

4. **Analyze** How does the arrival of Mr. Dussel heighten tensions in the Annex?

ACT TWO

Scene 1

In the darkness we hear Anne's Voice, again reading from the diary.

Anne's Voice. Saturday, the first of January, nineteen forty-four. Another new year has begun and we find ourselves still in our hiding place. We have been here now for one year, five months and twenty-five days. It seems that our life is at a standstill.

The curtain rises on the scene. It is late afternoon. Everyone is bundled up against the cold. In the main room Mrs. Frank *is taking down the laundry which is hung across the back.* Mr. Frank *sits in the chair down left, reading.* Margot *is lying on the couch with a blanket over her and the many-colored knitted scarf around her throat.* Anne *is seated at the center table, writing in her diary.* Peter, Mr. *and* Mrs. Van Daan, *and* Dussel *are all in their own rooms, reading or lying down.*

As the lights dim on, Anne's Voice *continues, without a break.*

Anne's Voice. We are all a little thinner. The Van Daans' "discussions" are as violent as ever. Mother still does not understand me. But then I don't understand her either. There is one great change, however. A change in myself. I read somewhere that girls of my age don't feel quite certain of themselves. That they become quiet within and begin to think of the miracle that is taking place in their bodies. I think that what is happening to me is so wonderful . . . not only what can be seen, but what is taking place inside. Each time it has happened I have a feeling that I have a sweet secret. (*We hear the chimes and then a hymn being played on the carillon outside.*) And in spite of any pain, I long for the time when I shall feel that secret within me again.

(*The buzzer of the door below suddenly sounds. Everyone is startled,* Mr. Frank *tiptoes cautiously to the top of the steps and listens. Again the buzzer sounds, in* Miep's *V-for-Victory signal.*)

Mr. Frank. It's Miep! (*He goes quickly down the steps to unbolt the door.* Mrs. Frank *calls upstairs to the* Van Daans *and then to* Peter.)

Mrs. Frank. Wake up, everyone! Miep is here! (Anne *quickly puts her diary away.* Margot *sits up, pulling the blanket around her shoulders.* Mr. Dussel *sits on the edge of his bed, listening, disgruntled.* Miep *comes up the steps, followed by* Mr. Kraler. *They bring flowers, books, newspapers, etc.* Anne *rushes to* Miep, *throwing her arms affectionately around her.*) Miep . . . and Mr. Kraler . . . What a delightful surprise!

Mr. Kraler. We came to bring you New Year's greetings.

Mrs. Frank. You shouldn't . . . you should have at least one day to yourselves. (*She goes quickly to the stove and brings down teacups and tea for all of them.*)

Anne. Don't say that, it's so wonderful to see them! (*sniffing at* Miep's *coat*) I can smell the wind and the cold on your clothes.

Miep (*giving her the flowers*). There you are. (*then to* Margot, *feeling her forehead*) How are you, Margot? . . . Feeling any better?

Margot. I'm all right.

Anne. We filled her full of every kind of pill so she won't cough and make a noise. (*She runs into her room to put the flowers in water.* Mr. *and* Mrs. Van Daan *come from upstairs. Outside there is the sound of a band playing.*)

Mrs. Van Daan. Well, hello, Miep. Mr. Kraler.

Mr. Kraler (*giving a bouquet of flowers to* Mrs. Van Daan). With my hope for peace in the New Year.

Peter (*anxiously*). Miep, have you seen Mouschi? Have you seen him anywhere around?

Miep. I'm sorry, Peter. I asked everyone in the neighborhood had they seen a gray cat. But they said no.

(Mrs. Frank *gives* Miep *a cup of tea.* Mr. Frank *comes up the steps, carrying a small cake on a plate.*)

Mr. Frank. Look what Miep's brought for us!

Mrs. Frank (*taking it*). A cake!

Mr. Van Daan. A cake! (*He pinches* Miep's *cheeks gaily and hurries up to the cupboard.*) I'll get some plates.

(Dussel, *in his room, hastily puts a coat on and starts out to join the others.*)

Mrs. Frank. Thank you, Miepia. You shouldn't have done it. You must have used all of your sugar ration for weeks. (*giving it to* Mrs. Van Daan) It's beautiful, isn't it?

Mrs. Van Daan. It's been ages since I even saw a cake. Not since you brought us one last year. (*without looking at the cake, to* Miep) Remember? Don't you remember, you gave us one on New Year's Day? Just this time last year? I'll never forget it because you had "Peace in nineteen forty-three" on it. (*She looks at the cake and reads.*) "Peace in nineteen forty-four!"

Miep. Well, it has to come sometime, you know. (*as* Dussel *comes from his room*) Hello, Mr. Dussel.

Mr. Kraler. How are you?

Mr. Van Daan (*bringing plates and a knife*). Here's the knife, *liefje.* Now, how many of us are there?

Miep. None for me, thank you.

Mr. Frank. Oh, please. You must.

Miep. I couldn't.

Mr. Van Daan. Good! That leaves one ... two ... three ... seven of us.

Dussel. Eight! Eight! It's the same number as it always is!

Mr. Van Daan. I left Margot out. I take it for granted Margot won't eat any.

Anne. Why wouldn't she!

160 **Mrs. Frank.** I think it won't harm her.

Mr. Van Daan. All right! All right! I just didn't want her to start coughing again, that's all.

Dussel. And please, Mrs. Frank should cut the cake.

Mr. Van Daan. What's the difference? ⎫
⎬ *Together*
170 **Mrs. Van Daan.** It's not Mrs. Frank's cake, is it, Miep? It's for all of us. ⎭

Dussel. Mrs. Frank divides things better.

Mrs. Van Daan (*going to* Dussel). What are you trying to say? ⎫
⎬ *Together*
Mr. Van Daan. Oh, come on! Stop wasting time! ⎭

Mrs. Van Daan (*to* Dussel). Don't I
180 always give everybody exactly the same? Don't I?

Mr. Van Daan. Forget it, Kerli.

Mrs. Van Daan. No. I want an answer! Don't I?

Dussel. Yes. Yes. Everybody gets exactly the same ... except Mr. Van Daan always gets a little bit more.

(Mr. Van Daan *advances on*
190 Dussel, *the knife still in his hand.*)

Mr. Van Daan. That's a lie!

(Dussel *retreats before the onslaught of the* Van Daans.)

Mr. Frank. Please, please! (*then to* Miep) You see what a little sugar cake does to us? It goes right to our heads!

Mr. Van Daan (*handing* Mrs. Frank *the knife*). Here you are,
200 Mrs. Frank.

Mrs. Frank. Thank you. (*then to* Miep *as she goes to the table to cut the cake*) Are you sure you won't have some?

Miep (*drinking her tea*). No, really, I have to go in a minute.

(*The sound of the band fades out in the distance.*)

Peter (*to* Miep). Maybe Mouschi
210 went back to our house ... they say that cats ... Do you ever get over there ... ? I mean ... do you suppose you could ... ?

Miep. I'll try, Peter. The first minute I get I'll try. But I'm afraid, with him gone a week ...

Dussel. Make up your mind, already someone has had a nice big dinner from that cat!

220 (Peter *is furious, inarticulate. He starts toward* Dussel *as if to hit him.* Mr. Frank *stops him.* Mrs. Frank *speaks quickly to ease the situation.*)

The Diary of Anne Frank: Act Two **327**

Mrs. Frank (*to* Miep). This is delicious, Miep!

Mrs. Van Daan (*eating hers*). Delicious!

Mr. Van Daan (*finishing it in one gulp*). Dirk's in luck to get a girl who can bake like this!

Miep (*putting down her empty teacup*). I have to run. Dirk's taking me to a party tonight.

Anne. How heavenly! Remember now what everyone is wearing, and what you have to eat and everything, so you can tell us tomorrow.

Miep. I'll give you a full report! Good-bye, everyone!

Mr. Van Daan (*to* Miep). Just a minute. There's something I'd like you to do for me. (*He hurries off up the stairs to his room.*)

Mrs. Van Daan (*sharply*). Putti, where are you going? (*She rushes up the stairs after him, calling hysterically.*) What do you want? Putti, what are you going to do?

Miep (*to* Peter). What's wrong?

Peter (*his sympathy is with his mother*). Father says he's going to sell her fur coat. She's crazy about that old fur coat.

Dussel. Is it possible? Is it possible that anyone is so silly as to worry about a fur coat in times like this?

Peter. It's none of your darn business . . . and if you say one more thing . . . I'll, I'll take you and I'll . . . I mean it . . . I'll . . .

(*There is a piercing scream from* Mrs. Van Daan *above. She grabs at the fur coat as* Mr. Van Daan *is starting downstairs with it.*)

Mrs. Van Daan. No! No! No! Don't you dare take that! You hear? It's mine! (*Downstairs* Peter *turns away, embarrassed, miserable.*) My father gave me that! You didn't give it to me. You have no right. Let go of it . . . you hear?

(Mr. Van Daan *pulls the coat from her hands and hurries downstairs.* Mrs. Van Daan *sinks to the floor, sobbing. As* Mr. Van Daan *comes into the main room the others look away, embarrassed for him.*)

Mr. Van Daan (*to* Mr. Kraler). Just a little—discussion over the advisability of selling this coat. As I have often reminded Mrs. Van Daan, it's very selfish of her to keep it when people outside are in such desperate need of clothing . . . (*He gives the coat to* Miep.) So if you will please to sell it for us? It should fetch a good price. And by the way, will you get me cigarettes. I don't care what kind they are . . . get all you can.

Miep. It's terribly difficult to get them, Mr. Van Daan. But I'll try. Good-bye.

(*She goes.* Mr. Frank *follows her down the steps to bolt the door after her.* Mrs. Frank *gives* Mr. Kraler *a cup of tea.*)

Mrs. Frank. Are you sure you won't have some cake, Mr. Kraler?

Mr. Kraler. I'd better not.

Mr. Van Daan. You're still feeling badly? What does your doctor say?

Mr. Kraler. I haven't been to him.

Mrs. Frank. Now, Mr. Kraler! . . .

Mr. Kraler (*sitting at the table*). Oh, I tried. But you can't get near a doctor these days . . . they're so busy. After weeks I finally managed to get one on the telephone. I told him I'd like an appointment . . . I wasn't feeling very well. You know what he answers . . . over the telephone . . . Stick out your tongue! (*They laugh. He turns to* Mr. Frank *as* Mr. Frank *comes back.*) I have some contracts here . . . I wonder if you'd look over them with me . . .

Mr. Frank (*putting out his hand*). Of course.

Mr. Kraler (*He rises*). If we could go downstairs . . . (Mr. Frank *starts ahead*, Mr. Kraler *speaks to the others.*) Will you forgive us? I won't keep him but a minute. (*He starts to follow* Mr. Frank *down the steps.*)

Margot (*with sudden foreboding*). What's happened? Something's happened! Hasn't it, Mr. Kraler?

(Mr. Kraler *stops and comes back, trying to reassure* Margot *with a pretense of casualness.*)

Mr. Kraler. No, really. I want your father's advice . . .

Margot. Something's gone wrong! I know it!

Mr. Frank (*coming back, to* Mr. Kraler). If it's something that concerns us here, it's better that we all hear it.

Mr. Kraler (*turning to him, quietly*). But . . . the children . . . ?

Mr. Frank. What they'd imagine would be worse than any reality.

(*As* Mr. Kraler *speaks, they all listen with intense apprehension.* Mrs. Van Daan *comes down the stairs and sits on the bottom step.*)

Mr. Kraler. It's a man in the storeroom . . . I don't know whether or not you remember him . . . Carl, about fifty, heavy-set, near-sighted . . . He came with us just before you left.

Mr. Frank. He was from Utrecht?

Mr. Kraler. That's the man. A couple of weeks ago, when I was in the storeroom, he closed the door and asked me . . . how's Mr. Frank? What do you hear from Mr. Frank? I told him I only knew there was a rumor that you were in Switzerland. He said he'd heard that rumor too, but he thought I might know something more. I didn't pay any attention to it . . . but then a thing happened yesterday . . . He'd brought some invoices to the office for me to sign. As I was going through them, I looked up. He was standing staring at the bookcase . . . your bookcase. He said he thought he remembered a door there . . . Wasn't there a door there that used to go up to the loft? Then he told

The Diary of Anne Frank: Act Two **329**

me he wanted more money. Twenty guilders¹ more a week.

Mr. Van Daan. Blackmail!

Mr. Frank. Twenty guilders? Very modest blackmail.

Mr. Van Daan. That's just the beginning.

Dussel (*coming to* Mr. Frank). You know what I think? He was the thief who was down there that night. That's how he knows we're here.

Mr. Frank (*to* Mr. Kraler). How was it left? What did you tell him?

Mr. Kraler. I said I had to think about it. What shall I do? Pay him the money? . . Take a chance on firing him . . . or what? I don't know.

Dussel (*frantic*). For God's sake don't fire him! Pay him what he asks . . . keep him here where you can have your eye on him.

Mr. Frank. Is it so much that he's asking? What are they paying nowadays?

Mr. Kraler. He could get it in a war plant. But this isn't a war plant. Mind you, I don't know if he really knows . . . or if he doesn't know.

Mr. Frank. Offer him half. Then we'll soon find out if it's blackmail or not.

Dussel. And if it is? We've got to pay it, haven't we? Anything he asks we've got to pay!

---

¹ **guilders** (gĭl´dərz): the basic monetary unit of the Netherlands at the time.

Mr. Frank. Let's decide that when the time comes.

Mr. Kraler. This may be all my imagination. You get to a point, these days, where you suspect everyone and everything. Again and again . . . on some simple look or word, I've found myself . . . (*The telephone rings in the office below.*)

Mrs. Van Daan (*hurrying to* Mr. Kraler). There's the telephone! What does that mean, the telephone ringing on a holiday?

Mr. Kraler. That's my wife. I told her I had to go over some papers in my office . . . to call me there when she got out of church. (*He starts out.*) I'll offer him half then. Goodbye . . . we'll hope for the best!

(*The group call their good-byes half-heartedly.* Mr. Frank *follows* Mr. Kraler, *to bolt the door below. During the following scene,* Mr. Frank *comes back up and stands listening, disturbed.*)

Dussel (*to* Mr. Van Daan). You can thank your son for this . . . smashing the light! I tell you, it's just a question of time now. (*He goes to the window at the back and stands looking out.*)

Margot. Sometimes I wish the end would come . . . whatever it is.

Mrs. Frank (*shocked*). Margot!

(Anne *goes to* Margot, *sitting beside her on the couch with her arms around her.*)

Margot. Then at least we'd know where we were.

Mrs. Frank. You should be ashamed of yourself! Talking that way! Think how lucky we are! Think of the thousands dying in the war, every day. Think of the people in concentration camps.

Anne (*interrupting*). What's the good of that? What's the good of thinking of misery when you're already miserable? That's stupid!

Mrs. Frank. Anne!

(*As* Anne *goes on raging at her mother,* Mrs. Frank *tries to break in, in an effort to quiet her.*)

Anne. We're young, Margot and Peter and I! You grownups have had your chance! But look at us . . . If we begin thinking of all the horror in the world, we're lost! We're trying to hold onto some kind of ideals . . . when everything . . . ideals, hopes . . . everything, are being destroyed! It isn't our fault that the world is in such a mess! We weren't around when all this started! So don't try to take it out on us!

(*She rushes off to her room, slamming the door after her. She picks up a brush from the chest and hurls it to the floor. Then she sits on the settee, trying to control her anger.*)

Mr. Van Daan. She talks as if we started the war! Did we start the war? (*He spots* Anne's *cake. As he starts to take it,* Peter *anticipates him.*)

Peter. She left her cake. (*He starts for* Anne's *room with the cake. There is silence in the main room.* Mrs. Van Daan *goes up to her room, followed by* Van Daan. Dussel *stays looking out the window.* Mr. Frank *brings* Mrs. Frank *her cake. She eats it slowly, without relish.* Mr. Frank *takes his cake to* Margot *and sits quietly on the sofa beside her.* Peter *stands in the doorway of* Anne's *darkened room, looking at her, then makes a little movement to let her know he is there.* Anne *sits up, quickly, trying to hide the signs of her tears.* Peter *holds out the cake to her.*) You left this.

Anne (*dully*). Thanks.

(Peter *starts to go out, then comes back.*)

Peter. I thought you were fine just now. You know just how to talk to them. You know just how to say it. I'm no good . . . I never can think . . . especially when I'm mad . . . That Dussel . . . when he said that about Mouschi . . . someone eating him . . . all I could think is . . . I wanted to hit him. I wanted to give him such a . . . a . . . that he'd . . . That's what I used to do when there was an argument at school . . . That's the way I . . . but here . . . And an old man like that . . . it wouldn't be so good.

Anne. You're making a big mistake about me. I do it all wrong. I say too much. I go too far. I hurt people's feelings . . .

(Dussel *leaves the window, going to his room.*)

Peter. I think you're just fine . . . What I want to say . . . if it wasn't for you around here, I don't know. What I mean . . .

(Peter *is interrupted by* Dussel's *turning on the light.* Dussel *stands in the doorway, startled to see* 540 Peter. Peter *advances toward him forbiddingly.* Dussel *backs out of the room.* Peter *closes the door on him.*)

Anne. Do you mean it, Peter? Do you really mean it?

Peter. I said it, didn't I?

Anne. Thank you, Peter!

(*In the main room* Mr. *and* Mrs. Frank *collect the dishes and take them to the sink, washing* 550 *them.* Margot *lies down again on the couch.* Dussel, *lost, wanders into* Peter's *room and takes up a book, starting to read.*)

Peter (*looking at the photographs on the wall*). You've got quite a collection.

Anne. Wouldn't you like some in your room? I could give you some. Heaven knows you spend enough 560 time in there . . . doing heaven knows what . . .

Peter. It's easier. A fight starts, or an argument . . . I duck in there.

Anne. You're lucky, having a room to go to. His lordship is always here . . . I hardly ever get a minute alone. When they start in on me, I can't duck away. I have to stand there and take it.

570 **Peter.** You gave some of it back just now.

Anne. I get so mad. They've formed their opinions . . . about everything . . . but we . . . we're still trying to find out . . . We have problems here that no other people our age have ever had. And just as you think you've solved them, something comes along and bang! 580 You have to start all over again.

Peter. At least you've got someone you can talk to.

Anne. Not really. Mother . . . I never discuss anything serious with her. She doesn't understand. Father's all right. We can talk about everything . . . everything but one thing. Mother. He simply won't talk about her. I don't think 590 you can be really intimate with anyone if he holds something back, do you?

Peter. I think your father's fine.

Anne. Oh, he is, Peter! He is! He's the only one who's ever given me the feeling that I have any sense. But anyway, nothing can take the place of school and play and friends of your own age . . . or near your 600 age . . . can it?

Peter. I suppose you miss your friends and all.

Anne. It isn't just . . . (*She breaks off, staring up at him for a second.*) Isn't it funny, you and I? Here we've been seeing each other every minute for almost a year and a half, and this is the first time we've ever really talked. It helps a lot to

have someone to talk to, don't you think? It helps you to let off steam.

Peter (*going to the door*). Well, any time you want to let off steam, you can come into my room.

Anne (*following him*). I can get up an awful lot of steam. You'll have to be careful how you say that.

Peter. It's all right with me.

Anne. Do you mean it?

Peter. I said it, didn't I?

(*He goes out.* Anne *stands in her doorway looking after him. As* Peter *gets to his door he stands for a minute looking back at her. Then he goes into his room.* Dussel *rises as he comes in, and quickly passes him, going out. He starts across for his room.* Anne *sees him coming, and pulls her door shut.* Dussel *turns back toward* Peter's *room.* Peter *pulls his door shut.* Dussel *stands there, bewildered, forlorn.*

The scene slowly dims out. The curtain falls on the scene. Anne's Voice comes over in the darkness . . . faintly at first, and then with growing strength.)

Anne's Voice. We've had bad news. The people from whom Miep got our ration books have been arrested. So we have had to cut down on our food. Our stomachs are so empty that they rumble and make strange noises, all in different keys. Mr. Van Daan's is deep and low, like a bass fiddle. Mine is high, whistling like a flute. As we all sit around waiting for supper, it's like an orchestra tuning up. It only needs Toscanini[2] to raise his baton and we'd be off in the Ride of the Valkyries.[3] Monday, the sixth of March, nineteen forty-four. Mr. Kraler is in the hospital. It seems he has ulcers. Pim says we are his ulcers. Miep has to run the business and us too. The Americans have landed on the southern tip of Italy. Father looks for a quick finish to the war. Mr. Dussel is waiting every day for the warehouse man to demand more money. Have I been skipping too much from one subject to another? I can't help it. I feel that spring is coming. I feel it in my whole body and soul. I feel utterly confused. I am longing . . . so longing . . . for everything . . . for friends . . . for someone to talk to . . . someone who understands . . . someone young, who feels as I do . . .

(*As these last lines are being said, the curtain rises on the scene. The lights dim on. Anne's Voice fades out.*)

Scene 2

It is evening, after supper. From outside we hear the sound of children playing. The "grownups," with the exception of Mr. Van Daan, *are all in the main room.*

---

[2] **Toscanini** (tŏs´-kə-nē´nē): Arturo Toscanini, a famous Italian orchestral conductor.

[3] **Ride of the Valkyries** (văl-kîr´əz): a moving passage from an opera by Richard Wagner, a German composer.

Mrs. Frank *is doing some mending.* Mrs. Van Daan *is reading a fashion magazine.* Mr. Frank *is going over business accounts.* Dussel, *in his dentist's jacket, is pacing up and down, impatient to get into his bedroom.* Mr. Van Daan *is upstairs working on a piece of embroidery in an embroidery frame.*

In his room Peter *is sitting before the mirror, smoothing his hair. As the scene goes on, he puts on his tie, brushes his coat and puts it on, preparing himself meticulously for a visit from* Anne. *On his wall are now hung some of* Anne's *motion picture stars.*

In her room Anne *too is getting dressed. She stands before the mirror in her slip, trying various ways of dressing her hair.* Margot *is seated on the sofa, hemming a skirt for* Anne *to wear.*

In the main room Dussel *can stand it no longer. He comes over, rapping sharply on the door of his and* Anne's *bedroom.*

Anne (*calling to him*). No, no, Mr. Dussel! I am not dressed yet. (Dussel *walks away, furious, sitting down and burying his head in his hands.* Anne *turns to* Margot.) How is that? How does that look?

Margot (*glancing at her briefly*). Fine.

Anne. You didn't even look.

Margot. Of course I did. It's fine.

Anne. Margot, tell me, am I terribly ugly?

Margot. Oh, stop fishing.

Anne. No. No. Tell me.

Margot. Of course you're not. You've got nice eyes . . . and a lot of animation, and . . .

Anne. A little vague, aren't you?

(*She reaches over and takes a brassière out of* Margot's *sewing basket. She holds it up to herself, studying the effect in the mirror. Outside,* Mrs. Frank, *feeling sorry for* Dussel, *comes over, knocking at the girls' door.*)

Mrs. Frank (*outside*). May I come in?

Margot. Come in, Mother.

Mrs. Frank (*shutting the door behind her*). Mr. Dussel's impatient to get in here.

Anne (*still with the brassière*). Heavens, he takes the room for himself the entire day.

Mrs. Frank (*gently*). Anne, dear, you're not going in again tonight to see Peter?

Anne (*dignified*). That is my intention.

Mrs. Frank. But you've already spent a great deal of time in there today.

Anne. I was in there exactly twice. Once to get the dictionary, and then three-quarters of an hour before supper.

Mrs. Frank. Aren't you afraid you're disturbing him?

Anne. Mother, I have some intuition.

Mrs. Frank. Then may I ask you this much, Anne. Please don't shut the door when you go in.

Anne. You sound like Mrs. Van Daan! (*She throws the brassière back in* Margot's *sewing basket and picks up her blouse, putting it on.*)

Mrs. Frank. No. No. I don't mean to suggest anything wrong. I only wish that you wouldn't expose yourself to criticism . . . that you wouldn't give Mrs. Van Daan the opportunity to be unpleasant.

Anne. Mrs. Van Daan doesn't need an opportunity to be unpleasant!

Mrs. Frank. Everyone's on edge, worried about Mr. Kraler. This is one more thing . . .

Anne. I'm sorry, Mother. I'm going to Peter's room. I'm not going to let Petronella Van Daan spoil our friendship.

(Mrs. Frank *hesitates for a second, then goes out, closing the door after her. She gets a pack of playing cards and sits at the center table, playing solitaire. In* Anne's *room* Margot *hands the finished skirt to* Anne. *As* Anne *is putting it on,* Margot *takes off her high-heeled shoes and stuffs paper in the toes so that* Anne *can wear them.*)

Margot (*to* Anne). Why don't you two talk in the main room? It'd save a lot of trouble. It's hard on Mother, having to listen to those remarks from Mrs. Van Daan and not say a word.

Anne. Why doesn't she say a word? I think it's ridiculous to take it and take it.

Margot. You don't understand Mother at all, do you? She can't talk back. She's not like you. It's just not in her nature to fight back.

Anne. Anyway . . . the only one I worry about is you. I feel awfully guilty about you.

(*She sits on the stool near* Margot, *putting on* Margot's *high-heeled shoes.*)

Margot. What about?

Anne. I mean, every time I go into Peter's room, I have a feeling I may be hurting you. (Margot *shakes her head.*) I know if it were me, I'd be wild. I'd be desperately jealous, if it were me.

Margot. Well, I'm not.

Anne. You don't feel badly? Really? Truly? You're not jealous?

Margot. Of course I'm jealous . . . jealous that you've got something to get up in the morning for . . . But jealous of you and Peter? No.

(Anne *goes back to the mirror.*)

Anne. Maybe there's nothing to be jealous of. Maybe he doesn't really like me. Maybe I'm just taking the place of his cat . . . (*She picks up a pair of short white gloves, putting them on.*) Wouldn't you like to come in with us?

Margot. I have a book.

(*The sound of the children playing outside fades out. In the main room*

Dussel *can stand it no longer. He jumps up, going to the bedroom door and knocking sharply.*)

Dussel. Will you please let me in my room!

Anne. Just a minute, dear, dear Mr. Dussel. (*She picks up her Mother's pink stole and adjusts it elegantly over her shoulders, then gives a last look in the mirror.*) Well, here I go . . . to run the gauntlet.[4] (*She starts out, followed by* Margot.)

Dussel (*as she appears—sarcastic*). Thank you so much.

(Dussel *goes into his room.* Anne *goes toward* Peter's *room, passing* Mrs. Van Daan *and her parents at the center table.*)

Mrs. Van Daan. My God, look at her! (Anne *pays no attention. She knocks at* Peter's *door.*) I don't know what good it is to have a son. I never see him. He wouldn't care if I killed myself. (Peter *opens the door and stands aside for* Anne *to come in.*) Just a minute, Anne. (*She goes to them at the door.*) I'd like to say a few words to my son. Do you mind? (Peter *and* Anne *stand waiting.*) Peter, I don't want you staying up till all hours tonight. You've got to have your sleep. You're a growing boy. You hear?

Mrs. Frank. Anne won't stay late. She's going to bed promptly at nine. Aren't you, Anne?

Anne. Yes, Mother . . . (*to* Mrs. Van Daan) May we go now?

Mrs. Van Daan. Are you asking me? I didn't know I had anything to say about it.

Mrs. Frank. Listen for the chimes, Anne dear.

(*The two young people go off into* Peter's *room, shutting the door after them.*)

Mrs. Van Daan (*to* Mrs. Frank). In my day it was the boys who called on the girls. Not the girls on the boys.

Mrs. Frank. You know how young people like to feel that they have secrets. Peter's room is the only place where they can talk.

Mrs. Van Daan. Talk! That's not what they called it when I was young.

(Mrs. Van Daan *goes off to the bathroom.* Margot *settles down to read her book.* Mr. Frank *puts his papers away and brings a chess game to the center table. He and* Mrs. Frank *start to play. In* Peter's *room,* Anne *speaks to* Peter, *indignant, humiliated.*)

Anne. Aren't they awful? Aren't they impossible? Treating us as if we were still in the nursery.

(*She sits on the cot.* Peter *gets a bottle of pop and two glasses.*)

Peter. Don't let it bother you. It doesn't bother me.

Anne. I suppose you can't really blame them . . . they think back

---

[4] **to run the gauntlet:** to endure a series of troubles or difficulties.

to what *they* were like at our age. They don't realize how much more advanced we are . . . When you think what wonderful discussions we've had! . . . Oh, I forgot. I was going to bring you some more pictures.

Peter. Oh, these are fine, thanks.

Anne. Don't you want some more? Miep just brought me some new ones.

Peter. Maybe later. (*He gives her a glass of pop and, taking some for himself, sits down facing her.*)

Anne (*looking up at one of the photographs*). I remember when I got that . . . I won it. I bet Jopie that I could eat five ice-cream cones. We'd all been playing ping-pong . . . We used to have heavenly times . . . we'd finish up with ice cream at the Delphi, or the Oasis, where Jews were allowed . . . there'd always be a lot of boys . . . we'd laugh and joke . . . I'd like to go back to it for a few days or a week. But after that I know I'd be bored to death. I think more seriously about life now. I want to be a journalist . . . or something. I love to write. What do you want to do?

Peter. I thought I might go off some place . . . work on a farm or something . . . some job that doesn't take much brains.

Anne. You shouldn't talk that way. You've got the most awful inferiority complex.

Peter. I know I'm not smart.

Anne. That isn't true. You're much better than I am in dozens of things . . . arithmetic and algebra and . . . well, you're a million times better than I am in algebra. (*with sudden directness*) You like Margot, don't you? Right from the start you liked her, liked her much better than me.

Peter (*uncomfortably*). Oh, I don't know.

(*In the main room* Mrs. Van Daan *comes from the bathroom and goes over to the sink, polishing a coffee pot.*)

Anne. It's all right. Everyone feels that way. Margot's so good. She's sweet and bright and beautiful and I'm not.

Peter. I wouldn't say that.

Anne. Oh, no, I'm not. I know that. I know quite well that I'm not a beauty. I never have been and never shall be.

Peter. I don't agree at all. I think you're pretty.

Anne. That's not true!

Peter. And another thing. You've changed . . . from at first, I mean.

Anne. I have?

Peter. I used to think you were awful noisy.

Anne. And what do you think now, Peter? How have I changed?

Peter. Well . . . er . . . you're . . . quieter.

(*In his room* Dussel *takes his pajamas and toilet articles and goes into the bathroom to change.*)

Anne. I'm glad you don't just hate me.

Peter. I never said that.

Anne. I bet when you get out of here you'll never think of me again.

Peter. That's crazy.

Anne. When you get back with all of your friends, you're going to say . . . now what did I ever see in that Mrs. Quack Quack.

Peter. I haven't got any friends.

Anne. Oh, Peter, of course you have. Everyone has friends.

Peter. Not me. I don't want any. I get along all right without them.

Anne. Does that mean you can get along without me? I think of myself as your friend.

Peter. No. If they were all like you, it'd be different.

(*He takes the glasses and the bottle and puts them away. There is a second's silence and then* Anne *speaks, hesitantly, shyly.*)

Anne. Peter, did you ever kiss a girl?

Peter. Yes. Once.

Anne (*to cover her feelings*). That picture's crooked. (Peter *goes over, straightening the photograph.*) Was she pretty?

Peter. Huh?

Anne. The girl that you kissed.

Peter. I don't know. I was blindfolded. (*He comes back and sits down again.*) It was at a party. One of those kissing games.

Anne (*relieved*). Oh. I don't suppose that really counts, does it?

Peter. It didn't with me.

Anne. I've been kissed twice. Once a man I'd never seen before kissed me on the cheek when he picked me up off the ice and I was crying. And the other was Mr. Koophuis, a friend of Father's who kissed my hand. You wouldn't say those counted, would you?

Peter. I wouldn't say so.

Anne. I know almost for certain that Margot would never kiss anyone unless she was engaged to them. And I'm sure too that Mother never touched a man before Pim. But I don't know . . . things are so different now . . . What do you think? Do you think a girl shouldn't kiss anyone except if she's engaged or something? It's so hard to try to think what to do, when here we are with the whole world falling around our ears and you think . . . well . . . you don't know what's going to happen tomorrow and . . . What do you think?

Peter. I suppose it'd depend on the girl. Some girls, anything they do's wrong. But others . . . well . . . it wouldn't necessarily be wrong with them. (*The carillon starts to strike nine o'clock.*) I've always thought that when two people . . .

Anne. Nine o'clock. I have to go.

Peter. That's right.

Anne (*without moving*). Good night.

(*There is a second's pause, then* Peter *gets up and moves toward the door.*)

Peter. You won't let them stop you coming?

Anne. No. (*She rises and starts for the door.*) Sometime I might bring my diary. There are so many things in it that I want to talk over with you. There's a lot about you.

Peter. What kind of things?

Anne. I wouldn't want you to see some of it. I thought you were a nothing, just the way you thought about me.

Peter. Did you change your mind, the way I changed my mind about you?

Anne. Well . . . You'll see . . .

(*For a second* Anne *stands looking up at* Peter, *longing for him to kiss her. As he makes no move she turns away. Then suddenly* Peter *grabs her awkwardly in his arms, kissing her on the cheek.* Anne *walks out dazed. She stands for a minute, her back to the people in the main room. As she regains her poise she goes to her mother and father and* Margot, *silently kissing them. They murmur their good nights to her. As she is about to open her bedroom door, she catches sight of* Mrs. Van Daan. *She goes quickly to her, taking her face in her hands and kissing her first on one cheek and then on the other. Then she hurries off into her room.* Mrs. Van Daan *looks after her, and then looks over at* Peter's *room. Her suspicions are confirmed.*)

Mrs. Van Daan (*She knows*). Ah hah!

(*The lights dim out. The curtain falls on the scene. In the darkness* Anne's Voice *comes faintly at first and then with growing strength.*)

Anne's Voice. By this time we all know each other so well that if anyone starts to tell a story, the rest can finish it for him. We're having to cut down still further on our meals. What makes it worse, the rats have been at work again. They've carried off some of our precious food. Even Mr. Dussel wishes now that Mouschi was here. Thursday, the twentieth of April, nineteen forty-four. Invasion fever is mounting every day. Miep tells us that people outside talk of nothing else. For myself, life has become much more pleasant. I often go to Peter's room after supper. Oh, don't think I'm in love, because I'm not. But it does make life more bearable to have someone with whom you can exchange views. No more tonight. P.S. . . . I must be honest. I must confess that I actually live for the next meeting. Is there anything lovelier than to sit under the skylight and feel the sun on your cheeks and have a darling boy in your arms? I admit now that I'm glad the Van Daans had a son and not a daughter. I've outgrown another dress. That's the third. I'm having to wear Margot's clothes after all. I'm working hard on my French and am now reading *La Belle Nivernaise*.

(*As she is saying the last lines—the curtain rises on the scene. The lights dim on, as* Anne's Voice *fades out.*)

Scene 3

It is night, a few weeks later. Everyone is in bed. There is complete quiet. In the Van Daans' room a match flares up for a moment and then is quickly put out. Mr. Van Daan, in bare feet, dressed in underwear and trousers, is dimly seen coming stealthily down the stairs and into the main room, where Mr. and Mrs. Frank and Margot are sleeping. He goes to the food safe and again lights a match. Then he cautiously opens the safe, taking out a half-loaf of bread. As he closes the safe, it creaks. He stands rigid. Mrs. Frank sits up in bed. She sees him.

Mrs. Frank (*screaming*). Otto! Otto! Komme schnell![5]

(*The rest of the people wake, hurriedly getting up.*)

Mr. Frank. Was ist los? Was ist passiert?[6]

(Dussel, *followed by* Anne, *comes from his room.*)

Mrs. Frank (*as she rushes over to* Mr. Van Daan). Er stiehlt das Essen![7]

Dussel (*grabbing* Mr. Van Daan). You! You! Give me that.

Mrs. Van Daan (*coming down the stairs*). Putti . . . Putti . . . what is it?

Dussel (*his hands on* Van Daan's *neck*). You dirty thief . . . stealing food . . . you good-for-nothing . . .

Mr. Frank. Mr. Dussel! For God's sake! Help me, Peter!

(Peter *comes over, trying, with* Mr. Frank, *to separate the two struggling men.*)

Peter. Let him go! Let go!

(Dussel *drops* Mr. Van Daan, *pushing him away. He shows them the end of a loaf of bread that he has taken from* Van Daan.)

Dussel. You greedy, selfish . . . !

(Margot *turns on the lights.*)

Mrs. Van Daan. Putti . . . what is it?

(*All of* Mrs. Frank's *gentleness, her self-control, is gone. She is outraged, in a frenzy of indignation.*)

Mrs. Frank. The bread! He was stealing the bread!

Dussel. It was you, and all the time we thought it was the rats!

Mr. Frank. Mr. Van Daan, how could you!

---

[5] ***Komme schnell!*** (kôm´e shněl´) German: Come quickly!

[6] ***Was ist los? Was ist passiert?*** (väs ĭst lôs´? väs ĭst päsērt´?) German: What's the matter? What has happened?

[7] ***Er stiehlt das Essen!*** (ĕr shtēlt´ däs ĕs´ən) German: He is stealing food!

Mr. Van Daan. I'm hungry.

Mrs. Frank. We're all of us hungry! I see the children getting thinner and thinner. Your own son Peter . . . I've heard him moan in his sleep, he's so hungry. And you come in the night and steal food that should go to them . . . to the children!

Mrs. Van Daan (*going to* Mr. Van Daan *protectively*). He needs more food than the rest of us. He's used to more. He's a big man.

(Mr. Van Daan *breaks away, going over and sitting on the couch.*)

Mrs. Frank (*turning on* Mrs. Van Daan). And you . . . you're worse than he is! You're a mother, and yet you sacrifice your child to this man . . . this . . . this . . .

Mr. Frank. Edith! Edith!

(Margot *picks up the pink woolen stole, putting it over her mother's shoulders.*)

Mrs. Frank (*paying no attention, going on to* Mrs. Van Daan). Don't think I haven't seen you! Always saving the choicest bits for him! I've watched you day after day and I've held my tongue. But not any longer! Not after this! Now I want him to go! I want him to get out of here!

Mr. Frank. Edith!

Mr. Van Daan. Get out of here? ⎫
Mrs. Van Daan. What do you mean? ⎬ *Together*

Mrs. Frank. Just that! Take your things and get out!

Mr. Frank (*to* Mrs. Frank). You're speaking in anger. You cannot mean what you are saying.

Mrs. Frank. I mean exactly that!

(Mrs. Van Daan *takes a cover from the* Franks' *bed, pulling it about her.*)

Mr. Frank. For two long years we have lived here, side by side. We have respected each other's rights . . . we have managed to live in peace. Are we now going to throw it all away? I know this will never happen again, will it, Mr. Van Daan?

Mr. Van Daan. No. No.

Mrs. Frank. He steals once! He'll steal again!

(Mr. Van Daan, *holding his stomach, starts for the bathroom.* Anne *puts her arms around him, helping him up the step.*)

Mr. Frank. Edith, please. Let us be calm. We'll all go to our rooms . . . and afterwards we'll sit down quietly and talk this out . . . we'll find some way . . .

Mrs. Frank. No! No! No more talk! I want them to leave!

Mrs. Van Daan. You'd put us out, on the streets?

Mrs. Frank. There are other hiding places.

Mrs. Van Daan. A cellar . . . a closet. I know. And we have no money left even to pay for that.

Mrs. Frank. I'll give you money. Out of my own pocket I'll give it gladly. (*She gets her purse from a shelf and comes back with it.*)

Mrs. Van Daan. Mr. Frank, you told Putti you'd never forget what he'd done for you when you came to Amsterdam. You said you could never repay him, that you . . .

Mrs. Frank (*counting out money*). If my husband had any obligation to you, he's paid it, over and over.

Mr. Frank. Edith, I've never seen you like this before. I don't know you.

Mrs. Frank. I should have spoken out long ago.

Dussel. You can't be nice to some people.

Mrs. Van Daan (*turning on* Dussel). There would have been plenty for all of us, if you hadn't come in here!

Mr. Frank. We don't need the Nazis to destroy us. We're destroying ourselves.

(*He sits down, with his head in his hands.* Mrs. Frank *goes to* Mrs. Van Daan.)

Mrs. Frank (*giving* Mrs. Van Daan *some money*). Give this to Miep. She'll find you a place.

Anne. Mother, you're not putting Peter out. Peter hasn't done anything.

Mrs. Frank. He'll stay, of course. When I say I must protect the children, I mean Peter too.

(Peter *rises from the steps where he has been sitting.*)

Peter. I'd have to go if Father goes.

(Mr. Van Daan *comes from the bathroom.* Mrs. Van Daan *hurries to him and takes him to the couch. Then she gets water from the sink to bathe his face.*)

Mrs. Frank (*while this is going on*). He's no father to you . . . that man! He doesn't know what it is to be a father!

Peter (*starting for his room*). I wouldn't feel right. I couldn't stay.

Mrs. Frank. Very well, then. I'm sorry.

Anne (*rushing over to* Peter). No, Peter! No! (Peter *goes into his room, closing the door after him.* Anne *turns back to her mother, crying.*) I don't care about the food. They can have mine! I don't want it! Only don't send them away. It'll be daylight soon. They'll be caught . . .

Margot (*putting her arms comfortingly around* Anne). Please, Mother!

Mrs. Frank. They're not going now. They'll stay here until Miep finds them a place. (*to* Mrs. Van Daan) But one thing I insist on! He must never come down here again! He must never come to this room where the food is stored! We'll divide what we have . . . an equal share for each! (Dussel *hurries over to get a sack of potatoes from the food safe.* Mrs. Frank *goes on, to* Mrs. Van Daan.) You can cook it here and take it up to him.

(Dussel *brings the sack of potatoes back to the center table.*)

Margot. Oh, no. No. We haven't sunk so far that we're going to fight over a handful of rotten potatoes.

Dussel (*dividing the potatoes into piles*). Mrs. Frank, Mr. Frank, Margot, Anne, Peter, Mrs. Van Daan, Mr. Van Daan, myself . . . Mrs. Frank . . .

(*The buzzer sounds in Miep's signal.*)

Mr. Frank. It's Miep! (*He hurries over, getting his overcoat and putting it on.*)

Margot. At this hour?

Mrs. Frank. It is trouble.

Mr. Frank (*as he starts down to unbolt the door*). I beg you, don't let her see a thing like this!

Mr. Dussel (*counting without stopping*). . . . Anne, Peter, Mrs. Van Daan, Mr. Van Daan, myself . . .

Margot (*to* Dussel). Stop it! Stop it!

Dussel. . . . . Mr. Frank, Margot, Anne, Peter, Mrs. Van Daan, Mr. Van Daan, myself, Mrs. Frank . . .

Mrs. Van Daan. You're keeping the big ones for yourself! All the big ones . . . Look at the size of that! . . . And that! . . .

(Dussel *continues on with his dividing.* Peter, *with his shirt and trousers on, comes from his room.*)

Margot. Stop it! Stop it!

(*We hear* Miep's *excited voice speaking to* Mr. Frank *below.*)

Miep. Mr. Frank . . . the most wonderful news! . . . The invasion has begun!

Mr. Frank. Go on, tell them! Tell them!

(Miep *comes running up the steps, ahead of* Mr. Frank. *She has a man's raincoat on over her nightclothes and a bunch of orange-colored flowers in her hand.*)

Miep. Did you hear that, everybody? Did you hear what I said? The invasion has begun! The invasion!

(*They all stare at* Miep, *unable to grasp what she is telling them.* Peter *is the first to recover his wits.*)

Peter. Where?

Mrs. Van Daan. When? When, Miep?

Miep. It began early this morning . . .

(*As she talks on, the realization of what she has said begins to dawn on them. Everyone goes crazy. A wild demonstration takes place.* Mrs. Frank *hugs* Mr. Van Daan.)

Mrs. Frank. Oh, Mr. Van Daan, did you hear that? (Dussel *embraces* Mrs. Van Daan. Peter *grabs a frying pan and parades around the room, beating on it, singing the Dutch National Anthem.* Anne *and* Margot *follow him, singing, weaving in and out among the excited grownups.* Margot *breaks away to take the flowers from* Miep *and distribute them to everyone. While this pandemonium is going on* Mrs. Frank *tries to make herself heard above the excitement.*)

Mrs. Frank (*to* Miep). How do you know?

Miep. The radio . . . The B.B.C.! They said they landed on the coast of Normandy!

Peter. The British?

Miep. British, Americans, French, Dutch, Poles, Norwegians . . . all of them! More than four thousand ships! Churchill spoke, and General Eisenhower! D-Day they call it!

Mr. Frank. Thank God, it's come!

Mrs. Van Daan. At last!

Miep (*starting out*). I'm going to tell Mr. Kraler. This'll be better than any blood transfusion.

Mr. Frank (*stopping her*). What part of Normandy did they land, did they say?

Miep. Normandy . . . that's all I know now . . . I'll be up the minute I hear some more! (*She goes hurriedly out.*)

Mr. Frank (*to* Mrs. Frank). What did I tell you? What did I tell you?

(Mrs. Frank *indicates that he has forgotten to bolt the door after* Miep. *He hurries down the steps.* Mr. Van Daan, *sitting on the couch, suddenly breaks into a convulsive sob. Everybody looks at him, bewildered.*)

Mrs. Van Daan (*hurrying to him*). Putti! Putti! What is it? What happened?

Mr. Van Daan. Please. I'm so ashamed.

(Mr. Frank *comes back up the steps.*)

Dussel. Oh, for God's sake!

Mrs. Van Daan. Don't, Putti.

Margot. It doesn't matter now!

Mr. Frank (*going to* Mr. Van Daan). Didn't you hear what Miep said? The invasion has come! We're going to be liberated! This is a time to celebrate!

(*He embraces* Mrs. Frank *and then hurries to the cupboard and gets the cognac and a glass.*)

Mr. Van Daan. To steal bread from children!

Mrs. Frank. We've all done things that we're ashamed of.

Anne. Look at me, the way I've treated Mother . . . so mean and horrid to her.

Mrs. Frank. No, Anneke, no.

(Anne *runs to her mother, putting her arms around her.*)

Anne. Oh, Mother, I was. I was awful.

Mr. Van Daan. Not like me. No one is as bad as me!

Dussel (*to* Mr. Van Daan). Stop it now! Let's be happy!

Mr. Frank (*giving* Mr. Van Daan *a glass of cognac*). Here! Here! Schnapps! L'chaim![8] (Van Daan *takes the cognac. They all watch him. He gives them a feeble smile.* Anne *puts up her fingers in a V-for-Victory sign. As* Van Daan *gives an answering V-sign, they are startled to hear a loud sob from behind them. It is* Mrs. Frank, *stricken with remorse. She is sitting on the other side of the room.*)

Mrs. Frank (*through her sobs*). When I think of the terrible things I said . . .

(Mr. Frank, Anne, *and* Margot *hurry to her, trying to comfort her.* Mr. Van Daan *brings her his glass of cognac.*)

---

[8] ***Schnapps!*** (shnäps) *German:* Brandy! ***L'chaim!*** (lə khä´yĭm) *Hebrew:* To life!

Mr. Van Daan. No! No! You were right!

Mrs. Frank. That I should speak that way to you! . . . Our friends! . . . Our guests! (*She starts to cry again.*)

Dussel. Stop it, you're spoiling the whole invasion!

(*As they are comforting her, the lights dim out. The curtain falls.*)

Anne's Voice (*faintly at first and then with growing strength*). We're all in much better spirits these days. There's still excellent news of the invasion. The best part about it is that I have a feeling that friends are coming. Who knows? Maybe I'll be back in school by fall. Ha, ha! The joke is on us! The warehouse man doesn't know a thing and we are paying him all that money! . . . Wednesday, the second of July, nineteen forty-four. The invasion seems temporarily to be bogged down. Mr. Kraler has to have an operation, which looks bad. The Gestapo have found the radio that was stolen. Mr. Dussel says they'll trace it back and back to the thief, and then, it's just a matter of time till they get to us. Everyone is low. Even poor Pim can't raise their spirits. I have often been downcast myself . . . but never in despair. I can shake off everything if I write. But . . . and that is the great question . . . will I ever be able to write well? I want to so much. I want to go on living even after my death. Another birthday has gone by, so now I am fifteen. Already I know what I want. I have a goal, an opinion.

(*As this is being said—the curtain rises on the scene, the lights dim on, and* Anne's Voice *fades out.*)

Scene 4

It is an afternoon a few weeks later . . . Everyone but Margot *is in the main room. There is a sense of great tension.*

Both Mrs. Frank *and* Mr. Van Daan *are nervously pacing back and forth,* Dussel *is standing at the window, looking down fixedly at the street below.* Peter *is at the center table, trying to do his lessons.* Anne *sits opposite him, writing in her diary.* Mrs. Van Daan *is seated on the couch, her eyes on* Mr. Frank *as he sits reading.*

The sound of a telephone ringing comes from the office below. They all are rigid, listening tensely. Mr. Dussel *rushes down to* Mr. Frank.

Dussel. There it goes again, the telephone! Mr. Frank, do you hear?

Mr. Frank (*quietly*). Yes. I hear.

Dussel (*pleading, insistent*). But this is the third time, Mr. Frank! The third time in quick succession! It's a signal! I tell you it's Miep, trying to get us! For some reason she can't come to us and she's trying to warn us of something!

Mr. Frank. Please. Please.

Mr. Van Daan (*to* Dussel). You're wasting your breath.

Dussel. Something has happened, Mr. Frank. For three days now Miep hasn't been to see us! And today not a man has come to work. There hasn't been a sound in the building!

Mrs. Frank. Perhaps it's Sunday. We may have lost track of the days.

Mr. Van Daan (to Anne). You with the diary there. What day is it?

Dussel (going to Mrs. Frank). I don't lose track of the days! I know exactly what day it is! It's Friday, the fourth of August. Friday, and not a man at work. (*He rushes back to* Mr. Frank, *pleading with him, almost in tears.*) I tell you Mr. Kraler's dead. That's the only explanation. He's dead and they've closed down the building, and Miep's trying to tell us!

Mr. Frank. She'd never telephone us.

Dussel (*frantic*). Mr. Frank, answer that! I beg you, answer it!

Mr. Frank. No.

Mr. Van Daan. Just pick it up and listen. You don't have to speak. Just listen and see if it's Miep.

Dussel (*speaking at the same time*). For God's sake . . . I ask you.

Mr. Frank. No. I've told you, no. I'll do nothing that might let anyone know we're in the building.

Peter. Mr. Frank's right.

Mr. Van Daan. There's no need to tell us what side you're on.

Mr. Frank. If we wait patiently, quietly, I believe that help will come.

(*There is silence for a minute as they all listen to the telephone ringing.*)

Dussel. I'm going down. (*He rushes down the steps.* Mr. Frank *tries ineffectually to hold him.* Dussel *runs to the lower door, unbolting it. The telephone stops ringing.* Dussel *bolts the door and comes slowly back up the steps.*) Too late. (Mr. Frank *goes to* Margot *in* Anne's *bedroom.*)

Mr. Van Daan. So we just wait here until we die.

Mrs. Van Daan (*hysterically*). I can't stand it! I'll kill myself! I'll kill myself!

Mr. Van Daan. For God's sake, stop it!

(*In the distance, a German military band is heard playing a Viennese waltz.*)

Mrs. Van Daan. I think you'd be glad if I did! I think you want me to die!

Mr. Van Daan. Whose fault is it we're here? (Mrs. Van Daan *starts for her room. He follows, talking at her.*) We could've been safe somewhere . . . in America or Switzerland. But no! No! You wouldn't leave when I wanted to. You couldn't leave your things. You couldn't leave your precious furniture.

Mrs. Van Daan. Don't touch me!

(*She hurries up the stairs, followed by* Mr. Van Daan. Peter, *unable to bear it, goes to his room.* Anne *looks after him, deeply concerned.* Dussel *returns to his post at the window.* Mr. Frank *comes back into the main room and takes a book, trying to read.* Mrs. Frank *sits near the sink, starting to peel some potatoes.* Anne *quietly goes to* Peter's *room, closing the door after her.* Peter *is lying face down on the cot.* Anne *leans over him, holding him in her arms, trying to bring him out of his despair.*)

Anne. Look, Peter, the sky. (*She looks up through the skylight.*) What a lovely, lovely day! Aren't the clouds beautiful? You know what I do when it seems as if I couldn't stand being cooped up for one more minute? I *think* myself out. I think myself on a walk in the park where I used to go with Pim. Where the jonquils and the crocus and the violets grow down the slopes. You know the most wonderful part about *thinking* yourself out? You can have it any way you like. You can have roses and violets and chrysanthemums all blooming at the same time . . . It's funny . . . I used to take it all for granted . . . and now I've gone crazy about everything to do with nature. Haven't you?

Peter. I've just gone crazy. I think if something doesn't happen soon . . . if we don't get out of here . . . I can't stand much more of it!

Anne (*softly*). I wish you had a religion, Peter.

Peter. No, thanks! Not me!

Anne. Oh, I don't mean you have to be Orthodox[9] . . . or believe in heaven and hell and purgatory and things . . . I just mean some religion . . . it doesn't matter what. Just to believe in something! When I think of all that's out there . . . the trees . . . and flowers . . . and seagulls . . . when I think of the dearness of you, Peter . . . and the goodness of the people we know . . . Mr. Kraler, Miep, Dirk, the vegetable man, all risking their lives for us every day . . . When I think of these good things, I'm not afraid any more . . . I find myself, and God, and I . . . (Peter *interrupts, getting up and walking away.*)

Peter. That's fine! But when I begin to think, I get mad! Look at us, hiding out for two years. Not able to move! Caught here like . . . waiting for them to come and get us . . . and all for what?

Anne. We're not the only people that've had to suffer. There've always been people that've had to . . . sometimes one race . . . sometimes another . . . and yet . . .

Peter. That doesn't make me feel any better!

Anne (*going to him*). I know it's terrible, trying to have any faith . . . when people are doing such horrible . . . But you know what I sometimes think? I think the world may be going through a

---

[9] **Orthodox:** Orthodox Jews who strictly observe Jewish laws and traditions.

phase, the way I was with Mother. It'll pass, maybe not for hundreds of years, but some day . . . I still believe, in spite of everything, that people are really good at heart.

Peter. I want to see something now . . . Not a thousand years from now! (*He goes over, sitting down again on the cot.*)

Anne. But, Peter, if you'd only look at it as part of a great pattern . . . that we're just a little minute in the life . . . (*She breaks off.*) Listen to us, going at each other like a couple of stupid grownups! Look at the sky now. Isn't it lovely? (*She holds out her hand to him. Peter takes it and rises, standing with her at the window looking out, his arms around her.*) Some day, when we're outside again, I'm going to . . .

(*She breaks off as she hears the sound of a car, its brakes squealing as it comes to a sudden stop. The people in the other rooms also become aware of the sound. They listen tensely. Another car roars up to a screeching stop.* Anne *and* Peter *come from* Peter's *room.* Mr. *and* Mrs. Van Daan *creep down the stairs.* Dussel *comes out from his room. Everyone is listening, hardly breathing. A doorbell clangs again and again in the building below.* Mr. Frank *starts quietly down the steps to the door.* Dussel *and* Peter *follow him. The others stand rigid, waiting, terrified.*

In a few seconds Dussel *comes stumbling back up the steps. He shakes off* Peter's *help and goes to his room.* Mr. Frank *bolts the door below, and comes slowly back up the steps. Their eyes are all on him as he stands there for a minute. They realize that what they feared has happened.* Mrs. Van Daan *starts to whimper.* Mr. Van Daan *puts her gently in a chair, and then hurries off up the stairs to their room to collect their things.* Peter *goes to comfort his mother. There is a sound of violent pounding on a door below.*)

Mr. Frank (*quietly*). For the past two years we have lived in fear. Now we can live in hope.

(*The pounding below becomes more insistent. There are muffled sounds of voices, shouting commands.*)

Men's Voices. *Auf machen! Da drinnen! Auf machen! Schnell! Schnell! Schnell! etc., etc.*[10]

(*The street door below is forced open. We hear the heavy tread of footsteps coming up.* Mr. Frank *gets two school bags from the shelves, and gives one to* Anne *and the other to* Margot. *He goes to get a bag for* Mrs. Frank. *The sound of feet coming up grows louder.* Peter *comes to* Anne, *kissing her good-bye, then he goes to his room to collect his things. The buzzer of their door starts to ring.* Mr. Frank *brings* Mrs. Frank *a bag. They stand together, waiting. We hear the thud of gun butts on the door, trying to break it down.*

---

[10] **Auf machen! . . . Schnell!** (ouf´ mäzкн´ən! dä drĭn´ən! ouf´ mäкн´ən! shnĕl! shnĕl! shnĕl!) **German:** Open up! Inside there! Open up! Quick! Quick! Quick!

Anne *stands, holding her school satchel, looking over at her father and mother with a soft, reassuring smile. She is no longer a child, but a woman with courage to meet whatever lies ahead.*

The lights dim out. The curtain falls on the scene. We hear a mighty crash as the door is shattered. After a second Anne's Voice *is heard.*)

Anne's Voice. And so it seems our stay here is over. They are waiting for us now. They've allowed us five minutes to get our things. We can each take a bag and whatever it will hold of clothing. Nothing else. So, dear Diary, that means I must leave you behind. Good-bye for a while. P.S. Please, please, Miep, or Mr. Kraler, or anyone else. If you should find this diary, will you please keep it safe for me, because some day I hope . . .

(*Her voice stops abruptly. There is silence. After a second the curtain rises.*)

Scene 5

It is again the afternoon in November, 1945. The rooms are as we saw them in the first scene. Mr. Kraler *has joined* Miep *and* Mr. Frank. *There are coffee cups on the table. We see a great change in* Mr. Frank. *He is calm now. His bitterness is gone. He slowly turns a few pages of the diary. They are blank.*

Mr. Frank. No more. (*He closes the diary and puts it down on the couch beside him.*)

Miep. I'd gone to the country to find food. When I got back the block was surrounded by police . . .

Mr. Kraler. We made it our business to learn how they knew. It was the thief . . . the thief who told them.

(Miep *goes up to the gas burner, bringing back a pot of coffee.*)

Mr. Frank (*after a pause*). It seems strange to say this, that anyone could be happy in a concentration camp. But Anne was happy in the camp in Holland where they first took us. After two years of being shut up in these rooms, she could be out . . . out in the sunshine and the fresh air that she loved.

Miep (*offering the coffee to* Mr. Frank). A little more?

Mr. Frank (*holding out his cup to her*). The news of the war was good. The British and Americans were sweeping through France. We felt sure that they would get to us in time. In September we were told that we were to be shipped to Poland . . . The men to one camp. The women to another. I was sent to Auschwitz. They went to Belsen. In January we were freed, the few of us who were left. The war wasn't yet over, so it took us a long time to get home. We'd be sent here and there behind the lines where

The Diary of Anne Frank: Act Two **351**

we'd be safe. Each time our train would stop . . . at a siding, or a crossing . . . we'd all get out and go from group to group . . . Where were you? Were you at Belsen? At Buchenwald? At Mauthausen? Is it possible that you knew my wife? Did you ever see my husband? My son? My daughter? That's how I found out about my wife's death . . . of Margot, the Van Daans . . . Dussel. But Anne . . . I still hoped . . . Yesterday I went to Rotterdam. I'd heard of a woman there . . . She'd been in Belsen with Anne . . . I know now.

(*He picks up the diary again, and turns the pages back to find a certain passage. As he finds it we hear* Anne's Voice.)

Anne's Voice. In spite of everything, I still believe that people are really good at heart.

(Mr. Frank *slowly closes the diary.*)

Mr. Frank. She puts me to shame. (*They are silent.*)

The Curtain Falls.

COLLABORATIVE DISCUSSION Mr. Frank read this from Anne's diary: "In spite of everything, I still believe that people are really good at heart." With a partner, discuss examples from the play that demonstrate that Anne really believed this to be true.

Analyze Dialogue in Drama

The story in a play is told mainly through dialogue, not only by the words characters speak but also by the way in which they say them. Through the dialogue, a playwright accomplishes different purposes:
- Dialogue propels the action in the story, moving the plot forward.
- Sometimes dialogue establishes a conflict that prompts characters to make a decision.
- Dialogue reveals different qualities, or **character traits,** of characters, because what people say and how they say it can reveal things such as fear, arrogance, doubt, or bravery.

Notice how the following dialogue increases tension in the play and reveals that Mr. Frank is forced to make a decision about a worker who may be blackmailing them:

Mr. Frank (*to* Mr. Kraler). How was it left? What did you tell him?

Mr. Kraler. I said I had to think about it. What shall I do? Pay him the money? . . . Take a chance on firing him . . . or what? I don't know.

As you analyze the dialogue, ask yourself, "What are these words explaining about the plot? What are they revealing about this character?"

Analyze Incidents in Drama

Playwrights usually tell events in **chronological order,** the order in which they occurred. They may, however, tell some events in a different order.

When an author interrupts the chronological order by describing something that took place at an earlier time, it is called a **flashback.** A flashback provides information that helps readers better understand a current situation. For example, in *The Diary of Anne Frank,* the first scene begins in November of 1945. Mr. Frank is speaking with Miep after World War II is over. The scene ends with a flashback as the audience hears words that Anne wrote in her diary during the war:

Our hiding place was to be upstairs in the building where Father used to have his business. Three other people were coming in with us . . . the Van Daans and their son Peter . . . Father knew the Van Daans but we had never met them . . .

As you analyze *The Diary of Anne Frank,* identify where the flashback ends.

Analyzing the Text

Cite Text Evidence   Support your responses with evidence from the text.

1. **Interpret** Reread lines 241–291 in Act Two. What does this part of the dialogue reveal about each of the Van Daans?

2. **Compare** Explain the differences between Peter and Anne's relationship in Act One and in Act Two.

3. **Cause/Effect** Examine the dialogue in lines 1167–1239 that describes the aftermath of Mr. Van Daan's theft. Explain the effect of this event and how it propels the action of the story.

4. **Infer** Mr. Frank says, "The invasion has come! We're going to be liberated!" What invasion is Mr. Frank speaking about?

5. **Analyze** Reread lines 1624–1651. What does this section of dialogue demonstrate about Mr. Frank and Mr. Dussel?

6. **Evaluate** Does the use of an extended flashback add or detract from the impact of this play? Explain your opinion.

Speaking and Listening

With a small group, choose a section from the play in which the dialogue provokes a character to make a decision. Consider how each character would sound. Rehearse the lines. Then stage a dramatic reading of the section that communicates clearly the characters' thoughts and feelings.

PERFORMANCE TASK

Speaking Activity: Response to Literature Choose three characters from the play, and plan a speech analyzing the character of each one. Use the character's words, actions, and interactions with others to support your analysis.

- Identify each character and explain his or her role in the play.
- Describe the character's physical appearance and age.
- Discuss positive character traits as well as any weaknesses.
- Explain the character's motivations, actions, and reactions in relation to others and to historical events.
- Analyze the character's attitudes and feelings and how these change or remain the same over time.

Anne Frank (1929–1945) *was 13 years old when she and her family went into hiding to avoid being sent to concentration camps by the Nazis. During the two years she spent living in an attic, she kept a diary, which she called "Kitty." After the war, Anne's father, the only family member to survive the concentration camps the family was eventually sent to, chose to publish the diary. The selection you are about to read consists of entries taken from throughout the work.*

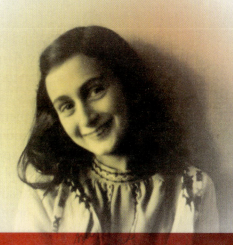

from The Diary of a Young Girl

Diary by Anne Frank

SETTING A PURPOSE As you read, think about which of Anne's thoughts and feelings are similar to that of any teenager and which are unique to her family's particularly dire, or urgent, situation.

WEDNESDAY, JANUARY 13, 1943

Dearest Kitty,

This morning I was constantly interrupted, and as a result I haven't been able to finish a single thing I've begun.

We have a new pastime, namely, filling packages with powdered gravy. The gravy is one of Gies & Co.'s[1] products. Mr. Kugler hasn't been able to find anyone else to fill the packages, and besides, it's cheaper if we do the job. It's the kind of work they do in prisons. It's incredibly boring and makes us dizzy and giggly.

Terrible things are happening outside. At any time of night and day, poor helpless people are being dragged out of their homes. They're allowed to take only a knapsack and a

---

[1] **Gies** (gēs) **& Co.:** the name of Mr. Frank's company in Amsterdam.

little cash with them, and even then, they're robbed of these possessions on the way. Families are torn apart; men, women and children are separated. Children come home from school to find that their parents have disappeared. Women return from shopping to find their houses sealed, their families gone. The Christians in Holland are also living in fear because their sons are being sent to Germany. Everyone is scared. Every night hundreds of planes pass over Holland on their way to German cities, to sow their bombs on German soil. Every hour hundreds, or maybe even thousands, of people are being killed in Russia and Africa. No one can keep out of the conflict, the entire world is at war, and even though the Allies[2] are doing better, the end is nowhere in sight.

As for us, we're quite fortunate. Luckier than millions of people. It's quiet and safe here, and we're using our money to buy food. We're so selfish that we talk about "after the war" and look forward to new clothes and shoes, when actually we should be saving every penny to help others when the war is over, to salvage whatever we can.

The children in this neighborhood run around in thin shirts and wooden shoes. They have no coats, no socks, no caps and no one to help them. Gnawing on a carrot to still their hunger pangs, they walk from their cold houses through cold streets to an even colder classroom. Things have gotten so bad in Holland that hordes of children stop passersby in the streets to beg for a piece of bread.

I could spend hours telling you about the suffering the war has brought, but I'd only make myself more miserable. All we can do is wait, as calmly as possible, for it to end. Jews and Christians alike are waiting, the whole world is waiting, and many are waiting for death.

Yours, Anne

---

[2] **Allies:** the group of countries that fought against Hitler and Germany.

Saturday, January 30, 1943

Dearest Kitty,

I'm seething with rage, yet I can't show it. I'd like to scream, stamp my foot, give Mother a good shaking, cry and I don't know what else because of the nasty words, mocking looks and accusations that she hurls at me day after day, piercing me like arrows from a tightly strung bow, which are nearly impossible to pull from my body. I'd like to scream at Mother, Margot, the van Daans, Dussel and Father too: "Leave me alone, let me have at least one night when I don't cry myself to sleep with my eyes burning and my head pounding. Let me get away, away from everything, away from this world!" But I can't do that. I can't let them see my doubts, or the wounds they've inflicted on me. I couldn't bear their sympathy or their good-humored derision. It would only make me want to scream even more.

Everyone thinks I'm showing off when I talk, ridiculous when I'm silent, **insolent** when I answer, cunning when I have a good idea, lazy when I'm tired, selfish when I eat one bit more than I should, stupid, cowardly, calculating, etc., etc. All day long I hear nothing but what an exasperating child I am, and although I laugh it off and pretend not to mind, I do mind. I wish I could ask God to give me another personality, one that doesn't antagonize everyone.

But that's impossible. I'm stuck with the character I was born with, and yet I'm sure I'm not a bad person. I do my best to please everyone, more than they'd ever suspect in a million years. When I'm upstairs, I try to laugh it off because I don't want them to see my troubles.

More than once, after a series of absurd **reproaches**, I've snapped at Mother: "I don't care what you say. Why don't you just wash your hands of me—I'm a hopeless case." Of course, she'd tell me not to talk back and virtually ignore me for two days. Then suddenly all would be forgotten and she'd treat me like everyone else.

insolent
(ĭn´ sə-lənt) *adj.* If someone is *insolent*, he or she is rude or disrespectful.

reproach
(rĭ-prōch´) *n.* A *reproach* is a scolding or blaming.

It's impossible for me to be all smiles one day and venomous³ the next. I'd rather choose the golden mean,⁴ which isn't so golden, and keep my thoughts to myself. Perhaps sometime I'll treat the others with the same contempt as they treat me. Oh, if only I could.

                                        Yours, Anne

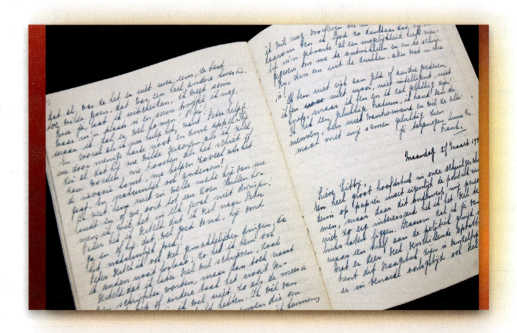

Anne Frank's diaries are on display at the Anne Frank House in Amsterdam, the Netherlands.

FRIDAY, FEBRUARY 5, 1943

Dearest Kitty,
Though it's been ages since I've written to you about the squabbles, there's still no change. In the beginning Mr. Dussel took our soon-forgotten clashes very seriously, but now he's grown used to them and no longer tries to **mediate**.

Margot and Peter aren't exactly what you'd call "young"; they're both so quiet and boring. Next to them, I stick out like a sore thumb, and I'm always being told, "Margot and Peter don't act that way. Why don't you follow your sister's example!" I hate that.

mediate
(mē′dē-āt′) v. If you *mediate* a conflict, you try to settle the differences.

---

³ **venomous** (vĕn′ə-məs): spiteful or bitter.
⁴ **golden mean:** the middle between two extremes.

I confess that I have absolutely no desire to be like Margot. She's too weak-willed and passive to suit me; she lets herself be swayed by others and always backs down under pressure. I want to have more spunk! But I keep ideas like these to myself. They'd only laugh at me if I offered this in my defense.

During meals the air is filled with tension. Fortunately, the outbursts are sometimes held in check by the "soup eaters," the people from the office who come up to have a cup of soup for lunch.

This afternoon Mr. van Daan again brought up the fact that Margot eats so little. "I suppose you do it to keep your figure," he added in a mocking tone.

Mother, who always comes to Margot's defense, said in a loud voice, "I can't stand that stupid chatter of yours a minute longer."

Mrs. van D. turned red as a beet. Mr. van D. stared straight ahead and said nothing.

Still, we often have a good laugh. Not long ago Mrs. van D. was entertaining us with some bit of nonsense or another. She was talking about the past, about how well she got along with her father and what a flirt she was. "And you know," she continued, "my father told me that if a gentleman ever got fresh, I was to say, 'Remember, sir, that I'm a lady,' and he'd know what I meant." We split our sides laughing, as if she'd told us a good joke . . .

Yours, Anne

Monday evening, November 8, 1943

Dearest Kitty,
If you were to read all my letters in one sitting, you'd be struck by the fact that they were written in a variety of moods. It annoys me to be so dependent on the moods here in the Annex, but I'm not the only one: we're all subject to them. If I'm engrossed in a book, I have to rearrange my thoughts before I can mingle with other people, because otherwise they might think I was strange. As you can see, I'm currently in the middle of a depression. I couldn't really tell you what set it off, but I think it stems from my cowardice, which confronts

me at every turn. This evening, when Bep was still here, the doorbell rang long and loud. I instantly turned white, my stomach churned, and my heart beat wildly—and all because I was afraid.

At night in bed I see myself alone in a dungeon, without Father and Mother. Or I'm roaming the streets, or the Annex is on fire, or they come in the middle of the night to take us away and I crawl under my bed in desperation. I see everything as if it were actually taking place. And to think it might all happen soon!

Miep often says she envies us because we have such peace and quiet here. That may be true, but she's obviously not thinking about our fear.

I simply can't imagine the world will ever be normal again for us. I do talk about "after the war," but it's as if I were talking about a castle in the air, something that can never come true.

I see the eight of us in the Annex as if we were a patch of blue sky surrounded by menacing black clouds. The perfectly round spot on which we're standing is still safe, but the clouds are moving in on us, and the ring between us and the approaching danger is being pulled tighter and tighter. We're surrounded by darkness and danger, and in our desperate search for a way out we keep bumping into each other. We look at the fighting down below and the peace and beauty up above. In the meantime, we've been cut off by the dark mass of clouds, so that we can go neither up nor down. It looms before us like an impenetrable wall, trying to crush us, but not yet able to. I can only cry out and implore, "Oh, ring, ring, open wide and let us out!"

Yours, Anne

THURSDAY, NOVEMBER 11, 1943

Dearest Kitty,

I have a good title for this chapter:

Ode to My Fountain Pen
In Memoriam

My fountain pen was always one of my most prized possessions; I valued it highly, especially because it had a thick nib, and I can only write neatly with thick nibs. It has led a long and interesting fountain-pen life, which I will summarize below.

When I was nine, my fountain pen (packed in cotton) arrived as a "sample of no commercial value" all the way from Aachen,[5] where my grandmother (the kindly donor) used to live. I lay in bed with the flu, while the February winds howled around the apartment house. This **splendid** fountain pen came in a red leather case, and I showed it to my girlfriends the first chance I got. Me, Anne Frank, the proud owner of a fountain pen.

When I was ten, I was allowed to take the pen to school, and to my surprise, the teacher even let me write with it. When I was eleven, however, my treasure had to be tucked away again, because my sixth-grade teacher allowed us to use only school pens and inkpots. When I was twelve, I started at the Jewish Lyceum and my fountain pen was given a new case in honor of the occasion. Not only did it have room for a pencil, it also had a zipper, which was much more impressive. When I was thirteen, the fountain pen went with me to the Annex, and together we've raced through countless diaries and compositions. I'd turned fourteen and my fountain pen was enjoying the last year of its life with me when ...

It was just after five on Friday afternoon. I came out of my room and was about to sit down at the table to write when I was roughly pushed to one side to make room for Margot and Father, who wanted to practice their Latin. The fountain pen remained unused on the table, while its owner, sighing, was forced to make do with a very tiny corner of the table, where she began rubbing beans. That's how we remove mold from the beans and restore them to their original state. At a quarter to six I swept the floor, dumped the dirt into a newspaper, along with the rotten beans, and tossed it into the stove.

> **splendid**
> (splĕn′dĭd) *adj.* If something is *splendid*, it is magnificent or very good.

---

[5] **Aachen** (ä′kən): a city in Germany.

A giant flame shot up, and I thought it was wonderful that the stove, which had been gasping its last breath, had made such a miraculous recovery.

All was quiet again. The Latin students had left, and I sat down at the table to pick up where I'd left off. But no matter where I looked, my fountain pen was nowhere in sight. I took another look. Margot looked, Mother looked, Father looked, Dussel looked. But it had vanished.

"Maybe it fell into the stove, along with the beans!" Margot suggested.

"No, it couldn't have!" I replied.

But that evening, when my fountain pen still hadn't turned up, we all assumed it had been burned, especially because celluloid is highly inflammable. Our darkest fears were confirmed the next day when Father went to empty the stove and discovered the clip, used to fasten it to a pocket, among the ashes. Not a trace of the gold nib was left. "It must have melted into stone," Father **conjectured**.

I'm left with one consolation, small though it may be: my fountain pen was cremated,[6] just as I would like to be someday!

conjecture
(kən-jĕk´ chər) *v.* If you *conjecture*, you guess or suppose.

Saturday, January 15, 1944

My dearest Kitty,

There's no reason for me to go on describing all our quarrels and arguments down to the last detail. It's enough to tell you that we've divided many things like meat and fats and oils and are frying our own potatoes. Recently we've been eating a little extra rye bread because by four o'clock we're so hungry for dinner we can barely control our rumbling stomachs.

Mother's birthday is rapidly approaching. She received some extra sugar from Mr. Kugler, which sparked off jealousy on the part of the van Daans, because Mrs. van D. didn't receive any on her birthday. But what's the point of boring you with harsh words, spiteful conversations and tears when you know they bore us even more?

---

[6] **cremated** (krē´ māt´ əd): burned to ashes.

Mother has expressed a wish, which isn't likely to come true any time soon: not to have to see Mr. van Daan's face for two whole weeks. I wonder if everyone who shares a house sooner or later ends up at odds with their fellow residents. Or have we just had a stroke of bad luck? At mealtime, when Dussel helps himself to a quarter of the half-filled gravy boat and leaves the rest of us to do without, I lose my appetite and feel like jumping to my feet, knocking him off his chair and throwing him out the door.

Are most people so stingy and selfish? I've gained some insight into human nature since I came here, which is good, but I've had enough for the present. Peter says the same.

The war is going to go on despite our quarrels and our longing for freedom and fresh air, so we should try to make the best of our stay here.

I'm preaching, but I also believe that if I live here much longer, I'll turn into a dried-up old beanstalk. And all I really want is to be an honest-to-goodness teenager!

Yours, Anne

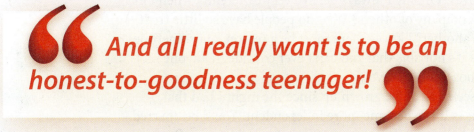

WEDNESDAY EVENING, JANUARY 19, 1944

Dearest Kitty,
I (there I go again!) don't know what's happened, but since my dream I keep noticing how I've changed. By the way, I dreamed about Peter again last night and once again I felt his eyes penetrate mine, but this dream was less vivid and not quite as beautiful as the last.

You know that I always used to be jealous of Margot's relationship with Father. There's not a trace of my jealousy left now; I still feel hurt when Father's nerves cause him to be unreasonable toward me, but then I think, "I can't blame you for being the way you are. You talk so much about the minds of children and adolescents, but you don't know the first thing about them!" I long for more than Father's affection, more than his hugs and kisses. Isn't it awful of me to be so preoccupied with myself? Shouldn't I, who want to be good and kind, forgive them first? I forgive Mother too, but every time she makes a sarcastic remark or laughs at me, it's all I can do to control myself.

I know I'm far from being what I should; will I ever be?

Anne Frank

PS. Father asked if I told you about the cake. For Mother's birthday, she received a real mocha cake, prewar quality,⁷ from the office. It was a really nice day! But at the moment there's no room in my head for things like that.

SATURDAY, JANUARY 22, 1944

Dearest Kitty,
Can you tell me why people go to such lengths to hide their real selves? Or why I always behave very differently when I'm in the company of others? Why do people have so little trust in one another? I know there must be a reason, but sometimes I think it's horrible that you can't ever confide in anyone, not even those closest to you.

It seems as if I've grown up since the night I had that dream, as if I've become more independent. You'll be amazed when I tell you that even my attitude toward the van Daans has changed. I've stopped looking at all the discussions and arguments from my family's biased point of view. What's brought on such a radical change? Well, you see, I suddenly realized that if Mother had been different, if she'd been a real mom, our relationship would have been very, very different. Mrs. van Daan is by no means a wonderful person, yet half the arguments could have been avoided if Mother hadn't been so hard to deal with every time they got onto a tricky subject. Mrs. van Daan does have one good point, though: you can talk to her. She may be selfish, stingy and underhanded, but she'll readily back down as long as you don't provoke her and make her unreasonable. This tactic doesn't work every time,

---

⁷ **prewar quality:** the better standard of goods before the war when there were no shortages of materials.

but if you're patient, you can keep trying and see how far you get.

All the conflicts about our upbringing, about not pampering children, about the food—about everything, absolutely everything—might have taken a different turn if we'd remained open and on friendly terms instead of always seeing the worst side.

I know exactly what you're going to say, Kitty. "But, Anne, are these words really coming from your lips? From you, who have had to put up with so many unkind words from upstairs? From you, who are aware of all the injustices?"

And yet they are coming from me. I want to take a fresh look at things and form my own opinion, not just ape my parents, as in the proverb "The apple never falls far from the tree." I want to reexamine the van Daans and decide for myself what's true and what's been blown out of proportion. If I wind up being disappointed in them, I can always side with Father and Mother. But if not, I can try to change their attitude. And if that doesn't work, I'll have to stick with my own opinions and judgment. I'll take every opportunity to speak openly to Mrs. van D. about our many differences and not be afraid—despite my reputation as a smart aleck—to offer my impartial opinion. I won't say anything negative about my own family, though that doesn't mean I won't defend them if somebody else does, and as of today, my gossiping is a thing of the past.

Up to now I was absolutely convinced that the van Daans were entirely to blame for the quarrels, but now I'm sure the fault was largely ours. We were right as far as the issues were concerned, but intelligent people (such as ourselves!) should have more insight into how to deal with others.

I hope I've got at least a touch of that insight, and that I'll find an occasion to put it to good use.

Yours, Anne

COLLABORATIVE DISCUSSION With a partner, discuss how Anne's ideas and reactions compare to those of you and your friends. Cite specific evidence from the text to support your ideas.

Analyze Text: Elements of a Diary

A **diary** is a daily record of a writer's thoughts, experiences, and feelings. While the term *journal* has a similar definition, diary entries are often composed in the form of a letter addressed to the diary itself, as they are in *The Diary of a Young Girl*. The first lines of *The Diary of a Young Girl* reveal many of a diary's main elements:

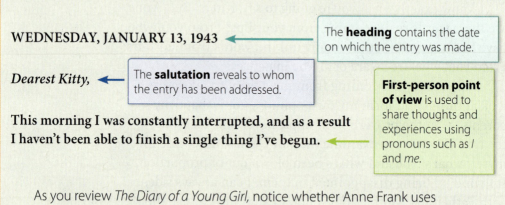

As you review *The Diary of a Young Girl,* notice whether Anne Frank uses the same elements with each diary entry.

Make Inferences

Though some writers intend to publish their diaries, most writers assume their diaries will remain private. As a result, certain explanations may be omitted. To make sense of the text, readers may need to make **inferences,** or logical guesses about meaning based on clues in the text and one's own knowledge. For example, look at this passage from *The Diary of a Young Girl*:

> This evening, when Bep was still here, the doorbell rang long and loud. I instantly turned white, my stomach churned, and my heart beat wildly—and all because I was afraid.

Anne does not explain why the sound of the doorbell frightens her, but you can make an inference about it.

Use your knowledge of the Franks' situation to make other inferences as you analyze the diary.

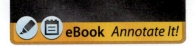

Analyzing the Text

Cite Text Evidence Support your responses with evidence from the text.

1. **Infer** Reread lines 5–26. What clues in the entry help readers make inferences about why "Mr. Kugler hasn't been able to find anyone else to fill the packages" of powdered gravy?

2. **Analyze** What is the effect of the repetition in Anne's statement that "All we can do is wait . . . Jews and Christians alike are waiting, the whole world is waiting, and many are waiting for death"?

3. **Infer** Read over lines 48–80. What is Anne's view of the tension between herself and her family? Consider how Anne's living conditions might contribute to her frustrations.

4. **Interpret** A **simile** makes a comparison between two unlike things using the word *like* or *as*. Reread lines 152–164. What does Anne Frank reveal about her perspective with her use of the simile "I see the eight of us in the Annex as if we were a patch of blue sky surrounded by menacing black clouds."

5. **Draw Conclusions** Reread lines 167–175. Notice that the elements of this entry differ from the others. Why might Anne Frank have used a slightly different form here?

6. **Compare** How does Anne compare her situation in the Annex to what others are facing, particularly to the other two young people there?

7. **Draw Conclusions** Over what span of time are the entries in this excerpt from the diary written? Explain how Anne's perspective has changed during this time.

PERFORMANCE TASK

Speaking Activity: Narrative
What does the story that Anne tells about her fountain pen reveal about her as a writer and a person? Perform this story as a skit for the class.

- Working in groups, analyze Anne's purpose for including the story of her pen. What makes the pen so special to her? Why is the pen especially important during her time in the Annex?

- As you prepare your skit, be sure to maintain Anne's style and use of details to describe the pen. Show how the events of the day led her to destroy her beloved pen.

- After performing the skit, discuss how Anne's narrative, voice, and vivid description helped to bring this story to life.

The Diary of a Young Girl 367

Critical Vocabulary

insolent   reproach   mediate
splendid   conjecture

Practice and Apply Explain your response to each question.

1. Which of the following might require someone to **mediate**? Why?
choices to end a disagreement   choices on a menu

2. Which of the following would you describe as **conjecture**? Why?
someone explaining   someone guessing

3. Which of the following would you describe as **insolent**? Why?
a disobedient child   a lost hiker

4. Which of the following would you describe as **splendid**? Why?
a lovely view   a challenging test

5. Which of the following would you describe as a **reproach**? Why?
a second draft of a story   a thorough scolding

Vocabulary Strategy: Connotation and Denotation

Many words have both a denotation and a connotation. A word's **denotation** is its dictionary definition. A word's **connotations** are the ideas and feelings associated with the word. Study this example from *The Diary of a Young Girl*:

> Things have gotten so bad in Holland that <u>hordes</u> of children . . . beg for a piece of bread.

While the denotation of *horde* is "a large group," the word's connotation suggests an out-of-control swarm that is desperate for food.

Practice and Apply Tell how the meaning of each sentence would change if the underlined word were replaced by the word in parentheses.

1. The families in the Annex had to be <u>stingy</u> with their food. (sparing)

2. The view from a certain window in the Annex was <u>splendid</u>. (fine)

3. Anne was bothered by the <u>conflicts</u> between the families. (battles)

Background *Anne Frank's* The Diary of a Young Girl *has become one of the most well-known books in the world, but it is not always recognized as a skillfully crafted piece of literature. Author* **Francine Prose** *(b. 1947), a successful novelist and nonfiction writer, researched the diary to learn more about how it was written, how it came to be published, and how it has been received over time. She published her findings in a book, from which this selection is excerpted.*

from ANNE FRANK: The Book, The Life, The Afterlife

Literary Criticism by Francine Prose

SETTING A PURPOSE Has *The Diary of a Young Girl* become a classic because of its author's tragically short life, or because of the quality of the writing? As you read, focus on the differing opinions about this question.

THE FIRST TIME I READ THE DIARY OF ANNE FRANK, I was younger than its author was when, at the age of thirteen, she began to write it. I can still picture myself sitting cross-legged on the floor of the bedroom in the house in which I grew up and reading until the daylight faded around me and I had to turn on the lamp. I lost track of my surroundings and felt as if I were entering the Amsterdam attic in which a Jewish girl and her family hid from the Nazis, and where, with the aid of their Dutch "helpers," they survived for two years and a month, until they were betrayed to the authorities, arrested, and deported. I was enthralled by Anne's vivid descriptions of her adored father, Otto; of her conflicts with her mother, Edith, and her sister, Margot; of her romance with Peter van Pels; and of her irritation with Hermann and Auguste van Pels and the dentist, Fritz Pfeffer, with whom the Franks shared the secret annex. I remember that when I finished the book, I went back to the first page and started again, and that I read and reread the diary until I was older than Anne Frank was when she died, at fifteen, in Bergen-Belsen.[1]

In the summer of 2005, I read the diary once more. I had just begun making notes for a novel that, I knew, would be narrated in the voice of a thirteen-year-old girl. Having written a book suggesting that writers seek guidance from a close and thoughtful reading of the classics, I thought I should follow my own advice, and it occurred to me that the greatest book ever written about a thirteen-year-old girl was Anne Frank's diary.

Like most of Anne Frank's readers, I had viewed her book as the innocent and spontaneous outpourings of a teenager. But now, rereading it as an adult, I quickly became convinced that I was in the presence of a consciously crafted work of literature. I understood, as I could not have as a child, how much art is required to give the impression of artlessness, how much control is necessary in order to seem natural, how almost nothing is more difficult for a writer than to find a narrative voice as fresh and unaffected as Anne Frank's. I appreciated, as I did not when I was a girl, her technical proficiency, the novelistic qualities of her diary, her ability to turn living people into characters, her observational powers, her eye for detail, her ear for dialogue and monologue, and the sense of pacing that guides her as she **intersperses** sections of reflection with dramatized scenes.

I kept pausing to marvel at the fact that one of the greatest books about the Nazi genocide[2] should have been written by a girl between the ages of thirteen and fifteen—not a demographic[3] we commonly associate with literary genius. How astonishing that a teenager could have written so intelligently and so movingly about a subject that continues to overwhelm the adult imagination. What makes it even more impressive is that this deceptively unassuming book focuses on a particular moment and on specific people, and at the same time speaks, in ways that seem timeless and universal,

intersperse
(ĭn′tər spûrs′) v.
If you *intersperse* something, you distribute it in different places.

---

[1] **Bergen-Belsen:** the Nazi concentration camp where Anne Frank was sent.
[2] **Nazi genocide:** the systematic killing of Jews by the Nazis.
[3] **demographic** (dĕm′ə-grăf′ĭk): part of a population.

about adolescence and family life. It tells the truth about certain human beings' **ineradicable** desire to exterminate the largest possible number of other human beings, even as it celebrates the will to survive and the determination to maintain one's decency and dignity under the most dehumanizing circumstances.

Anne Frank thought of herself not merely as a girl who happened to be keeping a diary, but as a writer. According to Hanneli Goslar, a childhood friend, Anne's passion for writing began when she was still in school. "Anne would sit in class between lessons and she would shield her diary and she would write and write. Everybody would ask her, 'What are you writing?' And the answer always was, 'It's none of your business.'" In April 1944, four months before the attic in which the Franks found **refuge** was raided by the Nazis, Anne Frank recorded her wish to become a writer. "If I haven't any talent for writing books or newspaper articles, well, then I can always write for myself.... I want to go on living even after my death! And therefore I am grateful to God for giving me this gift, this possibility of developing myself and of writing, of expressing all that is in me!"

Much has been made of how differently we see Anne Frank after the so-called *Definitive Edition* of her diary, published in 1995, restored certain passages that Otto Frank had cut from the version that appeared in Holland in 1947 and in the United States in 1952. In fact, though the *Definitive Edition* is almost a third longer than the first published version of *The Diary of a Young Girl*, the sections that were reinstated—barbed comments about Edith Frank and the Van Pelses, and other entries revealing the extent of Anne's curiosity about sexuality and about her body—don't substantially change our perception of her.

On the other hand, there is a scene in Miep Gies's memoir, *Anne Frank Remembered*, that actually *does* alter our image of Anne. Along with the other helpers, the employees of Opekta, Otto Frank's spice and pectin business, Miep risked her life to keep eight Jews alive for two years and a month, an experience she describes in a book that sharpens and enhances our sense of what the hidden Jews and their Dutch rescuers endured. The scene begins when Miep accidentally interrupts Anne while she is at work on her diary.

ineradicable
(ĭn´ĭ răd´ĭ-kə-bəl) *adj.* If something is *ineradicable*, it is impossible to remove.

refuge
(rĕf´yōoj) *n.* A *refuge* is shelter from danger.

> *I saw that Anne was writing intently, and hadn't heard me. I was quite close to her and was about to turn and go when she looked up, surprised, and saw me standing there. In our many encounters over the years, I'd seen Anne, like a chameleon, go from mood to mood, but always with friendliness. ...But I saw a look on her face at this moment that I'd never seen before. It was a look of dark concentration, as if she had a throbbing headache. The look pierced me, and I was speechless. She was suddenly another person there writing at that table.*

The Anne whom Miep observed *was* another person: a writer, interrupted.

In his 1967 essay, "The Development of Anne Frank," John Berryman[4] asked "whether Anne Frank has *had* any serious readers, for I find no indication in anything written about her that anyone has taken her with real seriousness." That is no longer completely true. In an **incisive** 1989 *New Yorker* essay, "Not Even a Nice Girl," Judith Thurman remarked on the skill with which Anne Frank constructed her narrative. A small number of critics and historians have called attention to Anne's **precocious** literary talent. In her introduction to the British edition of *The Tales from the House Behind*, a collection of Anne's fiction and her autobiographical compositions, the British author G. B. Stern wrote, "One thing is certain, that Anne was a writer in embryo." But is a "writer in embryo" the same as one who has emerged, at once newborn and mature?

The fact remains that Anne Frank has only rarely been given her due as a writer. With few exceptions, her diary has still never been taken seriously as literature, perhaps because it *is* a diary, or, more likely, because its author was a girl. Her book has been discussed as eyewitness testimony, as a war document, as a Holocaust narrative or not, as a book written during the time of war that is only **tangentially** about the war, and as a springboard for conversations about racism

incisive
(ĭn-sī′sĭv) *adj.* If something is *incisive*, it is penetrating, clear, and sharp.

precocious
(prĭ-kō′shəs) *adj.* If someone is *precocious*, the person is mentally advanced for his or her age.

tangential
(tăn-jĕn′shəl) *adj.* If something is *tangential*, it is only slightly connected.

---

[4] **John Berryman:** an American poet and scholar.

and intolerance. But it has hardly ever been viewed as a work of art.

Harold Bloom tells us why: "A child's diary, even when she was so natural a writer, rarely could sustain literary criticism. Since *this* diary is **emblematic** of hundreds of thousands of murdered children, criticism is irrelevant. I myself have no qualifications except as a literary critic. One cannot write about Anne Frank's *Diary* as if Shakespeare, or Philip Roth,[5] is the subject."

emblematic (ĕm′blə-măt′ĭk) *adj.* If something is *emblematic*, it is a symbol for something else.

> " *A child's diary, even when she was so natural a writer, rarely could sustain literary criticism.* "

The Dutch novelist Harry Mulisch attributed the diary's popularity to the fact that its young author died soon after writing it: "The work by this child is not simply *not* a work of art, but in a certain sense it is a work of art made by life itself: it is a found object. It was after all literally found among the debris on the floor after the eight characters departed . . . ." Writing in the *New Republic*, Robert Alter, a critic and biblical scholar, agreed: "I do not mean to sound **impervious** to the **poignancy** of the *Diary*. Still, many diaries of Jews who perished have been published that reflect a complexity of adult perspective and, in some instances, of a direct grappling with the barbarity[6] of Nazism; and these are absent from Anne Frank's writing . . . . Anne may have been a bright and admirably introspective girl, but there is not much in her diary that is emotionally demanding, and her reflections on the world have the quality of **banality** that one would expect from a 14-year-old. What makes the *Diary* moving is the shadow cast back over it by the notice of the death at the end. Try to imagine (as Philip Roth did, for other reasons, in *The Ghost Writer*) an Anne Frank who survived Bergen-Belsen, and, let us say, settled in Cleveland, became a journalist, married and

impervious (ĭm-pûr′vē-əs) *adj.* If something is *impervious*, it is impossible to penetrate.

poignant (poin′yənt) *adj.* If something is *poignant*, it is profoundly moving or touching.

banal (bə-năl′) *adj.* If something is *banal*, it is very commonplace, dull, and unoriginal.

---

[5] **Philip Roth:** an award-winning American novelist known for his depictions of American Jewish life.
[6] **barbarity** (bär-băr′ĭ-tē): savage cruelty or brutality.

had two children. Would anyone care about her wartime diary except as an account of the material circumstances of hiding out from the Nazis in Amsterdam?"

At once admiring of Anne's gifts and troubled by a sense of how they have been underestimated, I began to think it might be interesting and perhaps useful for students newly introduced to Anne's diary and for readers who have grown accustomed to seeing it in a certain light to consider her work from a more literary perspective. What aspects of the book have helped to ensure its long and influential afterlife? Why has Anne Frank become such an iconic figure for so many readers, in so many countries? What is it about her voice that continues to engage and move her audience? How have the various interpretations and versions of her diary—the Broadway play, the Hollywood film, the schoolroom lessons, the newspaper articles that keep her in the public eye— influenced our idea of who she was and what she wrote?

The book I imagined would address those questions, mostly through a close reading of the diary. Such a book would explore the ways in which Anne's diary found an enduring place in the culture and consciousness of the world. I would argue for Anne Frank's *talent as a writer*. Regardless of her age and her gender, she managed to create something that transcended[7] what she herself called "the unbosomings[8] of a thirteen-year-old" and that should be awarded its place among the great memoirs and spiritual confessions, as well as among the most significant records of the era in which she lived.

COLLABORATIVE DISCUSSION What do you think distinguishes an ordinary piece of writing from great literature? With a partner, discuss which of the author's reasons for considering Anne Frank's diary a work of art seem most convincing to you. Cite specific evidence from the text to support your ideas.

---

[7] **transcended** (trăn-sĕnd´əd): surpassed or went beyond the limits.
[8] **unbosoming** (ŭn-bŏŏz´əm-ing): revealing one's personal thoughts.

Determine Author's Point of View

An **author's viewpoint** is his or her position or attitude about a particular subject. This viewpoint is formed by the combination of ideas, values, feelings, and philosophy that influence and shape a writer's opinions. When determining an author's viewpoint, ask yourself,

- What opinions does the author express about this topic?
- What facts or other details suggest how the author feels?
- Are reasons provided to support a particular view?
- How has the author's background affected his or her attitudes?

Sometimes an author will mention the viewpoints of others. If these views are similar to the author's own, they may be used to support the author's opinions. If these viewpoints are different than the author's own, they may be presented so that the author can disprove them by offering a **counterargument**.

As you analyze the essay, look for clues to help you determine Francine Prose's viewpoint on the literary quality of Anne Frank's diary.

Analyze the Meanings of Words and Phrases

Every piece of writing has a particular tone. The **tone** expresses the author's attitude toward his or her subject. For example, a literary work might have a serious, humorous, sad, or respectful tone.

An author's selection of words, or **word choice,** contributes to the tone because words not only communicate ideas, they also convey specific feelings. Notice the word choice in this passage from *Anne Frank: The Book, the Life, the Afterlife*.

> I kept pausing to marvel at the fact that one of the greatest books about the Nazi genocide should have been written by a girl between the ages of thirteen and fifteen—not a demographic we commonly associate with literary genius. How astonishing that a teenager could have written so intelligently and so movingly about a subject that continues to overwhelm the adult imagination.

Words such as these help create a respectful, admiring tone.

Choose a passage from this selection and identify the words that contribute to the tone.

Analyzing the Text

Cite Text Evidence Support your responses with evidence from the text.

1. **Cite Evidence** What evidence in the essay demonstrates clearly that even as a young girl, Francine Prose loved the book *The Diary of Anne Frank*?

2. **Compare** Reread lines 29–43. Complete a chart like this one to show how the author's view of Anne Frank's diary changed over time. What might explain the change?

Prose's Viewpoint as a Child	Prose's Viewpoint as an Adult

3. **Draw Conclusions** How is the *Definitive Edition* of Anne Frank's diary different from the version that was originally published? Identify the evidence Prose provides to suggest why Anne's father made the decisions he did about the first edition.

4. **Evaluate** How does Francine Prose respond to John Berryman's view, expressed in lines 111–114, that Anne Frank never had any "serious readers"?

5. **Analyze** Why do you think Prose chose to include the quote from Robert Alter that appears in lines 150–166? Identify her counterargument to his view.

6. **Analyze** A **claim** is a writer's position on an issue. What is the main claim Prose makes about Anne Frank's writing?

PERFORMANCE TASK

Writing Activity: Analysis At the end of her essay, Francine Prose writes, "I would argue for Anne Frank's *talent as a writer.*" Do you think Prose has made a convincing argument? Write an analysis that explains why or why not.

- Work with a partner to analyze the argument. Remember to listen politely and to share ideas in a respectful way as you complete a graphic organizer showing Prose's claims and supporting evidence.

- Discuss whether the evidence Prose presents is relevant and sufficient and if her reasoning is sound.

- Next, work together to evaluate the author's tone and word choice. Do they strengthen her claims? Why or why not?

- When you are ready to write, begin your analysis by stating your view. Then support that view with evidence from the text.

Critical Vocabulary

intersperse	ineradicable	refuge	incisive
precocious	tangential	emblematic	impervious
poignant	banal		

Practice and Apply Use your understanding of the vocabulary words to answer each question.

1. Are birds likely to take **refuge** in a nest or in the sky?
2. Is an **incisive** news article insightful and clear or vague and confusing?
3. Would a **precocious** child write a note or a novel?
4. Which is **emblematic** of royalty, a star or a crown?
5. If you are **impervious** to bullies' taunts, will you remain calm or get upset?
6. Are bad habits eradicable or **ineradicable**?
7. Which has a **tangential** connection to astronomy, biology or astrology?
8. To **intersperse** a story with illustrations, would you place the drawings throughout the text or all at the end?
9. Would a **banal** TV commercial lead you to buy a product or not?
10. Would a **poignant** story be more likely to be forgotten or remembered?

Vocabulary Strategy: Latin Suffixes

You know that a **suffix** is a word part added to the end of a base word or a word root. The Latin suffixes *-able* and *-ible* form adjectives and mean "able to be," "capable of," or "worthy of." Look at this example from the text:

> It tells the truth about certain human beings' <u>ineradicable</u> desire to exterminate . . .

Knowing the meaning of the suffix *-able* can help you figure out that *ineradicable* means "not able to be eliminated."

Practice and Apply Find the word in each sentence that has the Latin suffix *-able* or *-ible*. Use the meaning of the suffix to help you write a definition of the word. Check each definition you write in a dictionary.

1. Anne Frank's vivid descriptions are enthralling and credible.
2. Critics find her writing commendable but do not consider it literature.
3. Is it conceivable that a teenager could write a great book about genocide?
4. Anne Frank made complex personal and historical events comprehensible.

Language Conventions: Use Ellipses

An **ellipsis** is a punctuation mark that consists of three dots, or periods. Ellipses are used to indicate an omission in text or a long pause.

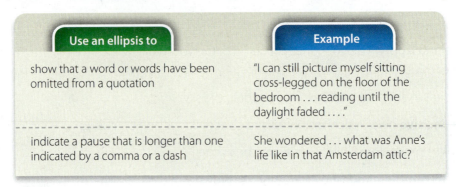

Use an ellipsis to	Example
show that a word or words have been omitted from a quotation	"I can still picture myself sitting cross-legged on the floor of the bedroom . . . reading until the daylight faded . . . ."
indicate a pause that is longer than one indicated by a comma or a dash	She wondered . . . what was Anne's life like in that Amsterdam attic?

Notice that when the omitted words are at the end of a sentence, the ellipsis are placed after the period or other end punctuation mark.

> **"In our many encounters over the years, I'd seen Anne, like a chameleon, go from mood to mood, but always with friendliness. . . . "**

Practice and Apply Rewrite the sentences. Add one or more ellipses to indicate a long pause or to take the place of the underlined words in the quotation.

1. She had an amazing gift as a writer a fresh voice technical proficiency.

2. "Anne Frank thought of herself not merely as a girl who happened to be keeping a diary, but as a writer. According to Hanneli Goslar, a childhood friend, Anne's passion for writing began when she was still in school."

3. "At once admiring of Anne's gifts and troubled by a sense of how they have been underestimated, I began to think it might be interesting and perhaps useful for students newly introduced to Anne's diary and for readers who have grown accustomed to seeing it in a certain light to consider her work from a more literary perspective."

4. "On the other hand, there is a scene in Miep Gies's memoir, *Anne Frank Remembered*, that actually *does* alter our image of Anne. Along with the other helpers, the employees of Opekta, Otto Frank's spice and pectin business, Miep risked her life to keep eight Jews alive for two years and a month, an experience she describes in a book that sharpens and enhances our sense of what the hidden Jews and their Dutch rescuers endured. The scene begins when Miep accidentally interrupts Anne while she is at work on her diary."

Background The first German concentration camps were built only for opponents of the Nazi Party. Later, these camps were also used to imprison Jews and other supposed enemies of the state. Auschwitz, the largest Nazi concentration camp, was opened in 1940 in southern Poland. Inside, prisoners were forced to do work for the Nazi government. Those who were unable to do useful work were killed. Over one million Jews were sent to Auschwitz. Most of them died inside its walls. The camp was finally abandoned by German soldiers as the Russian army advanced upon it in 1945.

After Auschwitz

Speech by Elie Wiesel

Elie Wiesel (b. 1928) *was born in Romania. After the Germans invaded his town, Wiesel and his family were sent to Auschwitz. Only Wiesel and two of his sisters survived. After the war, Wiesel moved to France and became a journalist. It was there that he wrote* Night, *a book about his experiences at Auschwitz. The book has sold millions of copies in many different languages. Wiesel later moved to the United States. There he devoted himself to ensuring that the deaths of millions of Jews in concentration camps would never be forgotten, and that other human beings would never be subjected to such crimes. In 1986, Wiesel was awarded the Nobel Peace Prize for his life's work.*

SETTING A PURPOSE The horrible crimes committed in Nazi concentration camps occurred long ago. As you read, think about why the author continues to reflect on these events. Why does he believe people need to be reminded of them? Write down any questions you have.

"*After Auschwitz, the human condition is not the same, nothing will be the same.*"

Here heaven and earth are on fire.

I speak to you as a man, who 50 years and nine days ago had no name, no hope, no future and was known only by his number, A7713.[1]

I speak as a Jew who has seen what humanity has done to itself by trying to exterminate an entire people and inflict suffering and humiliation and death on so many others.

In this place of darkness and malediction[2] we can but stand in awe and remember its stateless, faceless and nameless victims. Close your eyes and look: endless nocturnal processions are converging here, and here it is always night. Here heaven and earth are on fire.

Close your eyes and listen. Listen to the silent screams of terrified mothers, the prayers of anguished old men and women. Listen to the tears of children, Jewish children, a beautiful little girl among them, with golden hair, whose vulnerable tenderness has never left me. Look and listen as

---

[1] **A7713:** the identification number tattooed on Wiesel at Auschwitz.
[2] **malediction** (măl´ĭ-dĭk´shən): curse.

they quietly walk towards dark flames so gigantic that the planet itself seemed in danger.

All these men and women and children came from everywhere, a gathering of exiles drawn by death.

Yitgadal veyitkadash, Shmay Rabba.[3]

In this kingdom of darkness there were many people. People who came from all the occupied lands of Europe. And then there were the Gypsies and the Poles and the Czechs . . . It is true that not all the victims were Jews. But all the Jews were victims.

Now, as then, we ask the question of all questions: what was the meaning of what was so routinely going on in this kingdom of eternal night. What kind of demented mind could have invented this system?

And it worked. The killers killed, the victims died and the world was the world and everything else was going on, life as usual. In the towns nearby, what happened? In the lands nearby, what happened? Life was going on where God's creation was condemned to blasphemy[4] by their killers and their accomplices.

Yitgadal veyitkadash, Shmay Rabba.

Turning point or watershed,[5] Birkenau[6] produced a mutation[7] on a cosmic scale, affecting man's dreams and endeavours. After Auschwitz, the human condition is no longer the same. After Auschwitz, nothing will ever be the same.

Yitgadal veyitkadash, Shmay Rabba.

As we remember the solitude and the pain of its victims, let us declare this day marks our commitment to commemorate their death, not to celebrate our own victory over death.

---

[3] **Yitgadal veyitkadash, Shmay Rabba:** the words that begin a Jewish prayer for the dead.
[4] **blasphemy** (blăs´ fə-mē): a disrespect for religion.
[5] **watershed:** a place that marks a change of course or direction.
[6] **Birkenau:** the sub-camp at Auschwitz where prisoners were killed.
[7] **mutation** (myo͞o-ta´ shən): change.

As we reflect upon the past, we must address ourselves to the present and the future. In the name of all that is sacred in memory, let us stop the bloodshed in Bosnia, Rwanda and Chechnia; the vicious and ruthless terror attacks against Jews in the Holy Land.[8] Let us reject and oppose more effectively religious fanaticism and racial hate.

Where else can we say to the world *"Remember the morality of the human condition,"* if not here?

For the sake of our children, we must remember Birkenau, so that it does not become their future.

Yitgadal veyitkadash, Shmay Rabba: Weep for Thy children whose death was not mourned then: weep for them, our Father in heaven, for they were deprived of their right to be buried, for heaven itself became their cemetery.

COLLABORATIVE DISCUSSION Elie Wiesel delivered the speech you just read at a ceremony marking the 50th anniversary of the liberation of Auschwitz. With a partner, discuss whether you think his message was the right one for the occasion. Cite evidence from the text to support your thoughts.

---

[8] **Holy Land:** the ancient kingdom of Israel.

Analyze Word Choices

In "After Auschwitz," Elie Wiesel's goal is to persuade, or convince, his audience to adopt a particular viewpoint. To do so, he uses **persuasive techniques,** methods or devices designed to appeal to audiences' feelings and values and thus influence their opinions.

- An **emotional appeal** is a message that creates strong feelings in order to make a point. These appeals can tap into people's feelings such as fear, pity, or vanity. In this passage from his speech, Elie Wiesel appeals to feelings of sympathy and compassion for others.

  "Close your eyes and listen. Listen to the silent screams of terrified mothers, the prayers of anguished old men and women. Listen to the tears of children, Jewish children . . ."

- In an **ethical appeal,** a speaker or writer links a claim to a widely accepted value in order to gain moral support for the claim. In his speech, Wiesel appeals to the established belief that human beings should neither murder one another nor be indifferent to suffering.

  "And it worked. The killers killed, the victims died and the world was the world and everything else was going on, life as usual."

Speakers can also attempt to persuade listeners by using different rhetorical devices. **Rhetorical devices** are techniques writers use to enhance their arguments and communicate more effectively.

- **Repetition** is a rhetorical device in which a sound, word, phrase, clause, or line is repeated for emphasis or to give a text or speech a sense of unity. Repetition also helps reinforce meaning and can create an appealing rhythm, as in this example.

  "<u>After Auschwitz</u>, the human condition is no longer the same. <u>After Auschwitz</u>, nothing will ever be the same."

- **Parallelism** is the use of words, phrases, clauses, or lines that have a similar structure or grammatical form. Like repetition, parallelism can emphasize meaning and also produce a pleasing rhythm.

  "In this place of darkness and malediction we can but stand in awe and remember its <u>stateless</u>, <u>faceless</u> and <u>nameless</u> victims."

Study the persuasive techniques Elie Wiesel uses as you analyze his speech.

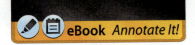

Analyzing the Text

Cite Text Evidence Support your responses with evidence from the text.

1. **Analyze** Wiesel's speech begins: "After Auschwitz, the human condition is not the same, nothing will be the same." Identify where similar language is repeated later in his speech. What is the effect of this repetition?

2. **Analyze** Reread lines 4–9. Identify two examples of parallelism in these lines and describe the effect of each.

3. **Interpret Imagery** Imagery consists of descriptive words and phrases that create sensory experiences for the reader. Wiesel writes: "Here heaven and earth are on fire." What image is he communicating? What effect does it have on the reader?

4. **Identify** Examine lines 51–60. What kind of appeal is Wiesel making in this part of his speech? What human values is he calling on his audience to consider?

5. **Identify** Reread lines 61–64. What kind of appeal is Wiesel making in this part of his speech? What human feelings is he tapping into to make his point?

6. **Evaluate** The sentence *Yitgadal veyitkadash, Shmay Rabba* is repeated three times in the speech. Is the use of this rhetorical device effective? Why or why not?

7. **Evaluate** Considering the author's purpose and audience, which persuasive techniques make the speech effective? Explain.

PERFORMANCE TASK

Speaking Activity: Discussion
Imagine that you have been put in charge of a museum exhibit about the Holocaust. Create a remembrance poster for the exhibit based on Elie Wiesel's speech.

- Choose two key quotes or ideas from the speech to highlight on your poster.
- Research the Holocaust, collecting information from print and digital sources.
- Select important facts, dates, quotes, and photographs to support the main points in Wiesel's speech.
- On the poster, include visuals such as a timeline or your own artwork or symbols.
- Describe your completed work to the class in an oral presentation. Discuss with classmates Wiesel's purpose and message and how your poster relates to them.

Background On September 1, 1939, Germany invaded Poland, triggering the start of World War II. The defeat of Poland was swift, and the occupation of the country that followed became one of the cruelest chapters of the war. After their downfall, many Polish soldiers and citizens were slaughtered by the German army. Surviving Polish political leaders, Jews, and others were later collected and sent to concentration camps to be killed or to work as slaves for the Nazis. By the end of the war, more than five million Poles had died.

There But for the Grace

Poem by Wisława Szymborska

Wisława Szymborska (1923–2012) *was born in a small town in western Poland. She was in high school when Germany invaded Poland. Despite the ban on high school education put in place by the Germans, Szymborska continued taking classes. Unlike many Poles, Szymborska was fortunate to avoid imprisonment and death at the hands of the Nazis. Szymborska has published more than a dozen collections of poetry. She has won numerous awards for her poetry, including the Nobel Prize for Literature in 1996.*

SETTING A PURPOSE As you read, think about the role that chance plays in a person's life. Write down any questions you have.

There But for the Grace

It could have happened.
It had to happen.
It happened sooner. Later.
Nearer. Farther.
5 It happened not to you.

You survived because you were the first.
You survived because you were the last.
Because you were alone. Because of people.
Because you turned left. Because you turned right.
10 Because rain fell. Because a shadow fell.
Because sunny weather prevailed.[1]

Luckily there was a wood.
Luckily there were no trees.
Luckily there was a rail, a hook, a beam, a brake,
15 a frame, a bend, a millimeter, a second.
Luckily a straw was floating on the surface.

Thanks to, because, and yet, in spite of.
What would have happened had not a hand, a foot,
by a step, a hairsbreadth[2]
20 by sheer coincidence.

So you're here? Straight from a moment still ajar?
The net had one eyehole, and you got through it?
There's no end to my wonder, my silence.
Listen
25 how fast your heart beats in me.

COLLABORATIVE DISCUSSION The speaker suggests that luck or chance plays a big part in survival. Do you agree? With a partner, discuss whether chance or determination is more likely to help a person in a difficult situation. Cite specific evidence from the text and your own knowledge or experiences to support your thoughts.

---

[1] **prevailed:** was common or frequent.
[2] **hairsbreadth:** a tiny space.

Analyze Sound Devices

Like songs, poems are meant to be heard. **Sound devices** are the use of certain words for their connection to the sense of hearing. Poets use various sound devices to convey meaning and mood, to draw attention to certain lines or images, to engage readers, and, sometimes, to unify a work.

Poets use a sound device called **rhythm** to bring out the musical quality of language, to emphasize ideas, and to create moods. Rhythm is a pattern of stressed and unstressed syllables in a line of poetry. Notice how the speaker in "There But for the Grace" emphasizes ideas with the rhythm of one-syllable words:

"Luckily there was a rail, a hook, a beam, a brake, . . ."

Poets also employ a variety of other sound devices to emphasize certain words or to unify a poem. The repetition of sounds, words, phrases, or lines often helps to reinforce meaning and create an appealing rhythm.

Sound Device	Definition	Example from the Poem
alliteration	repetition of consonant sounds at the beginnings of words	What would have happened had not a hand, a foot, . . .
assonance	repetition of vowel sounds within non-rhyming words	Because rain fell. Because a shadow fell. Because sunny weather prevailed.
consonance	repetition of consonant sounds within and at the ends of words	It happened sooner. Later. Nearer. Farther.
repetition	a technique in which a sound, word, phrase, or line is repeated for emphasis or unity	It could have happened. It had to happen. It happened sooner. Later.
parallelism	use of similar grammatical constructions to express ideas that are related or equal in importance	Luckily there was a wood. Luckily there were no trees.

Notice the impact of these sound devices as you continue to analyze "There But for the Grace." How does the poet's use of sound devices affect you as a reader?

Analyzing the Text

Cite Text Evidence Support your responses with evidence from the text.

1. **Interpret** What is the theme, or overall message, of this poem? Explain how the sound devices in the poem help to communicate that theme.

2. **Identify Patterns** Reread lines 6–7. What sound device is used in these lines, and what effect does it have?

3. **Analyze** Reread lines 8–11. How does the speaker use parallelism to emphasize chance?

4. **Cause/Effect** Examine line 16. Identify the sound device used, and explain how it affects the ending of the stanza.

5. **Infer** What two sound devices are used in the lines "by a step, a hairsbreadth / by sheer coincidence"? What impact does this combination of sound devices have?

6. **Evaluate** Reread stanzas 2 and 3. What does the poet do to establish rhythm in this part of the poem? How does that rhythm enhance the speaker's message?

7. **Draw Conclusions** The tone of a literary work expresses the writer's attitude toward his or her subject. Describe the overall tone of the poem, as well as the tone in line 23, "There's no end to my wonder, my silence."

PERFORMANCE TASK

Writing Activity: Analysis Respond to the poem by analyzing its connection to the topic of this collection.

- With a partner, discuss the poem's theme and how it relates to the themes present in other selections within the collection.
- Compare and contrast how similar ideas are presented across the texts.
- Identify the relationships you see between the poem's language and the events described in the other texts.
- Write one draft of your response, and then share it with your partner. Use your partner's feedback to improve and finalize your analysis.
- Publish your responses in a collection you can share with the whole class.

COLLECTION 5
PERFORMANCE TASK

Interactive Lessons
To help you complete this task, use:
- Writing Informative Texts
- Writing as a Process
- Conducting Research.

Research and Write an Informative Essay

In Collection 5 you read about the experiences that Anne Frank and others had when hiding from the Nazis. What was life like for other Jews and the people hiding them? In this activity, you will research and write an informative essay comparing Anne Frank's experiences to those of others during the Holocaust.

A successful informative essay
- provides an engaging introduction that clearly states the topic
- clearly organizes ideas and concepts to make connections
- includes facts, definitions, and examples that support ideas
- uses transitions to clarify relationships among ideas
- provides a conclusion that supports the central ideas

Mentor Text See how this example from *Anne Frank: The Book, The Life, The Afterlife* supports ideas with quotes.

> "A small number of critics and historians have called attention to Anne's precocious literary talent…the British author G. B. Stern wrote, 'One thing is certain, that Anne was a writer in embryo.'"

Visit hmhfyi.com to explore your topic and enhance your research.

PLAN

Formulate Ideas Prepare for research by jotting down questions that you will answer in your essay, such as how the experiences of others Jews and the people hiding them were similar to those of Anne Frank, and how they were different.

Gather Information Review *The Diary of Anne Frank* and other texts in the collection.

- What was it like to live in the Annex?
- How did the people in hiding obtain food and other supplies?
- What did people do to pass the time? How were their lives different during the week and on the weekends?
- What did helpers do, and what risks did they take?

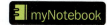

Use the annotation tools in your eBook to find evidence that supports your points about the living conditions in the Annex. Save each piece of evidence to your notebook.

ACADEMIC VOCABULARY

As you write your informative essay, be sure to use the academic vocabulary words.

communicate
draft
liberation
philosophy
publish

Collection Performance Task 389

Conduct Research Use both print and digital sources to investigate the experiences of other Jews and those of the people hiding them.

- Find facts, quotes, and examples that support or contradict the information you learned in the collection.
- Find library books using keyword or subject searches. Use a search engine or Internet directories to find Internet sources.

Organize Your Ideas Group related ideas together and create an outline of the central ideas and information for each paragraph.

> I. Use Roman numerals for main topics.
>   A. Indent and use capital letters for subtopics.
>   1. Indent and use numbers for supporting facts and details.
>   2. Indent and use numbers for supporting facts and details.
> II. Use Roman numerals for main topics.
>   B. Indent and use capital letters for subtopics.
>   1. Indent and use numbers for supporting facts and details.

Consider Your Purpose and Audience Think about who will read or listen to your essay, and what you want them to understand. What does the audience already know? What background information will they need?

Interactive Lessons
For help in drafting your essay, use
- Conducting Research: Taking Notes
- Writing Informative Texts: Organizing Ideas

PRODUCE

Draft Your Essay Review your notes and your outline as you begin your draft.

- Present the thesis statement clearly, previewing what is to follow. Include an unusual comment, fact, quote, or story to grab the reader's attention.
- Organize your information into paragraphs of similar information. Include relevant details, facts, and examples.
- Establish and maintain a formal style by using complete sentences with precise language. Avoid contractions and pronouns such as *I* and *you*.
- Include transition words and phrases such as *because, also, in addition, nearby,* and *finally* to clarify the relationships between ideas.
- Write a conclusion that follows from and supports your explanation.

Write your rough draft in *my*WriteSmart. Focus on getting your ideas down, rather than on perfecting your choice of language.

REVISE

Review Your Draft Have your partner or group of peers review your draft. Use the following chart to revise your draft.

Questions	Tips	Revision Techniques
Is the thesis statement clear?	**Underline** the thesis statement.	**Add** a thesis statement.
Does each paragraph have a main point related to the thesis?	**Highlight** the main point of each paragraph.	**Delete** unrelated ideas, or **rearrange** information into separate paragraphs.
Are there relevant supporting details for each point?	**Underline** facts, statistics, examples, and quotations that support your points.	**Add** more facts, statistics, examples, and quotations from your notes.
Are ideas organized logically? Do transitions connect ideas?	**Highlight** transitional words and phrases.	**Rearrange** sentences to organize ideas logically. **Add** transitions to connect ideas.
Does the conclusion summarize the topic and support the information presented?	**Underline** the summary. **Highlight** sentences that support information in the essay.	**Add** a summary of the topic. **Insert** sentences that support the information in the essay.

Have a partner or a group of peers review your draft in *my*WriteSmart. Ask your reviewers to note any ideas presented in your draft that need clarification or further support.

Interactive Lessons
For help in revising your essay, use
• Writing as a Process: Revising and Editing

Language Conventions: Condensing Ideas

Look for places where you can condense ideas to create precise and detailed sentences. Read the following passage from *The Diary of a Young Girl*.

> "Gnawing on a carrot to still their hunger pangs, they walk from their cold houses through cold streets to an even colder classroom."

Note how Anne Frank combines ideas about children gnawing on a carrot and the cold into one detailed, descriptive sentence.

PRESENT

Create a Finished Copy Finalize your essay and choose a way to share it with your audience. Consider these options:

- Give an oral report to classmates or community members.
- Record video or audio of you reading your essay aloud, and post the recording on an approved website.

PERFORMANCE TASK RUBRIC
INFORMATIVE ESSAY

	Ideas and Evidence	Organization	Language
4	• The thesis statement is clear and the introduction is appealing and informative. • The topic is well developed with relevant facts, concrete details, interesting quotations, and examples from reliable sources. • The concluding section capably summarizes the information presented.	• The organization is effective and logical throughout the essay. • Transitions successfully connect related ideas.	• The writing maintains a formal style throughout. • Language is strong and precise. • Ideas are condensed to create precise and detailed sentences. • Grammar, usage, and mechanics are correct.
3	• The thesis statement is present but the introduction could do more to grab readers' attention. • Some key points need more support from relevant facts, concrete details, quotations, and examples from reliable sources. • The concluding section summarizes the information presented.	• The organization is confusing in a few places. • A few more transitions are needed to connect related ideas.	• The style is inconsistent in a few places. • Language is too general in some places. • Some ideas are condensed to add detail to sentences. • Some errors in grammar, usage, and mechanics are repeated in the essay.
2	• The thesis statement is confusing, and the introduction is only partly informative and could be more engaging. • Most key points need more support in the form of relevant facts, concrete details, quotations, and examples from reliable sources. • The concluding section partially summarizes the information presented.	• The organization is logical in some places but often doesn't follow a pattern. • More transitions are needed throughout to connect related ideas.	• The style becomes informal in many places. • Overly general language is used in many places. • Many ideas are in separate sentences, instead of being combined. • Grammar, usage, and mechanics are incorrect in many places, but the writer's ideas are still clear.
1	• The thesis statement and introduction are missing. • Facts, details, quotations, and examples are from unreliable sources or are missing. • The essay lacks a concluding section.	• A logical organization is not used; information is presented randomly. • Transitions are not used, making the essay difficult to understand.	• The style is inappropriate for the essay. • Language is too general to convey the information. • Ideas are not combined. • Many errors in grammar, usage, and mechanics obscure the meaning of the writer's ideas.

COLLECTION 6

The Value of Work

“ Every job is a learning experience, and we can develop and grow in every one. ”

—Colin Powell

COLLECTION 6
The Value of Work

In this collection, you will explore the benefits and challenges that are part of being a worker.

COLLECTION PERFORMANCE TASK Preview

At the end of this collection, you will complete two performance tasks:

- You will write and present a narrative that reveals a lesson learned through a work experience.
- You will write an argument to support your views about whether it is important for teenagers to get work experience during their school years.

ACADEMIC VOCABULARY

Study the words and their definitions in the chart below. You will use these words as you discuss and write about the texts in this collection.

Word	Definition	Related Forms
commentary (kŏm´ən-tĕr´ē) *n.*	explanation or interpretation in the form of comments or observations	comment, commentator, commentaries
minors (mī´nərz) *n.*	people who have not reached legal adulthood	minority, minorities
occupation (ŏk´yə-pā´shən) *n.*	an activity that serves as one's source of income	occupy, occupational
option (ŏp´shən) *n.*	something chosen or available as a choice	optional, opt
style (stīl) *n.*	the way in which something is said, done, expressed, or performed	stylistic, styled, stylized

Mark Twain (1835–1910) *is the pen name of Samuel Clemens, who grew up in Missouri along the Mississippi River. Twain worked as a printer, riverboat captain, and a gold miner before finding his calling as a writer. In 1876, he published* The Adventures of Tom Sawyer, *which became one of his most famous works and contributed to his reputation as "the father of American literature." The excerpt included here takes place early in the book, when Tom has been commanded by his Aunt Sally to paint a fence.*

from The Adventures of Tom Sawyer

Novel by Mark Twain

SETTING A PURPOSE As you read, notice Tom's attitude toward his task. What lessons does he learn about work?

As you read, save new words to *myWordList*.

Tom's energy did not last. He began to think of the fun he had planned for this day, and his sorrows multiplied. Soon the free boys would come tripping along on all sorts of delicious expeditions, and they would make a world of fun of him for having to work—the very thought of it burnt him like fire. He got out his worldly wealth and examined it—bits of toys, marbles and trash; enough to buy an exchange of *work*, maybe, but not half enough to buy so much as half an hour of pure freedom. So he returned his straitened means to his pocket, and gave up the idea of trying to buy the boys. At this dark and hopeless moment an inspiration burst upon him! Nothing less than a great, magnificent inspiration.

He took up his brush and went **tranquilly** to work. Ben Rogers hove in sight presently—the very boy, of all boys, whose ridicule he had been dreading. Ben's gait[1] was the hop-skip-and-jump—proof enough that his heart was light and his anticipations high. He was eating an apple, and giving a long, melodious whoop at intervals, followed by a deep-toned ding-dong-dong, ding-dong-dong, for he was personating a steamboat. As he drew near he slackened speed, took the middle of the street, leaned far over to starboard,[2] and rounded-to ponderously and with laborious pomp and circumstance—for he was personating the 'Big Missouri,'[3] and considered himself to be drawing nine feet of water. He was boat, and captain, and engine-bells combined, so he had to imagine himself standing on his own hurricane deck giving the orders and executing them:

tranquil
(trăng′kwəl) *adj.* If something is *tranquil*, it is calm.

---

[1] **gait:** a rhythmical way of walking.
[2] **starboard:** the right side of a boat or ship.
[3] **Big Missouri:** the name of a riverboat.

'Stop her, sir! Ting-a-ling-ling.' The headway ran almost out, and he drew up slowly toward the sidewalk.

'Ship up to back! Ting-a-ling-ling!' His arms straightened and stiffened down his sides.

'Set her back on the stabboard! Ting-a-ling-ling! Chow! ch-chow-wow! Chow!' His right hand meantime describing stately circles, for it was representing a forty-foot wheel.

'Let her go back on the labboard! Ting-a-ling-ling! Chow-ch-chow-chow!' The left hand began to describe circles.

'Stop the stabboard! Ting-a-ling-ling! Stop the labboard! Come ahead on the stabboard! Stop her! Let your outside turn over slow! Ting-a-ling-ling! Chow-ow-ow! Get out that head-line! *Lively*, now! Come—out with your spring-line— what're you about there? Take a turn round that stump with the bight of it! Stand by that stage now—let her go! Done with the engines, sir! Ting-a-ling-ling! *Sh't! s'h't! s'h't!*' (trying the gauge-cocks).

Tom went on whitewashing—paid no attention to the steam-boat. Ben stared a moment, and then said:

'Hi-*yi! You're* up a stump,[4] ain't you?'

No answer. Tom **surveyed** his last touch with the eye of an artist; then he gave his brush another gentle sweep, and surveyed the result, as before. Ben ranged up alongside of him. Tom's mouth watered for the apple, but he stuck to his work. Ben said:

'Hello, old chap; you got to work, hey?'

Tom wheeled suddenly and said:

'Why, it's you. Ben! I warn't noticing.'

'Say—*I*'m going in a-swimming, *I* am. Don't you wish you could? But of course you'd druther[5] *work*—wouldn't you? Course you would!'

Tom **contemplated** the boy a bit, and said:

'What do you call work?'

'Why, ain't *that* work?'

Tom resumed his whitewashing, and answered carelessly:

'Well, maybe it is, and maybe it ain't. All I know is, it suits Tom Sawyer.'

survey
(sər-vā´) *v.* If you *survey* something, you inspect it.

contemplate
(kŏn´təm-plāt´) *v.* When you *contemplate*, you look at something attentively and thoughtfully.

---

[4] **up a stump:** an expression that means someone has a big problem.
[5] **druther:** rather.

'Oh, come now, you don't mean to let on that you *like* it?'

The brush continued to move.

'Like it? Well, I don't see why I oughtn't to like it. Does a boy get a chance to whitewash a fence every day?'

That put the thing in a new light. Ben stopped nibbling his apple. Tom swept his brush daintily back and forth—stepped back to note the effect—added a touch here and there—criticized the effect again—Ben watching every move, and getting more and more interested, more and more absorbed. Presently he said: 'Say, Tom, let *me* whitewash a little.'

Tom considered—was about to consent; but he altered his mind:

'No, no; I reckon it wouldn't hardly do, Ben. You see, Aunt Polly's awful **particular** about this fence—right here on the street, you know—but if it was the back fence I wouldn't mind, and *she* wouldn't. Yes, she's awful particular about this fence; it's got to be done very careful; I reckon there ain't one boy in a thousand, maybe two thousand, that can do it the way it's got to be done.'

'No—is that so? Oh, come now; lemme just try, only just a little. I'd let *you*, if you was me, Tom.'

'Ben, I'd like to, honest Injun; but Aunt Polly—well, Jim wanted to do it, but she wouldn't let him. Sid wanted to do it, and she wouldn't let Sid. Now, don't you see how I'm fixed? If you was to tackle this fence, and anything was to happen to it—'

'Oh, shucks; I'll be just as careful. Now lemme try. Say—I'll give you the core of my apple.'

'Well, here—No, Ben; now don't; I'm afeard—'

'I'll give you *all* of it!'

Tom gave up the brush with reluctance in his face but **alacrity** in his heart. And while the late steamer 'Big Missouri' worked and sweated in the sun, the retired artist sat on a barrel in the shade close by, dangled his legs, munched his apple, and planned the slaughter of more innocents. There was no lack of material; boys happened along every little while; they came to jeer, but remained to whitewash. By the time Ben was fagged out,[6] Tom had traded the next chance

particular
(pər-tĭk′yə-lər) *adj.*
If you are *particular* about something, you are fussy about it and pay attention to its details.

alacrity
(ə-lăk′rĭ-tē) *n. Alacrity* is cheerful willingness or eagerness.

---

[6] **fagged out:** tired.

> **"Tom gave up the brush with reluctance in his face but *alacrity* in his heart."**

to Billy Fisher for a kite, in good repair; and when *he* played out, Johnny Miller bought in for a dead rat and a string to swing it with; and so on, and so on, hour after hour. And when the middle of the afternoon came, from being a poor poverty-stricken boy in the morning, Tom was literally rolling in wealth. He had, beside the things before mentioned, twelve marbles, part of a jew's-harp,[7] a piece of blue bottle-glass to look through, a spool-cannon, a key that wouldn't unlock anything, a fragment of chalk, a glass stopper of a decanter,[8] a tin soldier, a couple of tadpoles, six fire-crackers, a kitten with only one eye, a brass door-knob, a dog-collar—but no dog—the handle of a knife, four pieces of orange-peel, and a **dilapidated** old window-sash. He had had a nice, good, idle time all the while—plenty of company—and the fence had three coats of whitewash on it! If he hadn't run out of whitewash, he would have bankrupted every boy in the village.

Tom said to himself that it was not such a hollow world, after all. He had discovered a great law of human action, without knowing it—namely, that in order to make a man

dilapidated
(dĭ-lăpʹĭ-dāʹtĭd) *adj.*
If something is *dilapidated*, it is falling apart.

---

[7] **jew's-harp:** a musical instrument that is held between the teeth and plucked to produce a sound.
[8] **glass stopper of a decanter:** the glass top of a special kind of bottle.

or a boy **covet** a thing, it is only necessary to make the thing difficult to **attain**. If he had been a great and wise philosopher, like the writer of this book, he would now have comprehended that Work consists of whatever a body is *obliged*[9] to do, and that Play consists of whatever a body is not obliged to do. And this would help him to understand why constructing artificial flowers or performing on a treadmill is work, while rolling ten-pins[10] or climbing Mont Blanc is only amusement. There are wealthy gentlemen in England who drive four-horse passenger-coaches twenty or thirty miles on a daily line in the summer, because the privilege costs them considerable money; but if they were offered wages for the service, that would turn it into work, and then they would resign.

The boy mused a while over the substantial change which had taken place in his worldly circumstances, and then wended[11] toward head-quarters to report.

covet
(kŭv´ĭt) *v.* If you *covet* something, you strongly wish for it.

attain
(ə-tān´) *v.* If you *attain* something, you gain it or achieve it.

COLLABORATIVE DISCUSSION With a partner, discuss what you think Tom learned from this work experience. What do you imagine the other boys learned? Cite specific evidence from the text to support your ideas.

---

[9] **obliged:** forced.
[10] **rolling ten-pins:** bowling.
[11] **wended:** proceeded or traveled.

Analyze Point of View

The **narrator** in a story or novel is the voice that is telling the story. The narrator may be a story character or an outside voice created by the author. The **point of view** in a story is the view or perspective from which the narrator tells events. When the narrator is an outside voice, the story is told from a **third-person point of view**. A third-person narrator may sometimes be **omniscient**, or all-knowing. An omniscient narrator

- knows everything about all the characters, including their thoughts and feelings
- knows everything about story events

An author's use of an omniscient narrator can create dramatic irony in a story. **Irony** is a special kind of contrast in which reality is the opposite of what it seems. In **dramatic irony,** the narrator reveals to readers something that a story character does not know. For example, in the following passage the reader knows something that Ben Rogers does not:

> Tom surveyed his last touch with the eye of an artist; then he gave his brush another gentle sweep, and surveyed the result, as before. Ben ranged up alongside of him. Tom's mouth watered for the apple, but he stuck to his work.

As you analyze the story, look for another example of how the third-person point of view creates dramatic irony.

Determine Meaning of Words and Phrases

The **style** of a literary work is the way in which the work is written. Style refers to how something is said rather than to what is said. Word choice, sentence structure, imagery, and tone all contribute to the style of a piece of writing.

Mark Twain's **humorous tone,** or amused attitude toward his subject, is part of his famous writing style. Notice the way Twain's word choice and use of irony create humor in this passage:

> Tom gave us the brush with reluctance in his face but alacrity in his heart. And while the late steamer 'Big Missouri' worked and sweated in the sun, the retired artist sat on a barrel . . . and planned the slaughter of more innocents.

Look for more examples of Twain's style as you analyze the text.

Analyzing the Text

Cite Text Evidence   Support your responses with evidence from the text.

1. **Identify** In lines 1–29, what words and phrases help you to determine the type of narrator telling this story? Identify the point of view being used.

2. **Summarize** Summarize Ben Rogers' sounds and movements in lines 20–44. Identify the phrases that best help you picture what he's doing.

3. **Analyze** The written conversation between two or more characters in a story is called **dialogue**. Analyze the dialogue between Tom and Ben that occurs in lines 53–94. What leads Ben to change his attitude about whitewashing the fence?

4. **Analyze** How does Mark Twain use dramatic irony to create humor? Give at least one specific example.

5. **Draw Conclusions** Reread lines 99–105. What conclusions can you draw about Tom's friends' attitudes toward work from this passage?

6. **Evaluate** Describe Mark Twain's writing style in this selection. In a chart like the one below, give examples of the word choices and use of irony that contribute to his style.

Word choice	Irony

7. **Evaluate** Reread lines 120–138. Do you think the message in this passage is serious or humorous, or some combination of both? Use examples from the text to explain your answer.

PERFORMANCE TASK

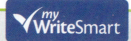

Writing Activity: Analysis Write an analysis that explains how the **theme**—the lesson or message— of this selection is developed through the character of Tom Sawyer.

- Work with a partner to create a character chart for Tom. In the left column, list his qualities. In the right column, list the passages from the text that demonstrate each quality.

- Next, determine the theme of the selection, drawing on the narrator's description of the lesson Tom learns.
- When you are ready, begin your analysis by stating the theme. Then, describe how the theme is developed in relation to Tom's thoughts, feelings, speech, and actions.

Critical Vocabulary

| tranquil | survey | contemplate | particular |
| alacrity | dilapidated | covet | attain |

Practice and Apply Use what you know about the Vocabulary words to answer the following questions.

1. When did you **contemplate** something very carefully? Why?
2. What have you worked hard to **attain**? Explain the steps you took.
3. When did someone **covet** something of yours? What happened?
4. What in your school or town has become **dilapidated**? Why?
5. What places do you think are **tranquil**?
6. When did you **survey** a situation before taking action? Why?
7. What is something that your teacher is **particular** about?
8. When did you begin a task with **alacrity**? Why?

Vocabulary Strategy: Verbal Irony and Puns

A **figure of speech** is a word or phrase that goes beyond the literal meanings of the words to create a special effect. Verbal irony and puns are two kinds of figures of speech. Verbal irony exists when someone knowingly exaggerates or says one thing while meaning another, such as in this example.

> "Say—I'm going in a swimming, I am. Don't you wish you could? But of course you'd druther *work*—wouldn't you?"

A **pun** is a humorous play on words. Some puns involve using different meanings of the same word, as in this passage where "played out" can mean "tired out; exhausted" or "finished play that was once considered work":

> "... Tom had traded the next chance to Billy Fisher for a kite, in good repair; and when he played out, Johnny Miller bought in for a dead rat and a string to swing it with ..."

Practice and Apply Identify the verbal irony or pun in each sentence and explain its meaning.

1. Ned said, "I just love working in the hot sun. When can we do this again?"
2. Billy Fisher was a minor character and remained one as an adult.
3. Kara read that Tom Sawyer tricked the boys. "What a good friend!" she remarked.
4. His friends none the wiser, Tom surveyed the results of his whitewashing.

Language Conventions: Interrogative Mood

The **mood of a verb** shows the status of the action or condition it describes. The following chart shows several kinds of verb moods and their purposes.

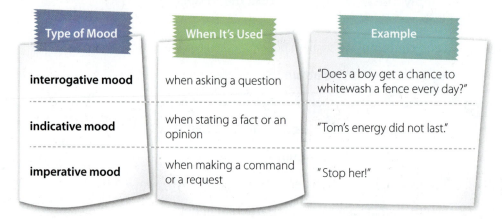

Type of Mood	When It's Used	Example
interrogative mood	when asking a question	"Does a boy get a chance to whitewash a fence every day?"
indicative mood	when stating a fact or an opinion	"Tom's energy did not last."
imperative mood	when making a command or a request	"Stop her!"

Sentences that use the **interrogative mood,** or the mood that asks a question, often invert the subject-verb order so that the helping verb comes before the subject. In the examples below, notice how the subject-verb order changes between the sentence in the indicative mood and the one in the interrogative mood.

Indicative mood: **You can earn a paycheck.**

Interrogative mood: **Can you earn a paycheck?**

Practice and Apply Identify the mood of the boldfaced verbs in each sentence. Then, rewrite each sentence using the interrogative mood.

1. Tom **will have** a moment of great inspiration.
2. Ben **scratched** his nose as he **stood** by the fence.
3. **Let** me whitewash a little!
4. **Give** Ben the brush, and then **watch** him work.
5. After a while, Tom **was rolling** in wealth.
6. **Trade** the tadpoles for a chance to whitewash the fence.

Gary Soto (b.1952) *was born to parents of Mexican decent in Fresno, California. His father died when he was five years old, and Soto worked in the fields and factories when he was young. He struggled in school, but he managed to enroll in college, where a book of poetry inspired him to begin writing. Much of Soto's poetry, fiction, and nonfiction reflects his experience growing up as a Mexican American.*

ONE LAST TIME

Memoir by Gary Soto

SETTING A PURPOSE As you read, notice Soto's experiences and attitudes about work. Think about how his family history affects the way he thinks about working.

Yesterday I saw the movie *Gandhi*[1] and recognized a few of the people—not in the theater but in the film. I saw my relatives, dusty and thin as sparrows, returning from the fields with hoes balanced on their shoulders. The workers were squinting, eyes small and veined, and were using their hands to say what there was to say to those in the audience with popcorn. . . . I didn't have any, though. I sat thinking of my family and their years in the fields, beginning with Grandmother who came to the United States after the Mexican revolution[2] to settle in Fresno where she met her

---

[1] **Gandhi** (gän´dē): a 1982 film biography of Mohandas Gandhi (1869–1948), an Indian spiritual and political leader who, through nonviolent struggle, forced England to grant India's independence.
[2] **Mexican revolution (1910–1920):** an armed conflict during which revolutionaries overthrew Mexico's longtime dictator and reformed the government.

One Last Time 405

husband and bore children, many of them. She worked in the fields around Fresno, picking grapes, oranges, plums, peaches, and cotton, dragging a large white sack like a sled. She worked in the packing houses, Bonner and Sun-Maid Raisin, where she stood at a conveyor belt passing her hand over streams of raisins to pluck out leaves and pebbles. For over twenty years she worked at a machine that boxed raisins until she retired at sixty-five.

Grandfather worked in the fields, as did his children. Mother also found herself out there when she separated from Father for three weeks. I remember her coming home, dusty and so tired that she had to rest on the porch before she trudged inside to wash and start dinner. I didn't understand the complaints about her ankles or the small of her back, even though I had been in the grape fields watching her work. With my brother and sister I ran in and out of the rows; we enjoyed ourselves and pretended not to hear Mother scolding us to sit down and behave ourselves. A few years later, however, I caught on when I went to pick grapes rather than play in the rows.

Mother and I got up before dawn and ate quick bowls of cereal. She drove in silence while I **rambled** on how everything was now solved, how I was going to make enough money to end our misery and even buy her a beautiful copper tea pot, the one I had shown her in Long's Drugs. When we arrived I was frisky and ready to go, self-consciously aware of my grape knife dangling at my wrist. I almost ran to the row the **foreman** had pointed out, but I returned to help Mother with the grape pans and jug of water. She told me to settle down and reminded me not to lose my knife. I walked at her side and listened to her explain how to cut grapes; bent down, hands on knees, I watched her demonstrate by cutting a few bunches into my pan. She stood over me as I tried it myself, tugging at a bunch of grapes that pulled loose like beads from a necklace. "Cut the stem all the way," she told me as last advice before she walked away, her shoes sinking in the loose dirt, to begin work on her own row.

I cut another bunch, then another, fighting the snap and whip of vines. After ten minutes of **groping** for grapes, my first pan brimmed with bunches. I poured them on the paper tray, which was bordered by a wooden frame that kept the grapes from rolling off, and they spilled like jewels from a

ramble
(răm´bəl) *v.* When you *ramble*, you talk at length in an aimless way

foreman
(fôr´mən) *n.* A *foreman* is the leader of a work crew.

grope
(grōp) *v.* When you *grope*, you reach about in an uncertain way.

pirate's chest. The tray was only half filled, so I hurried to jump under the vines and begin groping, cutting, and tugging at the grapes again. I emptied the pan, raked the grapes with my hands to make them look like they filled the tray, and jumped back under the vine on my knees. I tried to cut faster because Mother, in the next row, was slowly moving ahead. I peeked into her row and saw five trays gleaming in the early morning. I cut, pulled hard, and stopped to gather the grapes that missed the pan; already bored, I spat on a few to wash them before tossing them like popcorn into my mouth.

So it went. Two pans equaled one tray—or six cents. By lunchtime I had a trail of thirty-seven trays behind me while Mother had sixty or more. We met about halfway from our last trays, and I sat down with a grunt, knees wet from kneeling on dropped grapes. I washed my hands with the water from the jug, drying them on the inside of my shirt sleeve before I opened the paper bag for the first sandwich, which I gave to Mother. I dipped my hand in again to unwrap a sandwich without looking at it. I took a first bite and chewed it slowly for the tang of mustard. Eating in silence I looked straight ahead at the vines, and only when we were finished with cookies did we talk.

"Are you tired?" she asked.

"No, but I got a sliver from the frame," I told her. I showed her the web of skin between my thumb and index finger. She wrinkled her forehead but said it was nothing.

"How many trays did you do?"

I looked straight ahead, not answering at first. I recounted in my mind the whole morning of bend, cut, pour again and again, before answering a **feeble** "thirty-seven." No elaboration, no detail. Without looking at me she told me how she had done field work in Texas and Michigan as a child. But I had a difficult time listening to her stories. I played with my grape knife, stabbing it into the ground, but stopped when Mother reminded me that I had better not lose it. I left the knife sticking up like a small, leafless plant. She then talked about school, the junior high I would be going to that fall, and then about Rick and Debra, how sorry they would be that they hadn't come out to pick grapes because they'd have no new clothes for the school year. She stopped talking when she peeked at her watch, a bandless one she kept in her pocket. She

feeble
(fē´bəl) *adj.* If someone is *feeble*, the person is very weak.

got up with an *"Ay, Dios,"*[3] and told me that we'd work until three, leaving me cutting figures in the sand with my knife and dreading the return to work.

Finally I rose and walked slowly back to where I had left off, again kneeling under the vine and fixing the pan under bunches of grapes. By that time, 11:30, the sun was over my shoulder and made me squint and think of the pool at the Y.M.C.A. where I was a summer member. I saw myself diving face first into the water and loving it. I saw myself gleaming like something new, at the edge of the pool. I had to daydream and keep my mind busy because boredom was a terror almost as awful as the work itself. My mind went dumb with stupid things, and I had to keep it moving with dreams of baseball and would-be girlfriends. I even sang, however softly, to keep my mind moving, my hands moving.

I worked less hurriedly and with less vision. I no longer saw that copper pot sitting squat on our stove or Mother waiting for it to whistle. The wardrobe that I imagined, crisp and bright in the closet, numbered only one pair of jeans and two shirts because, in half a day, six cents times thirty-seven trays was two dollars and twenty-two cents. It became clear to me. If I worked eight hours, I might make four dollars. I'd take this, even gladly, and walk downtown to look into store windows on the mall and long for the bright madras[4] shirts from Walter Smith or Coffee's, but settling for two imitation ones from Penney's.

That first day I laid down seventy-three trays while Mother had a hundred and twenty behind her. On the back of an old envelope, she wrote out our numbers and hours. We washed at the pump behind the farm house and walked slowly to our car for the drive back to town in the afternoon heat. That evening after dinner I sat in a lawn chair listening to music from a transistor radio while Rick and David King played catch. I joined them in a game of pickle, but there was little joy in trying to avoid their tags because I couldn't get the fields out of my mind: I saw myself dropping on my knees under a vine to tug at a branch that wouldn't come off. In bed, when I closed my eyes, I saw the fields, yellow with kicked up dust, and a crooked trail of trays rotting behind me.

---

[3] *Ay, Dios* (ī dē-ōs´) **Spanish:** "Oh, God."

[4] **madras** (măd´rəs): cotton cloth, usually with a plaid pattern.

The next day I woke tired and started picking tired. The grapes rained into the pan, slowly filling like a belly, until I had my first tray and started my second. So it went all day, and the next, and all through the following week, so that by the end of thirteen days the foreman counted out, in tens mostly, my pay of fifty-three dollars. Mother earned one hundred and forty-eight dollars. She wrote this on her envelope, with a message I didn't bother to ask her about.

The next day I walked with my friend Scott to the downtown mall where we drooled over the clothes behind fancy windows, bought popcorn, and sat at a tier of outdoor fountains to talk about girls. Finally we went into Penney's for more popcorn, which we ate walking around, before we returned home without buying anything. It wasn't until a few days before school that I let my fifty-three dollars slip quietly from my hands, buying a pair of pants, two shirts, and a maroon T-shirt, the kind that was in style. At home I tried them on while Rick looked on enviously; later, the day before school started, I tried them on again wondering not so much if they were worth it as who would see me first in those clothes.

Along with my brother and sister I picked grapes until I was fifteen, before giving up and saying that I'd rather wear old clothes than **stoop** like a Mexican. Mother thought I was being stuck-up, even stupid, because there would be no clothes for me in the fall. I told her I didn't care, but when Rick and Debra rose at five in the morning, I lay awake in bed feeling that perhaps I had made a mistake but unwilling to change my mind. That fall Mother bought me two pairs of socks, a packet of colored T-shirts, and underwear. The T-shirts would help, I thought, but who would see that I had new underwear and socks? I wore a new T-shirt on the first day of school, then an old shirt on Tuesday, then another T-shirt on Wednesday, and on Thursday an old Nehru shirt[5] that was embarrassingly out of style. On Friday I changed into the corduroy pants my brother had handed down to me and slipped into my last new T-shirt. I worked like a magician, blinding my classmates, who were all clothes conscious and small-time social climbers, by arranging my wardrobe to make it seem larger than it really was. But by spring I had to do something—my blue jeans were almost silver and my shoes had lost their form, puddling like black ice around my feet. That spring of my sixteenth year, Rick and I decided to take a labor bus to chop cotton. In his old Volkswagen, which was more noise than power, we drove on a Saturday morning to West Fresno—or Chinatown as some call it—parked, walked slowly toward a bus, and stood gawking at the . . . blacks, Okies,[6] *Tejanos*[7] with gold teeth, . . . Mexican families, and labor **contractors** shouting "Cotton" or "Beets," the work of spring.

We boarded the "Cotton" bus without looking at the contractor who stood almost blocking the entrance. . . . We boarded scared. . . . We sat . . . looking straight ahead, and only glanced briefly at the others who boarded, almost all of them broken and poorly dressed in loudly mismatched clothes. Finally when the contractor banged his palm against the side of the bus, the young man at the wheel, smiling and talking in Spanish, started the engine, idled it for a moment while he adjusted the mirrors, and started off in slow chugs. Except for the windshield there was no glass in the windows,

stoop
(sto͞op) *v.* If you *stoop*, you bend forward and down from the waist.

contractor
(kŏn′trăk′tər) *n.* A *contractor* is a person who agrees to provide services for a specific price.

---

[5] **Nehru** (nā′ro͞o) **shirt:** an Indian-style shirt with a stand-up collar.
[6] **Okies** (ō′kēz): people from Oklahoma and other midwestern states who moved to California to find work during the Great Depression of the 1930s.
[7] *Tejanos* (tā-hä′nōs): Texans of Mexican ancestry.

so as soon as we were on the rural roads outside Fresno, the dust and sand began to be sucked into the bus, whipping about like **irate** wasps as the gravel ticked about us. We closed our eyes, clotted up our mouths that wanted to open with embarrassed laughter because we couldn't believe we were on that bus with those people and the dust attacking us for no reason.

When we arrived at a field we followed the others to a pickup where we each took a hoe and marched to stand before a row. Rick and I, self-conscious and unsure, looked around at the others who leaned on their hoes or squatted in front of the rows, almost all talking in Spanish, joking . . . all waiting for the foreman's whistle to begin work. Mother had explained how to chop cotton by showing us with a broom in the backyard.

"Like this," she said, her broom swishing down weeds. "Leave one plant and cut four—and cut them! Don't leave them standing or the foreman will get mad."

The foreman whistled and we started up the row stealing glances at other workers to see if we were doing it right. But after awhile we worked like we knew what we were doing, neither of us hurrying or falling behind. But slowly the clot of men, women, and kids began to spread and loosen. Even Rick pulled away. I didn't hurry, though. I cut smoothly and cleanly as I walked at a slow pace, in a sort of funeral march. My eyes measured each space of cotton plants before I cut. If I missed the plants, I swished again. I worked intently, seldom looking up, so when I did I was amazed to see the sun, like a broken orange coin, in the east. It looked blurry, unbelievable, like something not of this world. I looked around in amazement, scanning the eastern horizon that was a taut line jutted with an occasional mountain. The horizon was beautiful, like a snapshot of the moon, in the early light of morning, in the quiet of no cars and few people.

The foreman trudged in boots in my direction, stepping awkwardly over the plants, to inspect the work. No one around me looked up. We all worked steadily while we waited for him to leave. When he did leave, with a feeble complaint addressed to no one in particular, we looked up smiling under straw hats and bandanas.

irate
(ī-rāt´) *adj.* If you are *irate*, you are very angry.

By 11:00, our lunch time, my ankles were hurting from walking on clods[8] the size of hardballs. My arms ached and my face was dusted by a wind that was perpetual, always busy whipping about. But the work was not bad, I thought. It was better, so much better, than picking grapes, especially with the hourly wage of a dollar twenty-five instead of piece work. Rick and I walked sorely toward the bus where we washed and drank water. Instead of eating in the bus or in the shade of the bus, we kept to ourselves by walking down to the irrigation canal[9] that ran the length of the field, to open our lunch of sandwiches and crackers. We laughed at the crackers, which seemed like a cruel joke from our Mother, because we were working under the sun and the last thing we wanted was a salty dessert. We ate them anyway and drank more water before we returned to the field, both of us limping in exaggeration. Working side by side, we talked and laughed at our **predicament** because our Mother had warned us year after year that if we didn't get on track in school we'd have to work in the fields and then we would see. We mimicked Mother's whining voice and smirked at her smoky view of the future in which we'd be trapped by marriage and screaming kids. We'd eat beans and then we'd see.

Rick pulled slowly away to the rhythm of his hoe falling faster and smoother. It was better that way, to work alone. I could hum made-up songs or songs from the radio and think to myself about school and friends. At the time I was doing badly in my classes, mainly because of a difficult stepfather, but also because I didn't care anymore. All through junior high and into my first year of high school there were those who said I would never do anything, be anyone. They said I'd work like a donkey and marry the first Mexican girl that came along. I was reminded so often, verbally and in the way I was treated at home, that I began to believe that chopping cotton might be a lifetime job for me. If not chopping cotton, then I might get lucky and find myself in a car wash or restaurant or junkyard. But it was clear; I'd work, and work hard.

I cleared my mind by humming and looking about. The sun was directly above with a few soft blades of clouds against a sky that seemed bluer and more beautiful than our sky in the city. Occasionally the breeze flurried and picked up dust

predicament (prĭ-dĭk′ə-mənt) *n.* A *predicament* is an unpleasant situation from which it is difficult to free oneself.

---

[8] **clods:** hardened clumps of soil.
[9] **irrigation canal:** a ditch that brings water to crops.

Cotton field

so that I had to cover my eyes and screw up my face. The workers were hunched, brown as the clods under our feet, and spread across the field that ran without end—fields that were owned by corporations, not families.

I hoed trying to keep my mind busy with scenes from school and pretend girlfriends until finally my brain turned off and my thinking went fuzzy with boredom. I looked about, no longer mesmerized by the beauty of the landscape, . . . no longer dreaming of the clothes I'd buy with my pay. My eyes followed my chopping as the plants, thin as their shadows, fell with each strike. I worked slowly with ankles and arms hurting, neck stiff, and eyes stinging from the dust and the sun that glanced off the field like a mirror.

By quitting time, 3:00, there was such an excruciating pain in my ankles that I walked as if I were wearing snowshoes. Rick laughed at me and I laughed too, embarrassed that most of the men were walking normally and I was among the first timers who had to get used to this work. "And what about you . . ." I came back at Rick. His eyes were meshed red and his long hippie hair was flecked with dust and gnats and bits of leaves. We placed our hoes in the back of a pickup and stood in line for our pay, which was twelve fifty. I was amazed at the pay, which was the most I had ever earned in one day, and thought that I'd come back the next day, Sunday. This was too good.

Instead of joining the others in the labor bus, we jumped in the back of a pickup when the driver said we'd get to town sooner and were welcome to join him. We scrambled into the truck bed to be joined by a heavy-set and laughing *Tejano* whose head was shaped like an egg, particularly so because the bandana he wore ended in a point on the top of his head. He laughed almost demonically as the pickup roared up the dirt path, a gray cape of dust rising behind us. On the highway, with the wind in our faces, we squinted at the fields as if we were looking for someone. The *Tejano* had quit laughing but was smiling broadly, occasionally chortling tunes he never finished. I was scared of him, though Rick, two years older and five inches taller, wasn't. If the *Tejano* looked at him, Rick stared back for a second or two before he looked away to the fields.

I felt like a soldier coming home from war when we rattled into Chinatown. People leaning against car hoods stared, their necks following us, owl-like; . . . Chinese grocers stopped brooming their storefronts to raise their cadaverous faces at us. We stopped in front of the Chi Chi Club where Mexican music blared from the juke box and cue balls cracked like dull ice. The *Tejano*, who was dirty as we were, stepped awkwardly over the side rail, dusted himself off with his bandana, and sauntered into the club.

Rick and I jumped from the back, thanked the driver who said *de nada*[10] and popped his clutch, so that the pickup jerked and coughed blue smoke. We returned smiling to our car, happy with the money we had made and pleased that we had, in a small way, proved ourselves to be tough; that we worked as well as other men and earned the same pay.

We returned the next day and the next week until the season was over and there was nothing to do. I told myself that I wouldn't pick grapes that summer, saying all through June and July that it was for Mexicans, not me. When August came around and I still had not found a summer job, I ate my words, sharpened my knife, and joined Mother, Rick, and Debra for one last time.

COLLABORATIVE DISCUSSION How do you think Gary Soto's experiences working in the fields influenced his attitudes toward work? With a partner, discuss how those early work experiences might affect him as a writer. Cite specific evidence from the text to support your ideas.

---

[10] ***de nada*** (də nä´də) **Spanish:** "You're welcome—it's nothing."

Cite Evidence

Readers rely on more than an author's words to understand a text's complete meaning. Readers also draw conclusions about ideas that are not stated directly in a text. A **conclusion** is a statement of belief or a logical judgement made based on:

- evidence stated in the text
- inferences, or guesses, made about what the text does not say explicitly
- knowledge gained from personal experience
- reasoning that connects what you know and what you read

To help you draw a conclusion, you can fill in a statement like this:

"Based on _____ and _____, I believe _____ ."

Reread the first two paragraphs of "One Last Time" and draw a conclusion about Soto's attitude toward his family and the kind of work they did.

Analyze the Meanings of Words and Phrases

Authors choose words carefully to help readers imagine the things they are describing. **Imagery** is the use of descriptive words and phrases to create word pictures, or images. These images are formed through the use of **sensory details**, details that appeal to one or more of the five senses—sight, hearing, smell, taste, and touch.

Notice the many sensory details in these sentences from "One Last Time."

I cut another bunch, then another, fighting the snap and whip of vines. After ten minutes of groping for grapes, my first pan brimmed with bunches. I poured them on the paper tray, which was bordered by a wooden frame that kept the grapes from rolling off, and they spilled like jewels from a pirate's chest.

- snap and whip — Appeal to hearing and touch
- bordered by a wooden frame / jewels from a pirate's chest — Appeal to sight

Identify other words in the passage that appeal to the five senses, and continue to notice Soto's use of imagery and sensory details as you review the text.

Analyzing the Text

Cite Text Evidence Support your responses with evidence from the text.

1. **Compare** Examine lines 75–85. Identify statements that show how Soto feels about the work he's doing. What change has occurred in his attitude since he first arrived at the farm?

2. **Make Inferences** Reread lines 141–172 to draw conclusions about the author's attitude toward clothing when he was a teenager. What does he mean when he says "I worked like a magician"?

3. **Analyze** Use a chart like the one shown to identify sensory details in the paragraph that begins on line 182. What do these details help you to understand about Soto?

Sight	Hearing	Taste	Touch

4. **Analyze** Reread lines 299–310. Which sensory details help you imagine how the *Tejano* looks and sounds?

5. **Draw Conclusions** What type of agricultural work does Soto prefer? Draw a conclusion about why he has this preference.

6. **Draw Conclusions** What is Soto's attitude toward agricultural work? Express your ideas by filling in a statement like the following, expanding it as necessary: Based on _____ and _____, I believe Gary Soto thinks of agricultural work as _____ .

PERFORMANCE TASK

Speaking Activity: Presentation
With a small group, make a poster that illustrates the central idea of "One Last Time."

- First, work with your group to determine the central idea of the memoir. What is the main message you think Gary Soto wants to communicate? Discuss the imagery and events that support this idea.

- Next, make a poster. In the center, write the central idea. Then, create a collage of words and images from the selection that helps illustrate this idea. The images can be illustrations you draw or photos from other sources.

- Present your work to the class, explaining how the images and quotations in the poster connect to the central idea of the memoir.

Critical Vocabulary

ramble	foreman	grope	feeble
stoop	contractor	irate	predicament

Practice and Apply Complete each sentence in a way that shows the meaning of the vocabulary word.

1. The principal became **irate** because . . .
2. Each day the **foreman** at the factory has to . . .
3. My friend found himself in a **predicament** when . . .
4. Our neighbors hired a **contractor** because . . .
5. You have to **stoop** if you want to . . .
6. Henry still felt **feeble** because . . .
7. Be sure you don't **ramble** when . . .
8. Alissa had to **grope** for some candles because . . .

Vocabulary Strategy: Using a Dictionary

A **dictionary** is a reference work—either print or digital—that gives information about words. Notice the parts of a dictionary entry:

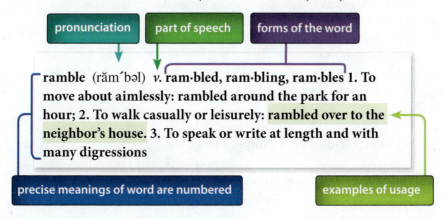

Practice and Apply Use a dictionary to look up the following words from "One Last Time." Then fill out a chart like the one shown.

Word	Pronunciation	Part of Speech	Guessed Definition	Dictionary Definition
elaboration (line 83)				
mesmerized (line 278)				
chortling (line 306)				

Language Conventions: Semicolons and Run-ons

A **run-on sentence** is made up of two or more independent clauses—or a group of words that contains a subject and predicate and can stand alone as a sentence—that are written as though they were one. Some run-ons have no punctuation within them, as in this example.

Incorrect: I didn't want to work I wanted to stay home.

Other run-ons may have independent clauses that are sepearted with a comma where a conjuncion or a semicolon is needed.

Incorrect: I thought I had enough clothes, I was wrong.

A **semicolon (;)** is a type of punctuation mark that can be used to separate the two independent clauses in a compound sentence.

Use a semicolon...	Example
...between two independent clauses when the relationship between the two clauses is very clear. The semicolon takes the place of a coordinating conjunction, such as *and, but, or,* or *nor*.	"At home I tried them on while Rick looked on enviously; later, the day before school started, I tried them on again wondering not so much if they were worth it as who would see me first in those clothes."
...before a conjunction to separate two independent clauses when one or both of the clauses contain commas.	He asked for new socks, T-shirts, and shoes; but what he really wanted was a phone.

One way to fix a run-on sentence is to break it into two separate sentences. Another way is to use a semicolon between the two independent clauses.

Correct: I didn't want to work. I wanted to stay home.

Correct: I thought I had enough clothes; I was wrong.

Practice and Apply Correct each sentence that has an error by rewriting it and adding a semicolon. If a sentence is already correct, write *correct*.

1. Soto and his friend went to the mall they drooled over clothes.
2. When Soto couldn't find another job, he ate his words, and he joined his mother, brother, and sister picking grapes.
3. Instead of joining the other workers in the labor bus, the boys jumped in the back of a pickup truck to get to town sooner.
4. Rick, Soto's brother, didn't appear to be sore, but his hair was flecked with dust, gnats, and bits of leaves.

Background In 2008, the United States entered into what many called the Great Recession, generally considered to be America's worst economic crisis since the Great Depression of the late 1920s and 1930s. A recession is a slowdown of economic activity. During a recession, people and businesses tend to spend less money, which contributes to a cycle of job losses and decreases in profits. The effects of the Great Recession were felt for years. At the time these arguments were written, the unemployment rate was high for adult workers and even higher for young workers.

Teens Need Jobs, Not Just Cash

Teens at Work

Argument by Anne Michaud | Argument from *The Record-Journal*

SETTING A PURPOSE As you read, consider the points each author makes about the importance of jobs for teenagers. Which reasons seem most valid to you?

I well remember how my first job made me feel: capable, creative, in charge. I was a summer counselor at a YMCA day camp, and still practically a kid myself, just out of 10th grade. I made a lot of mistakes.

As the arts and crafts counselor, I blew most of my $200 budget on Popsicle sticks and gimp.[1] We ran out of arts and crafts supplies halfway through the summer, and so taking long "nature walks" became our fallback. I wonder what the campers' parents thought.

10 Making mistakes like that is partly what early jobs are all about. We learn, and then make better decisions when the "real" job comes along.

---

[1] **gimp:** a narrow, flat braid used to make crafts such as a key chain.

So it's troubling that teens today are facing their third straight summer of bleak employment prospects—in fact, the worst since World War II, when the government began keeping track. In April, the jobless rate for 16-to 19-year-olds approached 25 percent. And the unemployment rate only counts those actively looking. Many are too discouraged by the dismal economy to try.

Parents may debate the merits of teens taking jobs bagging groceries versus studying or pursuing music, sports or college-level courses. But the poorest Americans don't have that choice, and to double down[2] on their woes, they are hit hardest by teen unemployment. Last summer, just one in five teenagers with annual family income below $20,000 had a job, according to a report by Northeastern University's Center for Labor Market Studies.

Not only aren't these teens earning needed cash—or learning the life lessons I got at the YMCA—but the joblessness they experience now may drag them down for years. One study in the United States and Britain said that 37-year-old men who had **sustained** a year of unemployment before age 23 made 23 percent less than their peers. The equivalent gap was 16 percent for women.

College graduates who took jobs beneath their education or outside of their fields often never got back to where they might have been, according to what the Japanese learned from their "lost decade" of economic doldrums[3] in the 1990s and early 2000s. When the Japanese economy recovered, employers preferred graduates fresh out of school, creating a generation that suffers higher rates of depression, heart attack and suicide, and lower life expectancy.[4]

These structural problems with capitalism—the ups and downs of the business cycle—should not be **borne** by individuals, but collectively. That's why we have unemployment insurance, for example.

Other countries seem to have a better understanding of this. Germany's **renowned** apprenticeship program, a training period of two to four years, attracts roughly two-

sustain
(sə-stān´) v.
When you *sustain* something, you keep it in existence or continue it.

borne
(bôrn) v. If something is *borne*, it is carried or supported.

renowned
(rĭ-nound´) adj.
If something is *renowned*, it is famous.

---

[2] **double down:** to increase one's bet to two times.
[3] **doldrums:** stagnations or slumps.
[4] **life expectancy:** the number of years that an individual is expected to live.

thirds of vocational school[5] students there. They're often hired afterward, one reason Germany has a far lower youth unemployment rate than us, at 9.5 percent. Firms and government share the apprenticeship expenses.

The Netherlands, also keen on **averting** a lost generation of workers, is dividing full-time private sector[6] jobs into two or three part-time ones, with government providing supplemental income for part-time workers. When the economy improves, Dutch 20-somethings will be ready with skills and experience.

The New York Youth Works program has the right idea. On Long Island, at least 64 employers have signed up. The program offers them tax credits for hiring low-income youth. Given that unemployment among teens is more than twice the 7.4 percent rate for adults on Long Island, we should expand this program.

When teens work, it teaches them independence, responsibility, a good work ethic[7] and how to get along with others. Our collective future depends on investing in their success.

avert
(ə-vûrt´) v. If you *avert* something, you prevent it from happening.

---

[5] **vocational school:** a school that teaches trades, such as plumbing or graphic design.
[6] **private sector:** the privately owned part of the economy that is not funded by the government.
[7] **work ethic:** the belief in the value of work.

Teens at Work
Online Editorial from *The Record-Journal*

To combat high national unemployment rates for teens, legislators[8] must craft more **initiatives** which help induce creation of summer and part-time work opportunities.

According to the U.S. Bureau of Labor Statistics, America's unemployment rate in 2011 for job-aspirants 16 to 19 years old was 24.4 percent, which does not include those who do not apply for openings. Since the Bureau began compiling such data in the late 1940s, last year's number was the second highest ever recorded. Worst of all time was 25.9 percent, in 2010. More must be done to address this issue.

Entire families can suffer when wages are not available for older kids. Many teenagers, fortunate enough to have work, contribute portions of paychecks to households' overall budgets. With fewer chances for adolescents to secure employment, steady sources of domestic income disappear. Moreover, when jobs are scarce, even youths who simply want discretionary money[9] must instead request finances from mom, dad or guardians, which places added levels of stress upon the family.

initiative
(ĭ-nĭsh´ə-tĭv) *n.*
An *initiative* is a beginning step in a plan.

> "Entire families can suffer when wages are not available for older kids."

One factor behind increased teen joblessness is that youths will often come up against experienced adults willing to work part-time for stable pay. While anyone's successful ascension[10] out of unemployment-status in this sluggish economy is positive, too much position-filling at newer generations' expense is **detrimental** long-term.

detrimental
(dĕt´rə-mĕn´tl) *adj.*
If something is *detrimental*, it causes damage or harm.

---

[8] **legislators:** lawmakers.
[9] **discretionary money:** money to be spent on things you want but do not need.
[10] **ascension:** rise.

For at part-time jobs is where most members of tomorrow's labor force will first learn valuable workplace skills. Delaying or denying this experience, crucial to one's ongoing professional development, will engender[11] negative economic **implications** in future decades. People who miss out on employment early may not reach full potential. Already, businesses nationwide report **deficiencies** in quantities of candidates who can fill positions which require advanced capabilities.

Teenagers' employment statistics have worsened also because of automated machines' replacement of personnel at low-level tasks—for example, grocery stores' self-scan aisles—and continued closures of businesses which utilize large staffs … Commendably, the White House and U.S. Department of Labor have begun a campaign to generate 250,000 private-sector jobs, with at least 100,000 being paid spots. While this is a start, even more government-backed employment stimulus[12] is necessary. Otherwise, a generation whose future is already threatened by the Great Recession's aftermath could fall even further behind—an unacceptable, dangerous prospect.

implication
(ĭm´plĭ-kā´shən) *n.*
An *implication* is a connection or consequence.

deficiency
(dĭ-fĭsh´ən-sē) *n.*
A *deficiency* is a lack or shortage of something.

COLLABORATIVE DISCUSSION Both authors mention the value of work experience for teenagers. With a partner, discuss whether the authors have convinced you that getting a job is more important than other school or sports activities you might enjoy. Cite specific evidence from the text to support your ideas.

---

[11] **engender:** produce or create.
[12] **employment stimulus:** funds, special programs, or other incentives provided by the government to generate new jobs or to encourage employers to hire more workers.

Delineate and Evaluate an Argument

"Teens Need Jobs, Not Just Cash" and "Teens at Work" both cite the need for the creation of more jobs for adolescents. Writing such as this that makes a claim and supports it with reasons and evidence is called an **argument**.

- A **claim** is the writer's position on an issue or problem. It is often stated directly at the beginning or end of an argument.
- **Support** consists of the reasons and evidence presented to prove the claim. Support may include explanations, specific facts, statistics, or examples.

A good argument anticipates opposing viewpoints and provides counterarguments to disprove them. **Counterarguments** are arguments made to oppose another argument. Notice this example in "Teens at Work."

> . . . youths will often come up against experienced adults willing to work part-time for stable pay. While anyone's successful ascension out of unemployment-status in this sluggish economy is positive, too much position-filling at newer generations' expense is detrimental long-term.

The reasons and evidence given in support of a claim must be **relevant,** or have some sensible connection. Writers may include information that appeals to readers' emotions, but is not really relevant to the claim. It is up to the reader to **evaluate,** or examine carefully, the support for the argument and determine whether it makes sense and is convincing.

Although "Teens Need Jobs, Not Just Cash" and "Teens at Work" both deal with the same topic and make similar claims, there are differences in the strength and relevance of the evidence. As you evaluate each claim, ask yourself the following questions:

- What claim is being made?
- What reasons and evidence are presented in support of the claim?
- Is the support presented in a way that makes sense?
- Are all the reasons and evidence relevant?
- Is an opposing argument addressed with a counterargument?

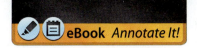

Analyzing the Text

Cite Text Evidence Support your responses with evidence from the texts.

1. **Interpret** In lines 1–12 of "Teens Need Jobs, Not Just Cash," the author includes an **anecdote,** a brief account of an interesting incident or event that is usually intended to entertain or make a point. What impact does this anecdote have on the tone of the article? Explain how it supports the author's claim.

2. **Interpret** What opposing viewpoint is presented in "Teens Need Jobs, Not Just Cash"? What counterargument does the author make?

3. **Evaluate** Reread lines 43–46 of "Teens Need Jobs, Not Just Cash." Is this information relevant as support for the author's claim about the need for jobs for teens? Why or why not?

4. **Analyze** In lines 5–10, why does the author of "Teens at Work" provide statistics about teen unemployment?

5. **Evaluate** Reread lines 26–34 of "Teens at Work." Are you convinced that early part-time work is important in developing a person's life-long career prospects?

6. **Evaluate** Briefly summarize the arguments made in each selection, making sure to include the main claim and support. Then tell which article you think presents the stronger argument and explain your opinion.

PERFORMANCE TASK

Speaking Activity: Argument In order to evaluate a claim made in an argument, you may need to do additional research. Develop an argument in which you present additional support that proves or disproves a claim made in one of the articles.

- Identify a claim that you will research.
- Use print and digital resources for your research.
- Display the results of your research in a graph or chart.
- Incorporate your findings into your argument and present it to the class. Be sure to use eye contact, appropriate volume, and clear pronunciation.

Critical Vocabulary

| sustain | borne | renowned | avert |
| initiative | detrimental | implication | deficiency |

Practice and Apply Use what you know about the Vocabulary words to answer the following questions.

1. Is a vitamin **deficiency detrimental** to your health? Why or why not?

2. If a dancer were **renowned** for his or her performing style, would you **avert** you eyes during a performance? Why or why not?

3. If you create an **initiative** to pass a law, what might **sustain** interest in it?

4. If most of the work on a project is **borne** by one or two people, what is the **implication** about other members of that project's team?

Vocabulary Strategy: Using Greek Suffixes

Suffixes—word parts added to the end of a root or base word—provide clues about the meaning of a word. For example, knowing that the Greek suffix -*ism* means "a practice, doctrine, or system" helps you define words such as *capitalism*. Look at this example from "Teens Need Jobs, Not Just Cash":

> These structural problems with capitalism—the ups and downs of the business cycle—should not be borne by individuals, but collectively.

The context of the sentence and the meaning of the suffix -*ism* help you to understand that the author is referring to an economic system.

When you encounter a suffixed word, follow these steps:
- Identify the meaning of the suffix.
- Look at the base word or word root and think about its meaning.
- Apply the meanings to define the word. Confirm your definition in a dictionary.

Practice and Apply Identify the -*ism* word or words in each sentence. Use the suffix meaning to define the word. Confirm your definition in a dictionary.

1. Which form of government is more authoritarian, socialism or communism?

2. The French painter Claude Monet was a pioneer of impressionism.

3. Teens are attracted to the gritty realism of the writer S. E. Hinton's novels.

4. The students' activism led to the occupation of the administration building.

ANCHOR TEXT: COMPARE POEMS

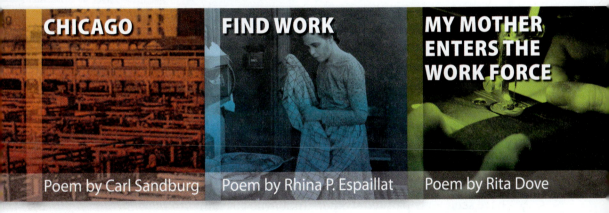

CHICAGO Poem by Carl Sandburg

FIND WORK Poem by Rhina P. Espaillat

MY MOTHER ENTERS THE WORK FORCE Poem by Rita Dove

Carl Sandburg (1878–1967) *was born in Galesburg, Illinois, to Swedish immigrant parents. After the eighth grade, Sandburg quit school so he could help support his family. He worked a variety of jobs, from shining shoes to delivering milk. Later, he began hopping on freight trains to explore the West. Eventually, Sandburg settled in Chicago. With the publication of his poetry collections* Chicago Poems, Cornhuskers, *and* Smoke and Steel, *Sandburg gained a reputation as a poet of the workers and common people.*

Rhina P. Espaillat (b. 1932) *was born in the Dominican Republic, but had to leave when her family was exiled for opposing the dictatorship in that country. Espaillat's family settled in New York City, where as a young girl she began writing poetry. She wrote in both English and Spanish, and has been published in both languages. Espaillat's collections of poetry have won her many prestigious literary awards.*

Rita Dove (b. 1952) *was the first African American to be named Poet Laureate of the United States, one of the highest official honors for American poets. Born in Akron, Ohio, Dove was encouraged to read by her parents and excelled at school. She was named a Presidential Scholar, one of the top one hundred high-school graduates in the country. Dove has published short stories and novels, as well as her award-winning collections of poetry. She has also written the lyrics for the songs of many renowned musical composers.*

SETTING A PURPOSE All of the poems you are about to read share a view about workers. As you read, think about what each of the poets suggests about the impact of workers on those around them.

Chicago
by Carl Sandburg

       Hog Butcher for the World,
       Tool Maker, Stacker of Wheat,
       Player with Railroads and the Nation's Freight Handler;
       Stormy, husky, brawling,
5   City of the Big Shoulders:

They tell me you are wicked and I believe them, for I
     have seen your painted women under the gas lamps
     luring the farm boys.
And they tell me you are crooked and I answer: Yes, it
     is true I have seen the gunman kill and go free to
     kill again.
And they tell me you are brutal and my reply is: On the faces
     of women and children I have seen the marks
     of wanton[1] hunger.
And having answered so I turn once more to those who
     sneer at this my city, and I give them back the sneer
     and say to them:
10 Come and show me another city with lifted head singing
     so proud to be alive and coarse and strong and cunning.
Flinging magnetic curses amid the toil of piling job on
     job, here is a tall bold slugger set vivid against the
     little soft cities;
Fierce as a dog with tongue lapping for action, cunning
     as a savage pitted against the wilderness,
       Bareheaded,
       Shoveling,
15   Wrecking,
       Planning,
       Building, breaking, rebuilding,

---

[1] **wanton:** without limitation.

Under the smoke, dust all over his mouth, laughing with
   white teeth,
Under the terrible burden of destiny laughing as a young
   man laughs,
20 Laughing even as an ignorant fighter laughs who has
   never lost a battle,
Bragging and laughing that under his wrist is the pulse, and
   under his ribs the heart of the people,
               Laughing!
Laughing the stormy, husky, brawling laughter of
   Youth, half-naked, sweating, proud to be Hog
25   Butcher, Tool Maker, Stacker of Wheat, Player with
   Railroads and Freight Handler to the Nation.

A view of the Chicago stockyards, where animals were kept before slaugther

Determine Meaning of Words and Phrases

Figurative language is language used in an imaginative way to communicate something beyond the literal meanings of the words. Poets use figurative language to create effects, to emphasize ideas, and to evoke emotions. Types of figurative language include the following.

- **Personification,** which gives human qualities to an animal, an object, or an idea. In the following lines from "Chicago," Sandburg personifies the city by giving it human characteristics, such as the ability to sing and feel pride.

  "Come and show me another city with lifted head singing so proud to be alive and coarse and strong and cunning."

- **Similes,** which compare things that are generally unlike by using the words *like* or *as*. In these lines, Sandburg uses similes to compare Chicago to a dog and to a savage:

  "Fierce as a dog with tongue lapping for action, cunning as a savage pitted against the wilderness"

Think about the effects of personification and similes as you analyze "Chicago."

Analyzing the Text

Cite Text Evidence   Support your responses with evidence from the text.

1. **Infer** Reread lines 1–5. What do the different names for Chicago tell you about the city's economy at the time this poem was written?

2. **Analyze** Examine lines 6–8. What three adjectives are used to describe Chicago? How does the poet counter this negative view in lines 9–10?

3. **Infer** Reread lines 12–17. What adjectives used to describe Chicago reveal the poet's attitude toward the residents of the city? Describe his attitude.

4. **Analyze** Identify three examples of personification in line 18 of the poem. What is the effect of these personifications?

5. **Analyze** Identify two similes in lines 19–20. What is the effect of these comparisons?

6. **Analyze** How is Chicago personified in line 21 of the poem?

Find Work
Poem by Rhina P. Espaillat

I tie my Hat—I crease my Shawl—
Life's little duties do—precisely
As the very least
Were infinite—to me—
—Emily Dickinson, #443

My mother's mother, widowed very young
of her first love, and of that love's first fruit,
moved through her father's farm, her country tongue
and country heart anaesthetized[1] and mute
with labor. So her kind was taught to do—
"Find work," she would reply to every grief—
and her one dictum,[2] whether false or true,
tolled heavy with her passionate belief.
Widowed again, with children, in her prime,
she spoke so little it was hard to bear
so much composure, such a truce with time
spent in the lifelong practice of despair.
But I recall her floors, scrubbed white as bone,
her dishes, and how painfully they shone.

---

[1] **anaesthetized:** made to feel numb or without feeling.
[2] **dictum:** saying or motto.

Analyze Structure

"Find Work" is a sonnet, which means "little song." More specifically, a **sonnet** is a 14-line poem that has a specific pattern of rhythm and rhyme.

The rhythmic pattern in a poem is called the **meter**. It is determined by the stressed and unstressed syllables in the words.

- Each unit of meter, known as a **foot,** consists of one stressed syllable and one or two unstressed syllables. A foot that is made up of an unstressed syllable followed by a stressed syllable is an **iamb**.
- Sonnets are often written in **iambic pentameter,** a meter in which each line is made up of five (penta) feet of iambs.
- To show the meter in a line of poetry, a stressed syllable is indicated by the symbol ´ and an unstressed syllable by the symbol ˘.

˘ ´ ˘ ´ ˘ ´ ˘ ´ ˘ ´
My mother's mother, widowed very young

˘ ´ ˘ ´ ˘ ´ ˘ ´ ˘ ´
of her first love, and of that love's first fruit,

The **rhyme scheme** in a poem is the pattern of end rhymes. A rhyme scheme is noted by assigning a letter of the alphabet, beginning with *a*, to each line. Lines that rhyme are given the same letter.

My mother's mother, widowed very young	a
of her first love, and of that love's first fruit,	b
moved through her father's farm, her country tongue	a
and country heart anaesthetized and mute	b

Many sonnets follow the rhyme scheme *abab, cdcd, efef, gg*. The last two lines are a **couplet,** or rhyming pair of lines. Notice the characteristics of a sonnet as you analyze "Find Work."

Analyzing the Text

Cite Text Evidence   Support your responses with evidence from the text.

1. **Identify Patterns** Use the symbols ´ and ˘ to mark the meter of lines 10–13 of the sonnet; use letters of the alphabet to identify the rhyme scheme. What type of rhythmic pattern, or meter, do these lines follow?

2. **Compare** How are the last two lines of "Find Work" different from the rest of the poem in form and content?

3. **Draw Conclusions** What role does work play in the life of the speaker's grandmother? Explain.

My Mother Enters the Work Force
Poem by Rita Dove

The path to ABC Business School
was paid for by a lucky sign:
ALTERATIONS, QUALIFIED SEAMSTRESS INQUIRE WITHIN.
Tested on sleeves, hers never puckered—puffed or sleek,
5 leg-o'-mutton or raglan—[1]
they barely needed the damp cloth
to steam them perfect.

Those were the afternoons. Evenings
she took in piecework,[2] the treadle machine
10 with its locomotive whir
traveling the lit path of the needle
through quicksand taffeta
or velvet deep as a forest.
And now and now sang the treadle,
15 *I know, I know....*

And then it was day again, all morning
at the office machines, their clack and chatter
another journey—rougher,
that would go on forever
20 until she could break a hundred words
with no errors—ah, and then

no more postponed groceries,
and that blue pair of shoes!

COLLABORATIVE DISCUSSION With a partner, discuss which of the poems speaks to you most directly about the subject of work. Cite specific evidence from the text to support your ideas.

---

[1] **leg-o'-mutton or raglan:** types of sleeves. A leg-of-mutton sleeve is wide at the top and narrow at the bottom. A raglan sleeve is cut so that it continues up to the collar.

[2] **piecework:** work paid for according to the amount done, not the time it takes.

Analyze Structure

Although sonnets and other types of poems follow an established structure, some poems have no special form at all. When a poem has no regular pattern of rhythm or rhyme, it is called **free verse**. The lines in a free verse poem flow more naturally and can create the effect of speech.

Just because a free verse poem doesn't have a set rhyme scheme or meter doesn't mean that the poem has no rhythm. Free verse poetry often
- achieves a rhythm that sounds more like everyday speech
- contains rhythmic sound effects, such as the repetition of sounds, words, or phrases

Look again at the first stanza of "My Mother Enters the Work Force." Notice whether the lines rhyme and whether they have a regular pattern of stressed and unstressed syllables. What is creating the rhythm in this stanza?

Analyzing the Text

Cite Text Evidence   Support your responses with evidence from the text.

1. **Infer** Who is the subject of this poem? Who is the speaker? Identify the lines that help you answer.

2. **Summarize** Give a brief summary of the events described in this poem.

3. **Analyze** A **metaphor** is a type of figurative language in which two things that are basically unlike one another are compared without using the words *like* or *as*. A **simile** is a comparison that uses like or as. Identify three examples of these types of figurative language in lines 9–16. In a chart like the one below, identify what is being compared in each. What is the impact of these metaphors?

Type of Figurative Language	What Is Being Compared

4. **Evaluate** Look again at lines 9–16. What is the effect of the personification of the sewing machine?

5. **Analyze** How might the effect of this poem have been different if it had been written with a regular pattern of rhythm and rhyme rather than as free verse?

ANCHOR TEXT: COMPARE POEMS

Compare and Contrast Structure

As you've learned, some forms of poetry follow set rules of rhyme, length, or meter while others do not. Poems that follow a fixed set of rules are known as **traditional forms**. Sonnets, odes, and epic poems are all traditional forms. Free verse poems are known as open forms because they take their shape and pattern from the poem's content.

Usually a poet chooses a specific form in order to convey something unique about the subject. For example, rhyming lines with a sing-song nature might convey a playful approach to the subject. In free verse, the poet uses different line lengths to create slow or fast rhythms that may emphasize certain aspects of the topic.

Compare these lines from the sonnet "Find Work" and the free verse poem "My Mother Enters the Work Force." What do you notice about the different rhythms?

from "Find Work":
**Widowed again, with children, in her prime,
she spoke so little it was hard to bear
so much composure, such a truce with time
spent in the lifelong practice of despair.**

from "My Mother Enters the Work Force":
**And then it was day again, all morning
at the office machines, their clack and chatter
another journey—rougher,
that would go on forever**

The characteristics of a sonnet and of free verse are noted in the chart. Think about how they might affect the way a subject is presented.

	Sonnet	Free Verse
Number of Lines	• 14 lines	• any number of lines
Meter/Rhythm	• regular pattern of rhythm • usually written in iambic pentameter	• no regular rhythmic pattern
Rhyme Scheme	• rhyme scheme is *abab, cdcd, efef, gg*	• no established rhyme scheme

Continue to compare the structures of the poems as you analyze "Chicago," "Find Work," and "My Mother Enters the Work Force."

Compare Texts 435

Analyzing the Text

Cite Text Evidence Support your responses with evidence from the texts.

1. **Identify Patterns** Of the three poems you just read, which two have the same form? Identify the characteristics that make these two poems similar in structure.

2. **Compare** Compare and contrast what the poems "Find Work" and "My Mother Enters the Work Force" have to say about the subject of work. What role does work serve for each of the mothers?

3. **Compare** In a Venn diagram like the one shown, compare and contrast the last two lines of "Find Work" with the last two lines of "My Mother Enters the Work Force."

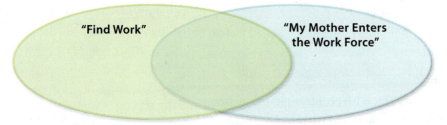

4. **Analyze** The **tone** of a literary work expresses the writer's attitude toward his or her subject. Identify several examples of words and phrases that help establish the tone in the poems "Chicago" and "Find Work." Compare the tone in the two poems.

5. **Analyze** How is the kind of figurative language found in "Chicago" similar to that in "My Mother Enters the Work Force"? Give examples.

PERFORMANCE TASK

Writing Activity: Compare and Contrast Essay Write an essay in which you compare and contrast two of the poems you just read.

- Choose two of the three poems to write about.
- To help plan your essay, create a Venn diagram in which you compare and contrast the theme, tone, structure, and use of language in the two poems.
- Use the notes from your diagram to write a comparison of the poems.
- Be sure your essay includes evidence from both poems to support your conclusions.

COLLECTION 6
PERFORMANCE TASK A

Interactive Lessons
To help you complete this task, use:
- *Writing Narratives*
- *Writing as a Process*
- *Giving a Presentation*

Present a Narrative

This collection includes narratives that explore the value of work. The excerpt from *The Adventures of Tom Sawyer* and "One Last Time," for example, relate tales of how two children—one fictional and one real—respond to the idea of work. In the following activity, you will script and present a narrative that reveals a lesson learned through an experience with work.

A successful narrative presentation

- establishes context, appropriate register, and point of view
- presents a logical sequence of events
- uses a variety of connecting and transitional words or phrases to link ideas and events
- employs narrative techniques to bring the story to life
- provides a conclusion that reflects on the experience

Mentor Text Note how this example from "One Last Time" establishes narrative context and point of view.

> " I remember her coming home, dusty and so tired that she had to rest on the porch before she trudged inside to wash and start dinner. I didn't understand the complaints about her ankles or the small of her back, even though I had been in the grape fields watching her work. . . . A few years later, however, I caught on when I went to pick grapes rather than play in the rows. "

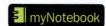 **myNotebook**

Use the annotation tools in your eBook to record text details that will help you generate ideas for your own narrative.

PLAN

Analyze the Texts Review and analyze the excerpt from *The Adventures of Tom Sawyer* and "One Last Time" from this collection and consider how they convey experiences related to work. Then think about a time that you or someone you know completed a job that taught something, even if that "learning experience" wasn't particularly enjoyable.

ACADEMIC VOCABULARY

As you share your experience with work, be sure to use the academic vocabulary words.

commentary
minors
occupation
option
style

Draft Your Ideas Draft ideas for your narrative and its context by outlining an experience with a job or task and the lesson it taught.

- Brainstorm ideas about a narrative you might present. What stories might you tell about your own experience with a job or task? What stories might you tell about the experience of someone you know? Which one would you most like to present?
- Outline your narrative's key events, sequencing them clearly so that your audience will understand what happened and recognize its significance.
- Decide on a point of view. Will you present events from a first-person point of view or a third-person point of view?

Interactive Lessons
For help in planning your presentation, use
- Giving a Presentation: Knowing Your Audience

PRODUCE

Script Your Narrative Review your outline, considering its clarity, your purpose, and the needs of your audience. Then script your narrative, remembering that your audience is going to listen to it, rather than read it.

- Establish an appropriate tone, or register. Is your narrative humorous, like Twain's, or formal, like Soto's?
- Use narrative techniques, such as realistic dialogue, effective pacing, vivid description, and sensory language to bring the story to life. Craft a conclusion that reflects on the meaning of the experience and communicates your point.

myWriteSmart
Write your rough draft in *myWriteSmart*. Focus on getting your ideas down, rather than perfecting your choice of language.

Interactive Lessons
For help drafting your presentation, use
- Writing Narratives: Narrative Techniques

Language Conventions: Realistic Dialogue Make sure that your narrative's dialogue sounds realistic. Read the following example from *The Adventures of Tom Sawyer*.

> 'But of course you'd druther *work*—wouldn't you? Course you would!'
>
> Tom contemplated the boy a bit, and said:
>
> 'What do you call work?'
>
> 'Why, ain't *that* work?'
>
> Tom resumed his whitewashing, and answered carelessly:
>
> 'Well, maybe it is, and maybe it ain't. All I know is, it suits Tom Sawyer.'

Note how Twain records the boys' language as it would sound to the ear. He includes their use of *ain't*, adds emphasis to *work* and *that*, and even includes brief interruptions, as if the conversation pauses while Tom considers responses to Ben's comments.

REVISE

Evaluate Your Narrative Have your partner or group of peers review your draft. Use the following chart to revise your narrative.

Ask your reviewers to note instances in your narrative where the dialogue could be more realistic.

Interactive Lessons
For help in revising your narrative, use
- Writing as a Process: Revising and Editing

Questions	Tips	Revision Techniques
Does the narrative establish context and point of view?	**Highlight** details that establish context. **Check** that your narrative is told from a consistent point of view.	**Add** details about where and when events take place. **Change** pronouns to make point of view consistent, as needed.
Does the narrative convey a logical sequence of events?	**Number** the events. **Check** that the sequence shows the actual order of events.	**Rearrange** events into the order in which they occurred. **Add** transitional words to link events.
Does the narrative include vivid description and realistic dialogue?	**Highlight** sensory details. **Underline** dialogue that advances the action.	**Elaborate** with sensory details, as needed. **Add** dialogue that reveals character and advances the action.
Does the narrative use appropriate pacing?	**Check** that the narrative does not drag or does not move too quickly.	**Add** sentence variety by combining sentences, combining verbs, and using a greater variety of verbs.
Does the conclusion include a reflection on the experience?	**Underline** the reflection on why the experience is meaningful.	**Add** a statement that explains the significance of the incident, as needed.

Practice Your Presentation Read your narrative aloud, marking places where you'll add emphasis, modify your pitch and tone, adjust your reading rate, or make any facial expressions or hand gestures.

PRESENT

Deliver Your Narrative Presentation Finalize your narrative and share it with your audience.

- Present your narrative as a speech to the class.
- Record your narrative as a webcast.

PERFORMANCE TASK A RUBRIC
NARRATIVE PRESENTATION

	Ideas and Evidence	Organization	Language
4	• The narrative conveys a real experience and its significance through an established context and well-chosen details. • Description and dialogue are used effectively. • The conclusion unfolds naturally and reflects on the experience.	• The narrative has a logical sequence that builds to a logical conclusion. • Well-chosen events result in effective pacing. • Transitions logically connect each event in the sequence. • Verbal and nonverbal elements effectively hold the audience's attention.	• The narrative successfully weaves in vivid details and sensory language. • The writer consistently maintains an effective point of view. • Sentence beginnings, lengths, and structures vary throughout. • Grammar, usage, and mechanics are correct, where appropriate.
3	• The narrative conveys a real experience and its significance. • Some well-chosen details are included. • More dialogue or description could be used. • The conclusion could be strengthened.	• The narrative has a sequence that leads to a conclusion, with some gaps in logic. • The narrative includes some extraneous events or omits some necessary events, resulting in ineffective pacing. • More transitions would make the sequence of events clearer. • Verbal and nonverbal elements sometimes hold the audience's attention.	• The narrative includes descriptive details and sensory language. • The writer mostly maintains an effective point of view. • Sentence beginnings, lengths, and structures vary somewhat. • Some errors in grammar, usage, or mechanics create distractions.
2	• The narrative conveys a real experience but needs more development and a clearer focus on its significance. • Details are lacking or irrelevant. • Dialogue and description are limited or lacking. • The conclusion is ineffective.	• The narrative has a confusing sequence caused by the inclusion of extraneous events or the omission of necessary events. • The narrative includes few transitions. • Missing events or information creates ambiguity. • Verbal and nonverbal elements are sparse or misplaced.	• The narrative needs more descriptive details or sensory language. • The point of view is inconsistent. • Sentence structures rarely vary, and some fragments or run-on sentences are present. • Multiple errors in grammar, usage, or mechanics create distractions.
1	• The narrative has no identifiable experience or focus on significance. • Details are vague or omitted. • Dialogue and description are not included. • A conclusion is not included.	• The narrative has no apparent sequence of events. • The narrative does not use transitions. • Verbal and nonverbal elements are not used or their inappropriate use detracts from the narrative.	• The narrative lacks descriptive details or sensory language. • The point of view is not established. • Repetitive sentence structure, fragments, and run-ons make the response hard to follow. • Significant errors in grammar, usage, or mechanics create confusion and misunderstanding.

COLLECTION 6
PERFORMANCE TASK B

Interactive Lessons
To help you complete this task, use:
- *Writing Arguments*
- *Writing as a Process*
- *Using Textual Evidence.*

Write an Argument

Write an argument that justifies your views about whether teenagers should gain work experience during their school years. Use evidence from the texts in the collection to support your position.

A successful argument
- contains an engaging introduction that establishes the claim
- supports the claim with credible reasons and evidence
- establishes and maintains a formal style
- includes a conclusion that follows from the argument

Mentor Text See how this example from "Teens at Work" uses evidence to support a claim and to argue against opposing views.

> "Entire families can suffer when wages are not available for older kids. Many teenagers, fortunate enough to have work, contribute portions of paychecks to households' overall budgets."

PLAN

Choose Your Position Revisit the points made in the texts in the collection. Do teenagers need work experience during their school years? Why or why not? Take a position you can argue.

Gather Information List reasons to explain your argument and consider how to distinguish your argument from alternate or opposing views. What counterclaims will you use to convince people? Use the annotation tools in your eBook to find evidence in the texts supporting your position. Save each piece of evidence to *my*Notebook, in a folder titled *Collection 6 Performance Task*.

ACADEMIC VOCABULARY

As you plan and write your argument, be sure to use the academic vocabulary words.

commentary
minors
occupation
option
style

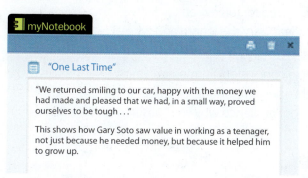

Organize Your Ideas A graphic organizer, such as a hierarchy chart, can help you plan and present your ideas logically. Place your claim in the top box, your reasons in the next row of boxes, and your evidence in the bottom row.

Interactive Lessons
To help you plan your argument, complete the following lessons in Writing Arguments:
• Reasons and Evidence
• Building Effective Support

Consider Your Purpose and Audience Think about your audience as you write. The development, organization, and style of your argument may be different for a group of classmates or friends than it would be for a group of adults.

> PRODUCE

Write Your Argument Use your notes and your graphic organizer as you begin your draft.

- Introduce your claim. Grab your readers' attention with a surprising or unexpected statistic, fact, or quotation.
- Sequence your reasons and evidence logically. Decide whether to begin or end with your strongest reason.
- Include relevant descriptions, facts, and details that emphasize your main points.
- Acknowledge opposing or alternate claims that others may have. Distinguish your claims from them, and include credible responses.
- Maintain a formal style, and use transition words and phrases such as *because, therefore,* and *for this reason* to clarify relationships between ideas. Vary the length and type of sentences as you write.
- Bring your argument to a conclusion. Summarize your viewpoint, repeating the most important reasons and evidence, and remind your audience why your position is the right one.

Write your rough draft in *my*WriteSmart. Focus on getting your ideas down, rather than on perfecting your choice of language.

Interactive Lessons
To help you draft your argument, complete the following lessons in Writing Arguments:
• Formal Style
• Concluding Your Argument

REVISE

Review Your Draft Have your partner or group of peers review your draft. Use the following chart to revise your draft.

Questions	Tips	Revision Techniques
Does the introduction contain a clear claim?	**Underline** the sentence that states the issue and the claim.	**Add** a claim, or **revise** the existing claim for clarity.
Is the claim supported by solid reasons and evidence?	**Highlight** each reason, and **underline** the evidence that supports it.	**Add** reasons, or insert evidence if needed. **Elaborate** to clarify evidence.
Are alternate or opposing claims addressed?	**Underline** opposing claims. **Highlight** sentences that address them.	**Add** persuasive responses to answer possible opposing claims.
Does the argument maintain a formal style?	**Highlight** contractions, casual slang, or informal language.	**Reword** contractions and **replace** informal language with precise, formal vocabulary.
Does the conclusion restate the claim?	**Underline** the restatement of the claim.	**Add** a sentence that restates the claim.

Have a partner or a group of peers review your draft in *my*WriteSmart. Ask your reviewers to note any reasons that do not support the claim well or that lack sufficient evidence.

Interactive Lessons
For help in revising your argument, use
- Writing as a Process: Revising and Editing

Language Conventions: Connect Ideas Look for opportunities to combine clauses to connect ideas. Read this passage from Gary Soto's "One Last Time."

> " By lunchtime I had a trail of thirty-seven trays behind me while Mother had sixty or more. "

Note how Soto uses words such as *by* and *while* to combine the ideas of what time it was, how many trays of grapes he had collected, and how many trays his mother had collected.

PRESENT

Create a Finished Copy Finalize your argument and choose a way to share it with your audience. Consider these options:

- Present your argument as an oral report.
- Post your argument as a blog on a classroom website.
- Hold a debate with someone with an opposing position.

PERFORMANCE TASK B RUBRIC
ARGUMENT

	Ideas and Evidence	Organization	Language
4	• The introduction immediately grabs the audience's attention; the claim clearly states a position on a topic. • Logical reasons and relevant evidence convincingly support the writer's claim. • Opposing or alternate claims are acknowledged and effectively addressed. • The concluding section effectively summarizes the claim.	• The reasons and evidence are organized logically and consistently throughout the argument. • Transitions effectively connect reasons and evidence to the writer's claim.	• The writer maintains a formal style. • Sentence beginnings, lengths, and structures vary and have a rhythmic flow. • Clauses are effectively combined to connect ideas. • Capitalization, punctuation, and other mechanics are correct. • Grammar and usage are correct.
3	• The introduction could do more to grab the audience's attention; the claim states a position. • Most reasons and evidence support the writer's claim, but they could be more convincing. • Opposing or alternate claims are acknowledged, but the responses need to be better developed. • The concluding section restates the claim.	• The organization of reasons and evidence is confusing in a few places. • A few more transitions are needed to connect reasons and evidence to the writer's claim.	• The style becomes informal in a few places. • Sentence beginnings, lengths, and structures vary somewhat. • Some clauses are combined to connect ideas. • Several capitalization and punctuation mistakes occur. • Some grammatical and usage errors are repeated in the argument.
2	• The introduction is ordinary; the claim identifies an issue, but the writer's position is not clearly stated. • The reasons and evidence are not always logical or relevant. • Opposing or alternate claims are acknowledged but not addressed logically. • The concluding section includes an incomplete summary of the claim.	• The organization of reasons and evidence is logical in some places, but it often doesn't follow a pattern. • Many more transitions are needed to connect reasons and evidence to the writer's claim.	• The style becomes informal in many places. • Sentence structures barely vary, and some fragments or run-on sentences are present. • Few ideas are clearly connected. • Several spelling and capitalization mistakes occur, and punctuation is inconsistent. • Grammar and usage are incorrect in many places.
1	• The introduction is missing. • Supporting reasons and evidence are missing. • Opposing or alternate claims are neither acknowledged nor addressed. • The concluding section is missing.	• A logical organization is not used; reasons and evidence are presented randomly. • Transitions are not used, making the argument difficult to understand.	• The style is inappropriate for the argument. • Repetitive sentence structure, fragments, and run-on sentences make the speech hard to follow. • Ideas are not connected. • Spelling and capitalization are often incorrect, and punctuation is missing. • Many grammatical and usage errors obscure the meaning of ideas.

Performance Task Reference Guide R2
- Writing an Argument R2
- Writing an Informative Essay R4
- Writing a Narrative R6
- Conducting Research R8
- MLA Citation Guidelines R10
- Participating in a Collaborative Discussion R12
- Debating an Issue R14

Reading Informational Texts: Patterns of Organization R16
1. Main Idea and Supporting Details R16
2. Chronological Order R17
3. Cause-Effect Organization R18
4. Compare-and-Contrast Organization R19
5. Problem-Solution Organization R21

Reading Arguments R22
1. Analyzing an Argument R22
2. Recognizing Proposition and Support Patterns R23
3. Recognizing Persuasive Techniques R23
4. Analyzing Logic and Reasoning R24
5. Evaluating Persuasive Texts R27

Grammar R29
Quick Reference
- Parts of Speech R29
- The Sentence and Its Parts R31
- Punctuation R32
- Capitalization R35

Grammar Handbook:
1. Nouns R36
2. Pronouns R36
3. Verbs R39
4. Modifiers R41
5. The Sentence and Its Parts R43
6. Phrases R44
7. Verbals and Verbal Phrases R45
8. Clauses R46
9. The Structure of Sentences R47
10. Writing Complete Sentences R48
11. Subject-Verb Agreement R49

Vocabulary and Spelling R53
1. Using Context Clues R53
2. Analyzing Word Structure R54
3. Understanding Word Origins R55
4. Synonyms and Antonyms R57
5. Denotation and Connotation R57
6. Analogies R57
7. Homonyms, Homographs, and Homophones R57
8. Words with Multiple Meanings R58
9. Specialized Vocabulary R58
10. Using Reference Sources R58
11. Spelling Rules R59
12. Commonly Confused Words R62

Glossary of Literary and Informational Terms R64

Using the Glossary R79

Pronunciation Key R79

Glossary of Academic Vocabulary R80

Glossary of Critical Vocabulary R81

Index of Skills R85

Index of Titles and Authors R95

Acknowledgments R96

Writing an Argument

Many of the Performance Tasks in this book ask you to craft an argument in which you support your ideas with text evidence. Any argument you write should include the following sections and characteristics.

Introduction

Clearly state your **claim**—the point your argument makes. As needed, provide context or background information to help readers understand your position. Note the most common opposing views as a way to distinguish and clarify your ideas. From the very beginning, make it clear for readers why your claim is strong; consider providing an overview of your reasons or a quotation that emphasizes your view in your introduction.

EXAMPLES

vague claim: We need fewer teenagers on the road.	**precise claim:** The state should raise the driving age to 18.
not distinguished from opposing view: There are plenty of people who don't want teenagers driving.	**distinguished from opposing view:** While some people think 16-year-olds are old enough to drive, the facts say otherwise.
confusing relationship of ideas: Teens want to drive. Many people drive cars.	**clear relationship of ideas:** By requiring teenagers to spend more time practicing their driving skills with their parents in the car, teenagers will be better prepared to get their licenses.

Development of Claims

The body of your argument must provide strong, logical reasons for your claim and must support those reasons with relevant evidence. A **reason** tells why your claim is valid; **evidence** provides specific examples that illustrate a reason. In the process of developing your claim you should also refute **counterclaims**, or opposing views, with equally strong reasons and evidence. To demonstrate that you have thoroughly considered your view, provide a well-rounded look at both the strengths and limitations of your claim and opposing claims. The goal is not to undercut your argument, but rather to answer your readers' potential objections to it. Be sure, too, to consider how much your audience may already know about your topic in order to avoid boring or confusing readers.

EXAMPLES

claim lacking reasons: Teenagers are bad drivers because they are young and irresponsible.	**claim developed by reasons:** Among the reasons to raise the driving age to 18 is that more driving errors occur when teenagers lack practice behind the wheel.
omission of limitations: People opposed to this idea deny that there is any downside to this plan.	**fair discussion of limitations:** Raising the driving age to 18 might cause some opponents to request that we require less permitting time and eliminate driver's education.
inattention to audience's knowledge: Teenage driving errors can damage a car, creating imbalances in the car's engine that are emphasized at high rpm, which might result in throwing a connecting rod through the sump.	**awareness of audience's knowledge:** Those unfamiliar with the movement to raise the driving age from 16 to 18 might not be aware that even rural communities favor raising the driving age to prevent fatal car crashes involving teenagers.

Links Among Ideas

Even the strongest reasons and evidence will fail to sway readers if it is unclear how the reasons relate to the central claim of an argument. Make the connections clear for your readers, using not only transitional words and phrases, but also using clauses and even entire sentences as a bridge between ideas you have already discussed and ideas you are introducing.

EXAMPLES

> **transitional word linking claim and reason:** The entire state will benefit from raising the driving age from 16 to 18 because teenagers will have more time to practice their driving.

> **transitional phrase linking reason and evidence:** A higher driving age will reduce accidents on the road. In fact, safety experts say that, "One in five 16-year-olds will have a reportable car crash within the first year."

> **transitional clause linking claim and counterclaim:** The safety benefits of raising the driving age are clear. Those opposed to such a measure might say that the inconvenience of driving 16-year-olds to after-school activities needs to be considered.

Appropriate Style and Tone

An effective argument is most often written in a direct and formal style. The style and tone you choose in an argument should not be an afterthought—the way you express your argument can either drive home your ideas or detract from them. Even as you argue in favor of your viewpoint, take care to remain objective in tone—avoid using loaded language when discussing opposing claims.

EXAMPLES

> **informal style:** The new law would help all state residents so everyone should be in favor of the measure.

> **formal style:** Because the law would help lower teenage driving accidents, making our roads safer, it is logical that state legislators would want to raise the driving age from 16 to 18.

> **biased tone:** It doesn't make any sense to not raise the driving age.

> **objective tone:** Arguments against this law have been refuted by statistics that show an increase in car accidents, many of which are fatal, among 16-year-olds.

> **inattention to conventions:** We need to get this law passed!

> **attention to conventions:** This law, which will greatly improve driving safety conditions in our state, needs to be considered by state lawmakers.

Conclusion

Your conclusion may range from a sentence to a full paragraph, but it must wrap up your argument in a satisfying way; a conclusion that sounds tacked-on helps your argument no more than providing no conclusion at all. A strong conclusion is a logical extension of the argument you have presented. It carries forth your ideas through an inference, question, quotation, or challenge.

EXAMPLES

> **inference:** Support for safer roadways begins with our youth.

> **question:** Who doesn't want to drive on roads that are safer?

> **quotation:** As Jay Giedd, chief of brain imaging in the child psychiatric unit at the National Institute of Mental Health, explains regarding a study he led on brain research, "A crucial part of the teen's brain, the area that peers ahead and considers consequences, remains undeveloped. That means careless attitudes and rash emotions often drive teen decisions."

> **challenge:** Laws of this type can be the difference between life and death.

Writing an Informative Essay

Most of the Performance Tasks in this book ask you to write informational or explanatory texts in which you present a topic and examine it thoughtfully, through a well-organized analysis of relevant content. Any informative or explanatory text that you create should include the following parts and features.

Introduction

Develop a strong **thesis statement**. That is, clearly state your **topic** and the **organizational framework** through which you will **connect** or **distinguish** elements of your topic. For example, you might state that your text will compare ideas, examine causes and effects, or explore a problem and its solutions.

EXAMPLE

Topic: Summer Jobs
Sample Thesis Statements
Compare-contrast: When deciding whether to take a summer job or not, consider the financial and career rewards or losses of working for a company or staying at home.
Cause-effect: While the causes of unemployment among teens, especially in a recession, aren't difficult to figure out, the consequences of not working might not be apparent right away.
Problem-solution: While our town faces a growing problem with joblessness among teenagers, we can get our youth back to work if businesses will step up and make a commitment to offer more apprenticeship programs.

Clarifying the organizational framework up front will help you organize the body of your text, suggest **headings** you can use to guide your readers, and help you identify **graphics** that you may need to clarify information. For example, if you compare and contrast the pros and cons of providing jobs for teens, you might create a chart like the one here to guide your writing. You could include the same chart in your paper as a graphic for readers. The row or column headings serve as natural paragraph headings.

	Working	Staying at Home
Finances	Earning income to save for college or a special purchase; ability to help their family pay bills, especially if mother or father is out of work	Missing out on income that could be used toward their college education or for discretionary purchases
Rewards	Learning a trade or skill that can be used in a future job; increased self-confidence	Opportunity to take summer school classes or to volunteer for an important cause

Development of the Topic

In the body of your text, flesh out the organizational framework you established in your introduction with strong supporting paragraphs. Include only support directly relevant to your topic. Don't rely on a single source, and make sure the sources you do use are reputable and current. The following table illustrates types of support you might use to develop aspects of your topic. It also shows how transitions link text sections, create cohesion, and clarify the relationships among ideas.

Performance Task Reference Guide

Types of Support in Explanatory/ Informative Texts	Uses of Transitions in Explanatory/ Informative Texts
Facts and examples: One cause of unemployment among teens is a recession; *for example,* older workers might be willing to take part-time jobs that otherwise would have gone to teenagers.	*One cause* signals the shift from the introduction to the body text in a cause-and-effect essay. *For example* introduces the support for the cause being cited.
Concrete details: *On the other hand,* teens might have a better chance at getting a job than an older person might, since the teen might work for less money because career experience is as important to them as income is.	*On the other hand* transitions the reader from one point of comparison to another in a compare-contrast essay.
Statistics: Turn to the U.S. Bureau of Labor Statistics if you doubt the scope of America's unemployment problem. According to the bureau, in 2011, the unemployment rate for job aspirants 16 to 19 years old was 24.4 percent.	The entire transitional sentence introduces the part of a problem-solution essay that demonstrates the existence of a problem.

You can't always include all of the information you'd like to in a short essay, but you can plan to point readers directly to useful **multimedia links** either in the body of or at the end of your essay.

Style and Tone

Use formal English to establish your credibility as a source of information. To project authority, use the language of the domain, or field, that you are writing about. However, be sure to define unfamiliar terms to avoid using jargon your audience may not know. Provide extended definitions when your audience is likely to have limited knowledge of the topic.

Using quotations from reputable sources can also give your text authority; be sure to credit the source of quoted material. In general, keep the tone objective, avoiding slangy or biased expressions.

> **Informal, jargon-filled, biased language:** Teenagers who do not try and find summer work are lazy and selfish, unwilling to take a job to help their families out in these hard economic times. These teens also have no regard for their future and don't take having a career seriously.

> **Extended definition in formal style and objective tone:** Teenagers' employment statistics have worsened because more businesses, such as grocery stores, are using automated machines for low-level tasks, replacing the need to hire workers. An automated machine, as defined by the dictionary, "is the use of control systems and information technologies reducing the need for human intervention."

Conclusion

Wrap up your essay with a concluding statement or section that sums up or extends the information in your essay.

EXAMPLES

> **Articulate implications:** Part-time jobs are where most teenagers will learn valuable workplace skills. Teens who don't have early job experience might miss out on crucial career and personal development and may never reach their full potential.

> **Emphasize significance:** Without a talented young work force, our nation's future is in jeopardy. Businesses throughout the U.S. are already reporting deficiencies in quantities of candidates who can fill positions that require advanced capabilities.

Writing a Narrative

When you are writing a fictional tale, an autobiographical incident, or a firsthand biography, you write in the narrative mode. That means telling a story with a beginning, a climax, and a conclusion. Though there are important differences between fictional and nonfiction narratives, you use similar processes to develop them.

Identify a Problem, Situation, or Observation

For a nonfiction narrative, dig into your memory bank for a problem you dealt with or an observation you've made about your life. For fiction, try to invent a problem or situation that can unfold in interesting ways.

EXAMPLES

Problem (nonfiction)	Last summer, I wanted to work enough so I could save money to go to France this year and learn French.
Situation (fiction)	Mary's mom confiscated the girl's cell phone after she learned Mary had gotten a ticket for texting while driving.

Establish a Point of View

Decide who will tell your story. If you are writing a reflective essay about an important experience or person in your own life, you will be the narrator of the events you relate. If you are writing a work of fiction, you can choose to create a first-person narrator or tell the story from the third-person point of view. In that case, the narrator can focus on one character or reveal the thoughts and feelings of all the characters. The examples below show the differences between a first- and third-person narrator.

First-person narrator (nonfiction)	Several thousand dollars is what I needed to go to France for two months. But I couldn't earn that much working at a summer camp, and no other jobs were available.
Third-person narrator (fiction)	Mary didn't want to wait to reply to her boyfriend's text about going out to dinner that night, so she quickly replied while driving to the store. Just before she hit the send button, she noticed flashing lights behind her. She looked in the rearview mirror and saw that a cop was pulling her over.

Gather Details

To make real or imaginary experiences come alive on the page, you will need to use narrative techniques like description and dialogue. The questions in the left column in the chart below can help you search your memory or imagination for the details that will form the basis of your narrative. You don't have to respond in full sentences, but try to capture the sights, sounds, and feelings that bring your narrative to life.

Who, What, When, Where?	Narrative Techniques
People: Who are the people or characters involved in the experience? What did they look like? What did they do? What did they say?	**Description:** The cop, who was not smiling, had an ominous look on his face as he approached my car. "Do you know why I am pulling you over?" he asked sternly. "No, officer, was I speeding?" I replied. "You were texting while driving, which is against the law, and because you were not paying attention while you were typing, you almost hit the car next to you," he explained. "Please get our your driver's license, car registration, and insurance."

continued

Who, What, When, Where?	Narrative Techniques
Experience: What led up to or caused the event? What is the main event in the experience? What happened as a result of the event?	**Description:** I loved being a camp counselor, but I knew earning $8 an hour would not be enough to save the money I needed to go to France. I created my own business mowing lawns. Several people in my neighborhood needed help with their yard work and were willing to pay me $15 an hour!
Places: When and where did the events take place? What were the sights, sounds, and smells of this place?	**Description:** I remember how intense the humidity was while I was mowing Mrs. Anderson's lawn. The air felt thick, as if I were trying to breathe through a straw stuck in the mud. The sun's heat was so severe that my skin felt hot to the touch.

Sequence Events

Before you begin writing, list the key events of the experience or story in chronological, or time, order. Place a star next to the point of highest tension—for example, the point at which a key decision determines the outcome of events. In fiction, this point is called the climax, but a gripping nonfiction narrative will also have a climactic event.

To build suspense—the uncertainty a reader feels about what will happen next—you'll want to think about the pacing or rhythm of your narrative. Consider disrupting the chronological order of events by beginning at the end, then starting over. Or interrupt the forward flow of events with a flashback, which takes the reader to an earlier point in the narrative.

Another way to build suspense is with multiple plot lines. For example, the personal narrative about the trip to France involves a second plot line in which the narrator realizes she needs a second job to afford to go overseas. Both plot lines intersect when the narrator starts her own business in order to raise money to travel.

Use Vivid Language

As you revise, make an effort to use vivid language. Use precise words and phrases to describe feelings and action. Use telling details to show, rather than directly state, what a character is like. Use sensory language that lets readers see, feel, hear, smell, and taste what you or your characters experienced.

First Draft	Revision
My dad, who supported my trip to France, encouraged me to start my own business.	My dad raised my chin with his right hand so I could look him in the eye as he said, "Terri, I am proud of you for having the initiative to start your own business." [telling details]
The temperature was soaring past 100 degrees for the fifth day in a row.	The relentless sun scorched my skin, turning it into blisters of pain. The only relief I felt was when I soothed my skin with cool aloe vera lotion. [precise words and phrases]
Mary was furious with her mother for taking her cell phone.	Mary slammed her door, rattling the photos hanging on the walls. She turned the lock and collapsed onto her bed. [sensory details]

Conclusion

At the conclusion of the narrative, you or your narrator will reflect on the meaning of the events. The conclusion should follow logically from the climactic moment of the narrative. The narrator of a personal narrative usually reflects on the significance of the experience—the lessons learned or the legacy left.

EXAMPLE

> As I stepped off the bus in Paris, all I could hear was the melody of French being spoken on the street. I looked left and saw a lovely outdoor cafe where people were reading and leisurely enjoying cafe au lait. In the distance was the majestic Eiffel Tower looking down on me as if to say, "You did it. You earned your way to France."

Conducting Research

The Performance Tasks in this book will require you to complete research projects related to the texts you've read in the collections. Whether the topic is stated in a Performance Task or is one you generate, the following information will guide you through your research project.

Focus Your Research and Formulate a Question

Some topics for a research project can be effectively covered in three pages; others require an entire book for a thorough treatment. Begin by developing a topic that is neither too narrow nor too broad for the time frame of the assignment. Also check your school and local libraries and databases to help you determine how to choose your topic. If there's too little information, you'll need to broaden your focus; if there's too much, you'll need to limit it.

With a topic in hand, formulate a research question; it will keep you on track as you conduct your research. A good research question cannot be answered in a single word. It should be open-ended. It should require investigation. You can also develop related research questions to explore your topic in more depth.

EXAMPLES

Possible topics for *The Diary of a Young Girl*	The Holocaust—too broad Holocaust victim Anne Frank—too narrow Anne's experience in the camps
Possible research question	To what degree are the settings and events in *The Diary of a Young Girl* based on fact?
Related questions	To what extent do historians agree or disagree on which aspects of *The Diary of a Young Girl* are real?

Locate and Evaluate Sources

To find answers to your research question, you'll need to investigate primary and secondary sources, whether in print or digital formats. **Primary sources** contain original, firsthand information, such as diaries, autobiographies, interviews, speeches, and eyewitness accounts. **Secondary sources** provide other people's versions of primary sources in encyclopedias, newspaper and magazine articles, biographies, and documentaries.

Your search for sources begins at the library and on the World Wide Web. Use **advanced search features** to help you find things quickly. Add a minus sign (–) before a word that should not appear in your results. Use an asterisk (*) in place of unknown words. List the name of and location of each possible source, adding comments about its potential usefulness. Assessing, or evaluating, your sources is an important step in the research process. Your goal is to use sources that are credible, or reliable and trustworthy.

Criteria for Assessing Sources	
Relevance: It covers the target aspect of my topic.	• How will the source be useful in answering my research question?
Accuracy: It includes information that can be verified by more than one authoritative source.	• Is the information up-to-date? Are the facts accurate? How can I verify them? • What qualifies the author to write about this topic? Is he or she an authority?
Objectivity: It presents multiple viewpoints on the topic.	• What, if any, biases can I detect? Does the writer favor one view of the topic?

Incorporating and Citing Source Material

When you draft your research project, you'll need to include material from your sources. This material can be **direct quotations, summaries,** or **paraphrases** of the original source material. Two well-known **style manuals** provide information on how to cite a range of print and digital sources: the *MLA Handbook for Writers of Research Papers* (published by the Modern Language Association) and Kate L. Turabian's *A Manual for Writers* (published by The University of Chicago Press). Both style manuals provide a wealth of information about conducting, formatting, drafting, and presenting your research, including guidelines for citing sources within the text (called parenthetical citations) and preparing the list of Works Cited, as well as correct use of the mechanics of writing. Your teacher will indicate which style manual you should use. The following examples use the format in the *MLA Handbook*.

Any material from sources must be completely documented, or you will be committing **plagiarism,** the unauthorized use of someone else's words or ideas. Plagiarism is not honest. As you take notes for your research project, be sure to keep complete information about your sources so that you can cite them correctly in the body of your paper. This applies to all sources, whether print or digital. Having complete information will also enable you to prepare the list of Works Cited. The list of Works Cited, which concludes your research project, provides author, title, and publication information for both print and digital sources. The following pages show the *MLA Handbook's* Works Cited citation formats for a variety of sources.

EXAMPLES

Direct quotation [The writer is citing comments made by eyewitnesses who had seen Anne Frank after she was apprehended by German police and transported to Auschwitz.]	In one interview with a friend of Anne Frank's, the friend states that, "... more often Anne displayed strength and courage. Her gregarious and confident nature allowed her to obtain extra bread rations for her mother, sister, and herself."
Summary [The writer is summarizing various accounts from prisoners that Anne Frank died of typhus while imprisoned at Bergen-Belsen.]	In the spring of 1945, nearly 20,000 prisoners, including Anne Frank, died after a typhus epidemic spread through the Bergen-Belsen concentration camp. A few weeks later, the camp was liberated by British troops.
Paraphrase [The writer is paraphrasing accounts from prisoners about Anne Frank's imprisonment, as well as interviews in the 1988 television documentary, *The Last Seven Months of Anne Frank*.]	Bloeme Evers-Emden, an Amsterdam native and schoolmate of Anne's, said she saw Anne while they were imprisoned in Auschwitz and confirmed that Anne had escaped being gassed because Anne had just turned 15. A majority of those gassed upon arriving at Auschwitz were younger than 15.

MLA Citation Guidelines

Today, you can find free websites that generate ready-made citations for research papers, using the information you provide. Such sites have some time-saving advantages when you're developing a Works Cited list. However, you should always check your citations carefully before you turn in your final paper. If you are following MLA style, use these guidelines to evaluate and finalize your work.

Books

One author

Lastname, Firstname. *Title of Book*. City of Publication: Publisher, Year of Publication. Medium of Publication.

Two authors or editors

Lastname, Firstname, and Firstname Lastname. *Title of Book*. City of Publication: Publisher, Year of Publication. Medium of Publication.

Three authors

Lastname, Firstname, Firstname Lastname, and Firstname Lastname. *Title of Book*. City of Publication: Publisher, Year of Publication. Medium of Publication.

Four or more authors

The abbreviation et al. means "and others." Use et al. instead of listing all the authors.

Lastname, Firstname, et al. *Title of Book*. City of Publication: Publisher, Year of Publication. Medium of Publication.

No author given

Title of Book. City of Publication: Publisher, Year of Publication. Medium of Publication.

An author and a translator

Lastname, Firstname. *Title of Book*. Trans. Firstname Lastname. City of Publication: Publisher, Year of Publication. Medium of Publication.

An author, a translator, and an editor

Lastname, Firstname. *Title of Book*. Trans. Firstname Lastname. Ed. Firstname Lastname. City of Publication: Publisher, Year of Publication. Medium of Publication.

Parts of Books

An introduction, a preface, a foreword, or an afterword written by someone other than the author(s) of a work

Lastname, Firstname. Part of Book. *Title of Book*. By Author of book's Firstname Lastname. City of Publication: Publisher, Year of Publication. Page span. Medium of Publication.

A poem, a short story, an essay, or a chapter in a collection of works by one author

Lastname, Firstname. "Title of Piece." *Title of Book*. Ed. Firstname Lastname. City of Publication: Publisher, Year of Publication. Page span. Medium of Publication.

A poem, a short story, an essay, or a chapter in an anthology of works by several authors

Lastname, Firstname. "Title of Piece." *Title of Book*. Ed. Firstname Lastname. City of Publication: Publisher, Year of Publication. Page range. Medium of Publication.

Magazines, Newspapers, and Encyclopedias

An article in a newspaper

Lastname, Firstname. "Title of Article." *Title of Book Periodical* Day Month Year: pages. Medium of Publication.

An article in a magazine

Lastname, Firstname. "Title of Article." *Title of Book Periodical* Day Month Year: pages. Medium of Publication.

An article in an encyclopedia

"Title of Article." *Title of Encyclopedia*. Year ed. Medium of Publication.

Miscellaneous Nonprint Sources

An interview

Lastname, Firstname. Personal interview. Day Month Year.

A video recording

Title of Recording. Producer, Year. Medium of Publication

Electronic Publications

A CD-ROM

"Title of Piece." *Title of CD*. Year ed. City of Publication: Publisher, Year of Publication. CD-ROM.

A document from an Internet site

Entries for online source should contain as much information as available.

Lastname, Firstname. "*Title of Piece*." Information on what the site is. Year. Web. Day Month Year (when accessed).

Participating in a Collaborative Discussion

Often, class activities, including the Performance Tasks in this book, will require you to work collaboratively with classmates. Whether your group will analyze a work of literature or try to solve a community problem, use the following guidelines to ensure a productive discussion.

Prepare for the Discussion

A productive discussion is one in which all the participants bring useful information and ideas to share. If your group will discuss a short story the class read, first re-read and annotate a copy of the story. Your annotations will help you quickly locate evidence to support your points. Participants in a discussion about an important issue should first research the issue and bring notes or information sources that will help guide the group. If you disagree with a point made by another group member, your case will be stronger if you back it up with specific evidence from your sources.

EXAMPLES

> **disagreeing without evidence:** I don't think horror stories like "The Tell-Tale Heart" are relevant today because people prefer to go and see a scary movie rather than take the time to read a horror story.
>
> **providing evidence for disagreement:** I disagree with Edgar Allan Poe's relevance today because I don't think students are inspired by horror tales in print. Students would rather watch a scary movie and enjoy the thrill of seeing and hearing the characters scream and run from whatever is chasing them. I think scary movies captivate people more than books from the 1800s do. I think books from that long ago are outdated when it comes to knowing what excites students and gets them scared. I mean how thrilling can an Edgar Allan Poe story be compared to seeing people running for their lives from decomposing zombies?

Set Ground Rules

The rules your group needs will depend on what your group is expected to accomplish. A discussion of themes in a poem will be unlikely to produce a single consensus; however, a discussion aimed at developing a solution to a problem should result in one strong proposal that all group members support. Answer the following questions to set ground rules that fit your group's purpose:

- What will this group produce? A range of ideas, a single decision, a plan of action, or something else?
- How much time is available? How much of that time should be allotted to each part of our discussion (presenting ideas, summarizing or voting on final ideas, creating a product such as a written analysis or speech)?
- What roles need to be assigned within the group? Do we need a leader, a note-taker, a timekeeper, or other specific roles?
- What is the best way to synthesize our group's ideas? Should we take a vote, list group members as "for" or "against" in a chart, or use some other method to reach consensus or sum up the results of the discussion?

Move the Discussion Forward

Everyone in the group should be actively involved in synthesizing ideas. To make sure this happens, ask questions that draw out ideas, especially from less-talkative members of the group. If an idea or statement is confusing, try to paraphrase it, or ask the speaker to explain more about it. If you disagree with a statement, say so politely and explain in detail why you disagree.

Performance Task Reference Guide

SAMPLE DISCUSSION

MIKE: Cindy, what do you think about horror tales? Are they scarier in a book or a movie?	*Question draws out quiet member*
CINDY: I had a hard time reading Poe's "The Tell-Tale Heart." My attention span may be short, but I am most engrossed in a plot when I am in a movie theater. I love clenching my friend's hand and screaming together.	*Response relates discussion to larger ideas*
PETER: I think horror stories like "The Tell-Tale Heart" can be suspenseful. I don't need to be in a theater to visualize what is going to happen. Poe's writing brings the plot's tension to life for me.	*Question challenges Cindy's conclusion*
CINDY: Yes, there are elements of Poe's story that are suspenseful but I don't get the same reaction as I do when I am at the movies, too afraid to look. That is a sensory experience I don't think a book can replicate.	*Response elaborates on ideas*
MOLLY: I can see the pros of going to a theater and feeding off of the audience's energy, but I do think "The Tell-Tale Heart" is still relevant today. It allows you to create the tale in your head and form conclusions about what is going to happen.	*Paraphrases idea and challenges it further based on evidence*

Respond to Ideas

In a diverse group, everyone may have a different perspective on the topic of discussion, and that's a good thing. Consider what everyone has to say, and don't resist changing your view if other group members provide convincing evidence for theirs. If, instead, you feel more strongly than ever about your view, don't hesitate to say so and provide reasons related to what those with opposing views have said. Before wrapping up the discussion, try to sum up the points on which your group agrees and disagrees.

SAMPLE DISCUSSION

MOLLY: OK, we have just a few more minutes. Can we try to reach an agreement?	*Molly and Mike try to summarize points of agreement*
MIKE: I think there are two positions—1) those who think scary stories are best seen in a theater and 2) those who think written stories allow you to use your imagination more.	
PETER: Yes, I think "The Tell-Tale Heart" is relevant today. I like how the story is organized and I find it interesting that we don't know who the narrator is.	*Peter maintains his position*
CINDY: I can understand what Peter is saying. I think if I gave the book more of a chance, I could let my imagination help to create the suspense.	*Cindy and Mike qualify their views based on what they have heard*
MIKE: That makes sense. Sometimes we need to use our minds more and not be so dependent on a movie. Poe's words and themes are scary, and we just need to use our imagination.	
MOLLY: I'm with Peter. I like Poe's prose. His words build suspense and they take you back in time to a different era.	*Molly supports her position by making a new connection*

Debating an Issue

The selection and collection Performance Tasks in this text will direct you to engage in debates about issues relating to the selections you are reading. Use the guidelines that follow to have a productive and balanced argument about both sides of an issue.

The Structure of a Formal Debate

In a debate, two teams compete to win the support of the audience about an issue. In a **formal debate**, two teams, each with two members, present their arguments on a given proposition or policy statement. One team argues for the proposition or statement and the other team argues against it. Each debater must consider the proposition closely and must research both sides of it. To argue convincingly either for or against a proposition, a debater must be familiar with both sides of the issue.

Plan the Debate

The purpose of a debate is to allow participants and audience members to consider both sides of an issue. Use these planning suggestions to hold a balanced and productive debate:

- **Identify Debate Teams** Form groups of six members based on the issues that the Performance Tasks include. Three members of the team will argue for the affirmative side of the issue—that is, they support the issue. The other three members will argue for the negative side of the issue—that is, they do not support the issue.
- **Appoint a Moderator** The moderator will present the topic and goals of the debate, keep track of the time, and introduce and thank the participants.
- **Research and Prepare Notes** Search texts you've read as well as print and online sources for valid reasons and evidence to support your team's claim. As with argument, be sure to anticipate possible opposing claims and compile evidence to counter those claims. You will use notes from your research during the debate.
- **Assign Debate Roles** One team member will introduce the team's claim and supporting evidence. Another team member will respond to questions and opposing claims in an exchange with a member of the opposing team. The last member will present a strong closing argument.

Hold the Debate

A formal debate is not a shouting match—rather, a well-run debate is an excellent forum for participants to express their viewpoints, build on others' ideas, and have a thoughtful, well-reasoned exchange of ideas. The moderator will begin by stating the topic or issue and introducing the participants. Participants should follow the moderator's instructions concerning whose turn it is to speak and how much time each speaker has.

- How effectively did the team rebut, or respond to, arguments made by the opposing team?
- Did the speakers maintain eye contact and speak at an appropriate rate and volume?
- Did the speakers observe proper debate etiquette—that is, did they follow the moderator's instructions, stay within their allotted time limits, and treat their opponents respectfully?

Formal Debate Format

Speaker	Role	Time
Affirmative Speaker 1	Present the claim and supporting evidence for the affirmative ("pro") side of the argument.	5 minutes
Negative Speaker 1	Ask probing questions that will prompt the other team to address flaws in the argument.	3 minutes
Affirmative Speaker 2	Respond to the questions posed by the opposing team and counter any concerns.	3 minutes

Speaker	Role	Time
Negative Speaker 2	Present the claim and supporting evidence for the negative ("con") side of the argument.	5 minutes
Affirmative Speaker 3	Summarize the claim and evidence for the affirmative side and explain why your reasoning is more valid.	3 minutes
Negative Speaker 3	Summarize the claim and evidence for the negative side and explain why your reasoning is more valid.	3 minutes

Evaluate the Debate

Use the following guidelines to evaluate a team in a debate:

- Did the team prove that the issue is significant? How thorough was the analysis?
- How did the team effectively argue that you should support their affirmative or negative side of the proposition or issue?
- How effectively did the team present reasons and evidence, including evidence from the texts, to support the proposition?

Reading Informational Texts: Patterns of Organization

Reading any type of writing is easier once you recognize how it is organized. Writers usually arrange ideas and information in ways that best help readers see how they are related. There are several common patterns of organization:

- main idea and supporting details
- chronological order
- cause-effect organization
- compare-and-contrast organization
- problem-solution organization

Writers also typically present arguments in ways that will help readers follow their reasoning.

1. Main Idea and Supporting Details

Main idea and supporting details is a basic pattern of organization in which a central idea about a topic is supported by details. The **main idea** is the most important idea about a topic that a particular text or paragraph conveys. **Supporting details** are words, phrases, or sentences that tell more about the main idea. The main idea may be directly stated at the beginning and then followed by supporting details, or it may be merely implied by the supporting details. It may also be stated after it has been implied by supporting details.

Strategies for Reading

- To find a stated main idea in a paragraph, identify the paragraph's topic. The topic is what the paragraph is about and can usually be summed up in one or two words. The word, or synonyms of it, will usually appear throughout the paragraph. Headings and subheadings are also clues to the topics of paragraphs.
- Look for the topic sentence, or the sentence that states the most important idea the paragraph conveys. It is often the first sentence in a paragraph; however, it may appear at the end.
- To find an implied main idea, ask yourself: Whom or what did I just read about? What do the details suggest about the topic?
- Formulate a sentence stating this idea and add it to the paragraph. Does your sentence convey the main idea?

Notice how the main idea is expressed in each of the following models.

Model:
Main Idea as the First Sentence

> On the second day of the heat wave, the temperature soared to a sweltering 110 degrees. [Main idea] The sun melted the tar of the newly paved driveway. It was almost impossible to escape the fumes, which caused him to hold his nose and breathe through his mouth. The air felt like a wet blanket smothering his lungs. Each breath was a struggle. [Supporting details]

Model:
Main Idea as the First Sentence

> His body tried to maintain a healthy temperature by producing large amounts of sweat. Because the air was so humid and there was no breeze, the sweat didn't evaporate and cool him at all. It just dripped unpleasantly, and he grew even hotter as he angrily tried to wipe it away. Despite losing all that water, he wasn't even thirsty. [Supporting details] Though he didn't know it, he was in danger of becoming dehydrated. [Main idea]

Model:
Implied Main Idea

As he walked along the street looking for something to drink, he began to feel lightheaded. He ignored the feeling for a few minutes, but then became so dizzy that he had to sit down. Soon he started to feel sick to his stomach. As he stretched out, he began to shiver. "How can I be cold when it's 110 degrees?" he wondered before he fainted.

> **Implied main idea:** He was dehydrated, which was a serious problem.

Practice and Apply

Read each paragraph, and then do the following:

1. Identify the main idea in the paragraph, using one of the strategies discussed on the previous page. Tell whether it is stated or implied.
2. Evaluate the pattern of organization used in the paragraph. Does it express the main idea effectively?

Community service is an important part of our school life. Every student is encouraged to participate in one of the many school-approved service options. No grades are given for the service work, but students record their hours and what type of service they perform. We can also choose to be involved in more than one type of service. Whatever we choose, we learn how much the people of our community appreciate our help and how much we enjoy helping others.

They never saw him. Now and then they heard whispered rumors to the effect that he was in the neighborhood. The woods were searched. The roads were watched. There was never anything to indicate his whereabouts. But a few days afterward, a goodly number of slaves would be gone from the plantation. Neither the master nor the overseer had heard or seen anything unusual in the quarter. Sometimes one or the other would vaguely remember having heard a whippoorwill call somewhere in the woods, close by, late at night. Though it was the wrong season for whippoorwills.
—Ann Petry, *Harriet Tubman: Conductor on the Underground Railroad*

2. Chronological Order

Chronological order is the arrangement of events in the order in which they happen. This type of organization is used in many short stories and novels, historical writing, biographies, and autobiographies. To show the order of events, writers use order words such as *after, next,* and *later* and time words and phrases that identify specific times of day, days of the week, and dates, such as *the next morning, Tuesday,* and *March 13, 2007.*

Strategies for Reading

- Scan the text for headings and subheadings that may indicate a chronological pattern of organization.
- Look for words and phrases that identify times, such as *in a year, three hours earlier, in AD 1066,* and *the next day.*
- Look for words that signal order, such as *first, afterward, then, during, later,* and *finally,* to see how events or steps are related.
- Note that a paragraph or passage in which ideas and information are arranged chronologically will have several words or phrases that indicate time order, not just one.
- Ask yourself: Are the events in the paragraph or passage presented in time order?

Notice the words and phrases that signal time order in the first two paragraphs of the following model.

Model:

Jackie Torrence, who was born **in 1944**, is the author of "Scary Stories." She **spent much of her childhood on a North Carolina farm**, where she grew up listening to traditional stories told by her grandfather. **Years later**, **while working as a librarian**, she was asked to read stories to some young children. She agreed, and the children were instantly captivated. **Before long**, Torrence **was invited to tell stories** in local and neighboring communities. Torrence, who was later dubbed "The Story Lady," went on to gain national prominence as a storyteller.

> Time words and phrases
>
> Events

3. Cause-Effect Organization

Cause-effect organization is a pattern of organization that shows causal relationships between events, ideas, and trends. Cause-effect relationships may be directly stated or merely implied by the order in which the information is presented. Writers often use the cause-effect pattern in historical and scientific writing. Cause-effect relationships may have several forms.

One cause with one effect

One cause with multiple effects

Multiple causes with a single effect

A chain of causes and effects

Strategies for Reading

- Look for headings and subheadings that indicate a cause-effect pattern of organization, such as "Effects of Food Allergies."
- To find the effect or effects, read to answer the question "What happened?"
- To find the cause or causes, read to answer the question "Why did it happen?"
- Look for words and phrases that help you identify specific relationships between events, such as *because, since, had the effect of, led to, as a result, resulted in, for that reason, due to, therefore, if...then,* and *consequently.*
- Look closely at each cause-effect relationship. Do not assume that because one event happened before another, the first event caused the second event.
- Use graphic organizers like the diagrams shown to record cause-effect relationships as you read.

Notice the words that signal causes and effects in the following model.

Model:
We're Destroying Our Rain Forests

According to a study done by Brazilian scientists, nearly 5 million acres of rain forest are disappearing a year. That's equal to seven football fields a minute.

The cause of this destruction is simple—cutting down trees. Every minute, around 2,000 trees are felled to create highways, railroads, and farms. Some trees, such as mahogany and teak, are harvested for their beautiful hardwood.

This destruction of the rain forests has wide-ranging effects on living things. About 30,000 plant species live in the Amazon rain forest alone. These plants provide important foods such as bananas, coffee, chocolate, and nuts, as well as medicinal compounds found nowhere else. Just four square miles of a rain forest shelters more than 550 species of birds, reptiles, and amphibians. Almost 100 species worldwide face extinction every day, many due to habitat loss in rain forests.

Rain forests also act as climate regulators, balancing the exchange of oxygen and carbon dioxide in the atmosphere and helping to offset global warming. The earth's well-being will suffer as a result of the rain forests' destruction.

It is crucial that steps be taken immediately to reduce the number of trees being cut down. If this destruction is not reversed, within 50 years, thriving rain forests will be no more than a memory.

Practice and Apply

Refer to the preceding model to do the following:

1. Use one of the graphic organizers on this page to show the multiple effects of cutting down trees described in the model.
2. List three words or phrases used to signal cause and effect in the last four paragraphs.

4. Compare-and-Contrast Organization

Compare-and-contrast organization is a pattern of organization that provides a way to look at similarities and differences in two or more subjects. A writer may use this pattern of organization to compare the important points or characteristics of two or more subjects. These points or characteristics are called **points of comparison.** There are two ways to develop compare-and-contrast organization:

Point-by-point organization—The writer discusses one point of comparison for both subjects, then goes on to the next point.

Subject-by-subject organization—The writer covers all points of comparison for one subject and then all points of comparison for the next subject.

Strategies for Reading

- Look in the text for headings, subheadings, and sentences that may suggest a compare-and-contrast pattern of organization, such as "Common Behaviors of Different Pets," to help you identify where similarities and differences are addressed.
- To find similarities, look for words and phrases such as *like, all, both, every,* and *in the same way.*
- To find differences, look for words and phrases such as *unlike, but, on the other hand, more, less, in contrast,* and *however.*
- Use a graphic organizer, such as a Venn diagram or a compare-and-contrast chart, to record points of comparison and similarities and differences.

Subject 1 | Both | Subject 2

	Subject 1	Subject 2
Point 1		
Point 2		
Point 3		

As you read the following models, use the signal words and phrases to identify the similarities and differences between the subjects and how the details are organized in each text.

Model 1

Mr. Frank and Mr. Van Daan

Moving into a tiny apartment with people you have never met is a sure way to discover your differences. In the play *The Diary of Anne Frank,* Mr. Frank and Mr. Van Daan are in a similar situation, but have very different personalities, behaviors, and relationships with their families.

Both men are Jews living in Nazi-occupied Amsterdam during World War II. Both have children: Mr. Frank, two daughters; and Mr. Van Daan, a son. They try to hide their families from the Nazis in the same apartment.

Despite these similarities, there are many differences between the two men. First, they have nearly opposite personalities. Mr. Van Daan is very concerned with appearances and wears expensive clothes. He can be kind, but often loses his temper. He also has strong opinions about the roles of men and women. For example, he acts embarrassed that his son Peter likes his pet cat and disapproves of Anne's outspokenness. He tells her, "A man likes a girl who'll listen to him once in a while."

In contrast, Mr. Frank doesn't seem to care about material things. He always stays calm and has compassion for other people. Even when Mr. Van Daan is caught stealing food, Mr. Frank tries to understand the man's behavior. Mr. Frank's attitude about women differs from Mr. Van Daan's as well. Mr. Frank never criticizes Anne for being unladylike; instead, he encourages her to be herself. He gives her a diary because he knows she loves to write, and he is proud of her creativity when she makes

Hanukkah presents for everyone. As Anne says about her father, "He's the only one who's ever given me the feeling that I have any sense."

The two men also respond differently to their situation. Mr. Van Daan is self-centered and believes he suffers more from hunger than the others. He even tries to take Anne's piece of cake. Mr. Frank, on the other hand, always puts the needs of others before his own. For example, he makes the newcomer, Dr. Dussel, feel welcome and gladly offers him food. He also risks his own safety to investigate when a robber enters the downstairs warehouse.

[Contrast words and phrases]

Mr. Frank and Mr. Van Daan relate differently with their families. Although Mr. and Mrs. Van Daan are close, they quarrel often. Mr. Van Daan criticizes his son's slowness and threatens to get rid of his beloved cat. In contrast, Mr. Frank shows only love and respect for his wife and daughters. Even when he scolds Anne, he does it privately and gently. After Anne hurts her mother's feelings, Mr. Frank tells her that parents "can only try to set a good example. The rest you must do yourself."

The differences between Mr. Frank and Mr. Van Daan in *The Diary of Anne Frank* far outnumber their similarities. Mr. Van Daan's selfishness endangers both families, while Mr. Frank's compassion and consideration help them all make the best of a terrible situation.

leaves of the yerba maté tree, it is traditionally brewed in hollow gourds, which are themselves called *matés*. The gourd is filled three-quarters full with leaves, and they are then covered with hot water. When the leaves have completely absorbed the moisture, more water is added. The brewed tea is then drunk through a tube with a strainer at one end called a *bombilla*. Yerba maté is sometimes served with milk, sugar, or lemon juice to cut its slight bitterness.

Yerba maté is thought to offer many health benefits. It is loaded with antioxidants that may boost the immune system and help prevent cancer. It also seems to aid digestion.

Green tea, on the other hand, is native to China and was exported to Japan in about AD 800. Unlike yerba maté, green tea usually is brewed in teapots. Only about a teaspoonful of leaves is used per pot. The leaves are steeped for only around two minutes—much less than the soaking time for yerba maté. Green tea has a very mild taste and generally is served plain in ceramic cups so the delicate taste can be savored.

[Contrast words and phrases]

Like yerba maté, green tea also is beneficial to health. Similarly rich in antioxidants, it has been reputed to lower cholesterol and blood sugar and also to relieve the pain of arthritis. So, the next time you have tea for two, try one of these two popular drinks—yerba maté and green tea.

[Comparison words and phrases]

Model 2

Two for Tea

Next to water, tea is the most popular drink worldwide. Served hot or iced, it comes in a variety of flavors to suit every taste. Yerba maté and green tea are two varieties that seem to suit the tastes of increasing numbers of people of all ages and nationalities.

Yerba maté is native to South America. Made from the dried

[Subjects]
[Comparison words and phrases]

Practice and Apply

Refer to the preceding models to do the following:

1. Find one similarity and one difference in the organization of these two models.
2. For each model, list three words or phrases that signal comparisons or contrasts.
3. Identify two points in each model that the writer compares or contrasts.
4. Make a Venn diagram or compare-and-contrast graphic to show the similarities and differences in one of the models.

5. Problem-Solution Organization

Problem-solution organization is a pattern of organization in which a problem is stated and analyzed and then one or more solutions are proposed and examined. This pattern of organization is often used in persuasive writing, such as editorials or proposals.

Strategies for Reading

- Look for an explanation of the problem in the first or second paragraph.
- Look for words such as *problem* and *reason* that may signal an explanation of the problem.
- To find the solution, ask: What suggestion does the writer offer to solve the problem?
- Look for words such as *propose, conclude,* and *answer* that may signal a solution.

Model

Teachers, administrators, school board members, and parents have begun expressing concerns that the foreign language students aren't getting enough practice using their languages in conversation.

Students read dialogues from their textbooks and respond to questions. They also use the language lab to get more practice speaking the language. The facilities are limited, though, and have to be used after school, which conflicts with other activities. Also, the language lab doesn't give them real-life experience with using the new language to listen to others, either.

One solution to this problem would be to establish language tables in the lunchroom. Students taking a given language would eat lunch at a specific table one day a week. For that time, they would speak only the foreign language.

This plan has several advantages. First, it doesn't require any additional equipment, staff, or materials. Second, it wouldn't take time away from other classes or activities. Language students have to eat lunch just like everyone else, so why not make it an enjoyable learning experience?

Setting up language tables would let students supplement their language skills while nourishing their bodies. That's a recipe for success!

Practice and Apply

Reread the model and then answer the following questions:

1. According to the model, what is the cause of the problem?
2. What solution does the writer offer? What words are a clue?

Reading Arguments

1. Analyzing an Argument

An **argument** expresses a position on an issue or problem and supports it with reasons and evidence. Being able to analyze and evaluate arguments will help you distinguish between claims you should accept and those you should not. A sound argument should appeal strictly to reason. However, arguments are often used in texts that also contain other types of persuasive devices. An argument includes the following elements:

- A **claim** is the writer's position on an issue or problem.
- **Support** is any material that serves to prove a claim. In an argument, support usually consists of reasons and evidence.
- **Reasons** are declarations made to justify an action, decision, or belief. For example: "My reason for walking so quickly is that I'm afraid I'll be late for class."
- **Evidence** consists of the specific references, quotations, facts, examples, and opinions that support a claim. Evidence may also consist of statistics, reports of personal experience, or the views of experts.
- A **counterargument** is an argument made to oppose another argument. A good argument anticipates the opposition's objections and provides counterarguments to disprove or answer them.

Claim	I need a larger allowance.
Reason	I don't have enough money to pay for my school lunches, fees, and transportation.
Evidence	I had to borrow money from my friend two weeks in a row to buy lunch.
Counter-argument	My parents say I just need to budget my allowance better, but they don't realize what my expenses are.

Practice and Apply

Read the following book review and use a chart like the one shown to identify the claim, reason, evidence, and counterargument.

Hatchet
Reviewed by Kristen Loos

What would you do if you suddenly found yourself in the middle of a wilderness with no one else around and only a hatchet to help you survive? That's what happens to Brian Robeson, a boy about my age, in Gary Paulsen's book *Hatchet*. Even if this sounds like a situation you'll never be in, *Hatchet* is worth reading for what it says about facing your fears.

After his parents get a divorce, Brian heads up to northern Canada to spend the summer with his dad. But the pilot flying the airplane has a heart attack, and Brian is forced to crash-land it by himself. From then on, he has to handle everything by himself.

From the beginning all the way to the end of the book, Brian faces big problems just to survive. He's a city kid, so he's used to opening up the refrigerator any time he wants to eat. Now, at the edge of the woods, he has to figure out things like how to be safe from wild animals and how to make a fire without matches. At first, he panics. He doesn't even know what to drink or how to find and prepare food. Even so, he doesn't give up.

One of the things I like about the book is how Brian changes. At first, he hopes he will be rescued very soon. He thinks he can hold out for a few days until his parents or a search party finds him. Then, when a plane flies over without seeing him, he realizes that he is really on his own. He learns to make tools to fish and hunt with and to depend on himself for everything he needs.

Some readers may not like the book because they think this is an unusual situation that most people will never have to face. I don't agree, though, because I think the real message is not just about being lost in the wilderness, but about bravely dealing with whatever challenges we face in our lives.

Reading Arguments

I'm not going to spoil the book for you by saying how it ends or whether Brian gets rescued. Read it yourself for an exciting adventure and some good lessons about surviving in the wilderness. I hope you enjoy it as much as I did.

2. Recognizing Proposition and Support Patterns

To find an author's claim, support, and counterarguments, it's helpful to identify the author's method for making his or her case. Here are two ways writers often make their cases:

- **Proposition and Support** The writer presents a **proposition,** which is a claim that recommends a policy, and two or three reasons for accepting the policy. For example, "Cigarette smoking should be banned in public places because it's bad for people's health and smelly." Then the writer supports each reason with evidence.
- **Strawman** The writer presents a proposition. Instead of supporting it, though, he or she sums up the other side's position and disproves it. Once that "strawman" has been defeated, the writer declares his or her proposition the best or only option.

Writers usually reveal how they are going to present their cases in the first few paragraphs of their work. Study the following paragraph to see how it signals that the argument to come will use a proposition and support pattern.

> **Model**
> Have you wanted to ride your bike to school but been frightened off by the car traffic? If so, you're not alone. **The city should create bike lanes on busy streets** because it would make cycling **safer and easier**.
>
> — Proposition
> — Support

The next paragraph introduces an editorial in which the writer uses the strawman method.

> **Model**
> **The city should create bike lanes on busy streets.** Opponents of bike lanes will tell you that **such lanes are a waste of money because drivers just ignore them**, but that's not true.
>
> — Proposition
> — Supposed argument against proposition

Practice and Apply

Now use the preceding models and instruction to help you identify the way in which the author of this next introduction plans to persuade her readers to adopt her proposition. Explain how you arrived at your conclusion.

> Every neighborhood should have a community garden. If the people in our neighborhood all had the chance to grow their own fruits, flowers, and vegetables in side-by-side garden plots, they would eat better, feel better, and get along better. Of course, not everyone would participate, but those who did would reap the benefits!

3. Recognizing Persuasive Techniques

Persuasive texts typically rely on more than just the **logical appeal** of an argument to be convincing. They also rely on ethical and emotional appeals and other **persuasive techniques**—devices that can convince you to adopt a position or take an action.

- **Ethical appeals** establish a writer's credibility and trustworthiness with an audience. When a writer links a claim to a widely accepted value, the writer not only gains moral support for that claim but also establishes himself or herself as a reputable, moral person readers can and should trust. For example, with the following appeal, the writer reminds readers of a value they should accept and suggests that if they share this value, then they should support the writer's position: "If you believe that all children deserve a good education, then vote for this legislation."

The following chart explains several other means by which a writer may attempt to sway you. Learn to recognize these techniques, and you are less likely to be influenced by them.

Persuasive Technique	Example
Bandwagon appeal Taps into people's desire to belong	Join the millions of health-conscious people who drink Wonder Water!
Testimonial Relies on endorsements from well-known people or satisfied customers	Send your game over the top with Macon Ace—the racket designed and used by tennis legend Sonja Macon.
Snob appeal Taps into people's desire to be special or part of an elite group	The best deserve only the best—you deserve Beautiful Bubbles bath soap.
Appeals to pity, fear, or vanity Use strong feelings, rather than facts, to persuade	Why go unnoticed when Pretty Face can make you the center of attention?

Sometimes persuasive techniques are misused to create rhetorical fallacies. A **rhetorical fallacy** is writing or speech that is false or misleading. For example, an athlete who endorses a line of athletic shoes would be misleading the public if he or she wears a different kind of shoe in competitions.

Practice and Apply

Identify the persuasive techniques used in this model.

A Dry Future?

One of the most talked-about books published this year is *Glass Half Empty*. This informative book paints a frightening picture of our dwindling water resources. In the next few decades, fresh drinking water may become more expensive and harder to find than gasoline! The author warns that competition for water will cause nations to go to war with each other. Over 40 scientists have spoken in praise of the book. If you care about the planet, rush out and get a copy of *Glass Half Empty*.

4. Analyzing Logic and Reasoning

While persuasive techniques may sway you to side with a writer, they should not be enough to convince you that an argument is sound. To determine the soundness of an argument, examine the argument's claim and support and the logic or reasoning that links them. Identifying the writer's mode of reasoning can help.

The Inductive Mode of Reasoning

When a person uses specific evidence to arrive at a generalization, that person is using **inductive reasoning.** Similarly, when a writer presents specific evidence first and then offers a generalization drawn from that evidence, the writer is making an **inductive argument.** Here is an example of inductive reasoning.

Specific Evidence
Fact 1 Wind and water wear away rocks over time.
Fact 2 Earthquakes and volcanoes create immediate and drastic changes in the land.
Fact 3 The slow movement of the continents and spreading of the sea floor create new landforms.
Generalization
Natural forces continually change the surface of the earth.

Strategies for Determining the Soundness of Inductive Arguments

Ask yourself the following questions to evaluate an inductive argument:

- **Is the evidence valid and sufficient support for the conclusion?** Inaccurate facts lead to inaccurate conclusions.
- **Does the conclusion follow logically from the evidence?** From the facts listed, the conclusion that Earth's core as well as its surface are constantly changing would be too broad.
- **Is the evidence drawn from a large enough sample?** These three facts are enough to support the claim. If you wanted to claim that these are the *only* forces that cause change, you would need more facts.

Reading Arguments

The Deductive Mode of Reasoning

When a person uses a **premise**, or general principle, to form a conclusion about a particular situation or problem, that person is using **deductive reasoning**. For example,

To drive a car well, all drivers must give driving their complete attention.	Premise, or general principle
▼	
Talking on a cell phone takes some of a person's attention.	The situation being observed or considered
▼	
Drivers shouldn't talk on cell phones while driving.	Conclusion (also considerd a deduction)

Similarly, a writer is making a **deductive argument** when he or she begins the argument with a claim that is based on a premise and then presents evidence to support the claim. For example, a writer might begin a deductive argument with the claim "Drivers should not talk on cell phones while they are driving."

Strategies for Determining the Soundness of Deductive Arguments

Ask yourself the following questions to evaluate a deductive argument:

- **Is the premise actually stated, or is it implied?** Writers often present deductive arguments without stating the premises. They just assume that readers will recognize and agree with the premises. So you may want to identify the premise for yourself.
- **Is the premise correct?** Don't assume it is true. Ask yourself whether it is really true.
- **Is the conclusion valid?** To be valid, a conclusion in a deductive argument must follow logically from the premise and the specific situation.

The following chart shows two conclusions drawn from the same premise.

All spiders have eight legs.	
Accurate Deduction	**Inaccurate Deduction**
The black widow is a spider, therefore it has eight legs.	An octopus has eight legs, therefore it is a spider.

An octopus has eight legs, but it belongs to a different category of animals than the spider.

Now, as you read the following model, pay attention to how the author arrives at her conclusion.

> The other day when I was waiting at the stoplight on my bike, I noticed that the car in front of me was in the right lane and had its right turn signal on. Wouldn't you have assumed, just like I did, that the driver was going to turn right? Well, I was wrong, and you probably would've been, too. As soon as the light turned green, the car swerved across two lanes and turned left.
>
> Then there was the surprise birthday party the neighborhood kids and I had for one of our friends. We'd managed to keep it a secret, so we all expected her to be really surprised and pleased. Instead, she was upset and embarrassed because she wasn't dressed properly for a party.
>
> It's dangerous to make assumptions about how other people will act. I've learned that the hard way!

Practice and Apply

Refer to the preceding model and instruction to do the following:

1. Identify the mode of reasoning used in the model.
2. In your own words, explain the difference between inductively and deductively organizing ideas.

Identifying Faulty Reasoning

Sometimes an argument at first appears to make sense but isn't valid because it is based on a **fallacy**. A fallacy is an error in logic. Learn to recognize these common fallacies.

Type of Fallacy	Definition	Example
Circular reasoning	Supporting a statement by simply repeating it in different words.	My mother is always busy because **she has too much to do.**
Either/or fallacy	A statement that suggests that there are only two choices available in a situation that really offers more than two options.	**Either** I grow two inches this summer **or** I'll never make any friends at my new school.
Oversimplification	An explanation of a complex situation or problem as if it were much simpler than it is.	**All you have to do to get good grades** is listen carefully in class.
Overgeneralization	A generalization that is too broad. You can often recognize overgeneralizations by the use of words such as *all, everyone, every time, anything, no one,* and *none*.	**Nobody** has as many chores as I do.
Hasty generalization	A conclusion drawn from too little evidence or from evidence that is biased.	I sneezed after taking a bite of the salad, so **I must be allergic to something in it.**
Stereotyping	A dangerous type of overgeneralization. Stereotypes are broad statements about people on the basis of their gender, ethnicity, race, or political, social, professional, or religious group.	**Artists are emotional** and **hard to get along with.**
Attacking the person or name-calling	An attempt to discredit an idea by attacking the person or group associated with it. Candidates often engage in name-calling during political campaigns.	The senator only supports this bill because he is **corrupt.**
Evading the issue	Responding to an objection with arguments and evidence that do not address its central point.	I forgot to get the milk, **but dairy products are hard to digest anyway.**
False cause	The mistake of assuming that because one event occurred after another event, the first event caused the second one to occur.	It rained this afternoon **because I left my umbrella at home.**
Non sequitur	A conclusion that does not follow logically from the "proof" offered to support it.	Mrs. Lewis will make Steve the baseball team captain. **He is already the captain of the volleyball team.**

Practice and Apply

Look for examples of logical fallacies in the following argument. Identify each one and explain why you identified it as such.

> Store clerks are so rude. A cashier was impatient with me in the supermarket the other day because I bought too much yogurt. They must train the employees to treat customers that way so more people will use the self-checkout lines. I need to budget more money for groceries.

5. Evaluating Persuasive Texts

Learning how to evaluate persuasive texts and identify bias will help you become more selective when doing research and also help you improve your own reasoning and arguing skills.

Strategies for Identifying Bias

Bias is an inclination for or against a particular opinion or viewpoint. A writer may reveal a strongly positive or negative bias on an issue by

- **presenting only one way** of looking at it
- **overlooking key information**
- **stacking more evidence on one side** of the argument than the other
- **using unfairly weighted evidence,** which is weak or unproven evidence that a writer treats as if it is more important than it really is
- **using loaded language,** which consists of words with strongly positive or negative connotations

EXAMPLE
At the Village Star, we bring you up-to-the-minute news. That's why so many people read our paper. (Someone who works for the paper is making the claim. *Up-to-the-minute* has very positive connotations. The writer also fails to mention important information: the paper is free.)

Strategies for Identifying Propaganda

Propaganda is any form of communication that is so distorted that it conveys false or misleading information. Logical fallacies such as name-calling, the either/or fallacy, and false causes are often used in propaganda. The following example shows false cause. The writer uses one fact to support a particular point of view but does not reveal another fact that does not support that viewpoint.

EXAMPLE
Since Jack Carter was elected mayor, unemployment has decreased by 25%. (The writer does not mention that it was the previous mayor, not Jack Carter, who was responsible for bringing in the new factory that provides the extra jobs.)

Strategies for Evaluating Evidence

It is important to have a set of standards by which you can evaluate persuasive texts. Use the questions below to help you critically assess facts and opinions that are presented as evidence.

- **Are the presented facts verifiable?** A **fact,** or **factual claim,** is a statement that can be proved by consulting a reliable source or doing research.
- **Are the presented opinions and commonplace assertions well informed?** An opinion is a statement of personal belief, feeling, or thought that does not require proof. A **commonplace assertion** is a statement that many people assume to be true but isn't necessarily so. When evaluating either type of statement, consider whether the author is knowledgeable about the topic and uses sound reasoning.
- **Is the evidence thorough and balanced?** Thorough evidence leaves no reasonable questions unanswered. Be alert to evidence that is weighted unfairly and contains loaded language or other signs of bias.
- **Is the evidence authoritative?** The people, groups, or organizations that provided the evidence should have credentials that support their authority.
- **Is it important that the evidence be current?** Where timeliness is crucial, as in the areas of medicine and technology, the evidence should reflect the latest developments in the areas.

Practice and Apply

Read the argument below. Identify the facts, opinions, and elements of bias.

> Ultra Bars are the tastiest and most efficient way to get your daily requirement of important nutrients. Our bodies need a well-balanced combination of protein, carbohydrates, fats, vitamins, minerals, and trace elements to function most effectively and make us feel our best. The ingredients in Ultra Bars have been chosen in the perfect proportion to ensure you get the maximum benefit. Best of all, they taste terrific. And they aren't just for athletes—ordinary people should carry these bars with them, too, for a quick boost throughout the day!

Strategies for Determining a Strong Argument

Make sure that all or most of the following statements are true:

- The argument presents a claim or controlling idea.
- The claim is connected to its support by a premise or generalization that most readers would readily agree with. Correct premise: *Doing your best will bring you personal pride.* Incorrect premise: *Doing your best will bring you success.*
- The reasons make sense.
- The reasons are presented in a logical and effective order.
- The claim and all reasons are adequately supported by sound evidence.
- The evidence is adequate, accurate, and appropriate.
- The logic is sound. There are no instances of faulty reasoning.
- The argument adequately anticipates and addresses readers' concerns and counterclaims with counterarguments.

Practice and Apply

Use the preceding criteria to evaluate the strength of the following proposal.

Model

Summary of Proposal

I propose that the city government create a park on the unused plot of land at the edge of town.

Need

We must preserve the natural beauty of the area for all to appreciate and enjoy.

Proposed Solution

The five-acre plot of land on the south side of town is now being considered for improvement.

Some people want to sell the land to a building developer. They say that doing this would be profitable for the town and also provide good housing for new residents.

It's true that the town could make money by developing the land. A park could also be a source of income, however.

The park would generate income in a number of ways. It could charge a small admission fee for summer concerts and other events. It also could lease the space to neighboring communities for their gatherings and to local food concessions and special-interest groups.

The cost of creating and maintaining a park is less than what it would bring in. Community groups already have agreed to donate plants, provide volunteers to landscape and take care of the grounds, create gazebos, and install benches, water fountains, and trashcans.

Without a park, we can't ensure the safety and health of our residents. It would have playgrounds and areas to bike, skate, picnic, and walk or jog. Unlike commercial and even residential buildings, parks do not encourage vandalism and graffiti. The chief of police has confirmed that parks are easier to supervise, too, because it isn't as hard to police them.

No one who cares about our community could fail to see how important it is to create this park.

Grammar

Writing that is full of mistakes can confuse or even annoy a reader. Punctuation errors in a letter might lead to a miscommunication and delay a reply. Sentence fragments might lower your grade on an essay. Paying attention to grammar, punctuation, and capitalization rules can make your writing clearer and easier to read.

Quick Reference: Parts of Speech

Part of Speech	Function	Examples
Noun	names a person, a place, a thing, an idea, a quality, or an action	
Common	serves as a general name, or a name common to an entire group	shadow, harmonica, paw, mistake
Proper	names a specific, one-of-a-kind person, place, or thing	Chinatown, Switzerland, Jupiter, Herbert
Singular	refers to a single person, place, thing, or idea	earthquake, laboratory, medication, outcome
Plural	refers to more than one person, place, thing, or idea	chemicals, splinters, geniuses, soldiers
Concrete	names something that can be perceived by the senses	calendar, basketball, ocean, snow
Abstract	names something that cannot be perceived by the senses	democracy, authority, beauty, fame
Compound	expresses a single idea through a combination of two or more words	self-esteem, mountaintop, firefighters, light bulb
Collective	refers to a group of people or things	team, family, class, choir
Possessive	shows who or what owns something	Pandora's, Strauss's, Franks', women's
Pronoun	takes the place of a noun or another pronoun	
Personal	refers to the person making a statement, the person(s) being addressed, or the person(s) or thing(s) the statement is about	I, me, my, mine, we, us, our, ours, you, your, yours, she, he, it, her, him, hers, his, its, they, them, their, theirs
Reflexive	follows a verb or preposition and refers to a preceding noun or pronoun	myself, yourself, herself, himself, itself, ourselves, yourselves, themselves
Intensive	emphasizes a noun or another pronoun	(same as reflexives)
Demonstrative	points to one or more specific persons or things	this, that, these, those

continued

Part of Speech	Function	Examples
Interrogative	signals a question	who, whom, whose, which, what
Indefinite	refers to one or more persons or things not specifically mentioned	both, all, most, many, anyone, everybody, several, none, some
Relative	introduces an adjective clause by relating it to a word in the clause	who, whom, whose, which, that
Verb	expresses an action, a condition, or a state of being	
Action	tells what the subject does or did, physically or mentally	find, know, clings, displayed, rises, crave
Linking	connects the subject to something that identifies or describes it	am, is, are, was, were, sound, taste, appear, feel, become, remain, seem
Auxiliary	precedes the main verb in a verb phrase	be, have, can, do, could, will, would, may, might
Transitive	directs the action toward someone or something; always has an object	She opened the **door**.
Intransitive	does not direct the action toward someone or something; does not have an object	The door **opened**.
Adjective	modifies a noun or pronoun	**slight** groan, **dying** gladiators, **ancient** sea, **two** pigtails
Adverb	modifies a verb, an adjective, or another adverb	**always** closed, **very** patiently, **more** pleasant, ran **quickly**
Preposition	relates one word to another word	at, by, for, from, in, of, on, to, with
Conjunction	joins words or word groups	
Coordinating	joins words or word groups used the same way	and, but, or, for, so, yet, nor
Correlative	used as a pair to join words or word groups used the same way	both . . . and, either . . . or, neither . . . nor
Subordinating	introduces a clause that cannot stand by itself as a complete sentence	although, after, as, before, because, when, if, unless
Interjection	expresses emotion	wow, ouch, hooray

Grammar

Quick Reference: The Sentence and Its Parts

The diagrams that follow will give you a brief review of the essentials of a sentence and some of its parts.

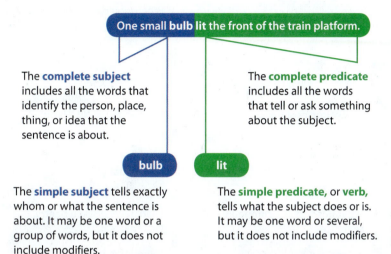

Every word in a sentence is part of a complete subject or a complete predicate.

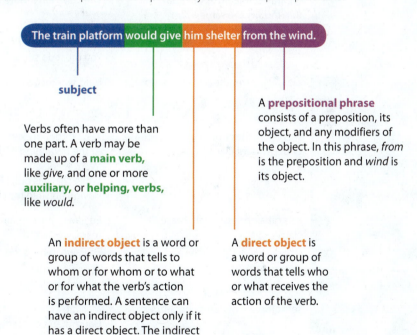

Grammar   **R31**

Quick Reference: Punctuation

Mark	Function	Examples
End Marks period, question mark, exclamation point	ends a sentence	We can start now**.** When would you like to leave**?** What a fantastic hit**!**
period	follows an initial or abbreviation **Exception:** postal abbreviations of states	Mrs. Dorothy Parker, Apple Inc., C. P. Cavafy, P.M., A.D., lb., oz., Blvd., Dr. NE (Nebraska), NV (Nevada)

period	follows a number or letter in an outline	I. Volcanoes
		   A. Central-vent
		      1. Shield

Comma	separates part of a compound sentence	I had never disliked poetry, but now I really love it.
	separates items in a series	Her humor, grace, and kindness served her well.
	separates adjectives of equal rank that modify the same noun	The slow, easy route is best.
	sets off a term of address	Maria, how can I help you? You must do something, soldier.
	sets off a parenthetical expression	Hard workers, as you know, don't quit. I'm not a quitter, believe me.
	sets off an introductory word, phrase, or dependent clause	Yes, I forgot my key. At the beginning of the day, I feel fresh. While she was out, I was here. Having finished my chores, I went out.
	sets off a nonessential phrase or clause	Ed Pawn, the captain of the chess team, won. Ed Pawn, who is the captain, won. The two leading runners, sprinting toward the finish line, finished in a tie.
	sets off parts of dates and addresses	Mail it by May 14, 2010, to the Hauptman Company, 321 Market Street, Memphis, Tennessee.
	follows the salutation and closing of a letter	Dear Jim, Sincerely yours,
	separates words to avoid confusion	By noon, time had run out. What the minister does, does matter. While cooking, Jim burned his hand.

continued

Mark	Function	Examples
Semicolon	separates items in a series that contain commas	We spent the first week of summer vacation in Chicago, Illinois; the second week in St. Louis, Missouri; and the third week in Albany, New York.
	separates parts of a compound sentence that are not joined by a coordinating conjunction	The last shall be first; the first shall be last. I read the Bible; however, I have not memorized it.
	separates parts of a compound sentence when the parts contain commas	After I ran out of money, I called my parents; but only my sister was home, unfortunately.
Colon	introduces a list	The names we wrote to were the following: Dana, John, and Will.
	introduces a long quotation	Abraham Lincoln wrote: "Four score and seven years ago, our fathers brought forth on this continent a new nation . . . ."
	follows the salutation of a business letter	To Whom It May Concern: Dear Leonard Atole:
	separates certain numbers	1:28 P.M., Genesis 2:5
Dash	indicates an abrupt break in thought	I was thinking of my mother—who is arriving tomorrow—just as you walked in.
Parentheses	enclose less important material	It was so unlike him (John is always on time) that I began to worry. The last World Series game (did you see it?) was fun.
Hyphen	joins parts of a compound adjective before a noun	The not-so-rich taxpayer won't stand for this!
	joins parts of a compound with *all-, ex-, self-,* or *-elect*	The ex-firefighter helped rescue him. Our president-elect is self-conscious.
	joins parts of a compound number (to ninety-nine)	Today is the twenty-fifth of November.
	joins parts of a fraction	My cup is one-third full.
	joins a prefix to a word beginning with a capital letter	I'm studying the U.S. presidents pre-1900. It snowed in mid-October.
	indicates that a word is divided at the end of a line	How could you have any reason-able expectations of getting a new computer?

continued

Mark	Function	Examples
Apostrophe	used with *s* to form the possessive of a noun or an indefinite pronoun	my friend's book, my friends' books, anyone's guess, somebody else's problem
	replaces one or more omitted letters in a contraction or numbers in a date	don't (omitted *o*), he'd (omitted *woul*), the class of '99 (omitted *19*)
	used with *s* to form the plural of a letter	I had two A's on my report card.
Quotation Marks	set off a speaker's exact words	"That, I'll do," Lemon said. "That," Lemon said, "I'll do." Did Lemon say, "That I'll do"? Lemon said, "That I'll do!"
	set off the title of a story, an article, a short poem, an essay, a song, or a chapter	I recited Wisława Szymborska's "There But for the Grace" at the assembly. Poe's "The Tell-Tale Heart" and Sandburg's "Chicago" held my interest. I enjoyed Jean Davies Okimoto's "My Favorite Chaperone."
Ellipses	replace material omitted from a quotation	"Her diary tells us that she … thought of ordinary things, such as going to school with other kids.…"
Italics	indicate the title of a book, a play, a magazine, a long poem, an opera, a film, or a TV series, or the name of a ship	***Harriet Tubman: Conductor on the Underground Railroad**, **The Diary of Anne Frank**, **TIME**, **The Magic Flute**,* the ***Iliad**, **Star Wars**, **60 Minutes**,* the ***Mayflower***

Quick Reference: Capitalization

Category	Examples
People and Titles	
Names and initials of people	Jack London, T. S. Eliot
Titles used before a name	Professor Holmes, Senator Long
Deities and members of religious groups	Jesus, Allah, Buddha, Zeus, Baptists, Roman Catholics
Names of ethnic and national groups	Hispanics, Jews, African Americans
Geographical Names	
Cities, states, countries, continents	Philadelphia, Kansas, Japan, Europe
Regions, bodies of water, mountains	the South, Lake Baikal, Mount Everest
Geographic features, parks	Great Basin, Yellowstone National Park
Streets and roads, planets	318 East Sutton Drive, Charles Court, Jupiter, Mars
Organizations, Events, Etc.	
Companies, organizations, teams	Ford Motor Company, Boy Scouts of America, St. Louis Cardinals
Buildings, bridges, monuments	Empire State Building, Eads Bridge, Washington Monument
Documents, awards	Declaration of Independence, Stanley Cup
Special named events	Mardi Gras, World Series
Government bodies, historical periods and events	U.S. Senate, House of Representatives, Middle Ages, Vietnam War
Days and months, holidays	Thursday, March, Thanksgiving, Labor Day
Specific cars, boats, trains, planes	Porsche, Carpathia, Southwest Chief, Concorde
Proper Adjectives	
Adjectives formed from proper nouns	French cooking, Spanish omelet, Edwardian age, Western movie
First Words and the Pronoun *I*	
First word in a sentence or quotation	This is it. He said, "Let's go."
First word of sentence in parentheses that is not within another sentence	The spelling rules are covered in another section. (Consult that section for more information.)
First words in the salutation and closing of a letter	Dear Madam, Very truly yours,
First word in each line of most poetry Personal pronoun *I*	Then am I A happy fly If I live or if I die.
First word, last word, and all important words in a title	"The Powwow at the End of the World," "New Immigrants Share Their Stories," "What Is the Horror Genre?"

1 Nouns

A **noun** is a word used to name a person, a place, a thing, an idea, a quality, or an action. Nouns can be classified in several ways.

For more information on different types of nouns, see **Quick Reference: Parts of Speech,** page R29.

1.1 COMMON NOUNS

Common nouns are general names, common to entire groups.

1.2 PROPER NOUNS

Proper nouns name specific, one-of-a-kind people, places, and things.

Common	Proper
legend, canyon, girl, city	Pecos Bill, Canyon de Chelly, Anne, Amsterdam

For more information, see **Quick Reference: Capitalization,** page R35.

1.3 SINGULAR AND PLURAL NOUNS

A noun may take a singular or a plural form, depending on whether it names a single person, place, thing, or idea or more than one. Make sure you use appropriate spellings when forming plurals.

Common	Proper
diary, valley, revolution, calf	diaries, valleys, revolutions, calves

For more information, see **Forming Plural Nouns,** page R60.

1.4 POSSESSIVE NOUNS

A **possessive noun** shows who or what owns something.

For more information, see **Forming Possessives,** page R61.

2 Pronouns

A **pronoun** is a word that is used in place of a noun or another pronoun. The word or word group to which the pronoun refers is called its **antecedent.**

2.1 PERSONAL PRONOUNS

Personal pronouns change their form to express person, number, gender, and case. The forms of these pronouns are shown in the following chart.

	Nominative	Objective	Possessive
Singular			
First Person	I	me	my, mine
Second Person	you	you	your, yours
Third Person	she, he, it	her, him, it	her, hers, his, its
Plural			
First Person	we	us	our, ours
Second Person	you	you	your, yours
Third Person	they	them	their, theirs

2.2 AGREEMENT WITH ANTECEDENT

Pronouns should agree with their antecedents in number, gender, and person.

If an antecedent is singular, use a singular pronoun.

> EXAMPLE: *Rachel wrote a* **detective story.** *It has a surprise ending.*

If an antecedent is plural, use a plural pronoun.

> EXAMPLES: *The* **characters** *have* **their** *motives for murder.*
> *Javier loves* **mysteries** *and reads* **them** *all the time.*

The gender of a pronoun must be the same as the gender of its antecedent.

EXAMPLE: *The **man** has to use all **his** wits to stay alive and solve the crime.*

The person of the pronoun must be the same as the person of its antecedent. As the chart in Section 2.1 shows, a pronoun can be in first-person, second-person, or third-person form.

EXAMPLE: ***You** want a story to grab **your** attention.*

Grammar Practice

Rewrite each sentence so that the underlined pronoun agrees with its antecedent.

1. The story's suspense kept readers interested in them.
2. My dog Riley chews my tennis ball so I put them in the garage.
3. Many fans lost them voices during the final minutes of the basketball tournament.
4. I brought my favorite sandwich to school and kept them in my locker until lunchtime.
5. You and her friends should go to the amusement park this weekend.

2.3 PRONOUN FORMS

Personal pronouns change form to show how they function in sentences. The three forms are the subject form, the object form, and the possessive form. For examples of these pronouns, see the chart in Section 2.1.

A **subject pronoun** is used as a subject in a sentence.

EXAMPLE: *The poem "Chicago" is about the U.S. city Chicago. **It** was written by Carl Sandburg.*

Also use the subject form when the pronoun follows a linking verb.

EXAMPLE: *The city of Chicago is defended against accusations that **it** exploits the working class.*

An **object pronoun** is used as a direct object, an indirect object, or the object of a preposition.

SUBJECT   OBJECT
***We** will give **them** to **her**.*
                    OBJECT OF PREPOSITION

A **possessive pronoun** shows ownership. The pronouns *mine, yours, hers, his, its, ours,* and *theirs* can be used in place of nouns.

EXAMPLE: *The city's resilient spirit is **its** best asset.*

The pronouns *my, your, her, his, its, our,* and *their* are used before nouns.

EXAMPLE: *The poem changed **my** view about life in big cities.*

WATCH OUT! Many spelling errors can be avoided if you watch out for *its* and *their.* Don't confuse the possessive pronoun *its* with the contraction *it's,* meaning "it is" or "it has." The homonyms *they're* (a contraction of *they are*) and *there* ("in that place") are often mistakenly used for *their.*

TIP To decide which pronoun to use in a comparison such as "He tells better tales than (*I* or *me*)," fill in the missing word(s): *He tells better tales than I tell.*

Grammar Practice

Write the correct pronoun form to complete each sentence.

1. The scary movie frightened (him, he).
2. Michael e-mailed a copy of the book report to (she, her).
3. My brother's car is fast but (it, its) engine is too loud.
4. (Me, I) got in trouble with my parents for talking on my cell phone while I was driving to the grocery store.
5. (We, Us) need to attend the soccer game and root on our team to victory!

2.4 REFLEXIVE AND INTENSIVE PRONOUNS

These pronouns are formed by adding *-self* or *-selves* to certain personal pronouns. Their forms are the same, and they differ only in how they are used.

A **reflexive pronoun** follows a verb or preposition and reflects back on an earlier noun or pronoun.

> EXAMPLES: *He likes himself too much.*
> *She is now herself again.*

Intensive pronouns intensify or emphasize the nouns or pronouns to which they refer.

> EXAMPLES: *They themselves will educate their children.*
> *You did it yourself.*

WATCH OUT! Avoid using hisself or theirselves. Standard English does not include these forms.

> NONSTANDARD: *Colorful desert flowers offer theirselves to the poem's speaker.*
> STANDARD: *Colorful desert flowers offer themselves to the poem's speaker.*

2.5 DEMONSTRATIVE PRONOUNS

Demonstrative pronouns point out things and persons near and far.

	Singular	Plural
Near	this	these
Far	that	those

2.6 INDEFINITE PRONOUNS

Indefinite pronouns do not refer to specific persons or things and usually have no antecedents. The chart shows some commonly used indefinite pronouns.

Singular	Plural	Singular or Plural	
another	both	all	none
anybody	few	any	some
no one	many	more	most
neither			

TIP Indefinite pronouns that end in *-one*, *-body*, or *-thing* are always singular.

> INCORRECT: *Did everybody play their part well?*

If the indefinite pronoun might refer to either a male or a female, *his or her* may be used to refer to it, or the sentence may be rewritten.

> CORRECT: *Did everybody play his or her part well?*
> *Did all the students play their parts well?*

2.7 INTERROGATIVE PRONOUNS

An **interrogative pronoun** tells a reader or listener that a question is coming. The interrogative pronouns are *who, whom, whose, which,* and *what*.

> EXAMPLES: *Who is going to rehearse with you?*
> *From whom did you receive the script?*

TIP *Who* is used as a subject; *whom* is used as an object. To find out which pronoun you need to use in a question, change the question to a statement.

> QUESTION: *(Who/Whom) did you meet there?*
> STATEMENT: *You met (?) there.*

Since the verb has a subject (*you*), the needed word must be the object form, *whom*.

> EXAMPLE: *Whom did you meet there?*

WATCH OUT! A special problem arises when you use an interrupter, such as *do you think,* within a question.

> EXAMPLE: *(Who/Whom) do you think will win?*

If you eliminate the interrupter, it is clear that the word you need is *who*.

2.8 RELATIVE PRONOUNS

Relative pronouns relate, or connect, adjective clauses to the words they modify in sentences. The noun or pronoun that a relative clause modifies is the antecedent of the relative pronoun. Here are the relative pronouns and their uses.

	Subject	Object	Possessive
Person	who	whom	whose
Thing	which	which	whose
Thing/Person	that	that	whose

Often, short sentences with related ideas can be combined by using a relative pronoun to create a more effective sentence.

SHORT SENTENCE: *Louisa May Alcott wrote* Hospital Sketches.

RELATED SENTENCE: Hospital Sketches *describes Alcott's experiences as a volunteer nurse.*

COMBINED SENTENCE: *Louisa May Alcott wrote* Hospital Sketches, *which describes her experiences as a volunteer nurse.*

Grammar Practice

Write the correct form of each incorrect pronoun.
1. Few would have volunteered her services like Alcott did.
2. For who did she risk her own life?
3. Everyone received their care from Alcott.
4. A wounded soldier proved hisself to be respectful.
5. Whom can read her diary without being moved?

2.9 PRONOUN REFERENCE PROBLEMS

The referent of a pronoun should always be clear. Avoid problems by rewriting sentences.

An **indefinite reference** occurs when the pronoun *it, you,* or *they* does not clearly refer to a specific antecedent.

UNCLEAR: *People appreciate* it *when they learn from an author's experiences.*

CLEAR: *People appreciate learning from an author's experiences.*

A **general reference** occurs when the pronoun *it, this, that, which,* or *such* is used to refer to a general idea rather than a specific antecedent.

UNCLEAR: *I picture myself in the author's situation.* This *helps me understand her reactions.*

CLEAR: *I picture myself in the author's situation.* Putting myself in her position *helps me understand her reactions.*

Ambiguous means "having more than one possible meaning." An **ambiguous reference** occurs when a pronoun could refer to two or more antecedents.

UNCLEAR: *Manuel urged Simon to edit* his *new film review.*

CLEAR: *Manuel urged Simon to edit* Manuel's *new film review.*

Grammar Practice

Rewrite the following sentences to correct indefinite, ambiguous, and general pronoun references.
1. Kerri told Kristen that she played well in the soccer game.
2. Everyone enjoyed the game and seeing their team win.
3. After the students left the locker rooms, the janitor cleaned them.
4. Before the game, the coach spoke to Kristen and she looked unhappy.

3 Verbs

A **verb** is a word that expresses an action, a condition, or a state of being.

For more information, see **Quick Reference: Parts of Speech,** page R29.

3.1 ACTION VERBS

Action verbs express mental or physical activity.

EXAMPLE: *Otto Frank* comforted *his family.*

3.2 LINKING VERBS

Linking verbs join subjects with words or phrases that rename or describe them.

EXAMPLE: *They* were *in hiding during the war.*

3.3 PRINCIPAL PARTS

Action and linking verbs typically have four principal parts, which are used to form verb tenses. The principal parts are the **present,** the **present participle,** the **past,** and the **past participle.**

Action verbs and some linking verbs also fall into two categories: regular and irregular. A **regular verb** is a verb that forms its past and past participle by adding *-ed* or *-d* to the present form.

Present	Present Participle	Past	Past Participle
jump	(is) jumping	jumped	(has) jumped
solve	(is) solving	solved	(has) solved
grab	(is) grabbing	grabbed	(has) grabbed
carry	(is) carrying	carried	(has) carried

An **irregular verb** is a verb that forms its past and past participle in some other way than by adding *-ed* or *-d* to the present form.

Present	Present Participle	Past	Past Participle
begin	(is) beginning	began	(has) begun
solve	(is) breaking	broke	(has) broken
grab	(is) going	went	(has) gone

3.4 VERB TENSE

The **tense** of a verb indicates the time of the action or the state of being. An action or state of being can occur in the present, the past, or the future. There are six tenses, each expressing a different range of time.

The **present tense** expresses an action or state that is happening at the present time, occurs regularly, or is constant or generally true. Use the present participle.

NOW: *That snow* looks *deep.*
REGULAR: *It* snows *every day.*
GENERAL: *Snow* falls.

The **past tense** expresses an action that began and ended in the past. Use the past participle.

EXAMPLE: *The storyteller* finished *his tale.*

The **future tense** expresses an action or state that will occur. Use **shall** or **will** with the present participle.

EXAMPLE: *They* will attend *the next festival.*

The **present perfect tense** expresses an action or state that (1) was completed at an indefinite time in the past or (2) began in the past and continues into the present. Use **have** or **has** with the past participle.

EXAMPLE: *Poetry* has inspired *many readers.*

The **past perfect tense** expresses an action in the past that came before another action in the past. Use **had** with the past participle.

EXAMPLE: *He* had built *a fire before the dog ran away.*

The **future perfect tense** expresses an action in the future that will be completed before another action in the future. Use **shall have** or **will have** with the past participle.

EXAMPLE: *They* will have read *the novel before they see the movie version of the tale.*

TIP A past-tense form of an irregular verb is not used with an auxiliary verb, but a past-participle main irregular verb is always used with an auxiliary verb.

INCORRECT: *I have saw her somewhere before.* (*Saw* is the past-tense form of an irregular verb and shouldn't be used with *have.*)
CORRECT: *I have seen her somewhere before.*
INCORRECT: *I seen her somewhere before.* (*Seen* is the past participle of an irregular verb and shouldn't be used without an auxiliary verb.)

3.5 PROGRESSIVE FORMS

The progressive forms of the six tenses show ongoing actions. Use forms of **be** with the present participles of verbs.

PRESENT PROGRESSIVE: *Anne* is arguing *her case.*

PAST PROGRESSIVE: *Anne was arguing her case.*

FUTURE PROGRESSIVE: *Anne will be arguing her case.*

PRESENT PERFECT PROGRESSIVE: *Anne has been arguing her case.*

PAST PERFECT PROGRESSIVE: *Anne had been arguing her case.*

FUTURE PERFECT PROGRESSIVE: *Anne will have been arguing her case.*

WATCH OUT! Do not shift from tense to tense needlessly. Watch out for these special cases.

- In most compound sentences and in sentences with compound predicates, keep the tenses the same.

  INCORRECT: *She defied him, and he scolds her.*

  CORRECT: *She defied him, and he scolded her.*

- If one past action happens before another, do shift tenses.

  INCORRECT: *They wished they started earlier.*

  CORRECT: *They wished they had started earlier.*

Grammar Practice

Rewrite each sentence, using a form of the verb in parentheses. Identify each form that you use.

1. Frederick Douglass (write) a letter to Harriet Tubman in which he (praise) her.
2. He (say) that she (do) much to benefit enslaved people.
3. People (remember) her work with the Underground Railroad forever.
4. Both Douglass and Tubman (appear) in the history books that kids study.
5. They (inspire) seekers of justice for many years to come.

Rewrite each sentence to correct an error in tense.

1. When she went to the plantations, Tubman's signal has been the spiritual "Go Down Moses."
2. She is leading the slaves all the way from Maryland to Canada, and brought them to freedom.
3. Although she never will have been to Canada, she went bravely on.
4. They arrived safe and sound, but Tubman leaves for the South again.
5. Her life's work for the next six years had began.

3.6 ACTIVE AND PASSIVE VOICE

The voice of a verb tells whether its subject performs or receives the action expressed by the verb. When the subject performs the action, the verb is in the **active voice.** When the subject is the receiver of the action, the verb is in the **passive voice.**

Compare these two sentences:

ACTIVE: *Walt Whitman wrote "O Captain! My Captain!"*

PASSIVE: *"O Captain! My Captain!" was written by Walt Whitman.*

To form the passive voice, use a form of *be* with the past participle of the verb.

WATCH OUT! Use the passive voice sparingly. It can make writing awkward and less direct.

AWKWARD: *"The Monkey's Paw" is a short story that was written by W. W. Jacobs.*

BETTER: *W. W. Jacobs wrote the short story "The Monkey's Paw."*

There are occasions when you will choose to use the passive voice because

- you want to emphasize the receiver: *The king was shot.*
- the doer is unknown: *My books were stolen.*
- the doer is unimportant: *French is spoken here.*

4 Modifiers

Modifiers are words or groups of words that change or limit the meanings of other words. Adjectives and adverbs are common modifiers.

4.1 ADJECTIVES

Adjectives modify nouns and pronouns by telling which one, what kind, how many, or how much.

> WHICH ONE: *this, that, these, those*
> EXAMPLE: *This poem uses no capital letters.*
> WHAT KIND: *electric, bright, small, open*
> EXAMPLE: *An open flame would kill the moth.*
> HOW MANY: *one, several, both, none, each*
> EXAMPLE: *The moth wants one moment of beauty.*
> HOW MUCH: *more, less, enough, as much*
> EXAMPLE: *I think the cockroach has more sense than the moth.*

4.2 PREDICATE ADJECTIVES

Most adjectives come before the nouns they modify, as in the examples above. A **predicate adjective,** however, follows a linking verb and describes the subject.

> EXAMPLE: *My friends are very intelligent.*

Be especially careful to use adjectives (not adverbs) after such linking verbs as *look, feel, grow, taste,* and *smell.*

> EXAMPLE: *The bread smells wonderful.*

4.3 ADVERBS

Adverbs modify verbs, adjectives, and other adverbs by telling where, when, how, or to what extent.

> WHERE: *The children played outside.*
> WHEN: *The author spoke yesterday.*
> HOW: *We walked slowly behind the leader.*
> TO WHAT EXTENT: *He worked very hard.*

Adverbs may occur in many places in sentences, both before and after the words they modify.

> EXAMPLES: *Suddenly the wind shifted.*
> *The wind suddenly shifted.*
> *The wind shifted suddenly.*

4.4 ADJECTIVE OR ADVERB?

Many adverbs are formed by adding *-ly* to adjectives.

> EXAMPLES: *sweet, sweetly; gentle, gently*

However, *-ly* added to a noun will usually yield an adjective.

> EXAMPLES: *friend, friendly; woman, womanly*

4.5 COMPARISON OF MODIFIERS

Modifiers can be used to compare two or more things. The form of a modifier shows the degree of comparison. Both adjectives and adverbs have **comparative** and **superlative** forms.

The **comparative form** is used to compare two things, groups, or actions.

> EXAMPLES: *His father's hands were stronger than his own.*
> *My father was more courageous than I am.*

The **superlative form** is used to compare more than two things, groups, or actions.

> EXAMPLES: *His father's hands were the strongest in the family.*
> *My father was the most courageous of us all.*

4.6 REGULAR COMPARISONS

Most one-syllable and some two-syllable adjectives and adverbs have comparatives and superlatives formed by adding *-er* and *-est.* All three-syllable and most two-syllable modifiers have comparatives and superlatives formed with *more* or *most.*

Modifier	Comparative	Superlative
small	smaller	smallest
thin	thinner	thinnest
sleepy	sleepier	sleepiest
useless	more useless	most useless
precisely	more precisely	most precisely

> **WATCH OUT!** Note that spelling changes must sometimes be made to form the comparatives and superlatives of modifiers.
>
> EXAMPLES: *friendly, friendlier* (Change *y* to *i* and add the ending.)
> *sad, sadder* (Double the final consonant and add the ending.)

4.7 IRREGULAR COMPARISONS

Some commonly used modifiers have irregular comparative and superlative forms. They are listed in the chart. You may wish to memorize them.

Modifier	Comparative	Superlative
good	better	best
bad	worse	worst
far	farther *or* further	farthest *or* furthest
little	less *or* lesser	least
many	more	most
well	better	best
much	more	most

4.8 PROBLEMS WITH MODIFIERS

Study the tips that follow to avoid common mistakes:

Farther and Further Use *farther* for distances; use *further* for everything else.

Double Comparisons Make a comparison by using *-er/-est* or by using *more/most*. Using *-er* with *more* or using *-est* with *most* is incorrect.

INCORRECT: *I like her more better than she likes me.*

CORRECT: *I like her better than she likes me.*

Illogical Comparisons An illogical or confusing comparison results when two unrelated things are compared or when something is compared with itself. The word *other* or the word *else* should be used when comparing an individual member to the rest of a group.

ILLOGICAL: *The cockroach is smarter than any insect.* (implies that the cockroach isn't an insect)

LOGICAL: *The cockroach is smarter than any other insect.* (identifies that the cockroach is an insect)

Bad vs. Badly *Bad,* always an adjective, is used before a noun or after a linking verb. *Badly,* always an adverb, never modifies a noun. Be sure to use the right form after a linking verb.

INCORRECT: *Ed felt badly after his team lost.*

CORRECT: *Ed felt bad after his team lost.*

DANGLING: *Looking out the window, his brother was seen driving by.*

CLEARER: *Looking out the window, Josh saw his brother driving by.*

Grammar Practice

Choose the correct word or words from each pair in parentheses.
1. Mark Twain's attempt at studying the law did not go (good, well).
2. That wasn't the (worse, worst) of his many occupations, however.
3. He actually wasn't a (bad, badly) riverboat pilot.
4. He didn't have (no, any) confidence as a newspaper editor.
5. Still, that turned out to be the (more, most) satisfying job he ever had.

Grammar Practice

Rewrite each sentence that contains a misplaced or dangling modifier. Write "correct" if the sentence is written correctly.
1. Mark Twain discovered that he was a good storyteller working as an editor.
2. Twain often added exciting details to his stories.
3. It didn't matter to Twain whether all of the details were true in his articles.
4. He wrote 16 different articles about a single hay wagon in the paper.
5. When all else failed, he made up events.

5 The Sentence and Its Parts

A **sentence** is a group of words used to express a complete thought. A complete sentence has a subject and a predicate.

For more information, see **Quick Reference: The Sentence and Its Parts,** page R31.

5.1 KINDS OF SENTENCES

There are four basic types of sentences.

Type	Definition	Example
Declarative	states a fact, a wish, an intent, or a feeling	This poem is about Abraham Lincoln.
Interrogative	asks a question	Did you understand the metaphor?
Imperative	gives a command or direction	Read it more closely.
Exclamatory	expresses strong feeling or excitement	Whitman really admired Lincoln!

5.2 COMPOUND SUBJECTS AND PREDICATES

A compound subject consists of two or more subjects that share the same verb. They are typically joined by the coordinating conjunctions *and* or *or*.

EXAMPLE: *A short story or novel will keep you engaged.*

A compound predicate consists of two or more predicates that share the same subject. They too are usually joined by a coordinating conjunction such as *and, but,* or *or*.

EXAMPLE: *The class finished all the poetry but did not read the short stories.*

5.3 COMPLEMENTS

A **complement** is a word or group of words that completes the meaning of the sentence. Some sentences contain only a subject and a verb. Most sentences, however, require additional words placed after the verb to complete the meaning of the sentence. There are three kinds of complements: direct objects, indirect objects, and subject complements.

Direct objects are words or word groups that receive the action of action verbs. A direct object answers the question *what* or *whom*.

EXAMPLES: *Ellis recited the poem.* (Recited what?)
His performance entertained the class. (Entertained whom?)

Indirect objects tell to whom or what or for whom or what the actions of verbs are performed. Indirect objects come before direct objects. In the following examples, the indirect objects are highlighted.

EXAMPLES: *The teacher gave the speech a good grade.* (Gave to what?)
He showed his father the teacher's comments. (Showed to whom?)

Subject complements come after linking verbs and identify or describe the subjects. A subject complement that names or identifies a subject is called a **predicate nominative.** Predicate nominatives include **predicate nouns** and **predicate pronouns.**

EXAMPLES: *My friends are very hard workers.*
The best writer in the class is she.

A subject complement that describes a subject is called a **predicate adjective.**

EXAMPLE: *The pianist appeared very energetic.*

6 Phrases

A **phrase** is a group of related words that does not contain a subject and a predicate but functions in a sentence as a single part of speech.

6.1 PREPOSITIONAL PHRASES

A **prepositional phrase** is a phrase that consists of a preposition, its object, and any modifiers of the object. Prepositional phrases that modify nouns or pronouns are called **adjective phrases.** Prepositional phrases that modify verbs, adjectives, or adverbs are **adverb phrases.**

ADJECTIVE PHRASE: *The central character of the story is a villain.*

ADVERB PHRASE: *He reveals his nature in the first scene.*

6.2 APPOSITIVES AND APPOSITIVE PHRASES

An **appositive** is a noun or pronoun that identifies or renames another noun or pronoun. An **appositive phrase** includes an appositive and modifiers of it. An appositive usually follows the noun or pronoun it identifies.

An appositive can be either **essential** or **nonessential.** An **essential appositive** provides information that is needed to identify what is referred to by the preceding noun or pronoun.

EXAMPLE: *The biography is about the courageous African American abolitionist Harriet Tubman.*

A **nonessential appositive** adds extra information about a noun or pronoun whose meaning is already clear. Nonessential appositives and appositive phrases are set off with commas.

EXAMPLE: *The story, a biography, describes how activists rescued people from slavery.*

7 Verbals and Verbal Phrases

A **verbal** is a verb form that is used as a noun, an adjective, or an adverb. A **verbal phrase** consists of a verbal along with its modifiers and complements. There are three kinds of verbals: **infinitives, participles,** and **gerunds.**

7.1 INFINITIVES AND INFINITIVE PHRASES

An **infinitive** is a verb form that usually begins with *to* and functions as a noun, an adjective, or an adverb. An **infinitive phrase** consists of an infinitive plus its modifiers and complements.

NOUN: *To show bravery is challenging.* (subject)
Harriet Tubman did not want to obey the laws of slavery. (direct object)

Her greatest trait was to become too courageous. (predicate nominative)

ADJECTIVE: *That was a trait to admire.* (adjective modifying *trait*)

ADVERB: *She joined the Underground Railroad to satisfy her anger.* (adverb modifying *created*)

Because *to* often precedes infinitives, it is usually easy to recognize them. However, sometimes *to* may be omitted.

EXAMPLE: *Her husband helped her [to] forgive herself.*

7.2 PARTICIPLES AND PARTICIPIAL PHRASES

A **participle** is a verb form that functions as an adjective. Like adjectives, participles modify nouns and pronouns. Most participles are present-participle forms, ending in *-ing,* or past-participle forms ending in *-ed* or *-en.* In the examples below, the participles are highlighted.

MODIFYING A NOUN: *The dying man had a smile on his face.*

MODIFYING A PRONOUN: *Frustrated, everyone abandoned the cause.*

Participial phrases are participles with all their modifiers and complements.

MODIFYING A NOUN: *The dogs searching for survivors are well trained.*

MODIFYING A PRONOUN: *Having approved your proposal, we are ready to act.*

7.3 DANGLING AND MISPLACED PARTICIPLES

A participle or participial phrase should be placed as close as possible to the word that it modifies. Otherwise the meaning of the sentence may not be clear.

MISPLACED: *The boys were looking for squirrels searching the trees.*

CLEARER: *The boys searching the trees were looking for squirrels.*

A participle or participial phrase that does not clearly modify anything in a sentence is called a **dangling participle.**

A dangling participle causes confusion because it appears to modify a word that it cannot sensibly modify. Correct a dangling participle by providing a word for the participle to modify.

DANGLING: *Running like the wind*, my hat fell off. (The hat wasn't running.)

CLEARER: *Running like the wind*, I lost my hat.

7.4 GERUNDS AND GERUND PHRASES

A **gerund** is a verb form ending in *-ing* that functions as a noun. Gerunds may perform any function nouns perform.

SUBJECT: *Jogging* is my favorite exercise.
DIRECT OBJECT: My sister loves *jogging*.
INDIRECT OBJECT: She gave *jogging* a try last year.
SUBJECT COMPLEMENT: Their real passion is *jogging*.
OBJECT OF PREPOSITION: The effects of *jogging*.

Gerund phrases are gerunds with all their modifiers and complements.

SUBJECT: *Using the Underground Railroad* was Tubman's plan.
OBJECT OF PREPOSITION: *She flourished greatly* after defying the slave owners.
APPOSITIVE: Her family, *remembering Tubman's courage and determination*, admired her.

Grammar Practice

Rewrite each sentence, adding the type of phrase shown in parentheses.

1. I read an excerpt from Anne Frank's diary. (infinitive phrase)
2. Anne was able to maintain her faith in other people. (gerund phrase)
3. Peter Van Daan eventually became Anne's good friend. (appositive phrase)
4. The Nazis found the Franks' hiding place. (prepositional phrase)
5. I know more about World War II. (participial phrase)

8 Clauses

A **clause** is a group of words that contains a subject and a predicate. There are two kinds of clauses: main and subordinate.

8.1 MAIN AND SUBORDINATE CLAUSES

A **main (independent) clause** can stand alone as a sentence.

MAIN CLAUSE: I enjoyed "Marigolds."

A sentence may contain more than one main clause.

EXAMPLE: I read it twice, and I gave it to a friend.

In the preceding example, the coordinating conjunction *and* joins two main clauses.

For more coordinating conjunctions, see Quick Reference: Parts of Speech, page R29.

A **subordinate (dependent) clause** cannot stand alone as a sentence. It is subordinate to, or dependent on, a main clause.

EXAMPLE: *After I read it*, I recommended it to my friends.

The highlighted clause cannot stand by itself.

8.2 ADJECTIVE CLAUSES

An **adjective clause** is a subordinate clause used as an adjective. It usually follows the noun or pronoun it modifies.

EXAMPLE: The lesson *that the story tells* is about understanding the vulnerabilities of adulthood.

Adjective clauses are typically introduced by the relative pronouns *who, whom, whose, which,* and *that.*

For more information, see Relative Pronouns, page R38.

EXAMPLE: Lizabeth, *who was angered by her father's crying*, tore up her neighbor's flowerbed.

An adjective clause can be either essential or nonessential. An **essential adjective clause** provides information that is necessary to identify the preceding noun or pronoun.

> **EXAMPLE:** *She enjoyed disturbing John Burke who would curse at her.*

A **nonessential adjective clause** adds additional information about a noun or pronoun whose meaning is already clear. Nonessential clauses are set off with commas.

> **EXAMPLE:** *The marigolds, which were brilliant shades of yellow and gold, were destroyed by the children.*

8.3 ADVERB CLAUSES

An **adverb clause** is a subordinate clause that is used to modify a verb, an adjective, or an adverb. It is introduced by a subordinating conjunction.

For examples of subordinating conjunctions, see **Noun Clauses**, page R47.

Adverb clauses typically occur at the beginning or end of sentences.

> **MODIFYING A VERB:** *When he got bored, Nick told stories.*
>
> **MODIFYING AN ADVERB:** *Most people study more than Bob does.*
>
> **MODIFYING AN ADJECTIVE:** *He was excited because a cyclone was forming.*

TIP An adverb clause should be followed by a comma when it comes before a main clause. When an adverb clause comes after a main clause, a comma may not be needed.

8.4 NOUN CLAUSES

A **noun clause** is a subordinate clause that is used as a noun. A noun clause may be used as a subject, a direct object, an indirect object, a predicate nominative, or the object of a preposition. Noun clauses are introduced either by pronouns, such as *that, what, who, whoever, which,* and *whose,* or by subordinating conjunctions, such as *how, when, where, why,* and *whether.*

For more subordinating conjunctions, see **Quick Reference: Parts of Speech,** page R29.

TIP Because the same words may introduce adjective and noun clauses, you need to consider how a clause functions within its sentence. To determine if a clause is a noun clause, try substituting *something* or *someone* for the clause. If you can do it, it is probably a noun clause.

> **EXAMPLES:** *I know whose woods these are.* ("I know *something.*" The clause is a noun clause, a direct object of the verb *know.*)
> *Give a copy to whoever wants one.* ("Give a copy to *someone.*" The clause is a noun clause, an object of the preposition *to.*)

9 The Structure of Sentences

When classified by their structure, there are four kinds of sentences: simple, compound, complex, and compound-complex.

9.1 SIMPLE SENTENCES

A **simple sentence** is a sentence that has one main clause and no subordinate clauses.

> **EXAMPLES:** *Sam ran to the theater.*
> *Max waited in front of the theater.*

A simple sentence may contain a compound subject or a compound verb.

> **EXAMPLES:** *Sam and Max went to the movie.* (compound subject)
> *They clapped and cheered at their favorite parts.* (compound verb)

9.2 COMPOUND SENTENCES

A **compound sentence** consists of two or more main clauses. The clauses in compound sentences are joined with commas and coordinating conjunctions (*and, but, or, nor, yet, for, so*) or with semicolons. Like simple sentences, compound sentences do not contain any subordinate clauses.

EXAMPLES: *Sam likes action movies, but Max prefers comedies.*
The actor jumped from one building to another; he barely made the final leap.

9.3 COMPLEX SENTENCES

A **complex sentence** consists of one main clause and one or more subordinate clauses.

EXAMPLES: *One should not complain unless one has a better solution.*
Mr. Neiman, who is an artist, sketched pictures until the sun went down.

9.4 COMPOUND-COMPLEX SENTENCES

A **compound-complex sentence** contains two or more main clauses and one or more subordinate clauses. Compound-complex sentences are both compound and complex.

COMPOUND: *All the students knew the answer, yet they were too shy to volunteer.*

COMPOUND-COMPLEX: *All the students knew the answer that their teacher expected, yet they were too shy to volunteer.*

9.5 PARALLEL STRUCTURE

When you write sentences, make sure that coordinate parts are equivalent, or **parallel**, in structure. For instance, be sure items you list in a series or contrast for emphasis are parallel.

NOT PARALLEL: *I want to lose weight, becoming a musician, and good grades.* (*To lose weight* is an infinitive phrase, *becoming a musician* is a gerund phrase, and *grades* is a noun.)

PARALLEL: *I want to lose weight, to become a musician, and to get good grades.* (*To lose, to become,* and *to get* are all infinitives.)

NOT PARALLEL: *I not only want to lose weight, I'm keeping it off, too.* (*To lose weight* is an infinitive phrase; *keeping it off* is a gerund phrase.)

PARALLEL: *I not only want to lose weight, I want to keep it off, too.* (*To lose weight* and *to keep it off* are both infinitive

phrases. To make them both infinitive, it is necessary to change *am* to an action verb. Now the contrast set up by *not only* adds emphasis to the second part of the statement.)

Grammar Practice

Revise each sentence to make its parts parallel.

1. Jewell Parker Rhodes wrote "Block Party" about her old neighborhood and to publish a memoir of it.
2. In the story, she mentions many colorful characters, riding her bike with her sister, and watching the world from her front stoop.
3. With her friends, Rhodes played hide and seek in the laundry hanging out to dry, would slide down the banisters in the house, and rode a red tricycle through the kitchen.
4. A block party is when the street is closed off to traffic, hydrants were turned on by the fire department, and the neighbors gather for a picnic.
5. Rhodes went on to earn degrees in drama criticism, English, and a third degree in creative writing.
6. She now writes novels, nonfiction, and even for magazines!

10 Writing Complete Sentences

Remember, a sentence is a group of words that expresses a complete thought. In writing that you wish to share with a reader, try to avoid both sentence fragments and run-on sentences.

10.1 CORRECTING FRAGMENTS

A **sentence fragment** is a group of words that is only part of a sentence. It does not express a complete thought and may be confusing to a reader or listener. A sentence fragment may be lacking a subject, a predicate, or both.

FRAGMENT: *Worried about not doing well.* (no subject)

CORRECTED: *Laura worried about not doing well.*

FRAGMENT: *Her mother and father.* (no predicate)

CORRECTED: *Her mother and father were both highly successful.*

FRAGMENT: *In a gentle way.* (neither subject nor predicate)

CORRECTED: *They tried to encourage her in a gentle way.*

In your writing, fragments may be a result of haste or incorrect punctuation. Sometimes fixing a fragment will be a matter of attaching it to a preceding or following sentence.

FRAGMENT: *Laura did her best. But never felt satisfied.*

CORRECTED: *Laura did her best but never felt satisfied.*

10.2 CORRECTING RUN-ON SENTENCES

A **run-on sentence** is made up of two or more sentences written as though they were one. Some run-ons have no punctuation within them. Others may have only commas where conjunctions or stronger punctuation marks are necessary.

Use your judgment in correcting run-on sentences, as you have choices. You can change a run-on to two sentences if the thoughts are not closely connected. If the thoughts are closely related, you can keep the run-on as one sentence by adding a semicolon or a conjunction.

RUN-ON: *She joined more clubs her friendships suffered.*

MAKE TWO SENTENCES: *She joined more clubs. Her friendships suffered.*

RUN-ON: *She joined more clubs they took up all her time.*

USE A SEMICOLON: *She joined more clubs; they took up all her time.*

ADD A CONJUNCTION: *She joined more clubs, but they took up all her time.*

WATCH OUT! When you form compound sentences, make sure you use appropriate punctuation: a comma before a coordinating conjunction, a semicolon when there is no coordinating conjunction. A very common mistake is to use a comma alone instead of a comma and a conjunction. This error is called a *comma splice*.

INCORRECT: *He finished the job, he left the village.*

CORRECT: *He finished the job, and he left the village.*

11 Subject-Verb Agreement

The subject and verb in a clause must agree in number. Agreement means that if the subject is singular, the verb is also singular, and if the subject is plural, the verb is also plural.

11.1 BASIC AGREEMENT

Fortunately, agreement between subjects and verbs in English is simple. Most verbs show the difference between singular and plural only in the third person of the present tense. In the present tense, the third-person singular form ends in **-s**.

Present-Tense Verb Forms	
Singular	Plural
I sleep	we sleep
you sleep	you sleep
she he it sleeps	they sleep

11.2 AGREEMENT WITH *BE*

The verb **be** presents special problems in agreement, because this verb does not follow the usual verb patterns.

Forms of *Be*			
Present Tense		Past Tense	
Singular	Plural	Singular	Plural
I am	we are	I was	we were
you are	you are	you were	you were
she he it is	they are	she he it was	they were

Grammar R49

11.3 WORDS BETWEEN SUBJECT AND VERB

A verb agrees only with its subject. When words come between a subject and a verb, ignore them when considering proper agreement. Identify the subject and make sure the verb agrees with it.

> EXAMPLES: *Whipped cream* served with berries *is* my favorite sweet.
>
> A *study* by scientists *recommends* eating berries.

11.4 AGREEMENT WITH COMPOUND SUBJECTS

Use plural verbs with most compound subjects joined by the word *and.*

> EXAMPLE: *My father and his friends play chess every day.*

To confirm that you need a plural verb, you could substitute the plural pronoun *they* for *my father and his friends.*

If a compound subject is thought of as a unit, use a singular verb. Test this by substituting the singular pronoun *it.*

> EXAMPLE: *Peanut butter and jelly [it] is my brother's favorite sandwich.*

Use a singular verb with a compound subject that is preceded by *each, every,* or *many a.*

> EXAMPLE: *Each novel and short story seems grounded in personal experience.*

When the parts of a compound subject are joined by *or, nor,* or the correlative conjunctions *either . . . or* or *neither . . . nor,* make the verb agree with the noun or pronoun nearest the verb.

> EXAMPLES: *Cookies or ice cream is my favorite dessert.*
> *Either Cheryl or her friends are being invited.*
> *Neither ice storms nor snow is predicted today.*

11.5 PERSONAL PRONOUNS AS SUBJECTS

When using a personal pronoun as a subject, make sure to match it with the correct form of the verb *be.* (See the chart in Section 11.2.) Note especially that the pronoun *you* takes the forms *are* and *were,* regardless of whether it is singular or plural.

> **WATCH OUT!** *You is* and *you was* are nonstandard forms and should be avoided in writing and speaking. *We was* and *they was* are also forms to be avoided.
>
> INCORRECT: *You was* a good student.
> CORRECT: *You were* a good student.
> INCORRECT: *They was* starting a new school.
> CORRECT: *They were* starting a new school.

11.6 INDEFINITE PRONOUNS AS SUBJECTS

Some indefinite pronouns are always singular; some are always plural.

Singular Indefinite Pronouns			
another	either	neither	one
anybody	everybody	nobody	somebody
anyone	everyone	no one	someone
anything	everything	nothing	something
each	much		

> EXAMPLES: *Each* of the writers *was given* an award. *Somebody* in the room upstairs *is sleeping.*

Plural Indefinite Pronouns			
both	few	many	several

> EXAMPLES: *Many* of the books in our library *are* not in circulation. *Few have been returned* recently.

Still other indefinite pronouns may be either singular or plural.

Singular or Plural Indefinite Pronouns		
all	more	none
any	most	some

The number of the indefinite pronoun *any* or *none* often depends on the intended meaning.

> EXAMPLES: *Any* of these topics *has* potential for a good article. (any one topic)
> *Any* of these topics *have* potential for good articles. (all of the many topics)

The indefinite pronouns *all, some, more, most,* and *none* are singular when they refer to quantities or parts of things. They are plural when they refer to numbers of individual things. Context will usually provide a clue.

> EXAMPLES: *All* of the flour *is* gone. (referring to a quantity)
> *All* of the flowers *are* gone. (referring to individual items)

11.7 INVERTED SENTENCES

A sentence in which the subject follows the verb is called an **inverted sentence.** A subject can follow a verb or part of a verb phrase in a question, a sentence beginning with *here* or *there,* or a sentence in which an adjective, an adverb, or a phrase is placed first.

> EXAMPLES: There clearly *are* far too many *cooks* in this kitchen.
> What *is* the correct *ingredient* for this stew?
> Far from the frazzled cooks *stands* the *master chef*.

TIP To check subject-verb agreement in some inverted sentences, place the subject before the verb. For example, change *There are many people* to *Many people are there.*

11.8 SENTENCES WITH PREDICATE NOMINATIVES

In a sentence containing a predicate noun (nominative), the verb should agree with the subject, not the predicate noun.

> EXAMPLES: The *poems* of Walt Whitman *are* a unique record of U.S. history. (Poems is the subject—not *record*—and it takes the plural verb *are*.)

> One unique *record* of U.S. history is the poems of Walt Whitman. (The subject is *record*—not *poems*—and it takes the singular verb *is*.)

11.9 DON'T AND DOESN'T AS AUXILIARY VERBS

The auxiliary verb *doesn't* is used with singular subjects and with the personal pronouns *she, he,* and *it.* The auxiliary verb *don't* is used with plural subjects and with the personal pronouns *I, we, you,* and *they.*

> SINGULAR: *Doesn't* the *poem* "O Captain! My Captain!" sound almost like a news report?
> *It doesn't* sound like a poem, even though it rhymes.
> PLURAL: *People don't* know enough about United States President Abraham Lincoln. *Don't they* think history is important?

11.10 COLLECTIVE NOUNS AS SUBJECTS

Collective nouns are singular nouns that name groups of persons or things. *Team,* for example, is the collective name of a group of individuals. A collective noun takes a singular verb when the group acts as a single unit. It takes a plural verb when the members of the group act separately.

> EXAMPLES: Our team usually wins. (The team as a whole wins.)
> The faculty vote differently on most issues. (The individual members of the faculty vote.)

11.11 RELATIVE PRONOUNS AS SUBJECTS

When the relative pronoun *who, which,* or *that* is used as a subject in an adjective clause, the verb in the clause must agree in number with the antecedent of the pronoun.

> SINGULAR: The story *that affects me the most* is "The Diary of a Young Girl."

The antecedent of the relative pronoun *that* is the singular *poem*; therefore, *that* is singular and must take the singular verb *affects.*

PLURAL: *Rita Dove and Audre Lorde are African-American poets* who write about life's issues.

The antecedent of the relative pronoun *who* is the plural compound subject *Rita Dove and Audre Lorde.* Therefore *who* is plural, and it takes the plural verb *write.*

Grammar Practice

Locate the subject in each sentence below. Then choose the correct verb form.

1. Mark Twain's novel *The Adventures of Tom Sawyer* (describes, describe) the escapades of a young boy growing up in a Mississippi River town.
2. (Doesn't, Don't) Tom have to whitewash a fence as punishment for playing hooky from school?
3. Nobody (realizes, realize) that Tom is tricking them into doing his work.
4. Tom falls in love with a new girl in town and (persuade, persuades) her to kiss him.
5. Huckleberry Finn and Tom (goes, go) to the graveyard and witness a murder.
6. Tom and his friend run away to an island to (become, becomes) pirates.
7. Tom (returns, return) home one night.
8. When Muff Potter's trial (begin, begins) Tom testifies.
9. Muff Potter is acquitted and the real murderer, Injun Joe, (flees, flee) the courtroom.
10. Tom and Huckleberry Finn (find, finds) buried treasure in a haunted house.

Vocabulary and Spelling

By learning and practicing vocabulary strategies, you'll know what to do when you encounter unfamiliar words while reading. You'll also know how to refine the words you use for different situations—personal, school, and work. Learning basic spelling rules and checking your spelling in a dictionary will help you spell words that you may not use frequently.

1 Using Context Clues

The context of a word is made up of the punctuation marks, words, sentences, and paragraphs that surround the word. A word's context can give you important clues about its meaning.

1.1 GENERAL CONTEXT

Sometimes you need to determine the meaning of an unfamiliar, ambiguous, or novel word by reading all the information in a passage.

> Stop teasing me! Just because you are a better tennis player than I am doesn't mean you should belittle my abilities.

You can figure out from the context that belittle means "make something less than it is."

1.2 IDIOMS, SLANG, AND FIGURATIVE LANGUAGE

An **idiom** is an expression whose overall meaning differs from the meaning of the individual words.

> A nasty case of the flu kept me under the weather. (Under the weather means "tired and sickly.")

Slang is informal language in which made-up words and ordinary words are used to mean something different from their meanings in formal English.

> I'm going to jazz up this salad with some walnuts. (Jazz up means "make more interesting.")

Figurative language is language that communicates meaning beyond the literal meaning of the words.

> The lone desert monument was like a sentinel standing guard. (Lone and standing guard help describe a sentinel.)

1.3 specific context clues

Sometimes writers help you understand the meanings of unfamiliar, ambiguous, or novel words by providing specific clues such as those shown in the chart.

Specific Context Clues		
Type of Clue	**Key Words/ Phrases**	**Example**
Definition or restatement of the meaning of the word	or, which is, that is, in other words, also known as, also called	Olympic gymnasts are very *limber,* or **flexible.**
Example following an unfamiliar word	such as, like, as if, for example, especially, including	We collected *kindling,* such as **dry twigs and branches,** to start the fire.
Comparison with a more familiar word or concept	as, like, also, similar to, in the same way, likewise	Kari's face was *luminous,* **like the rays of the sun.**
Contrast with a familiar word or experience	unlike, but, however, although, on the other hand, on the contrary	The summer was *sultry,* but the fall was **dry and cool.**
Cause-and-effect relationship in which one term is familiar	because, since, when, consequently, as a result, therefore	When the *tree fell across the road,* it **obstructed** traffic.

2 Analyzing Word Structure

Many words can be broken into smaller parts. These word parts include base words, roots, prefixes, and suffixes.

2.1 BASE WORDS

A **base word** is a word part that by itself is also a word. Other words or word parts can be added to base words to form new words.

2.2 ROOTS

A **root** is a word part that contains the core meaning of the word. Many English words contain roots that come from older languages such as Greek, Latin, Old English (Anglo-Saxon), and Norse. Knowing the meaning of the word's root can help you determine the word's meaning.

Root	Meaning	Example
aud (Latin)	hear	audio, audition
voc (Latin)	voice	vocal, invoke
mem, ment (Latin)	mind	memory, mental, mention
chron (Greek)	time	chronic, synchronize
gram (Greek)	something written	telegram, grammar
gen (Greek)	race, family	genesis, genre, genius
angr (Old Norse)	painfully constricted, sorrow	anger, anguish

2.3 PREFIXES

A **prefix** is a word part attached to the beginning of a word or word root. Most prefixes come from Greek, Latin, or Old English.

Prefix	Meaning	Example
mid-	middle, center	midnight
pro-	forward	proceed, procession
uni-	one	uniform, unicycle
tele-	view	telescope
multi-	many, much	multimedia, multivitamins

2.4 SUFFIXES

A **suffix** is a word part that appears at the end of a root or base word to form a new word. Some suffixes do not change word meaning. These suffixes are

- added to nouns to change the number of persons or objects
- added to verbs to change the tense
- added to modifiers to change the degree of comparison

Suffix	Meaning	Example
-s, -es	to change the number of a noun	lock + s = locks
-d, -ed, -ing	to change verb tense	stew + ed = stewed
-er, -est	to indicate comparison in modifiers	mild + er = milder soft + est = softest

Other suffixes can be added to the root or base to change the word's meaning. These suffixes can also determine a word's part of speech.

Suffix	Meaning	Example
-age	amount	footage
-able, -ible	able, inclined to	readable, tangible
-ant, -ent	a specific state or condition	pleasant, different

Strategies for Understanding Unfamiliar Words

- Look for any prefixes or suffixes. Remove them so that you can concentrate on the base word or the root.
- See if you recognize any elements—prefix, suffix, root, or base—of the word. You may be able to guess its meaning by analyzing one or two elements.
- Think about the way the word is used in the sentence. Use the context and the word parts to make a logical guess about the word's meaning.
- Look in a dictionary to see whether you are correct.

3 Understanding Word Origins

3.1 DEVELOPMENT OF THE ENGLISH LANGUAGE

During the past 2,000 years or so, English has developed from a language spoken by a few Germanic tribes into a language that is more widely spoken and written than any other in the world. Some experts, in fact, call today's English the first truly global language. Its most valuable characteristic is its ability to change and grow, adopting new words as the need arises. The history of the English language can be divided into three main periods.

Old English About the year AD 449, Germanic people who lived on the European continent along the North Sea began a series of invasions into Britain. At that time, Britain was inhabited by the Celts, whose native language was Gaelic. Over a period of years, the raiders conquered and settled in Britain. The conquerors, known today as the Anglo-Saxons, prospered in Britain. In time, Britain became "Engla land," and the Anglo-Saxon languages evolved into "Englisc," or what modern scholars call Old English.

Old English was very different from the English we speak today. It was harsher in sound, had no silent letters, and was written phonetically. Few examples of Old English remain in our current English vocabulary. Those that do exist, however, are common words for people, places, things, and actions.

man (*mann*)   wife (*wif*)   child (*cild*)
house (*hus*)   meat (*mete*)   drink (*drincan*)
sleep (*slæpan*)   live (*libban*)   fight (*feohtan*)

In the sixth and seventh centuries, missionaries from Rome and other Christian cities arrived in England, bringing with them their knowledge of religion and ancient languages. Among the most influential figures was St. Augustine, who converted thousands of Anglo-Saxons, including a king, to Christianity. As the Anglo-Saxons accepted this faith, they also accepted words from Latin and Greek.

Latin	Greek
candle	alphabet
cup	angel
priest	box
noon	demon
scripture	school

During the late eighth century, Viking invaders from Denmark and Norway settled in northeast England. As a result, Scandinavian words became part of Old English.

sky	knife	are
steak	leg	birth
they	skin	seat
window	them	their

Middle English The Norman Conquest brought great changes to England and its language. In 1066, England was defeated by the Normans, a people from an area in France. Their leader, William the Conqueror, staged a successful invasion of England and became the nation's new monarch. With William on the throne of England, Norman French became the language of the English court, government business, nobility, and scholars. Eventually, French words were adopted in everyday vocabulary as well.

The language that evolved is called Middle English. Middle English was not as harsh-sounding as Old English and borrowed many words from Norman French.

attorney	joint	mallet
baron	jolly	marriage
chivalry	laundry	merchandise
gown	lodge	petty

Norman French itself borrowed thousands of words from Latin and Greek, as well as from ancient Indian and Semitic languages. Consequently, Middle English also contained many of these foreign terms.

Latin	Greek	Indian	Semitic
language	circle	ginger	camel
library	hour	jungle	cinnamon
money	lantern	orange	coffee
serpent	leopard	sugar	lion
square	magnet	pepper	syrup

Modern English By the late 1400s, Middle English began to develop into Modern English. The various pronunciations, word forms, and spellings common to Middle English were becoming more uniform. One invention that aided this process was the printing press. Introduced to London around 1476, the printing press allowed printers to standardize the spellings of common English words. As a result, readers and writers of English became accustomed to following "rules" of spelling and grammar.

During this period, the English vocabulary also continued to grow as new ideas and discoveries demanded new words. As the English began to colonize and trade with other areas of the world, they borrowed foreign words. In time, the English vocabulary grew to include words from diverse languages, such as French, Dutch, Spanish, Italian, Portuguese, and Chinese. Many of these words stayed the way they were in their original languages.

French	Dutch	Spanish	Italian
ballet	boss	canyon	diva
beret	caboose	rodeo	carnival
mirage	dock	taco	spaghetti
vague	skate	tornado	studio

Portuguese	Chinese	Japanese	Native American
cashew	chow	kamikaze	caribou
mango	ginseng	karaoke	moccasin
jaguar	kung fu	sushi	papoose
yam	kow tow	tsunami	tomahawk

Today, the English language is still changing and absorbing new words. It is considered the international language of science and technology. It is also widely used in business and politics.

3.2 DICTIONARY AS A SOURCE OF WORD ORIGINS

Many dictionary entries provide information about a word's origin. This information often comes at the end of an entry, as in this example.

> **ge•om•e•try** (jē-ŏmʹĭ-trē) *n., pl.* **-tries**
> **1.** The mathematics of the properties, measurement, and relationships of points, lines, angles, surfaces, and solids. **2.** Configuration; arrangement. **3.** A physical arrangement suggesting geometric forms or lines. [From Greek *geōmetriā*, from *geōmetrein*, to measure land.]

3.3 WORD FAMILIES

Words that have the same root make up a word family and have related meanings. The charts below show some common Greek and Latin roots. Notice how the meanings of the example words are related to the meanings of their roots.

Latin Root	*circum*, around or about
English	**circumference** the boundary line of a circle
	circumnavigation the act of moving completely around
	circumstance a condition or fact surrounding an event
Greek Root	*monos*, **single or alone**
English	**monopoly** exclusive control by one group
	monologue a speech delivered by one person
	monotonous sounded or spoken in a single unvarying tone
French Root	*caval*, **a horse**
English	**calvary** troops trained to fight on horseback
	cavalcade a procession of riders or horse-drawn carriages

Vocabulary and Spelling

TIP Once you recognize a root in one English word, you will notice the same root in other words. Because these words develop from the same root, all words in the word family are similar in meaning.

4 Synonyms and Antonyms

4.1 SYNONYMS

Positive	Negative
slender	scrawny
thrifty	cheap
young	immature

A **synonym** is a word with a meaning similar to that of another word. You can find synonyms in a thesaurus or a dictionary. In a dictionary, synonyms are often given as part of the definition of the word. The following word pairs are synonyms:

satisfy/please   occasionally/sometimes
rob/steal   schedule/agenda

4.2 ANTONYMS

An **antonym** is a word with a meaning opposite that of another word. The following word pairs are antonyms:

accurate/incorrect   similar/different
fresh/stale   unusual/ordinary

5 Denotation and Connotation

5.1 DENOTATION

A word's dictionary meaning is called its **denotation.** For example, the denotation of the word *thin* is "having little flesh; spare; lean."

5.2 CONNOTATION

The images or feelings you connect to a word add a finer shade of meaning, called **connotation.** The connation of a word goes beyond its basic dictionary definition. Writers use connotations of words to communicate positive or negative feelings.

Make sure you understand the denotation and connotation of a word when you read it or use it in your writing.

6 Analogies

An **analogy** is a relationship between pairs of words. In an analogy question on a test, the words in one pair relate to each other the same way as the words in a second pair, one of which you have to choose. To complete an analogy, identify the relationship between the words in the first pair. Then choose the word that will cause the words in the second pair to relate to the other in the same way.

Analogies are often written as follows—

  cheap : expensive :: humid : dry

If the analogy is read out loud, you would say, "cheap is to expensive as humid is to dry."

There are various ways the word pairs in an analogy can be related.

- Words can be related because they are opposites, or antonyms, as in the example above.
- Words can be related because they are similar, or synonyms.
  tired : exhausted :: talkative : chatty
- Words can be related by function. If the first pair of words contains a noun and its function, the second pair should also.
  helmet : protection :: lamp : illumination
- Words can be related by description. If the first pair or words contains a noun and a word that describes it, the second pair should also.
  rain : wet :: lettuce : green

7 Homonyms, Homographs, and Homophones

7.1 HOMONYMS

Homonyms are words that have the same spelling and sound but have different meanings.

The snake shed its skin in the shed behind the house.

Shed can mean "to lose by natural process," but an identically spelled word means "a small structure."

Sometimes only one of the meanings of a homonym may be familiar to you. Use context clues to help you figure out the meaning of an unfamiliar word.

7.2 HOMOGRAPHS

Homographs are words that are spelled the same but have different meanings and origins. Some are also pronounced differently, as in these examples.

Please close the door. (klōz)

That was a close call. (klōs)

If you see a word used in a way that is unfamiliar to you, check a dictionary to see if it is a homograph.

7.3 HOMOPHONES

Homophones are words that sound alike but have different meanings and spellings. The following homophones are frequently misused:

it's/its   they're/their/there
to/too/two   stationary/stationery

Many misused homophones are pronouns and contractions. Whenever you are unsure whether to write *your* or *you're* and *who's* or *whose*, ask yourself if you mean *you are* and *who is/has*. If you do, write the contraction. For other homophones, such as *fair* and *fare,* use the meaning of the word to help you decide which one to use.

8 Words with Multiple Meanings

Some words have acquired additional meanings over time that are based on the original meaning.

I had to be replaced in the cast of the play because of the cast on my arm.

These two uses of cast have different meanings, but both of them have the same origin. You will find all the meanings of cast listed in one entry in the dictionary.

9 Specialized Vocabulary

Specialized vocabulary is special terms suited to a particular field of study or work. For example, science, mathematics, and history all have their own technical or specialized vocabularies. To figure out specialized terms, you can use context clues and reference sources, such as dictionaries on specific subjects, atlases, or manuals.

10 Using Reference Sources

10.1 DICTIONARIES

A **general dictionary** will tell you not only a word's definitions but also its pronunciation, parts of speech, and history and origin, or etymology.

① tan·gi·ble ② (tăn´jə-bəl) ③ *adj.*
1a. Discernible by the touch; palpable. **b.** Possible to touch. **c.** Possible to be treated as fact; real or concrete. **2.** Possible to understand or realize. **3.** Relating to or being property of a physical nature, such as land, objects, and goods. [Late Latin *tangibilis,* from Latin *tangere,* to touch] ⑤

① Entry word
② Pronunciation
③ Part of speech
④ Definitions
⑤ Etymology

A **specialized dictionary** focuses on terms related to a particular field of study or work. Use a dictionary to check the spelling of any word you are unsure of in your English class and other classes as well.

10.2 THESAURI

A **thesaurus** (plural, *thesauri*) is a dictionary of synonyms. A thesaurus can be especially helpful when you find yourself using the same modifiers over and over again.

10.3 SYNONYM FINDERS

A **synonym finder** is often included in wordprocessing software. It enables you to highlight a word and be shown a display of its synonyms.

10.4 GLOSSARIES

A **glossary** is a list of specialized terms and their definitions. It is often found in the back of a book and sometimes includes pronunciations. Many textbooks contain glossaries. In fact, this textbook has three glossaries: the **Glossary of Literary and Informational Terms,** the **Glossary of Academic Vocabulary,** and the **Glossary of Critical Vocabulary.** Use these glossaries to help you understand how terms are used in this textbook.

11 Spelling Rules

11.1 WORDS ENDING IN A SILENT E

Before adding a suffix beginning with a vowel or **y** to a word ending in a silent **e,** drop the **e** (with some exceptions).

    amaze + -ing = amazing
    love + -able = lovable
    create + -ed = created
    nerve + -ous = nervous

Exceptions: *change + -able = changeable; courage + -ous = courageous*

When adding a suffix beginning with a consonant to a word ending in a silent **e,** keep the **e** (with some exceptions).

    late + -ly = lately
    spite + -ful = spiteful
    noise + -less = noiseless
    state + -ment = statement

Exceptions: *truly, argument, ninth, wholly, awful, and others*

When a suffix beginning with **a** or **o** is added to a word with a final silent **e,** the final **e** is usually retained if it is preceded by a soft **c** or a soft **g.**

    bridge + -able = bridgeable
    peace + -able = peaceable
    outrage + -ous = outrageous
    advantage + -ous = advantageous

When a suffix beginning with a vowel is added to words ending in **ee** or **oe,** the final, silent **e** is retained.

    agree + -ing = agreeing
    free + -ing = freeing
    hoe + -ing = hoeing
    see + -ing = seeing

11.2 WORDS ENDING IN Y

Before adding most suffixes to a word that ends in **y** preceded by a consonant, change the **y** to **i.**

    easy + -est = easiest
    crazy + -est = craziest
    silly + -ness = silliness
    marry + -age = marriage

Exceptions: *dryness, shyness,* and *slyness*

However, when you add **-ing,** the **y** does not change.

    empty + -ed = emptied   but
    empty + -ing = emptying

When adding a suffix to a word that ends in **y** preceded by a vowel, the **y** usually does not change.

    play + -er = player
    employ + -ed = employed
    coy + -ness = coyness
    pay + -able = payable

11.3 WORDS ENDING IN A CONSONANT

In one-syllable words that end in one consonant preceded by one short vowel, double the final consonant before adding a suffix beginning with a vowel, such as **-ed** or **-ing.** These are sometimes called 1+1+1 words.

    dip + -ed = dipped
    set + -ing = setting
    slim + -est = slimmest
    fit + -er = fitter

The rule does not apply to words of one syllable that end in a consonant preceded by two vowels.

    feel + -ing = feeling
    peel + -ed = peeled
    reap + -ed = reaped
    loot + -ed = looted

In words of more than one syllable, double the final consonant when (1) the word ends with one consonant preceded by one vowel and (2) when the word is accented on the last syllable.

   be·gin´ per·mit´ re·fer´

In the following examples, note that in the new words formed with suffixes, the accent remains on the same syllable:

   be·gin´ + -ing = be·gin´ning = beginning
   per·mit´ + -ed = per·mit´ted = permitted

Exceptions: In some words with more than one syllable, though the accent remains on the same syllable when a suffix is added, the final consonant is nevertheless not doubled, as in the following examples:

   tra´vel + er = tra´vel·er = traveler
   mar´ket + er = mar´ket·er = marketer

In the following examples, the accent does not remain on the same syllable; thus, the final consonant is not doubled:

   re·fer´ + -ence = ref´er·ence = reference
   con·fer´ + -ence = con´fer·ence = conference

11.4 PREFIXES AND SUFFIXES

When adding a prefix to a word, do not change the spelling of the base word. When a prefix creates a double letter, keep both letters.

   dis- + approve = disapprove
   re- + build = rebuild
   ir- + regular = irregular
   mis- + spell = misspell
   anti- + trust = antitrust
   il- + logical = illogical

When adding **-ly** to a word ending in **l**, keep both **l**'s. When adding **-ness** to a word ending in **n**, keep both **n**'s.

   careful + -ly = carefully
   sudden + -ness = suddenness
   final + -ly = finally
   thin + -ness = thinness

11.5 FORMING PLURAL NOUNS

To form the plural of most nouns, just add **-s**.

   prizes dreams circles stations

For most singular nouns ending in **o**, add **-s**.

   solos halos studios photos pianos

For a few nouns ending in **o**, add **-es**.

   heroes tomatoes potatoes echoes

When the singular noun ends in **s, sh, ch, x,** or **z**, add **-es**.

   waitresses brushes ditches
   axes buzzes

When a singular noun ends in **y** with a consonant before it, change the **y** to **i** and add **-es**.

army—armies	**candy—candies**
baby—babies	**diary—diaries**
ferry—ferries	**conspiracy—conspiracies**

When a vowel (**a, e, i, o, u**) comes before the **y**, just add **-s**.

boy—boys	**way—ways**
array—arrays	**alloy—alloys**
weekday—weekdays	**jockey—jockeys**

For most nouns ending in **f** or **fe**, change the **f** to **v** and add **-es** or **-s**.

life—lives	**shelf—shelves**
thief—thieves	**loaf—loaves**
calf—calves	**knife—knives**

For some nouns ending in **f**, add **-s** to make the plural.

   roofs chiefs reefs beliefs

Some nouns have the same form for both singular and plural.

   deer sheep moose salmon trout

For some nouns, the plural is formed in a special way.

man—men	**goose—geese**
ox—oxen	**woman—women**
mouse—mice	**child—children**

For a compound noun written as one word, form the plural by changing the last word in the compound to its plural form.

   stepchild—stepchildren
   firefly—fireflies

If a compound noun is written as a hyphenated word or as two separate words, change the most important word to the plural form.

> brother-in-law—brothers-in-law
> life jacket—life jackets

11.6 FORMING POSSESSIVES

If a noun is singular, add **'s**.

> mother—my mother's car
> Ross—Ross's desk

Exception: The **s** after the apostrophe is dropped after *Jesus', Moses',* and certain names in classical mythology (*Zeus'*). These possessive forms can thus be pronounced easily.

If a noun is plural and ends with **s**, add an apostrophe.

> parents—my parents' car
> the Santinis—the Santinis' house

If a noun is plural but does not end in **s**, add **'s**.

> people—the people's choice
> women—the women's coats

11.7 SPECIAL SPELLING PROBLEMS

Only one English word ends in *-sede: supersede.* Three words end in *-ceed: exceed, proceed,* and *succeed.* All other verbs ending in the sound "seed" are spelled with *-cede.*

> concede precede recede secede

In words with **ie** or **ei,** when the sound is long **e** (as in *she*), the word is spelled **ie** except after **c** (with some exceptions).

i before *e*	thief	relieve	field
	piece	grieve	pier
except after *c*	conceit	perceive	ceiling
	receive	receipt	
Exceptions:	either	neither	weird
	leisure	seize	

12 Commonly Confused Words

Words	Definitions	Examples
accept/ except	The verb *accept* means "to receive" or "to believe." *Except* is usually a preposition meaning "excluding."	Did the teacher **accept** your report? Everyone smiled for the photographer **except** Jody.
advice/ advise	*Advise* is a verb. *Advice* is a noun naming that which an *adviser* gives.	I **advise** you to take that job. Whom should I ask for **advice**?
affect/effect	As a verb, *affect* means "to influence." *Effect* as a verb means "to cause." If you want a noun, you will almost always want *effect*.	How deeply did the news **affect** him? The students tried to **effect** a change in school policy. What **effect** did the acidic soil produce in the plants?
all ready/ already	*All ready* is an adjective meaning "fully ready." *Already* is an adverb meaning "before" or "by this time."	He was **all ready** to go at noon. I have **already** seen that movie.
desert/ dessert	*Desert* (dĕz´ərt) means "a dry, sandy, barren region." *Desert* (dĭ-zûrt´) means "to abandon." *Dessert* (dĭ-zûrt´) is a sweet, such as cake.	The Sahara, in North Africa, is the world's largest **desert**. The night guard did not **desert** his post. Alison's favorite **dessert** is chocolate cake.
among/ between	*Between* is used when you are speaking of only two things. *Among* is used for three or more.	**Between** ice cream and sherbet, I prefer the latter. Gary Soto is **among** my favorite authors.
bring/take	*Bring* is used to denote motion toward a speaker or place. *Take* is used to denote motion away from such a person or place.	**Bring** the books over here, and I will **take** them to the library.
fewer/less	*Fewer* refers to the number of separate, countable units. *Less* refers to bulk quantity.	We have **less** literature and **fewer** selections in this year's curriculum.
leave/let	*Leave* means "to allow something to remain behind." *Let* means "to permit."	The librarian will **leave** some books on display but will not **let** us borrow any.
lie/lay	To *lie* is "to rest or recline." It does not take an object. *Lay* always takes an object.	Rover loves to **lie** in the sun. We always **lay** some bones next to him.
loose/lose	*Loose* (lōōs) means "free, not restrained." *Lose* (lōōz) means "to misplace" or "to fail to find."	Who turned the horses **loose**? I hope we won't **lose** any of them.

passed/past	**Passed** is the past tense of pass and means "went by." **Past** is an adjective that means "of a former time." **Past** is also a noun that means "time gone by."	We **passed** through the Florida Keys during our vacation. My **past** experiences have taught me to set my alarm. Ebenezer Scrooge is a character who relives his **past**.
than/then	Use **than** in making comparisons. Use **then** on all other occasions.	Ramon is stronger **than** Mark. Cut the grass and **then** trim the hedges.
two/too/to	**Two** is the number. **Too** is an adverb meaning "also" or "very." Use **to** before a verb or as a preposition.	Meg had **to** go **to** town, **too**. We had **too** much reading **to** do. **Two** chapters is **too** many.
their/there/they're	**Their** means "belonging to them." **There** means "in that place." **They're** is the contraction for "they are."	**There** is a movie playing at 9 P.M. **They're** going to see it with me. Sakara and Jessica drove away in **their** car after the movie.

Glossary of Literary and Informational Terms

Act An act is a major division within a play, similar to a chapter in a book. Each act may be further divided into smaller sections, called scenes. Plays can have as many as five acts. *The Diary of Anne Frank* has two acts.

Adventure Story An adventure story is a literary work in which action is the main element. An adventure novel usually focuses on a main character who is on a mission and is facing many challenges and choices.

Alliteration Alliteration is the repetition of consonant sounds at the beginning of words. Note the repetition of the *s* sound in this line: **S**uddenly **S**arah **s**ighed and **s**ank down on the **s**and.
See also Consonance.

Allusion An allusion is a reference to a famous person, place, event, or work of literature. In "The Drummer Boy of Shiloh" by Ray Bradbury, the general makes an allusion to the poet Henry Wadsworth Longfellow.

Analogy An analogy is a point-by-point comparison between two things that are alike in some respect. Often, writers use analogies in nonfiction to explain unfamiliar subjects or ideas in terms of familiar ones.
See also Extended Metaphor; Metaphor; Simile.

Anecdote An anecdote is a brief account of an interesting incident or event that is usually intended to entertain or make a point.

Antagonist The antagonist is a force working against the protagonist, or main character, in a story, play, or novel. The antagonist is usually another character but can be a force of nature, society itself, or an internal force within the main character.
See also Protagonist.

Appeal to Authority An appeal to authority is an attempt to persuade an audience by making reference to people who are experts on a subject.

Argument An argument is speaking or writing that expresses a position, or makes a claim, and supports it with reasons and evidence. An argument often takes into account other points of view, anticipating and answering objections that opponents might raise.
See also Claim; Counterargument; Evidence.

Assonance Assonance is the repetition of vowel sounds within nonrhyming words. An example of assonance is the repetition of the short *a* sound in the following line: The boy threw an apple at the animal.

Assumption An assumption is an opinion or belief that is taken for granted. It can be about a specific situation, a person, or the world in general. Assumptions are often unstated.

Author's Message An author's message is the main idea or theme of a particular work.
See also Main Idea; Theme.

Author's Perspective An author's perspective is the unique combination of ideas, values, feelings, and beliefs that influences the way the writer looks at a topic. Tone, or attitude, often reveals an author's perspective.
See also Author's Purpose; Tone.

Author's Position An author's position is his or her opinion on an issue or topic.
See also Claim.

Author's Purpose A writer usually writes for one or more of these purposes: to express thoughts or feelings, to inform or explain, to persuade, and to entertain.
See also Author's Perspective.

Autobiography An autobiography is a writer's account of his or her own life. In almost every case, it is told from the first-person point of view. Generally, an autobiography focuses on the most significant events and people in the writer's life over a period of time.
See also Memoir.

Ballad A ballad is a type of narrative poem that tells a story and was originally meant to be sung or recited. Because it tells a story, a ballad has a setting, a plot, and characters. Traditional ballads are written in four-line stanzas with regular rhythm and rhyme. Folk ballads were composed orally and handed down by word of mouth. These ballads usually tell about ordinary people who have unusual adventures or perform daring deeds. A literary ballad is a poem written by a poet in imitation of the form and content of a folk ballad.

Bias In a piece of writing, the author's bias is the side of an issue that he or she favors. Words with extremely positive or negative connotations are often a signal of an author's bias.

Bibliography A bibliography is a list of related books and other materials used to write a text. Bibliographies can be good sources for further study on a subject.

See also Works Consulted.

Biography A biography is the true account of a person's life, written by another person. As such, biographies are usually told from a third-person point of view. The writer of a biography usually researches his or her subject in order to present accurate information. The best biographers strive for honesty and balance in their accounts of their subjects' lives.

Blank Verse Blank verse is unrhymed poetry written in iambic pentameter. That is, each line of blank verse has five pairs of syllables. In most pairs, an unstressed syllable is followed by a stressed syllable. The most versatile of poetic forms, blank verse imitates the natural rhythms of English speech. Much of Shakespeare's drama is in blank verse.

Career Development Documents Career development documents are texts such as business letters and job applications, often to help a person advance in a career. In general, career development documents are brief, to the point, clear, courteous, and professional.

Cast of Characters In the script of a play, a cast of characters is a list of all the characters in the play, usually in order of appearance. It may include a brief description of each character.

Cause and Effect Two events are related by cause and effect when one event brings about, or causes, the other. The event that happens first is the **cause**; the one that follows is the **effect**. Cause and effect is also a way of organizing an entire piece of writing. It helps writers show the relationships between events or ideas.

Character Characters are the people, animals, or imaginary creatures who take part in the action of a work of literature. Like real people, characters display certain qualities, or character traits, that develop and change over time, and they usually have motivations, or reasons, for their behaviors.

Central character: Central or main characters are the most important characters in literary works. Generally, the plot of a short story focuses on one main character, but a novel may have several main characters.

Minor characters: The less important characters in a literary work are known as minor characters. The story is not centered on them, but they help carry out the action of the story and help the reader learn more about the main character.

Dynamic character: A dynamic character is one who undergoes important changes as a plot unfolds. The changes occur because of the character's actions and experiences in the story. The changes are usually internal and may be good or bad. Main characters are usually, though not always, dynamic.

Static character: A static character is one who remains the same throughout a story. The character may experience events and have interactions with other characters, but he or she is not changed because of them.

See also Characterization; Character Traits.

Characterization The way a writer creates and develops characters is known as characterization. There are four basic methods of characterization:

- The writer may make direct comments about a character through the voice of the narrator.
- The writer may describe the character's physical appearance.
- The writer may present the character's own thoughts, speech, and actions.
- The writer may present thoughts, speech, and actions of other characters.

See also Character; Character Traits.

Character Traits Character traits are the qualities shown by a character. Traits may be physical (brown eyes) or expressions of personality (shyness). Writers reveal the traits of their characters through methods of characterization. Sometimes writers directly state a character's traits, but more often readers need to infer traits from a character's words, actions, thoughts, appearance, and relationships. Examples of words that describe traits include *courageous, humble, generous,* and *wild.*

Chronological Order Chronological order is the arrangement of events by their order of occurrence. This type of organization is used in fictional narratives and in historical writing, biography, and autobiography.

Claim In an argument, a claim is the writer's position on an issue or problem. Although an argument focuses on supporting one claim, a writer may make more than one claim in a text.

Clarify Clarifying is a strategy that helps readers understand or make clear what they are reading. Readers usually clarify by rereading, reading aloud, or discussing.

Classification Classification is a pattern of organization in which objects, ideas, and/or information are presented in groups, or classes, based on common characteristics.

Cliché A cliché is an overused expression. "Better late than never" and "hard as nails" are common examples. Good writers generally avoid clichés unless they are using them in dialogue to indicate something about a character's personality.

Climax The climax stage is the point of greatest interest in a story or play. The climax usually occurs toward the end of a story, after the reader has understood the conflict and become emotionally involved with the characters. At the climax, the conflict is resolved and the outcome of the plot usually becomes clear.

See also Plot.

Comedy A comedy is a dramatic work that is light and often humorous in tone, usually ending happily with a peaceful resolution of the main conflict.

Compare and Contrast To compare and contrast is to identify the similarities and differences of two or more subjects. Compare and contrast is also a pattern of organizing an entire piece of writing.

Conclusion A conclusion is a statement of belief based on evidence, experience, and reasoning. A valid conclusion is one that logically follows from the facts or statements upon which it is based.

Conflict A conflict is a struggle between opposing forces. Almost every story has a main conflict—a conflict that is the story's focus. An **external conflict** involves a character who struggles against a force outside him- or herself, such as nature, a physical obstacle, or another character. An **internal conflict** is one that occurs within a character. A **cultural conflict** is a struggle that arises because of differing values, customs, or circumstances between groups of people.

See also Plot.

Connect Connecting is a reader's process of relating the content of a text to his or her own knowledge and experience.

Connotation A word's connotations are the ideas and feelings associated with the word, as opposed to its dictionary definition. For example, the word *mother,* in addition to its basic meaning ("a female parent"), has connotations of love, warmth, and security.

Consonance Consonance is the repetition of consonant sounds within and at the end of words, as in "lo<u>n</u>ely after<u>n</u>oo<u>n</u>." Consonance is unlike rhyme in that the vowel sounds preceding or following the repeated consonant sounds differ. Consonance is often used together with alliteration, assonance, and rhyme to create a musical quality, to emphasize certain words, or to unify a poem.

See also Alliteration.

Consumer Documents Consumer documents are printed materials that accompany products and services. They usually use text features to provide information about the use, care, operation, or assembly of the product or service they accompany. Some common consumer documents are applications, contracts, warranties, manuals, instructions, labels, brochures, and schedules.

Contemporary Literature Contemporary literature consists of works by authors who are currently writing today or who wrote in the recent past.

Context Clues When you encounter an unfamiliar word, you can often use context clues to understand it. Context clues are the words or phrases surrounding the word that provide hints about the word's meaning.

Counterargument A counterargument is an argument made to oppose another argument. A good argument anticipates opposing viewpoints and provides counterarguments to disprove them.

Couplet A couplet is a rhymed pair of lines. A couplet may be written in any rhythmic pattern.
See also Stanza.

Credibility Credibility is the believability or trustworthiness of a source and the information it provides.

Critical Essay *See* Essay.

Critical Review A critical review is an evaluation or critique by a reviewer, or critic. Types of reviews include film reviews, book reviews, music reviews, and art show reviews.

Database A database is a collection of information that can be quickly and easily accessed and searched and from which information can be easily retrieved. It is frequently presented in an electronic format.

Debate A debate is an organized exchange of opinions on an issue. In school settings, debate is usually a formal contest in which two opposing teams defend and attack a proposition.
See also Argument.

Deductive Reasoning Deductive reasoning is a way of thinking that begins with a generalization, presents a specific situation, and then moves forward with facts and evidence toward a logical conclusion. The following passage has a deductive argument embedded in it: "All students in the math class must take the quiz on Friday. Since Lana is in the class, she had better show up." This deductive argument can be broken down as follows: generalization—All students in the math class must take the quiz on Friday; specific situation—Lana is a student in the math class; conclusion—Therefore, Lana must take the math quiz.

Denotation A word's denotation is its dictionary definition.
See also Connotation.

Description Description is writing that helps a reader to picture events, objects, and characters. To create descriptions, writers often use imagery—words and phrases that appeal to the reader's senses.

Dialect A dialect is a form of a language that is spoken in a particular place or by a particular group of people. Dialects may feature unique pronunciations, vocabulary, and grammar.

Dialogue Dialogue is written conversation between two or more characters. Writers use dialogue to bring characters to life and to give readers insights into the characters' qualities, traits, and reactions to other characters. In fiction, dialogue is usually set off with quotation marks. In drama, stories are told primarily through dialogue.

Diary A diary is a daily record of a writer's thoughts, experiences, and feelings. As such, it is a type of autobiographical writing. The terms *diary* and *journal* are often used to mean the same thing.

Dictionary *See* Reference Works.

Drama A drama, or play, is a form of literature meant to be performed by actors in front of an audience. In a drama, the characters' dialogue and actions tell the story. The written form of a play is known as a script. A script usually includes dialogue, a cast of characters, and stage directions that give instructions about performing the drama. The person who writes the drama is known as the playwright or dramatist.

Dramatic Irony *See* Irony.

Draw Conclusions To draw a conclusion is to make a judgment or arrive at a belief based on evidence, experience, and reasoning.

Dynamic Character See Character.

Editorial An editorial is an opinion piece that usually appears on the editorial page of a newspaper or as part of a news broadcast. The editorial section of the newspaper presents opinions rather than objective news reports.

See also Op/Ed Piece.

Either/Or Fallacy An either/or fallacy is a statement that suggests that there are only two choices available in a situation when in fact there are more than two.

Elegy An elegy is an extended meditative poem in which the speaker reflects on death—often in tribute to a person who has died recently—or on an equally serious subject. Most elegies are written in formal, dignified language and are serious in tone.

Emotional Appeal An emotional appeal is a message that creates strong feelings in order to make a point. An appeal to fear is a message that taps into people's fear of losing their safety or security. An appeal to pity is a message that taps into people's sympathy and compassion for others to build support for an idea, a cause, or a proposed action. An appeal to vanity is a message that attempts to persuade by tapping into people's desire to feel good about themselves.

Encyclopedia See Reference Works.

Epic An epic is a long narrative poem on a serious subject, presented in an elevated or formal style. It traces the adventures of a great hero whose actions reflect the ideals and values of a nation or race. Epics address universal concerns, such as good and evil, life and death, and sin and redemption.

Essay An essay is a short work of nonfiction that deals with a single subject. There are many types of essays. An **expository essay** presents or explains information and ideas. A **personal essay** usually reflects the writer's experiences, feelings, and personality. A **persuasive essay** attempts to convince the reader to adopt a certain viewpoint. A **critical essay** evaluates a situation or a work of art.

Ethical Appeal In an ethical appeal, a writer links a claim to a widely accepted value in order to gain moral support for the claim. The appeal also creates an image of the writer as a trustworthy, moral person.

Evaluate To evaluate is to examine something carefully and to judge its value or worth. Evaluating is an important skill. A reader can evaluate the actions of a particular character, for example. A reader can also form opinions about the value of an entire work.

Evidence Evidence is a specific piece of information that is offered to support a claim. Evidence can take the form of a fact, a quotation, an example, a statistic, or a personal experience, among other things.

Exaggeration An extreme overstatement of an idea is called an exaggeration. It is often used for purposes of emphasis or humor.

Exposition Exposition is the first stage of a typical story plot. The exposition provides important background information and introduces the setting and the important characters. The conflict the characters face may also be introduced in the exposition, or it may be introduced later, in the rising action.

See also Plot.

Expository Essay See Essay.

Extended Metaphor An extended metaphor is a figure of speech that compares two essentially unlike things at some length and in several ways. It does not contain the words *like* or *as*.

See also Metaphor.

External Conflict See Conflict.

Fable A fable is a brief tale told to illustrate a moral or teach a lesson. Often the moral of a fable appears in a distinct and memorable statement near the tale's beginning or end.

See also Moral.

Fact Versus Opinion A fact is a statement that can be proved, or verified. An opinion, on the other hand, is a statement that cannot be proved because it expresses a person's beliefs, feelings, or thoughts.

See also Generalization; Inference.

Fallacy A fallacy is an error—usually in reasoning. Typically, a fallacy is based on an incorrect inference or a misuse of evidence.

See also Either/Or Fallacy; Logical Appeal; Overgeneralization.

Falling Action The falling action is the stage of the plot in which the story begins to draw to a close. The falling action comes after the climax and before the resolution. Events in the falling action show the results of the important decision or action that happened at the climax. Tension eases as the falling action begins; however, the final outcome of the story is not yet fully worked out at this stage.

See also Climax; Plot.

Fantasy Fantasy is a type of fiction that is highly imaginative and portrays events, settings, or characters that are unrealistic. The setting might be a nonexistent world, the plot might involve magic or the supernatural, and the characters might have superhuman powers.

Farce Farce is a type of exaggerated comedy that features an absurd plot, ridiculous situations, and humorous dialogue. The main purpose of a farce is to keep an audience laughing. Comic devices typically used in farces include mistaken identity, wordplay (such as puns and double meanings), and exaggeration.

Faulty Reasoning *See* Fallacy.

Feature Article A feature article is an article in a newspaper or magazine about a topic of human interest or lifestyles.

Fiction Fiction is prose writing that tells an imaginary story. The writer of a fictional work might invent all the events and characters or might base parts of the story on real people and events. The basic elements of fiction are plot, character, setting, and theme. Fiction includes both short stories and novels.

See also Novel; Short Story.

Figurative Language Figurative language is language that communicates meanings beyond the literal meanings of words. In figurative language, words are often used to symbolize ideas and concepts they would not otherwise be associated with. Writers use figurative language to create effects, to emphasize ideas, and to evoke emotions. Simile, metaphor, extended metaphor, hyperbole, and personification are examples of figurative language.

See also Hyperbole; Metaphor; Onomatopoeia; Personification; Simile.

First-Person Point of View *See* Point of View.

Flashback In a literary work, a flashback is an interruption of the action to present events that took place at an earlier time. A flashback provides information that can help a reader better understand a character's current situation.

Foil A foil is a character who provides a striking contrast to another character. By using a foil, a writer can call attention to certain traits possessed by a main character or simply enhance a character by contrast.

Folklore The traditions, customs, and stories that are passed down within a culture are known as its folklore. Folklore includes various types of literature, such as legends, folk tales, myths, trickster tales, and fables.

See also Fable; Folk Tale; Myth.

Folk Tale A folk tale is a story that has been passed from generation to generation by word of mouth. Folk tales may be set in the distant past and involve supernatural events. The characters in them may be animals, people, or superhuman beings.

Foreshadowing Foreshadowing occurs when a writer provides hints that suggest future events in a story. Foreshadowing creates suspense and makes readers eager to find out what will happen.

Form The structure or organization of a work of writing is often called its form. The form of a poem includes the arrangement of its words and lines on the page.

Free Verse Free verse is poetry that does not contain regular patterns of rhythm or rhyme.

The lines in free verse often flow more naturally than do rhymed, metrical lines and therefore achieve a rhythm more like that of everyday speech. Although free verse lacks conventional meter, it may contain various rhythmic and sound effects, such as repetitions of syllables or words. Free verse can be used for a variety of subjects.

See also Meter; Rhyme.

Generalization A generalization is a broad statement about a class or category of people, ideas, or things based on a study of, or a belief about, only some of its members.

See also Overgeneralization; Stereotyping.

Genre The term *genre* refers to a category in which a work of literature is classified. The major genres in literature are fiction, nonfiction, poetry, and drama.

Government Publications Government publications are documents produced by government organizations. Pamphlets, brochures, and reports are just some of the many forms these publications take. Government publications can be good resources for a wide variety of topics.

Graphic Aid A graphic aid is a visual tool that is printed, handwritten, or drawn. Charts, diagrams, graphs, photographs, captions, and maps are examples of graphic aids.

Graphic Organizer A graphic organizer is a "word picture"—a visual illustration of a verbal statement—that helps a reader understand a text. Charts, tables, webs, and diagrams can all be graphic organizers. Graphic organizers and graphic aids can look the same. However, graphic organizers and graphic aids do differ in how they are used. Graphic aids help deliver important information to students using a text. Graphic organizers are actually created by students themselves. They help students understand the text or organize information.

Hero A hero is a main character or protagonist in a story. In older literary works, heroes tend to be better than ordinary humans. They are typically courageous, strong, honorable, and intelligent. They are protectors of society who hold back the forces of evil and fight to make the world a better place. In modern literature, a hero may simply be the most important character in a story. Such a hero is often an ordinary person with ordinary problems.

Historical Context The historical context of a literary work refers to the social conditions that inspired or influenced its creation. To understand and appreciate certain works, the reader must relate them to particular events in history.

Historical Document Historical documents are writings that have played a significant role in human events. The Declaration of Independence, for example, is a historical document.

Historical Dramas Historical dramas are plays that take place in the past and are based on real events. In many of these plays, the characters are also based on real historical figures. The dialogue and the action, however, are mostly created by the playwright.

Historical Fiction A short story or a novel can be called historical fiction when it is set in the past and includes real places and real events of historical importance.

How-To Book A how-to book explains how to do something—usually an activity, a sport, or a household project.

Humor Humor is a quality that provokes laughter or amusement. Writers create humor through exaggeration, amusing descriptions, irony, and witty and insightful dialogue.

Hyperbole Hyperbole is a figure of speech in which the truth is exaggerated for emphasis or humorous effect.

Idiom An idiom is an expression that has a meaning different from the meaning of its individual words. For example, "to go to the dogs" is an idiom meaning "to go to ruin."

Imagery Imagery consists of descriptive words and phrases that re-create sensory experiences for the reader. Imagery usually appeals to one or more of the five senses— sight, hearing, smell, taste, and touch—to help the reader imagine exactly what is being described. Note the appeals to sight, taste, and touch in the following lines: The aroma of popcorn drew me to the bright red concession stand.

Implied Main Idea *See* Main Idea.

Index The index of a book is an alphabetized list of important topics covered in the book and the page numbers on which they can be found. An index can be used to quickly find specific information about a topic.

Inductive Reasoning Inductive reasoning is the process of logical reasoning that starts with observations, examples, and facts and moves on to a general conclusion or principle.

Inference An inference is a logical guess that is made based on facts and one's own knowledge and experience.

Informational Text Informational text is writing that provides factual information. It often explains an idea or teaches a process. Examples include news reports, science textbooks, software instructions, and lab reports.

Internal Conflict *See* Conflict.

Internet The Internet is a global, interconnected system of computer networks that allows for communication through e-mail, listservs, and the World Wide Web. The Internet connects computers and computer users throughout the world.

Interview An interview is a conversation conducted by a writer or reporter in which facts or statements are elicited from another person, recorded, and then broadcast or published.

Irony Irony is a special kind of contrast between appearance and reality—usually one in which reality is the opposite of what it seems. One type of irony is **situational irony,** a contrast between what a reader or character expects and what actually exists or happens. Another type of irony is **dramatic irony,** where the reader or viewer knows something that a character does not know. **Verbal irony** exists when someone knowingly exaggerates or says one thing and means another.

Journal A journal is a periodical publication issued by a legal, medical, or other professional organization. The term may also be used to refer to a diary or daily record.

See also Diary.

Legend A legend is a story handed down from the past about a specific person, usually someone of heroic accomplishments. Legends usually have some basis in historical fact.

Limerick A limerick is a short, humorous poem composed of five lines. It usually has the rhyme scheme ***aabba,*** created by two rhyming couplets followed by a fifth line that rhymes with the first couplet. A limerick typically has a sing-song rhythm.

Limited Point of View *See* Point of View.

Line The line is the core unit of a poem. In poetry, line length is an essential element of the poem's meaning and rhythm. Line breaks, where a line of poetry ends, may coincide with grammatical units. However, a line break may also occur in the middle of a grammatical unit, therefore creating a meaningful pause or emphasis. Poets use a variety of line breaks to play with sense, grammar, and syntax and thereby create a wide range of effects.

Loaded Language Loaded language consists of words with strongly positive or negative connotations intended to influence a reader's or listener's attitude.

Logical Appeal A logical appeal is a way of writing or speaking that relies on logic and facts. It appeals to people's reasoning or intellect rather than to their values or emotions. Flawed logical appeals—that is, errors in reasoning—are called logical fallacies.

See also Fallacy.

Lyric Poetry A lyric poem is a short poem in which a single speaker expresses personal thoughts and feelings. Most poems other than dramatic and narrative poems are lyric poems. In ancient Greece, lyric poetry was meant to be sung. Modern lyrics are usually not intended for singing, but they are characterized by strong melodic rhythms. Lyric poetry has a variety of forms and covers many subjects, from love and death to everyday experiences.

Main Idea The main idea is the central or most important idea about a topic that a writer or speaker conveys. It can be the central idea of an entire work or of just a paragraph. Often, the main idea of a paragraph is expressed in a topic sentence. However, a main idea may just be implied, or suggested, by details. A main idea is typically supported by details.

Make Inferences *See* Inference.

Memoir A memoir is a form of autobiographical writing in which a writer shares his or her personal experiences and observations of significant events or people. Often informal or even intimate in tone, memoirs usually give readers insight into the impact of historical events on people's lives.

See also Autobiography.

Metaphor A metaphor is a comparison of two things that are basically unlike but have some qualities in common. Unlike a simile, a metaphor does not contain the words *like* or *as*.

See also Extended Metaphor; Figurative Language; Simile.

Meter Meter is a regular pattern of stressed and unstressed syllables in a poem. The meter of a poem emphasizes the musical quality of the language. Each unit of meter, known as a **foot**, consists of one stressed syllable and one or two unstressed syllables. In representations of meter, a stressed syllable is indicated by the symbol (´); an unstressed syllable by the symbol (˘). The four basic types of metrical feet are the iamb, an unstressed syllable followed by a stressed syllable (˘´); the trochee, a stressed syllable followed by an unstressed syllable (´˘); the anapest, two unstressed syllables followed by a stressed syllable (˘˘´); and the dactyl, a stressed syllable followed by two unstressed syllables (´˘˘).

See also Rhythm.

Minor Character *See* Character.

Monitor Monitoring is the strategy of checking your comprehension as you read and modifying the strategies you are using to suit your needs. Monitoring often includes the following strategies: questioning, clarifying, visualizing, predicting, connecting, and rereading.

Mood Mood is the feeling or atmosphere that a writer creates for the reader. Descriptive words, imagery, and figurative language all influence the mood of a work.

See also Tone.

Moral A moral is a lesson that a story teaches. A moral is often stated at the end of a fable. Other times, the moral is implied.

See also Fable.

Motivation *See* Character.

Myth A myth is a traditional story, usually concerning some superhuman being or unlikely event, that was once widely believed to be true. Frequently, myths were attempts to explain natural phenomena, such as solar and lunar eclipses or the cycle of the seasons. For some peoples, myths were both a kind of science and a religion. In addition, myths served as literature and entertainment, just as they do for modern-day audiences.

Narrative Nonfiction Narrative nonfiction is writing that reads much like fiction, except that the characters, setting, and events are based on real life.

Narrative Poetry Poetry that tells a story is called narrative poetry. Like fiction, a narrative poem contains characters, a setting, and a plot. It might also contain such elements of poetry as rhyme, rhythm, imagery, and figurative language.

Narrator The narrator is the voice that tells a story. Sometimes the narrator is a character in the story. At other times, the narrator is an outside voice created by the writer. The narrator is not the same as the writer. An **unreliable narrator** is one who tells a story or interprets events in a way that makes readers doubt what he or she is saying. An unreliable narrator is usually a character in the story. The narrator may be unreliable for a number of different reasons. For example, the narrator may not have all the facts or may be too young to understand the situation.

See also Point of View.

News Article A news article is writing that reports on a recent event. In newspapers, news articles are usually brief and to the point,

Glossary of Literary and Informational Terms

presenting the most important facts first, followed by more detailed information.

Nonfiction Nonfiction is writing that tells about real people, places, and events. Unlike fiction, nonfiction is mainly written to convey factual information. Nonfiction includes a wide range of writing—newspaper articles, letters, essays, biographies, movie reviews, speeches, true-life adventure stories, advertising, and more.

Novel A novel is a long work of fiction. Like a short story, a novel is the product of a writer's imagination. Because a novel is considerably longer than a short story, a novelist can develop the characters and story line more thoroughly.

See also Fiction.

Ode An ode is a type of lyric poem that deals with serious themes, such as justice, truth, or beauty. Odes appeal to both the imagination and the intellect, and many commemorate events or praise people or elements of nature.

Omniscient Point of View *See* Point of View.

Onomatopoeia Onomatopoeia is the use of words whose sounds echo their meanings, such as *buzz, whisper, gargle,* and *murmur*. As a literary technique, onomatopoeia goes beyond the use of simple echoing words. Skilled writers, especially poets, choose words whose sounds intensify images and suggest meaning.

Op/Ed Piece An op/ed piece is an opinion piece that typically appears opposite ("op") the editorial page of a newspaper. Unlike editorials, op/ed pieces are written and submitted by readers.

Oral Literature Oral literature consists of stories that have been passed down by word of mouth from generation to generation. Oral literature includes folk tales, legends, and myths. In more recent times, some examples of oral literature have been written down or recorded so that the stories can be preserved.

Organization *See* Pattern of Organization.

Overgeneralization An overgeneralization is a generalization that is too broad. You can often recognize overgeneralizations by the appearance of words and phrases such as *all, everyone, every time, any, anything, no one,* or *none*. An example is "None of the city's workers really cares about keeping the environment clean." In all probability, there are many exceptions. The writer can't possibly know the feelings of every city worker.

Overview An overview is a short summary of a story, a speech, or an essay.

Parallel Episodes Parallel episodes occur when elements of a plot are repeated several times in the course of a story. Fairy tales often employ parallel episodes, as in the examples of "Goldilocks and the Three Bears" and "The Three Little Pigs."

Paraphrase Paraphrasing is the restating of information in one's own words.

See also Summarize.

Part-by-Part Order Part-by-part order is a pattern of organization in which one idea or group of ideas suggests another, which suggests another, and so on until the end.

Pattern of Organization The term *pattern of organization* refers to the way ideas and information are arranged and organized. Patterns of organization include cause and effect, chronological, compare and contrast, classification, part-by-part, and problem-solution, among others.

See also Cause and Effect; Chronological Order; Classification; Compare and Contrast; Part-by-Part Order; Problem-Solution Order; Sequential Order.

Periodical A periodical is a magazine or other publication that is issued on a regular basis.

Personal Essay *See* Essay.

Personification The giving of human qualities to an animal, object, or idea is known as personification.

See also Figurative Language.

Persuasion Persuasion is the art of swaying others' feelings, beliefs, or actions. Persuasion normally appeals to both the mind and the emotions of the reader.

See also Appeal to Authority; Emotional Appeal; Ethical Appeal; Loaded Language; Logical Appeal.

Persuasive Essay *See* Essay.

Play *See* Drama.

Playwright *See* Drama.

Plot The series of events in a story is called the plot. The plot usually centers on a **conflict,** or struggle, faced by the main character. The action that the characters take to solve the problem builds toward a **climax** in the story. At this point, or shortly afterward, the problem is solved and the story ends. Most story plots have five stages: exposition, rising action, climax, falling action, and resolution.

See also Climax; Conflict; Exposition; Falling Action; Rising Action.

Poetry Poetry is a type of literature in which words are carefully chosen and arranged to create certain effects. Poets use a variety of sound devices, imagery, and figurative language to express emotions and ideas.

See also Alliteration; Assonance; Ballad; Free Verse; Imagery; Meter; Narrative Poetry; Rhyme; Rhythm; Stanza.

Point of View Point of view refers to the method of narration used in a short story, novel, narrative poem, or work of nonfiction. In a work told from a **first-person** point of view, the narrator is a character in the story. In a work told from a **third-person** point of view, the narrative voice is outside the action, not one of the characters. If a story is told from a **third-person omniscient,** or all-knowing, point of view, the narrator sees into the minds of all the characters. If events are relayed from a **third-person limited** point of view, the narrator tells what only one character thinks, feels, and observes.

See also Narrator.

Predict Predicting is a reading strategy that involves using text clues to make a reasonable guess about what will happen next in a story.

Primary Source *See* Source.

Prior Knowledge Prior knowledge is the knowledge a reader already possesses about a topic. This information might come from personal experiences, expert accounts, books, films, or other sources.

Problem-Solution Order Problem-solution order is a pattern of organization in which a problem is stated and analyzed and then one or more solutions are proposed and examined.

Prop The word *prop,* originally an abbreviation of the word *property,* refers to any physical object that is used in a drama.

Propaganda Propaganda is any form of communication that is so distorted that it conveys false or misleading information to advance a specific belief or cause.

Prose The word *prose* refers to all forms of writing that are not in verse form. The term may be used to describe very different forms of writing—short stories as well as essays, for example.

Protagonist A protagonist is the main character in a story, play, or novel. The protagonist is involved in the main conflict of the story. Usually, the protagonist undergoes changes as the plot runs its course.

Public Document Public documents are documents that were written for the public to provide information that is of public interest or concern. They include government documents, speeches, signs, and rules and regulations.

See also Government Publications.

Radio Play A radio play is a drama that is written specifically to be broadcast over the radio. Because the audience is not meant to see a radio play, sound effects are often used to help listeners imagine the setting and the action. The stage directions in the play's script indicate the sound effects.

Recurring Theme *See* Theme.

Reference Works Reference works are sources that contain facts and background information on a wide range of subjects. Most reference works are good sources of reliable information because they have been reviewed by experts. The following are some common reference works: encyclopedias, dictionaries, thesauri, almanacs, atlases, and directories.

Repetition Repetition is a technique in which a sound, word, phrase, or line is repeated for emphasis or unity. Repetition often helps to reinforce meaning and create an appealing rhythm.

See also Alliteration; Sound Devices.

Resolution *See* Falling Action.

Review *See* Critical Review.

Rhetorical Question Rhetorical questions are those that have such obvious answers that they do not require a reply. Writers often use them to suggest that their claim is so obvious that everyone should agree with it.

Rhyme Rhyme is the occurrence of similar or identical sounds at the end of two or more words, such as *suite, heat,* and *complete.* Rhyme that occurs within a single line of poetry is internal rhyme. Rhyme that occurs at the ends of lines of poetry is called end rhyme. End rhyme that is not exact but approximate is called slant rhyme, or off rhyme.

Rhyme Scheme A rhyme scheme is a pattern of end rhymes in a poem. A rhyme scheme is noted by assigning a letter of the alphabet, beginning with *a,* to each line. Lines that rhyme are given the same letter.

Rhythm Rhythm is a pattern of stressed and unstressed syllables in a line of poetry. Poets use rhythm to bring out the musical quality of language, to emphasize ideas, and to create moods. Devices such as alliteration, rhyme, assonance, and consonance often contribute to creating rhythm.

See also Meter.

Rising Action The rising action is the stage of the plot that develops the conflict, or struggle. During this stage, events occur that make the conflict more complicated. The events in the rising action build toward a climax, or turning point.

See also Plot.

Scanning Scanning is the process used to search through a text for a particular fact or piece of information. When you scan, you sweep your eyes across a page, looking for key words that may lead you to the information you want.

Scene In a drama, the action is often divided into acts and scenes. Each scene presents an episode of the play's plot and typically occurs at a single place and time.

See also Act.

Scenery Scenery is a painted backdrop or other structures used to create the setting for a play.

Science Fiction Science fiction is fiction in which a writer explores unexpected possibilities of the past or the future, using known scientific data and theories as well as his or her creative imagination. Most science fiction writers create believable worlds, although some create fantasy worlds that have familiar elements.

See also Fantasy.

Scope Scope refers to a work's focus. For example, an article about Austin, Texas, that focuses on the city's history, economy, and residents has a broad scope. An article that focuses only on the restaurants in Austin has a narrower scope.

Screenplay A screenplay is a play written for film.

Script The text of a play, film, or broadcast is called a script.

Secondary Source *See* Source.

Sensory Details Sensory details are words and phrases that appeal to the reader's senses of sight, hearing, touch, smell, and taste.

See also Imagery.

Sequential Order Sequential order is a pattern of organization that shows the order of steps or stages in a process.

Setting The setting of a story, poem, or play is the time and place of the action. Sometimes the setting is clear and well-defined. At other times, it is left to the reader's imagination. Elements of setting include geographic location, historical period (past, present, or future), season, time of day, and culture.

Setting a Purpose The process of establishing specific reasons for reading a text is called setting a purpose.

Short Story A short story is a work of fiction that centers on a single idea and can be read in one sitting. Generally, a short story has one main conflict that involves the characters and keeps the story moving.

See also Fiction.

Sidebar A sidebar is additional information set in a box alongside or within a news or feature article. Popular magazines often make use of sidebars.

Signal Words In a text, signal words are words and phrases that help show how events or ideas are related. Some common examples of signal words are *and, but, however, nevertheless, therefore,* and *in addition.*

Simile A simile is a figure of speech that makes a comparison between two unlike things using the words *like* or *as*: My heart is pounding like a jackhammer.

See also Figurative Language; Metaphor.

Situational Irony *See* Irony.

Sonnet A sonnet is a poem that has a formal structure, containing 14 lines and a specific rhyme scheme and meter. A sonnet often consists of three quatrains, or four-line units, and a final couplet. The sonnet, which means "little song," can be used for a variety of subjects.

See also Couplet; Rhyme Scheme.

Sound Devices Sound devices, or uses of words for their connection to the sense of hearing, can convey meaning and mood or unify a work. Some common sound devices are **alliteration, assonance, consonance, meter, onomatopoeia, repetition, rhyme,** and **rhythm.**

See also Alliteration; Assonance; Consonance; Meter; Onomatopoeia; Repetition; Rhyme; Rhythm.

Source A source is anything that supplies information. **Primary sources** are materials created by people who witnessed or took part in the event they supply information about. Letters, diaries, autobiographies, and eyewitness accounts are primary sources. **Secondary sources** are those made by people who were not directly involved in the event or even present when it occurred. Encyclopedias, textbooks, biographies, and most news articles are examples of secondary sources.

Speaker In poetry, the speaker is the voice that "talks" to the reader, similar to the narrator in fiction. The speaker is not necessarily the poet.

Speech A speech is a talk or public address. The purpose of a speech may be to entertain, to explain, to persuade, to inspire, or any combination of these purposes.

Stage Directions In the script of a play, the instructions to the actors, director, and stage crew are called the stage directions. Stage directions might suggest scenery, lighting, sound effects, and ways for actors to move and speak. Stage directions often appear in parentheses and in italic type.

Stanza A stanza is a group of two or more lines that form a unit in a poem. Each stanza may have the same number of lines, or the number of lines may vary.

See also Couplet; Form; Poetry.

Static Character *See* Character.

Stereotype In literature, characters who are defined by a single trait are known as stereotypes. Such characters do not usually demonstrate the complexities of real people. Familiar stereotypes in popular literature include the absent-minded professor and the busybody.

Stereotyping Stereotyping is a dangerous type of overgeneralization. It can lead to unfair judgments of people based on their ethnic background, beliefs, practices, or physical appearance.

Structure The structure of a work of literature is the way in which it is put together. In poetry, structure involves the arrangement of words and lines to produce a desired effect. One structural unit in poetry is the stanza. In prose, structure involves the arrangement of such elements as sentences, paragraphs, and events.

Style A style is a manner of writing. It involves how something is said rather than what is said.

Subplot A subplot is an additional, or secondary, plot in a story. The subplot contains its own conflict, which is often separate from the main conflicts of the story.

Glossary of Literary and Informational Terms

Summarize To summarize is to briefly retell the main ideas of a piece of writing in one's own words.

See also Paraphrase.

Support Support is any information that helps to prove a claim.

Supporting Detail *See* Main Idea.

Surprise Ending A surprise ending is an unexpected plot twist at the end of a story. The surprise may be a sudden turn in the action or a piece of information that gives a different perspective to the entire story.

Suspense Suspense is a feeling of growing tension and excitement felt by a reader. Suspense makes a reader curious about the outcome of a story or an event within a story. A writer creates suspense by raising questions in the reader's mind. The use of foreshadowing is one way that writers create suspense.

See also Foreshadowing.

Symbol A symbol is a person, a place, an object, an animal, or an activity that stands for something beyond itself. For example, a flag is a colored piece of cloth that stands for a country. A white dove is a bird that represents peace.

Synthesize To synthesize information means to take individual pieces of information and combine them in order to gain a better understanding of a subject.

Tall Tale A tall tale is a humorously exaggerated story about impossible events, often involving the supernatural abilities of the main character.

Text Feature Text features are elements of a text, such as boldface type, headers, and subheaders, that help organize and call attention to important information. Italic type, bulleted or numbered lists, sidebars, and graphic aids such as charts, tables, timelines, captions, illustrations, and photographs are also considered text features.

Theme A theme is a message about life or human nature that the writer shares with the reader. In many cases, readers must infer what the writer's message is. One way of figuring out a theme is to apply the lessons learned by the main characters to people in real life.

    Recurring themes: Themes found in a variety of works. For example, authors from different backgrounds might express similar themes having to do with the importance of family values.

    Universal themes: Themes that are found throughout the literature of all time periods.

See also Moral.

Thesaurus *See* Reference Works.

Thesis Statement A thesis statement is the main proposition that a writer attempts to support in a piece of writing. It serves as the controlling idea of the composition.

Third-Person Point of View *See* Point of View.

Title The title of a piece of writing is the name that is attached to it. A title often refers to an important aspect of the work.

Tone The tone of a literary work expresses the writer's attitude toward his or her subject. Words such as *angry, sad,* and *humorous* can be used to describe different tones.

See also Author's Perspective; Mood.

Topic Sentence The topic sentence of a paragraph states the paragraph's main idea. All other sentences in the paragraph provide supporting details.

Tragedy A tragedy is a dramatic work that presents the downfall of a dignified character or characters involved in historically or socially significant events. The events in a tragic plot are set in motion by a decision that is often an error in judgment on the part of the hero. Succeeding events are linked in a cause-and-effect relationship and lead inevitably to a disastrous conclusion, usually death.

Traits *See* Character Traits.

Treatment The way a topic is handled in a work is referred to as its treatment. Treatment includes the form the writing takes as well as the writer's purpose and tone.

Turning Point *See* Climax.

Understatement Understatement is a technique of creating emphasis by saying less than is actually or literally true. It is the opposite of **hyperbole**, or exaggeration. Understatement is often used to create a humorous effect.

Universal Theme *See* Theme.

Unreliable Narrator *See* Narrator.

Verbal Irony *See* Irony.

Visualize Visualizing is the process of forming a mental picture based on written or spoken information.

Voice The term *voice* refers to a writer's unique use of language that allows a reader to "hear" a human personality in the writer's work. Elements of style that contribute to a writer's voice can reveal much about the author's personality, beliefs, and attitudes.

Website A website is a collection of "pages" on the World Wide Web that is usually devoted to one specific subject. Pages are linked together and accessed by clicking hyperlinks or menus, which send the user from page to page within a website. Websites are created by companies, organizations, educational institutions, branches of the government, the military, and individuals.

Word Choice The success of any writing depends on the writer's choice of words. Words not only communicate ideas but also help describe events, characters, settings, and so on. Word choice can make a writer's work sound formal or informal, serious or humorous. A writer must choose words carefully depending on the goal of the piece of writing. For example, a writer working on a science article would probably use technical, formal words; a writer trying to establish the setting in a short story would probably use more descriptive words.

See also Style.

Workplace Document Workplace documents are materials that are produced or used within a work setting, usually using text features to aid in the functioning of the workplace. They include job applications, office memos, training manuals, job descriptions, and sales reports.

Works Cited The term *works cited* refers to a list of all the works a writer has referred to in his or her text. This list often includes not only books and articles but also Internet sources.

Works Consulted The term *works consulted* refers to a list of all the works a writer consulted in order to create his or her text. It is not limited just to those works cited in the text.

See also Bibliography.

Pronunciation Key

Using the Glossary

This glossary is an alphabetical list of vocabulary words found in the selections in this book. Use this glossary just as you would a dictionary—to determine the meanings, parts of speech, pronunciation, and syllabication of words. (Some technical, foreign, and more obscure words in this book are not listed here but are defined for you in the footnotes that accompany many of the selections.)

Many words in the English language have more than one meaning. This glossary gives the meanings that apply to the words as they are used in the selections in this book. Words closely related in form and meaning are listed together in one entry (for instance, *consumption* and *consume*), and the definition is given for the first form.

The following abbreviations are used to identify parts of speech of words:

adj. adjective *adv.* adverb *n.* noun *v.* verb

Each word's pronunciation is given in parentheses. A guide to the pronunciation symbols appears in the Pronunciation Key below. The stress marks in the Pronunciation Key are used to indicate the force given to each syllable in a word. They can also help you determine where words are divided into syllables.

For more information about the words in this glossary or for information about words not listed here, consult a dictionary.

Pronunciation Key

Symbol	Examples	Symbol	Examples	Symbol	Examples
ă	pat	m	mum	ûr	urge, term, firm, word, heard
ā	pay	n	no, sudden* (sud'n)	v	valve
ä	father	ng	thing	w	with
âr	care	ŏ	pot	y	yes
b	bib	ō	toe	z	zebra, xylem
ch	church	ô	caught, paw	zh	vision, pleasure, garage
d	deed, milled	oi	noise	ə	about, item, edible, gallop, circus
ĕ	pet	ŏŏ	took	ər	butter
ē	bee	ōō	boot		
f	fife, phase, rough	ŏŏr	lure		
g	gag	ôr	core		
h	hat	ou	out		
hw	which	p	pop		
ĭ	pit	r	roar		
ī	pie, by	s	sauce		
îr	pier	sh	ship, dish		
j	judge	t	tight, stopped		
k	kick, cat, pique	th	thin		
l	lid, needle* (nēd'l)	th	this		
		ŭ	cut		

Sounds in Foreign Words

Symbol	Examples
KH	German ich, ach; Scottish loch
N	French bon (bôN)
œ	French feu, œuf; German schön
ü	French tu; German über

* In English the consonants *l* and *n* often constitute complete syllables by themselves.

Stress Marks

The relevant emphasis with which the syllables of a word or phrase are spoken, called stress, is indicated in three different ways. The strongest, or primary, stress is marked with a bold mark (´). An intermediate, or secondary, level of stress is marked with a similar but lighter mark (´). The weakest stress is unmarked. Words of one syllable show no stress mark.

Glossary of Academic Vocabulary

access (ăk´sĕs) *n.* a way of approaching or making use of

civil (sĭv´əl) *adj.* of, or related to, citizens and their relations with each other and the state

commentary (kŏm´ən-tĕr´ē) *n.* explanation or interpretation in the form of comments or observations

communicate (kə-myoo´nĭ-kāt´) *v.* to convey information or exchange ideas

contribute (kən-trĭb´yoot) *v.* to give or supply for a common purpose

convention (kən-vĕn´shən) *n.* a practice or procedure widely used by a group; a custom

debate (dĭ-bāt´) *v.* to engage in arguments by discussing opposing points

deduce (dĭ-doos´) *v.* to reach a conclusion or decision through reasoning

demonstrate (dĕm´ən-strāt´) *v.* to show clearly and deliberately

document (dŏc´yə-mənt) *n.* written or printed paper that provides evidence or information

draft (drăft) *n.; v.* early versions or stages of a written document or plan; to write such a version

immigrate (ĭm´ĭ-grāt´) *v.* to enter and settle in a new country

liberation (lĭb´ə-rā´shən) *n.* the act of freeing or the state of being free

license (lī´səns) *n.* a document that is issued as proof of legal permission to do something

minors (mī´nərz) *n.* people who have not reached legal adulthood

occupation (ŏk´yə-pā´shən) *n.* an activity that serves as one's source of income

option (ŏp´shən) *n.* something chosen or available as a choice

philosophy (fĭ-lŏs´ə-fē) *n.* the underlying theory or set of ideas related to life as a whole

predict (prĭ-dĭkt´) *v.* to tell about in advance, especially on the basis of special knowledge

psychology (sī-kŏl´ə-jē) *n.* the study of mental processes and behaviors

publish (pŭb´lĭsh) *v.* to prepare and issue a book or other material to the public

reaction (rē-ăk´shən) *n.* a response to something

relocate (rē-lō´kāt) *v.* to move to a new place

shifting (shĭft´ĭng) *adj.* changing attitudes, judgments, or emphases

style (stīl) *n.* the way in which something is said, done, expressed, or performed

sufficient (sə-fĭsh´ənt) *adj.* being enough, or as much as needed

summary (sŭm´ə-rē) *n.* a condensed, or shorter, report that includes the main points of a text or event

symbolize (sĭm´bə-līz´) *v.* to serve as a symbol of, or represent something else

technique (tĕk-nēk´) *n.* the systematic or orderly procedure by which a task is accomplished

trend (trĕnd) *n.* the general direction of something; a current style

Glossary of Critical Vocabulary

alacrity (ə-lăk′rĭ-tē) *n.* *Alacrity* is cheerful willingness or eagerness.

anecdote (ăn′ĭk-dōt′) *n.* An *anecdote* is a short account of an incident.

apprehension (ăp′rĭ-hĕn′shən) *n.* *Apprehension* is the fear or dread of the future.

arbitrary (är′bĭ-trĕr′ē) *adj.* If something is *arbitrary*, it is determined by chance or whim.

askew (ə-skyo͞o′) *adj.* When something is *askew*, it is off center.

attain (ə-tān′) *v.* If you *attain* something, you gain it or achieve it.

audacity (ô-dăs′ĭ-tē) *n.* *Audacity* is shameless daring or boldness.

autonomous (ô-tŏn′ə-məs) *adj.* If someone is *autonomous*, the person is independent and not controlled by outside forces.

avert (ə-vûrt′) *v.* If you *avert* something, you prevent it from happening.

banal (bə-năl′) *adj.* If something is *banal*, it is very commonplace, dull, and unoriginal.

bane (bān) *n.* A *bane* is a cause of death, destruction, or ruin.

boon (bo͞on) *n.* A *boon* is a gift or benefit.

borne (bôrn) *v.* If something is *borne*, it is carried or supported.

bravado (brə-vä′dō) *n.* *Bravado* is a false show of bravery.

cajole (kə-jōl′) *v.* When you *cajole*, you coax or urge gently.

chide (chīd) *v.* To *chide* is to scold or correct in some way.

cohort (kō′hôrt′) *n.* A *cohort* is a group or band of people.

commence (kə-mĕns′) *v.* When things *commence*, they begin or start.

compensation (kŏm′pən-sā′shən) *n.* *Compensation* is something, such as money, that is received as payment.

conceive (kən-sēv′) *v.* When you *conceive* an idea, you think of it.

condole (kən-dōl′) *v.* If you *condole* with someone, you express sympathy or sorrow.

confluence (kŏn′flo͞o-əns) *n.* A *confluence* is a gathering or joining together in one place.

conjecture (kən-jĕk′chər) *v.* If you *conjecture*, you guess or suppose.

contemplate (kŏn′təm-plāt′) *v.* When you *contemplate*, you look at something attentively and thoughtfully.

contractor (kŏn′trăk′tər) *n.* A *contractor* is a person who agrees to provide services for a specific price.

coup (ko͞o) *n.* A *coup* is the sudden overthrow of a government by a group of people.

covet (kŭv′ĭt) *v.* If you *covet* something, you strongly wish for it.

credulity (krĭ-do͞o′lĭ-tē) *n.* *Credulity* is a tendency to believe too readily.

crevice (krĕv′ĭs) *n.* A *crevice* is a narrow crack.

deficiency (dĭ-fĭsh′ən-sē) *n.* A *deficiency* is a lack or shortage of something.

degradation (dĕg′rə-dā′shən) *n.* *Degradation* is the condition of being brought to a lower level or humiliated.

denunciation (dĭ-nŭn′sē-ā′shən) *n.* A *denunciation* is the public condemnation of something as wrong or evil.

derision (dĭ-rĭzh′ən) *n.* *Derision* is jeering laughter or ridicule.

despondent (dĭ-spŏn′dənt) *adj.* Someone who is *despondent* feels a loss of hope or confidence.

detrimental (dĕt′rə-mĕn′tl) *adj.* If something is *detrimental*, it causes damage or harm.

diffuse (dĭ-fyo͞os′) *adj.* If something is *diffuse*, it is very spread out or scattered.

dilapidated (dĭ-lăp′ĭ-dā′tĭd) *adj.* If something is *dilapidated*, it is falling apart.

disheveled (dĭ-shĕvʹəld) *adj.* When something is *disheveled*, it is messy or untidy.

dispatcher (dĭs-pă̆chʹər) *n.* A *dispatcher* is a person who sends out vehicles according to a schedule.

dispel (dĭ-spĕlʹ) *v.* When you *dispel* something, you drive it away.

dispossess (dĭsʹpə-zĕsʹ) *v.* To *dispossess* someone is to deny him or her possession of something.

egregious (ĭ-grēʹjəs) *adj.* If something is *egregious*, it is very bad or offensive.

eloquence (ĕlʹə-kwəns) *n.* *Eloquence* is the ability to speak powerfully and persuasively.

emblematic (ĕmʹblə-mătʹĭk) *adj.* If something is *emblematic*, it is a symbol for something else.

evoke (ĭ-vōkʹ) *v.* When you *evoke* something, you summon it.

expiration (ĕkʹspə-rāʹshən) *n.* *Expiration* is the act of exhaling or breathing out.

exuberance (ĭg-zōōʹbər-əns) *n.* *Exuberance* is a condition of unrestrained joy.

fate (fāt) *n.* *Fate* is a power that is thought to determine the course of events.

feeble (fēʹbəl) *adj.* If someone is *feeble*, the person is very weak.

foreman (fôrʹmən) *n.* A *foreman* is the leader of a work crew.

grimace (grĭmʹĭs) *n.* A *grimace* is a facial expression of pain or disgust.

grope (grōp) *v.* When you *grope*, you reach about in an uncertain way.

hypocritical (hĭpʹə-krĭtʹĭ-kəl) *adj.* If someone is *hypocritical*, the person is false or deceptive.

impervious (ĭm-pûrʹvē-əs) *adj.* If something is *impervious*, it is impossible to penetrate.

impetuous (ĭm-pĕchʹōō-əs) *adj.* If someone is *impetuous*, he or she acts without thinking things through.

implication (ĭmʹplĭ-kāʹshən) *n.* An *implication* is a connection or consequence.

impotent (ĭmʹpə-tənt) *adj.* If someone is *impotent*, he or she is lacking strength or vigor.

inadequate (ĭn-ădʹĭ-kwĭt) *adj.* If something is *inadequate*, it is insufficient or not enough.

incisive (ĭn-sīʹsĭv) *adj.* If something is *incisive*, it is penetrating, clear, and sharp.

ineradicable (ĭnʹĭ-rădʹĭ-kə-bəl) *adj.* If something is *ineradicable*, it is impossible to remove.

initiative (ĭ-nĭshʹə-tĭv) *n.* An *initiative* is a beginning step in a plan.

insolent (ĭnʹsə-lənt) *adj.* If someone is *insolent*, he or she is rude or disrespectful.

instill (ĭn-stĭlʹ) *v.* When you *instill* something, you supply it gradually.

intensify (ĭn-tĕnʹsə-fī) *v.* If you *intensify* something, you make it grow in strength.

intersperse (ĭnʹtər-spûrsʹ) *v.* If you *intersperse* something, you distribute it in different places.

irate (ī-rātʹ) *adj.* If you are *irate*, you are very angry.

jubilation (jōōʹbə-lāʹshən) *n.* *Jubilation* is the act of celebrating.

justify (jŭsʹtə-fī) *v.* If you *justify* something, you prove it is right or valid.

legitimately (lə-jĭtʹə-mĭt-lē) *adv.* When you do something *legitimately*, you do it lawfully.

linger (lĭngʹgər) *v.* When you *linger*, you remain or stay longer.

looter (lōōtʹər) *n.* A *looter* is someone who steals during a war or riot.

mediate (mēʹdē-āt) *v.* If you *mediate* a conflict, you try to settle the differences.

muted (myōōʹtĭd) *adj.* When something is *muted*, it is softened or muffled.

natal (nātʹl) *adj.* If something is *natal*, it relates to birth.

naturalize (năchʹər-ə-līzʹ) *v.* When governments *naturalize* people, they grant them full citizenship.

Glossary of Critical Vocabulary

nominal (nŏm´ə-nəl) *adj.* Something that is *nominal* is small or insignificant.

notion (nō´shən) *n.* A *notion* is a belief or opinion.

novice (nŏv´ĭs) *n.* A *novice* is a beginner.

oppress (ə-prĕs´) *v.* When you *oppress* someone, you overwhelm or crush them.

ostensible (ŏ-stĕn´sə-bəl) *adj.* If something is *ostensible*, it is apparent or supposed.

paradox (păr´ə-dŏks´) *n.* A *paradox* is a true statement that seems like it would not be true.

parallel (păr´ə-lĕl´) *adj.* If things are *parallel*, they have comparable or similar parts.

particular (pər-tĭk´yə-lər) *adj.* If you are *particular* about something, you are fussy about it and pay attention to its details.

peril (pĕr´əl) *n.* A *peril* is something that is dangerous.

pernicious (pər-nĭsh´əs) *adj.* If something is *pernicious*, it is very harmful or destructive.

perpetual (pər-pĕch´ōō-əl) *adj.* If something is *perpetual*, it lasts for a very long time.

persecution (pûr´sĭ-kyōō´shən) *n. Persecution* is the harsh treatment of others, often due to race or religion.

perverse (pər-vûrs´) *adj.* If something is *perverse*, it is stubbornly contrary, wrong, or harmful.

poignant (poin´yənt) *adj.* If something is *poignant*, it is profoundly moving or touching.

precocious (prĭ-kō´shəs) *adj.* If someone is *precocious*, the person is mentally advanced for his or her age.

predicament (prĭ-dĭk´ə-mənt) *n.* A *predicament* is an unpleasant situation from which it is difficult to free oneself.

predominate (prĭ-dŏm´ə-nāt´) *v.* If ideas or things *predominate*, they are the most common.

prosaic (prō-zā´ĭk) *adj.* If something is *prosaic*, it is dull or ordinary.

provisions (prə-vĭzh´ənz) *n. Provisions* are a stock of necessary supplies, such as food.

prudence (prōōd´ns) *n. Prudence* is the wise handling of practical matters.

quest (kwĕst) *n.* A *quest* is a search.

ramble (răm´bəl) *v.* When you *ramble*, you talk at length in an aimless way.

recap (rē-kăp´) *v.* To *recap* an event is to retell or summarize it.

refuge (rĕf´yōōj) *n.* A *refuge* is a shelter from danger.

renowned (rĭ-nound´) *adj.* If something is *renowned*, it is famous.

repatriate (rē-pā´trē-āt´) *v.* To *repatriate* people is to return them to the country in which they were born.

reproach (rĭ-prōch´) *n.* A *reproach* is a scolding or blaming.

requisite (rĕk´wĭ-zĭt) *adj.* Something that is *requisite* is needed or essential.

resignation (rĕz´ĭg-nā´shən) *n. Resignation* is the acceptance of something that is inescapable.

resolute (rĕz´ə-lōōt´) *adj.* If you are *resolute*, you are firm or determined.

resonate (rĕz´ə-nāt´) *v.* When ideas *resonate*, they have a great effect or impact.

retribution (rĕt´rə-byōō´shən) *n. Retribution* is something given in repayment, usually as a punishment.

ruffian (rŭf´ē-ən) *n.* A *ruffian* is a thug or a gangster.

scuffle (skŭf´əl) *n.* A *scuffle* is a disorderly fight.

secede (sĭ-sēd´) *v.* When you *secede*, you formally withdraw from an organization or association.

solemn (sŏl´əm) *adj.* If an event is *solemn*, it is deeply serious.

splendid (splĕn´dĭd) *adj.* If something is *splendid*, it is magnificent or very good.

sponsor (spŏn´sər) *v.* If you *sponsor* someone, you support his or her admission into a group.

squalor (skwŏl´ər) *n.* *Squalor* is a filthy, shabby, and wretched condition, as from poverty.

stifle (stī´fəl) *v.* If you *stifle* something, you smother it.

stoicism (stō´ĭ-sĭz´əm) *n.* *Stoicism* is indifference to pleasure or pain, or a lack of visible emotion.

stoop (sto͞op) *v.* If you *stoop*, you bend forward and down from the waist.

strew (stro͞o) *v.* If you *strew* something, you spread it here and there, or scatter it.

stun (stŭn) *v.* To *stun* someone is to make him or her feel shocked or dazed.

succumb (sə-kŭm´) *v.* To *succumb* is to give in to an overwhelming force.

sullen (sŭl´ən) *adj.* *Sullen* people show silent resentment.

survey (sər-vā´) *v.* If you *survey* something, you inspect it.

sustain (sə-stān´) *v.* When you *sustain* something, you keep it in existence or continue it.

tangential (tăn-jĕn´shəl) *adj.* If something is *tangential*, it is only slightly connected.

telecommunications (tĕl´ĭ-kə-myo͞o´nĭ-kā´shəns) *n.* *Telecommunications* are the electronic systems that telephones and other electronic devices use to send information.

throng (thrông) *n.* A *throng* is a large group of people.

thwart (thwôrt) *v.* If you *thwart* something, you stop it from happening.

tranquil (trăng´kwəl) *adj.* If something is *tranquil*, it is calm.

tumult (to͞o´mŭlt´) *n.* A *tumult* is a disorderly disturbance.

unabated (ŭn´ə-bā´tĭd) *adj.* If something is *unabated*, it keeps its full force without decreasing.

unmoor (ŭn-mo͝or´) *v.* if you *unmoor* something, you release it from a place.

vehemently (vē´ə-mənt-lē) *adv.* If you do something *vehemently*, you do it with intense emotion.

vengeance (vĕn´jəns) *n.* *Vengeance* is a punishment given in return for a wrong.

vex (vĕks) *v.* If you *vex* someone, you annoy that person.

vindication (vĭn´dĭ-kā´shən) *n.* *Vindication* is the evidence or proof that someone's claim is correct.

whimper (hwĭm´pər) *v.* To *whimper* is to sob or let out a soft cry.

Index of Skills

A

abstract nouns, R29
Academic Vocabulary, 2, 79, 83, 88, 133, 137, 142, 203, 207, 212, 269, 273, 278, 389, 394, 437, 441. *See also* Glossary of Academic Vocabulary
act, of a play, 324, R64
action verbs, R30, R39
active voice, 70, 246, R41
activities
   media activity, 124, 268
   research activity, 51
   speaking activity, 78, 103, 130, 164, 174, 202, 233, 244, 354, 367, 384, 416, 425
   writing activity, 28, 38, 68, 96, 118, 149, 196, 226, 260, 376, 388, 402, 436
add details, 209
adjective clauses, R46–R47
adjective phrases, R44–R45
adjectives, R30, R42
   comparative forms of, R42–R43
   infinitives as, 228
   predicate, R43
   proper, R35
   superlative forms of, R42–R43
adventure stories, R64
adverb clauses, R47
adverb phrases, R44
adverbs, R30, R42
   vs. adjectives, R42
   comparatives, R42–R43
   infinitives as, 228
   superlatives, R42–R43
advertisements, 263
affirmative side, in debates, R14
alliteration, 387, R64
allusions, 68, 77, 118, 173, 196, R64
almanac, R74
ambiguous references, R39
analogies, 103, R57, R64. *See also* metaphors; similes
analysis. *See also* literary analysis
   writing activity, 376, 388, 402
Analyze Diverse Media, 267
Analyze Media, 73
analyzing
   arguments, R22
   autobiography, 148
   author's purpose, 149
   characters, 27
   connotative meanings, 195
   dialogue, 353, 402
   diary, 366
   drama, 324, 353, 354

historical fiction, 173
incidents in drama, 353
information, 259
media, 265
memoirs, 68
nonfiction elements, 50
plot, 27
poetry, 202, 430, 434, 436
point of view, 95, 401
sound devices, 387
stories, 27, 117, 173, 225
structure, 148, 163, 195, 201, 432, 434
suspense, 95
symbols, 226
text, 67, 129, 163, 366, 367
theme, 118, 402
tone, 103, 436
word choices, 383
word meanings, 67, 102, 375, 415
Analyzing the Media, 74, 124, 265, 267, 268
Analyzing the Text, 28, 37, 38, 51, 68, 78, 96, 103, 118, 130, 149, 164, 174, 196, 202, 226, 233, 244, 255, 258, 260, 324, 354, 367, 376, 384, 388, 402, 416, 425, 430, 434, 436
anecdotes, 425, R64
animation, 73, 265
Annotate It!, 28, 38, 68, 78, 96, 118, 130, 149, 164, 174, 196, 202, 226, 233, 255, 258, 260, 324, 354, 367, 376, 384, 388, 402, 416, 425, 430, 432, 434
antagonists, R64
antecedent, R36–R37
antonyms, 165, R57
apostrophes, R34
appeals
   to authority, R64
   bandwagon, R24
   emotional, 383, R23, R68
   ethical, 383, R23
   identifying, 384
   logical, R71
   to pity, fear, or vanity, R23, R68
appositive phrases, R45
appositives, R45
arguments, 133–136, 424, 425, R22, R64
   analyzing, R22
   audience for, 134, 442
   choosing position for, 441
   claims in, 243, 424, R22
   conclusions in, R25
   counterarguments in, 102, 103, 243, 244, 375, 424, 425, R22, R67

delineating, 424
delivering, 135
developing, 274
draft of, 134–135
elements of successful, 133, 441
evaluating, 135, 243, 244, 424, 425, 443, R27
evidence in, 134, 243, 424
gathering information for, 133, 441
linking ideas in, R3
logic and reasoning in, R24–R27
organization of, 134, 442
Performance Task Rubric, 136, 444
planning, 133–134, 441–442
position for, 133
practicing, 135
presenting, 443
purpose of, 134, 442
reading, R22–R28
recognizing persuasive techniques in, R23
research for, 134
revising, 443
speaking, 133–136
strategies for determining strong, R28
style and tone for, R3
support for, 424
tracing, 243
visuals for, 135
writing activity, 260
writing, 441–444, R2–R3
articles
   editorials, 274, R68
   feature, R69
   news, R72–R73
assonance, 387, R64
As You View, 72, 122, 264, 266
audience
   for argument, 134, 442
   considering your, 80, 84, 134, 138, 269, 273–274, 390, 442
   for informative essay, 80, 390
   for literary analysis, 138, 269
   for multimedia campaign, 273–274
   for personal narrative, 84
   target, 265
author's background, 3, 31, 53, 75, 89, 99, 105, 125, 143, 151, 167, 177, 199, 213, 229, 279, 355, 369, 379, 385, 395, 405, 427
author's craft, 163
author's message, R64
author's perspective, R64
author's position, R64. *See also* claims
author's purpose, 129, 148, R64
   analyzing, 149

Index of Skills   **R85**

author's viewpoint, 102, 375
autobiography, 148, R64
auxiliary verbs, R40, R51

B

ballads, R64
bandwagon appeals, R24
bar graphs, 50
base words, R54
bias, R27, R65
biased language, R5
biased tone, R3, R5
bibliography, R65. *See also* works cited
biography, 163, R65
brainstorming, 84, 438
bulleted lists, 50

C

camera filters, 123
camera shots, 123
capitalization
  first words, R35
  geographical names, R35
  I, R35
  organizations and events, R35
  people and titles, R35
  proper adjectives, R35
  quick reference, R35
career development documents, R65
cast of characters, 324, R65
cause and effect relationships, 148, R65
cause-effect organization, R4, R18
central ideas. *See also* theme
  determining, 37, 255
  for literary analysis, 270
  summarizing, 260
  supporting details for, 37, 255
characterization, 27, 163, R65
characters, 27, R65
  antagonists, R64
  cast of, 324
  dialogue by, 27
  dynamic, R65
  foils, R69
  main, R65
  minor, R65
  motivations of, 225
  static, R65
  and theme, 225
character sketches, 354
character traits, 353, R65
charts, 50, 51, 52, 74, 103, 164, 208, 268, 402
chronological order, 37, 353, R7, R17, R66
circle graphs, 50
circular reasoning, R26
citations, R10–R11

Cite Text Evidence, 28, 38, 51, 68, 74, 78, 96, 103, 118, 124, 130, 149, 164, 174, 196, 202, 226, 233, 244, 255, 258, 260, 265, 267, 268, 324, 354, 367, 376, 384, 388, 402, 415, 416, 425, 430, 436
claims, 243, 424, R66. *See also* arguments; thesis statement
  author's, R23
  counterclaims, R2, R28
  debating, R14–R15
  developing, R2–R3
  evaluating, 424
  evidence for, 243, 424
  factual, R27
  introducing, R2
  linking ideas to, R3
  support for, 243, 424, R15, R23, R77
  vague, R2
clarifying, R66
classification, R66
classroom discussions, R12–R13
clauses, R46
  adjective, R46
  adverb, R47
  essential adjective, R46–R47
  independent, 418, R46
  nonessential adjective, R47
  noun, R47
  subordinate, R46
  transitional, R3
cliché, R66
climax, 27, R7, R66
close-up shots, 123
Collaborative Discussion, 26, 36, 49, 66, 72, 76, 94, 101, 116, 122, 128, 147, 162, 172, 194, 200, 203–206, 224, 242, 257, 266, 352, 365, 374, 382, 386, 400, 414, 423, 433
collaborative discussions, 203–206, R12–R13
  conducting, 205
  elements of successful, 203
  gathering information for, 203
  ground rules for, 203, R12
  moving forward in, R12
  Performance Task Rubric, 206
  preparing for, 203–204, R12
  presenting, 205
  producing, 204–205
  purpose of, 204
  responding to ideas in, R13
  revising, 205
  writing draft of, 204
collective nouns, R29, R51
colons, R33
color, use of, 267
comedy, R66
commas, 132, R32
comma splices, R49

commonly confused words, R62–R63
common nouns, R29, R36
commonplace assertions, R27
comparative form, R42
compare-and-contrast organization, 195, R16, R19–R20, R66
Compare Media, 263, 268
Compare Poems, 427, 435
Compare Texts, 247, 259
comparisons
  as context clues, R53
  double, R43
  illogical, R43
  irregular, R43
  points of comparison, R19
  regular, R42
  speaking activity, 233
complements, R44
complete predicate, R31
complete subject, R31
complex sentences, R48
compound-complex sentences, R48
compound nouns, R29
compound predicates, R44
compound sentences, 418, R47
compound subjects, R44, R50
conclusions
  drawing, 51, 415, R68
  of arguments, R3
  of essays, R5
  of narratives, R7
concrete details, R5
concrete nouns, R29
condensing ideas, 139, 391
conditional mood, 166
conflict, 27, 225, R66, R74
conjunctions, R30
  coordinating, R30
  correlative, R30
  subordinating, R30
connecting, R66
connecting ideas, 81, 270, 443
connotations, 195, 368, R57, R66
consonance, 387
consumer documents, R66
content-area vocabulary, R58
context clues, 29, 150, 197, R67
  to interpret figures of speech, 175
  types of, R53
  using, R53
contrast, as context clue, R53
controlling idea. *See* thesis statement
coordinating conjunctions, R30
correlative conjunctions, R30
counterarguments, 102, 103, 243, 244, 375, 424, 425, R22, R67
counterclaims, R2, R28
couplets, 432, R67
credibility, R5, R67

Index of Skills

credible sources, R8
criteria, 129
   for argument, 133, 441
   for collaborative discussion, 203
   for informative essay, 79, 389
   for literary analysis, 137, 138, 269
   for multimedia campaign, 273
   for narrative, 437
   for personal narrative, 83
critical essays, R67
critical review, R67
Critical Vocabulary, 29, 39, 52, 69, 97, 119, 131, 150, 165, 175, 197, 227, 245, 261, 368, 377, 403, 417, 426. *See also* Glossary of Critical Vocabulary
critique, of documentary, 74

D

dangling participles, R45
dashes, R33
database, R67
debates, R14–R15, R67
   affirmative side in, R14
   evaluating, R15
   format of, R15
   holding, R14
   moderators of, R14
   negative side in, R15
   planning, R14
   roles in, R15
   speaking activity, 103, 244
   structure of formal, R15
   teams for, R14
declarative sentences, R44
deductive reasoning, 258, R25, R67
demonstrative pronouns, R29, R38
denotations, 195, 368, R57, R67
dénouement. *See* falling action
description, R6, R67
details
   concrete, R5
   gathering, R6
   quotations from experts, 255
   sensory, 85, 415, 416, R75
   supporting, 37, 255, R16
   determining
      author's viewpoint, 102, 375
      central ideas, 37, 255
      theme, 117, 118, 225, 232
      word meanings, 29, 77, 173, 201, 401, 430
diagrams, 50
dialect, R67
dialogue, 353, 402, R67
   in drama, 324, 353
   realistic, 438
diary, 366, R67
dictionaries, 417, R58
direct objects, 198, R31, R44
direct quotations, R9

discussion
   collaborative, R12–R13
   Collaborative Discussion, 26, 36, 49, 66, 72, 76, 94, 101, 116, 128, 147, 162, 172, 194, 200, 203–206, 224, 242, 257, 266, 352, 365, 374, 382, 386, 400, 414, 423, 429, 433
   group, 208, R12–R13
   speaking activity, 78, 130, 174, 384
documentary films, 71–74
   animation in, 73
   evaluating, 73, 74
   motive for making, 73
   purpose of, 73
   stills in, 73
   summarizing, 74
   techniques used in, 73
   voice-overs in, 73
documents
   consumer, R66
   government, R74
   historical, R70
   public, R74
domain-specific words, 261
double comparison, R43
drafts, 80–81, 84, 138–139, 204, 208–209, 270, 274, 390–391, 439, 442
   of arguments, 134–135, 442
   of editorials, 274
   of informative essays, 80–81, 390–391
   of literary analysis, 138–139, 208–209, 270
   of narratives, 439
   of personal narratives, 84
   revising, 81, 85, 139, 209, 271, 275, 391, 439, 443
drama, R67
   acts in, 324, R64
   cast of characters in, 324
   dialogue in, 324, 353
   flashbacks in, 353
   historical, R70
   incidents in, 353
   playwrights, 324
   scenes in, 324, R75
   script for, 324
   sequencing of events in, 353
   stage directions for, 324
   structure of, 324
   tragedy, R77
dramatic irony, 401
drawing conclusions. *See* conclusions
dynamic characters, R65

E

eBook, 28, 38, 51, 68, 78, 96, 103, 118, 130, 149, 164, 174, 196, 202, 226, 233, 255, 258, 260, 265, 268, 324,
354, 367, 376, 384, 388, 402, 416, 425, 430, 432, 434
editorials, R68
   writing, 274
effect, R65
either/or fallacy, R68
elegy, 201
ellipses, 378, R34
emotional appeals, 383, R23, R68
end rhyme, R75
epic poems, 435, R75
essays, R68
   central idea of, 37
   compare and contrast, 436
   conclusion, R5
   critical, R67
   drafts of, 80–81, 390–391
   expository, R68
   informative, 79–82, 389–392, R4–R5
   outlines for, 80
   personal, 37, R73
   persuasive, R74
   presenting, 81
   purpose and audience for, 80
   revising, 81, 391
   visuals for, 80
   writing activity, 436
ethical appeals, 383, R68
etymologies, R58
evading the issue, R26
evaluating, R68
   allusions, 196
   arguments, 243, 244, 424, 425, 443, R27
   author's reasoning, 258
   debates, R25
   documentary, 73, 74
   drama, 354
   evidence, R27
   films, 123, 124
   media, 73, 123, 268
   poetry, 202, 388
   public service announcements, 265
   source material, 204
   speeches, 135, 384
   text, 255, 260, 376
   tone, 78, 402
   writing style, 402
evidence, R68. *See also* cite text evidence
   evaluating, R27
   irrelevant, 243
   from media, 74, 265, 267, 268
   relevant, 243, 424
   to support claims, 243, R2, R12
exclamation points, R32
exclamatory sentences, R44
explanation, writing activity, 51
exposition, 27, R68

extended definitions, R5
extended metaphors, 201, R68
external conflict, R68

F

fables, R68
facts, 255, 259, R5
factual claims, R27
fact versus opinion, R68
fallacies, R26, R69
falling action, 27, R69
false causation, R26
fantasy, R69
faulty reasoning, R26
fear, appeals to, 383, R24, R68
feature article, R69
fiction, R69. *See also* short stories
    fantasy, R69
    historical, 173, R70
    horror, 130, 133, 137
    science fiction, R75
figurative language, 67, 201, 233, 367, 434, 430, 436, R53, R76. *See also* metaphors, personification, similes; style
figures of speech, 175, 403
films
    animation in, 265
    camera filters in, 123
    camera shots used in, 123
    documentary, 71–74
    evaluating, 123, 124
    lighting in, 123
    music in, 123
    narrator in, 265
    public service announcement, 264
    sound elements of, 265
    summarizing, 124
    techniques used in, 122, 123
    visual elements of, 265
first drafts. *See* drafts
first-person narrator, R6
first-person point of view, 95, R69
flashbacks, 353, R7, R69
flow charts, 84
foils, R69
folk ballads, R64–R65
folklore, R69
folk tales, R69
foot (meter), 432
foreign words, R55–R56
foreshadowing, 117, R69
form, R69
formal debates, R14–R15
fragments, sentence, 262, R48
free verse, 434, 435, R69
future perfect progressive tense, R40–R41
future perfect tense, R40

future progressive tense, R41
future tense, R40
fyi, 2, 88, 142, 212, 278, 394

G

general dictionary, R58
generalization, R70
    hasty, R26
    overgeneralization, R26, R73
general references, R39
genre, R70
gerund phrases, R46
gerunds, 198, R46
glossaries, 39, R59
Glossary of Academic Vocabulary, R80
Glossary of Critical Vocabulary, R81
Glossary of Literary and Informational Terms, R64–R78
government publications, R70
grammar. *See also* Language Conventions; parts of speech
    capitalization, R35
    handbook, R36–R52
    parts of speech, R29
    punctuation, R32–R34
    sentence parts, R31
    sentences, R31
graphics, 50, 134, R70
graphic organizers, 27, R70
    flow charts, 80, 84
    hierarchy charts, 134, 138, 270, 274, 442
    timelines, 38
    Venn diagrams, 436
graphics, 267, R4
graphs, 50
Greek prefixes, 52
Greek roots, 245, R54
Greek suffixes, 426
group discussions, 208, R12–R13

H

hasty generalization, R26
headers, 50, R4
helping verbs, R31
heroes, R70
hierarchy charts, 134, 138, 270, 274, 442
high-angle shots, 123
historical documents, R70
historical drama, R70
historical fiction, 173, R70
HISTORY™, 41, 53, 105, 143, 151, 167, 279, 379
homonyms, R57–R58
homophones, R57–R58
horror genre, 133, 137
how-to books, R70
humor, R70

humorous tone, 401
hyperbole, R70, R78
hyphens, R33

I

iamb, 432
iambic pentameter, 432
ideas. *See also* central ideas
    linking, in arguments, R3
    main, R72
idioms, 175, R53, R70
illogical comparisons, R43
imagery, 67, 84, R70
    interpreting, 96, 384
    and mood, 173
    in poetry, 77
    use of, 415
imperative mood, 30, 176, 246, 404
imperative sentences, R44
indefinite pronouns, R30, R38, R50
indefinite references, R39
independent clauses, 418, R46
index, R71
indicative mood, 176, 246, 404
indirect objects, R31, R44
inductive reasoning, 258, R24, R71
inferences, 77, R71
    about character motivations, 225
    about drama, 354
    about media, 267
    about poetry, 77, 78, 232, 233, 388, 430, 434
    about public service announcements, 265
    about similes, 68
    about stories, 28, 226
    about text, 38, 51, 96, 118, 130, 164, 226, 366, 367, 416
    about theme, 117, 232
infinitive phrases, 228, R45
infinitives, 228, R45
informal tone, R3
informational texts, R71
    reading, R16–R21
    writing, R4
informative essays, 79–82, 196, 389–392, R68
    audience for, 80, 390
    determining topic for, 79–80
    drafts of, 80–81, 390–391
    elements of successful, 79, 389
    gathering information for, 389–390
    ideas for, 79
    organization, 80, 390
    outlines for, 80, 390
    Performance Task Rubric, 82, 392
    planning, 79–80, 389–390
    presenting, 81, 391
    purpose of, 80, 390
    research for, 80, 390

revising, 81, 391
    visuals for, 80
intensive pronouns, R29, R37
Interactive Lessons, 80, 81, 84, 134, 135, 138, 139, 203, 205, 208, 209, 270, 271, 274, 390, 391, 438, 439, 442, 443
interjections, R30
internal conflict, R71
internal rhyme, R75
Internet, R71
interrogative mood, 404
interrogative pronouns, R30, R38
interrogative sentences, R44
interviews, R71
intransitive verbs, R30
inverted sentences, R51
irony, 202, 401
    dramatic, 401
    situational, 38
    verbal, 403
irregular verbs, R40
irrelevant evidence, 243
italics, R34

J

jargon, R5
journal, R71

L

Language Conventions
    active and passive voice, 70
    add details, 209
    commas, 132
    condensing ideas, 139, 391
    conditional mood, 166
    connecting ideas, 81, 270, 443
    dashes, 98
    details and sensory language, 85
    ellipses, 378
    fragments, 262
    gerunds, 198
    imperative mood, 30
    indicative mood, 176
    infinitives, 228
    interrogative mood, 404
    participles, 40
    realistic dialogue, 438
    run-on sentences, 418
    semicolons, 418
    shifts in voice and mood, 246
    subject-verb agreement, 104
    subjunctive mood, 120
    using transitions, 135
    words ending in *y*, 234
Latin prefixes, 69
Latin roots, 119, R54
Latin suffixes, 227, 377
legend, R71. *See also* myths
lighting, in film, 123

limerick, R71
linking verbs, R30, R39
lists
    bulleted, 50
    colons before, R33
literary analysis, 137–140, 207–210, 269–272
    audience for, 138, 269
    central idea for, 270
    choosing story for, 137
    criteria for, 138
    draft of, 138–139, 208–209, 270
    elements of successful, 137, 207, 269
    and group discussions, 208
    Performance Task Rubric, 140, 210, 272
    planning, 208
    presenting, 139, 209, 271
    purpose of, 138, 269
    research for, 207
    revising, 139, 209, 271
    writing activity, 149, 226
literary criticism
    author's purpose in, 129
    definition of, 129
literary techniques
    alliteration, 387, R64
    allusion, 68, 77, 118, 173, 196, R64
    assonance, 387, R64
    cliché, R66
    foreshadowing, 117, R69
    hyperbole, R70 R78
    idioms, 175, R53, R70
    imagery, 67, 77, 84, 415, R70
    irony, 38, 202, 401, 403
    metaphors, 67, 201, 434, R72
    onomatopoeia, R73
    personification, 233, 430, 434, R73
    puns, 403
    rhetorical devices, 383, 384
    similes, 67, 68, 233, 367, 430, 434, R76
    symbols, 173, 225, 226, R77
literature
    oral, R73
    response to, 202, 203–206, 233, 354
loaded language, R27, R71
logic
    analyzing, in arguments, R24–R26
    circular, R24
logical appeals, R71
logical arguments, R71
logical fallacies, R27
low-angle shots, 123
lyric poetry, R71

M

main characters, R65
main idea, R16, R72. *See also* central

ideas
    implied, R17
main verb, R31
A Manual for Writers (Turabian), R9
media. *See also* media elements and techniques; media genres and types
    analyzing, 73, 74, 124, 265, 267
    comparing, 247, 268
    evaluating, 73, 123, 268
    evidence from, 74, 265, 267, 268
    message of, 265
    motive for, 73
    oral information in, 268
    persuasive techniques, 265
    purpose of, 73
    quantitative information in, 268
    statistics in, 267
    target audience, 265
media activity
    posters, 38
    public service announcements, 268
    storyboards, 124
    videos, 74
Media Analysis, 71, 121, 263
media elements and techniques,
    animation, 73
    camera filters, 123
    camera shots, 123
    close-up shot, 123
    color, 267
    graphics, 267
    high-angle shot, 123
    lighting, 123
    low-angle shot, 123
    music, 123
    narrator, 265
    point-of-view shot, 123
    sound elements, 265
    stills, 73
    storyboard, 124
    visual elements, 265, 267
    voice-over, 73
media genres and types
    documentaries, 71–74
    films, 121–124
    public service announcement film, 263–265, 268
    public service announcement poster, 263, 266–268
memoirs, 67, R72
Mentor Text, 79, 83, 84, 133, 137, 389, 437, 441
metaphors, 67, 201, 434, R72
    extended, 201, R68
meter, 432, 435, R72
minor characters, R65
MLA Handbook for Writers of Research Papers (MLA), R9
moderators, debate, R14

Modern Language Association (MLA), R9
modifiers, R41–R42
　adjectives, R30, R42
　adverbs, R30, R42
　comparisons, R42
　dangling, R43
　misplaced, R43
　problems with, R43
monitoring, R72
mood, of story, 173, R72
mood, of verb
　conditional, 166
　imperative, 30, 176, 246, 404
　indicative, 176, 246, 404
　interrogative, 404
　shifts in, 246
　subjunctive, 120, 176
moral, R72
motivations, of characters, 225
motives
　commercial, 73
　of documentary filmmaker, 73
　political, 73
　social, 73
multimedia campaign, 273–276
　audience for, 273–274
　developing argument for, 274
　elements of successful, 273
　gathering information for, 273
　multiple formats for, 275
　Performance Task Rubric, 276
　planning, 273–274
　presenting, 275
　producing, 274–275
　purpose of, 273–274
　research for, 273
　revising, 275
multimedia links, R5
multiple-meaning words, R58
multiple plot lines, R7
music, in film, 123
*my*Notebook, 3, 79, 83, 89, 133, 137, 143, 204, 207, 213, 269, 273, 279, 389, 395, 437, 441
myths, 117, R72
*my*WordList, 3, 89, 143, 213, 279, 395
*my*WriteSmart, 28, 38, 51, 68, 74, 78, 80, 81, 84, 85, 96, 103, 118, 124, 130, 134, 135, 138, 139, 149, 164, 174, 196, 202, 204, 205, 208, 209, 226, 233, 268, 270, 271, 274, 275, 354, 367, 376, 384, 388, 390, 391, 402, 416, 425, 436, 438, 442, 443

N

narrative, presenting, 437–440
　audience for, 438
　drafts of, 439
　elements of successful, 437
　Performance Task Rubric, 440
　planning, 437–438
　point of view for, 438
　presenting, 439
　purpose of, 438
　revising, 439
　writing, 437–440
narrative, speaking activity, 367
narrative, writing activity, 96
narrative nonfiction, R72
narrative poetry, R72
narrative techniques, R6. *See also* literary techniques
narrator, R6, R72
　analyzing, 96
　in film, 265
　omniscient, 401
　in personal narratives, 83
　and point of view, 95, 401
　unreliable, 95, R72
news article, R72
nonessential adjective clauses, R47
nonessential appositives, R45
nonfiction elements, 50
noun clauses, R47
nouns, R29, R36
　abstract, R29
　collective, R29, R36
　common, R29, R36
　compound, R29
　concrete, R29
　infinitives as, 228
　plural, 234, R29, R36, R60
　possessive, R29, R36, R61
　predicate, 198, R44
　proper, R29, R36
　singular, R29, R36
novels, R73

O

objective tone, R3, R5
object of preposition, 198
object pronouns, R37
objects
　direct, 198, R31, R44
　indirect, R31, R44
observations, identifying, in writing narratives, R6
odes, 435, R73
omniscient narrators, 401
onomatopoeia, R73
op-ed pieces, R73
oral information, 268
oral literature, R73
organization
　for arguments, 134, 442
　for informational texts, R16–R21
organizational patterns, R16–R21, R73

cause and effect, 148, R18
chronological order, 37, 38, 353, R17, R66
compare and contrast, 195, R19
　point-by-point, R19
　problem-solution, R21, R74
　subject-by-subject, R19
outlines, creating, 80, 390
overgeneralization, R26, R73
oversimplification, R26
overview, R73

P

pacing, 438, R7
parallelism, 163, 383, 387, R48
paraphrasing, R9, R73
parentheses, R33
parenthetical citations, R9
participle phrases, R45
participles, 40, 198, R45
　dangling, R45
　misplaced, R45
　past, 40
　present, 40
parts of speech, R29–R30
passive voice, 70, 246, R41
past participles, 40, R39
past perfect progressive tense, R40
past perfect tense, R39
past principal part, R39
past progressive tense, R40
past tense, R39
pattern of organization, R73
patterns, identifying, 196, 324, 388, 436
patterns of organization. *See* organizational patterns
Performance Task, end of collection
　argument, 133–136, 441–444
　collaborative discussion, 203–206
　informative essay, 79–82, 389–392
　literary analysis, 137–140, 207–210, 269–272
　multimedia campaign, 273–276
　narrative presentation, 437–440
　personal narrative, 83–86
　Plan, Produce, Revise, Present, 79–81, 83–85, 133–135, 137–139, 203–205, 207–209, 269–271, 273–275, 389–391, 437–439, 441–443
Performance Task, selection
　media activity, 74, 124, 268
　research activity, 51
　speaking activity, 78, 103, 130, 164, 174, 202, 233, 244, 354, 367, 384, 416, 425
　writing activity, 28, 38, 68, 96, 118, 149, 196, 226, 260, 376, 388, 402, 436

Index of Skills

Performance Task Rubric
  argument, 136, 444
  collaborative discussion, 206
  informative essay, 82, 392
  literary analysis, 140, 210, 272
  multimedia campaign, 276
  narrative presentation, 440
  personal narrative, 86
periodicals, R73
periods, R32
personal essays, 37, R73
  audience for, 84
  drafts of, 84
  elements of successful, 83
  images in, 84
  Performance Task Rubric, 86
  personal narratives, 83–86
  planning, 83–84
  presenting, 85
  purpose of, 84
  revising, 85
  sequence of events in, 83–84
  situation, establishing, 83
personal pronouns, R29, R36, R50
personification, 233, 430, 434, R73
persuasion, R73
persuasive essays, R68
persuasive techniques, 265, 383, 384
persuasive texts
photographs, 50
phrases, R44
  adjective, R44
  adverb, R44
  appositives, R45
  gerund, R45
  infinitive, 228, R45
  participle, R45
  prepositional, R31, R44
  verbal, R45
pity, appeals to, 383, R24, R68
plagiarism, R9
Plan, Produce, Revise, Present. *See under* Performance Task, end of collection
plays. *See* drama
playwrights, 324
plot, 27, R74
  conflict in, 27, 225, R74
  elements of, 27
  falling action in, 27, R69
  multiple plot lines, R7
  resolution in, 27
  rising action in, 27
  theme and, 225
plural nouns, R29, R36, R60
poetic elements and devices. *See also* poetic form; poetry
  alliteration, 387
  allusions, 77
  consonance, 387

couplets, 432
meter, 432, 435
parallelism, 387
personification, 233
repetition, 78, 387
rhyme, R75
rhyme scheme, 432, 435
rhythm, 387, R75
similes, 434
sound devices, 387, 388, R76
speaker, 77, 232, R76
stanza, R76
theme, 232
tone, 78, 201, 436
poetic form. *See also* poetic elements; poetry
  elegy, 201
  epic, 435, R68
  free verse, 434, 435
  narrative, R72
  odes, 435
  sonnets, 432, 435, R76
  traditional forms, 435
poetry, R74
  analyzing, 430, 434, 436
  choral reading of, 202
  comparing, 427, 435
  determining meanings in, 77
  inferences about, 77, 78, 232, 233, 388, 430, 434
  interpreting, 78, 202, 388
  metaphors in, 434
  structure of, 201, 432, 434
point-by-point organization, R19
point of view, R74. *See also* narrator
  analyzing, 95, 401
  first-person, 95, R74
  identifying, 402
  for narrative, 438
  objective, R74
  subjective, R74
  third-person, 95, 401, R74
point-of-view shots, 123
points of comparison, R19
possessive nouns, R29, R36, R61
possessive pronouns, R37
poster
  media activity, 38
  public service announcement, 266
  writing activity, 196
predicate
  adjectives, R42
  complete, R31
  compound, R44
  nominatives, R44, R51
  nouns, 198, R44
  pronouns, R44
predicting, R74
prefixes, R54, R60
  Greek, 52

Latin, 69
prepositional phrases, R31, R44
prepositions, R30
  objects of, 198
presentations
  narrative, 437–440
  speaking activity, 416
present participles, 40, R39
present perfect progressive tense, R41
present perfect tense, R40
present principal part, R40
present progressive tense, R41
present tense, R40
primary sources, R74
prior knowledge, R74
problem-solution order, R4, R21, R74
pronouns, R29, R36
  antecedent agreement, R36–R37
  demonstrative, R29, R38
  forms, R37
  indefinite, R30, R38
  intensive, R29, R37
  interrogative, R30, R38
  object, R37
  personal, R29, R36, R50
  possessive, R37
  predicate, R44
  reference problems, R39
  reflexive, R29, R37
  relative, R30, R38, R51–R52
  subject, R37
pronunciation key, R79
propaganda, R27, R74
proper adjectives, R35
proper nouns, R29, R36
props, R74
prose, R74
protagonists, R74
public documents, R74
punctuation
  apostrophes, R34
  colons, R33
  commas, 132, R32
  dashes, 98, R33
  ellipses, 378, R34
  exclamation points, R32
  hyphens, R33
  parentheses, R33
  periods, R32
  question marks, R32
  quick reference, R32–R34
  quotation marks, R34
  semicolons, 418, R33
  use of, 163
puns, 403

Q

quantitative information, 268
question marks, R32
questions

research, R8
rhetorical, R75
quotation marks, R34
quotations, 255
  colons before, R33
  direct, R9

R

radio play, R74
reading
  arguments, R22–R28
  informational texts, R16–R21
reasoning
  circular, R26
  deductive, 258, R25, R67
  evaluating author's, 258
  faulty, R26
  inductive, 258, R24, R71
reasons, to support claims, R2
recurring themes, R74
reference works, R58, R74
  bibliography, R65
  dictionaries, 417, R67
  glossaries, 39, R59
  synonym finders, R58
  thesaurus, 97, R58
reflexive pronouns, R29, R37
regular verbs, R40
relative pronouns, R30, R38, R51
  as subjects, R51–R52
relevant evidence, 243, 424
repetition, 78, 383, 387, R74
reports
  writing activity, 68, 118
rereading, 28, 38, 51, 78, 96, 118, 130, 133, 137, 149, 164, 196, 201, 202, 207, 226, 233, 255, 258, 260, 269, 324, 354, 367, 376, 384, 388, 402, 415, 416, 425, 430
research
  conducting, 80, 134, 196, 204, 207, 273, 390, R8
  focus of, R8
  formulating question for, R8
research questions, R8
research study, example, 41–49
resolution, 27. *See also* falling action
response to literature, 202, 203–206, 233, 354
rhetorical devices, 383, 384
rhetorical questions, R75
rhyme, R75
rhyme scheme, 432, 435, R75
rhythm, 387, R75
rising action, 27
roots, R54
  Greek, 245
  Latin, 119
rough drafts. *See* drafts
rubric. *See* Performance Task Rubric

run-on sentences, 418, R48–R49

S

scanning, R75
scenery, R75
scenes, 324, R75
science fiction, R75
screenplays, R75
scripts, 324, R75
secondary sources, R8, R75
semicolons, 418, R33
sensory details, 415, 416, R75
sensory language, R7
sentence fragments, 262, R48
sentences
  complements, R44
  complete, writing, R48–R49
  complex, R48
  compound, 418, R47
  compound-complex, R48
  compound subjects and predicates, R44
  declarative, R44
  exclamatory, R44
  imperative, R44
  interrogative, R44
  inverted, R57
  parallel structure in, R48
  parts of, R31, R43
  with predicate nominatives, R51
  run-on, 418, R48–R49
  simple, R47
  structure of, R47–R48
  subject-verb agreement in, 104, R49–R50
  syntax, 102, 163
  topic, R77
  types of, R44
  variety in, 163
sequential order, R75
setting, 173, 225, R75
Setting a Purpose, 3, 31, 41, 53, 71, 75, 89, 99, 105, 121, 125, 143, 151, 167, 177, 199, 213, 229, 235, 247, 263, 279, 355, 369, 379, 385, 395, 405, 419, 427
short stories, R75
sidebars, R76
signal words, R76
similes, 67, 68, 233, 367, 430, 434, R76
situational irony, 38
slang, R53
snob appeal, R24
sonnets, 432, 435, R76
sound devices, 387, 388, R76
sound elements, 265
sources, R76
  citing, R9
  credible, R8
  evaluating, R8

  incorporating into research paper, R9
  locating, R8
  primary, R8, R74
  secondary, R8, R75
speaker, of poem, 77, 232, R76
speaking activity
  argument, 425
  choral reading, 202
  debate, 103, 244
  discussion, 78, 130, 174, 384
  narrative, 367
  presentation, 416
  response to literature, 233, 354
  speech, 164
Speaking and Listening, 96, 149, 174, 233, 354
specialized dictionary, R58
specialized vocabulary, R58
speeches, R76
  argument, 133–136
  delivering, 135
  evaluating, 135, 384
  practicing, 134
  speaking activity, 164
  visuals for, 135
  writing, 134
spelling rules
  plural nouns, forming, R60
  possessives, forming, R61
  prefixes, R60
  special spelling problems, R61
  suffixes, R60
  words ending in a consonant, R59–R60
  words ending in silent *e*, R59
  words ending in *y*, R59
stage directions, 324, R76
stanza, R76
static characters, R65
statistics, 255, 267, R5
stereotypes, R76
stereotyping, R26, R76
stills, in documentary, 73
storyboards, 124
Stream to Start, 2, 88, 142, 212, 278, 394
style, 102, 401, R76
  for arguments, R3
  elements of, 102, 103
  and figurative language, 102
  formal, R5
  for informative essay, R5
  of literary work, 401
  and syntax, 102
  and tone, 401
  and word choice, 102
style manuals, R9
subheadings, 50
subject-by-subject organization, R19

R92 Student Resources

Index of Skills

subject complements, R44
subject pronouns, R37
subjects
  collective nouns as, R51
  complete, R31
  compound, R44, R50
  gerunds as, 198
  indefinite pronouns as, R50
  personal pronouns as, R50
  plural, 104
  relative pronouns as, R51
  singular, 104
subject-verb agreement, 104
  basic, R49
  with *be*, R49
  with collective nouns, R51
  with compound subjects, R50
  don't and *doesn't* as auxiliary verbs, R51
  with indefinite pronouns, R50
  inverted sentences, R51
  with personal pronouns, R50
  with predicate nominatives, R51
  with relative pronouns, R51
  with words between subject and verb, R50
subject-verb order, 404
subjunctive mood, 120, 176
subordinate clause, R46
subordinating conjunction, R30
subtitles, 50
suffixes, 131, R54, R60
  Greek, 426
  Latin, 227, 377
summarizing, 129, R77. *See also* paraphrasing
  central ideas, 260
  documentary, 74
  films, 124
summary, writing activity, 28
superlative form, R42
support
  for claims, 424, R16, R77
  types of, R5
supporting details, 37, 255, R16
surprise endings, R77
suspense, 95, 117, R7, R77
symbols, 173, 225, 226, R77
synonym finders, R58
synonyms, 97, R57
syntax, 102, 163
synthesize, R77

T

take/bring, R62
tall tales, R77
target audience, 265
tense, verb, R40
testimonials, R24

text features, 50, R77
  bulleted list, 50
  graphics, 50
  headers, 50
  subheaders, 50
  subtitles, 50
theme, R77
  analyzing, 402
  clues to, 225
  determining, 117, 118, 225, 232
  inferences about, 117
  of poem, 232
  recurring, R77
  universal, 117, R77
thesaurus, 97, R58
thesis statement, 79–82, 138–140, 208–210, 269–271, 390–392, R4, R77
third-person narrator, R6
third-person point of view, 95, 401, R74
timelines, 38
time order. *See* chronological order
titles, 225, R77
tone, 436, R77
  of argument, R3
  biased, R3, R5
  of elegy, 201
  formal, R5
  humorous, 401
  informal, R3
  for informative essay, R5
  objective, R3, R5
  of poem, 78, 436
  and word choice, 375, 401
topic sentence, R77
trace, an argument, 243
traditional forms, 435
tragedy, R77
transitions, 135, R4–R5
transitive verbs, R30

U

understatement, R78
universal themes, 117, R77
unreliable narrators, 95, R72

V

vanity, appeals to, 383, R24, R68
Venn diagrams, 436
verbal irony, 403
verbal phrases, R45
verbals, 40, 198, 228, R45
verbs, R30, R39
  action, R30, R39
  active and passive voice, 70, 246
  auxiliary, R30, R31, R51
  conditional mood, 166
  gerunds, 198, R45
  helping, R31

imperative mood, 30, 176, 246, 404
indicative mood, 176, 246, 404
infinitives, 228
interrogative mood, 404
intransitive, R30
irregular, R40
linking, R30, R39
main, R31
mood of, 30, 120, 166, 176, 246, 404
participles, R45
passive voice, R41
principal parts, R39
progressive forms, R40
regular, R40
subject-verb agreement, 104, R49
subject-verb order, 404
subjunctive mood, 120, 176
tenses, R40
transitive, R30
voice of, 246
video. *See also* films
  creating, 74
  public service announcement, 264
viewpoint, author's, 102, 375
visual aids, 50, 80, 134
visual elements, 265, 267
visualize, R78
vivid language, R7
vocabulary
  Academic Vocabulary, 2, 79, 83, 88, 133, 137, 142, 203, 207, 212, 269, 273, 278, 389, 394, 437, 441
  commonly confused words, R62–R63
  Critical Vocabulary, 29, 39, 52, 69, 97, 119, 131, 150, 165, 175, 197, 227, 245, 261, 368, 377, 403, 417, 426
  specialized, R58
  strategies for understanding, R54
Vocabulary Strategy
  connotations, 368
  context clues, 29, 150, 197, R53
  denotations, 368
  dictionary, using, 417
  domain-specific words, 261
  figures of speech, 175
  glossary, using, 39
  Greek prefixes, 52
  Greek roots, 245
  Greek suffixes, 426
  Latin prefixes, 69
  Latin roots, 119
  Latin suffixes, 227, 377
  puns, 403
  suffixes, 131
  thesaurus, using, 97
  verbal irony, 403
  word relationships, 165

voice, of verb
   active, 70, 246
   passive, 70, 246
   shifts in, 246
voice, of writer, R78
voice-over, 73

W

website, R78
word choice, 102, 163, 195, 375, 383, 401, R78
word families, R56
word meanings
   analyzing, 67, 102, 375, 415
   antonyms, 165
   connotations, 195, 368
   denotations, 195, 368
   determining, 29, 77, 150, 173, 197, 201, 401, 430
   interpreting, 196
   and prefixes, 52, 69
   and suffixes, 227, 377, 426
   and word roots, 119, 245
word origins, R56
word structure, R54
workplace documents, R78
works cited, R9, R78
works consulted, R78
writing
   arguments, 133–136, 441–444, R2–R3
   complete sentences, R48–R49
   drafts, 80–81, 84, 134–135, 138–139, 204, 208–209, 270, 274, 390–391, 439, 442
   editorials, 274
   informative essays, 79–82, 389–392
   informative texts, R4–R5
   literary analysis, 137–140, 207–210, 269–272
   narrative presentation, 337–340
   narratives, R6–R7
   outlines, 80, 390
   personal narratives, 83–86
writing activity
   analysis, 376, 388, 402
   argument, 260
   compare and contrast essay, 436
   explanation, 51
   informative report, 260
   literary analysis, 149, 226
   narrative, 96
   poster, 196
   report, 118
   summary, 28
Writing and Research, 196
writing style. *See* style

Index of Titles and Authors

A
Adventures of Tom Sawyer, The, 395
After Auschwitz, 379
Alexie, Sherman, 75
Anne Frank: The Book, the Life, the Afterlife, 369
Aubrey, Allison, 247

B
Benoît, Jean-Pierre, 31
Bittle, Scott, 41
Bloody Times: The Funeral of Abraham Lincoln and the Manhunt for Jefferson Davis, 177
Bonne Année, 31
Bradbury, Ray, 167

C
Cheng, Jenny Diamond, 235
Chicago, 428
Collier, Eugenia, 213

D
Davis, Robert, 247
Diary of a Young Girl, The, 355
Diary of Anne Frank, The, 279
Douglass, Frederick, 143
Dove, Rita, 427
Driving Distracted, 266
Drummer Boy of Shiloh, The, 167

E
Espaillat, Rhina, P., 427

F
Fatal Car Crashes Drop for 16-Year-Olds, Rise for Older Teens, 256
Find Work, 431
Frank, Anne, 355

G
Goodrich, Frances, 279

H
Hackett, Albert, 279
Hanging Fire, 230
Harriet Tubman: Conductor on the Underground Railroad, 151
Hofer, Barbara, 235

I
Is 16 Too Young to Drive a Car?, 247

J
Jacobs, W. W., 105

K
Kitman, Jamie Lincoln, 235

L
Latehomecomer, The, 53
Lorde, Audre, 229

M
Marigolds, 213
Michaud, Anne, 419
Monkey's Paw, The, 105
Monkey's Paw, The (film clip), 121
Mora, Pat, 229
My Favorite Chaperone, 3
My Mother Enters the Work Force, 433

N
Narrative of the Life of Frederick Douglass, an American Slave, 143
New Immigrants Share Their Stories (documentary), 71

O
O Captain! My Captain!, 200
Okimoto, Jean Davies, 3
One Last Time, 405

P
Petry, Ann, 151
Place to Call Home, A, 41
Poe, Edgar Allan, 89
Powwow at the End of the World, The, 75
Prose, Francine, 369

R
Rochkind, Jonathan, 41
Russell, Sharon A., 125

S
Sandburg, Carl, 427
Scary Tales, 99
Soto, Gary, 405
Steinberg, Laurence, 235
Swanson, James L., 177
Szymborska, Wisława, 385

T
Teenagers, 231
Teens at Work, 422
Teens Need Jobs, Not Just Cash, 419
Tell-Tale Heart, The, 89
There But for the Grace, 386
Thompson, Michael, 235
Torrence, Jackie, 99
Twain, Mark, 395

W
Wiesel, Elie, 379
What Is the Horror Genre?, 125
When Do Kids Become Adults?, 235
Whitman, Walt, 199

Y
Yang, Kao Kalia, 53
Your Phone Can Wait, 263

Acknowledgments

"After Auschwitz" by Elie Wiesel. Text copyright © 1995 by Elie Wiesel. Reprinted by permission of Elie Wiesel.

Excerpt from *The American Heritage Dictionary of the English Language, Fifth Edition*. Text copyright © 2011 by Houghton Mifflin Harcourt. Adapted and reprinted by permission of Houghton Mifflin Harcourt Publishing Company.

Excerpt from *Anne Frank: The Book, the Life the Afterlife* by Francine Prose. Text copyright © 2009 by Francine Prose. Reprinted by permission of HarperCollins Publishers.

"Better Training for New Drivers" by Jamie Lincoln Kitman from *The New York Times*, May 28, 2012. Text copyright © 2012 by the New York Times. Reprinted by permission of PARS International on behalf of the New York Times. All rights reserved.

Excerpt from *Bloody Times: The Funeral of Abraham Lincoln and the Manhunt for Jefferson Davis* by James L. Swanson. Text copyright © 2011 by James L. Swanson. Reprinted by permission of HarperCollins Publishers.

Excerpt from "Bonne Année" by Jean-Pierre Benoît from *The Butterfly's Way: Voices From the Haitian Dyaspora in the United States* edited by Edwidge Danticat. Text copyright © 2001 by Jean-Pierre Benoit. Reprinted by permission of Jean-Pierre Benoit.

"Chicago" from *Chicago Poems* by Carl Sandburg. Text copyright © 1944 by Carl Sandburg. Reprinted by permission of Houghton Mifflin Harcourt Publishing Company.

Excerpt from *The Diary of a Young Girl: The Definitive Edition* by Anne Frank, edited by Otto H. Frank and Mirjam Pressler and translated by Susan Massotty. Translation copyright © 1995 by Doubleday, a division of Random House, Inc. Reprinted by permission of Doubleday, a division of Random House, Inc. and Penguin Group UK. Any third party use of this material, outside of this publication, is prohibited. Interested parties must apply directly to Random House, Inc. for permission.

The Diary of Anne Frank by Frances Goodrich and Albert Hackett. Text copyright © 1956 by Albert Hackett, Frances Goodrich Hackett, and Otto Frank. Reprinted by permission of Random House, Inc. Any third party use of this material, outside of this publication, is prohibited. Interested parties must apply directly to Random House, Inc. for permission.

"The Drummer Boy of Shiloh" by Ray Bradbury, originally published in the *Saturday Evening Post*. Text copyright © 1960 by the Curtis Publishing Company, renewed 1988 by Ray Bradbury. Reprinted by permission of Don Congdon Associates, Inc.

"Fatal Crashes Drop For 16-Year-Olds, Rise For Older Teens" by Allison Aubrey, originally broadcast on NPR's *Morning Edition*® on September 14, 2011. Text copyright © 2011 by National Public Radio, Inc. Reprinted by permission of NPR®.

"Find Work" by Rhina P. Espaillat from *Poetry Magazine*, February 1999. Text copyright © 1999 by Rhina P. Espaillat. Reprinted by permission of the Rhina P. Espaillat.

"Hanging Fire" from *The Collected Poems of Audre Lorde* by Audre Lorde. Text copyright © 1978 by Audre Lorde. Reprinted by permission of W.W. Norton & Company, Inc. and Charlotte Sheedy Literary Agency on behalf of the author's estate.

Excerpts from *Harriet Tubman: Conductor on the Underground Railroad* by Ann Petry. Text copyright © 1955 by Ann Petry, renewed in 1983 by Ann Petry. Reprinted by permission of Russell & Volkening as agents for the author.

"Is 16 Too Young to Drive a Car?" by Robert Davis from *USA Today*, March 2, 2005. Text copyright © 2012 by USA Today. Reprinted by permission of PARS International on behalf of USA Today. All rights reserved.

Excerpt from *The Latehomecomer: A Hmong Family Memoir* by Kao Kalia Yang. Text copyright © 2008 by Kao Kalia Yang. Reprinted by permission of The Permissions Company on behalf of Coffee House Press.

"Leave the Voting Age Alone" by Jenny Diamond Cheng from *The New York Times*, May 28, 2012. Text copyright © 2012 by Jenny Diamond Cheng. Reprinted by permission of Jenny Diamond Cheng.

"Mandatory Service to Become an Adult" by Michael Thompson from *The New York Times*, May 28, 2012. Text copyright © 2012 by Michael Thompson. Reprinted by permission of Michael Thompson.

"Marigolds" by Eugenia Collier, originally published in *Negro Digest*, Vol. XIX, No 1, Nov. 1969. Reprinted in *Breeder and Other Stories* by Eugenia Collier, 1994. Text copyright © 1969 by Eugenia Collier. Reprinted by permission of Eugenia Collier.

"My Favorite Chaperone" by Jean Davis Okimoto from *First Crossing: Stories About Teen Immigrants* edited by Donald R. Gallo. Text copyright © 2004 by Jean Davis Okimoto. Reprinted by permission of Jean Davis Okimoto.

"My Mother Enters the Work Force" from *On the Bus with Rosa Parks* by Rita Dove. Text copyright © 1999 by Rita Dove. Reprinted by permission of W. W. Norton & Company, Inc.

"One Last Time" from *Living Up the Street* by Gary Soto. Text copyright © 1985 by Gary Soto. Reprinted by permission of Gary Soto.

"A Parent's Role in the Path to Adulthood" by Barbara Hofer from *The New York Times*, May 28, 2012. Text copyright © 2012 by Barbara Hofer. Reprinted by permission of Barbara Hofer.

Excerpt adapted from *A Place to Call Home: What Immigrants Say Now About Life in America* by Scott Bittle and Jonathan Rochkind. Text copyright © 2009 by Public Agenda. Reprinted by permission of Public Agenda.

"The Powwow at the End of the World" from *The Summer of Black Widows* by Sherman Alexie. Text copyright © 1996

Acknowledgments

by Sherman Alexie. Reprinted by permission of Hanging Loose Press.

"Scary Tales" from *Jackie Torrence: The Magic of Creating Stories and the Art of Telling Them* by Jackie Torrence. Text copyright © 1998 by Jackie Torrence. Reprinted by permission of Eleanor Qadirah, on behalf of The Estate of Jackie Torrence.

"Teenagers" from *My Own True Name: New and Selected Poems for Young Adults* by Pat Mora. Text copyright © 2000 by Arte Público Press-University of Houston. Reprinted by permission of Arte Público Press-University of Houston.

"Teens at Work," by Kyle Swartz, from the *Record-Journal*, May 14, 2012. Text copyright © 2012 by the Record Journal. Reprinted by permission of Record-Journal Publishing Co., Meriden, CT.

"Teens Need Jobs, Not Just Cash" by Anne Michaud, originally published as "Summer jobs and the lost generation" from *Newsday* July 12, 2012. Text copyright © 2012. Reprinted by permission of PARS International on behalf of Newsday. All rights reserved.

"There But for the Grace" by Wisława Szymborska from *Sounds, Feelings, Thoughts: Seventy Poems by Wisława Szymborska* translated and introduced by Magnus J. Krynski and Robert A. Maguire. Text copyright © 1981 by Princeton University Press. Reprinted by permission of Princeton University Press.

Excerpt from "What is the Horror Genre?" by Stephen King from *Stephen King: a Critical Companion* by Sharon A. Russell. Text copyright © 1996 by Sharon A. Russell. Reprinted by permission of Copyright Clearance Center.

"What the Brain Says About Maturity" by Laurence Steinberg from *The New York Times*, May 28, 2012. Text copyright © 2012 by the New York Times. Reprinted by permission of PARS International on behalf of the New York Times. All rights reserved.